PAUL DURAND-RUEL AND THE MODERN ART MARKET

INVENTING IMPRESSIONISM

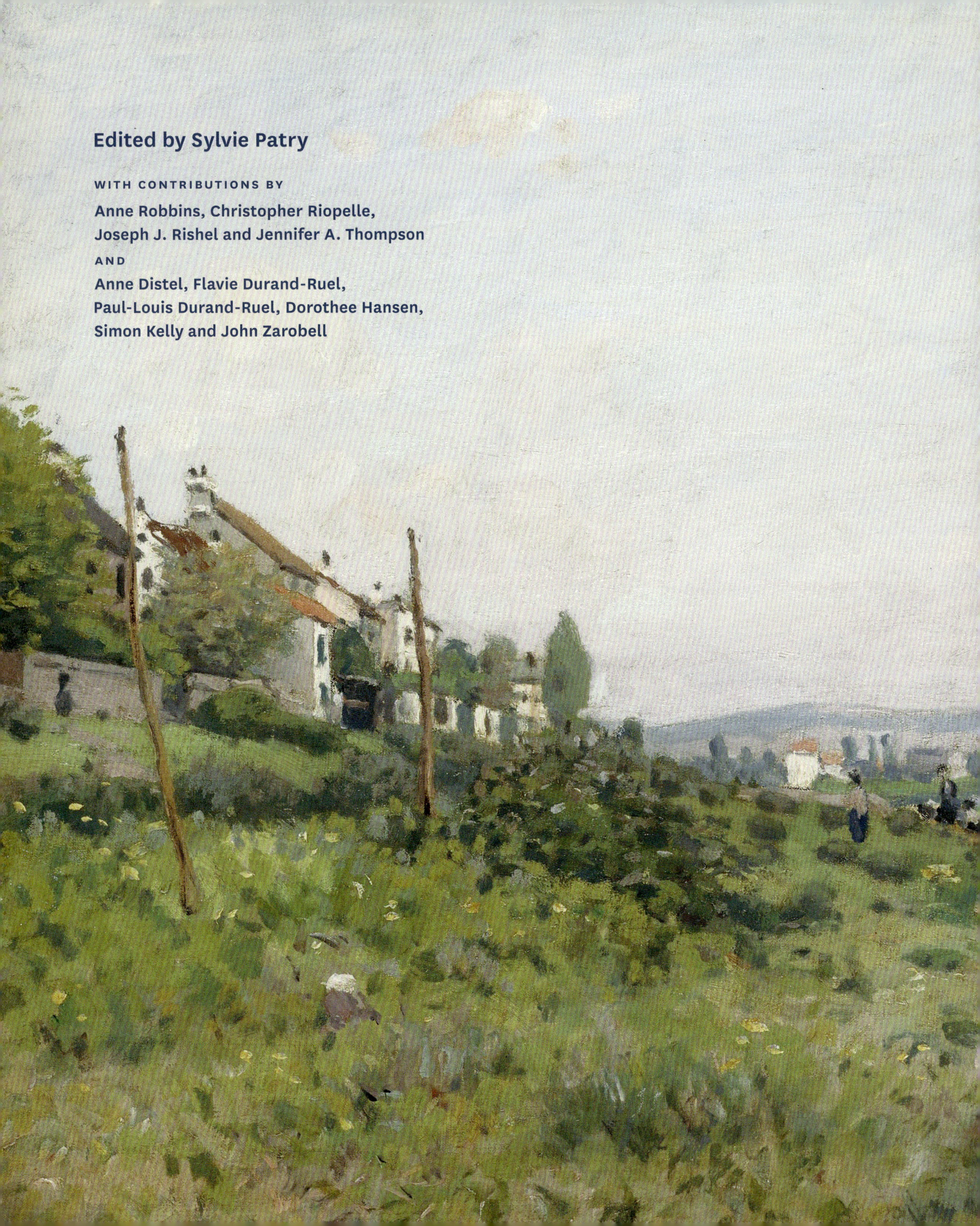

Edited by Sylvie Patry

WITH CONTRIBUTIONS BY

Anne Robbins, Christopher Riopelle,
Joseph J. Rishel and Jennifer A. Thompson

AND

Anne Distel, Flavie Durand-Ruel,
Paul-Louis Durand-Ruel, Dorothee Hansen,
Simon Kelly and John Zarobell

PAUL DURAND-RUEL AND THE MODERN ART MARKET

INVENTING IMPRESSIONISM

NATIONAL GALLERY COMPANY, LONDON
DISTRIBUTED BY YALE UNIVERSITY PRESS

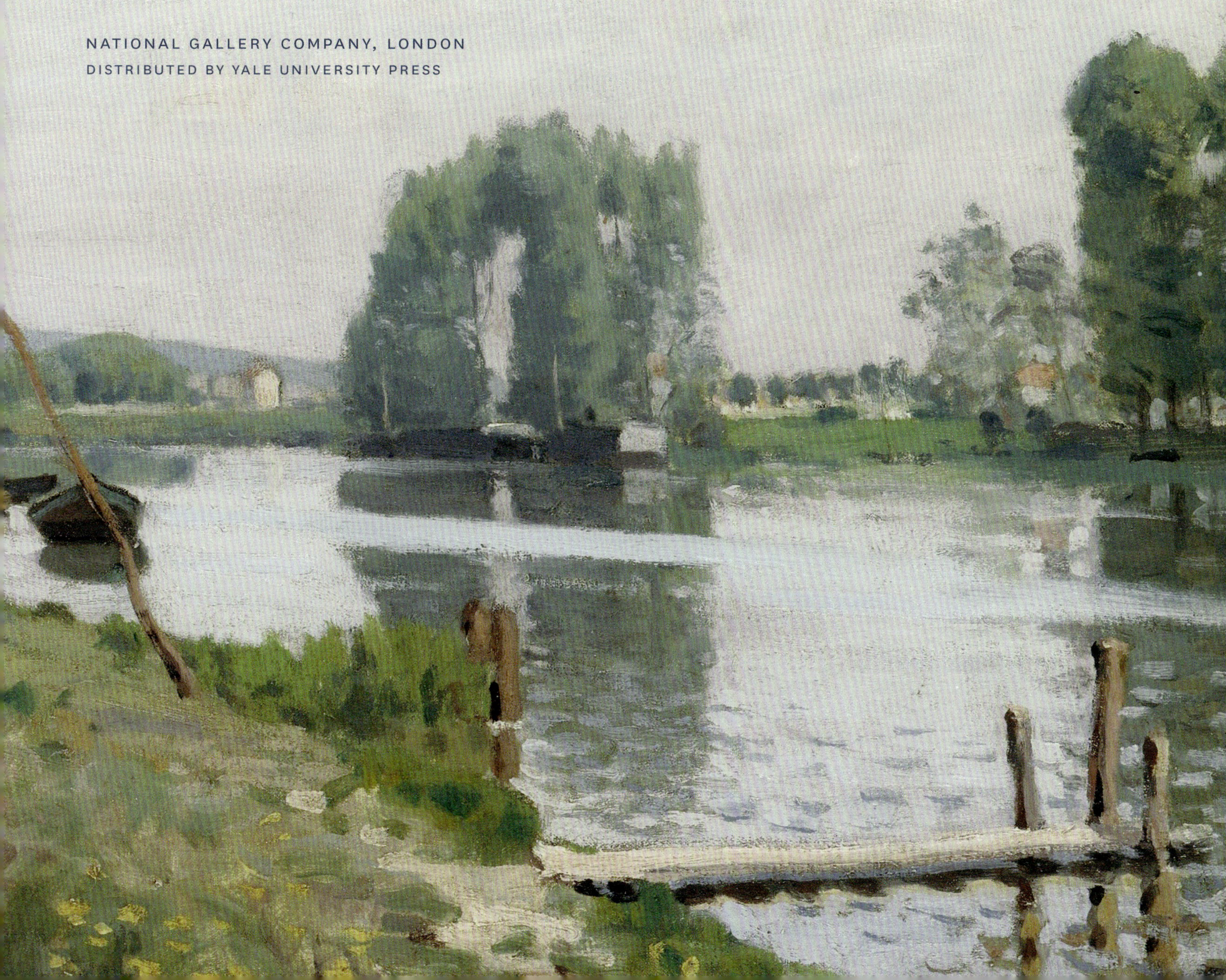

Published to accompany the exhibition

Paul Durand-Ruel:
Le Pari de l'Impressionnisme
Musée du Luxembourg, Paris (Sénat)
9 October 2014 – 8 February 2015

Inventing Impressionism:
Paul Durand-Ruel and the Modern Art Market
The National Gallery, London
4 March – 31 May 2015

Discovering the Impressionists:
Paul Durand-Ruel and the New Painting
Philadelphia Museum of Art
24 June – 13 September 2015

This exhibition was organised by The National Gallery, London, the Philadelphia Museum of Art and Réunion des musées nationaux – Grand Palais in collaboration with the Musée d'Orsay, Paris.

This catalogue is produced with support from the Pilkington Anglo-Japanese Cultural Foundation.

This catalogue first published in France in 2014 by Réunion des musées nationaux – Grand Palais, Paris to accompany the French exhibition at the Musée du Luxembourg.

This edition published in Great Britain in 2015 by
National Gallery Company Limited
St Vincent House
30 Orange Street
London WC2H 7HH
www.nationalgallery.co.uk

HB ISBN 9781857095845
1038743

PB ISBN 9781857095852
1038742

British Library Cataloguing-in-Publication Data.
A catalogue record is available from the British Library.

Library of Congress Control Number: 2014956220

PUBLISHER Jan Green
PROJECT EDITOR Rachel Giles
EDITOR Caroline Bugler
PICTURE RESEARCHER Anna Siebert
PRODUCTION Jane Hyne and Penny Le Tissier
DESIGNER Philip Lewis

Origination by DL Imaging, London
Printed and bound in Italy by Conti TipoColor, Florence

All measurements give height before width.

Translation from French into English by Laura Bennett and from German into English by Edward Neather.

FRONT COVER Pierre-Auguste Renoir, *Portrait of Mademoiselle Legrand*, 1875; detail of fig. 86
BACK COVER Alfred Sisley, *View of the Thames: Charing Cross Bridge*, 1874; detail of fig. 121
FRONTISPIECE Alfred Sisley, *L'Ile Saint-Denis*, 1872; detail of fig. 8
PAGE 6 Pierre-Auguste Renoir, *Paul Durand-Ruel*, 1910; detail of fig. 125

CONTENTS

FOREWORD

Monet, Pissarro, Degas, Renoir, Sisley, Morisot, Manet, Cassatt. These are the names of the painters we associate with the movement known as Impressionism that originated in Paris in the 1860s. Today they are world-famous, but it is important to remember that the initial reaction to their innovative work was largely hostile. It took careful planning, courage and persistence to present Impressionism to the public, to win over influential critics, to sell paintings to adventurous private collectors and then to place them in public museums.

Among those who were willing to champion the artists of this new movement was the Parisian art dealer Paul Durand-Ruel (1831–1922). Although he might have enjoyed a prosperous career selling the finest works by Delacroix, Corot and the Barbizon masters of an earlier generation – expanding an already-successful business his father had begun – for Durand-Ruel this was not enough. In 1870–1 he met fellow-exiles Monet and Pissarro in London and experienced a kind of conversion to the 'new painting'. From that point forward Durand-Ruel became an indefatigable champion of these two artists and many of their contemporaries, buying their works as quickly as they were produced. When financial adversity forced him to curtail his purchases, he used his considerable organisational skills to mount group and monographic exhibitions that kept Impressionism in the public eye. Conservative in manner as well as in politics, Durand-Ruel nonetheless crafted audacious strategies – including auctions, publications, the purchase of works in partnership with other dealers and, most critically, an astute decision to promote Impressionism internationally – for selling the works of the artists he represented and convincing collectors to take greater risks. He, as much as anyone, invented the market for contemporary art as it continues to function today.

Remarkably, nearly 12,000 paintings by Monet, Renoir, Pissarro, Degas and others passed through Durand-Ruel's hands. Some were bought and sold within a few days, while others remained with him for years and were sent to exhibitions across Europe, Russia and the United States, as he patiently built and then sustained new markets for the work of the artists he championed. Among the most important of these was America, which Durand-Ruel would claim had saved him because collectors there embraced Impressionism with fewer prejudices than tradition-bound Europeans. Indeed, the initial success he enjoyed in America in the mid-1880s demonstrated the importance of new markets and of the expansion of his clientele beyond the small but fervent group of French collectors and supporters of the Impressionists.

This exhibition, an international effort involving institutions and scholars in France, the United Kingdom, the United States and Germany – the four countries in which Durand-Ruel was most active – traces the fascinating story of this great dealer's embrace of avant-garde painting and the ways in which he sought to persuade a sometimes sceptical world of its enduring value. It is fitting that this publication and the exhibition it accompanies have been organised jointly by the Musée d'Orsay in collaboration with the Réunion des musées nationaux – Grand Palais, Paris, the National Gallery, London and the Philadelphia Museum of Art because our holdings of works by the Impressionists bear the indelible stamp of Durand-Ruel's influence on the advancement of this movement. In this regard, the development of this project was a collaborative effort, and one that has benefited enormously from cooperation of many other institutions and individuals who generously agreed to lend works from their collections.

We are indebted to the Durand-Ruel family, and to the Durand-Ruel Archives, for making available the documentation on which this exhibition is based. Their commitment to the project and contributions to this catalogue are of broad significance to our understanding of Impressionism, and at the same time deeply personal. Without their encouragement and support, this important chapter in the history of the movement could not have been written, and for that we are extremely grateful.

JEAN-PAUL CLUZEL
Président, Réunion des musées nationaux – Grand Palais, Paris

GUY COGEVAL
Président de l'Etablissement public des Musées d'Orsay et de l'Orangerie

NICHOLAS PENNY
Director, The National Gallery, London

TIMOTHY RUB
The George D. Widener Director and Chief Executive Officer, Philadelphia Museum of Art

A Note on Abbreviations and Currency

The handwritten sources, archival material, bibliographic references, exhibition catalogues, sales catalogues and catalogues raisonnés quoted in the texts and notes have been abbreviated. The note 'cat. "00"' refers to an exhibited work.

Reference is often made to sources from the Galerie Durand-Ruel Archives. The term 'daybook' refers to the registers (known in French as '*brouillards*') in which the daily operations of the gallery were noted down. The term 'stock' followed by a number refers to a number assigned by the gallery when a work was purchased. These numbers, which do not always follow the registers, are only cited here if they have already been published, refer to pictures from public collections, or allow the history of a work to be documented in a new way. The deposit numbers designate works put on deposit at the gallery. The points of reference described below allow us to put the prices quoted into the context of the time.

France

In the early 1870s, Durand-Ruel bought pictures by Monet, Sisley, Pissarro and Renoir for between 100 and 200 francs each, and a Degas for between 500 and 1,000 francs. In 1873, the State paid 20,000 francs for *The Cock Fight* by Gérôme (Musée d'Orsay, Paris), a successful artist. The average annual wage of a labourer in 1872 was 884 francs, and the annual salary by law of a primary school teacher was 700 francs (Crozet 1991; Marchand and Thélot 1997). In 1874, Paul Durand-Ruel's annual salary was 18,000 francs. In the early 1880s, prices for buying and selling Impressionist pictures began to rise. In 1880, the average price of a Monet canvas was 300 francs; that of a Renoir ranged between 150 and 700 francs, but the following year Durand-Ruel bought *Girl with a Cat* (fig. 35) from him for 2,500 francs. The average annual wage of a labourer was then 1,035 francs, while that of a primary school teacher was 900 francs. Durand-Ruel's monthly salary was 1,500 francs (excluding expert assessments); that of his employees was between 200 and 300 francs (ADR, daybooks).

Around 1900, prices for Impressionist works began to reach record levels: in 1893, Durand-Ruel sold Degas's *Horses before the Stands* (fig. 61) for 30,000 francs; in 1905, he sold *Cliffs at Pourville, Morning* (private collection, United States) for 20,000 francs and *Leaving the Conservatory* by Renoir (The Barnes Collection, Philadelphia) to the Prince de Wagram for 24,000 francs. The annual salary by law of a primary school teacher was 1,500 francs and a labourer's annual wage was 1,152 francs. In 1903, Monet registered an annual income of 105,000 francs.

Great Britain

Durand-Ruel's first transactions in London were recorded in francs: this was the case for *The Avenue, Sydenham* by Pissarro (fig. 58), which was bought for 400 francs. In 1872, Durand-Ruel sold Degas's *The Dance Foyer of the Opera at rue Le Peletier* (fig. 62) for 4,200 francs (£168). This sum was not insignificant for an Impressionist picture at that time, but remained well below those achieved by great Victorian paintings, the record having been set by *Captive Andromache* (Manchester Art Gallery) by Lord Leighton, President of the Royal Academy, which sold for £4,000 in the 1880s, or six times the price hoped for by Durand-Ruel for Renoir's *Dance at Bougival* (fig. 5) at his London exhibition in 1883 (£600). The price of this Renoir nevertheless represented several years of work for a construction labourer. *Ile de la Loge* by Sisley (fig. 80), one of the cheapest works, cost £72, or the equivalent of eight months' work for the same labourer. The average annual salary at that time amounted to £660; an office employee earned between £200 and £500 and a man's suit cost about £2 (Daunton 2007).

United States

In the 1880s, when Durand-Ruel first brought Impressionist paintings to America, he sold works by Monet for as much as $1,500, while Renoirs and Pissarros generally went for $400 to $800. This translates into prices ranging from 2,000 to 7,500 francs since the exchange rate was five francs to the dollar for much of the nineteenth century. In 1889, the Havemeyers bought a Decamps (*The Good Samaritan*, Metropolitan Museum of Art, New York) for $11,000 (New York 1993, p. 323). Within a decade, prices rose substantially; in June 1896, Bertha and Potter Palmer of Chicago purchased a Manet (*The Races at Longchamp*, Art Institute of Chicago) for $9,000 and a Degas pastel (*The Mante Family*, Philadelphia Museum of Art) for $5,000 (AIC, curatorial files). In the same period, an American factory worker made between $400 and $500 a year, a skilled worker such as a carpenter or tailor earned between $700 and $900 annually, and clerks made about $1,200 (Licht 1995, pp. 183–4). In comparison, the Chief of Police for the city of Philadelphia had an annual salary of $2,325 in 1886 (Coolidge 1887, p. 275).

Abbreviations

The abbreviations of the catalogues raisonnés can be found on p. 286.

AAA	Archives of American Art, Washington
AIC	Art Institute of Chicago
ADM	*L'Art dans les deux mondes*
ADR	Archives Durand-Ruel, Paris
AM	Archives municipales, Paris
AMN	Archives des musées nationaux, Paris
AMR	Archives du musée Rodin, Paris
AMRBAB, FST	Archives des musées royaux des beaux-arts de Belgique, Fonds des Salons triennaux
AP	Archives de Paris
BCMN	Bibliothèque centrale des musées nationaux, Paris
BnF	Bibliothèque nationale de France, Paris
BnF, Est.	Bibliothèque nationale de France, Paris, département des Estampes et de la Photographie
CAC	*La Chronique des arts et de la curiosité*
GBA	*Gazette des beaux-arts*
GR	Getty Research Institute, Los Angeles
GUL	Glasgow University Library
GUW	Glasgow University Whistler (see Select Bibliography)
INHA	Institut national d'histoire de l'art, Paris
MMD	Musée Maurice Denis, Saint-Germain-en-Laye
MO	Musée d'Orsay, Paris

ACKNOWLEDGEMENTS

This exhibition and catalogue would not have been possible without the continued support of Paul-Louis Durand-Ruel, President of Durand-Ruel & Cie, and Flavie Durand-Ruel Mouraux, who works alongside him. We would like to express our deepest appreciation for the invaluable assistance they have given us throughout this project. The individual acknowledgements offered by the authors of this catalogue are indicative of the extent of our debt to the Archives Durand-Ruel, so remarkably preserved and so vital to researchers, thanks to Charles Durand-Ruel, Caroline Durand-Ruel Godfroy, Paul-Louis Durand-Ruel and Flavie Durand-Ruel Mouraux, as well as Claire Durand-Ruel Snollaerts.

The curators of the exhibition would also like to thank the heads of their institutions for the trust placed in them: Guy Cogeval, Nicholas Penny and Timothy Rub, as well as Jean-Paul Cluzel.

An impetus for the National Gallery's involvement in the exhibition came from the late Paul Josefowitz. As early as February 2007 he made a point of introducing National Gallery curators to members of the Durand-Ruel family, proclaiming that the time had come for a major exhibition devoted to Paul Durand-Ruel, and that that exhibition needed to be seen in London, which played such an important role in the story. Until his untimely death in March 2013 Paul followed planning for the exhibition with his usual enthusiasm and acuity. The National Gallery owes him yet another of many debts.

John Zarobell has also supported the genesis and development of this project since 2007. We are grateful to him for his enthusiastic collaboration. In Paris, Philippe Thiébaut encouraged this project when it was still in its infancy. Sylvie Patry would also like to thank Sylvie Patin, Catherine Chevillot, Caroline Mathieu and Marie-Paule Vial. In addition, we would like to express our gratitude to Monique Nonne, who carried out extensive research and shared it with us throughout the preparation of this project.

For their contributions to the catalogue we would like to thank François Blanchetière, Ashley Boulden, Anne Distel, Claire Durand-Ruel Snollaerts, Isabelle Gaëtan, Dorothee Hansen, Sarah Herring, Simon Kelly, Monique Nonne, Naina Saligram and John Zarobell. The catalogue has also benefited from the expertise and attentive care of Jan Green, Rachel Giles, Caroline Bugler, Anna Siebert, Suzanne Bosman, Jane Hyne and Penny Le Tissier.

We would also like to extend our sincere thanks to all those who worked on the exhibition and catalogue in a variety of ways: Bill Acquavella, Sébastien Allard, Elsa Badie Modiri, Ronnie Baer, Joseph Baillio, Nienke Bakker, Stéphane Bayard, Véronique Beauregard, Emily Beeny, Giovanna Bertazzoni, Sophie Boegly, Stéphanie de Brabander, Xavier Bray, Jo Briggs, Aimée Brown Price, Caroline Campbell, Philippe Casset, Line Clausen Pedersen, Alan Crookham, Barbara Dawson, Philipp Demandt, Thomas Denenberg, Claire Denis, Stéphanie Deschamps-Tan, Lloyd DeWitt, Douglas Druick, Annie Dufour, Mark Evans, Hélène Flon, Françoise Fur, Gianna Furia, Vanessa Fusco, Thomas Galifot, Christian Garoscio, Hubertus Gaßner, Chantal Georgel, Véronique Gérard-Powell, Albert Godycki, Fiona Gomez, Allison Goudie, Deanna Griffin, Stephen Gritt, Gloria Groom, Claire Hallinan, Amélie Hardivillier, Rebecca Hast, Claire Hayat, Gill Hart, Jane Holmes, Dominique Jacquot, David Jaffé, Megumi Jingaoka, Kimberly A. Jones, Franck Joubin, Sophie Jugie, Larry Keith, Eva Keochakian, Leah Kharibian, Anabelle Kienle Ponka, Véronique Kientzy, Daniel Koep, Dorothy Kosinski, Felix Krämer, Teresa Krasny, Flore de La Doucette, Paul Lang, Clémence Laurent, Marie-Caroline Le Guen, Antoinette Le Normand-Romain, Marie-Josèphe Le Sueur de Trémaudan, Sophie Le Tarnec, Louise Lippincott, Dominique Lobstein, Isabelle Loric, Laurence Madeline, Marie-Blanche Maillard, Cécile Maisonneuve, Agnès Marconnet, Jean-Luc Martinez, Annabelle Mathias, Véronique Mattiussi, Nathalie Mengelle, Anne-Charlotte Ménoret, Mitchell Merling, Odile Michel, Ula Michlowicz, Gabrielle Montarnal, Mary Morton, Kaoru Murakami, Helena Newman, Josephine Nielsen-Bergqvist, Patrick Noon, Liberté Nuti, Stéphane Paccoud, Édouard Papet, Helena Patsiamanis, Ronald Pickvance, Caroline Porter, Elizabeth Prettejohn, Catherine Putz, Richard Rand, Eliza Rathbone, Camille Richer, William Robinson, Marie-Claire Rodriguez, Léa Saint-Raymond, Marie-Pierre Salé, Marie-Amélie zu Salm-Salm, Arnika Schmidt, Patrice Schmidt, Bill Scott, Karen Serres, George T. M. Shackelford, Fabienne Stahl, Laurent Stanich, Anne-Laure Sol, Susan Stein, Richard Thomson, Letizia Treves, Béatrice Tupinier, Maite van Dijk, Ernst Vegelin van Claerbergen, Hélène Voigt, Linda Whiteley, Juliet Wilson-Bareau and Coline Zellal.

We would like to express our deep gratitude to all those collectors who wished to remain anonymous but consented to be a part of this exhibition with generous loans. Works from private collections have been entrusted to us thanks to the support of teams from Christie's, both in Europe and the United States. We would also like to thank Colin B. Bailey, Director of the Fine Arts Museums of San Francisco, for his assistance.

SYLVIE PATRY, ANNE ROBBINS, CHRISTOPHER RIOPELLE, JOSEPH J. RISHEL AND JENNIFER A. THOMPSON

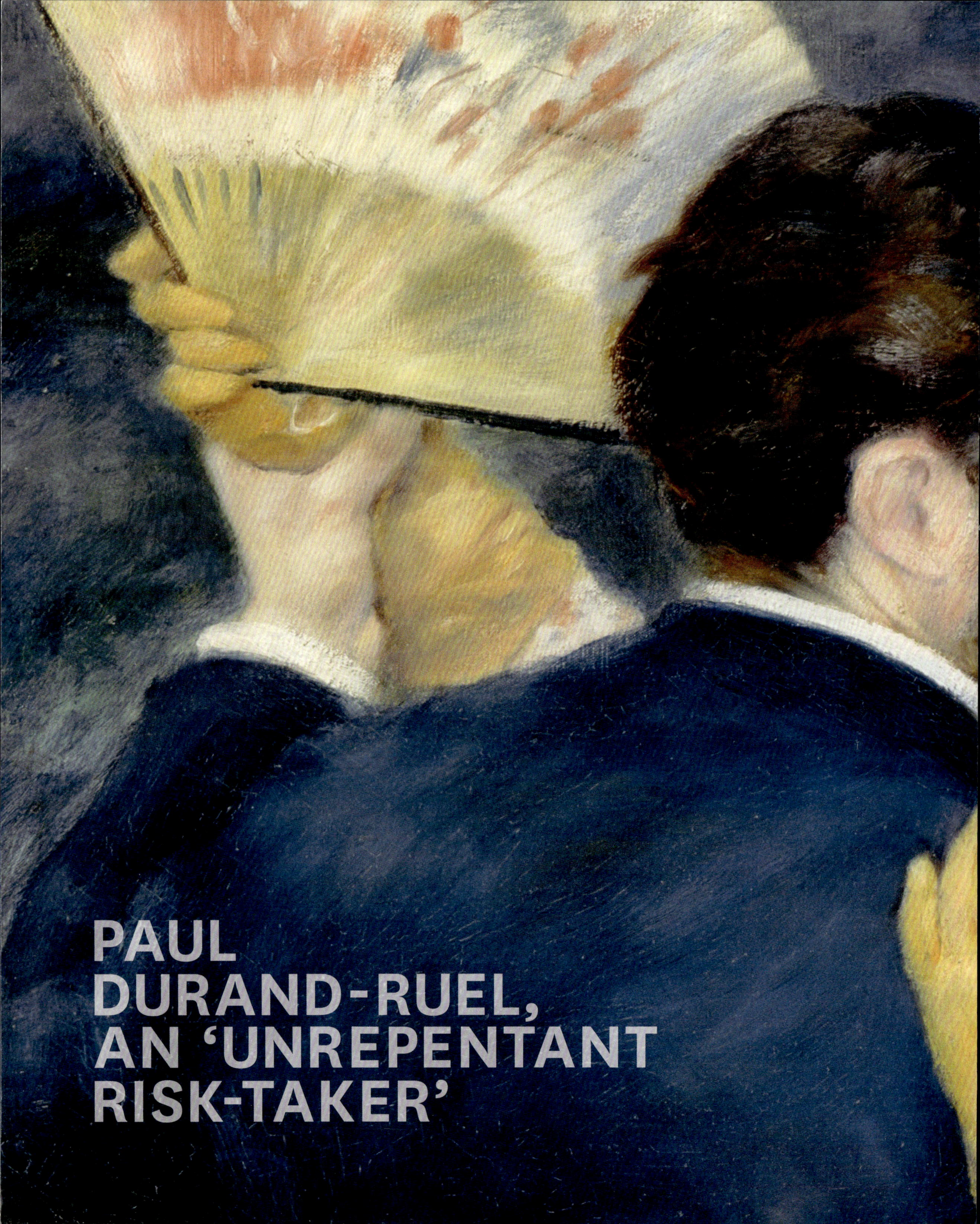

PAUL DURAND-RUEL, AN ‘UNREPENTANT RISK-TAKER’

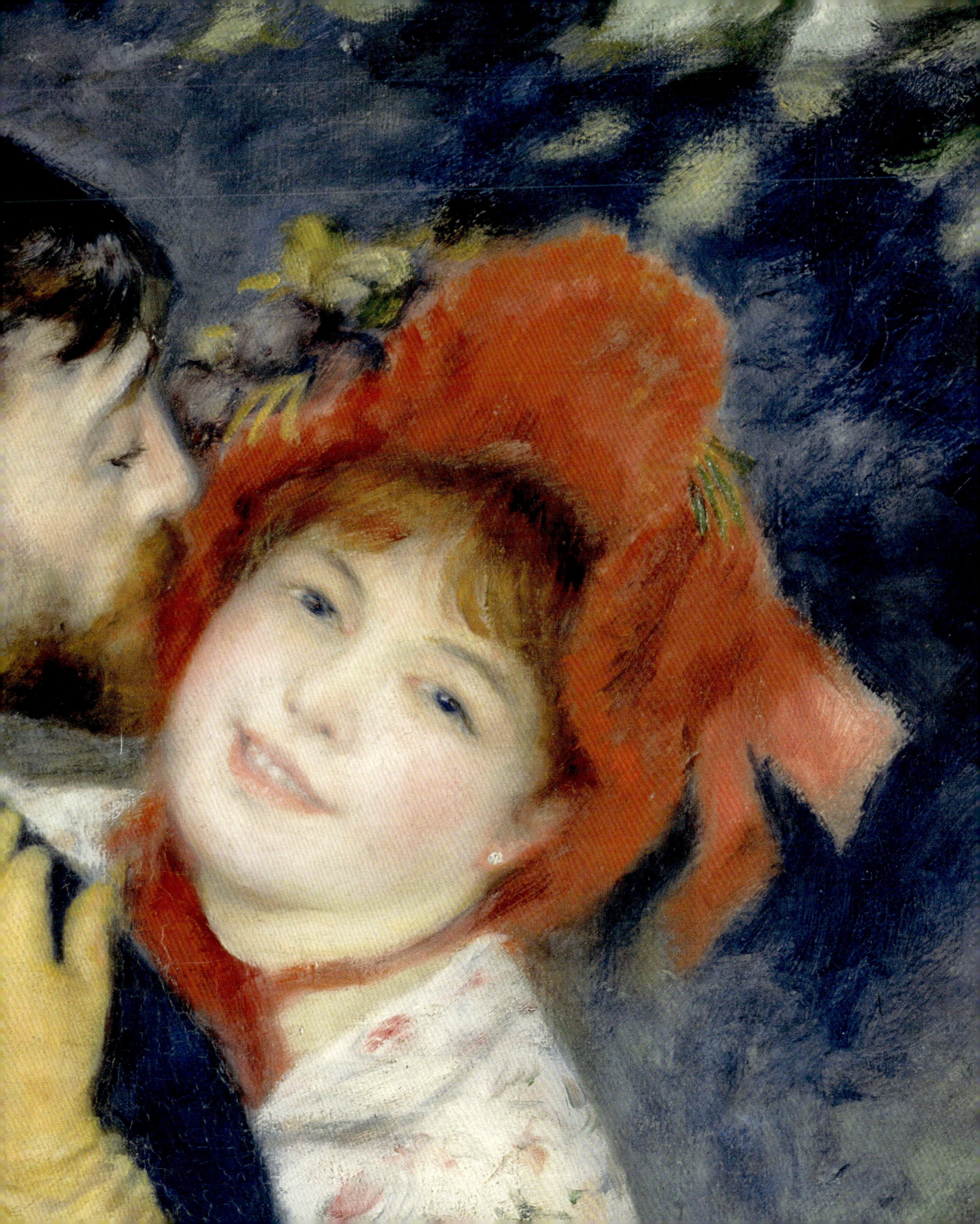

Paul Durand-Ruel, an 'Unrepentant Risk-taker'

Sylvie Patry, Anne Robbins, Christopher Riopelle, Joseph J. Rishel and Jennifer A. Thompson

'No name of a non-artist is more closely bound up with the history of Impressionism than that of Paul Durand-Ruel,' declared the distinguished art historian John Rewald in 1943.[1] His assessment of Durand-Ruel as more than an art dealer – as loyal friend, fierce advocate and courageous backer of the Impressionists – has remained little altered in the discourse on Impressionism for seven decades. It has been estimated that in his lifetime Durand-Ruel bought some 1,500 Renoirs, more than 1,000 Monets, 800 Pissarros, more than 400 Degas's, almost 400 Sisleys and Cassatts, and 200 Manets.[2] An exhibition devoted to the dealer and his relationships with Monet, Renoir, Pissarro, Sisley, Manet, Degas, Morisot, Cassatt and Cézanne offers an invitation to dive into the heart of Impressionism, and provides an opportunity for a detailed study of this exceptional art dealer's contribution to the movement. With these goals in the mind, the Musée d'Orsay, The National Gallery, London, and the Philadelphia Museum of Art embarked on planning such a project, an exercise that arose almost organically from collections that are in their own ways connected to Durand-Ruel. That the Durand-Ruel Gallery was innately international in its clientele, aspirations and efforts, makes it fitting that an exhibition devoted to it should be shared by the three countries in which Paul Durand-Ruel was most active: France, England and America.

Durand-Ruel in Paris, London and Philadelphia

The Musée d'Orsay holds almost 100 paintings purchased, sold or exhibited by the Durand-Ruel Gallery – nearly a quarter of the museum's Impressionist collections. These works reflect Paul Durand-Ruel's taste, and his commitment not just to Delacroix, Rousseau, Decamps, Courbet, Boudin, Fantin-Latour and Puvis de Chavannes, but also, and importantly, to Monet, Renoir, Degas, Pissarro and Sisley. For the most part, the Impressionist pictures joined the collections of the Musée du Luxembourg or the Louvre (though they are now kept at the Musée d'Orsay) at the turn of the century, thanks to the generosity of collectors such as Etienne Moreau-Nélaton, Isaac de Camondo and Antonin Personnaz. These men compiled their collections in part at the Durand-Ruel Gallery, from the 1890s onwards, sometimes following advice from the dealer, whose crucial role became apparent when these collections were later offered to museums. Until the early 1890s, the Musée du Luxembourg, at that time the museum for living artists, did not exhibit a single work by the Impressionists, whose paintings still provoked controversy. When 38 pictures and pastels by Manet, Degas, Monet, Pissarro, Sisley and Cézanne were accepted by the museum in 1894 as part of the bequest left by Gustave Caillebotte, it was the first time a significant number of Impressionist works had entered a French public collection. By contrast, at the turn of the century, the Durand-Ruel Gallery was hailed by some as a 'second Louvre'[3] and the dealer's apartment, which was open to visitors, was described as 'the most wonderful museum of contemporary painting in France' (figs 3 and 4).[4] Paul Signac wrote in 1899: 'It's true, when you go into Durand-Ruel's you would think you were at the Louvre – and I dare to compare Renoir's *Luncheon of the Boating Party* to *The Wedding Feast at Cana*. And to think that people have yelled in front of it!'[5]

Although the National Gallery has a more limited number of works – approximately 40 – that passed through Durand-Ruel's hands or were exhibited by him, they illustrate key stages in the dealer's career, such as his meeting with Monet and Pissarro in London (see figs 58, 113 and 115) and the opening of his gallery's first international branch. These paintings also provide a glimpse into the turbulent and often controversial story of the arrival of Impressionism in British collections, as demonstrated by the fate of Monet's *Lavacourt under*

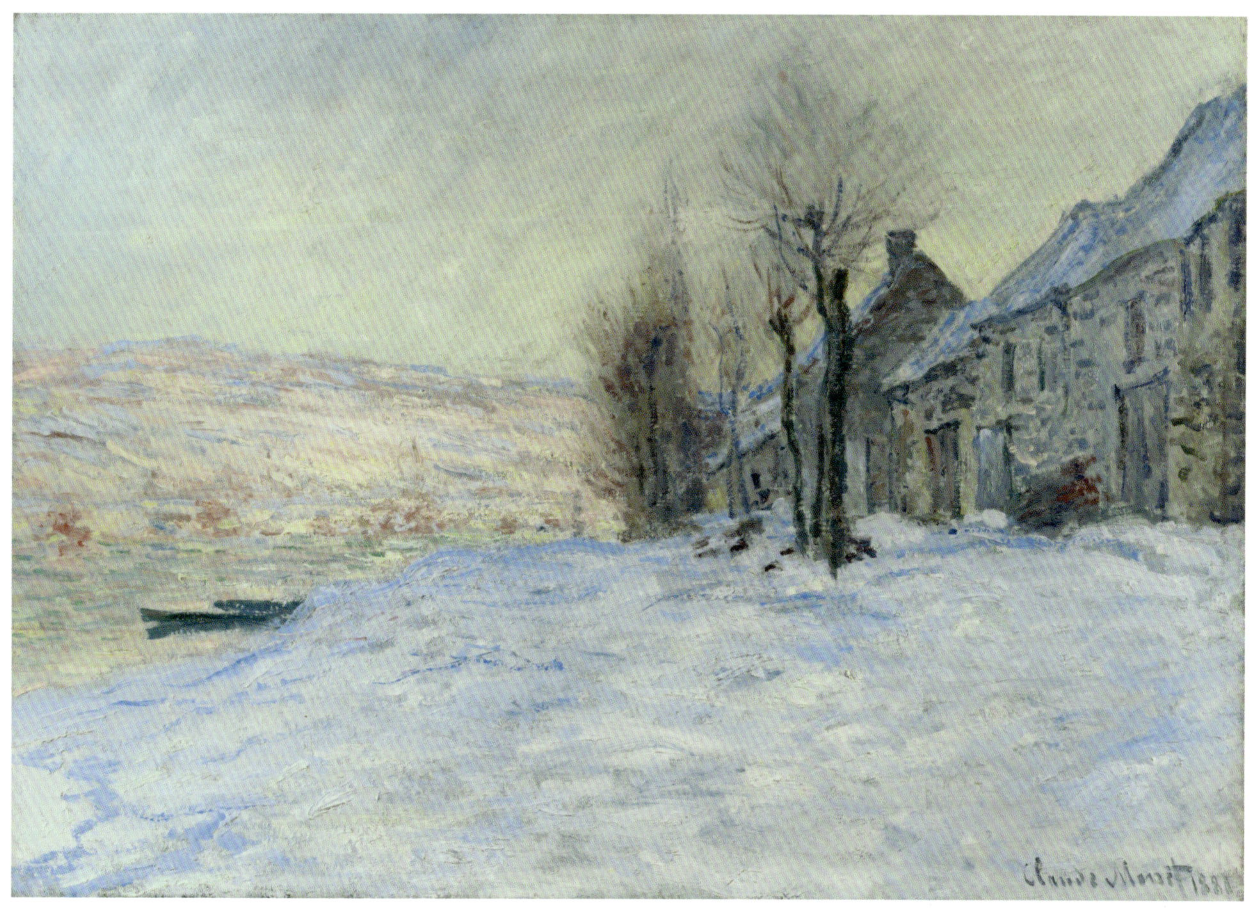

Snow (fig. 1). The picture was exhibited at the Grafton Galleries in London in 1905 as part of the epoch-making exhibition organised by Durand-Ruel, which drew attention to the lack of such modern foreign paintings in British public collections.[6] A public subscription was launched to support the gift of the picture to the National Gallery. However, the Gallery trustees had let it be known that they would not accept the picture, and a Boudin was presented instead. The picture eventually selected, Boudin's *Entrance to Trouville Harbour* (fig. 2), had not been exhibited at the Grafton Galleries but was purchased from another collection, in order to prevent any suspicion of collusion with the dealer. As for the Monet, Durand-Ruel sold it to Hugh Lane and it entered the National Gallery 10 years later, when Lane went down on the *Lusitania*, leaving his important collection of modern paintings – in large part assembled through Durand-Ruel – to the National Gallery. Soon joined by works that had also passed through the Durand-Ruel Gallery (see fig. 42), the pictures of the Lane bequest form the embryo of the National Gallery's so-called modern collection, where they attest to Durand-Ruel's presence behind the scenes.

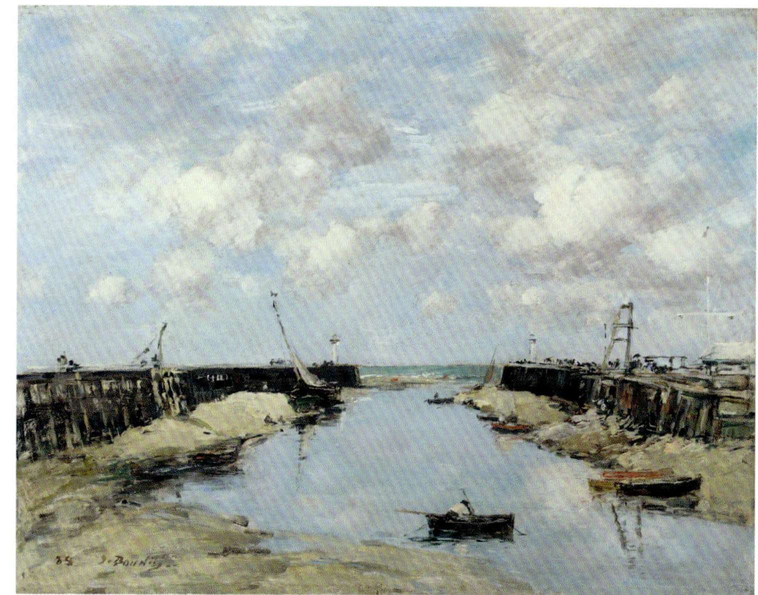

FIG. 1
Claude Monet
Lavacourt under Snow, about 1878–81
Oil on canvas, 59.7 × 80.6 cm
The National Gallery, London
[cat. 41]

FIG. 2
Eugène Boudin
The Entrance to Trouville Harbour, 1888
Oil on mahogany, 32.4 × 40.9 cm
The National Gallery, London
[cat. 3]

Philadelphia played a central role in the formation of artistic taste in America. Residents of the city were some of Durand-Ruel's earliest clients, beginning in the late 1860s and early 1870s when local businessmen bought Romantic and Barbizon paintings during regular visits to the Paris gallery, a tradition that continued with the next generation who favoured Impressionism. The dealer benefited in particular from the assistance of Mary Cassatt, born in Pennsylvania and raised in Philadelphia, who encouraged her brother Alexander, Vice-President of the Pennsylvania Railroad and one of the greatest entrepreneurs of the age, and other American collectors, to buy Impressionist paintings. Consequently, the Philadelphia Museum of Art owns over 100 works that passed through the gallery, and its impressive collection of Impressionist paintings, like that of many American museums, is inextricably linked with Durand-Ruel. The gallery further helped to shape Philadelphia collections in its close work with Dr Albert C. Barnes, who was such a loyal customer that he wrote to Durand-Ruel in 1915, 'my collection is practically an annex of your business'.[7]

Durand-Ruel today

The Impressionist collections in Paris, London and Philadelphia demonstrate how Durand-Ruel's business determined a taste that is still evident today. As such, this exhibition follows in the wake of recent shows that have explored the vital role played by influential 'intermediaries', as Chastel and Pomian have called them[8]: Theo van Gogh, the brother of the painter and head of Goupil's Paris branch from 1881 to 1890 (Amsterdam and Paris, 1999–2000), Goupil & Co. (Bordeaux, New York and Pittsburgh, 2000), Ambroise Vollard (New York, Chicago and Paris, 2006–7) and, most recently, Daniel-Henry Kahnweiler (Villeneuve d'Ascq, 2013–14). These exhibitions reflect art history's growing interest in dealers, long viewed in anecdotal terms or with a financial fascination and kept – legitimately – at a distance for fear that exhibitions and publications might appear to endorse commercial undertakings.

In the case of Durand-Ruel, the gallery stopped selling paintings in 1974 and its role to date has been seen in a largely historical context. Indeed, dealers are now regarded as lying at the heart of social, economic, cultural, quantitative history and geography (relating to the movement of works of art, for example), but also vital to the history of taste and collections. This approach emphasises the place held by those involved in the 'art world',[9] and the significant role that circulation, presentation and diffusion of works play in the creation of aesthetic values and pantheons long held to be absolute. Recent studies of the business strategies employed by publishers and entertainment entrepreneurs are comparable in many respects to those of art dealers. Research into the business side of art has been bolstered by access to new sources.[10] For the period in question here, the archives of Vollard,[11] Goupil & Co.[12] and Duveen[13], to be joined by Knoedler[14] and Agnew, which are still being researched, are invaluable.[15] New research has led to greater understanding and the discovery of many dealers, and has established in the first half of the nineteenth century – rather than the second half – the emergence of a contemporary art market based on an entrepreneurial and financial model.[16] Ultimately, these investigations have weakened the link, long considered organic, between modern art and the dealer system.

It was against the backdrop of this new material and of first-hand archival research that our project developed. Despite isolated tributes paid to Durand-Ruel in 1943 by the New York gallery, in 1970 in both Hamburg and New York, and in 1974 by the Durand-Ruel Gallery in Paris, Paul Durand-Ruel has never been the subject of an exhibition. Yet he was hailed in 1904 by the English painter Wynford Dewhurst, one of the first historians of Impressionism, as 'the most celebrated of all the Parisian art dealers'.[17] In 1892, Georges Lecomte's *L'Art impressionniste*, the first overview of the movement since that carried out by Théodore Duret in 1878, gave prominence to the dealer. Lecomte wished to write a 'complete history' of the movement and did so in a volume devoted to the private collection of Durand-Ruel.[18] Illustrated with 36 engravings by Lauzet and printed by the gallery, this luxurious book was part history, part promotional tool, as complimentary copies were given to Durand-Ruel's clients and colleagues. Following in the footsteps of Gustave Geffroy, Lecomte established the broad outlines of an account of Durand-Ruel, one that culminated in a Balzacian portrait published by Arsène Alexandre in 1911 in the German avant-garde review *Pan*, followed by the obituaries that appeared in 1922. These underscored the dealer's pioneering role; his unwavering faith in the value of Impressionism and in the so-called Barbizon School; his infallible tenacity in the face of hostility from the public, critics and institutions; and his eventual triumph. As if echoing one of the vocations of the dealer's youth, this description often makes use of religious vocabulary and celebrates the 'apostolate' or the 'high priest of Impressionism'.[19] According to Duret, who had not mentioned Durand-Ruel in his *Histoire des peintres impressionnistes* of 1878, and introduced him only in the 1906 edition:[20] 'he is not a dealer in pictures but an apostle, a prophet'.[21]

In these early portraits, the faith of the 'missionary of Impressionism',[22] to use Renoir's expression, implied bad business sense. In 1920 Felix Fénéon published an interview with Durand-Ruel as part of a series on important collectors, in which the dealer stated: 'I was, in short, a bad dealer in paintings, because I never liked what sold, and what I liked, I never managed to sell'.[23] Close study of the gallery, however, negates this paradoxical assertion. Durand-Ruel provided a wealth of information to Fénéon, a sort of prelude to or reworking of his memoirs, which the dealer began in around 1910. An indispensable resource, Durand-Ruel's recollections were partly printed in 1912,[24] and again in 1939, when *Les Archives de l'impressionnisme* by Lionello Venturi was published by the Durand-Ruel Gallery.[25] Venturi outlined the history of the gallery and studied the Impressionists' relationships with Durand-Ruel,[26] gathering letters and documents that highlighted the extraordinary richness of the gallery's archives. These are to Impressionism what the Vatican is to Raphael, Venturi asserted at the beginning of his volume.[27] In a similar fashion, the gallery partially funded the preparation of the monumental and still authoritative *History of Impressionism* by John Rewald in 1946.[28] Photographs of works that passed through the Durand-Ruel galleries also served as a visual reservoir for research, fuelling the interwar publications on Impressionism. The firm therefore found itself intimately connected to the very writing of the history of the movement and to its visual diffusion, while becoming a vital source for establishing provenances and preparing catalogues raisonnés of Impressionist painters and collections.

The era of eye-witness accounts was followed by studies drawn from the Durand-Ruel Archives, sometimes undertaken by the dealer's descendants, notably Charles Durand-Ruel, Caroline Durand-Ruel Godfroy, Claire Durand-Ruel Snollaerts, Paul-Louis Durand-Ruel and Flavie Durand-Ruel Mouraux, who have devoted themselves to understanding and conserving this precious resource since 1974. Meanwhile, from the 1960s onwards, Paul Durand-Ruel became a central figure in the sociology of art, which was nevertheless based on second-hand documentation. In his pioneering work of 1967, *Le Marché de la peinture en France*, Raymonde Moulin saw Durand-Ruel as the 'entrepreneur' *par*

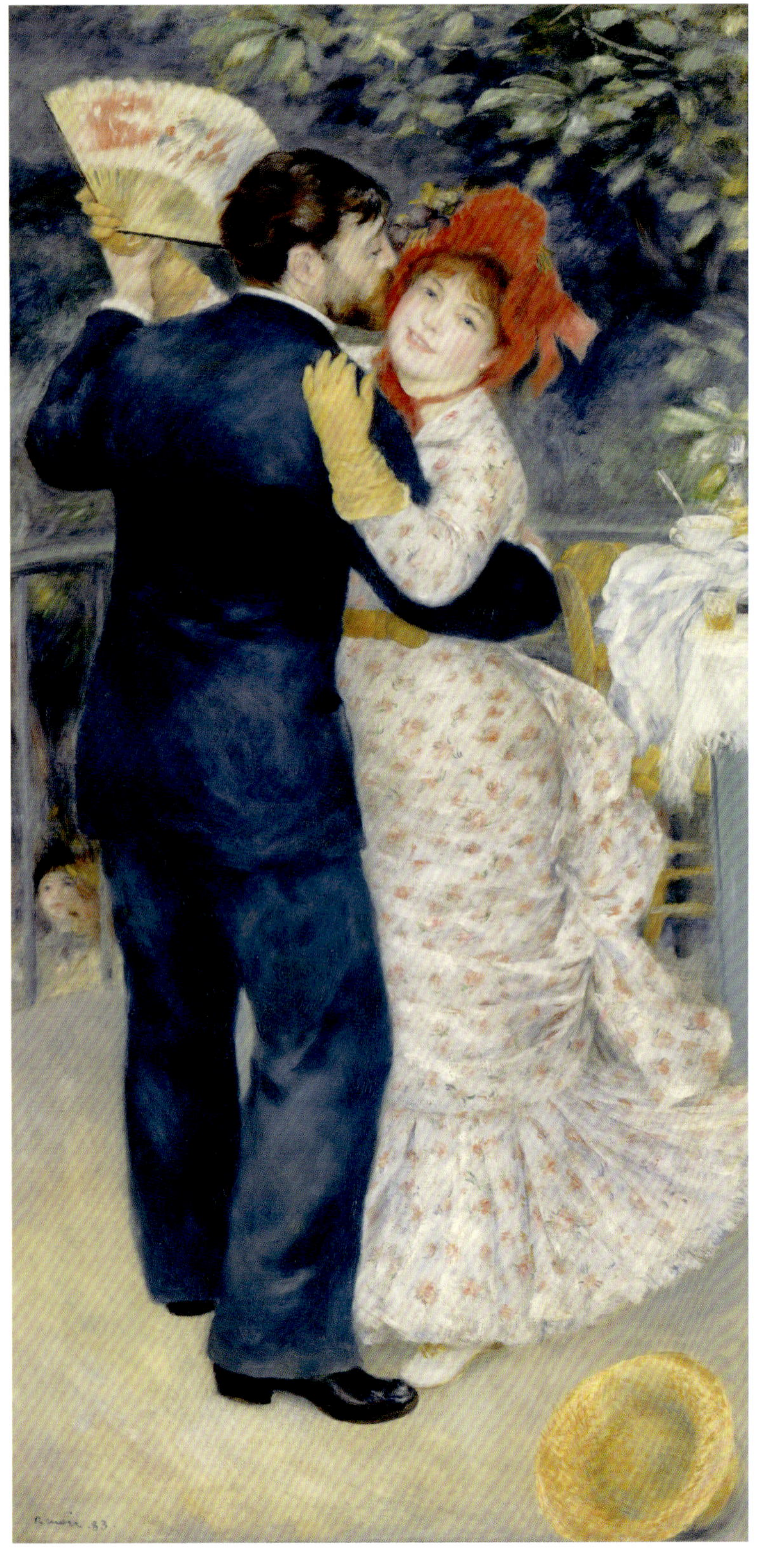

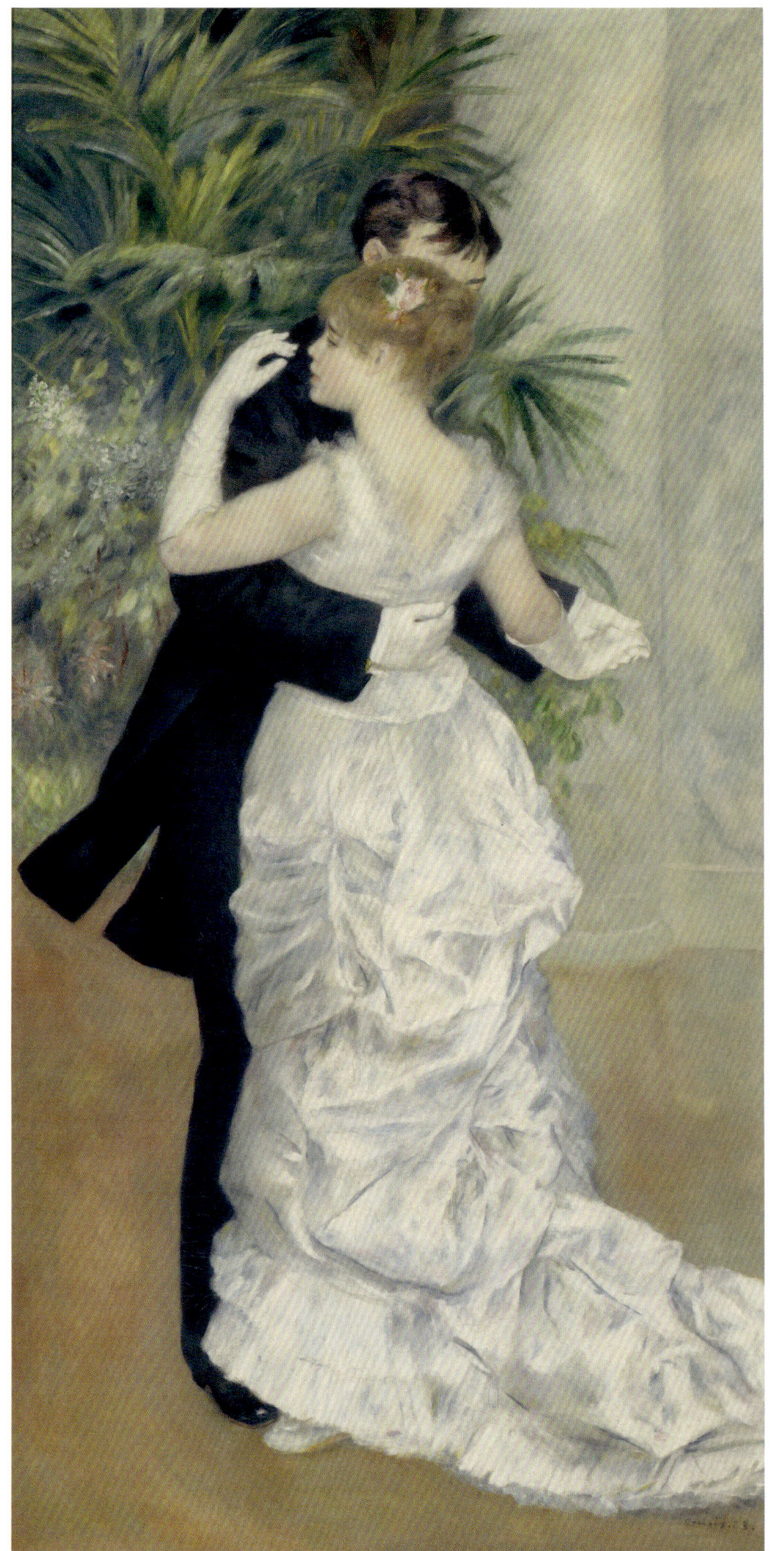

FIG. 3
Pierre-Auguste Renoir
Dance in the Country, 1883
Oil on canvas, 180 × 89 cm
Musée d'Orsay, Paris
[cat. 79]

FIG. 4
Pierre-Auguste Renoir
Dance in the City, 1883
Oil on canvas, 180 × 90 cm
Musée d'Orsay, Paris
[cat. 80]

FIG. 5
Pierre-Auguste Renoir
Dance at Bougival, 1883
Oil on canvas, 181.9 × 98.1 cm
Museum of Fine Arts, Boston
[cat. 81]

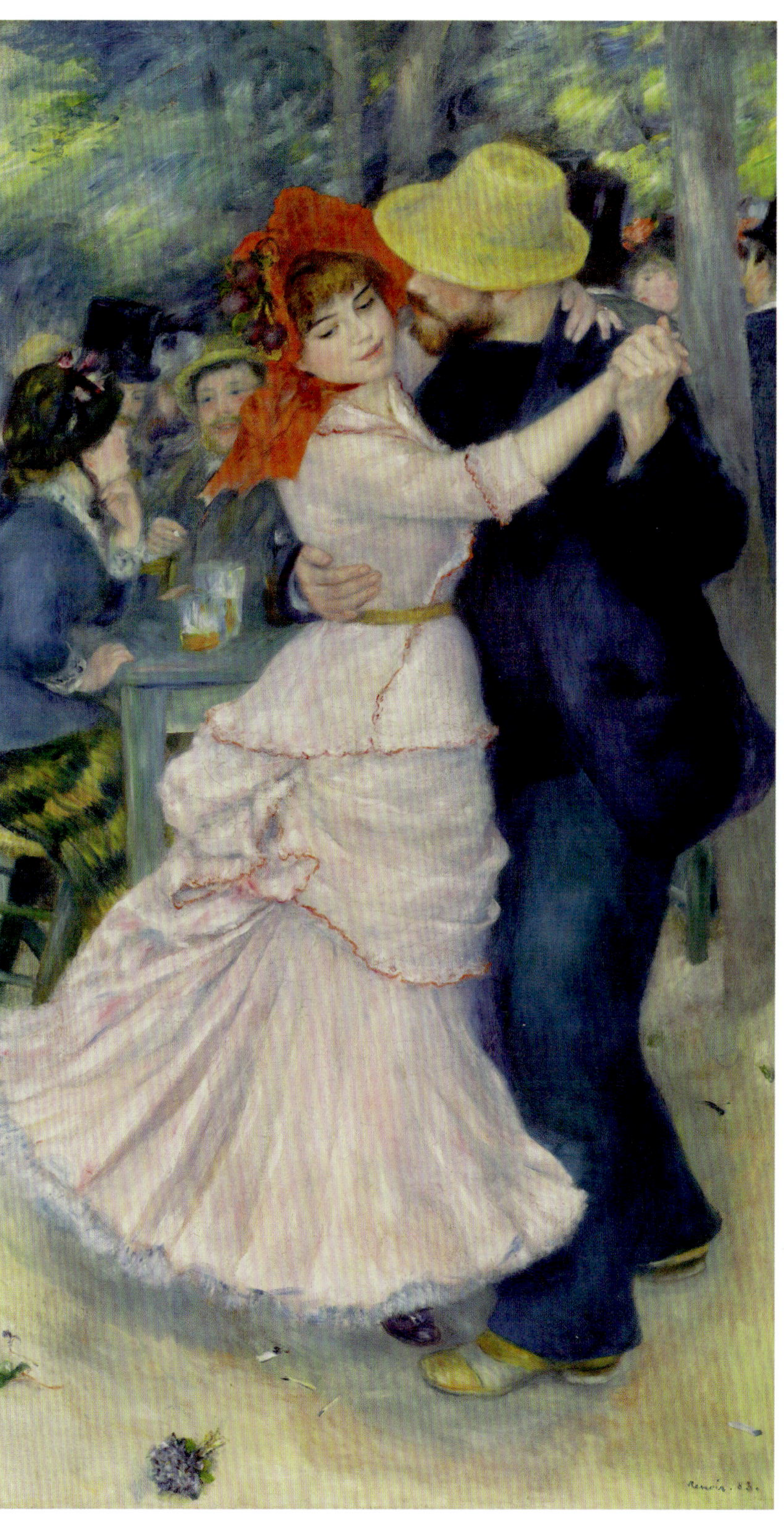

excellence and the 'first of the great modern dealers'.[29] Moulin followed in the footsteps of Harrison and Cynthia White, who in their famous *Canvases and Careers* of 1965,[30] regarded Durand-Ruel as the linchpin of the 'dealer-critic' system, a new vehicle for artistic legitimation that defined artists' careers, supplanting the Academy and the Salon. Innovative and stimulating, these publications have prompted more recent studies by Robert Jensen, David Galenson and Nicholas Green, who have analysed the establishment of new commercial 'strategies' as constituent parts of the construction of modernism. They have questioned the head-on collision between the dealer system and the official system, which was further qualified by Jean-Paul Bouillon and Pierre Vaisse. Important archival research carried out by Linda Whiteley and by Anne Distel, as well as the commendable biography of Durand-Ruel by Pierre Assouline, the only one to date, round out our extremely summary review of pertinent scholarship.

Methods and approaches

The aim of this exhibition and the accompanying catalogue is to enrich and renew our knowledge and understanding of a figure who occupies a key position in the history of art and who still provides a lively example to dealers today. We want to look beyond the myth of Durand-Ruel's heroic isolation and reopen the glorious chapter of the discovery and promotion of Impressionism in the light of these approaches and discoveries made in the gallery's archives. A project of this kind could not have been conceived without the support of Paul-Louis Durand-Ruel and Flavie Durand-Ruel Mouraux, who acted as our guides through the archives of their ancestor: their collaboration goes well beyond their involvement as authors of this catalogue. The archival material was sometimes so rich and required such delicate interpretation that we gave priority to two approaches: a careful reading of the *brouillards* (daybooks) that logged the gallery's activities, and document its evolution and transition from the late 1860s to the early 1880s, and selective surveys of stock books and other volumes that record purchases, sales, deposits and clients. Although admirably preserved, the Durand-Ruel Archives are not exhaustive: they begin in 1864 and are incomplete for the first half of the 1870s, for example. The records do not offer the same degree of detail for the whole period, making it impossible to extract comprehensive and accurate quantitative data. We relied on additional sources: contemporary press reports and archives both in France and abroad. Unsurprisingly, the full range of material accumulated for the project could not be included in this catalogue. Above all, we wanted to anchor our investigation in a corpus of works. We believe that such an approach – far from suggesting aesthetic relativism or diminishing the part played by the artist – considers the conditions of artistic creation and therefore enriches our understanding of the works of art, and ultimately, our enjoyment. Credited with a double 'invention', that of Impressionism and the profession of the modern art dealer, Paul Durand-Ruel occupies a central position in the cultural history of art and taste, one on which paintings retain their pre-eminent position.

The works of art

By focusing on Paul Durand-Ruel's support of the Impressionists and, to a lesser extent, of the School of 1830, our project has not attempted to cover all his activities. His trade in Old Masters is readily apparent in the archives from the 1860s and includes momentous purchases and sales, such as the extraordinary *Assumption of the Virgin* by El Greco, which he sold to the Art Institute of Chicago in 1906. In addition to eighteenth-century French painting, Durand-Ruel was particularly interested in the Dutch and Spanish schools, visiting the Netherlands and Spain on several occasions for business purposes, and shaping his highly personal taste for their artistic traditions. He particularly admired Rembrandt, whose *Saul and David* he sold in 1898 to Abraham Bredius, after trying to find a buyer for it in New York and Chicago. (The erudite collector and director of the Mauritshuis in The Hague placed the painting on deposit at the museum before bequeathing it to the institution.) Durand-Ruel also admired El Greco (in addition to his great coup in the sale of the *Assumption*, he sold a Saint Francis to Hugh Lane in 1913)[31] and Goya, selling a Goya portrait to the Louvre in 1903 for the not insubstantial sum of 30,000 francs.[32] These painters and schools of painting were subject to a critical re-evaluation and attracted the interest of the artists championed by Durand-Ruel. Alexandre, who was the first to draw attention to this aspect of the dealer's business – one that is yet to be fully studied – saw in it Durand-Ruel's taste for 'bold cutting-edge works',[33] whatever the period in question.

When it came to the painting of his own time, Durand-Ruel did not restrict himself to the 'moderns', demonstrating an eclectic blend of personal taste and pragmatism: 'I have been and still am a friend of Bouguereau, Cabanel, Bonnat and Baudry ... But was it any reason to despise such great artists as Millet, Corot, Delacroix, Rousseau and Courbet, and leave them neglected?',[34] he declared in 1885. In vogue in the 1860s and 1870s, genre painters such as Scheffer, Escosura, Caille, Zamacoïs, Béranger, Lévy, Toulmouche (a relative of Monet whose work was taken on by Durand-Ruel well before his own) and Hugues Merle, who was close to the dealer and from whom he commissioned portraits of himself and his wife (see figs 137 and 138), were essential to the life of the gallery and its economic stability. 'These pieces were purchased even before they had been painted',[35] noted Charles Blanc. In 1872, Durand-Ruel bought a picture from Merle for 10,000 francs, compared to the 100 or 200 francs he might have paid for a Pissarro or Monet.[36] For the most part, it was genre paintings that were sent to London or Brussels until the early 1880s, and in 1887 for the second exhibition in New York. There were established dealers such as McLean, Agnew, Tedesco and Hollender as well as an international clientele for these works, which Durand-Ruel was sometimes able to sell for more than 10,000 francs in the late 1870s and early 1880s. Based on a commercial model not dissimilar to that of Goupil, but lacking the industrial scale, based on worldwide distribution of images.[37] Durand-Ruel also sold replicas, engravings and photographs taken from his pictures: reproductions of Merle's *Maternal Love* and *First Thorns* and Toulmouche's *The Marriage of Reason* sold for between five and 20 francs each, and were great successes at the gallery. The gallery's *Recueil d'estampes*, the collections of etchings that promoted its stock between 1873 and 1875, included 30 works by such artists as Boulard, Héreau, Roybet, Meissonier and Lévy, but only 21 by the Impressionists. Durand-Ruel's interest in the Orientalists, including Fromentin, Huguet and Frère, should also be stressed. The Durand-Ruel Gallery's business in Algeria (it organised exhibitions in Oran and Algiers in 1880) and its links with the *Société des peintres orientalistes*, which exhibited at the gallery between 1895 and 1900, may have been an extension of this interest. In the 1870s and 1880s, Durand-Ruel continued to visit artists' workshops before the Salon, where he would sometimes purchase pictures; in addition, he assisted painters in selecting works to be sent to the Salon, and certain artists, such as Whistler, Viel-Castel (1881), Lays and Maincent (1882), were listed as domiciled at the gallery in the *livret*, or official catalogue.[38] Although Durand-Ruel began to sell his pictures by Bouguereau to Petit in 1866 – Durand-Ruel's father had been the artist's main dealer[39] – he continued to sell Bouguereau from time to time.

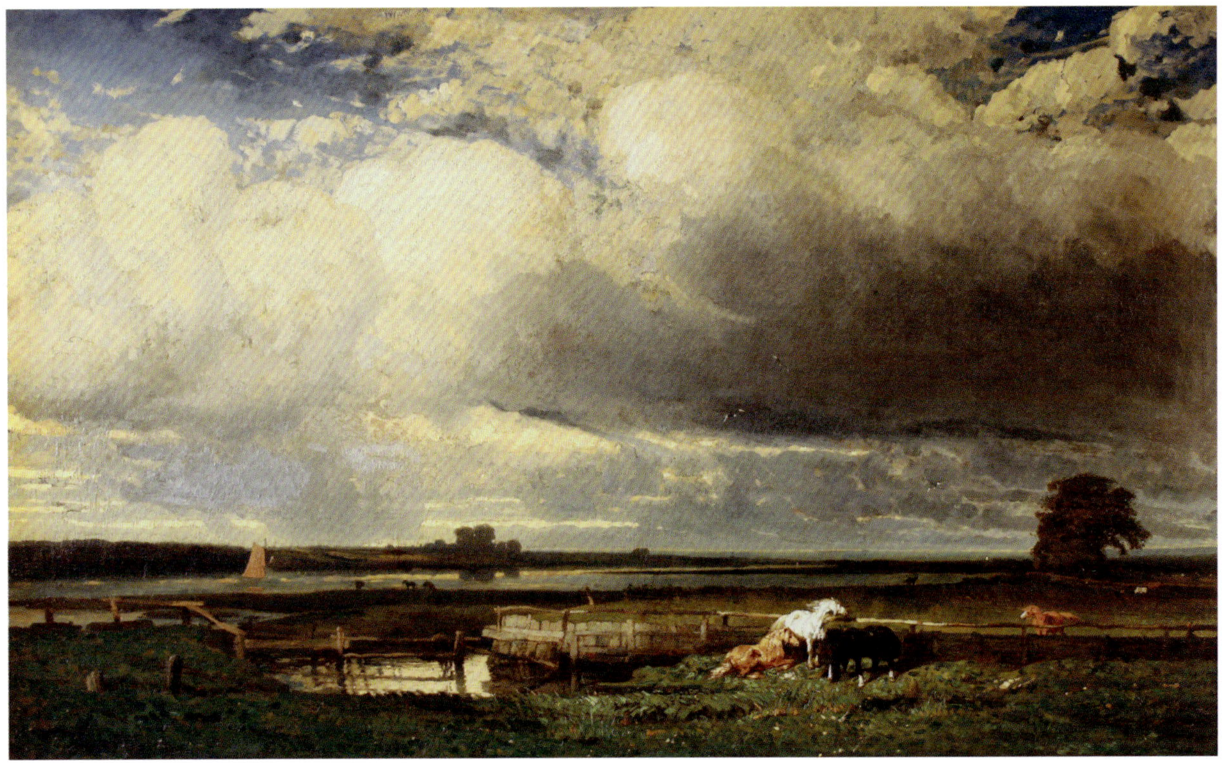

He wrote to Monet in 1883: 'This cheque is the price of a Bouguereau. You see that I have to sell bad painting to live, and to support my friends'.[40] The share made up by these painters, who were less of a financial burden than Corot, Delacroix and Rousseau, for example, became increasingly marginal during the 1870s,[41] and when Durand-Ruel had new capital at his disposal in the early 1880s, he admittedly purchased works by Vervée and Damoye and other lesser-known artists, but above all the Impressionists from 1881–2.[42]

The absence here of these artists, some of whom have now been forgotten, does not point to a desire on our part to hide any 'mistakes' made by the dealer,[43] but to the need to understand what it was that marked out his activity, vision and taste (see Paul-Louis Durand-Ruel and Flavie Durand-Ruel's essay, this book). Research undertaken for this project confirms that Durand-Ruel forged his identity as a dealer and collector with what he called the '*belle école de 1830*', followed by the painting of Manet and the Impressionists. In his eyes, the two generations were linked not only by aesthetic affinities but by the shared experience of a time lag between the creation of their works and their recognition and success. The gallery's commercial operations and exhibitions reflected, and may even have contributed to, the sense of continuity between these generations.

The exercise of choosing the corpus of artists for our exhibition and catalogue called for a drastic selection from among the thousands of pictures that passed through the gallery. Durand-Ruel's admiring description of the 'School of 1830' referred to Delacroix, as well as Corot, Millet, Rousseau, Diaz, Troyon, Daubigny and even his 'great friend Jules Dupré',[44] from whom he purchased the sumptuous *Landscape near Southampton* (fig. 6) for the considerable sum of 44,100 francs at the same time as Delacroix's *Sardanapalus* (see fig. 20), which he bought for 96,000 francs at the Wilson sale in 1873. Aware of the injustices we might commit, but trusting in the light that would be shed by Simon Kelly in his catalogue essay, we assembled a group of significant works by Delacroix, Rousseau, Corot and Courbet.

The Impressionists have been defined as the principal artists who took part in the exhibitions of the group between 1874 and 1886, with the exception of Caillebotte. This painter did indeed give some of his works to the dealer to exhibit, and the gallery hosted the posthumous tribute paid to him in 1895, but Durand-Ruel did not sell Caillebotte's work thereafter. To the Impressionists, we have added Manet, a tutelary figure whose fate at the hands of Durand-Ruel is indivisible from that of his younger colleagues. On the other hand, with the exception of Boudin (fig. 2) and Daubigny (see fig. 116) these precursors, who like Jongkind were extremely well-represented in Durand-Ruel's stock, have had to be passed over. Similarly, artists of the next generation, such as Maxime Maufra, André Moret, Georges d'Espagnat and Gustave Loiseau, who Durand-Ruel considered successors to the Impressionists, have not been included here; they are part of the much broader question of the gallery's role in the context of Post-Impressionism and the emergence of competitors such as Vollard, discussed in this catalogue by Joseph J. Rishel. Finally, Durand-Ruel's championing of new, innovative artists included Puvis de Chavannes, whose works he began to purchase at the same time as the Impressionists in 1872 (fig. 7) and to whom he would devote an important retrospective in 1887. The very nature of Puvis's production, as a painter of mural decorations, nevertheless involves different commercial practices than those of the Impressionists. Overall, we cannot stress enough that Durand-Ruel's role as

FIG. 6
Jules Dupré
Landscape near Southampton, 1835
Oil on canvas, 115 × 184 cm
Musée d'art et d'histoire Louis-Senlecq, l'Isle-Adam

FIG. 7
Pierre-Cécile Puvis de Chavannes
Peace, 1867
Oil on canvas, 108.9 × 148.6 cm
Philadelphia Museum of Art, Pennsylvania

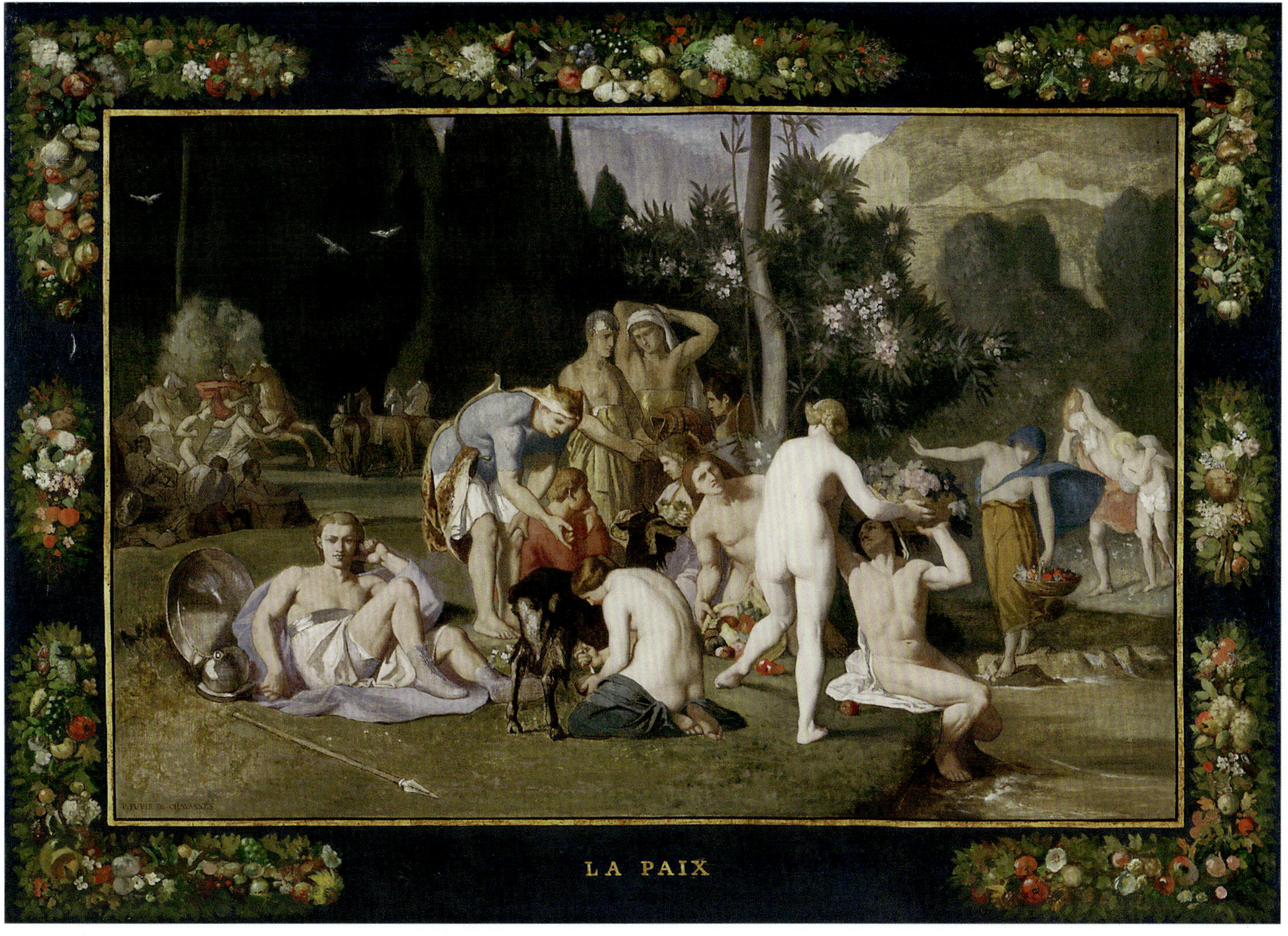

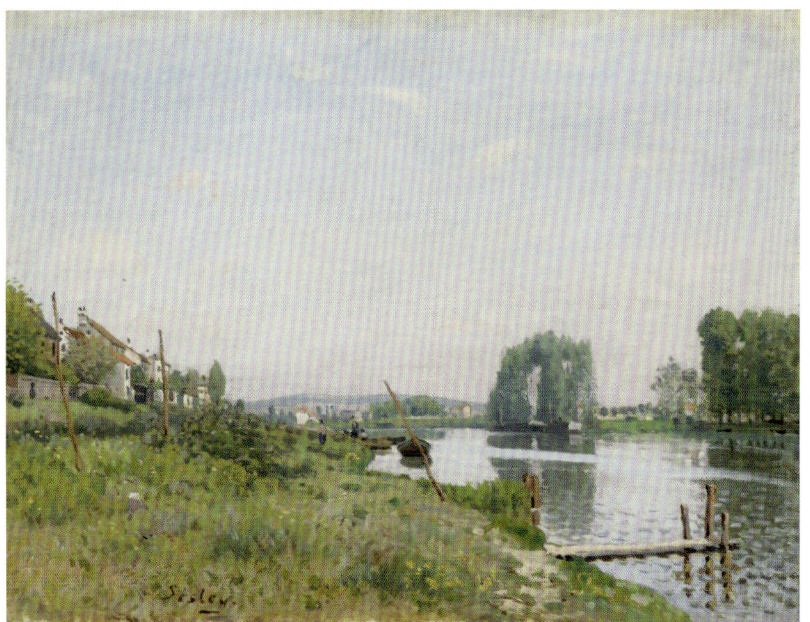

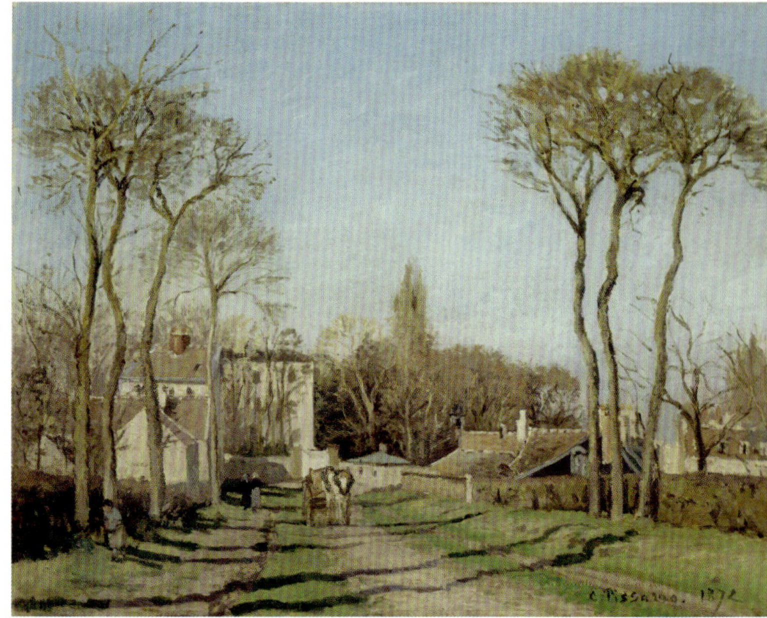

PAUL DURAND-RUEL, AN 'UNREPENTANT RISK-TAKER'

a dealer in modernity was not limited merely to the Impressionist avant-garde.

The balance among the artists selected strives to reflect the stock and choices of the dealer at different points in his career, while posing the question of his taste, which we have tried to identify through transactions, correspondence and his memoirs. As the viewer walks through the exhibition, they will notice the dominance of Renoir and Monet, whereas Cézanne, whose works Durand-Ruel modestly purchased in the 1890s, and Morisot, whose works were rarer on the market, are less in evidence. Degas is present throughout the exhibition, in keeping with the regular contact he maintained with the gallery, although this is less documented by correspondence. Although Durand-Ruel bought Impressionist paintings *en masse*, he had stated preferences and promoted some works more than others, sometimes keeping a distance, as with the Ingresque pictures by Renoir, who showed his *Large Bathers* (1887, Philadelphia Museum of Art) with Georges Petit, or Pissarro's Neo-Impressionist pictures and Dutch landscapes. 'This is not what I expected of you ... you were not at ease painting in a new country and the harmonies do not seem quite as accurate as usual',[45] the dealer wrote to Pissarro in 1894. Although the works displayed at the exhibition's three venues are present for the reasons explained in each catalogue entry, the overall selection, despite remaining subjective and dependent on the loans obtained, is an attempt to recreate a visual world, a taste perhaps, as well as the nature and evolution of the relationships between Durand-Ruel and the Impressionists.

Exhibition structure

As our starting point, we have chosen the late 1860s, when Paul Durand-Ruel, who in 1865 had succeeded his father as the head of a gallery with an international reputation, began to make his mark. He strengthened the presence of the so-called Barbizon School (Kelly, this book) and moved the gallery to the heart of the Parisian art market, to 16, rue Laffitte/11, rue Le Peletier, nicknamed *la rue des tableaux*, the street of pictures. His annual rent of 30,000 francs indicates the dealer's optimism and ambition for his gallery, which kept this address until 1924, two years after his death. Purchases and sales gradually began to take precedence over the rental of works, a widespread practice evident in the archives, albeit in a more residual fashion, until the 1880s. The same evolution can be noticed in the declining sale of artist supplies, photographs, engravings, sculptures[46] and religious items, as well as framing and restoration work. The gallery sometimes handled exhibition labels for certain clients or took care of

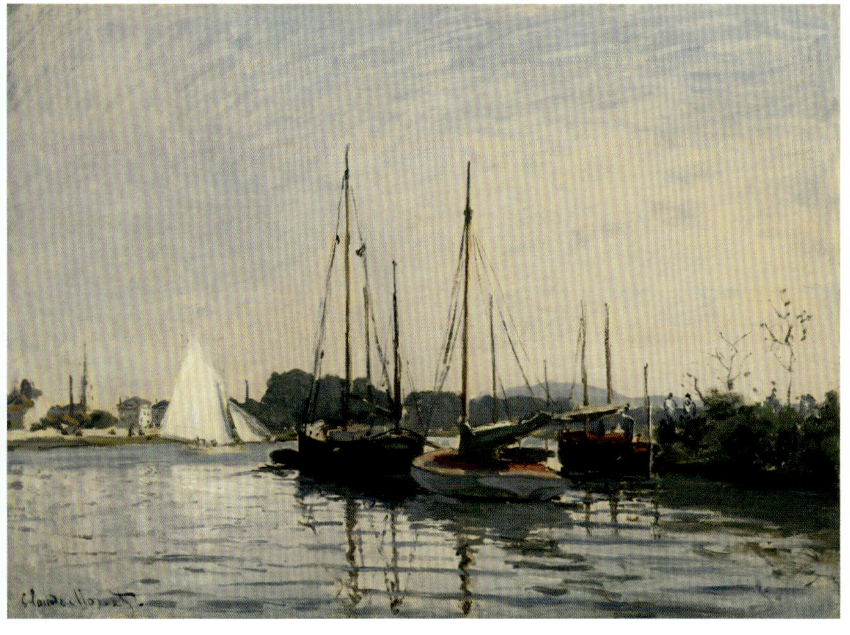

FIG. 8
Alfred Sisley
L'Ile Saint-Denis, 1872
Oil on canvas, 50.5 × 65 cm
Musée d'Orsay, Paris
[cat. 90]

Camille Pissarro
Entrance to the Village of Voisins, 1872
Oil on canvas, 46 × 55.5 cm
Musée d'Orsay, Paris
[cat. 63]

Claude Monet
Pleasure Boats, 1872–3
Oil on canvas, 49 × 65 cm
Musée d'Orsay, Paris
[cat. 35]

hanging their collections. This great diversity of activity and clientele, which saw French and European aristocracy, Parisian bourgeoisie, American collectors, religious institutions and provincial notables rub shoulders, began to change in the early 1870s.

The time Durand-Ruel spent in London in 1870–1, studied here by Anne Robbins, did indeed mark a break, due to his meeting Monet and Pissarro in the city, but also because of his immersion in the English market, with which the gallery had been in contact since the early nineteenth century through the art dealer John Arrowsmith.[47] Durand-Ruel's return to Paris confirmed the redirection initiated in England, and continued with his discovery and support for the 'new' painting through the purchase of works by Manet, Degas, Sisley and Renoir in 1872. Although the turning point of 1870–1 was decisive for the dealer, it was somewhat late in the day if we consider that these artists had been exhibiting at the Salon since the mid-1860s. Monet had been particularly successful in 1866 with *Camille* (see fig. 107) and Manet enjoyed a reputation for scandal, which did not prevent Zola from heralding his commercial success, anticipating the model used by Durand-Ruel in 1872: 'I am so sure that Manet will be one of the masters of tomorrow that I should believe I had made a good bargain, had I the money, in buying all his canvases today. In fifty years they will sell for fifteen or twenty times more'.[48] Dealers had begun to take an interest in the Impressionists in the 1860s: Cadart supported Monet's debut, as well as Morisot and Manet, who also experienced their early success at his gallery – Cadart exhibited Manet's *Battle of the U.S.S. 'Kearsarge'* in 1864 (see fig. 21), for example.[49] The same can be said of Beugniet and Détrimont, with whom Morisot was in contact in 1867–8, as well as 'Père' Martin, Febvre, from whom Durand-Ruel bought *Boy with a Sword* (see fig. 91), and Latouche, who exhibited works by Monet and sold Pissarros, Sisleys and Boudins to Durand-Ruel in 1872.[50] Durand-Ruel was therefore part of a pre-existing but hesitant commercial network, which he turned on its head, not by making one-off purchases, but through the acquisition of 10 or 20 pictures a year from Sisley, Monet and Pissarro (fig. 8; Distel, Zarobell, this book). This section of the exhibition brings together an exceptional collection of fresh and luminous pictures painted with an evident freedom in the footsteps of Corot; Durand-Ruel was the only dealer to exhibit such paintings in significant numbers in the early 1870s in Paris and London, where they were strategically mixed with works by recognised and unthreatening artists.

The archives also tell us that this phase was brief, quickly followed by a crisis that threatened the gallery's existence. Galenson and Jensen have already pointed

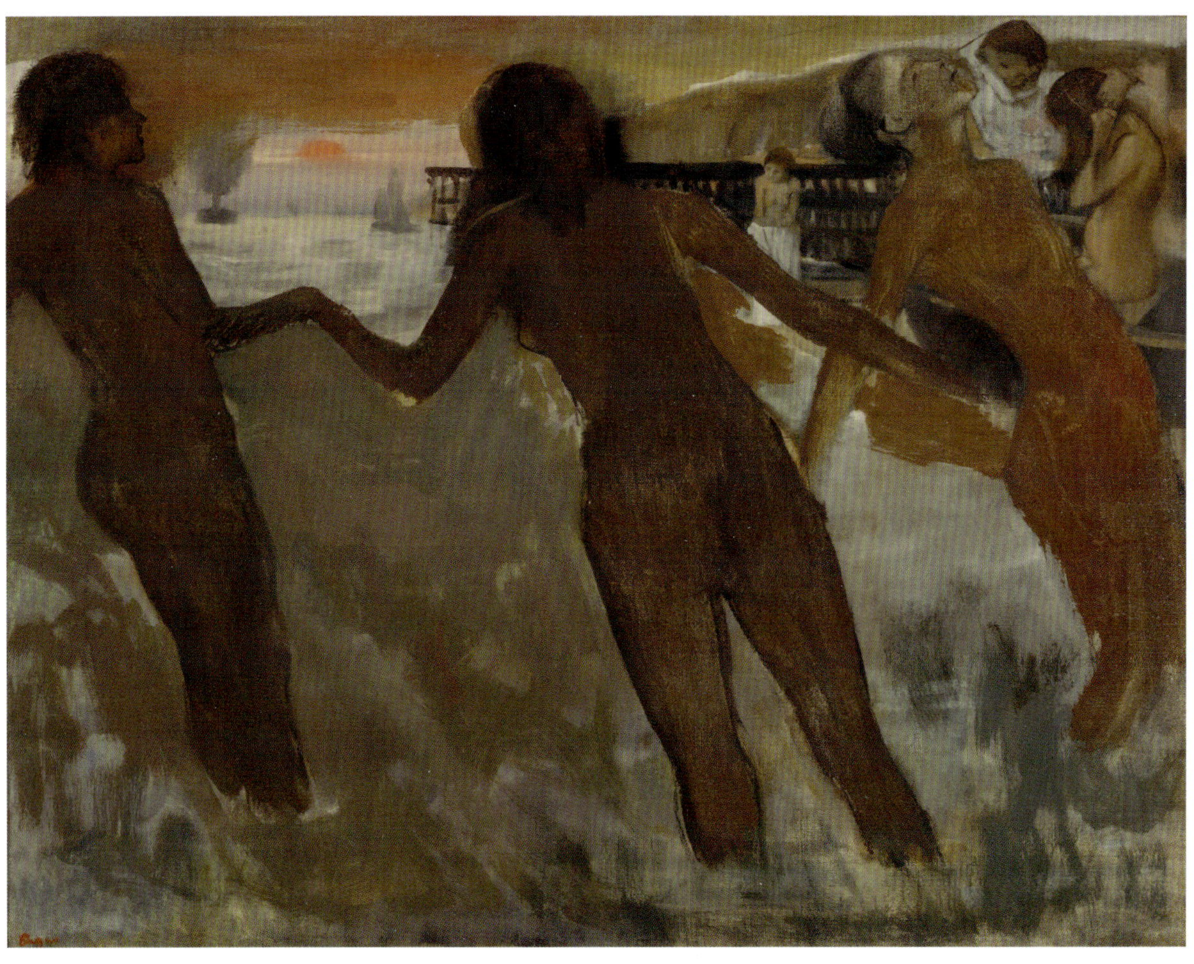

PAUL DURAND-RUEL, AN 'UNREPENTANT RISK-TAKER'

out that the dealer was in fact absent from the history of Impressionism at its most crucial points as he ceased purchasing from 1875 to 1881 – during five of the group's eight collective exhibitions. The gallery's activity slowed in all areas: fewer than 10 sales were recorded in 1879–80. Durand-Ruel purchased 18 pictures at the first and disastrous sale organised by Renoir, Monet, Morisot and Sisley in 1875,[51] but refused to organise the following one: 'The particularly unusual circumstances in which I momentarily find myself are forcing me to exercise great restraint and often prevent me from doing what I would like ... There may be compensation for you in taking a man who is not accused of being your accomplice, as I am'.[52] However, he rented out three rooms in his gallery to the Impressionists for their second collective exhibition in 1876 (figs 9 and 10) for the sum of 1,500 francs.[53] The exhibition was accompanied by a brochure written by the critic and novelist Edmond Duranty. Considered the movement's only manifesto, it was entitled *La Nouvelle Peinture. A propos du groupe d'artistes qui expose dans les galeries Durand-Ruel* (The New Painting: On the Group of Artists Exhibiting in the Durand-Ruel Gallery) and publicly associated the painters with their 'accomplice'. The event gave rise to a number of articles, and the gallery was visited by Henry James, August Strindberg and Stéphane Mallarmé, who subsequently wrote about Impressionism for the first time. This episode is our first case study, which illustrates the importance of exhibitions to the dealer's work. Durand-Ruel's exhibitions were in fact designed as a way of promoting his painters, and the series he organised in 1883, when he was experiencing another financial crisis, is revealing. The difficulties encountered and the meagre commercial results of the monographic exhibitions on Boudin, Monet, Renoir, Pissarro and Sisley (Patry, this book), contrast with the success of the solo exhibitions of Renoir, Pissarro and Monet in 1891–2, which heralded the recognition of Impressionism. For example, *Young Girls at the Piano* by Renoir, the first Impressionist purchase for the Musée du Luxembourg,

FIG. 9
Edgar Degas
Peasant Girls bathing in the Sea at Dusk, about 1869–75
Oil on canvas, 65 × 84 cm
Private collection, Ireland
[cat. 14]

FIG. 10
Camille Pissarro
Farm at Montfoucault, 1874
Oil on canvas, 60 × 73.5 cm
Musées d'Art et d'Histoire, Geneva
[cat. 67]

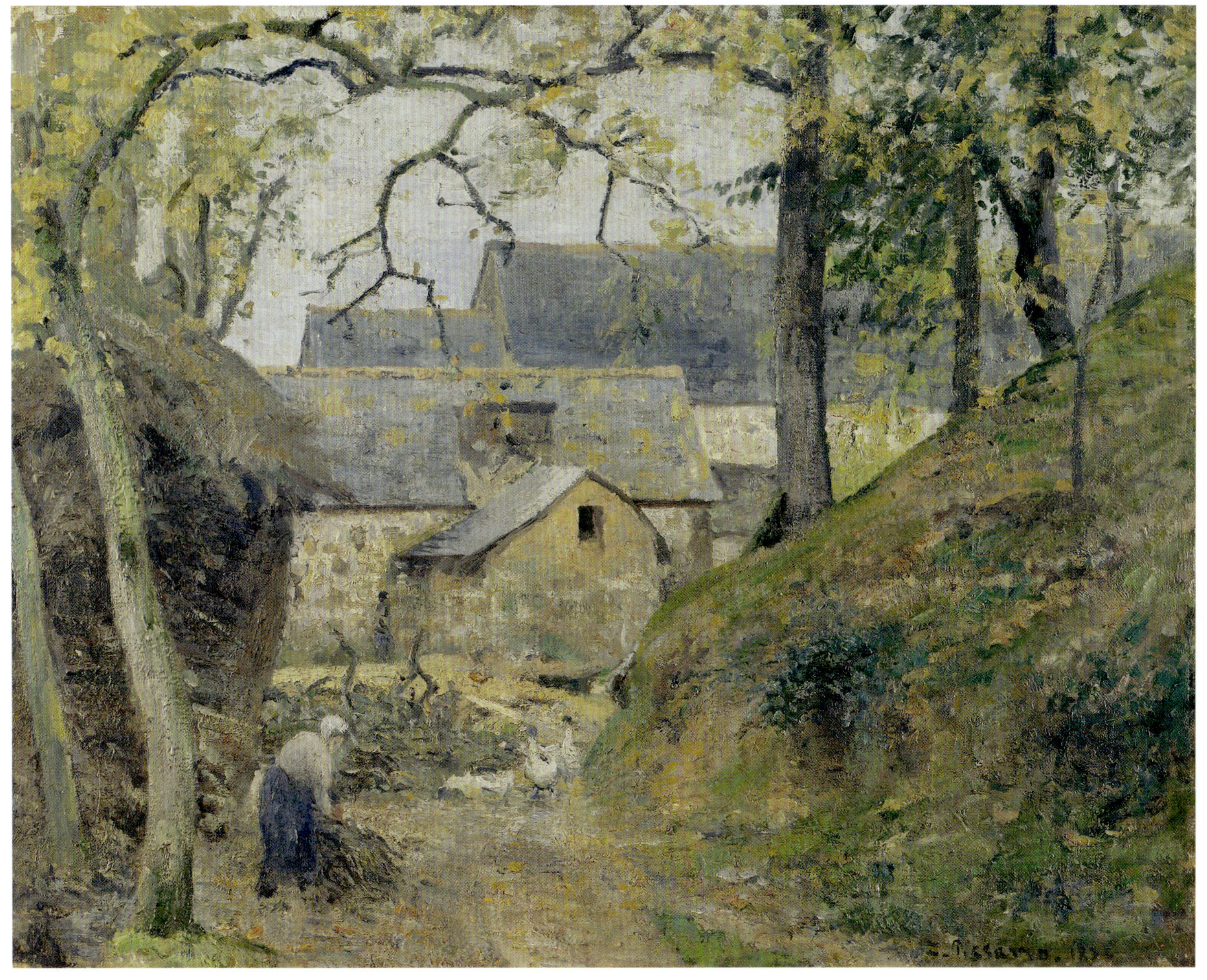

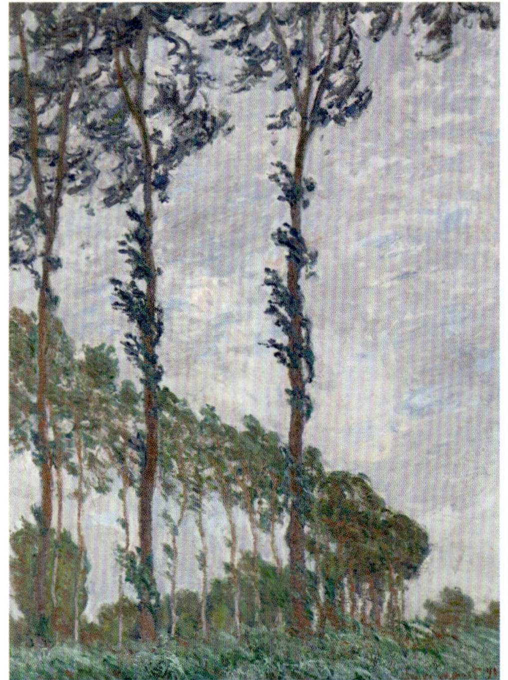

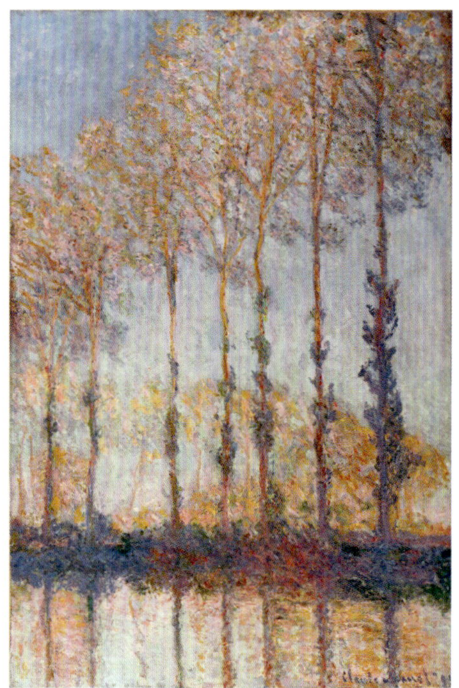

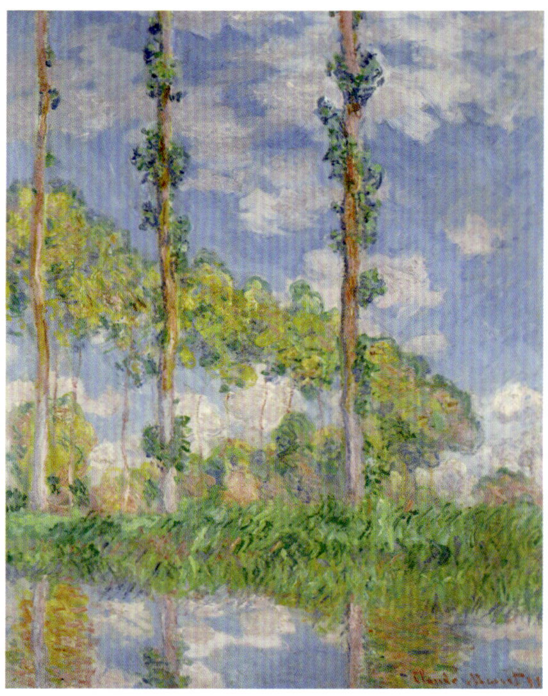

was exhibited in the gallery before being hung in the museum in 1892. The case of Monet is particularly significant to this turnaround and is our second case study: with the Poplars series that marked the rise in the artist's popularity, the gallery space also became an essential component of an aesthetic project in which the pictures were designed to be viewed together (figs 11–14).

The international spread of Impressionism

In Durand-Ruel's eyes, the march towards recognition came about through the conquest of new markets, and we have chosen to devote a large section of the exhibition and this catalogue to the international expansion of the avant-garde art trade. Durand-Ruel relentlessly pursued opportunities in Germany, England, North America, Austria, Belgium, Holland, Russia and Sweden. Loans to exhibitions in London, Vienna and Chicago, exhibitions in the galleries of his colleagues – McLean, Gurlitt and Eastman Chase – or in hotels in the United States and Germany, efficiently introduced the Impressionists to foreign markets (Robbins, Hansen, Thompson, this book). Preceded by Knoedler, Goupil, and more modestly Cadart, who sent an 'enormous cargo' of works by Courbet, Rousseau and Corot to New York, Boston and Philadelphia[54] in 1865 and 1866, and Legrand in 1878, Durand-Ruel was neither the only nor the first to take this route,[55] but the above attempts were short-lived and cannot be compared to the energy and persistence of his efforts. The only rival of similar international calibre at that time was Goupil & Co. (which became Boussod, Valadon & Co. in 1884), based in Paris, The Hague, London, Berlin, Brussels, Vienna and New York, which began to show Impressionist pictures in 1885.[56] This exhibition demonstrates the extent to which the Durand-Ruel Gallery's international expansion was crucial to the gradual acceptance of Impressionism, particularly in the United States, with the 1886 exhibition and the opening of a branch in New York in 1887. Our research (Thompson, this book) also outlines an image of a gallery less focused on New York than previously thought, as Durand-Ruel courted markets in Chicago and Boston in 1888, as well as Pittsburgh and Denver during the following decade. The gallery's relationships with collectors, particularly the Philadelphia-based networks around the merchant Adolph Borie and Alexander Cassatt's colleagues in the rail industry, and in Chicago, with the socially active Bertha and Potter Palmer, Martin A. Ryerson, Charles Hutchinson, Charles

FIG. 11
Claude Monet
Wind Effect, Sequence of Poplars, 1891
Oil on canvas, 100 × 74 cm
Musée d'Orsay, Paris
[cat. 56]

FIG. 12
Claude Monet
Poplars on the Bank of the Epte River, 1891
Oil on canvas, 100.3 × 65.2 cm
Philadelphia Museum of Art, Pennsylvania
[cat. 53]

FIG. 13
Claude Monet
Poplars in the Sun, 1891
Oil on canvas, 93 × 73.5 cm
The National Museum of Western Art, Tokyo
[cat. 57]

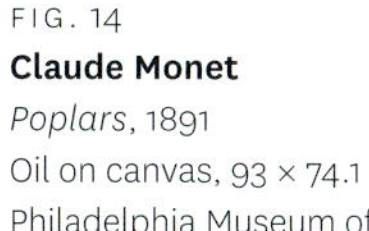

FIG. 14
Claude Monet
Poplars, 1891
Oil on canvas, 93 × 74.1 cm
Philadelphia Museum of Art, Pennsylvania
[cat. 58]

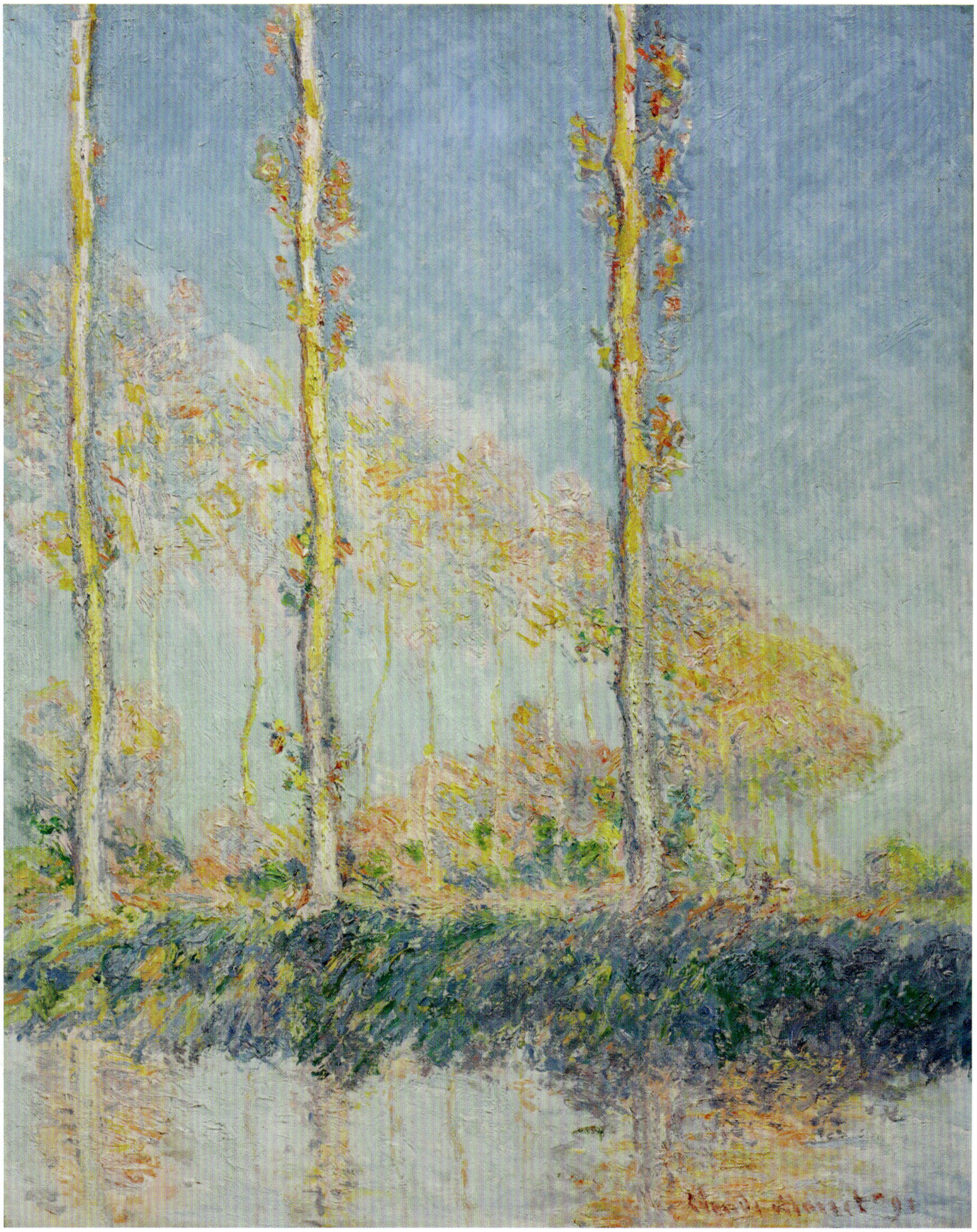

T. Yerkes and others, contributed to forging and diffusing a taste for Impressionism, which became a fashionable 'must-have' for any enlightened connoisseur.

Our assessment also reveals that the eventual success of Durand-Ruel was more mixed and precarious than his memoirs and other retrospective accounts have suggested. The early years of expansion abroad were marked by debts, financial difficulties, unfavourable reviews, and exhibitions or auctions that saw significant quantities of works left unsold. Although these various international experiences were of limited, if any, financial benefit, they allowed Durand-Ruel to patiently cultivate collectors one by one, so much so that by the late 1890s hundreds of Impressionist pictures had been purchased by individuals as well as by museums in Europe and the United States. The dealer in fact saw museums as a different kind of customer, selling works to them at lower or non-existent margins in order to recruit new clients from among their visitors. 'Museums are our best publicity', he declared to Cassirer,[57] his intermediary in Germany, where the particularly close relationship between Durand-Ruel and certain collectors, such as Hugo von Tschudi, has been studied by Dorothee Hansen in this catalogue.

France was a different case. For the period in question, only the Musée des Beaux-Arts in Lyon purchased Impressionist paintings from Durand-Ruel (fig. 15).[58] The dealer and his early biographers made the opposition of the Beaux-Arts administration part of his myth, while in truth the situation was more complex. Although Durand-Ruel did not force open the doors of museums by donating Impressionist pictures, as did some of his best clients, such as Isaac de Camondo or François Depeaux in Rouen, he sold *Dance at Bougival* to the latter on the condition that the work would eventually be given to the Rouen museum (fig. 5). He was sometimes able to recommend a purchase, suggesting a Millet or selling two large Duprés in 1881, for example,[59] or by working on behalf of his painters, as revealed in a letter from Boudin: 'I have an official commission!... Yes, my friend, the Under-secretary asked for me through Durand-Ruel, who shamed him into giving me this commission'.[60] Relations nevertheless remained distant between the dealer, a Catholic monarchist, and the institutions of the Third Republic. By intervening too much, Durand-Ruel could have been suspected of further bolstering the popularity and prices of his artists. Investigations into his practice of sending 'modern' Impressionist pictures outside Paris and to provincial clientele has yet to be carried out: apart from Saulnier in Bordeaux, Flornoy in Nantes, Vasnier in Reims, Depeaux in Rouen, and Van der Velde and Senn in Le Havre, other more modest connections also existed, such as with Lespiault, the director of the local museum in Nérac, a small market town in Lot-et-Garonne, who rented a Sisley in 1884,[61] as well as with exhibitions and local *salons*, which further research in years to come will no doubt help clarify.[62] A study of the Durand-Ruel Archives reveals the importance of circulating works, something that was critical for their reception as well as for their dissemination, if we accept, like Durand-Ruel, that their meaning changed depending on the context in which they were displayed.

The connections between Durand-Ruel's public and private convictions is another theme of our exhibition. Beginning in the mid-1880s, the Durand-Ruel family apartment located at 35, rue de Rome in Paris became 'a small museum of Impressionism'.[63] The dealer commissioned decorative panels from Monet for it (see figs 26–32) and in 1885 a visit to the personal collection made a powerful impression on the New York entrepreneur James Sutton. The dealer assembled almost 370 works for himself, including Renoir's famous *Luncheon of the Boating Party*, now the jewel in the crown of the Phillips Collection, Washington (see fig. 33). It was in the family dining room, during a lunch with

FIG. 15
Pierre-Auguste Renoir
Woman playing a Guitar, 1896–7
Oil on canvas, 81 × 65 cm
Musée des Beaux-Arts, Lyon
[cat. 82]

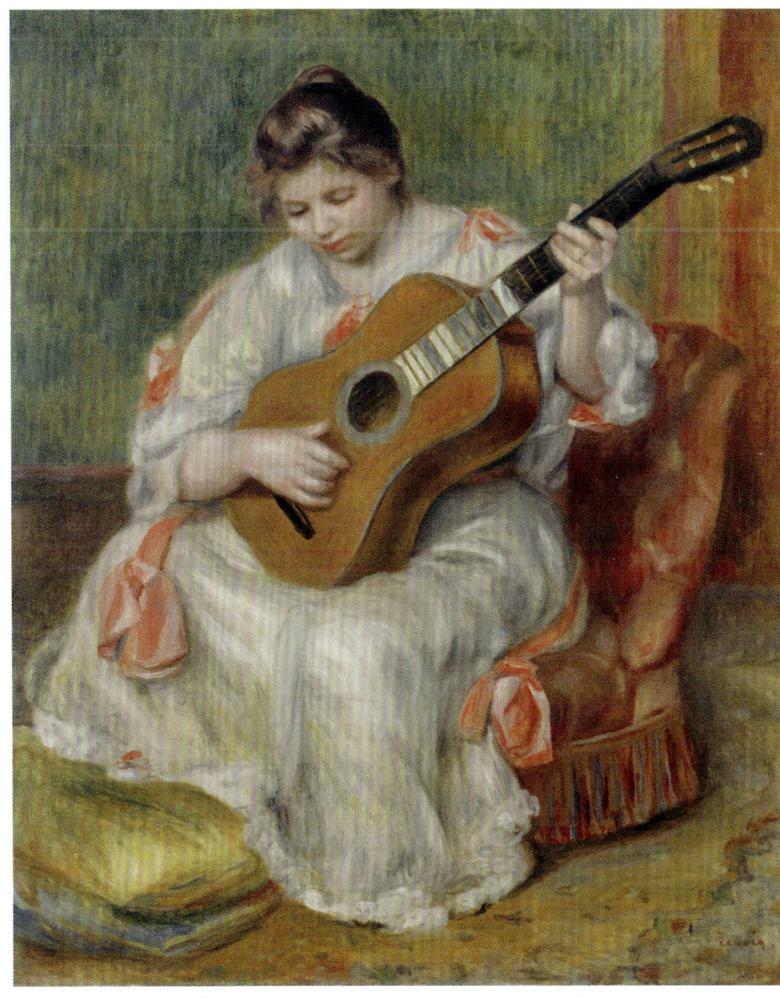

Joseph Durand-Ruel in 1923, that Duncan and Marjorie Phillips fell under the spell of the picture, buying it some months later.[64] In 1898, the dealer began opening his apartment to visitors; opening times and entrance fees were even listed in the famous Baedeker guide to Paris in 1900.[65]

A 'magnificent act of faith'[66] and a place in which to showcase works, the family apartment married the private and commercial spheres. We find a similar combination in the exhibition Durand-Ruel organised at the Grafton Galleries in London in 1905, which we have chosen as the culmination of the period under examination. With 315 works, including 196 from his personal collection, this retrospective of Impressionism was the most complete ever organised, intended to establish its importance by offering a historical reading of the movement (the majority of the artists exhibited were no longer alive). Its importance has long been underestimated. Douglas Cooper accounted it a 'failure',[67] not without reason, as only a handful of works found buyers. His particular analysis reveals the broader tendency among British and British-based critics and connoisseurs of French Modernism to give the central role in the history of the reception of this art to Roger Fry – who organised his exhibition *Manet and the Post-Impressionists* in 1910, in the same Grafton Galleries – and to his disciple Samuel Courtauld. Our research qualifies this view by pointing out that five years before Fry's show, Durand-Ruel had exhibited in the Grafton Galleries not eight Manets, as in the 1910 exhibition, but no fewer than 19, including the study for *Bar at the Folies-Bergère* (see fig. 118). The large picture at the Courtauld Gallery in London, which was not included, was however part of Fry's 1910 exhibition, lent by a consortium that included Durand-Ruel himself.[68] The French dealer's role in making modern foreign painting available to the British public should be fully acknowledged.

The preparation of this catalogue has also provided an opportunity to gain a better understanding of the history of particular works of art. Some passed through the gallery briefly, others remained for several decades prior to being sold, but not before being exhibited in France and abroad, used as collateral, photographed or recommended to collectors. These methods were all part of what Durand-Ruel called his '*essais*' – tactics employed in order to 'impose' (as he put it) his 'highly original and highly knowledgeable'[69] painters, in keeping with his new concept of being a dealer. Although this exhibition cannot claim to exhaust as vast and fascinating a subject as the relationship between Durand-Ruel and Impressionism, we hope it will be a step towards a new portrait of a truly visionary dealer, an 'unrepentant risk-taker'[70] as his friend Mirbeau described him.

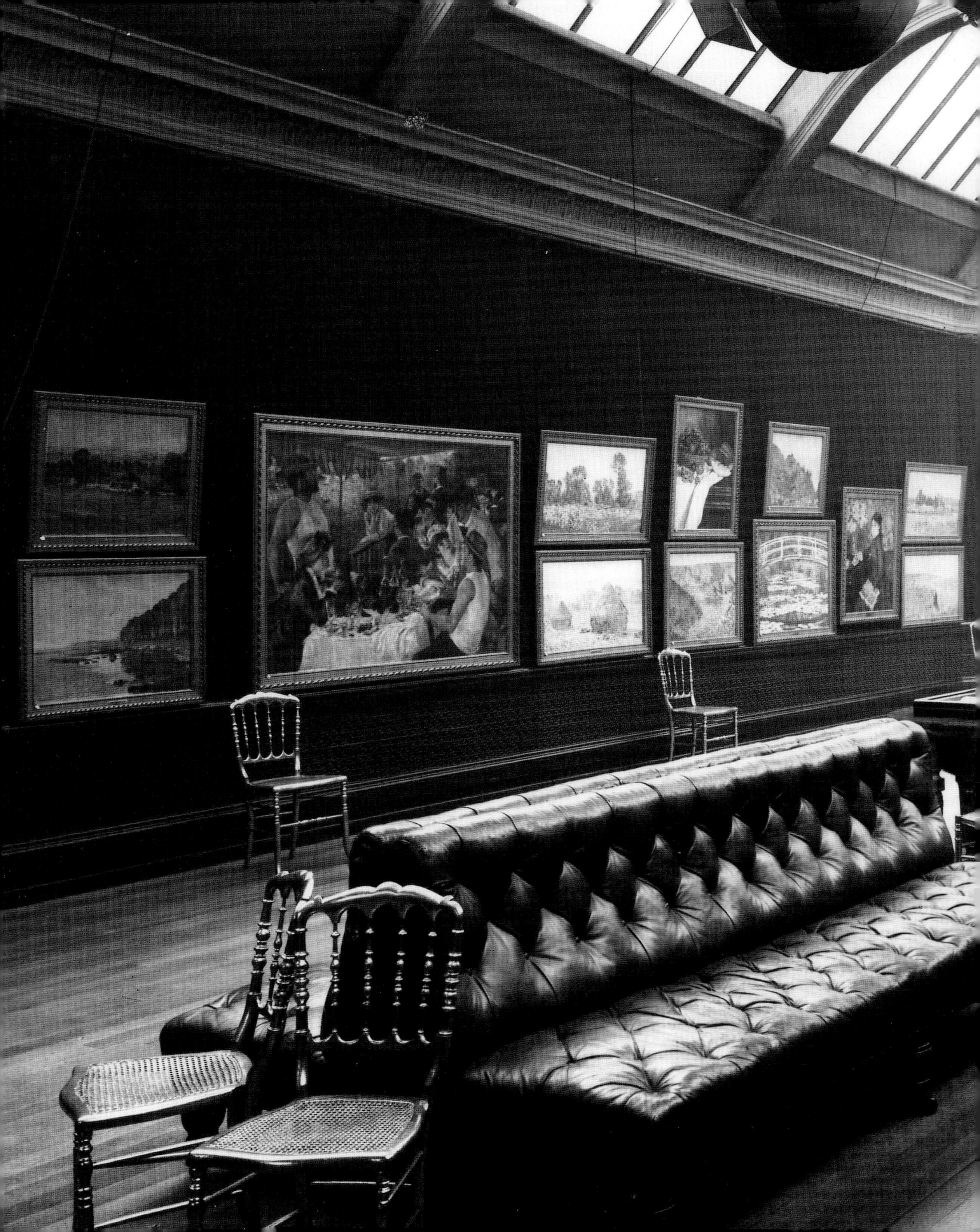

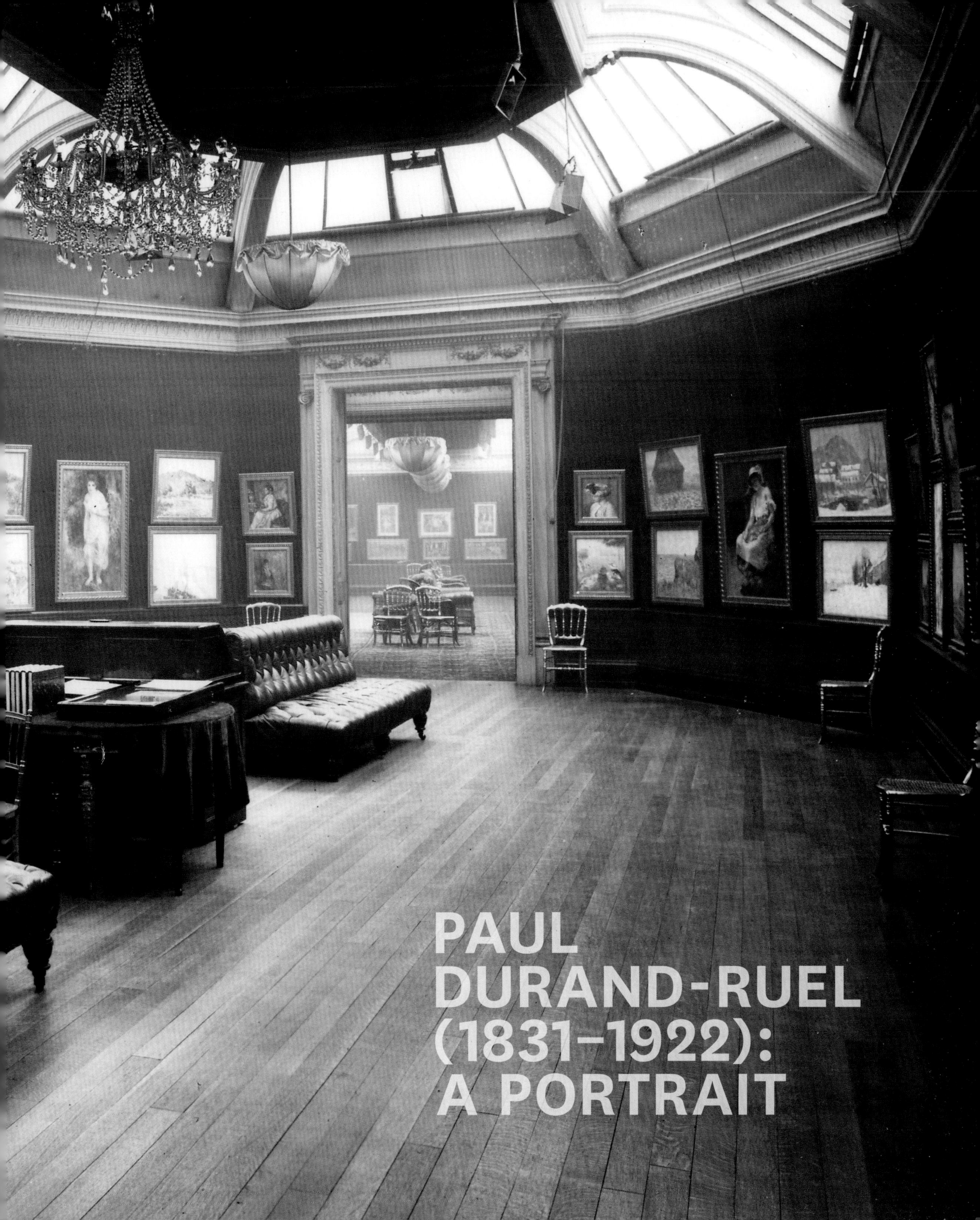

PAUL DURAND-RUEL (1831–1922): A PORTRAIT

Paul Durand-Ruel (1831–1922): A Portrait

Paul-Louis Durand-Ruel and
Flavie Durand-Ruel

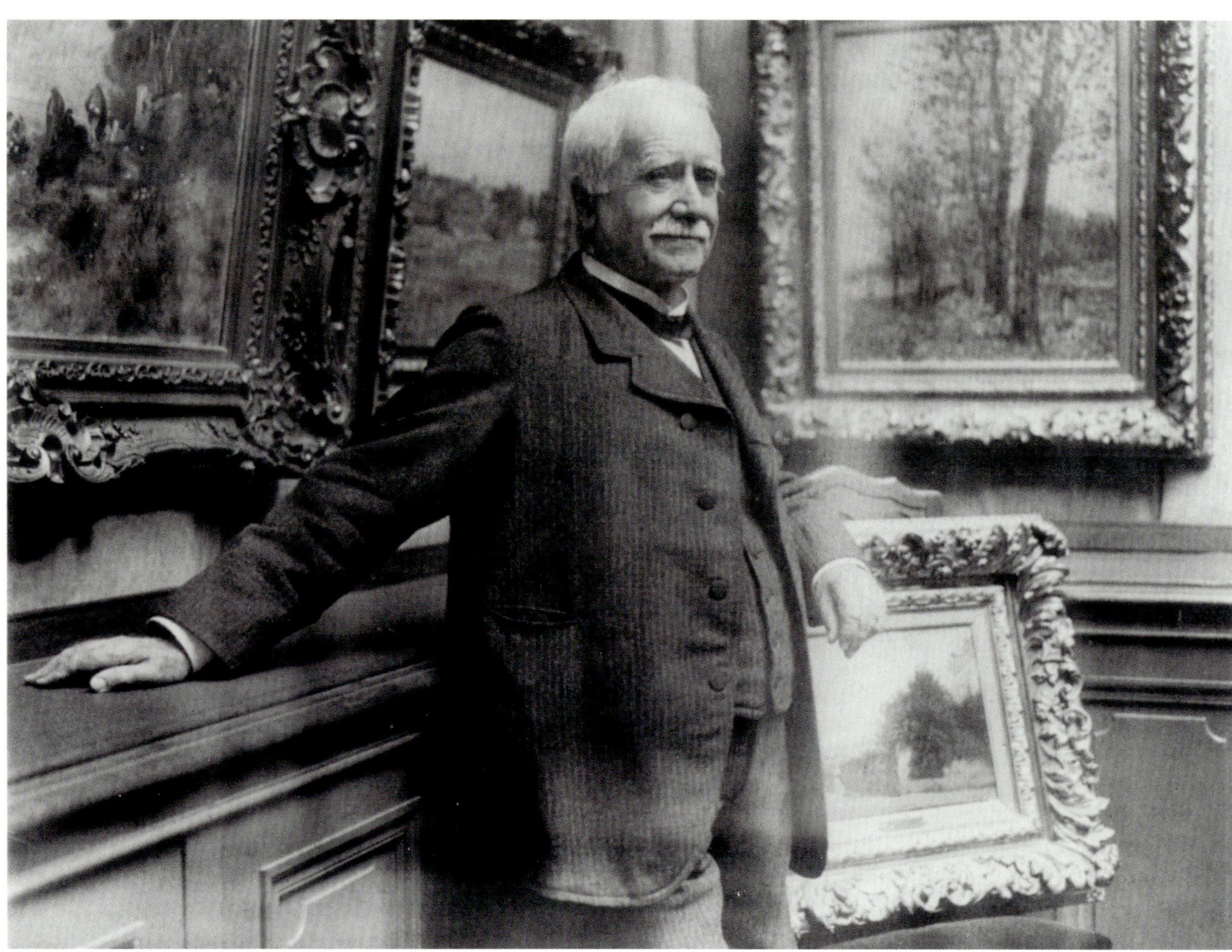

FIG. 16
Paul Durand-Ruel in his gallery, taken by Dornac, about 1910
Silver gelatin print
Archives Durand-Ruel

FIG. 17
The grand salon with *Dance in the City* by Renoir
Photograph
Archives Durand-Ruel

'The principal works by these innovators should be on display at the Palais du Luxembourg. But instead, its walls are decorated with banalities. M. Durand-Ruel has done what the State, disdainful of this new art, was unable to do. For the delight of his eyes and the charm of what lies within, with the steadfast passion of an enlightened collector, he has assembled the canvases most representative of the talent of these painters. He has created the most wonderful museum of contemporary painting in France.' These words were written by Gustave Geffroy, quoted by Georges Lecomte in 1892 in the introduction to his book *L'Art impressionniste d'après la collection privée de M. Durand-Ruel.*[1] Yet Paul Durand-Ruel would say the following of his collection: 'Do not congratulate me for having assembled this Impressionist collection ... it is to the collectors that we should be grateful. Which pictures do they reject at first, regardless of the painter? Those in which there is an abundance of the alleged defects that later come to be known as characteristic qualities. Whenever I kept a picture of this kind on display for too long, I would lose patience and take it home. This is the reason why there are so many highly original works here'.[2]

Paul Durand-Ruel's collection is a wonderful tribute to the artists he discovered, supported, defended and exhibited, despite opposition from all sides for more than 20 years, before their talent was recognised by the public and art institutions. A great innovator, both in his artistic tastes and strategy as a dealer, Durand-Ruel revolutionised the history of art. A champion of the artists of the 1830 and Barbizon Schools in particular, Durand-Ruel defended them for more than 10 years before their art was accepted. Thereafter, he discovered and promoted the Impressionists with the same fervour. He would say of these artists: 'They cannot be found on the benches of the Ecole des Beaux-Arts or in academic

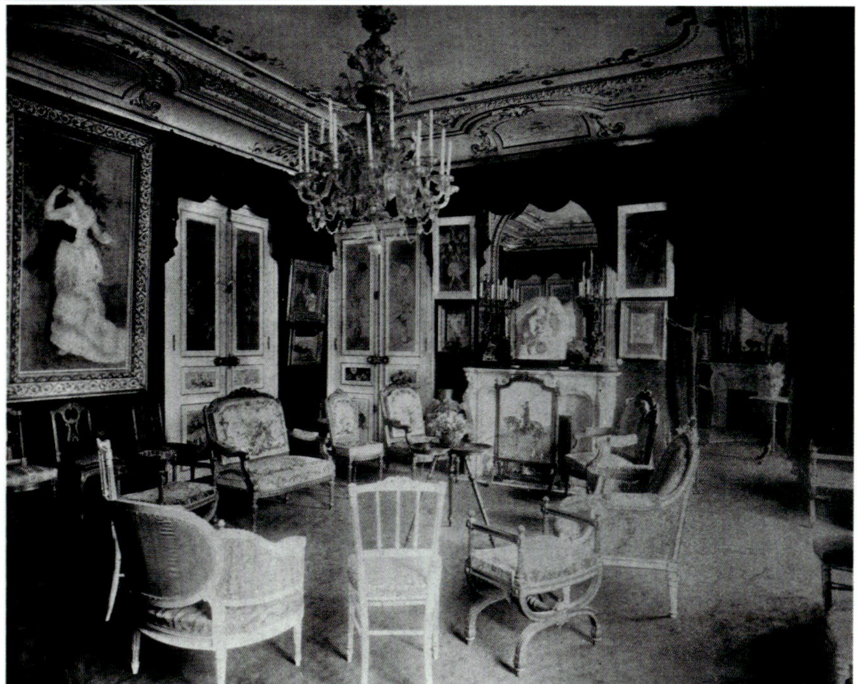

circles. They will be found among artists who seek for inspiration only within themselves, by contemplating the ever-renewed wonders of nature, and by closely studying masterful works'.[3]

Origins of the dynasty

Paul Durand-Ruel's character and convictions were handed down from his family. His maternal grandfather, François Hyacinthe Ruel (born in 1760), was a royal notary in Belgentier (Var), near Toulon, when the French Revolution broke out in 1789; the young public official was forced to emigrate to Italy with his family, where he made a living by giving French lessons. After returning to France a little too early,

RUE ET PORTE SAINT-JACQUES, N° 174, A PARIS,
VENTE ET LOCATION
DE LAVIS ET AQUARELLES.

DURAND-RUEL,
MARCHAND DE PAPIERS,

Tient la Fourniture des Bureaux et des Colléges, et tout ce qui concerne le Commerce de la PAPETERIE. Grand Assortiment d'Objets relatifs à la Peinture, au Lavis et au Dessin; Couleurs à l'huile; Toiles, Brosses, Palettes, Chevalets, Boîtes de campagne; Couleurs anglaises de Newman's, Cartons de Bristol et d'ivoire, Papier anglais et de Chine, Sepia de Rome, Ivoire pour Miniature, Cartons tendus, Bordures dorées, Encre de Chine, Pinceaux fins pour Lavis, Godets, Styratores, Passe-Partout, etc.

Nota. Il fait l'Encadrement, se charge de l'Impression en Taille-Douce et en Lithographie, et expédie pour la Province et l'Étranger.

FIG. 18
Advertisement for the shop owned by Jean Durand and Marie Ruel
Printed on paper
Archives Durand-Ruel

he was imprisoned under Robespierre but saved from the guillotine by the Thermidorian Reaction. He then settled in Paris, where he became secretary to Maréchal Soult and later secretary at the Ecole de Droit. Stories of these events left Paul Durand-Ruel with a hatred of the French Revolution and a profound attachment to the monarchy.

In order to provide for their daughter Marie Ferdinande, in 1825 François Hyacinthe Ruel and his wife purchased the stock of a large stationery shop located at 174, rue Saint-Jacques from friends, the Guillot associates; the shop was managed by a particularly competent employee, Jean Marie Fortuné Durand. The young couple liked each other and got married, joining their surnames to form the trading name 'Durand-Ruel'.[4] Jean Durand came from a family of winemakers from Solers (Seine-et-Marne) that had also been displaced by the events of 1789.

A passionate monarchist, Paul Durand-Ruel missed no opportunity to rail against 'the dreadful revolution of 1789'[5] or to deplore universal suffrage: 'In a democracy, everything goes awry and the blind claim to be steering the boat. The result is clear to see'.[6] But his patriotism forced him to overcome these differences of opinion; he maintained a friendly relationship with Clemenceau, despite their opposing political views. He wrote to 'The Tiger' when he was appointed prime minister in the dark days of 1917: 'Dear Sir, I am requested by many artists and lovers of art, all of whom are excellent Catholics and patriots as we all should be, to express our ardent good wishes for the success of your sublime mission to restore the inner peace that will facilitate, with God's protection, the final victory over our enemies. Your old friend, Paul Durand-Ruel'.[7] After the death of the art dealer, Clemenceau wrote: 'Durand-Ruel spared Monet much grief by freeing him to remain himself, despite the harassment of mediocrities. We owe him a debt of gratitude'.[8]

A Catholic and a patriot, Paul Durand-Ruel was an *antidreyfusard* (alongside Degas, Renoir and Rodin, but in opposition to Monet and Pissarro). However, this position did not prevent him, right in the midst of the '*affaire*', from inviting Pissarro, who was Jewish, to the wedding of his eldest son, Joseph,[9] or from instigating joint deals with the Bernheim-Jeunes.

A militant Catholic

The faith of the Durands was just as strong as that of the Ruels. Young Paul (born in 1831) would remain a practising Catholic throughout his life, something that would lead to his arrest in 1881[10] for protesting against laws suppressing religious congregations. However, his militancy was devoid of sectarianism and he championed artists regardless of their political ideas or religious beliefs. This allowed him to illegally conceal works the Communard Gustave Courbet entrusted to him in 1873 in an attempt to prevent their confiscation by the State, and to support both the atheist republican, Claude Monet, and the Jewish anarchist, Camille Pissarro.

Paul Durand-Ruel's committed Catholicism, which inspired and supported him throughout his life, was in keeping with the teachings of Lamennais, Ozanam and Albert de Mun. Very strict when it came to doctrine (he attended Mass every morning), Durand-Ruel's attention was focused on those around him: 'The fortune that divine Providence has placed in our hands does not belong to us; this should never be forgotten, we are merely those who dispense it ... It is precisely because a great many of those who possess wealth have forgotten

FIG. 19
Charles-François Daubigny
The main showroom of the Durand-Ruel Gallery, 1845
Etching, 21.5 × 13 cm
Archives Durand-Ruel

these truths that the poor too often have plausible reasons to complain and pretexts to revolt'.[11] And also: 'We are on this earth, not for our amusement and to think only of ourselves and our loved ones, but to do good all around us, within the limits of our power. This is why I so admired the articles by M. de Mun and his apostolate among workers and young people'.[12] It is clear that Durand-Ruel was not a man to bind himself to the dominant ideology: a militant monarchist under the Republic[13] and a militant Catholic under an anti-clerical regime, he displayed the same profound conviction in his defence of controversial painters.

The early days of the Durand-Ruel Gallery

Paul Durand-Ruel learnt the art dealer's trade from his father. In 1825, Jean Durand-Ruel decided to add artists' materials to his stock and agreed to the principle of exchanging supplies for works. This trade in pictures soon became sizeable. Jean Durand-Ruel was in tune with the artists of his time; he was interested in the English watercolourists whose works he exhibited, including Bonington. He also appreciated the work of his contemporaries, such as Daumier, Barye and the painters of the Barbizon School, who his son would later defend with body and soul. The Durand-Ruel Gallery specialised in contemporary painting and grew in

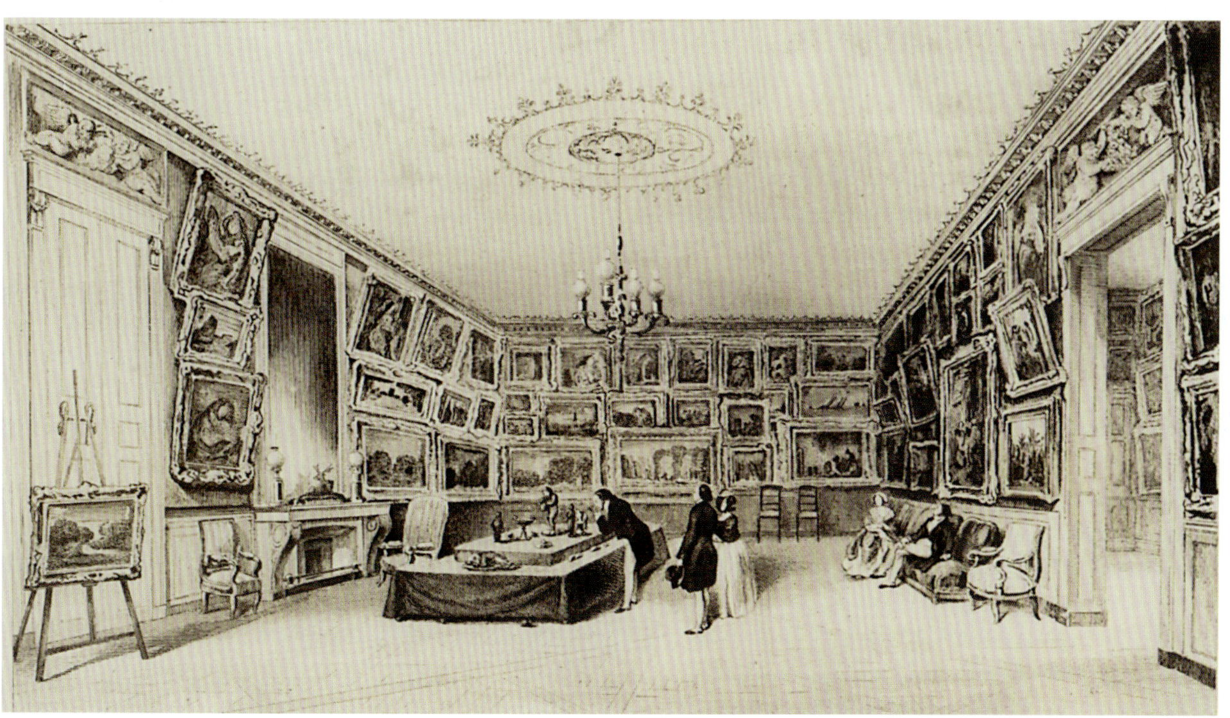

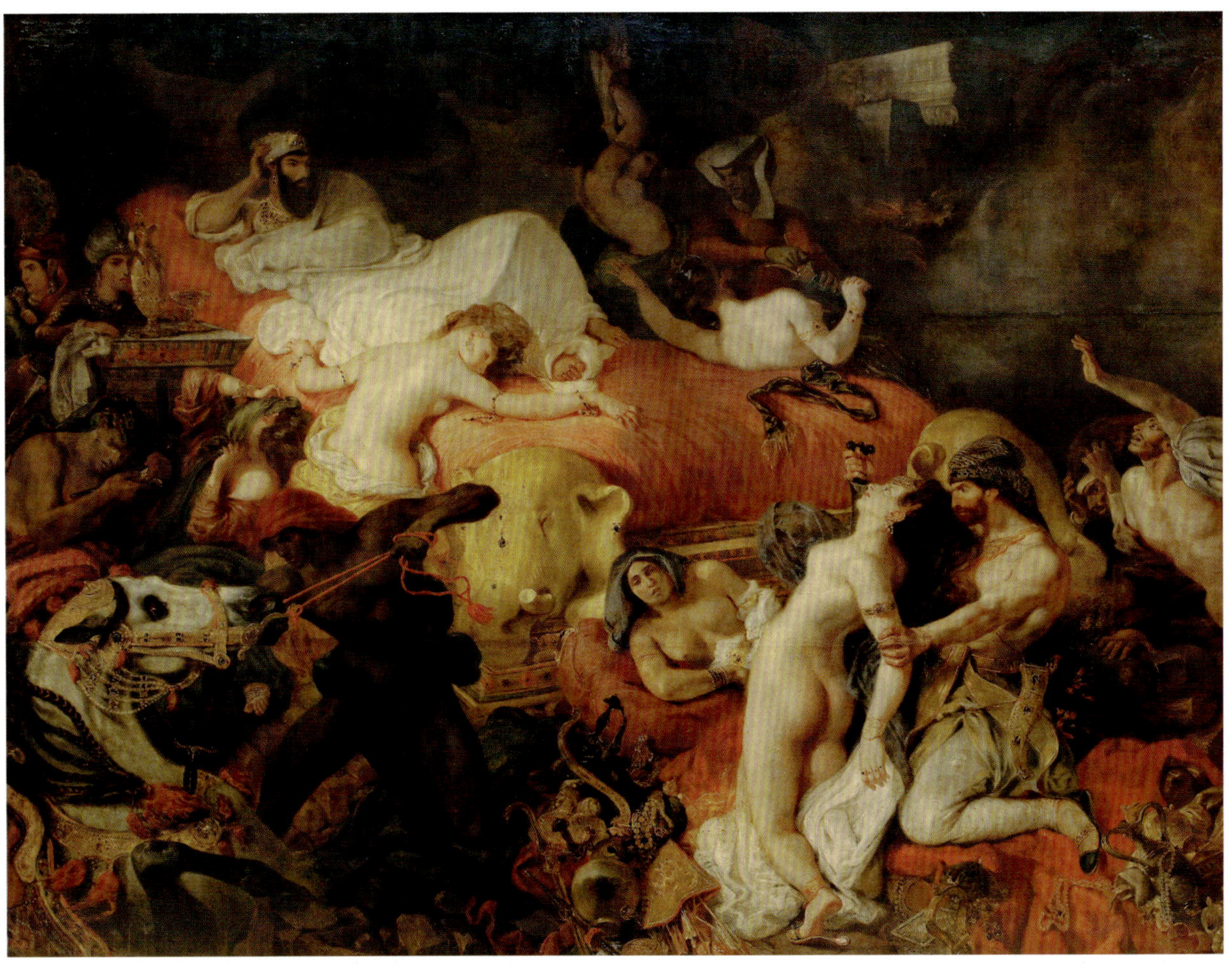

PAUL DURAND-RUEL (1831–1922): A PORTRAIT

reputation, so much so that both artists and clients began to visit more regularly.[14] In 1845, Jean Durand-Ruel published a large collection of reproductions of 120 works,[15] including four by Delacroix – *The Jewish Wedding in Morocco*[16] from the 1841 Salon among others[17] – six by Dupré and one by Diaz. On the frontispiece, a magnificent engraving by Charles-François Daubigny[18] (fig. 19) shows the gallery's main showroom, providing a helpful overview of its size and the style of hanging at the time. (The pictures are very close to one another and cover the walls from floor to ceiling, as was the case at the Salon; bronzes by Barye are positioned on a central table and on the fireplace.) The young Paul lived his life surrounded by artists and their works – his bedroom was sometimes decorated with pictures that were too new to be shown to the public.[19] Jean Durand-Ruel also offered works for hire, a trade that was more lucrative than sales.[20] Clients hired pictures, sometimes for evening receptions in order to impress their guests, or for a month so they could have the picture copied. In high society at that time, it was considered the done thing for one's daughter to have a basic understanding of painting or watercolour, but letting her attend an art school, or even visit the Louvre to copy works by the masters, was out of the question. Paul Durand-Ruel continued his father's business until 1870; he abandoned selling stationery and hiring out paintings, as it took up too much time and prevented him from devoting himself fully to his artists.

The birth of a vocation

At first, the difficulties experienced by his parents, particularly during the revolution of 1848, which saw business plummet and the shop put at risk, did not encourage the young Paul Durand-Ruel to embrace a career as an art dealer. He was attracted by other vocations, both military and missionary. However, despite entering the Ecole Militaire de Saint-Cyr in 1851,[21] he later resigned to assist his father, who was exhausted by disease and hardship. He visited the collections at the Louvre, as well as public auction exhibitions; he also travelled. He set off for the provinces and other parts of Europe, selling works and also roaming the museums,[22]

FIG. 20
Eugène Delacroix
The Death of Sardanapalus, 1827
Oil on canvas, 392 × 496 cm
Musée du Louvre, Paris

educating his eye in the process. But the real starting point for his vocation as an art dealer was marked by the Universal Exhibition of 1855. Paul Durand-Ruel, aged 24 at the time, felt a flood of admiration for Delacroix's work; the artist had 35 high-profile works on display in a room that was almost entirely dedicated to his painting. As the art dealer wrote in his *Memoirs*: 'It was the triumph of modern art over academic art … they permanently opened my eyes and reinforced the idea that I might, perhaps, in my own humble way, be of some service to true artists by helping to make them better understood and appreciated'[23] Won over by the genius of Delacroix, he would go on to purchase more than 60 of his works between 1868 and 1883,[24] including *The Death of Sardanapalus* (fig. 20), a 'key work' that he acquired at a public sale 'to audience applause for 96,000 francs'.[25] These purchases bear witness to the dealer's boldness and the originality of his strategy, which included supporting the work of the artists he believed in by pushing up their prices at public auctions. The promotion of works internationally was another of his principles. *The Death of Sardanapalus* was exhibited in Vienna[26] and London in 1873,[27] in Paris in 1878,[28] and in New York in 1887,[29] without success. The dealer failed to sell it until 1879, when it was sold at a loss to the Scottish industrialist James Duncan for 50,000 francs. Enthusiastically committed to championing the artists of the 1830 School (including Delacroix, Corot, the Barbizon School, Courbet and Daumier), all of whom were maligned by the critics of the time, Paul Durand-Ruel remained the principal buyer of their works and succeeded in having them accepted by the public from the late 1860s onwards.

Like his father, Paul Durand-Ruel learnt how to authenticate and value works. He appeared as an expert alongside the auctioneer at a public auction for the first time in 1863 at the age of 32; the *Gazette des Beaux-Arts* described the event on its first page: 'It was his debut in the delicate career of the expert appraiser, and he accomplished it with brilliance. M. Durand-Ruel *fils* … has seen many of the best modern paintings on their progress through his father's gallery, and so they are familiar to him. This question is of the utmost importance where false attributions and fakes are concerned. M. Durand-Ruel would seem to us to personify all the qualities of tact and honour'.[30]

Meeting the future Impressionists

At the outbreak of the Franco-Prussian War, on 8 September 1870 Paul Durand-Ruel left for London, where he rented premises to exhibit works by French artists. Located at 168, New Bond Street, this gallery was inopportunely named the 'German Gallery'. London would be the location for some of the dealer's most crucial meetings. In January 1871, Charles-François Daubigny introduced him to Claude Monet with the following comment: 'This artist will surpass us all'.[31] The dealer, who had already caught glimpses of Monet's paintings at previous Salons,[32] purchased his works and exhibited them immediately.[33] Some days later, Pissarro visited the gallery and delivered a canvas in the absence of Durand-Ruel. The dealer wrote to him immediately: 'The painting you have brought me is charming and I am sorry I was not at the gallery to compliment you myself. Please tell me how much you would like for it, and please be so kind as to send me others as soon as you are able to. I must try to sell many of them for you here'.[34]

After the signing of the armistice in 1871, Durand-Ruel returned to Paris, where he was to experience a tragic loss. One evening, after a visit to the Opéra, his wife, Eva Lafon, contracted pneumonia and died some days later,[35] aged not quite 30 and carrying the couple's sixth child. Durand-Ruel found himself a widower at the age of 40, with five children under nine; he would never

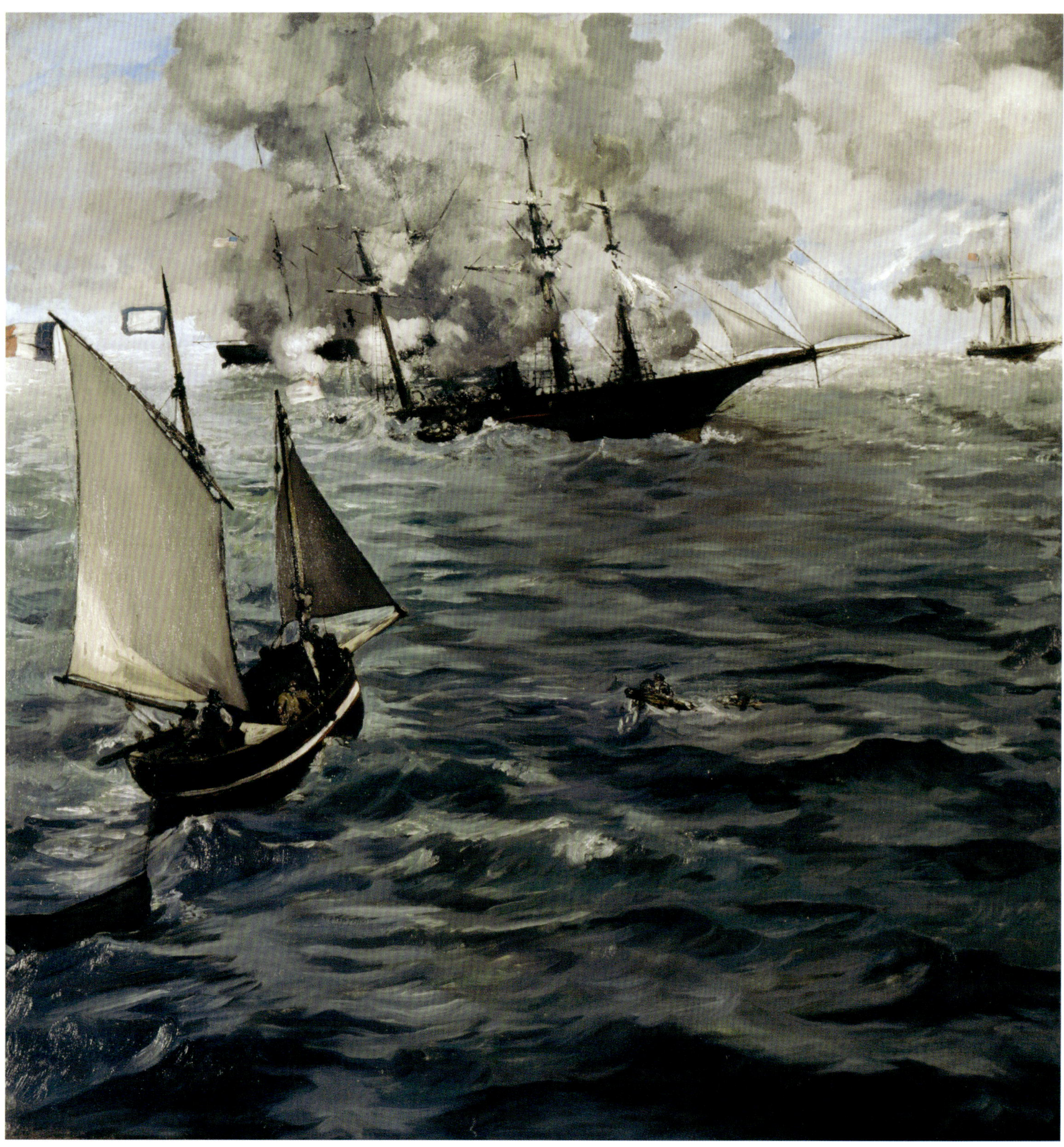

FIG. 21
Edouard Manet
The Battle of the U.S.S. 'Kearsarge' and the C.S.S. 'Alabama', 1864
Oil on canvas, 137.8 × 128.9 cm
Philadelphia Museum of Art, Pennsylvania
[cat. 23]

remarry and became increasingly devoted to his artists and their art. In the following months, he met friends and colleagues of Monet and Pissarro: Degas, from whom he would purchase his first works in January 1872 (*The Dance Foyer*, *The Orchestra at the Opéra*), Puvis de Chavannes in February (*Hope*), Renoir (*The Pont des Arts*) (see fig. 141) and Sisley (*The Way to Church*) in March, Boudin in May (*On the Shore*, Salon of 1872), and Morisot in July (*The Jetty*).

Although Manet had sold only very few paintings, in 1872 the dealer discovered two of his pictures in the studio of the Belgian painter, Alfred Stevens – *The Salmon* (see fig. 53) and *Moonlight at the Port of Boulogne* (see fig. 54) – which he purchased immediately. Some days later, Durand-Ruel visited Manet in his studio and bought 23 of his works at once, including *The Battle of the U.S.S. 'Kearsarge' and the C.S.S. 'Alabama'* (fig. 21) and *The Reader* (see fig. 52). It was as if the dealer had been hit by a thunderbolt. Later, when Edouard Manet's heirs were dealing with the sale of the artist's studio, his mother remarked: 'The sale of our dear Edouard's pictures must be done intelligently.... It would be enormously ungrateful not to give the responsibility to Durand-Ruel, who was an admirer of Edouard and his first buyer.[36]

The crisis of Impressionism

Durand-Ruel's devotion to the new school of painting soon resulted in a series of setbacks:

> All my efforts were thwarted by the violent campaign mounted against Manet, Monet, Renoir, Sisley, Degas and Puvis de Chavannes, and other artists whose works I had the audacity to show in my galleries. Attacked and reviled by upholders of the academy and old doctrines, by the most established art critics, by the entire press and by most of my colleagues, they were beginning to become the laughing stock of the salons and the public... Myself, guilty of having exhibited and daring to champion such works, I was treated as a madman and a person of bad faith. Little by little, the trust I had succeeded in inspiring disappeared and my best clients began to question me. 'How can you', they would say, 'after being one of the first to have loved the 1830 School, now praise these pictures in which there is not a shred of quality?' On several occasions, they predicted I would end my days in Charenton.[37]

Heavily in debt,[38] Durand-Ruel was forced to sell off his extensive stock of Barbizon School paintings,[39] which he was only able to do through brokers, as his name scared away potential buyers. He avoided bankruptcy by coming to an arrangement with his creditors, but in 1874 he virtually had to stop purchasing works from his Impressionist friends.

Of the second exhibition of the Impressionist group, held in April 1876 at the Durand-Ruel Gallery, the influential art critic of the *Figaro*, Albert Wolff, wrote:

> Following upon the burning of the Opera-House, a new disaster has fallen upon the quarter. There has just been opened at Mr Durand-Ruel's an exhibition of what is said to be painting... Five or six lunatics, of whom one is a woman, have chosen to exhibit their works. There are people who burst into laughter in front of these objects. Personally I am saddened by them. These so-called artists style themselves Intransigents, Impressionists.[40]

Paul Durand-Ruel enjoyed some financial respite in 1880 when the Banque de l'Union Générale granted him credit. His purchasing of Impressionist works began again in earnest, but the bank collapsed in 1882 and he was forced to repay his loans. Facing financial ruin once again, he wrote: 'I had to raise cash from everywhere ... I sublet the apartment ... Only one person agreed to lend me money – based on the price of the frames and not the value of the pictures'.[41] He was forced to ask his creditors for a moratorium for a second time in 1884, just as he had done in 1874.

Collectors, the majority of Durand-Ruel's clients, remained rare.[42] Despite all these difficulties, the dealer persisted. He remained faithful to his exhibition strategy as the only way to gain recognition for his new artists. As Renoir wrote to him in 1885, while Durand-Ruel was being attacked in the press by an unscrupulous competitor in the case of a forgery he had nothing to do with: 'Do what they may, they [the public, press and art dealers] will never destroy your true quality: your love of art and your defence of living artists. In the future, it will be your claim to fame.'[43] This dedication to his contemporary artists held true throughout his life: 'A quite common mistake, and one that we have an excellent opportunity to rectify, involves the dating, one might say, of M. Durand-Ruel and his originality to the Impressionism period. If he had died in 1870, he would have been considered the most fervent champion of the 1830 School and would have died in bankruptcy. If he had died in 1886, he would also have left behind him the memory of a man who had bankrupted himself for the Impressionists; this would have made all the difference, not in terms of the effects he had but on the perspective of history'.[44]

The recognition of an intuition

Paul Durand-Ruel's salvation, and that of the Impressionists, came from America. In 1885, he received an all-expenses-paid invitation to exhibit in New York from James Sutton, Director of the American Art Association. Durand-Ruel set sail with 300 pictures, despite the reluctance of some sceptical artists: Puvis de Chavannes refused to take part, while Monet was concerned about seeing his pictures 'leave the country for the land of the Yankees'.[45] But the American artist Mary Cassatt assisted her dealer in this undertaking; she introduced him to her childhood friend Louisine Havemeyer and her husband Henry Osborne Havemeyer, the 'Sugar King'. The two were among the greatest enthusiasts of the paintings of Manet and the Impressionists, and would become loyal clients of Durand-Ruel, thanks to whom they would also purchase works by Old Masters such as El Greco's *View of Toledo*, now in the Metropolitan Museum of Art in New York, and *Portrait of a Cardinal (Nino de Guevara)* by Goya.

Durand-Ruel was already recognised in the United States as the champion of the Barbizon School.[46] The public and collectors alike flocked without preconceptions to his exhibition in New York in 1886, placing their trust in the dealer, who wrote in his *Memoirs*:

> The show drew crowds of the curious, and unlike what happened in Paris, it triggered no fuss or stupid comments and sparked no protest. Press coverage was unanimously favourable and many articles of praise appeared in all the papers in New York and all large cities in the United States.[47] Art lovers and the general public came not to laugh, but to find out about the notorious paintings that had created such a stir in Paris. And since I was almost as well known in America as in France for having been one of the early defenders of the great artists of the School of 1830, people came without the least prejudice to study closely the works of my new friends, which they assumed must have some qualities because I was backing them.[48]

It was the first time an Impressionist exhibition had been well received by the public and the press, so much so that its run had to be extended and moved to larger premises. The Havemeyers were joined by new collectors.[49]

Encouraged, Durand-Ruel organised another exhibition in New York the following year, and opened a gallery in the city in 1888. Lean times had come to an end; in 1894, he would repay all his debts. In the wake of this American success, the Europeans would finally be convinced.

In 1905, Durand-Ruel organised an exhibition at the Grafton Galleries in London that remains to this day the largest and finest exhibition of Impressionist painting: *Pictures by Boudin, Cézanne, Degas, Manet, Monet, Morisot, Pissarro, Renoir, Sisley*, including 315 works from among the painters' greatest masterpieces [see fig. 164].

The principles and methods of Paul Durand-Ruel

The methods used by Durand-Ruel were in stark contrast to those of his competitors. As an art dealer, his approach was based on seven entirely new principles: the protection of the art first and foremost; the exclusivity of the artists' work; the founding of art reviews; the marriage of the worlds of art and finance;[50] the staging of solo rather than group exhibitions;[51] a network of international galleries; and regular unrestricted access to his galleries and apartment. Throughout his career, Durand-Ruel applied these principles in order to gain recognition for the artists' work in the face of a lack of understanding on the part of the public, official artistic circles and the majority of the collectors of the period.

Moral as well as financial support

In 1873,[52] the art dealer began paying the future Impressionists a monthly sum against their works, allowing them the freedom to work without fear for the future. Durand-Ruel also settled bills from their suppliers and tailors, their rent and fees charged by their doctors. These gentleman's agreements (no contracts were ever signed) guaranteed Durand-Ruel exclusivity over the artists' creativity (or the right to be the first to see their work), allowing him to bolster prices. He wrote to Monet in 1882, following an exhibition he had organised in his Paris gallery: 'You know I asked for high prices. I could have asked for half, but I would not have sold any more and would not have been able to fix the pictures in the minds of the collectors in the same way.'[53] But in 1885, when Durand-Ruel's finances were depleted, Monet challenged his policy of exclusivity and exhibited at competing galleries, such as that of Georges Petit. Monet believed, sometimes rightly, that exclusivity was not necessarily the best commercial strategy when it came to raising the asking price of his works. However, Durand-Ruel was the first art dealer to believe in the works of the Impressionists, of whom he was, for a long time and to a considerable extent, their principal client. As his personality dictated, Durand-Ruel accepted the prices suggested by the artists, who passed information among themselves and sometimes asked the dealer to set the prices himself, convinced he would offer higher sums than those they would have dared to claim. In the 1860s, Durand-Ruel did indeed double his asking prices. Jules Dupré 'couldn't get over it.'[54]

But the support Durand-Ruel gave his artists was not simply financial, it was also moral. A sincere man of integrity, Durand-Ruel was close to the artists and helped them whatever the circumstances. He had to reassure the eternally dissatisfied Monet on many an occasion. For example, on 18 September 1992 the terribly downhearted artist wrote to the dealer from Pourville: 'You will find I am lacking in courage but I can hold on no longer and am completely discouraged. After some days of fine weather, it has begun to rain once more. Yet again, I must set aside my unfinished studies. I am going mad and have taken against my canvases: a large painting of flowers I had just finished; I destroyed it along with three or four canvases that I punctured and

FIG. 22
Pierre-Auguste Renoir
Charles and Georges Durand-Ruel, 1882
Oil on canvas, 61 × 81 cm
Private collection
[cat. 77]

FIG. 23
Pierre-Auguste Renoir
Joseph Durand-Ruel, 1882
Oil on canvas, 81 × 65 cm
Private collection
[cat. 76]

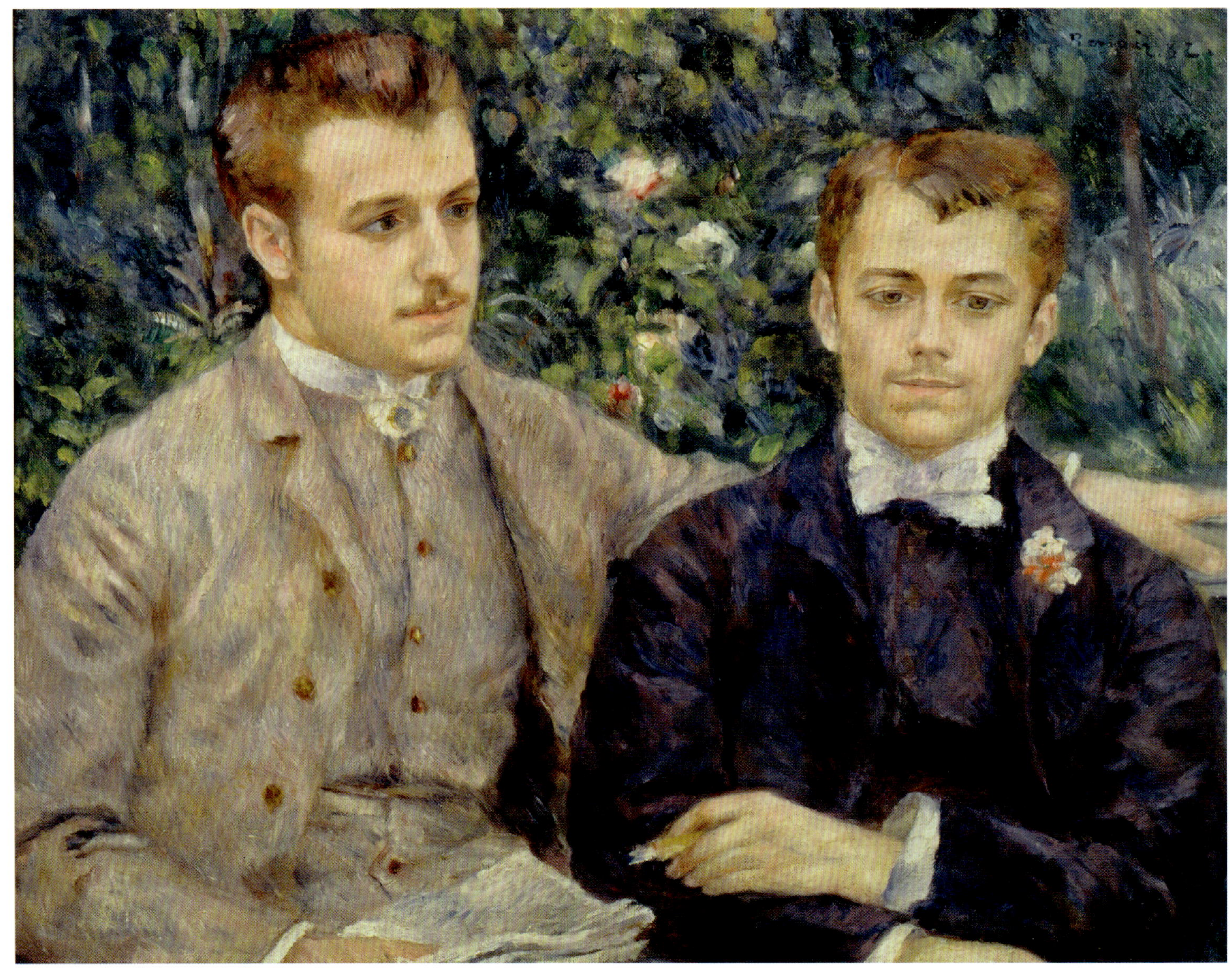

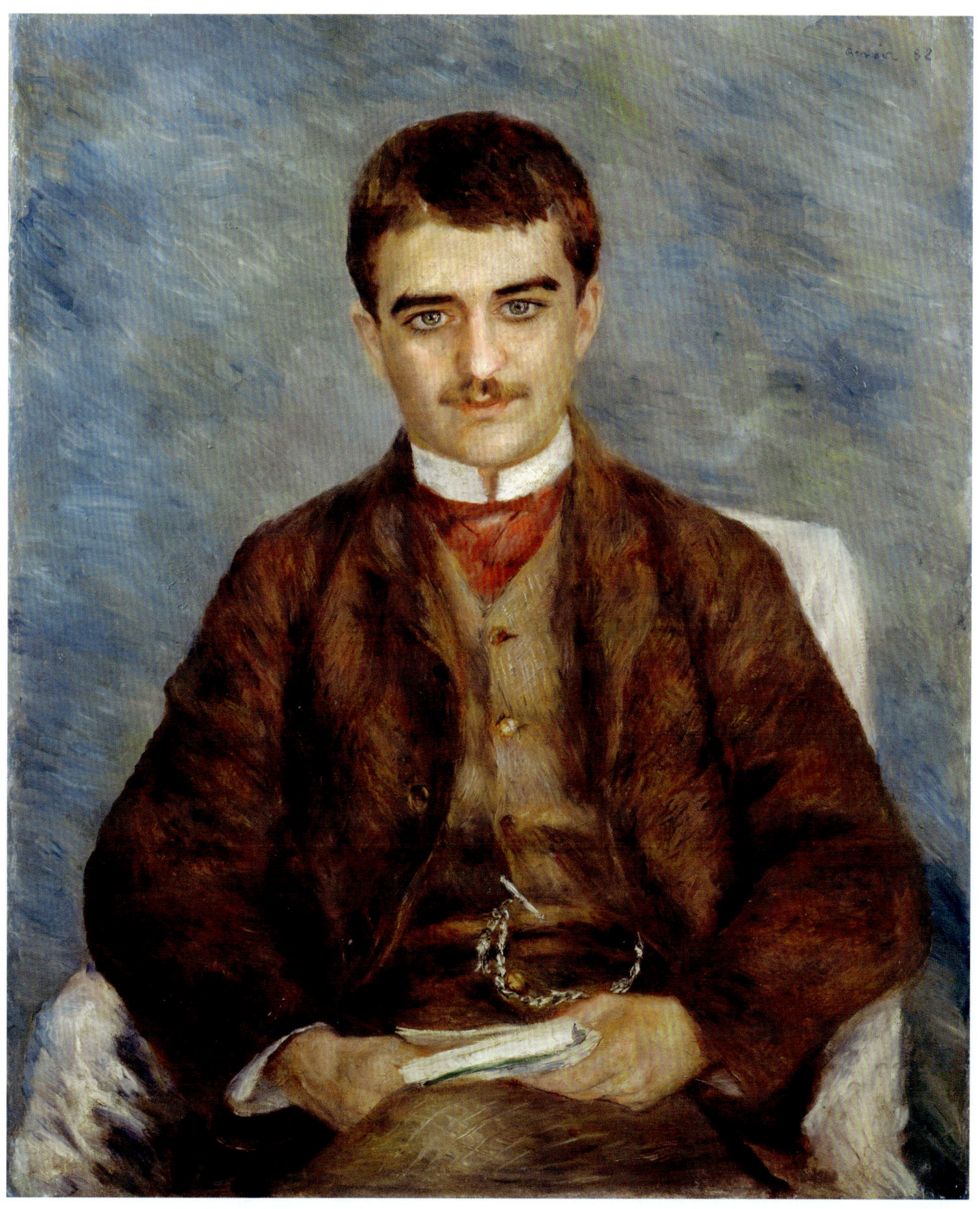

FIG. 24
Pierre-Auguste Renoir
The Daughters of Paul Durand-Ruel, Marie-Thérèse and Jeanne, 1882
Oil on canvas, 81.3 × 65.4 cm
Chrysler Museum of Art, Norfolk, Virginia
[cat. 78]

scratched. It is absurd, I realise that'.[55] Durand-Ruel replied to the letter the very same day: 'I am sending the 1,500 francs you asked for. I would also like to be able to send you some courage to overcome the many difficulties you are facing at every turn … The challenges you are undergoing will be useful to you. It is adversity that gives rise to the best lessons; do not believe you have learnt nothing in your struggle against nature'. Durand-Ruel also invited Monet to work at his home: 'My apartment on rue de Rome has a large salon you could use as a studio, a room like any other, where you could paint still-life pictures. To rest from his studies of nature, Corot has created a host of masterpieces in his studio. Why should you not do the same?'[56]

In his *Memoirs*, the dealer detailed just how much he learnt from the artists themselves. Durand-Ruel believed in their creative genius and guided them very little; he suggested to Pissarro: 'Look for attractive subjects; this contributes greatly to success. Leave the figures to one side for the moment, or use them as accessories. I think there is a much better chance of selling landscapes'.[57] He advised Monet to travel in search of new horizons: 'I have often told you about Venice. There is Holland, where the blue skies will not attract you at this time of year, but where you may find new insights'.[58] To Boudin, he wrote: 'When it comes to choosing subjects for your pictures, do exactly as you please. It is much better to follow your inspiration'.[59]

These sincere and profound relationships based on trust went well beyond the usual connections between an artist and his dealer. In 1884, Renoir wrote to Durand-Ruel, who was experiencing serious financial difficulties at the time: 'If you need me, please consider me entirely at your disposal, whatever may occur. I will always be loyal to you … If you are obliged to make sacrifices when it comes to the paintings, regret nothing. I will paint other, better ones for you'.[60] The relationship between the dealer and several of his artists was one of real friendship and their families would mix regularly. Renoir chose Durand-Ruel's third son, Georges (fig. 22), as godfather to his son Jean, the future film director. Durand-Ruel asked Puvis de Chavannes and Degas to be witnesses at the marriage of his eldest son Joseph (fig. 23), and at those of his two daughters, Marie-Thérèse and Jeanne (fig. 24).

Prints as promotion

Reviving an initiative introduced by his father in 1845, in 1873 Paul Durand-Ruel published a collection of engravings and etchings, a *Recueil d'estampes gravées à l'eau forte*,[61] which was intended to contain illustrations of all the works that had passed through his hands. The publication remained incomplete for financial reasons, although 300 etchings of works predominantly by the 1830 School were eventually published;[62] 26 by Delacroix, including *The Death of Sardanapalus*; 28 by Corot, including *The Bridge at Mantes*; 28 by Millet, including *The Angelus*; and 21 by Théodore Rousseau, including *The Forest in Winter at Sunset* (see fig. 47). Seven pictures by Courbet, including *The Woman in the Waves* (fig. 25); seven by Manet, including *Boy with a Sword* (see fig. 91); two by Degas, four by Monet, five by Pissarro, three by Sisley and six by Puvis de Chavannes, including *Hope*, also appeared. Durand-Ruel founded two art reviews: the *Revue internationale de l'art et de la curiosité*, published from 15 January 1869 until 15 August 1870 (interrupted by the war) and *L'Art dans les deux mondes*, published from November 1890 until July 1891. Too costly, neither review survived for more than two years. Alongside Georges Lecomte's book, *L'Art impressionniste d'après la collection privée de M. Durand-Ruel*, which was published in 1892, these publications allowed Durand-Ruel not only to raise the profile of his young protégés but also

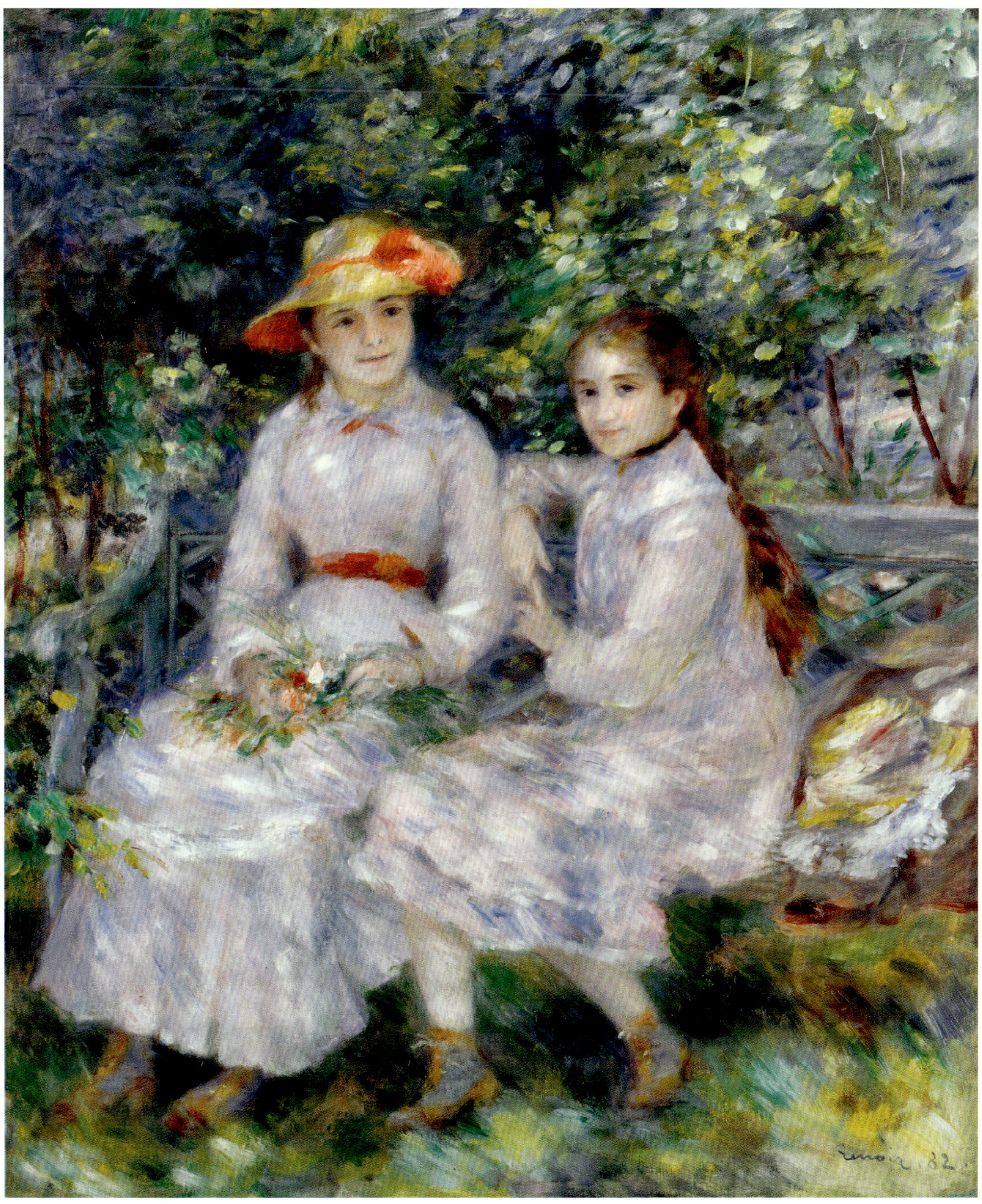
Renoir. 82.

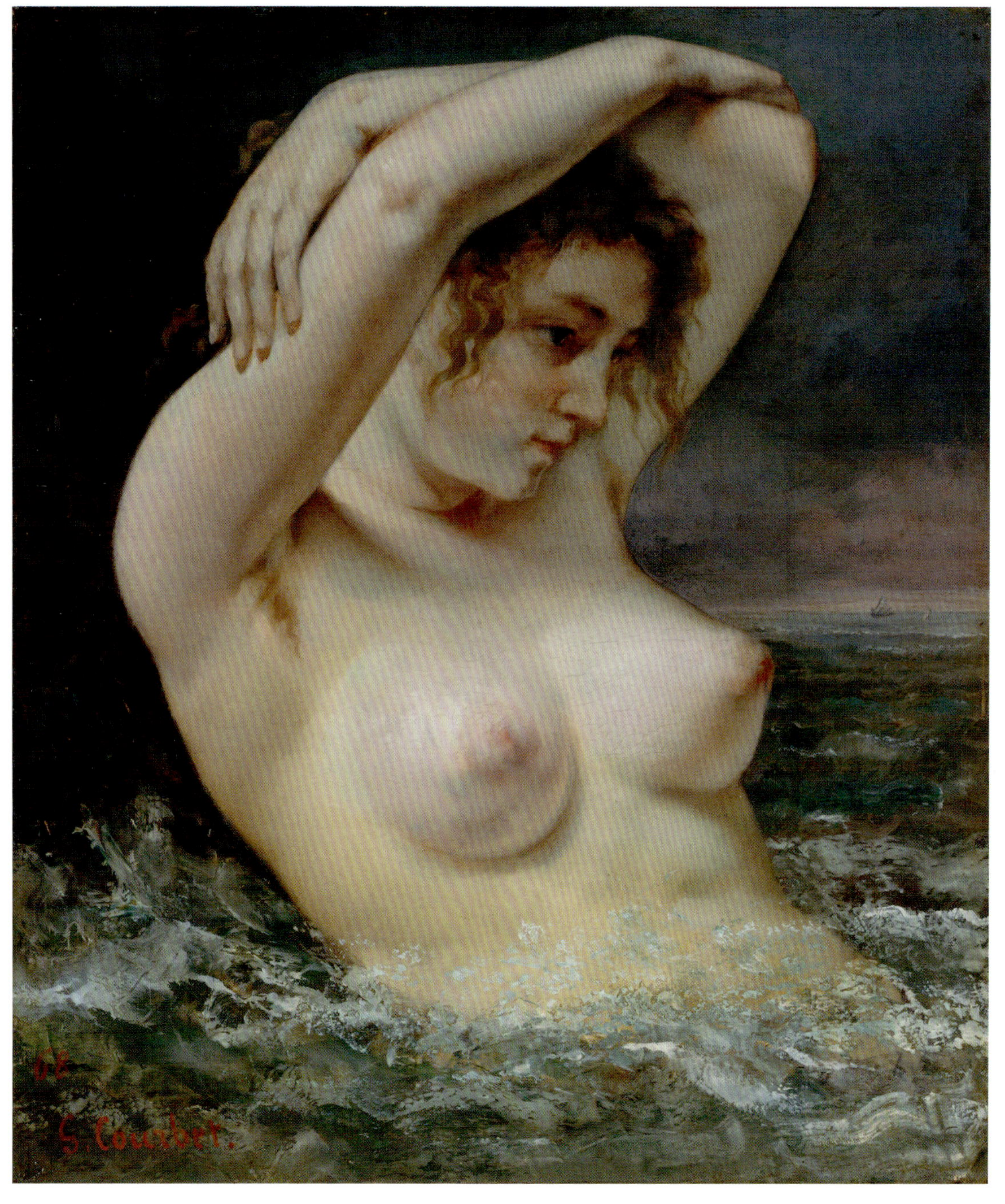
68
G. Courbet.

FIG. 25
Gustave Courbet
Woman in the Waves, 1868
Oil on canvas, 65.4 × 54 cm
The Metropolitan Museum of Art, New York
[cat. 8]

to retain clients and attract new collectors. He also paid great attention to his exhibition catalogues, for which he called upon great art critics and authors to write the prefaces, including Arsène Alexandre,[63] Théodore Duret,[64] Gustave Geffroy,[65] Georges Lecomte,[66] Stéphane Mallarmé,[67] Roger Marx,[68] Octave Mirbeau,[69] and Emile Zola.[70]

The marriage of art and finance

Durand-Ruel had only limited capital at his disposal and, to implement his policy of buying to excess, was forced to appeal to financial backers or external financiers.[71]

Exhibitions all over the world

In 1883, Durand-Ruel mounted a series of solo exhibitions in a change from the usual practice of staging group shows: Boudin in February, Monet in March, Renoir in April, Pissarro in May and Sisley in June. The dealer made an initial attempt with the Impressionists in America, in Boston in 1883,[72] and then in Germany, at the Fritz Gurlitt Gallery in Berlin. No pictures were sold at either of these first two exhibitions.[73] He staged an exhibition in London in the same year, at the Dowdeswell & Dowdeswell Gallery, where a single picture by Degas was eventually sold. Despite the lack of success of these exhibitions, Durand-Ruel continued to provide his artists with moral support, as well as financial support whenever possible. His relationship of trust with his artists endured and in 1892 he even succeeded in convincing the most difficult among them, Degas, to stage the only solo exhibition to take place in France during his lifetime at the Durand-Ruel Gallery,[74] which would attract a Japanese clientele.[75] Between 1870 and 1922, the year of his death, Durand-Ruel staged more than 200 exhibitions (solo or group) in Paris and almost 130 in New York. He also took part in a number of exhibitions around the world,[76] and sent hundreds of works to Germany, to his colleague Paul Cassirer, between 1898 and 1914. It was for these overseas dealings that in 1920, two years before his death, Paul Durand-Ruel was awarded the Légion d'Honneur, not for his services to fine arts but to foreign trade.

His sons and grandsons would go on to hold 205 exhibitions in New York before 1949 (the year the New York gallery closed) and 370 in Paris before 1974 (since when the Maison Durand-Ruel, which is still active today, has concentrated on managing the Impressionist archives).

A network of international galleries

In addition to his base in Paris, Durand-Ruel opened galleries outside France: he maintained a presence in London from 1870 to 1875, in Brussels from 1871 to 1875 and in New York from 1888 to 1949. In all his galleries, he attached great importance to lighting – using gas or electricity in the early days (the spotlights were impressive), and later illuminating the works with daylight filtered through glass panels.

In 1891, Durand-Ruel began to systematically photograph the works that passed through his galleries; his stock books were constantly updated and the many registers were carefully conserved. These images and documents are now a key resource for research at the Durand-Ruel Archives.

Access to his galleries and apartment

Always aiming to promote the talent of the French artists he championed, Durand-Ruel allowed access to his Paris apartment. In 1892, a Paris magazine reported that it was 'entirely decorated with his favourite painters, the Impressionists, and that [visitors] invariably left with inflamed eyes'.[77] Renoir triumphed in the apartment's

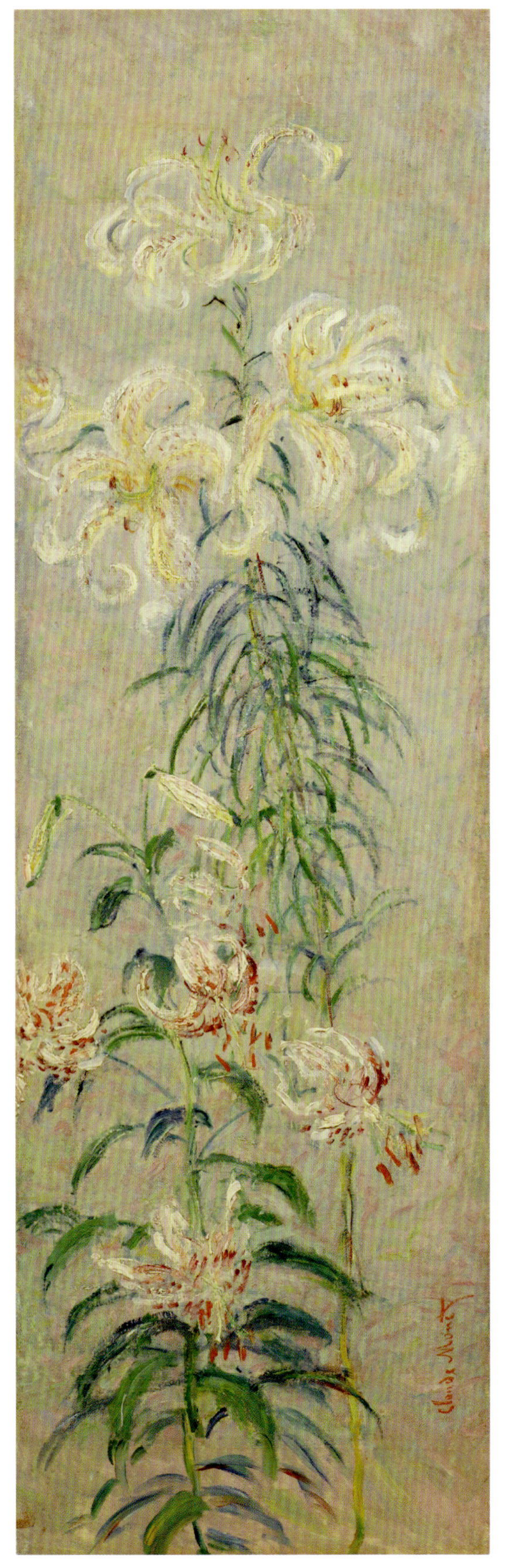

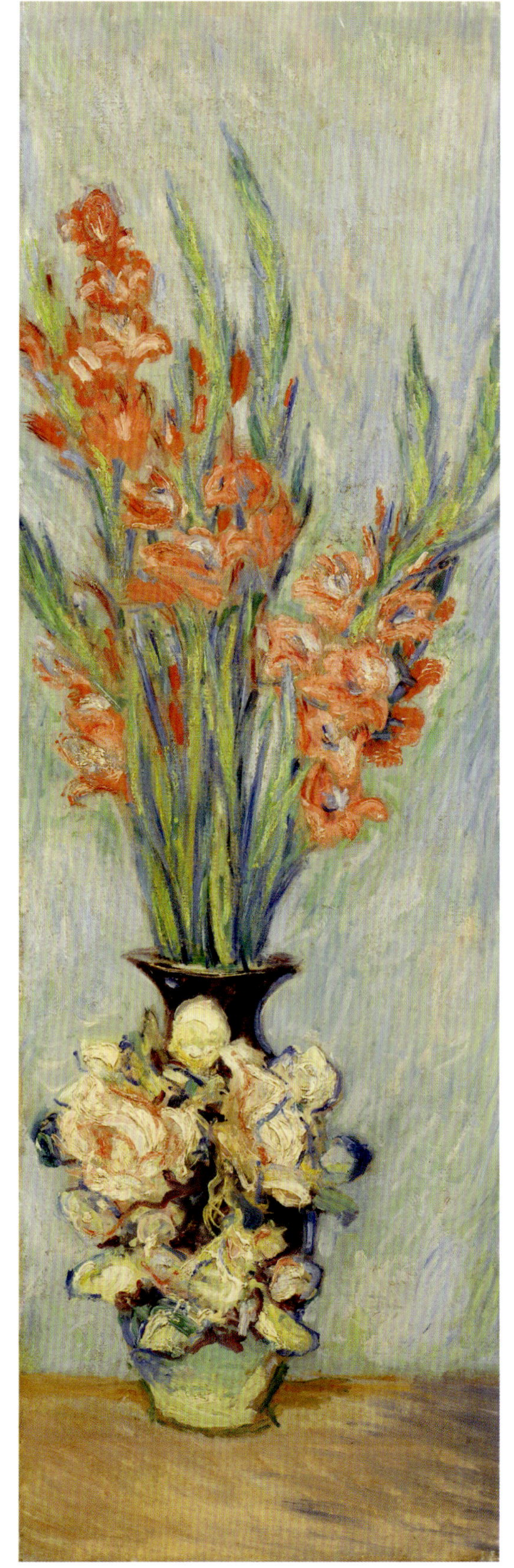

FIG. 26
Claude Monet (*facing, left*)
Japanese Lilies, 1883
Oil on canvas, door panel, 119.5 × 37 cm
Private collection
[cat. 47]

FIG. 27
Claude Monet (*facing, right*)
Gladioli, 1883
Oil on canvas, door panel, 128 × 37 cm
Private collection
[cat. 48]

FIG. 30
Claude Monet (*right*)
Door panels (overall view)
Private collection

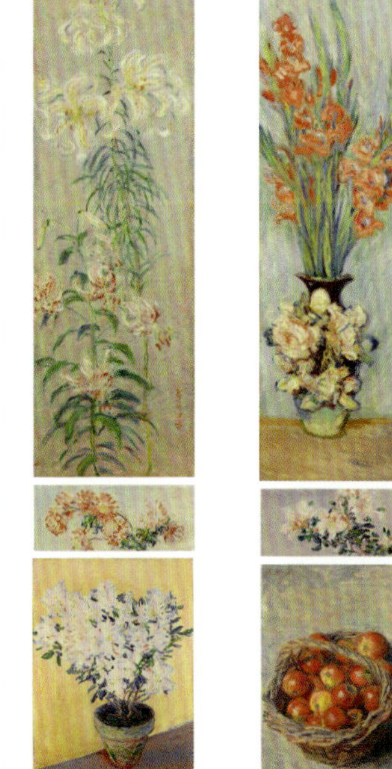

FIG. 28
Claude Monet
Chrysanthemums, 1883
Oil on canvas, door panel, 16.5 × 40 cm
Private collection
[cat. 49]

FIG. 29
Claude Monet
Branches of White and Pink Azaleas, 1883
Oil on canvas, door panel, 16.5 × 41 cm
Private collection
[cat. 50]

FIG. 31
Claude Monet
Pot of White Azaleas, 1883
Oil on canvas, door panel, 50.5 × 37 cm
Private collection
[cat. 51]

FIG. 32
Claude Monet
Basket of Apples, 1883
Oil on canvas, door panel, 50.5 × 37.8 cm
Private collection
[cat. 52]

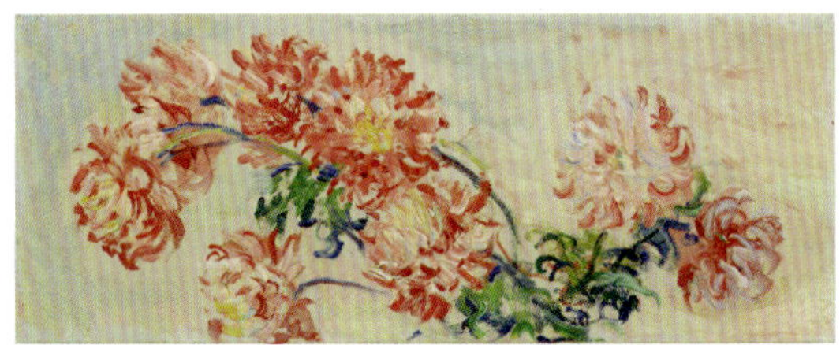

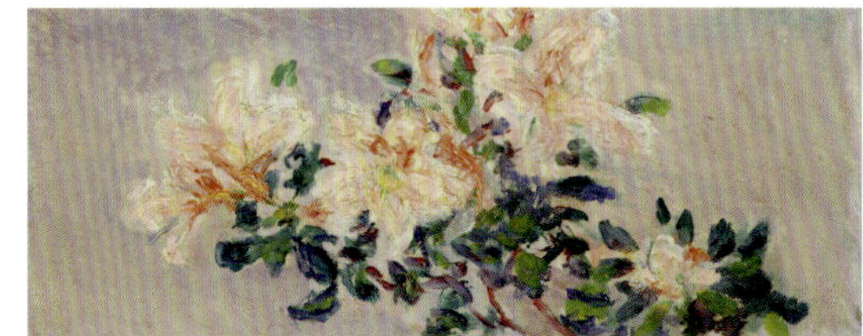

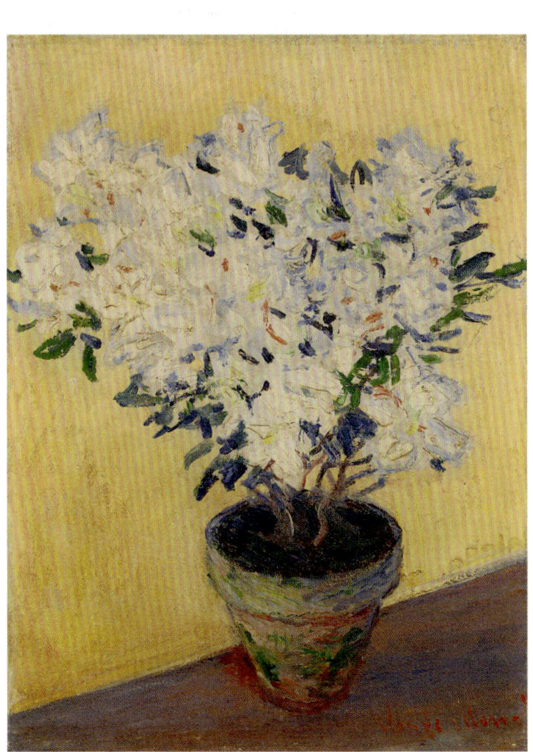

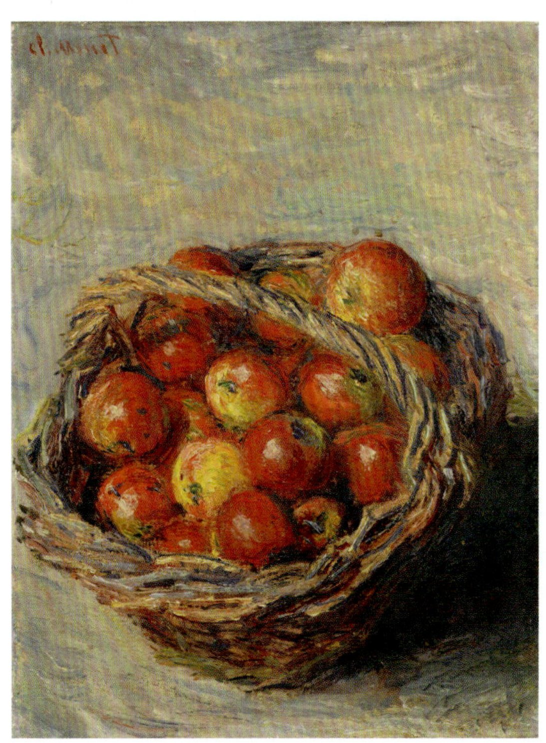

FIG. 33
Pierre-Auguste Renoir
Luncheon of the Boating Party,
1880–1
Oil on canvas, 130.2 × 175.6 cm
The Phillips Collection,
Washington, DC

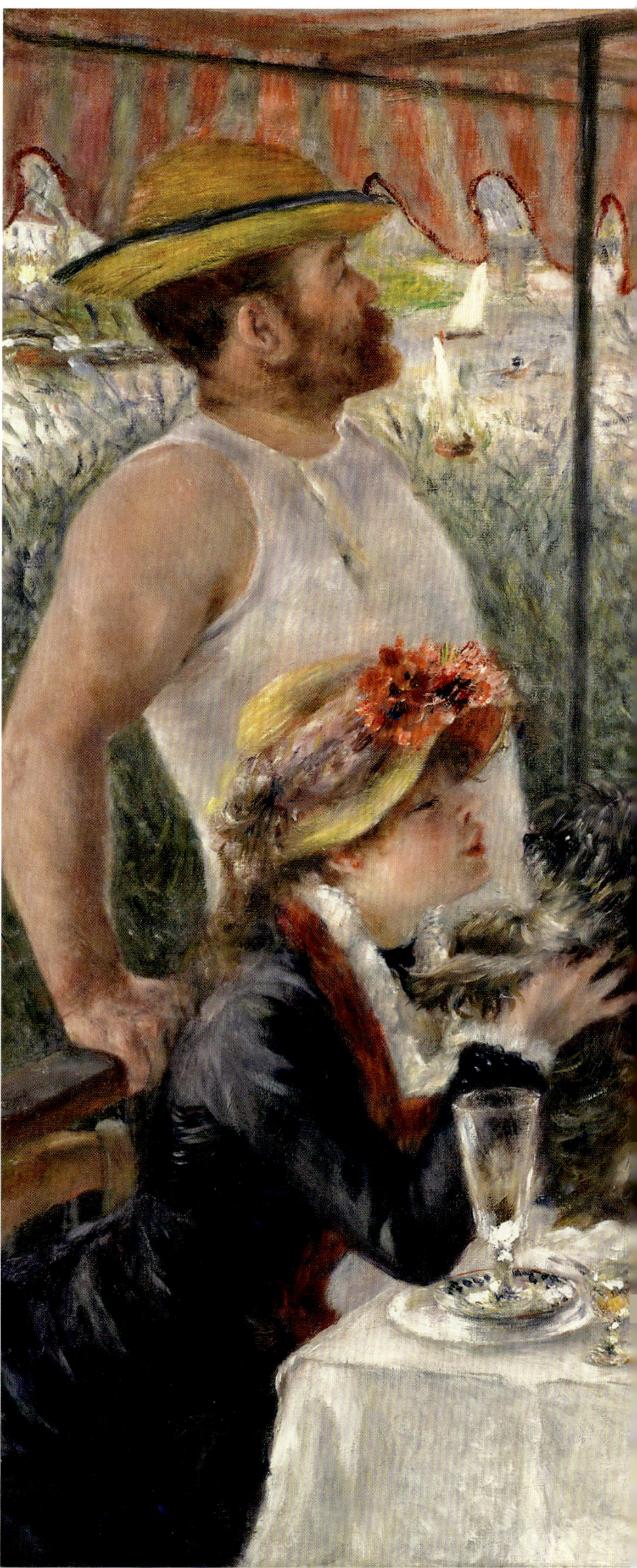

grand salon, with *Dance in the Country* and *Dance in the City* (see figs 3 and 4) hung opposite one another, next to *Girl with a Cat* (fig. 35), and followed by a *Spinner*[78] by Puvis de Chavannes, above a *Port* by Boudin. Renoir's *Mussel Fishers at Berneval* hung on the other wall,[79] between double doors decorated with six panels of flowers and fruits painted by Monet (figs 26–32). Visitors could also admire more intimate scenes, such as a *Maternity*[80] by Mary Cassatt or a marble by Rodin, *Young Mother in the Grotto* (see cat. 84).[81] The study was adorned with *The Spanish Ballet*[82] and a *Guitar Player*[83] by Manet. On another wall hung Monet's *Débâcle*,[84] with *Before the Race*[85] by Degas above, and a tigress by Barye and *Horses in a Meadow*[86] by Degas below. In the dining room, Renoir's famous *Luncheon of the Boating Party*[87] had pride of place (fig. 33). In 1898, callers were only required to give notice the day before a visit. In 1901, finally falling victim to their own success, the gallery made visits possible only on Tuesdays (the museums' weekly closing day) between two and four in the afternoon.[88] The family apartment was a valuable working tool for Durand-Ruel, who received clients, hosted dinners and exhibited works in a home setting, striving to appeal to potential buyers. Located at 35, rue de Rome, it was near the Gare Saint-Lazare, where the dealer would catch the train to visit Monet at Giverny (fig. 34). He would also visit Mary Cassatt in the Oise and Renoir in Cagnes.

PAUL DURAND-RUEL (1831–1922): A PORTRAIT

Paul Durand-Ruel worked with his family, first with his father, then with his sons Joseph (1862–1928), Charles (1865–1892) and Georges (1866–1931). His sons and his grandchildren Pierre (1899–1961) and Charles (1905–1985) shared responsibility for business at the Paris and New York galleries, taking turns to work six months in each city. Following in the family footsteps, they championed the Impressionists and Federico Zandomeneghi, as well as a new stable of artists – Albert André, Eugène Durenne, Georges d'Espagnat,

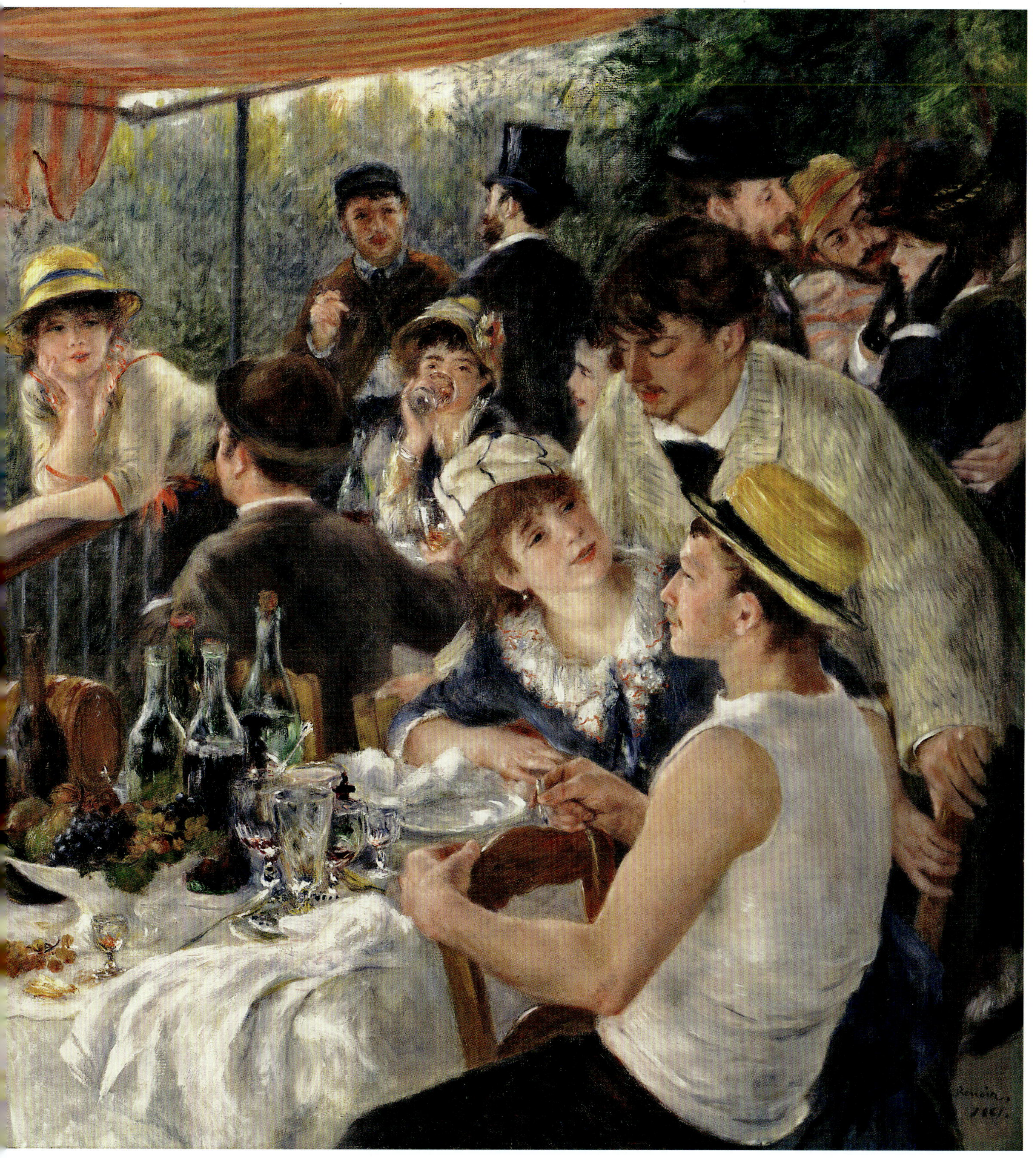
Renoir.
1881.

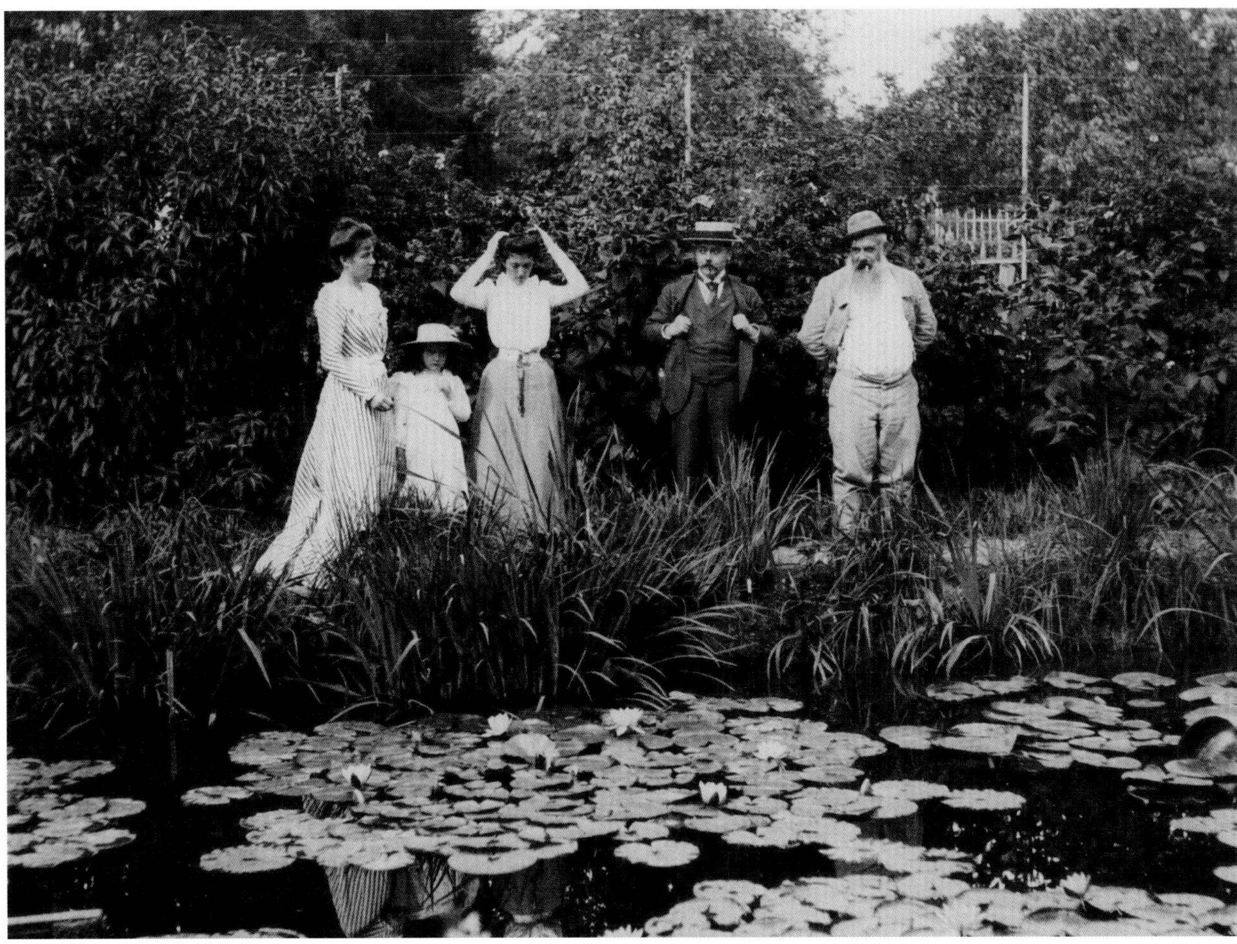

Gustave Loiseau, Maxime Maufra and Henry Moret – exhibiting them all internationally.

In 1911, more than 40 years after the dealer's discovery of the Impressionists, the art critic Arsène Alexandre described Paul Durand-Ruel:

> To start with, he is simplicity itself. No other famous Parisian is more approachable than he. Anyone can find him, at any time of the day, in his office on rue Laffitte, before the half-open door pushed by countless artists, art lovers, anonymous tourists, and curious passersby every year. Up stands a man of average height with round, clean-shaven face crowned by short gray hair and punctuated by a bottlebrush moustache and bushy eyebrows that are serious and questioning even as they quiver with mischief.... Much irony; few long words, no long sentences. On the other hand, there is every mark of uncommon obstinacy, of an unyielding yet nonviolent will that is imposed with a smile. Such is this white little man dressed in black, a man who never dwells on an unfavourable opinion, who receives with such urbanity, and who chats so pleasantly.[89]

PAUL DURAND-RUEL (1831–1922): A PORTRAIT

At the end of his life, Durand-Ruel found himself able to state: 'At last the Impressionist masters triumphed just as the generation of 1830 had. My madness had been wisdom. To think that, had I passed away at 60, I would have died debt-ridden and bankrupt, surrounded by a wealth of underrated treasures.'[90]

Two years after the art dealer's death, Monet told Marc Elder: 'We would have died of hunger without Durand-Ruel, all we impressionists. We owe him everything. He persisted, stubborn, risking bankruptcy twenty times in order to back us. The critics dragged us through the mud, but he, he was even worse! They wrote, "These people are crazy but a dealer who buys their work is even crazier!"'[91]

FIG. 34
Germaine Hoschedé, Lili Butler, Mme Joseph Durand-Ruel, Georges Durand-Ruel, Claude Monet at the water-lily pond in Giverny, 1900
Photograph
Archives Durand-Ruel

FIG. 35
Pierre-Auguste Renoir
Girl with a Cat, 1880
Oil on canvas, 120.3 × 92 cm
Sterling and Francine Clark Art Institute, Williamstown, Massachusetts
[cat. 74]

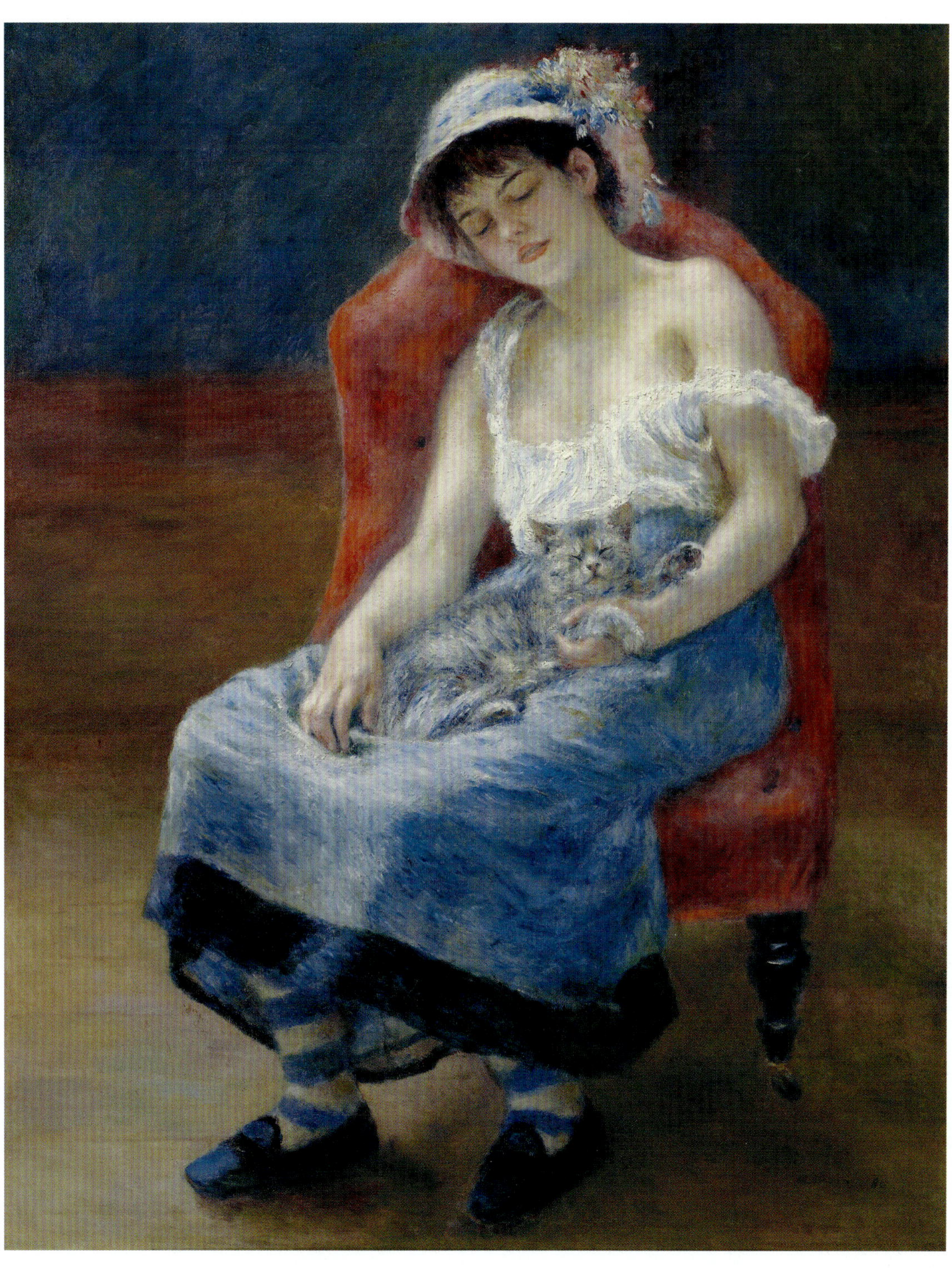

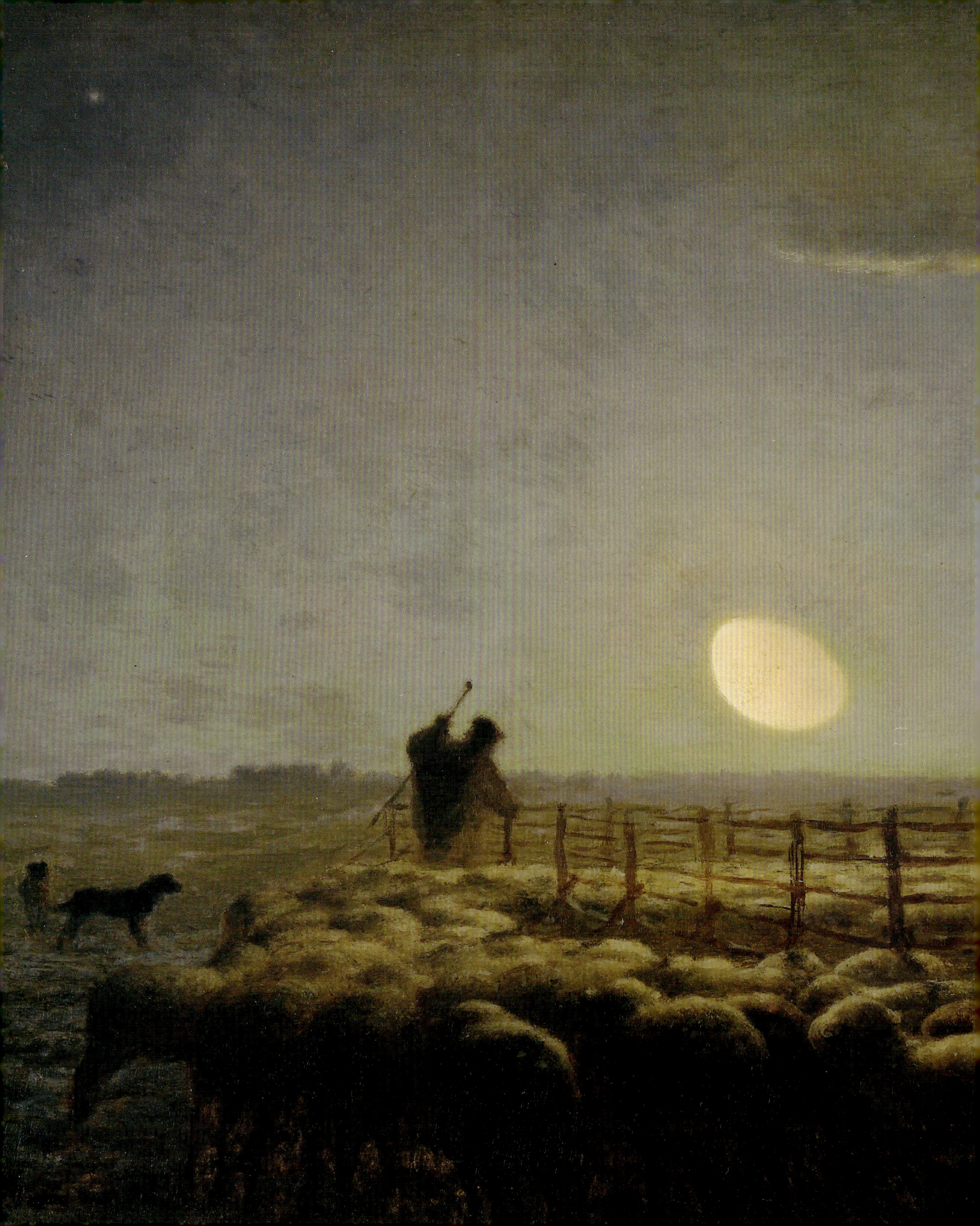

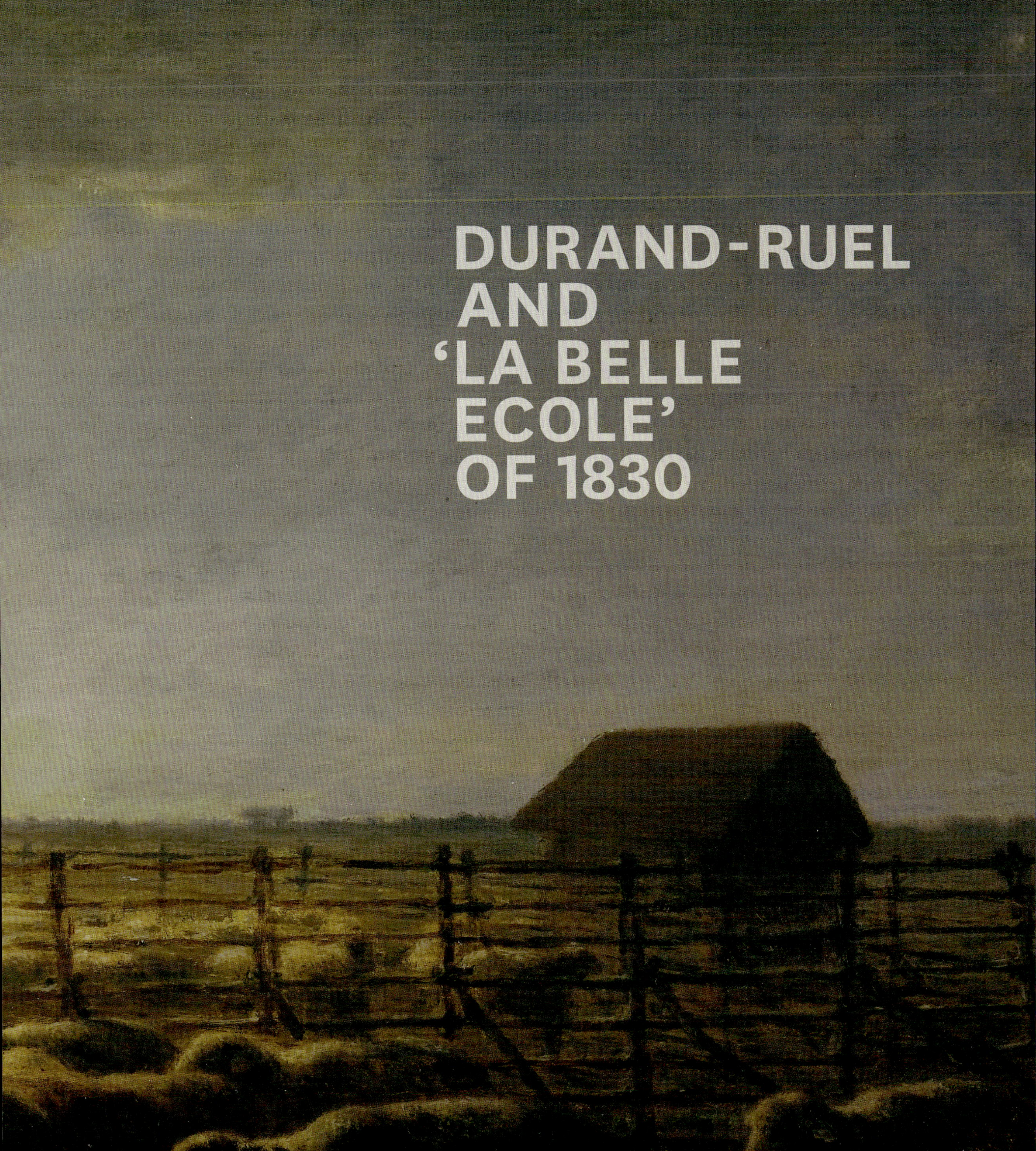
DURAND-RUEL
AND
'LA BELLE
ECOLE'
OF 1830

Durand-Ruel and 'La Belle Ecole' of 1830

Simon Kelly

In his *Memoirs*, Paul Durand-Ruel wrote that his career had been dominated by two campaigns: the first to raise the value of 'the beautiful School of 1830', and the second to increase support for his cherished Impressionists.[1] These campaigns are inextricably linked and his tactics for supporting the School of 1830 provide essential context – and often important precedents – for his patronage of the Impressionists. Yet his support of the School of 1830 – principally the nature-based work of Jean-Baptiste-Camille Corot, Théodore Rousseau and Jean-François Millet – is far less well known. This essay explores the strategies that Durand-Ruel used to elevate the value – both economic and aesthetic – of their work. It also situates their painting within the context of the dealer's patronage of two other major artists who were closely linked for him with these landscape painters: Eugène Delacroix and Gustave Courbet. To what extent did Durand-Ruel's efforts to promote all of these artists enjoy success and, more broadly, to what extent did his approaches transform the contemporary art market in nineteenth-century France?

In examining Durand-Ruel's patronage of the School of 1830, this essay focuses on the pivotal years of the late 1860s and early 1870s when the dealer was particularly active in collecting the work of these artists, after he took over his father's firm in 1865. By 1874, he had fallen into financial difficulties and he collected little of their work until the early 1880s, when his fortunes once again improved. Thereafter, he would work hard to promote their painting, particularly in America, but never with the same intensity as those earlier years when he was in close personal contact with the artists and when he essentially shaped many of his approaches to dealing. At a time when the market in contemporary art was still relatively modest, Durand-Ruel offered a newly ambitious model of a modern dealer.[2] That he was able to do so was largely due to his receiving very substantial but unorthodox loans, particularly from the Middle-Eastern banker Charles Edwards. These were offered at a very high rate of interest, and there was an agreement that paintings from Durand-Ruel's stock would be used as guarantees. Not only did the loans allow Durand-Ruel to acquire the work of the School of 1830 on a previously unprecedented scale, but they also financed his move to an enormous and prestigious new gallery space on the corner of the rue Laffitte in 1869.

Durand-Ruel later presented himself as an ingénue in business, affirming that he was motivated above all by a love of art. He certainly carried a missionary zeal to promote the artists in his stable, and this may have been underpinned by his strong religious beliefs. Yet his methods were far from ingenuous. Nicholas Green first highlighted the range of these approaches, noting in particular the dealer's collaboration with critics at a time when the artist biography was emerging as a distinct literary genre.[3] Robert Jensen has also looked more broadly at Durand-Ruel's business as anticipating modern dealing practices not only in France but also internationally, providing a model, for example, for the German dealer Paul Cassirer.[4] Linda Whiteley has noted the eclecticism of Durand-Ruel's early taste, which also embraced the more academic work of Bouguereau.[5] As we shall see, Durand-Ruel used a range of approaches in his dealing: the monopolisation of the artists in his stable to raise their prices; the consistent setting of sale records for their work at auction; the spectacular one-person or group retrospective; the use of the artist biography to raise collector interest and further legitimise his work; and the promotion of work not only in France but also on an international stage through an exhibition circuit across Europe and America. All these methods would be pursued in his support of the Impressionists, but they were first developed in his patronage of the School of 1830.

FIG. 36
Attributed to
André-Adolphe-Eugène Disdéri
Salon Carré (Delacroix gallery at the Universal Exhibition, Paris), 1855
Photograph
Fine Arts Museums of San Francisco, California

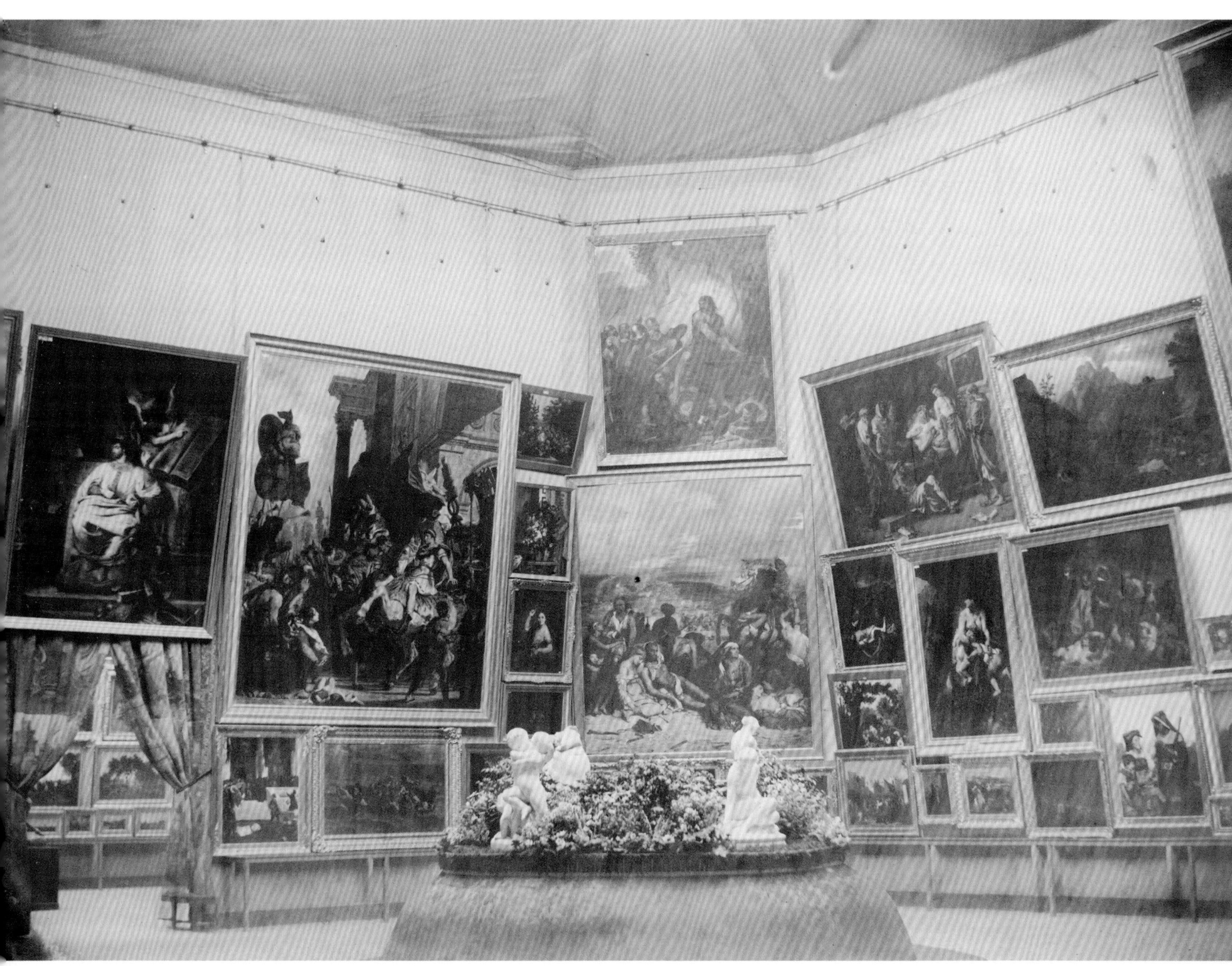

The 'Genius' of Eugène Delacroix

Durand-Ruel's collecting of the School of 1830 is closely linked to his support for Delacroix. The older artist had, indeed, been a crucial inspiration for many of these landscape painters through his experiments with colour, tone and gestural touch. Durand-Ruel had a 'limitless admiration' for the 'genius' of Delacroix's work from an early age.[6] He would have seen major works by Delacroix such as *Medea* (Musée des Beaux-Arts, Lille) and *The Jewish Wedding* (Musée du Louvre, Paris) on view in his father's gallery. He also remembered the overwhelming impact of Delacroix's retrospective at the 1855 Universal Exhibition (fig. 36), which shone with an 'incomparable brightness', making him determined to become an art dealer.[7]

From 1866 until 1872, Durand-Ruel bought 102 works by Delacroix in concert with his fellow dealer Hector Brame, also a great admirer of the artist. He described the former actor Brame as 'a very active, ardent and excellent seller' but pointedly also noted that his financial resources were limited.[8] Their acquisitions (on a 50/50 basis) covered the full range of the artist's output, from history painting (fig. 37) to Orientalist subjects (fig. 38) to landscape, and oil painting to water-colour, and began with *The Assassination of the Bishop of Liège* (fig. 39), purchased on 19 October, 1866. Generally they sold on their purchases rapidly but at relatively minor profits. Sometimes they were a little more successful, as in the case of a batch of prestigious works acquired from the collector Bouruet-Aubertot in the summer of 1868, which included *The Abduction of Rebecca* (Metropolitan Museum of Art, New York).[9]

After the Franco-Prussian War, Durand-Ruel made his most important Delacroix purchases on his own.[10] In February 1872, he bought the lyrical *Four Seasons* series (São Paulo Museum of Art) from Brame, perhaps in a show of one-upmanship over his partner.[11] Most spectacularly, he acquired Delacroix's great Salon painting, *The Death of Sardanapalus* (see fig. 20) at auction on 21 March 1873 for a sale record for the artist of 96,000 francs,[12] outbidding representatives of the State who had hoped to acquire the work for the Musée du Luxembourg. He subsequently sought to promote this key painting by exhibiting it abroad at his saleroom in England as well as in Vienna at the time of the 1873 International Exhibition.[13] In so doing, he became the leading French dealer in the artist's work internationally. He was, however, unable to find a buyer (perhaps because of its lascivious subject matter) and would ultimately sell the work some six years later at a very considerable loss of nearly 50,000 francs.[14] Overall, Durand-Ruel's success in dealing in Delacroix was mixed, perhaps because he was purchasing the work of an already well-established, dead artist. He would enjoy greater success in his acquisitions of the living painters of the School of 1830, from whom he bought directly.

FIG. 37
Eugène Delacroix
Interior of a Dominican Convent in Madrid, 1831
Oil on canvas, 130.2 × 161.9 cm
Philadelphia Museum of Art, Pennsylvania
[cat. 18]

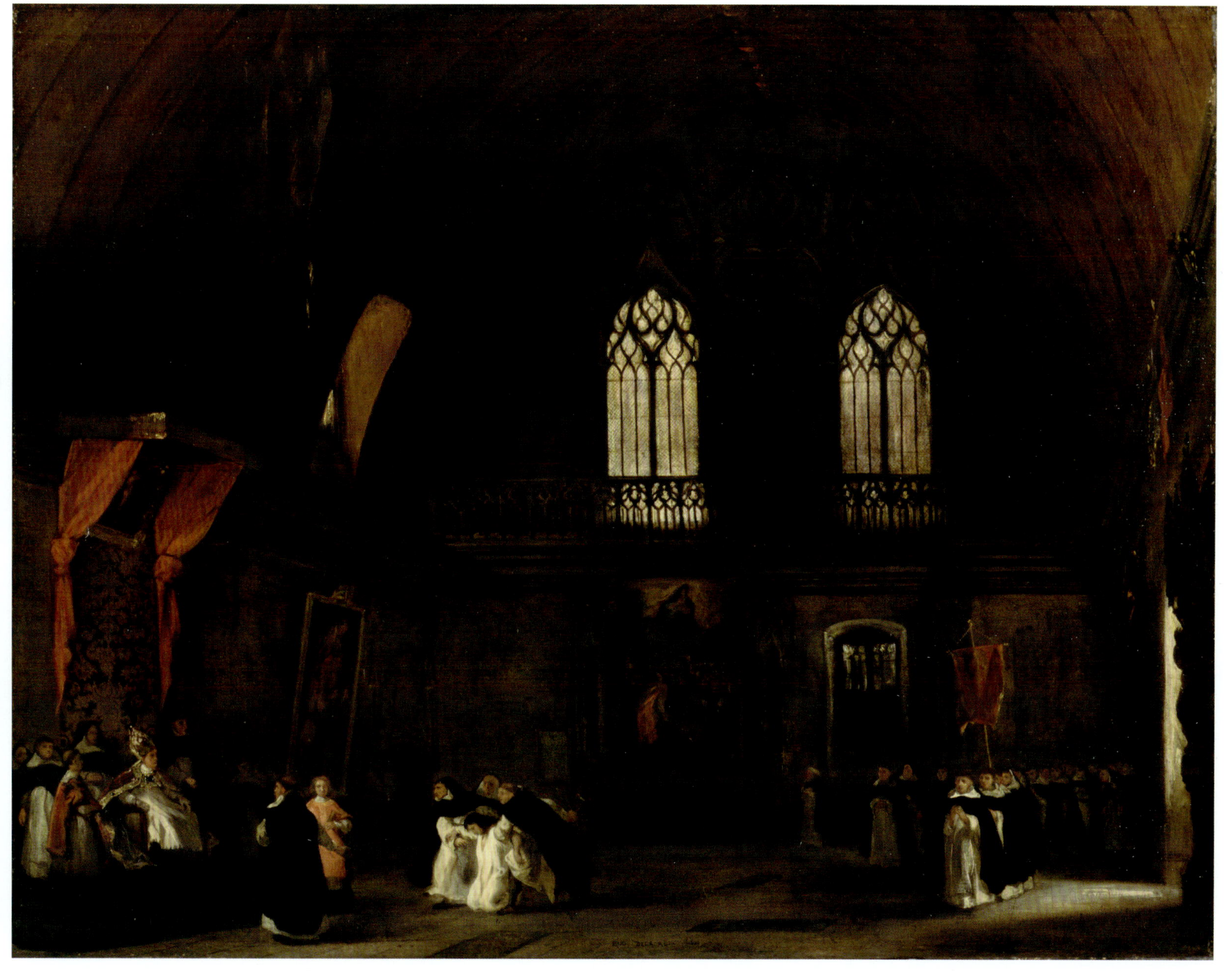

FIG. 38
Eugène Delacroix
Arab Horses Fighting in a Stable, 1860
Oil on canvas, 64.5 × 81 cm
Musée d'Orsay, Paris
[cat. 19]

FIG. 39
Eugène Delacroix
The Assassination of the Bishop of Liège, 1829
Oil on canvas, 91 × 116 cm
Musée du Louvre, Paris

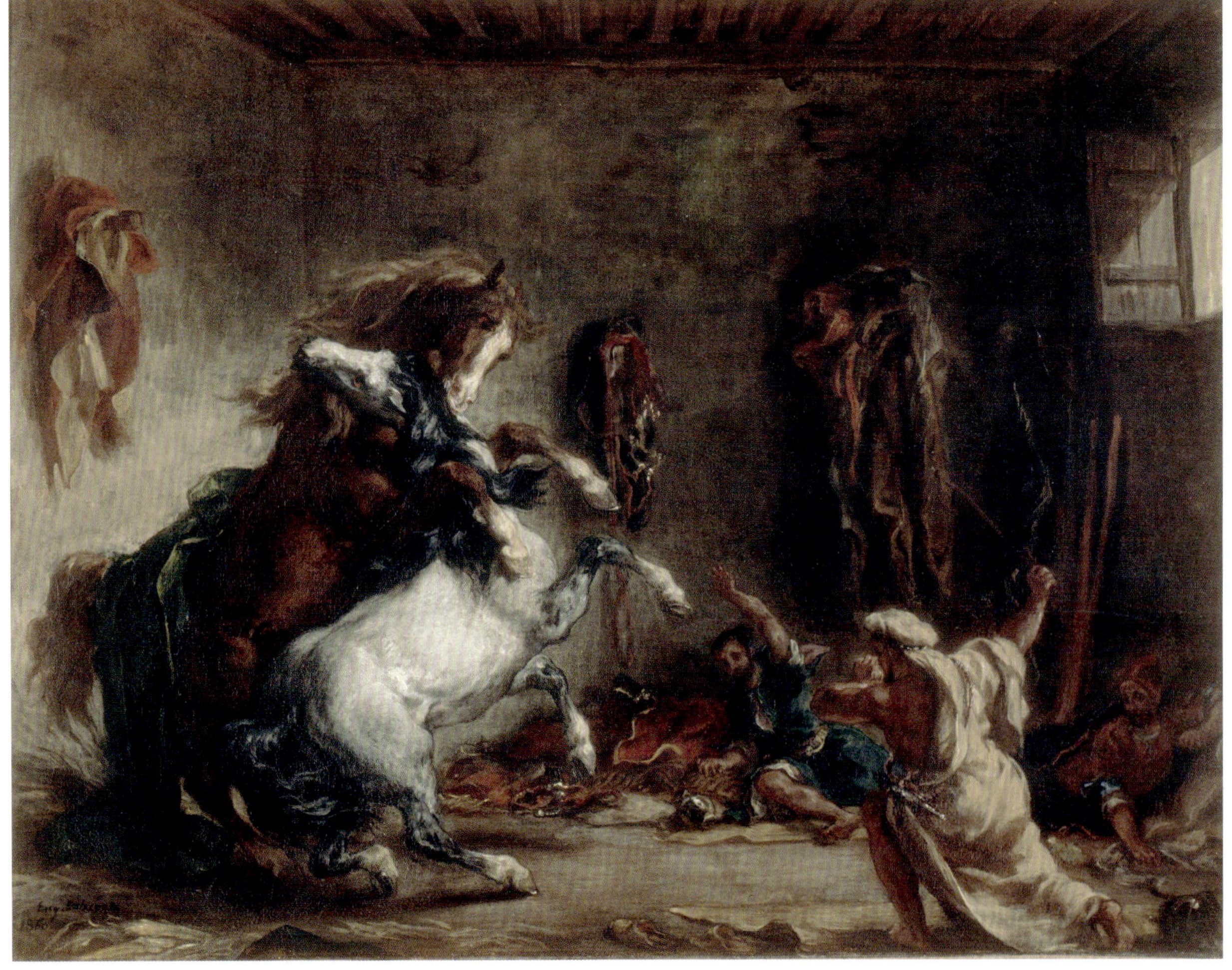

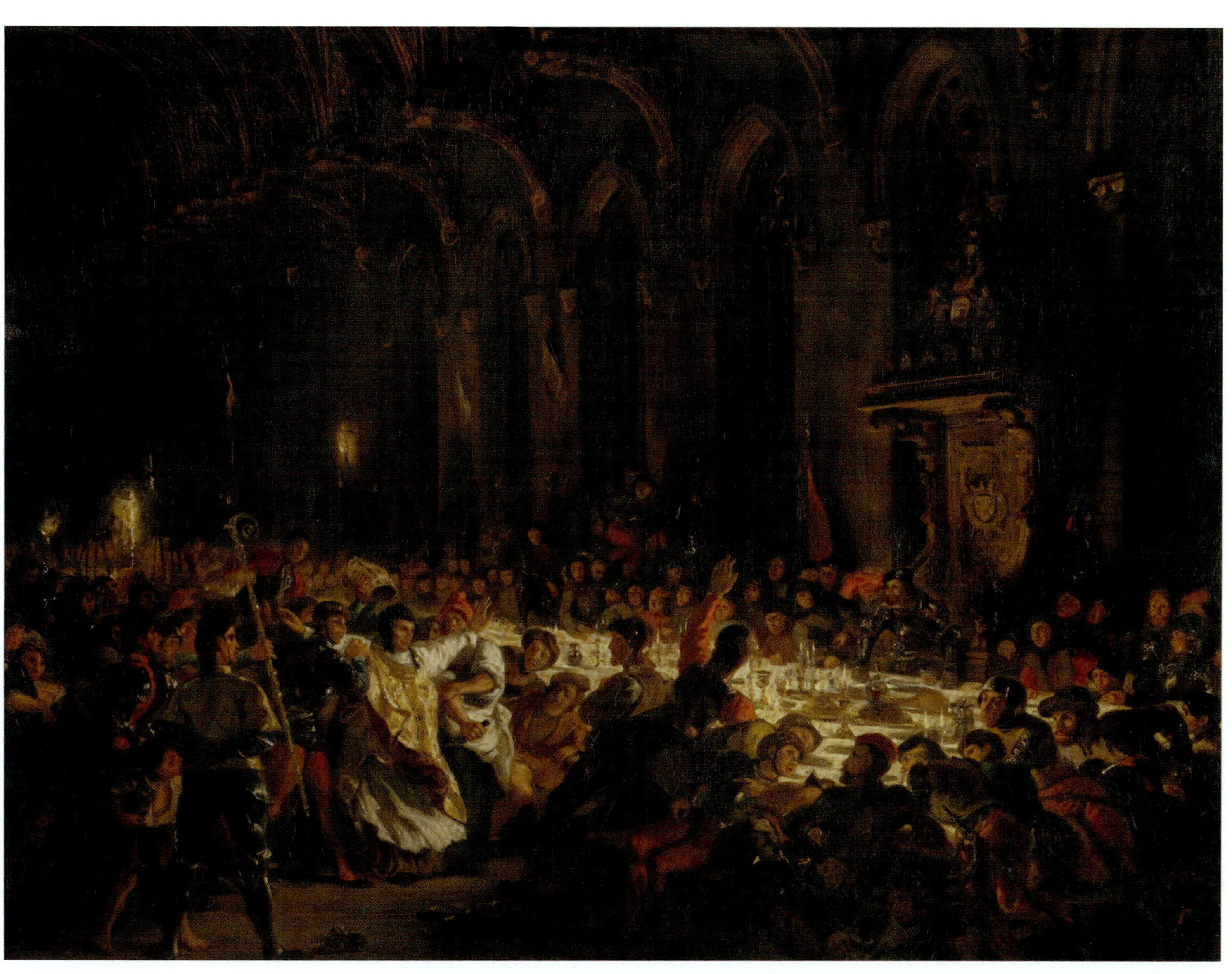

FIG. 40
Jean-Baptiste-Camille Corot
Ruins of the Château of Pierrefonds, about 1840–5, re-worked about 1866–7
Oil on canvas, 74.5 × 106.4 cm
Cincinnati Art Museum, Illinois
[cat. 7]

FIG. 41
Jean-Baptiste-Camille Corot
The Bridge at Mantes, 1868–70
Oil on canvas, 38 × 55 cm
Musée du Louvre, Paris

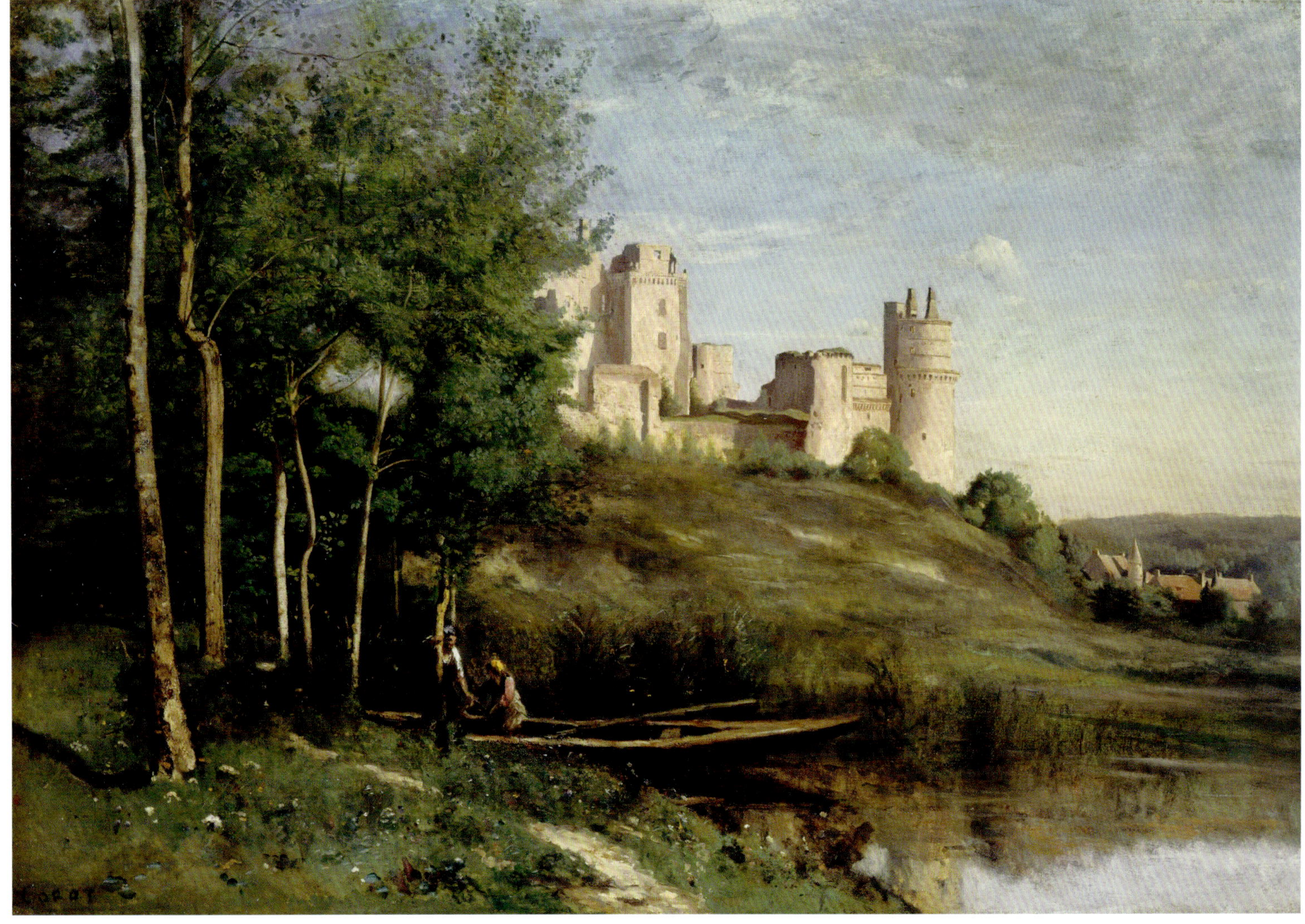

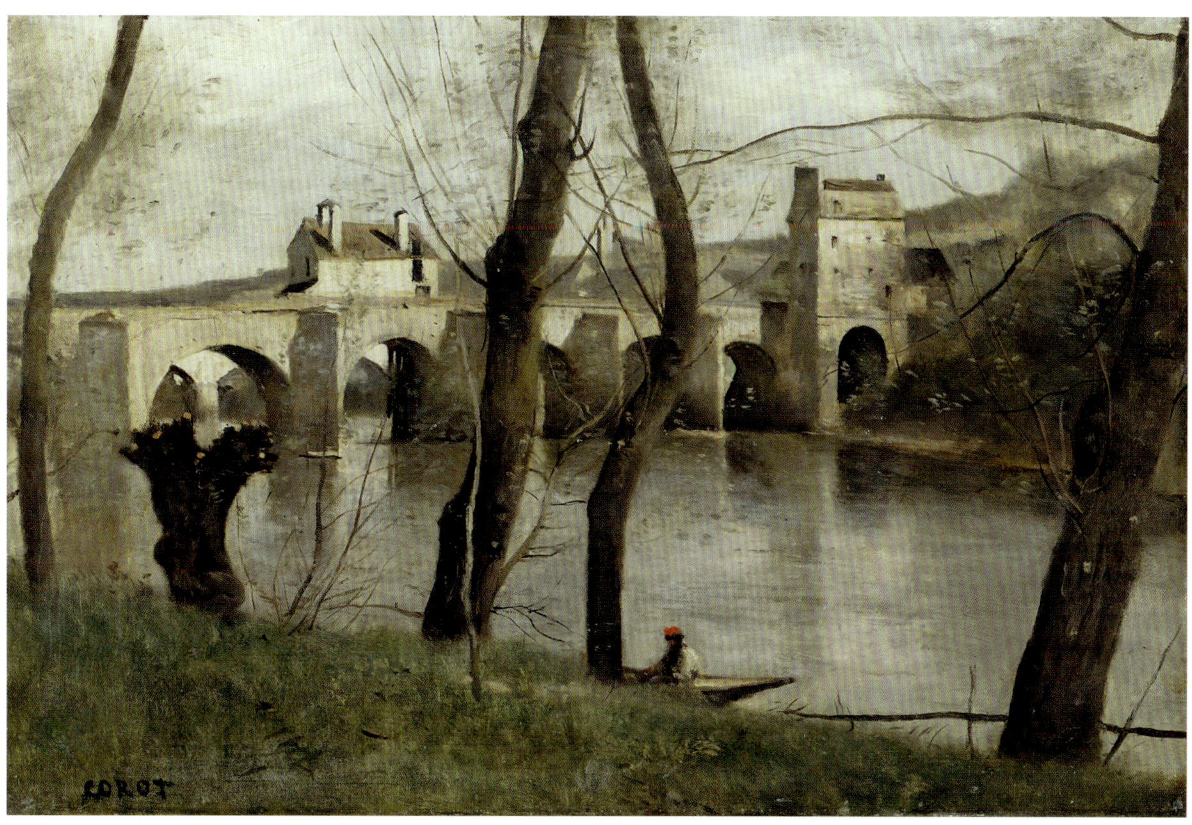

Jean-Baptiste-Camille Corot

Durand-Ruel later wrote that the only artist that he admired as much as Delacroix was Jean-Baptiste-Camille Corot, arguably the leading figure in the School of 1830.[15] In the late 1860s, in concert with Brame, he purchased many works from Corot, including such major Salon paintings as *Macbeth* (Wallace Collection, London) as well as naturalistic views of sites around France.[16] Between 1866 and 1873, he bought 225 works by the artist on his own, as he undertook a systematic campaign to build up a monopoly over Corot's work.[17] Indeed, Corot purchases appear more regularly in stock books from the early 1870s than those of any other artist.[18] Durand-Ruel bought large numbers of pictures from his fellow dealers and collectors (including the luminous *Bridge at Mantes* (fig. 41)[19] as well as directly from Corot. He remembered that he was a regular visitor to the artist's studio, where he purchased major paintings such as *The Destruction of Sodom* (Metropolitan Museum of Art, New York), for which he paid the substantial sum of 15,000 francs, and intimate portraits including *Woman Reading* (Musée des Beaux-Arts, Lyon).[20] Many of these acquisitions were sent to his London gallery or to Hourquebie, his representative in his Brussels gallery. The period from 1870 until 1875 was, indeed, a period of early affluence in Durand-Ruel's career when he maintained offices in both of these capitals.

Durand-Ruel sought to promote an overall, encyclopaedic view of Corot's multi-faceted production (fig. 40). In this, he differed from earlier dealers, who had generally focused on particular areas in the artist's output such as his outdoor sketches, which had enjoyed a vogue among rue Laffitte dealers since the 1850s. Generally, however, Durand-Ruel made only modest gains on these purchases, usually selling them on soon after at a profit of around 20–30%. Occasionally, he made more substantial profits, as in the case of the *Dance of the Nymphs* (private collection, Robaut 1627), acquired for 6,500 francs in 1871 and sold on for twice that amount.[21] Durand-Ruel's respect for Corot was evident shortly before the artist's death, when he was instrumental in commissioning a medal, sculpted by Geoffroy-Dechaume, to honour the painter. This was awarded in the gallery on the rue Laffitte and the artist, deeply touched, was apparently moved to tears.[22]

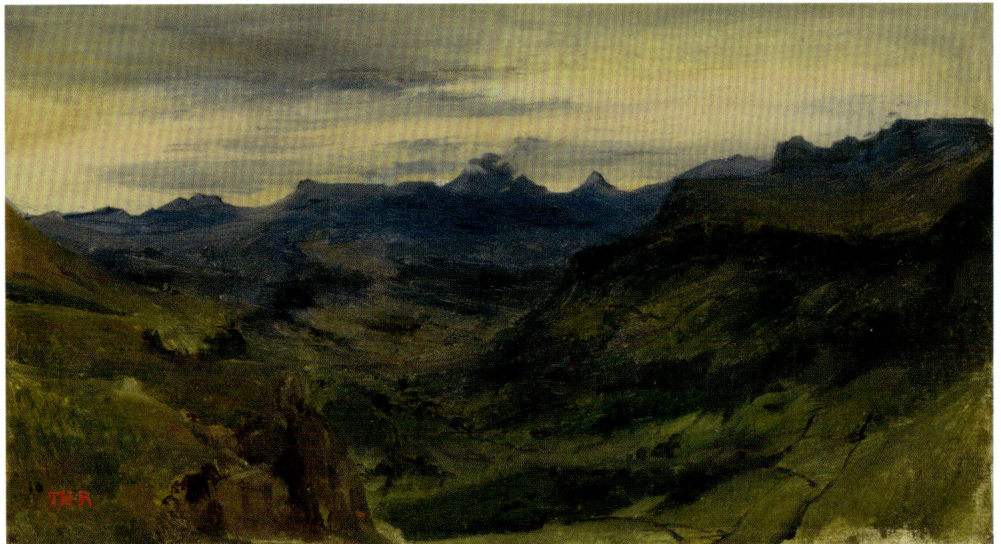

Théodore Rousseau

Durand-Ruel also much admired the work of Théodore Rousseau,[23] (fig. 43) and remembered that as a young man he often saw the painter, who helped to form his artistic judgment.[24] He also remembered the artist's desolation after the one-man sale of his paintings in 1850, when large numbers were bought in and returned to the Durand-Ruel Gallery.[25] In the autumn of 1866, he and Brame visited Rousseau at Barbizon where they saw much of his work in his studio: Millet noted that the artist entertained them with lunch.[26] Soon after, the dealers acquired the *Interior of Wood with Cows* (Musée d'Orsay, Paris), which was subsequently shown at the 1867 Salon.[27] Their most spectacular purchase from Rousseau, however, was a group of 91 works, consisting principally of plein-air oil sketches, for a combined sum of 100,000 francs; this acquisition was made between March and June 1867. It was a considerable gamble at a time when Durand-Ruel was still not financially secure – the dealer later remembered that his accountant counselled him not to make the deal – while Rousseau's sketches were also little known (figs 42 and 44). However, it was a far-sighted move, particularly as the individual values assigned to each sketch were often low. The dealer's strategy chimed with a growing interest in artistic personality with the rise of the artist biography: these sketches served as the best indicator of the artist's direct engagement with nature. In the years and months to come, Durand-Ruel was able to sell them for very considerable profits. The sketch *The Grotto of Port-en-Bessin* (private collection, S 135), for example, acquired for 500 francs, remained in his stock for more than five years, when he sold it at a five-fold profit of 2,500 francs.[28] Durand-Ruel was quite willing to keep his works in stock for long periods of time, aware that rushed sales could damage an artist's prices. He and Brame were also proactive in generating collector interest in the sketches, particularly through the organisation of an exhibition of Rousseau's work in the gentleman's club, the Cercle de la rue de Choiseul, in the summer of 1867, at the same time as the Paris Universal Exhibition. This included 109 paintings, with 80 sketches and several larger-scale preparatory works, all highlighting the complexity of the artist's working methods and providing exceptional insight into his process. The two dealers commissioned a catalogue introduction from the critic Philippe Burty, which described these sketches as the very 'key' to the artist's whole production.[29]

Following Rousseau's death in December 1867, Durand-Ruel sought to promote the artist's prices at auction. Most notably, he and Brame bought the artist's early masterpiece, *Avenue of Chestnut Trees* (fig. 46), at the sale of the Turkish collector, Khalil Bey, for the very substantial sum of 27,100 francs, a new auction record for the artist.[30] This was a painting that they had in fact recently sold to Bey for around half that amount.[31] In buying back the picture, they made an important public statement about the new level of prices for Rousseau's work at the very time when they were building up a

FIG. 42
Théodore Rousseau
The Valley of Saint-Vincent, 1830
Oil on paper laid on canvas,
18.2 × 32.4 cm
The National Gallery, London
[cat. 85]

FIG. 43
Théodore Rousseau
View of Mont Blanc, seen from La Faucille, about 1863–7
Oil on canvas, 91.4 × 118.4 cm
Minneapolis Institute of Arts, Minnesota
[cat. 87]

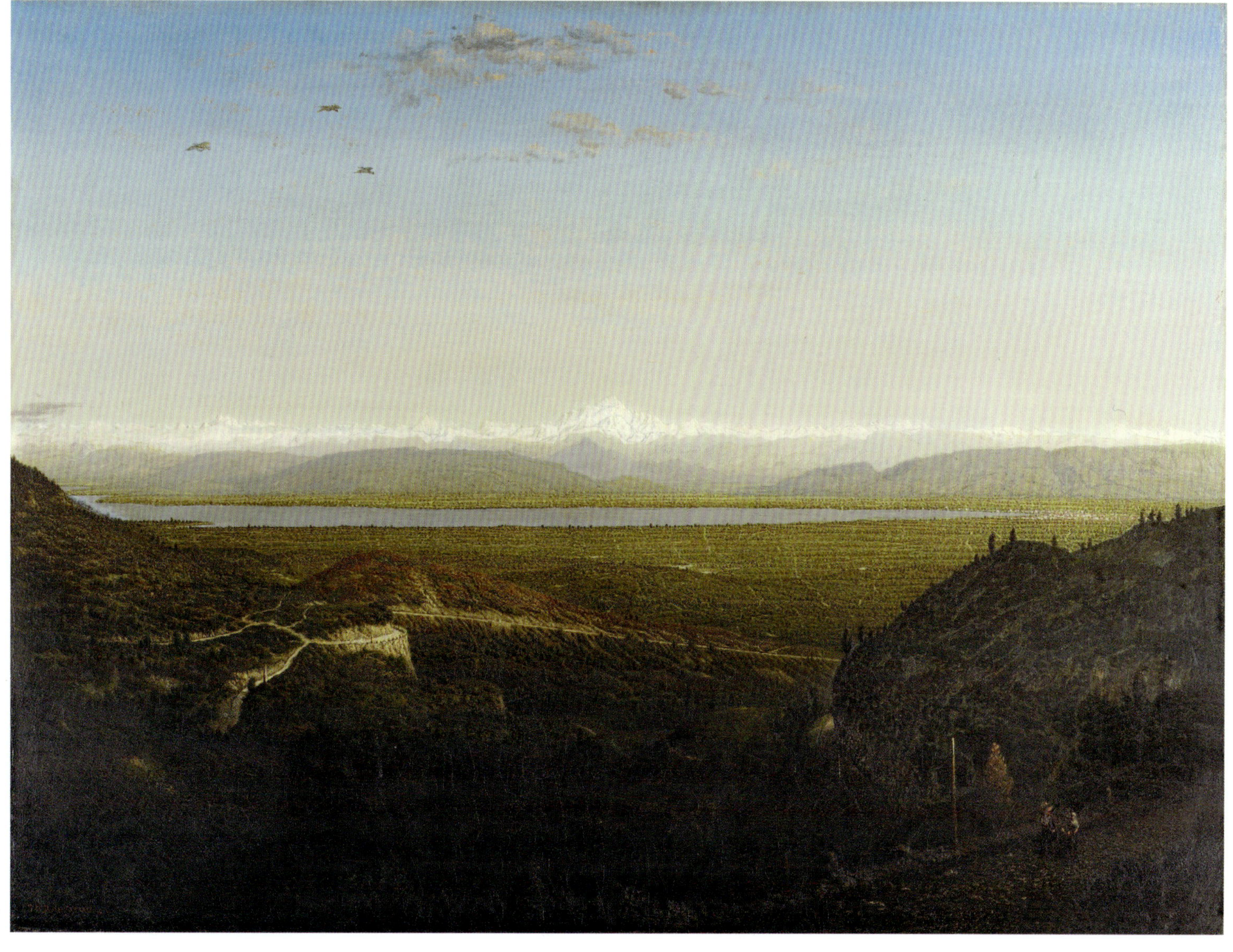

FIG. 44
Théodore Rousseau
Clearing in the High Forest of Fontainebleau, 1866
Oil on wood, 28 × 53 cm
Musée d'Orsay, Paris

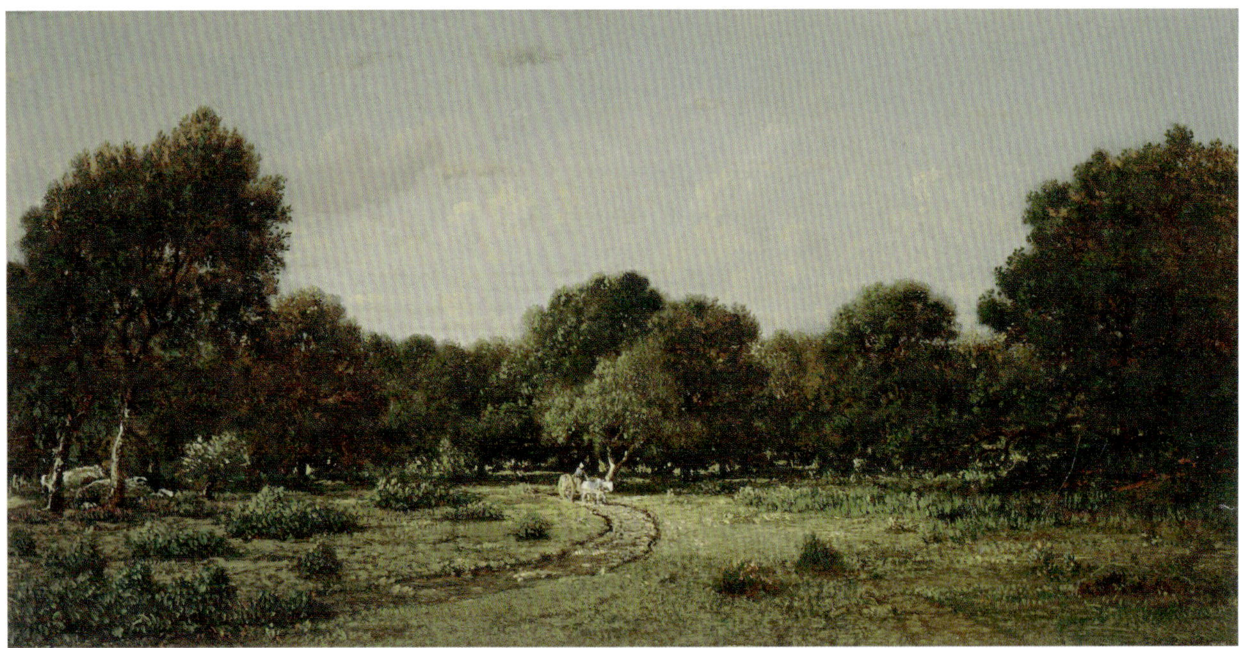

FIG. 45
Théodore Rousseau
The Old Park at Saint-Cloud, about 1831–2
Oil on canvas, 66.6 × 82.5 cm
National Gallery of Canada, Ottawa
[cat. 86]

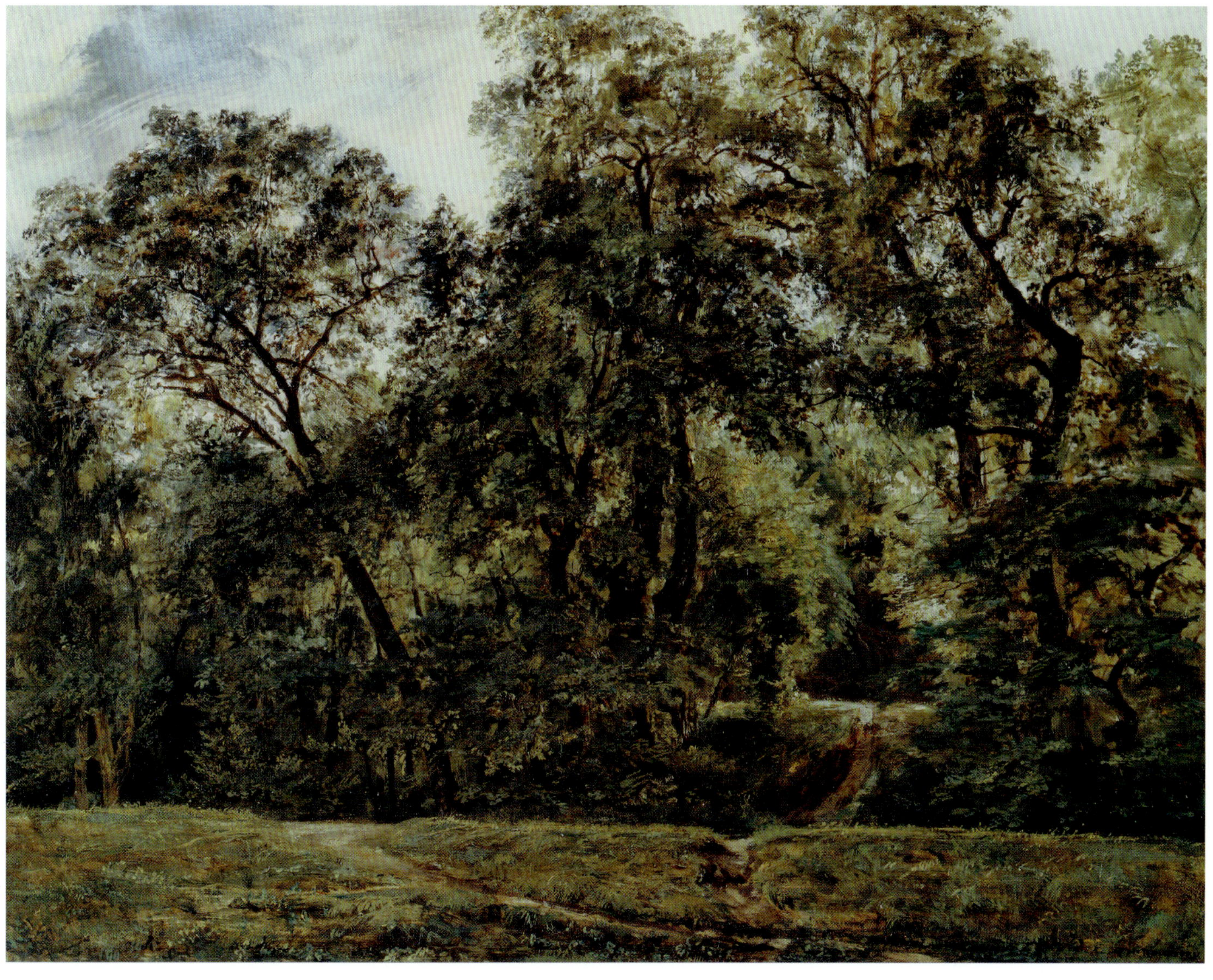

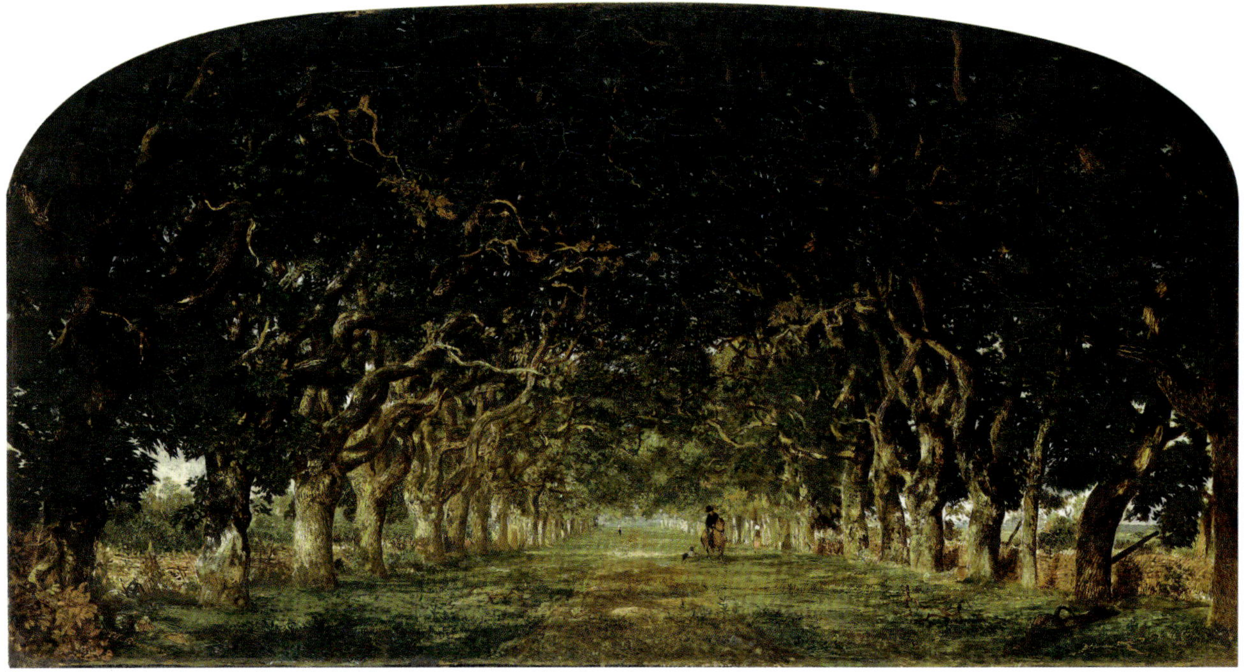

monopoly on his pictures. Despite their short-term loss, they were soon able to sell the work on at profit.[32] Durand-Ruel and Brame were subsequently the largest buyers at Rousseau's posthumous sale in April 1868, acquiring most notably the incandescent *The Forest in Winter at Sunset* (fig. 47).[33]

Durand-Ruel recognised the importance of developing a critical and intellectual discourse around an artist's work as a means of increasing its economic value. In January 1869, he established a monthly arts magazine, *La Revue internationale de l'art et de la curiosité*, with the purpose of encouraging supportive articles on the artists in his stable. The magazine was distributed around Europe in Paris, London, Turin and Florence, Vienna and Frankfurt. The critic Alfred Sensier published his memories of Théodore Rousseau in serial form from July 1869 until August 1870, when the review was abruptly halted by the Franco-Prussian War (with the final article still to be published). These memories played a crucial role in shaping public perceptions of Rousseau's personality. Sensier presented the artist as a tormented and unjustly neglected outsider – 'le malheureux supplicié'[34] – as well as a pantheist in exceptionally close touch with nature. Both of these constructions served to encourage collector interest in the artist's work (fig. 45). Sensier's articles on Rousseau were brought together in a book, *Souvenirs sur Théodore Rousseau*, also published by Durand-Ruel, in 1872. In April that year, the dealer sent 25 copies of the book to prominent dealers and critics such as Brame and Burty as well as the Belgian dealer Arthur Stevens, and critic Gustave Frédéric of *l'Indépendance belge*.[35]

At the same time, Durand-Ruel organised an innovative public programme, including a lecture series in 1870 in his new gallery space on the rue Laffitte. Here, Sensier gave a lecture on the history of French landscape painting, subsequently published in the *Revue internationale* in July 1870.[36] Surrounded by Rousseau's work – most notably *The Forest in Winter* – the critic argued that it was the culmination of a long national landscape tradition, dating back to the Middle Ages and continuing through Poussin to the present day. *The Forest in Winter* was also a work to which Durand-Ruel was deeply attached personally, and he bought it for his private collection in February 1872.[37] It is possible that he was drawn to this work of solemn, metaphysical power by his religious upbringing (he attended church regularly until his death), as well as his early interest in becoming a missionary.

FIG. 46
Théodore Rousseau
Avenue of Chestnut Trees, 1837–42
Oil on canvas, 79 × 144 cm
Musée du Louvre, Paris

FIG. 47
Théodore Rousseau
The Forest in Winter at Sunset, about 1846–67
Oil on canvas, 162.6 × 260 cm
The Metropolitan Museum of Art, New York

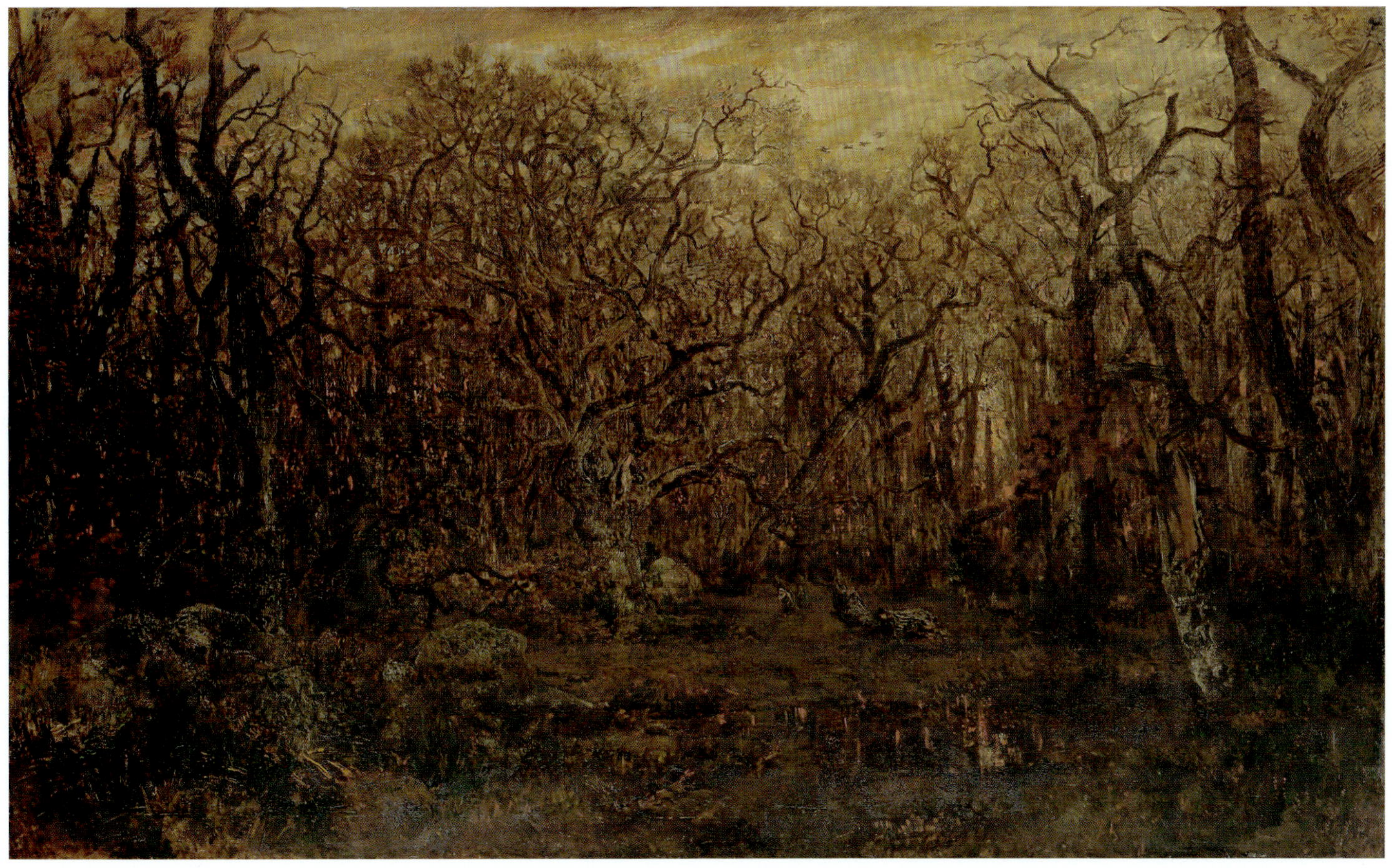

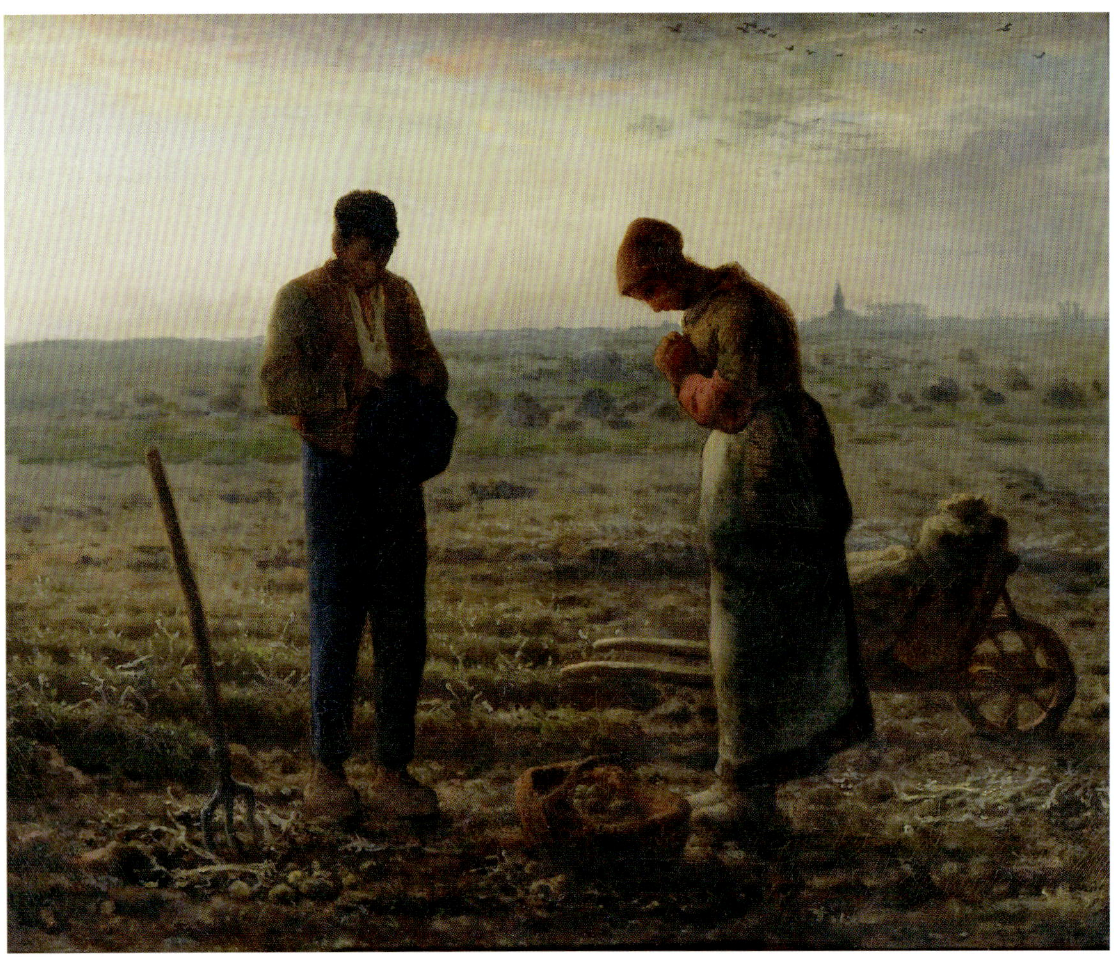

Jean-François Millet

Durand-Ruel was also a major supporter of Jean-François Millet, whom he had known from the 1840s when his father had purchased neo-rococo images from the artist. In the autumn of 1866, he and Brame offered Millet an exclusive contract to secure the artist's annual production in return for a yearly sum of 30,000 francs.[38] Though the painter refused their offer, they continued to buy works, often directly from him, such as *The Geese* (private collection, Japan, MN 241).

DURAND-RUEL AND 'LA BELLE ECOLE' OF 1830

During the Franco-Prussian War, Durand-Ruel regularly sent money from London to Millet at Cherbourg. At a time of difficulty for the artist, this support led to a new level of friendship between the men. Millet wrote in 1871, 'It's impossible for me to imagine how we could have survived if Durand-Ruel had not asked for paintings. He proved our saviour.'[39] Following his return to Paris after the war, Durand-Ruel began to collect Millet's work with a new intensity, seeking to establish a monopoly over the artist's production. His support of Millet was particularly spectacular in 1872, when he spent the enormous sum of 390,950 francs on the artist's work.[40] He now systematically bought up Millet's most important pictures from other dealers and collectors (notably Emile Gavet), including *The Angelus* (fig. 48), *The Shepherd* (Yamanashi Prefectural Museum of Art, Japan) and *Death and the Woodcutter* (Ny Carlsberg Glyptotek, Copenhagen).[41] He also acquired the artist's recent landscapes, such as the grand and now destroyed painting *Winter*. These newly acquired pictures were all showcased in a special exhibition in his galleries and 'very much admired', as noted by Sensier.[42] In May 1872, the dealer also bought 34 paintings by Millet from Sensier's spectacular collection, most notably *The Sower* (Yamanashi Prefectural Museum of Art).[43] Durand-Ruel also asked Millet to send him all his new pictures – 'everything you do' – including work on a newly ambitious scale.[44] Among the paintings he received were luminous landscapes with dramatic high horizon lines such as *Shepherdess Spinning* (Art Institute of Chicago, Illinois) and *The Turkey Herder* (Metropolitan

FIG. 48
Jean-François Millet
The Angelus, 1857–59
Oil on canvas, 55.5 cm × 66 cm
Musée d'Orsay, Paris

FIG. 49
Jean-François Millet
The Sheepfold, Moonlight
about 1856–8
Oil on panel, 45.3 × 63.4 cm
The Walters Art Museum, Baltimore
[cat. 28]

Museum of Art, New York). He paid 12,300 francs for the latter, selling it on soon after at a very considerable profit for 30,000 francs.[45]

Durand-Ruel promoted Millet's work hard on the international exhibition circuit, putting on significant displays in his London galleries and at the 1873 Vienna International Exhibition (which included *The Sower*, Yamanashi Prefectural Museum of Art).[46] He also made sustained efforts to push Millet's prices at the auction house. In April 1872, he set a sale record for Millet by buying the atmospheric *Sheepfold, Moonlight* for 20,000 francs (fig. 49). A year later, at the Laurent-Richard sale, he paid another record of 38,500 francs for the intimate genre scene *Woman by Lamplight* (Frick Collection, New York). As had been the case in his support of Rousseau, here he bought back a work that he had supplied himself.[47] After this sale, Sensier wrote to Millet:

> Durand has bought back your two paintings [*Woman by Lamplight* and *Laundrywoman*]. Collombel [Durand-Ruel's representative] pushed them for Durand, who wanted to see an increase ... This brave Durand knows no obstacles and affirms that your paintings must increase to the prices of Meissonier. There's nothing wrong with that, but will he be able to do it?[48]

The years to come would provide an affirmative answer to Sensier's rhetorical question. Millet's prices would rise to an extent that they would exceed those of Meissonier, making him the most expensive painter of the nineteenth century, an elevation in large part due to Durand-Ruel.

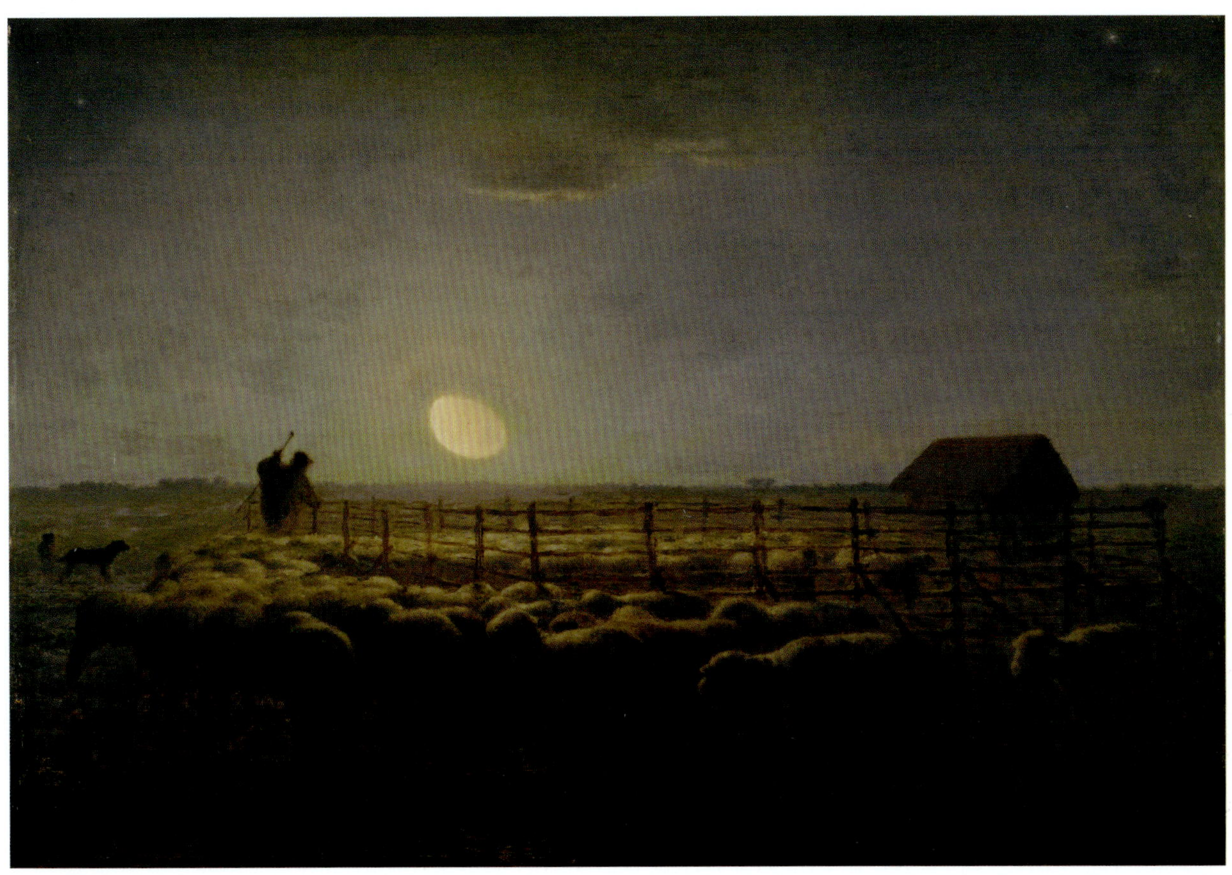

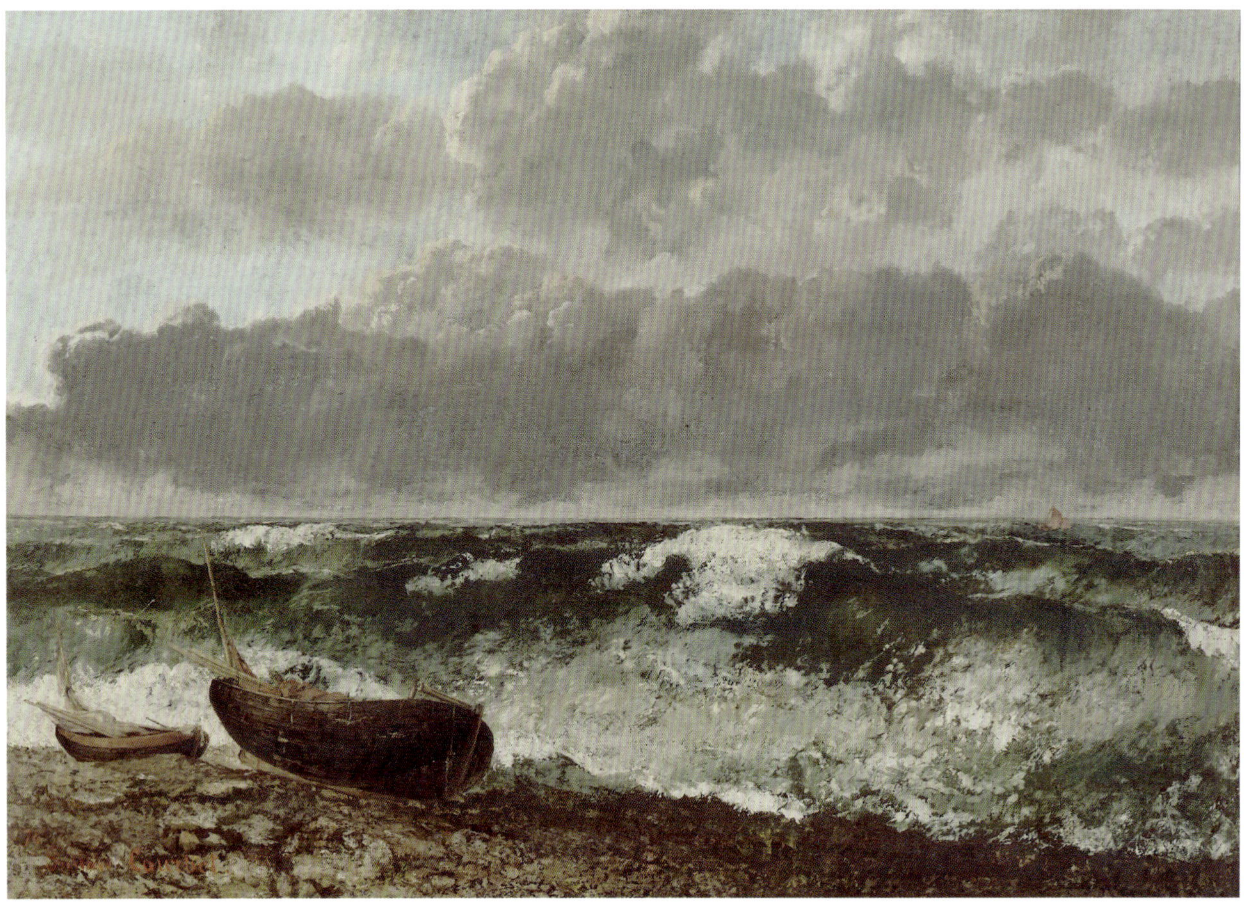

Gustave Courbet

In the early 1870s, Durand-Ruel's aggressive and expansive collecting of the School of 1830 also focused on the closely related work of Gustave Courbet. Previously, he had bought a small number of pictures by the artist in concert with Brame, but now he greatly expanded his purchases. Durand-Ruel's conservative, Catholic and royalist politics contrasted with those of the radical left-wing Courbet, but did not prevent his extensive support. At the time of the Franco-Prussian War, when Courbet's Parisian studio was threatened with bombardment by Prussian guns, Durand-Ruel sheltered the artist's major works, such as *The Burial at Ornans* and *The Studio* (both Musée d'Orsay, Paris). Soon after, he showed his open-mindedness in acquiring the anti-clerical *Return from the Fair* (original now lost), which he sold on immediately at a 50% profit.[49]

Durand-Ruel's purchases now concentrated on landscapes, many of which were acquired in large batches directly from Courbet's studio (fig. 51). In April 1872, he bought a group of 26 paintings including *The Great Oak* (Musée Courbet, Ornans) and the 1870 Salon work, *The Wave* (fig. 50): he paid 6,000 francs for the latter, selling it on immediately at almost two-and-a-half times the price for 15,000 francs.[50] Early the following year, he bought another batch of 24 pictures including marines and Franche-Comté views such as *The Grotto of Source of the Loue* (Getty Art Museum, Los Angeles).[51] Durand-Ruel also orchestrated Courbet's exhibition of paintings in Vienna at the time of the 1873 International Exhibition.[52] Courbet's own gratitude to the dealer was sincere.[53]

FIG. 50
Gustave Courbet
The Wave, 1870
Oil on canvas, 116.5 × 160 cm
Musée d'Orsay, Paris

FIG. 51
Gustave Courbet
Still Life with Apples, 1872
Oil on canvas, 59.4 × 73.5 cm
The Mesdag Collection,
The Hague
[cat. 9]

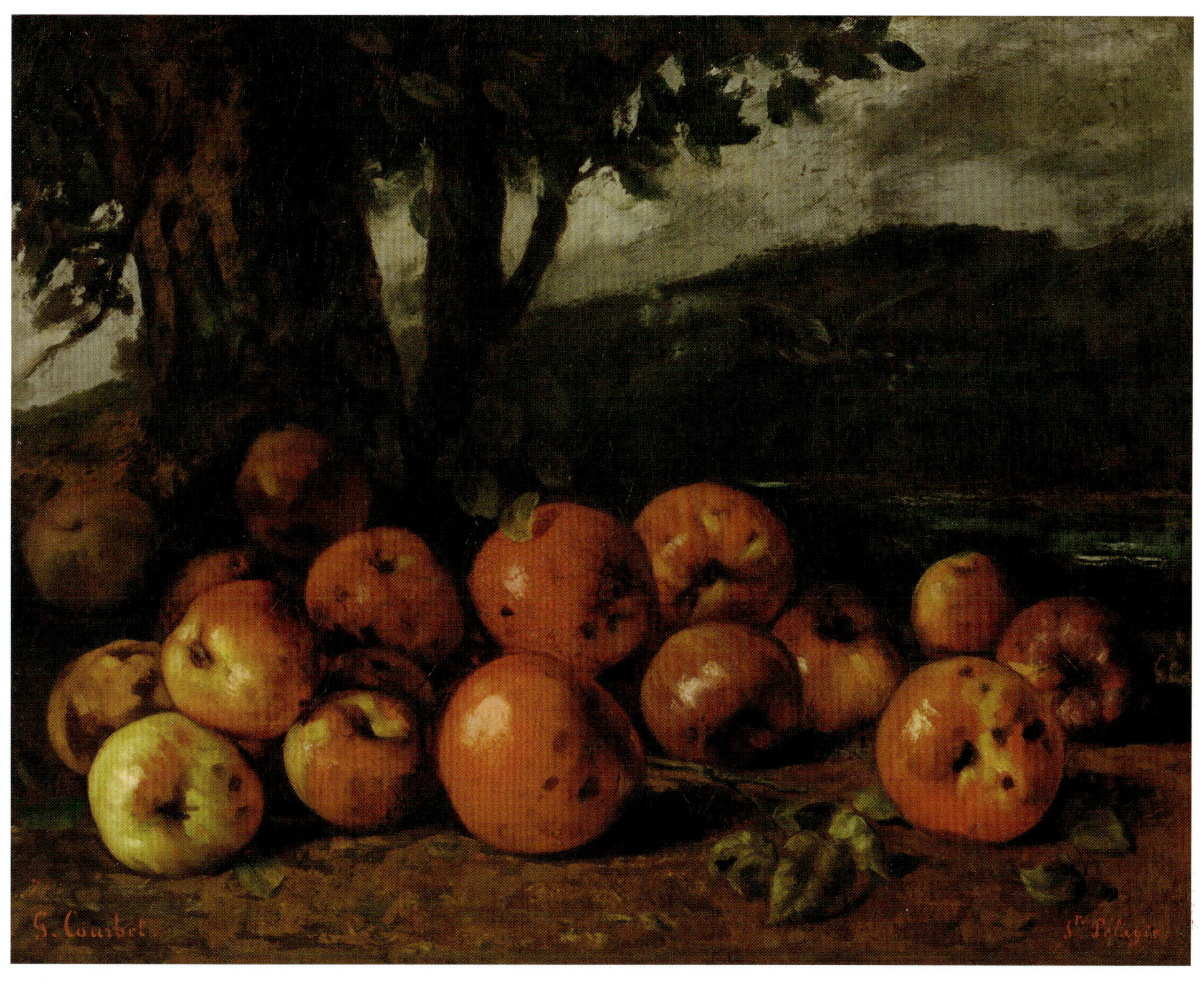

Jules Dupré, Charles-François Daubigny and others

In the late 1860s and early 1870s, Durand-Ruel also bought significant numbers of works from other artists of the 1830 School, including the forest views of Narcisse-Virgile Diaz de la Peña and the rural genre scenes of Constant Troyon, often paying particularly high prices for the latter artist.[54] He was a major supporter of Jules Dupré, whom his father had also patronised extensively and whom he described as 'my great friend'.[55] Durand-Ruel acquired landscapes and marines by Dupré, sometimes from collectors (in the spring of 1870, he bought 12 works from the opera singer Jean-Baptiste Faure) and sometimes from the artist.[56] The extant correspondence from Dupré to Durand-Ruel at the time of the Franco-Prussian War suggests their closeness. Dupré had fled his studio at L'Isle-Adam at this time and retreated to the Normandy Coast at Cayeux. He described his struggles over the development of his thickly impasted marines, as well as his desolation at the takeover of his studio: 'I have heard that Prussian officers passed the night in my salon in playing piano music'.[57] He also referred to Durand-Ruel's (sadly lost) letters of friendship: 'Continue to write to me as you are doing, your excellent letters do me good and give me courage.'[58] He continued, 'I need them because I have days of profound sadness.'[59]

Durand-Ruel also bought the marines and river views of Charles-François Daubigny, developing his association with this artist when the two men stayed in London at the same time during the Franco-Prussian War (and where he was introduced to Monet by Daubigny).[60] There had, indeed, been a long-standing association between the Durand-Ruel family and Daubigny, who had produced an image (see fig. 19) of the family gallery as early as 1845.

The 1878 Exhibition

Durand-Ruel's financial problems of the mid-1870s hindered his continued purchases, but he was nonetheless able to continue to promote the work of the School of 1830. Most notably, in 1878 he organised a spectacular retrospective exhibition of their painting at the same time as the Universal Exhibition, Paris, where their works were largely overlooked in the official display.[61] Borrowing pictures from his circle of private collectors (many of which he had sold himself), he assembled an enormous show in his rue Laffitte galleries, containing 382 works with 88 paintings by Corot (including *The Port of La Rochelle*, Yale University Art Gallery), 61 by Millet (including *The Angelus* and *Four Seasons*), 33 by Rousseau (including *Forest in Winter*), 32 by Delacroix (including *The Death of Sardanapalus*) and many other works by Courbet, Daubigny and Dupré.[62] This was the largest exhibition that he ever organised of work by the School of 1830 and summed up his commitment to their output.[63]

Durand-Ruel later noted that the show did not attract large crowds, but he also wrote that it had a considerable impact among 'people of taste'.[64] It received several significant critical reviews in the Parisian press, with most praising the dealer for organising an exhibition that surpassed the official display. Durand-Ruel noted that seeing so many works by these artists together had a major impact on collectors and dealers, providing an important catalyst for the increase in auction prices of the School of 1830 in the years around 1880. In 1881, for example, Millet's *Angelus*, the highlight of the artist's 1878 display, sold at the John W. Wilson sale for 160,000 francs – a new sale record.

The Legacy of Durand-Ruel

In his *Memoirs*, Durand-Ruel stated his aim to raise the value of the work of the School of 1830, and he undoubtedly succeeded. The late 1860s and early 1870s represented an especially remarkable period in his patronage. In purely financial terms, his involvement with the School of 1830 dominated his business during these years and he bought the most important pictures by all of the painters.[65] Durand-Ruel engaged with the work and personality of these artists on a deeply visceral level, responding strongly to the meditative quality of their painting, and arguably showing an intensity of engagement with their art that he never demonstrated with the Impressionists. He also, of course, realised the possibilities that their work offered for speculation. These painters were all relatively established when he patronised them and he paid far more for their work than the early career Impressionists (at this time he paid around 300 francs for a landscape by Monet), but he also made far greater profits. He regularly made two-fold returns on Corot, and even more substantial profits on the large batches of landscapes that he acquired from the studios of Rousseau and Courbet. His greatest investments were directed at the expensive work of Millet, and here he regularly made large profits of up to two-and-a-half times the cost price.

Durand-Ruel's signal promotion of the School of 1830 also had wider ramifications in its impact on the market for contemporary art. The strategies that the dealer used to raise the value of the work of the School all provided a newly ambitious model of art dealing, particularly for later prominent dealers such as Ambroise Vollard. His monopolisation of Corot, Millet and Rousseau set an example for the future, as did his extensive collaboration with critics such as Sensier and Burty. His consistent setting of sale records for Rousseau, Millet and Delacroix was also notable, as was his innovative use of the one-man and group retrospective. His willingness to send work abroad emphasised the importance of a global outlook. Recent writing on the structures of the nineteenth-century French art market has sought to shift the emphasis away from dealers as catalysts in effecting change in the nineteenth-century art world: instead, it has been argued that artists themselves were the principal agents of change, as in the artist-organised Impressionist shows.[66] Yet the case of Durand-Ruel highlights the continuing centrality of the art dealer in generating market growth in contemporary art in nineteenth-century France. Durand-Ruel's strategies in supporting the School of 1830 anticipate dealing methods that have become crucial to the structures and practices of the modern art market.

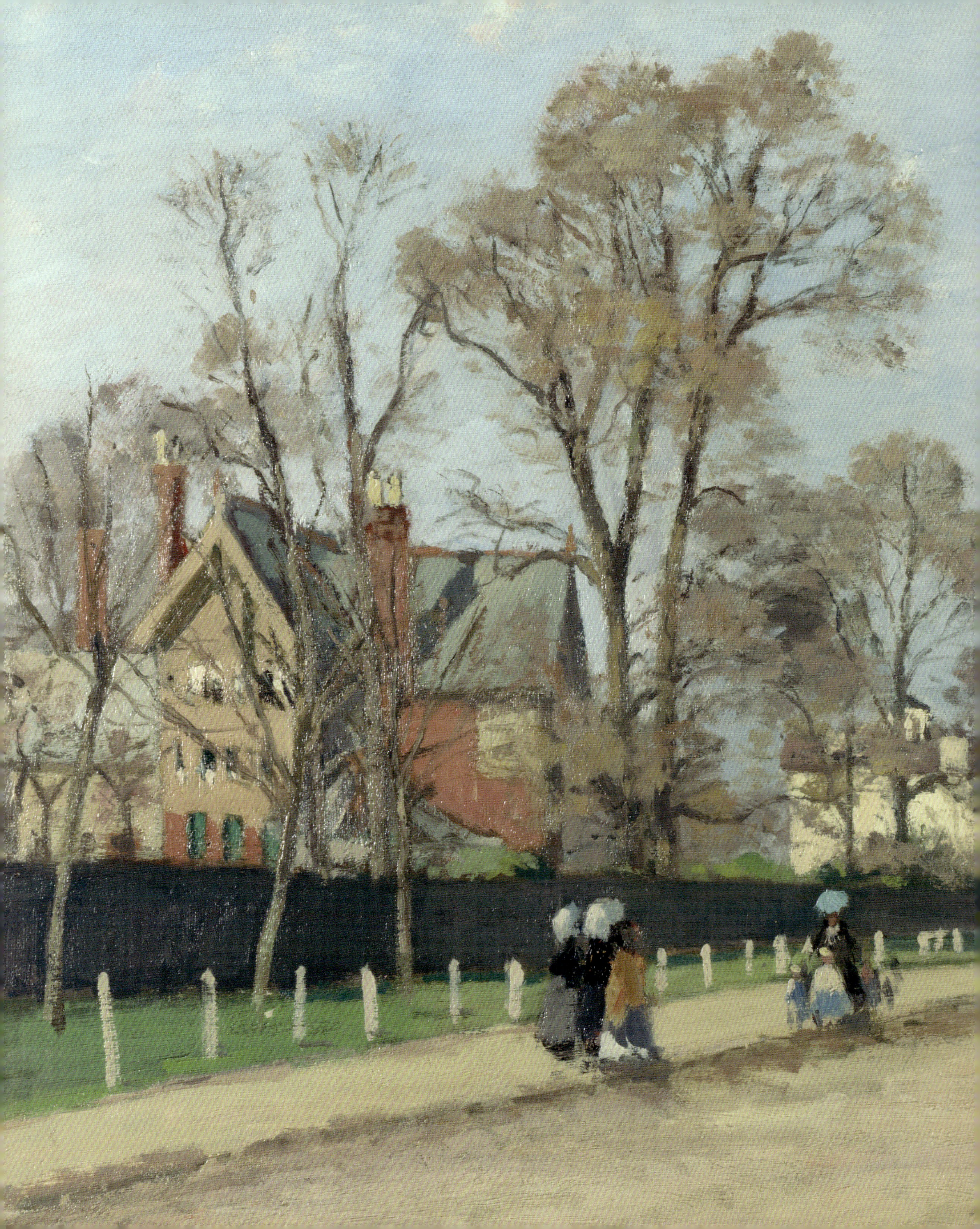

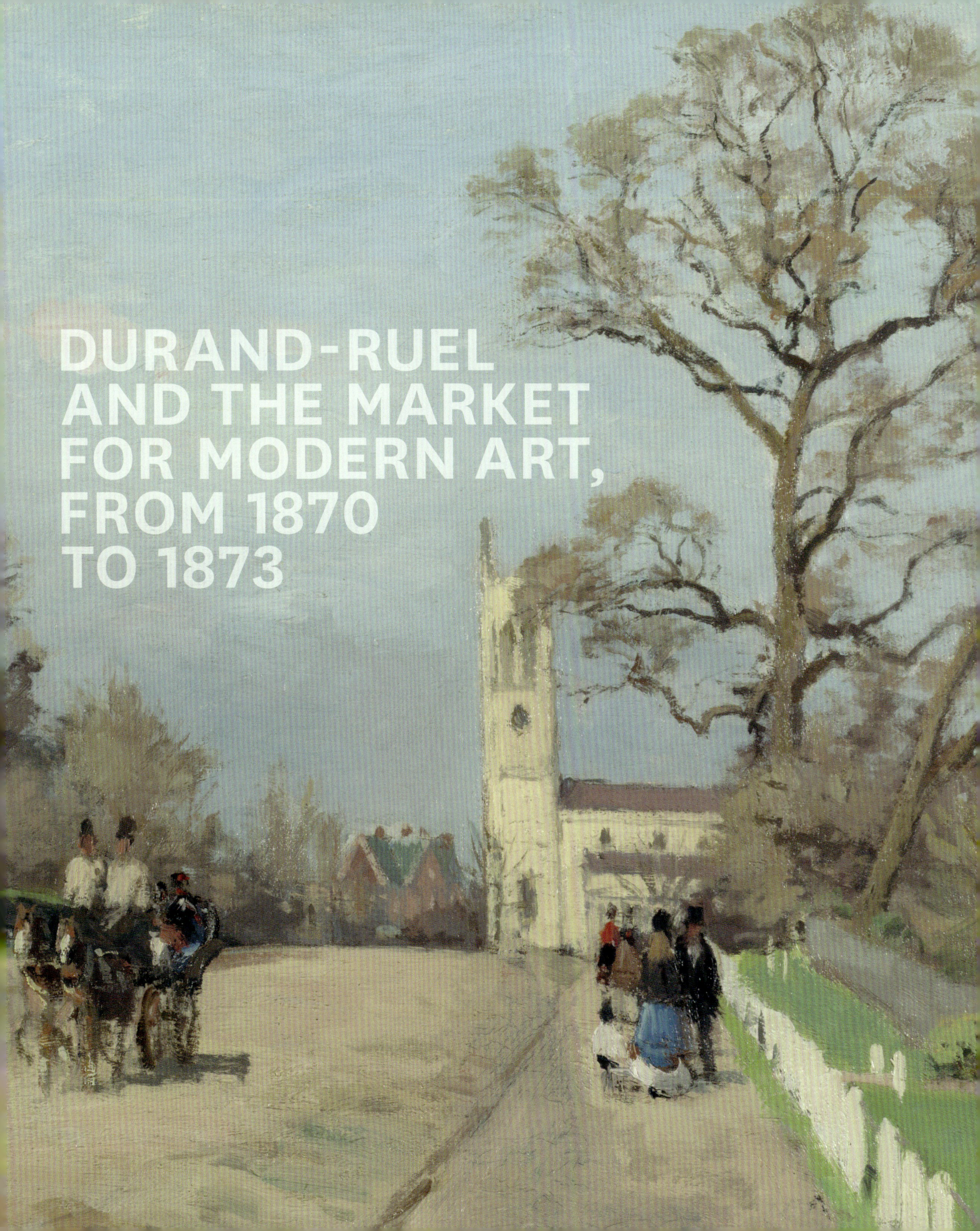
DURAND-RUEL
AND THE MARKET
FOR MODERN ART,
FROM 1870
TO 1873

Durand-Ruel and the Market for Modern Art, from 1870 to 1873

John Zarobell

In the years between 1870 and 1873, Paul Durand-Ruel introduced many innovations to the art market which, as Nicholas Green[1] and Robert Jensen[2] among others have asserted, were in keeping with the broader developments of his time. His approach blended the evangelisation of progress pursued by the followers of Saint-Simon and students of the Ecole Polytechnique (Second-Empire industrialists among them) with a level of connoisseurship in relation to the evolving conditions of modern art. The question that Durand-Ruel answered so deftly was how to evaluate what was being made by the artists of his day in order to determine what works and which artists would endure as symbols of their generation. His consistent engagement with contemporary artists led to an effort to finance their production (or at least allow them to continue it). In order to sustain that effort over time, he needed not only financial backers, but also the means to generate value from the elusive class of contemporary artists who stood outside the academic system and sought to renew French art through their innovations. It was in this spirit that he took up Edouard Manet (fig. 52) and some of the Impressionist artists during this period, consistently buying their works even though there was practically no one to sell them to. His mission was to create value, and he staked much of his business on his ability to do so, accumulating over the course of his career works by Manet, Monet and Pissarro, as well as Sisley, Renoir and Degas. Though he met the Impressionists in 1871 and collected their work consistently after that, it was not until 1886, with his first exhibition in New York, that Durand-Ruel would begin to reap the rewards of his undying commitment to this generation of artists.

In his article on the economic transformation of the artistic field in France in the second half of the nineteenth century, Nicholas Green begins with a discussion of the Edwards sale of 37 lots held at the Hôtel Drouot on 7 March 1870.[3] This sale is a perfect illustration of how the economics of modern art distribution and consumption are connected to the creation of individual masters and, more generally, cultural value within the field of art history. This is because Charles Edwards, whose collection had been acquired from Paul Durand-Ruel in the previous two years, was actually the dealer's creditor. According to Durand-Ruel's own account, Edwards had drawn him into a speculative venture to allow him capital to acquire artworks, but also to inflate the values of some of Durand-Ruel's most cherished artists, such as Delacroix, Rousseau and Millet, in whose paintings he had already made a considerable investment.[4]

Green's ground-breaking article positions Durand-Ruel as a new kind of speculator in modern art, whose techniques had been inherited from a group of adventurous and manipulative financiers such as the Péreire brothers, who had thrived under Louis-Napoléon's Second Empire.[5] Whether the dealer followed their lead or not, Isaac Péreire was in fact an occasional customer of the gallery.[6] Yet there are other ways to see Durand-Ruel's contributions to the history of art and art dealing. Recent literature has allowed new perspectives to emerge, demonstrating that many of Durand-Ruel's innovations were presaged by developments in both England[7] and Belgium.[8] As Jan Dirk Baetens has observed: 'The traditional assumption of the almost messianic uniqueness of Durand-Ruel therefore seems to be founded on a lack of documentary evidence on art dealing in the earlier decades of the nineteenth century.'[9]

This rejoinder to Green and others who have described Durand-Ruel as an originator of the market for modern art is instructive and useful to our understanding of the evolution of the modern art market, but it does not explain how Durand-Ruel, unlike predecessors such as Gustave Coûteaux and Ernest Gambart,

FIG. 52
Edouard Manet
The Reader, 1861
Oil on canvas, 99.7 × 81.3 cm
Saint Louis Art Museum, Missouri
[cat. 21]

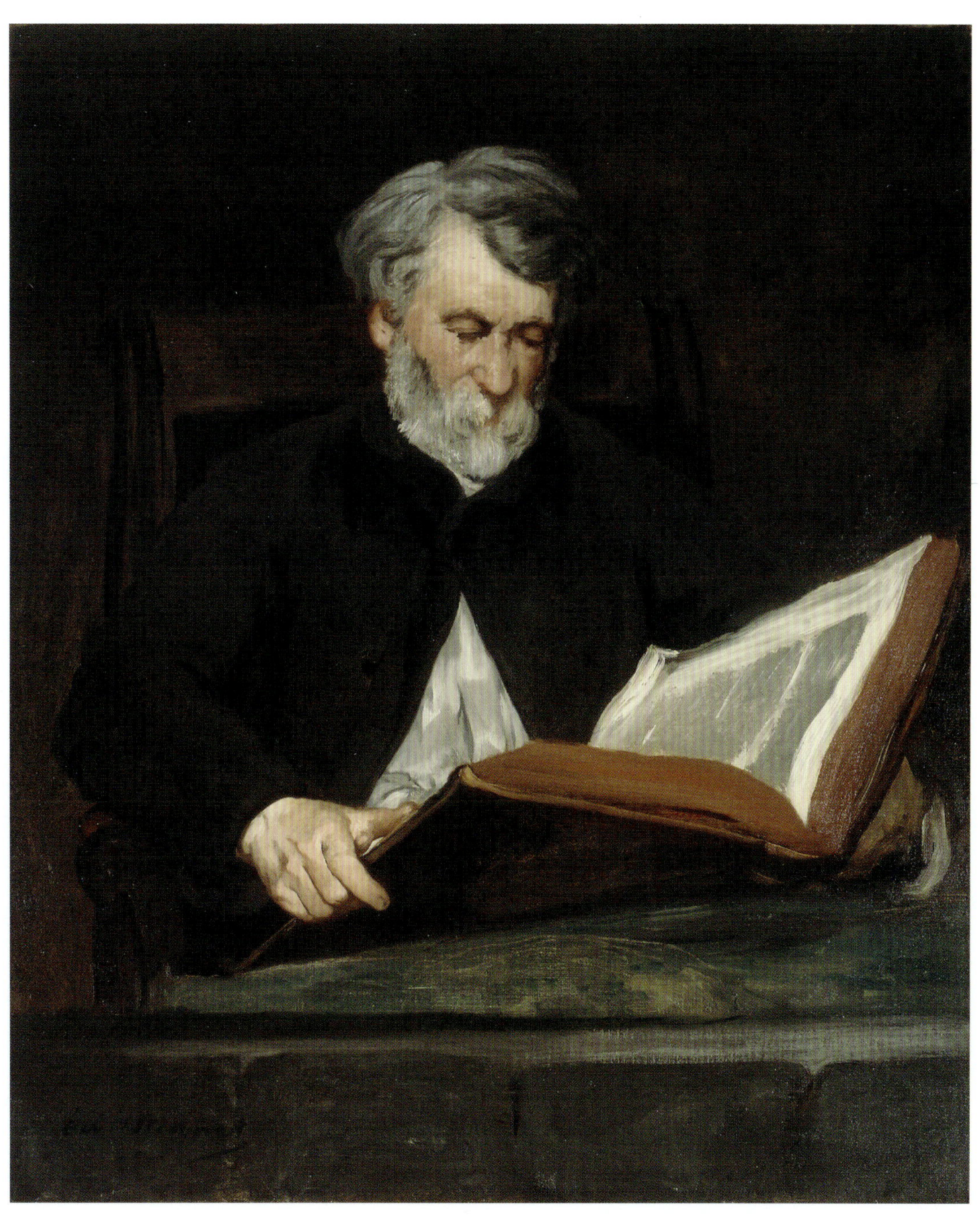

managed to make a living selling art that most collectors simply did not want. Whether one considers Durand-Ruel speculative or not, his signal achievement was to have made a fortune selling Impressionist art, despite the fact that critics and the official art establishment were primarily against it. Even among Durand-Ruel's latter-day champions, none have reconstructed the essential details of his financing of the gallery, nor have they explained how his business practices contributed to the development of modern art. This essay seeks to clarify some specifics of Durand-Ruel's business techniques and how they contributed to the careers of Manet and the Impressionists.

The importance of how Durand-Ruel's gallery was financed cannot be overestimated, but Edwards is only one part in the complex story. There are a number of specific innovations that Durand-Ruel borrowed from the world of finance that he applied in the commercial domain of the art gallery. The question is why they are important to a consideration of his role in the history of modern art, particularly in this period of the early 1870s, before the Impressionist artists assembled themselves into a group and mounted a series of exhibitions.

For Green, Durand-Ruel's economic innovations are a means of situating him within his epoch, but they are intimately connected in his account to the development of individuality as a marketable commodity and the rising significance of landscape painting. This essay offers a somewhat different analysis, showing how Durand-Ruel played a role – perhaps even a major one – in producing a new paradigm of what is now called 'contemporary' art. This new development, neither patronage nor commercialism exclusively, produced an alternative way of generating value through market mechanisms as a means to support alternatives to the accepted aesthetic canon of the Académie. In effect, Durand-Ruel succeeded in ending the monopoly the academy held on aesthetic value.

Promoting modern art

In his *Memoirs*, originally written before 1911, Durand-Ruel stated that Edwards offered him capital in exchange for a selection of paintings chosen by him for Edwards's fashionable apartment on the new boulevard Haussmann. He would later sell these at auction, resulting in mutual benefit. It is interesting that Durand-Ruel was using as collateral against the loan paintings by modern masters who were seen as anti-establishment, certain of whom were still alive and continuing to produce – though there were works by Goya in the Edwards sale as well. Although the market for Barbizon artists and French Romantics did exist, it was still embryonic, and Durand-Ruel's admission that this sale generated considerable interest among collectors is telling.[10] The nature of this financial arrangement was speculative on both sides, with Edwards charging interest but signalling that his promotion of these artists would secure enhanced values that would benefit Durand-Ruel. For the dealer, the capital allowed him to start a journal and to make major acquisitions from the studios of Barbizon painters.[11] More importantly, it allowed him to establish higher values for a group of artists, long supported by the Durand-Ruel firm, who operated primarily outside of the academy-centred, state-funded art system. Sales through the Hôtel Drouot auction house were another means to value works that competed with the system of honours and medals provided by the Académie des Beaux-Arts through the annual (or biannual) Salon. For Robert Jensen, this made Durand-Ruel the prototype of the ideological, as opposed to speculative, dealer.[12]

Before recounting the relationship that Durand-Ruel developed with the Impressionists in the years between 1871 and 1873, it is worth reviewing some of the ways that his commercial establishment echoed the business practices among French bankers and industrialists of his time. A few observations help to bring a new perspective to his entrepreneurial methods.[13]

A number of authors – including White and White, who first addressed the 'dealer-critic' system in nineteenth-century France – have discussed Durand-Ruel's use of publications as a means to promote his gallery, his artists and his collection.[14] Green has pointed out that this promotional tool was used in the financial sector, and that it was Edwards's financing that made it possible for Durand-Ruel to publish the short-lived *Revue internationale de l'art et de la curiosité*. This journal presented substantial writing on art with news about art events and it served two interlocking purposes: to substantiate Durand-Ruel's claim to be a disinterested supporter of art and art history (a connoisseur) as well as to promote his business interests indirectly by enhancing the stature of the artists whose paintings he held in stock (sometimes in collaboration with them). It also drew the public's attention to sales from which he would benefit. While Durand-Ruel's role in the Hôtel Drouot is well known,[15] the various ways he employed the auction house to shore up his own business practices is a complex topic worthy of further investigation elsewhere.

This pairing of interest with disinterest is hardly new in the history of publications and, as Guy Palmade shows, Second-Empire bankers and industrialists, such as the Péreires and Mirès, started their own journals (*La Liberté* and *Le Journal des Chemins de Fer*, respectively) not only to promote general knowledge about their business practices but also to stimulate investments in their enterprises.[16] But Durand-Ruel copied these predecessors in inspired ways. At the time of the Edwards sale, a preview was published in the *Revue* by the author Jean Ravenel, who praised the works to be auctioned in extravagant terms. Concerning the works by Delacroix, Rousseau and Dupré, he wrote: 'They are almost all important and significant because they represent our modern masters at their apogee and greatest power.'[17] Such praise was perhaps justified for some of the works on sale, but it also served to entice speculators to invest in untested works. A particularly long section in Ravenel's article is devoted to describing the works of Jules Dupré, for example. The author also notes that an earlier article had been devoted to the collection in Edwards's apartment by the editor of the journal, Ernest Feydeau, and a report was published after the sale. Knowing Durand-Ruel's arrangement with Edwards, it would seem that both of these articles were part of the self-promotional aspect of the *Revue*.

It is worth remembering that Jean Ravenel was the pen name of the author Alfred Sensier, a longtime friend, associate and biographer of Rousseau and eventually of Millet. Sensier held a significant number of Barbizon works himself, which he sold to Durand-Ruel in April 1872, including nine Rousseaus and 19 Millets.[18] In his *Memoirs*, the dealer lists far more works acquired from Sensier, so this must be only the first instalment of what he eventually acquired.[19] Thus Sensier, the author, was also destined to benefit from the rise in prices for the School of 1830 that the Edwards sale established. As for Feydeau – a literary polymath who wrote on every subject from travel in Algeria to women's toiletries – his *Mémoires d'un coulissier* (Memoirs of a Stockjobber) published in 1873 is significant because it describes his years working for the famous banking house Maison Laffitte. In other words, Durand-Ruel did not simply take lessons from the financial world, he hired in its staff.

One of his borrowings from the world of finance was the business practice of adjustment, which involves making strategic alliances with other bankers to share control of a market.[20] Whether or not Durand-Ruel heard about this practice from Feydeau, he was in the habit of collaborating with his competitors before, during and after this period, often in order to corner an emerging market. The shared accessions of works by Rousseau and Millet[21] are the clearest manifestation of this practice, but there are many other instances enumerated in the Durand-Ruel archives that have not yet been investigated. Of course, dealers would buy and sell paintings from one another, whether Old Masters, modern masters or contemporary artists, but there were also a considerable number of instances in which works would be let out to middlemen or small-time dealers who thought they had a market for them. This strategy was particularly important for the Impressionist artists in the mid-1870s, when a nascent market for their work was fuelled by their group exhibitions.

It is instructive to look at how Durand-Ruel managed such investments and relationships in the early 1870s. There were speculators in the art trade, of course, and while most stuck to tried and true artists, a handful like the opera star Jean-Baptiste Faure speculated on contemporary artists, particularly Manet but also the Impressionists.[22] On 3 February 1872, Durand-Ruel cut a deal with Faure that was noted in his daybook. A painting by Constant Troyon, a Barbizon artist who had died in 1865, entitled *Cows* and valued at 36,000 francs, was let out to Faure. Under the record was written: 'The profits will be shared between him and M. Durand if he sells the painting.'[23] This exchange demonstrates that Durand-Ruel made deals not just with other dealers and financial backers, but with speculative collectors as well.

In fact, the network of professionals with whom Durand-Ruel did business was an international group, and his partnerships with dealers such as the German Paul Cassirer formed at the end of the century were prefigured by his connections with foreign dealers, collectors and middlemen in this early period. Durand-Ruel kept galleries in London between 1870 and 1875 and in Brussels from 1871 to 1875, and he cultivated business contacts in both these locations as well as sending works to his galleries abroad. This had the advantage of putting his considerable stock of paintings before new eyes and promoting his business to an international clientele. There was a serious escalation in foreign investment in France from the middle of the century, so Durand-Ruel's activities abroad once again fitted with the behaviour of French investors and industrialists at that time. The innovation of bringing French art to an international market was not his – he was preceded by Goupil Gallery and their representative in New York, Knoedler, who sold reproductions and eventually paintings[24] – but he strategically relocated to London during the Franco-Prussian War, and there he was able to mount impressive exhibitions in the so-called German Gallery, which continued until 1875. These exhibitions grouped established conventional artists with more adventurous ones and sought to entice a new clientele through a mixed presentation of official art, middle-of-the road and modernist paintings. Even the young Monet and Pissarro, whom he met in London, were included in his second hanging alongside more established Barbizon names.[25] Works by Manet were also shipped over to London to be shown among other contemporary French paintings.

One final technique learned from Second-Empire financiers is relevant to Durand-Ruel's gallery during this period, namely the practice of creating monopolies.[26] In this context, his role is somewhat elusive, because while he did not sign 'his' artists to exclusive contracts, he did attempt to derive a commanding position in the market for their works by absorbing a stock of paintings. While this strategy paid off in the end, it proved to be exceptionally risky, since in order to generate value for these works he had to make sure that the prices did not fall below a certain level, and this often required him to buy more works by artists in whom he was heavily invested if they came up at auction. It cost him dearly to acquire the most significant works by certain of his artists (he paid 30,000 francs for Millet's *Angelus* in 1872), but when he was right (and history has proven him to be) it was a worthwhile investment. At times, Durand-Ruel's *Memoirs* read like a history of successful

FIG. 53
Edouard Manet
The Salmon, 1869
Oil on canvas, 71.8 × 89.9 cm
Shelburne Museum, Vermont
[cat. 25]

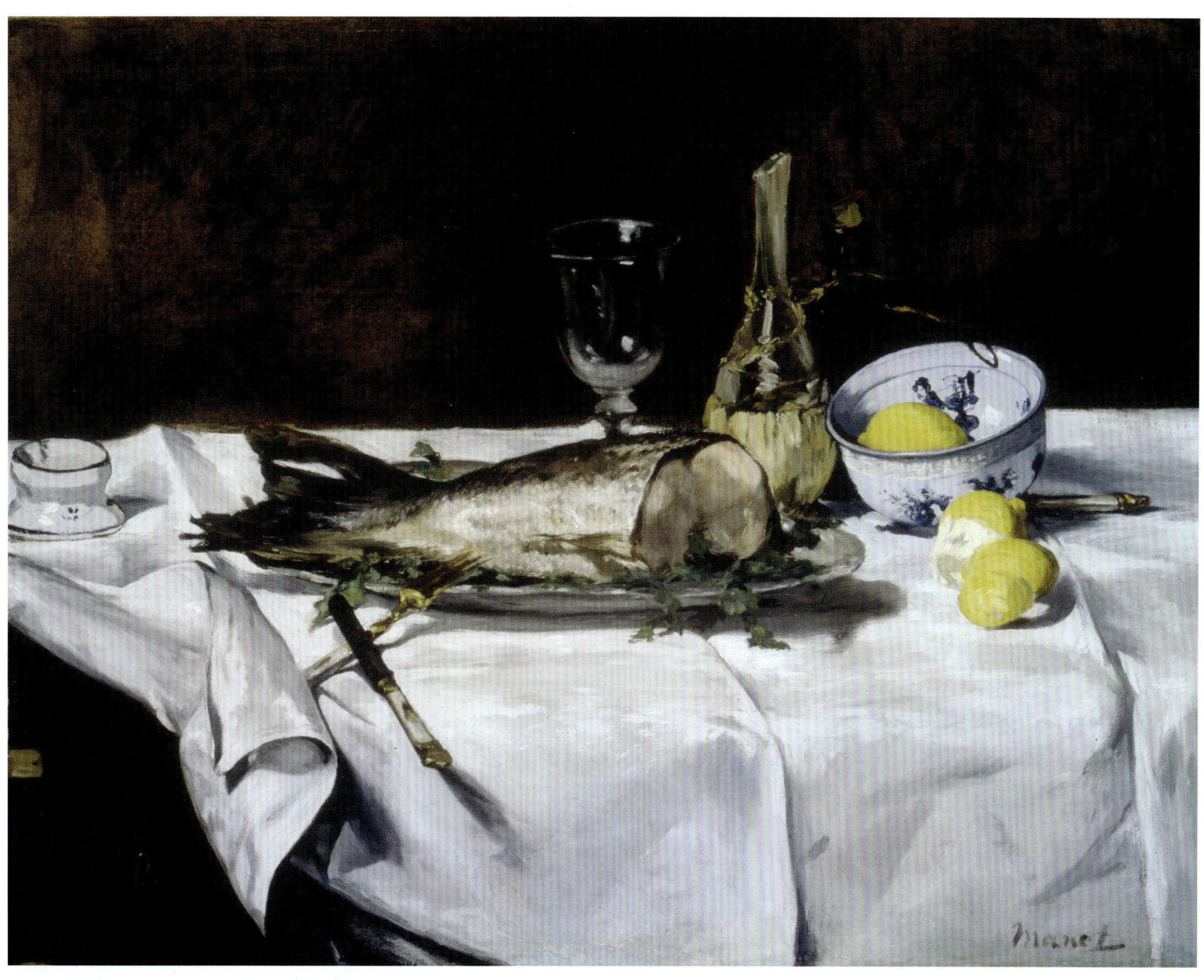

FIG. 54
Edouard Manet
Moonlight at the Port of Boulogne, 1868
Oil on canvas, 81.5 × 101 cm
Musée d'Orsay, Paris
[cat. 24]

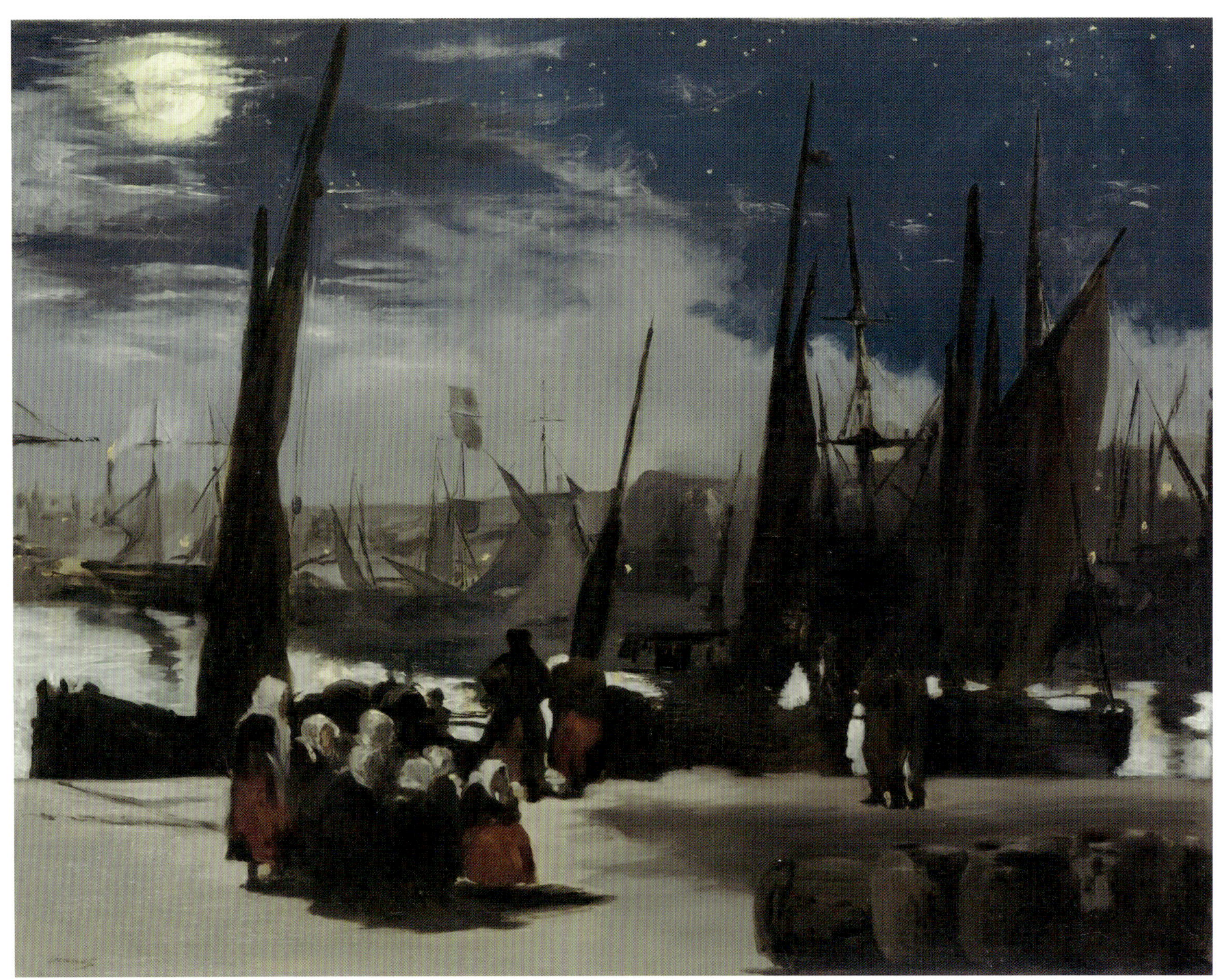

conquests, of buying low and selling unbelievably high by the end of the century, but it must be remembered that this was a generation after he had made his investments. The payoff was huge but it was proportional to the risk involved, and the money he spent to keep his business going is beyond calculation and more than once pushed him to the edge of bankruptcy. To this end, he sought backers and eventually capitalised his gallery as a company with public shares through the Société générale des arts in 1869 and again in 1880.[27]

The Manet purchase

Perhaps Durand-Ruel's boldest attempt to monopolise the work of an emerging artist during this period was the Manet purchase of 1872. This is a well-documented interaction[28] and there is little new that can be added here, but it is worth reviewing the details because they reveal Durand-Ruel's unique business methods as well as the kinds of links he forged with artists. This much is clear: in January 1872, Durand-Ruel spotted two Manet canvases at the studio of Alfred Stevens (*The Salmon*, fig. 53) and *Moonlight at the Port of Boulogne*, fig. 54), which he proceeded to purchase. The same month he visited Manet's studio, where he agreed to buy 21 more paintings – most of Manet's extant production – for a total of 35,000 francs. A few more Manet pictures turn up in the later stock books, but this is where things get less clear. In his *Memoirs*, Durand-Ruel claims to have bought five more paintings for 16,000 francs, but only three are listed in the stock books. In the account book for this period, all the payments of the 35,000 francs are clarified but not the 16,000. Interestingly, it took Durand-Ruel a year to pay off Manet, with instalments beginning in January and more in February, March, April, October and November of 1872. He made some payments with cash, and some with a bill that could be cashed in at a later date. The last sum of 525 francs was covered when Durand-Ruel bought a picture for Manet on his account.[29]

A few observations are in order. First, Manet was the subject of a great deal of argument and gossip, but he was not a marketable artist at the time that Durand-Ruel made this purchase, so it is clear that the dealer was banking on the future market for his work in 1872. In that sense, it was speculative (what else could one call it?) but it was not the kind of speculation that could be turned around for an easy profit. It is almost as if Durand-Ruel was investing in history and, needless to say, he was right. But his business was selling art, not history, so this was a very long-term investment. His commitment to Manet's work shows that he was the kind of dealer who took risks on contemporary artists and faithfully supported them despite a weak or non-existent market for their works. Of the 21 paintings listed together in the Durand-Ruel stock book from 1872 to 1876, only two sold before the book expired, *Flowers* (RW I-86) and *Beach at Boulogne* (RW I-148).[30] He did take Manet works on commission in later years but he did not continue to buy from the artist regularly, as with the Impressionists. Further, it is worth noting that since he neither paid all at once nor in cash, he may not have had a significant amount of cash to hand at the time. Though he had financial backing, he was effectively living day to day. Whether or not it was intentional, this created a lasting relationship with the artist through a flurry of communications and payments. Durand-Ruel kept Manet in the loop and developed a long-standing relationship that served both of their interests.

One last discovery from the archives will put this into perspective. When Durand-Ruel was preparing to send a group of 37 works to show at his gallery in London on 20 March 1872, he added one Manet work that was not in his stock, titled simply '*Le Balcon*' (*The Balcony*, fig. 55) and valued alone at 25,000 francs. Perhaps this is one of the pictures that Manet had been

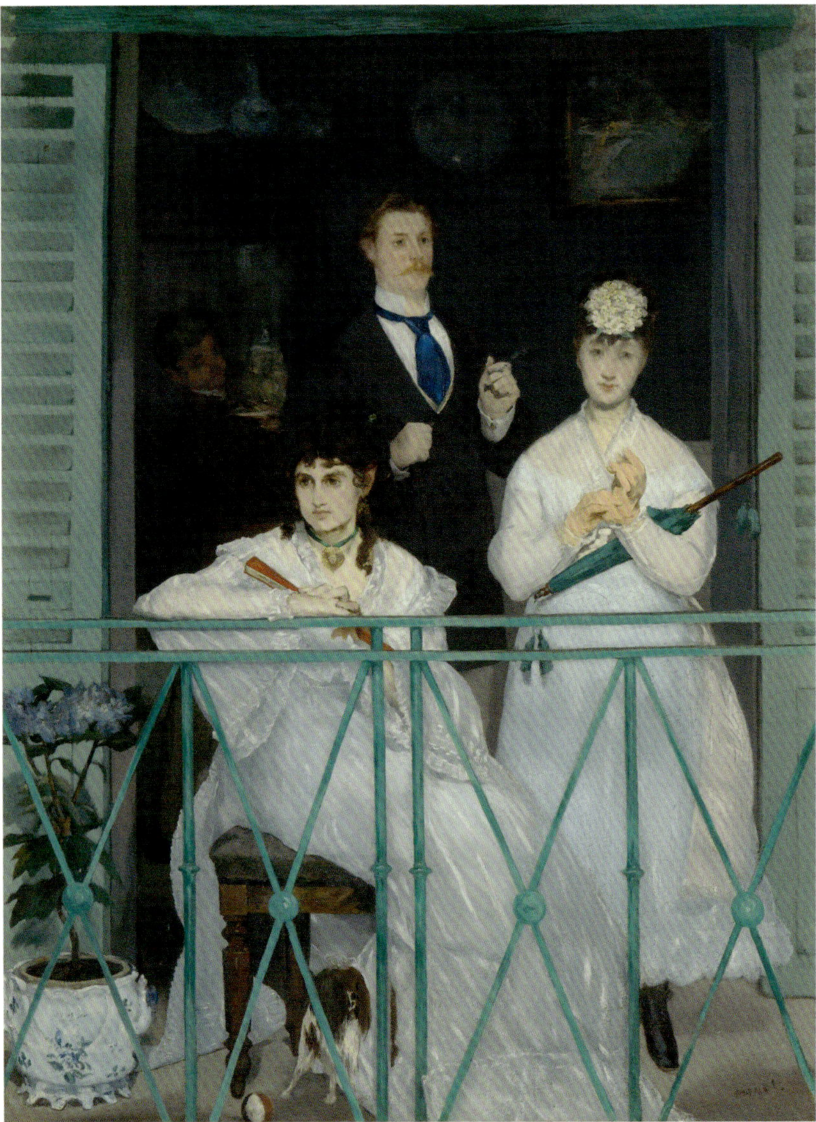

FIG. 55
Edouard Manet
The Balcony, 1868–9
Oil on canvas, 170 × 124.5 cm
Musée d'Orsay, Paris

unwilling to part with when Durand-Ruel had come calling three months earlier, but Manet entrusted it to him to send to London. The interesting point is that this picture is listed neither in the stock books nor the account books. The fact that such an important commission was 'off the books' suggests that Durand-Ruel had exceptional access to artists' works but that he did not always record paintings coming in and going out. It is fascinating to imagine that the works registered in his accounts may only have been a portion of what actually passed through his hands.

Encounters with the Impressionists

When examining Durand-Ruel's relationships with the Impressionists in these early years, it is important to note that despite the wealth of material in the Durand-Ruel archives there is much that is unknown. Correspondence before 1874 is thin[31] and there are no formal contracts, so the historian is left to piece together the fragments of a relationship that had developed into full bloom by the time that Durand-Ruel was documenting his affairs more carefully, in the 1880s and 1890s. It is clear that Durand-Ruel was introduced to Monet and Pissarro in London.[32] It is also known that Durand-Ruel bought pictures from Monet and Pissarro, but there are no London stock books, so these transactions can only be traced by post-dated notations in the Paris stock books. John House noted that Durand-Ruel's first recorded purchase of a Monet was at the London gallery in June 1871, a painting titled *Trouville*, which was also sold in London (*Breakwater at Trouville, Low Tide*, fig. 56). This is the only record that confirms any sale of Monet's pictures in London at the time.[33] House

FIG. 56
Claude Monet
Breakwater at Trouville, Low Tide, 1870
Oil on canvas, 54 × 65.7 cm
Szépművészeti Múzeum, Budapest

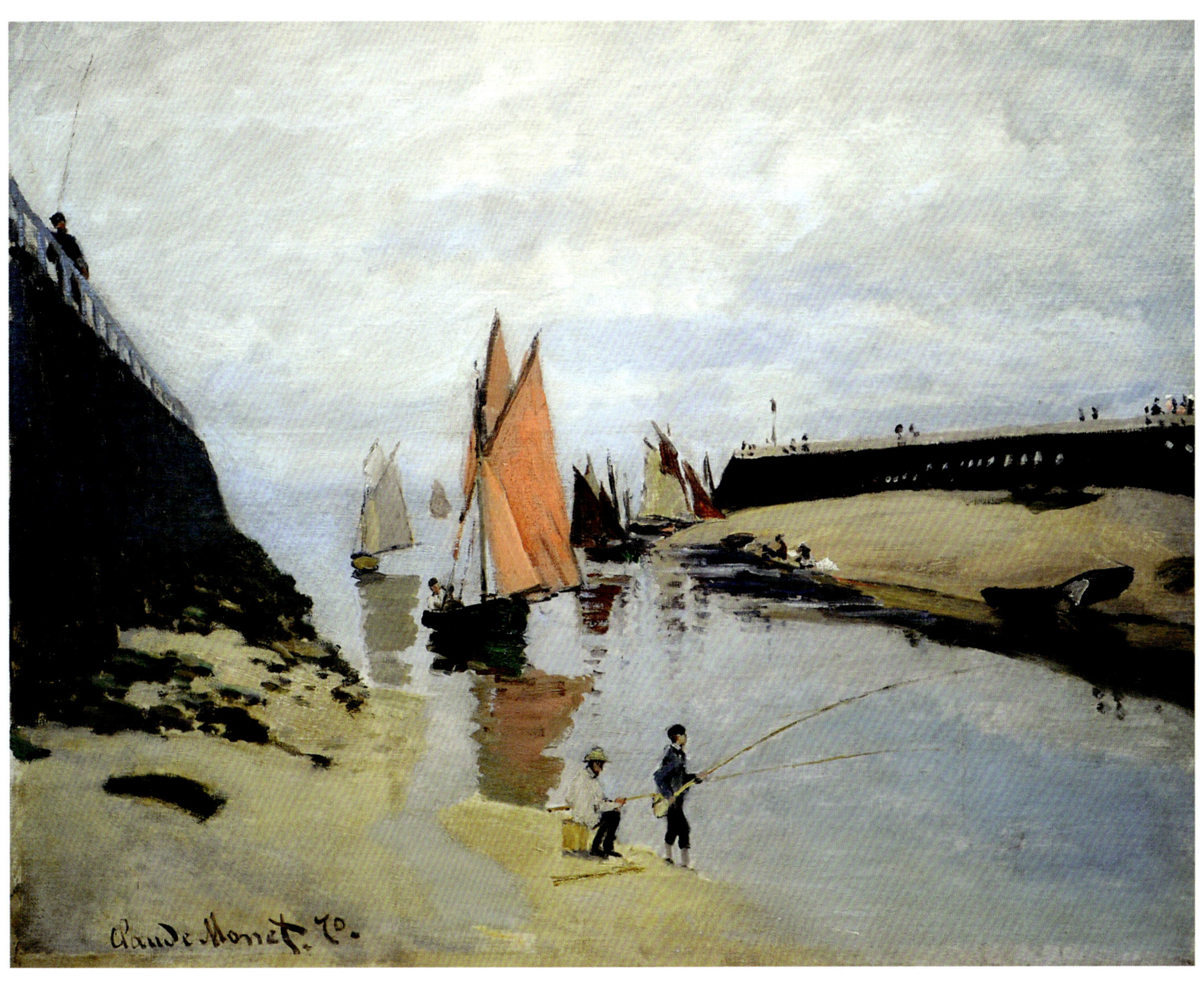

also noted that Durand-Ruel bought four pictures from Pissarro in London. In a letter from Pissarro to Duret of 5 June 1871,[34] the artist notes that Durand-Ruel had bought two pictures (one of these is *The Avenue, Sydenham* (fig. 58) and the other is either *Winter Landscape near Norwood*, W 185 or *Snowy Landscape at South Norwood*, W 187). The other purchases must have taken place later.[35]

Based on a typewritten list preserved in the Durand-Ruel archives, it seems that both artists were included in the second hanging of the 'First Annual Exhibition in London of Pictures: The Contribution of the Society of French Artists' at the German Gallery in March 1871. Among 144 paintings, there is one Monet listed (no. 36, *Entrance to Trouville Harbour*, W 154) and two Pissarros (no. 38, *Snow Effect* and no. 41, *View in Upper Norwood*).[36] As House has noted, Durand-Ruel also included three works by Monet and two by Pissarro in the French section that he organised for the International Exhibition held in South Kensington in 1871. The most prominent of these pictures, *Meditation* (*Madame Monet on the Sofa*, fig. 57), was painted in London and was subsequently purchased by Durand-Ruel in 1873.[37]

When they all returned to France, Monet and Pissarro are reported to have introduced Durand-Ruel to their friends such as Sisley, Renoir and Degas. In retrospect, it would appear that core of the next generation was now complete and Durand-Ruel's support for the Impressionists had begun. This story makes sense but there is no way to confirm these significant social and professional alliances. The best evidence available is the transactions that Durand-Ruel recorded in his stock books. These reveal varying levels of support for these artists, as well as different prices paid and different strategies for acquiring their works. Monet certainly received the most money, with purchases totalling 9,000 francs in 1872 and 19,000 in 1873.[38] Pissarro and Sisley (fig. 59) received more modest, if continual, support and Degas seems to have sold work to Durand-Ruel rarely, more often depositing works with him for sale. Renoir is listed only once in the stock or account books before the end of 1873.[39] Another point of interest is that Durand-Ruel was willing to buy works by Degas (fig. 62) from others at prices higher than he was paying the other artists for their work.

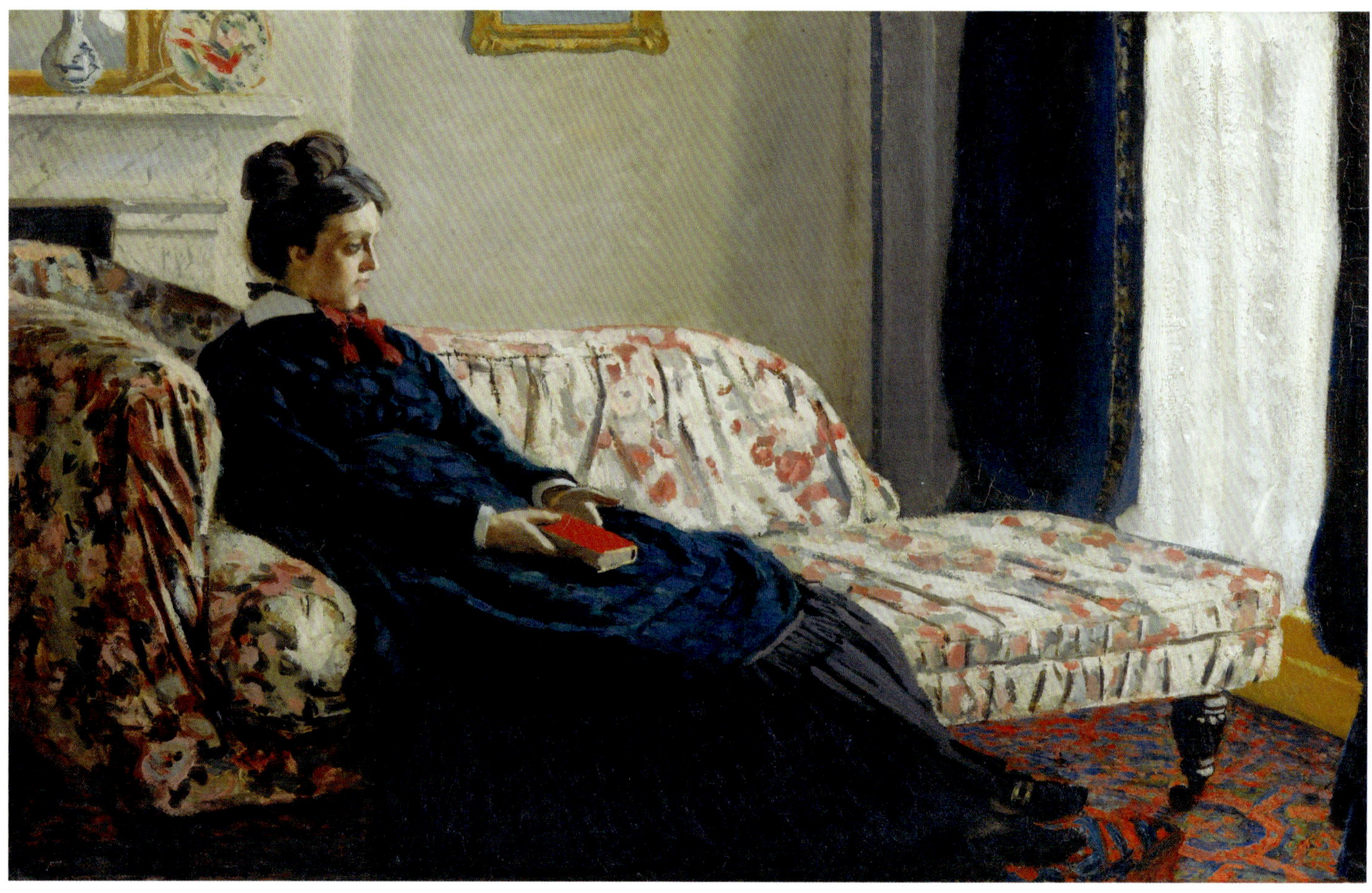

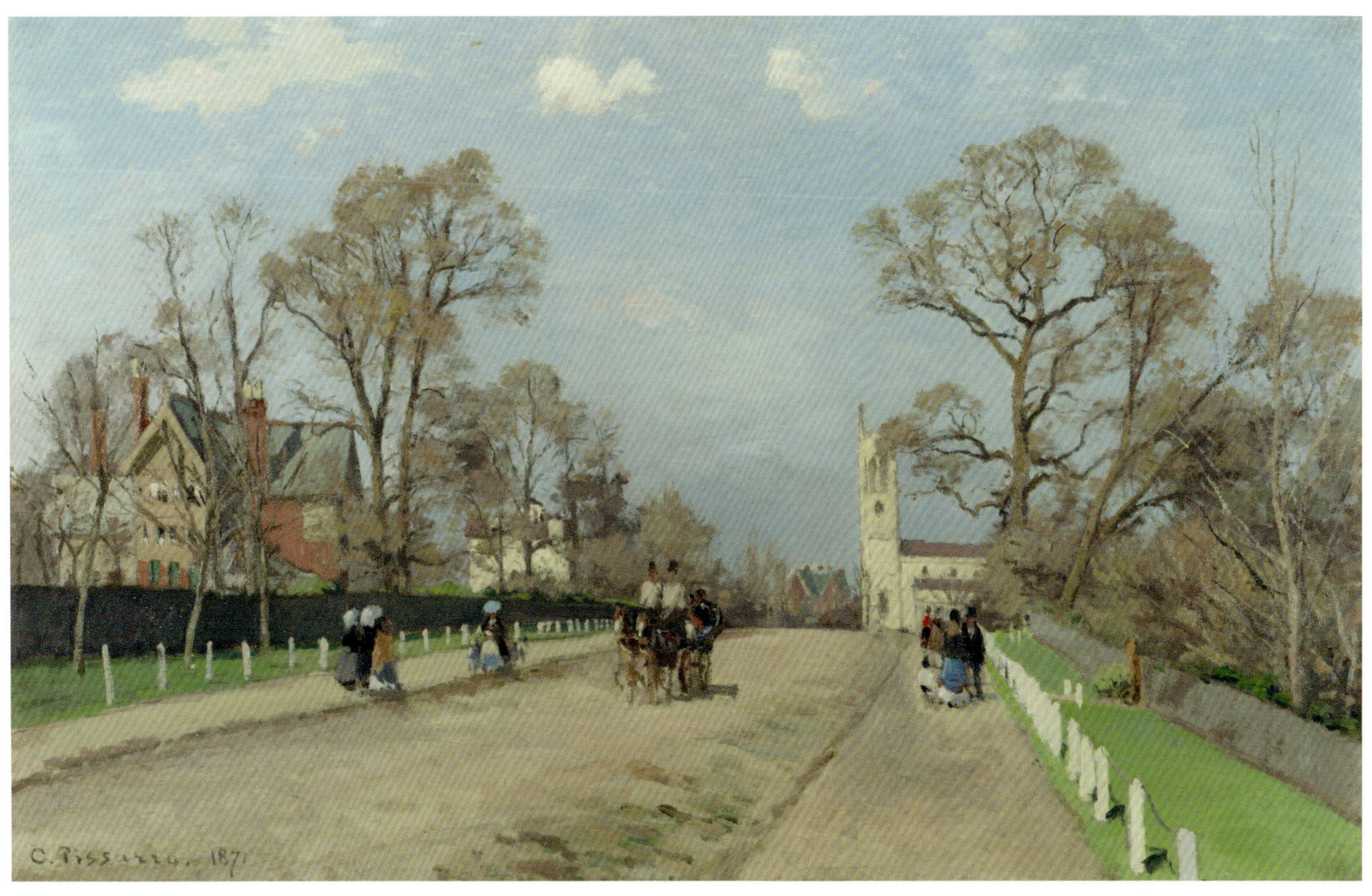

FIG. 57
Claude Monet
Meditation (*Madame Monet on the Sofa*), about 1871
Oil on canvas, 48.2 × 74.5 cm
Musée d'Orsay, Paris
[cat. 32]

FIG. 58
Camille Pissarro
The Avenue, Sydenham, 1871
Oil on canvas, 48 × 73 cm
The National Gallery, London
[cat. 62]

FIG. 59
Alfred Sisley
The Bridge at Villeneuve-la-Garenne, 1872
Oil on canvas, 49.5 × 65.4 cm
The Metropolitan Museum of Art, New York
[cat. 89]

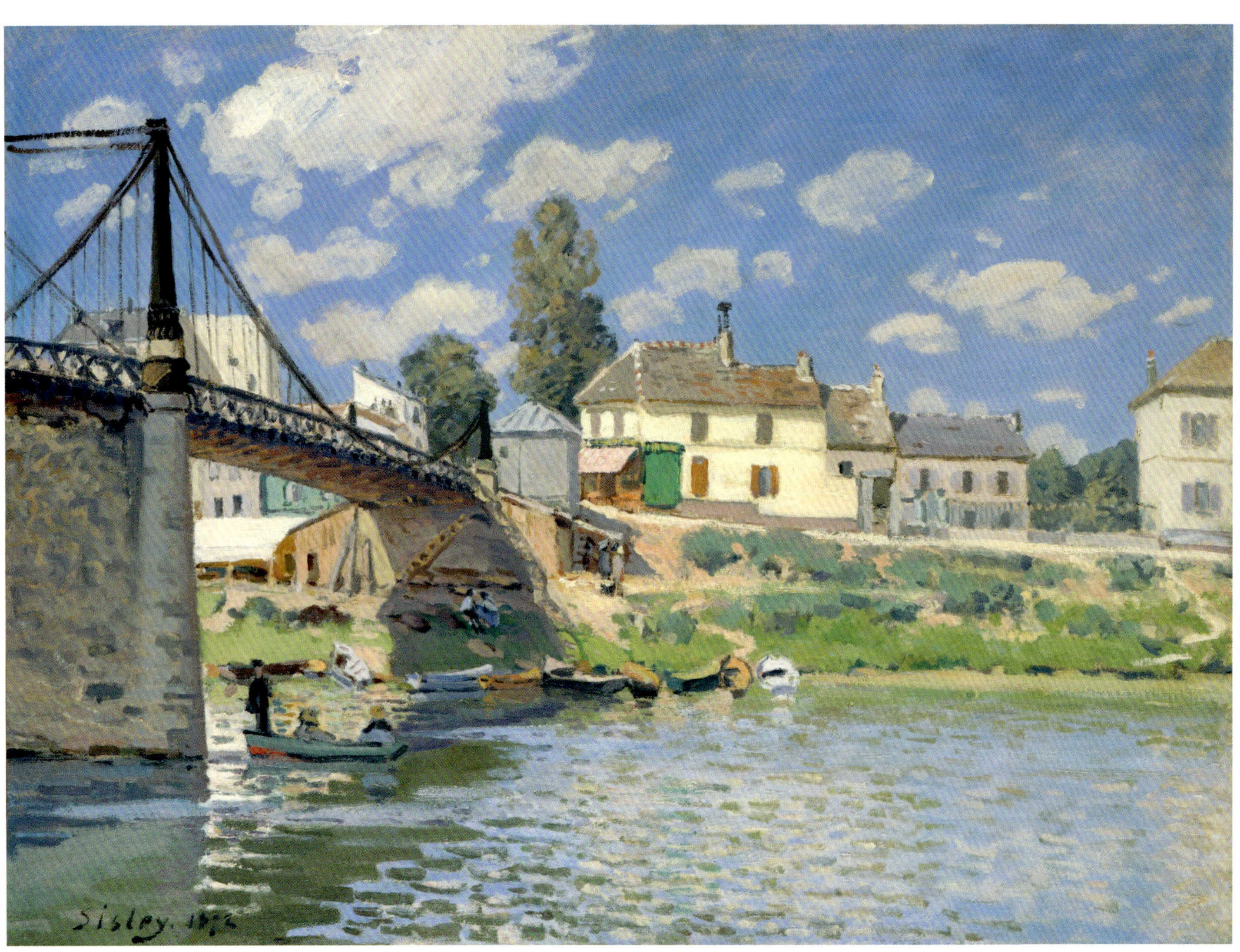

FIG. 60
Durand-Ruel Gallery
stock book, 1872–6
Photograph
Archives Durand-Ruel

One page from the stock book of 1872 (fig. 60) will put Durand-Ruel's support for these artists into perspective. No. 1128 in the book is a Degas picture, *Courses au Bois de Boulogne.* This could be *Horses before the Stands* (fig. 61), bought from Reitlinger for 1,400 francs. On the same page are four Monet landscapes (nos. 1140–3) bought for 300 francs each. Later that month, another Degas is bought from Reitlinger for 1,150 francs (no. 1156), as well as three landscapes by Sisley for 200 francs each. Unfortunately, the stock book does not list any titles for these paintings except for the three Sisleys, but two Monets have been identified in subsequent research: *Houses and Canal at Zaandam, Holland* (W 185) and *Windmills in Holland* (W 171, private collection). Among these paintings, only one Monet (*Houses and Canal at Zaandam*) sold (for 500 francs to Beriot) before 1876, when the stock book expires. On the next page, the dealer buys two Pissarro paintings for 200 francs apiece and he manages to sell one of these to Vaisse for 300 francs.[40] Because Reitlinger, Beriot and Vaisse turn up frequently in these stock books, it would appear that all of them were dealers or brokers involved in the trade, so it seems like there was not yet a real customer base for these works. More importantly, Durand-Ruel was obviously acquiring these works rapidly and was not able to sell them (fig. 67), so he was taking on stock – a process he continued for many years.

A careful look at the account books reveals exactly how Durand-Ruel supported these artists. There are numerous letters from artists requesting money from him, and such inquiries make it seem as if Durand-Ruel was paying them stipends so they could continue to paint, but it is clear that the dealer held them to account. As far as Monet is concerned, in February Durand-Ruel bought two paintings from him for 1,600 francs each – they must have been large since this was a higher price than

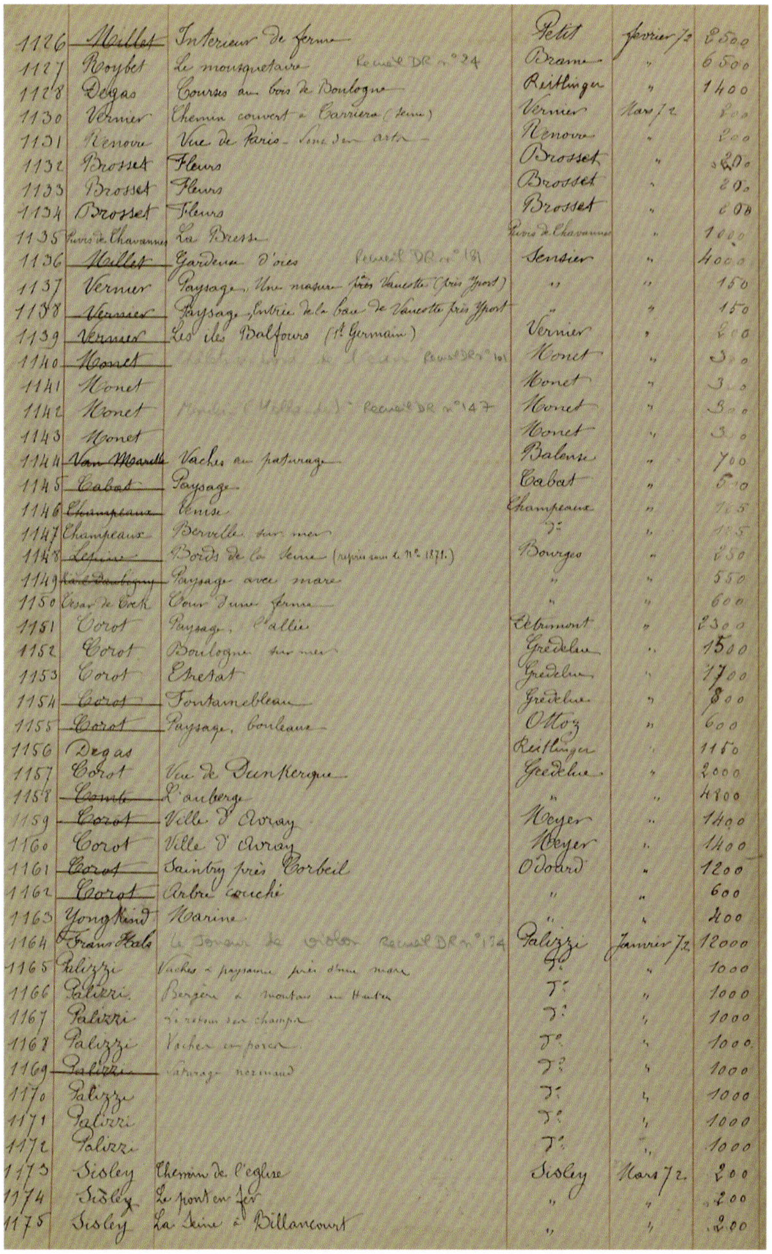

FIG. 61
Edgar Degas
Horses before the Stands, 1866–8
Oil (essence) on paper laid down on canvas, 46 × 61 cm
Musée d'Orsay, Paris
[cat. 11]

FIG. 62
Edgar Degas
The Dance Foyer of the Opera at rue Le Peletier, 1872
Oil on canvas, 32.7 × 46.3 cm
Musée d'Orsay, Paris
[cat. 12]

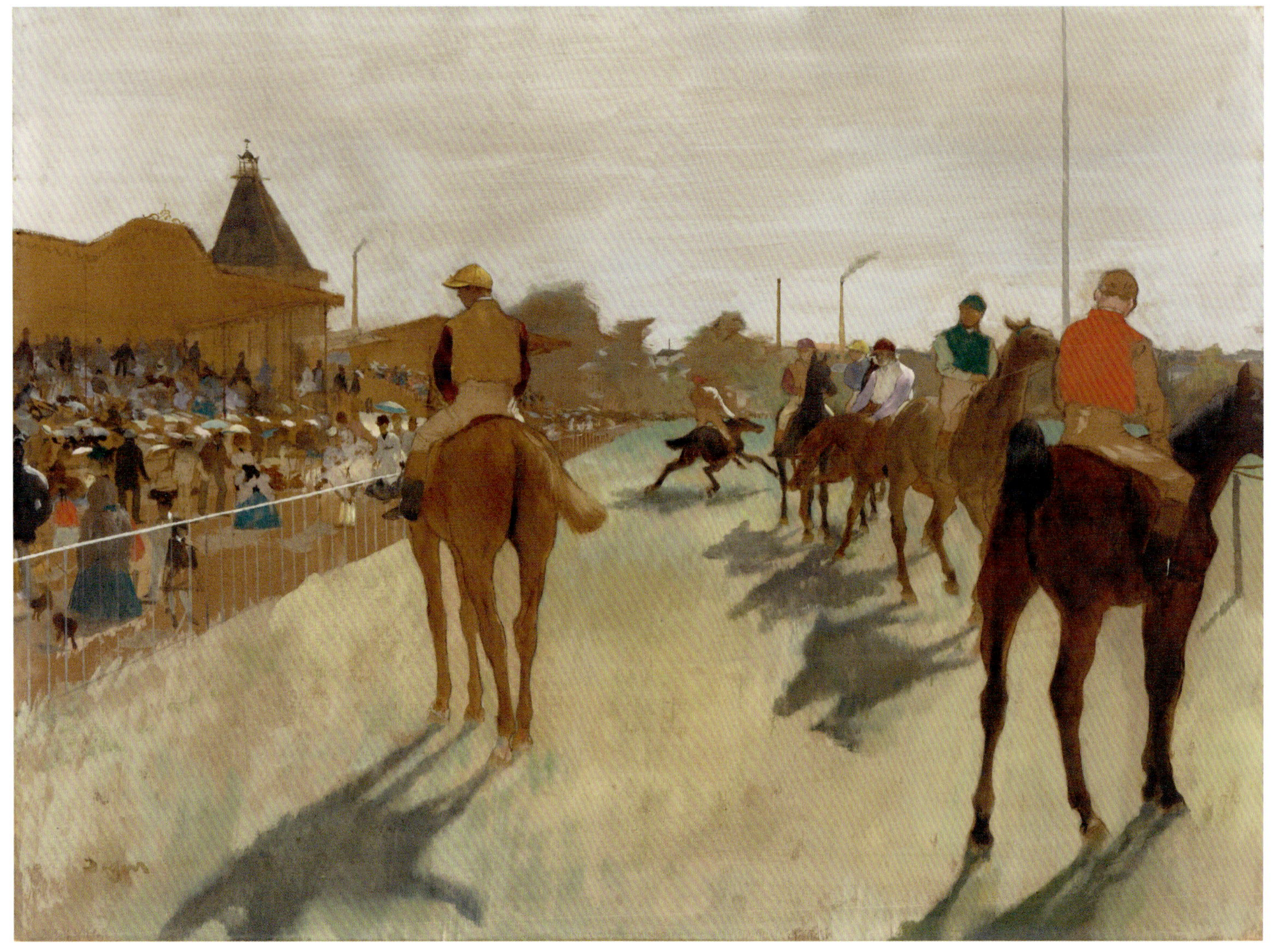

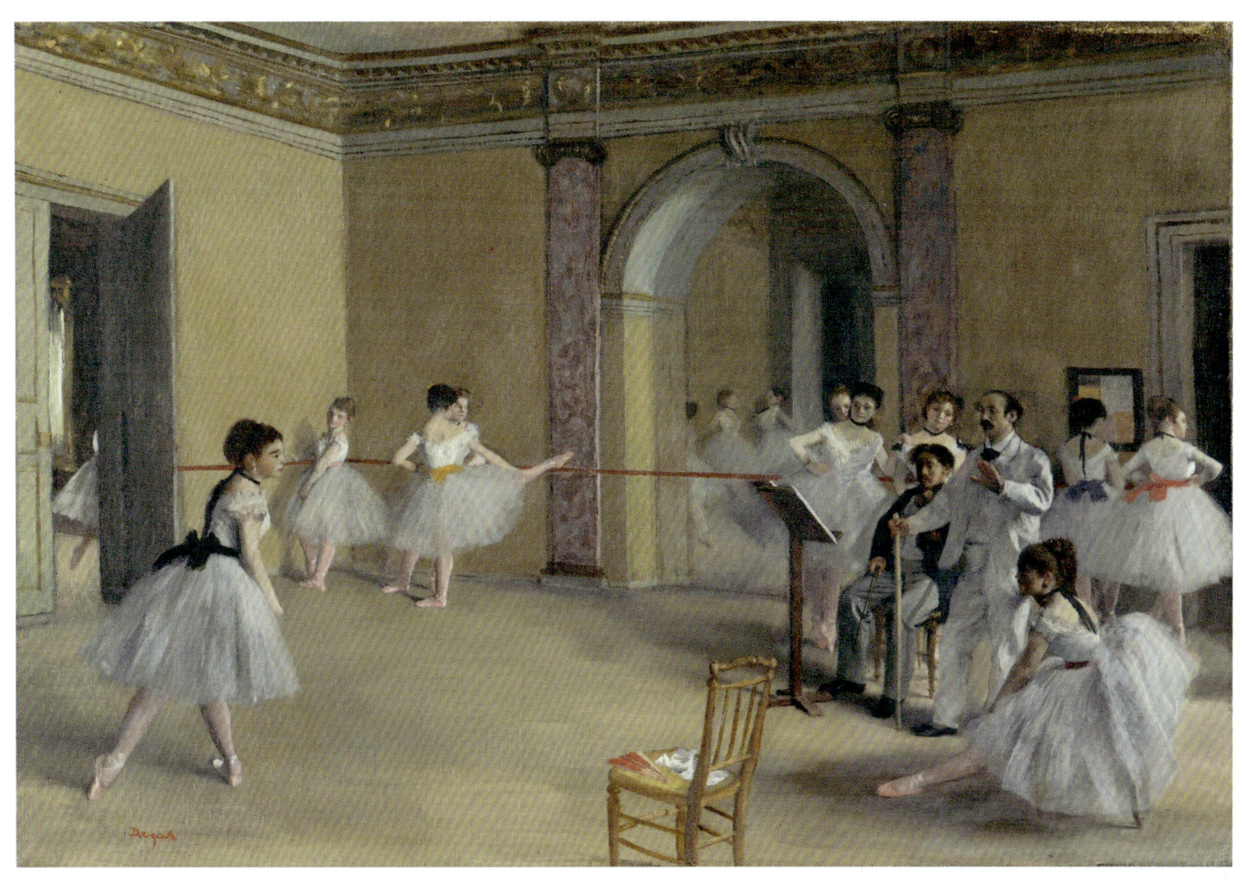
Degas

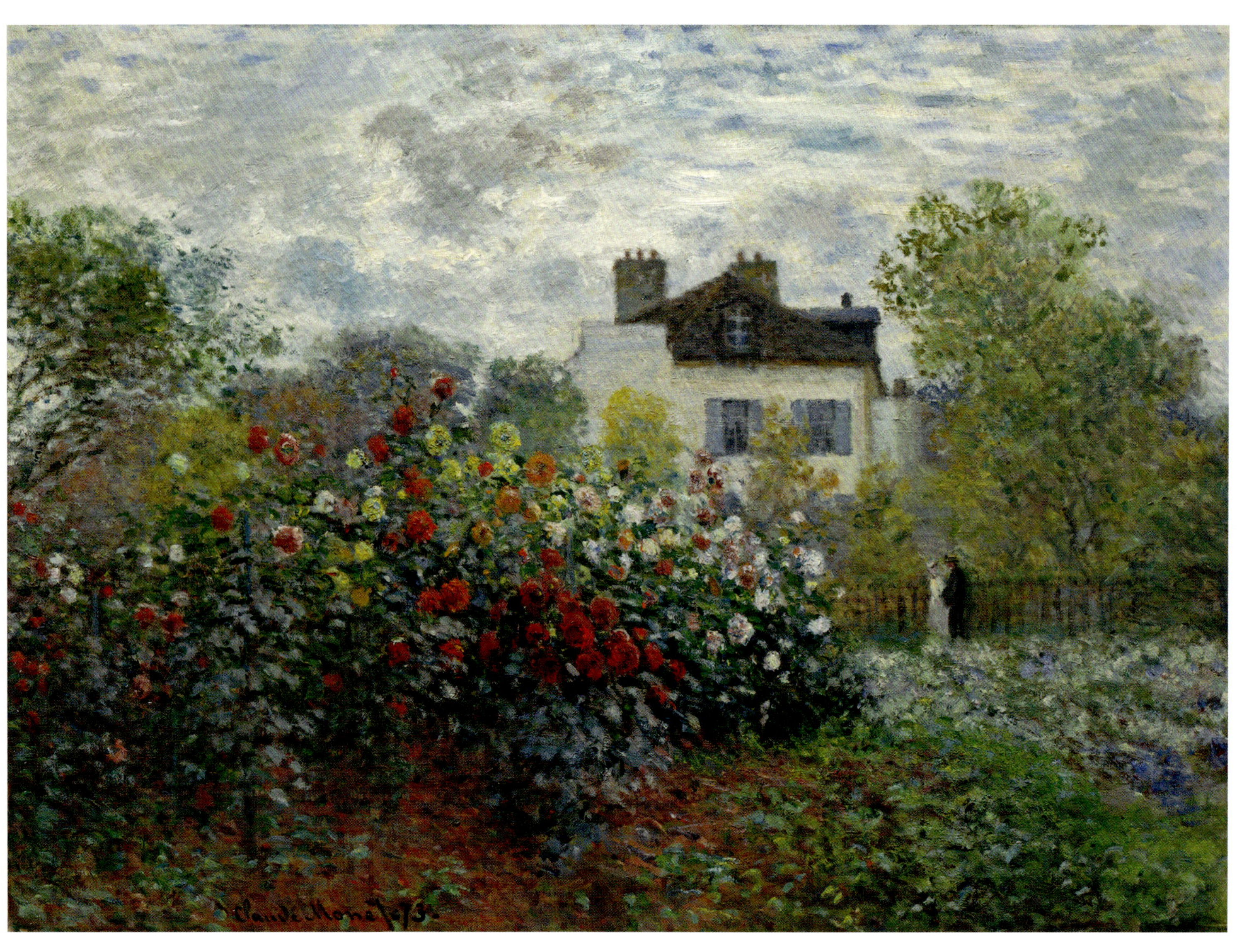

FIG. 63
Claude Monet
The Artist's Garden in Argenteuil (*A Corner of the Garden with Dahlias*), 1873
Oil on canvas, 61 × 82.5 cm
National Gallery of Art, Washington, DC
[cat. 38]

FIG. 64
Claude Monet
Railroad Bridge, Argenteuil, 1873
Oil on canvas, 54.3 × 73.3 cm
Philadelphia Museum of Art, Pennsylvania
[cat. 37]

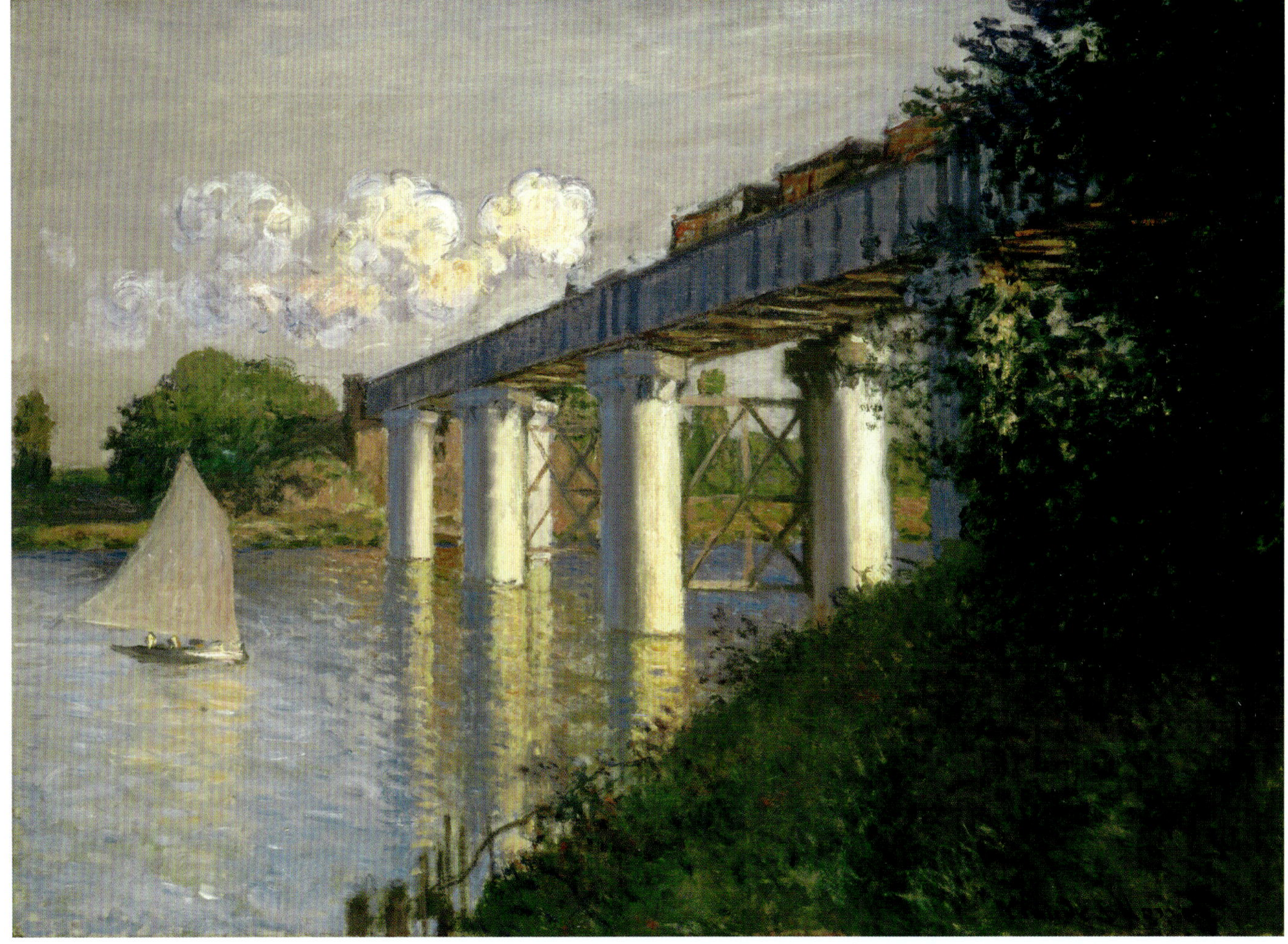

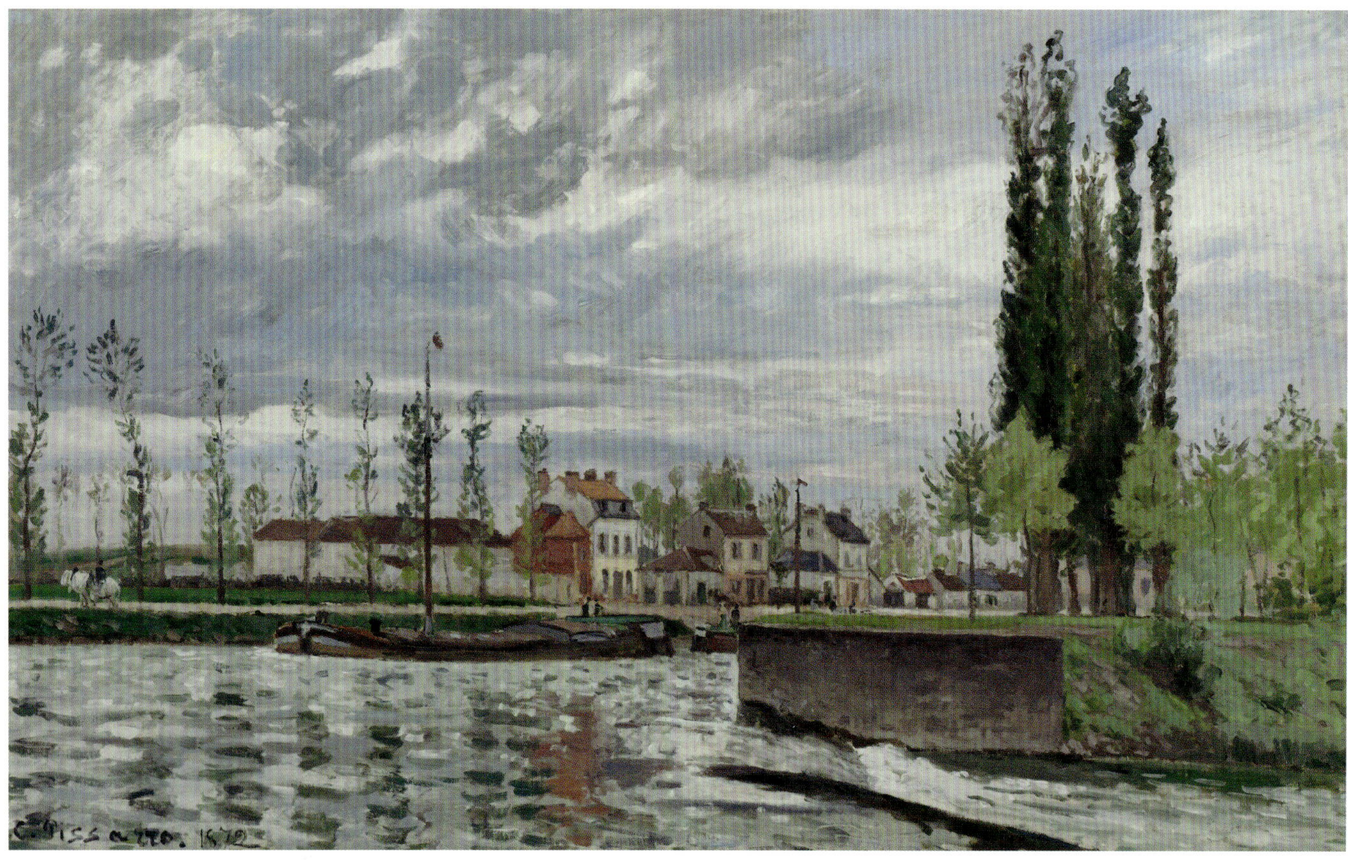

normal – and cash payments are made to Monet almost every ensuing month in 1872, supporting the stipend hypothesis. Sometimes payments are sent on the same day paintings are received (7 March and 30 September), but at other times money goes out before paintings are sent and vice versa. At the end of the year, it all adds up to more than 10,000 francs exchanged (more than Monet listed in his own account books), but it is notable that Monet was painting faster than Durand-Ruel was paying him. The same situation can be seen with Pissarro, but the exchanges involve less money overall, demonstrating that Monet was always more commercially viable than Pissarro, or at least more prolific.[41] (figs 63, 64, 65 and 66).

Durand-Ruel's support of these artists was more than just commercial, however. Beyond including them in exhibitions in London, he sought to introduce them to the public through another major publication project he conceived during this period, the *Recueil d'estampes gravées à l'eau-forte,* with a preface by Armand Silvestre.[42] This three-volume collection, including 300 reproduction engravings of paintings in the Durand-Ruel collection, was intended to shore up the gallery's reputation, so it is all the more notable that works by Manet, Monet and Pissarro in the dealer's hands are presented in these volumes. This represents the philosophy of promoting younger, untested artists, put forward in his *Memoirs*. By mixing in their work with more established masters, whether in an exhibition context or in a publication, he sought to give it a credence that it had not found at the Salon. Since the *Recueil* included Goya, David, Delacroix and Courbet, as well as Manet, Monet and Pissarro, he was also placing the work of the younger artists in the historical continuum embodied in his collection, not just a commercial environment. The truly striking fact is that these younger artists are still the core of the art-historical canon for nineteenth-century France. Though other artists were included who have long been forgotten, this book presages the historical development of the Impressionists, before their first group exhibition, as the artists of their epoch.

FIG. 65
Camille Pissarro
The Lock at Pontoise, 1872
Oil on canvas, 53 × 83 cm
The Cleveland Museum of Art, Ohio
[cat. 64]

FIG. 66
Camille Pissarro
The Crossroads, Pontoise, or
Square at the Old Cemetery, Pontoise, 1872
Oil on canvas, 55 × 91 cm
Carnegie Museum of Art, Pittsburgh
[cat. 65]

FIG. 67
Camille Pissarro
Apples and Pears in a Round Basket, 1872
Oil on canvas, 45.7 × 55.2 cm
The Henry and Rose Pearlman Foundation, on long-term loan to the Princeton University Art Museum
[cat. 66]

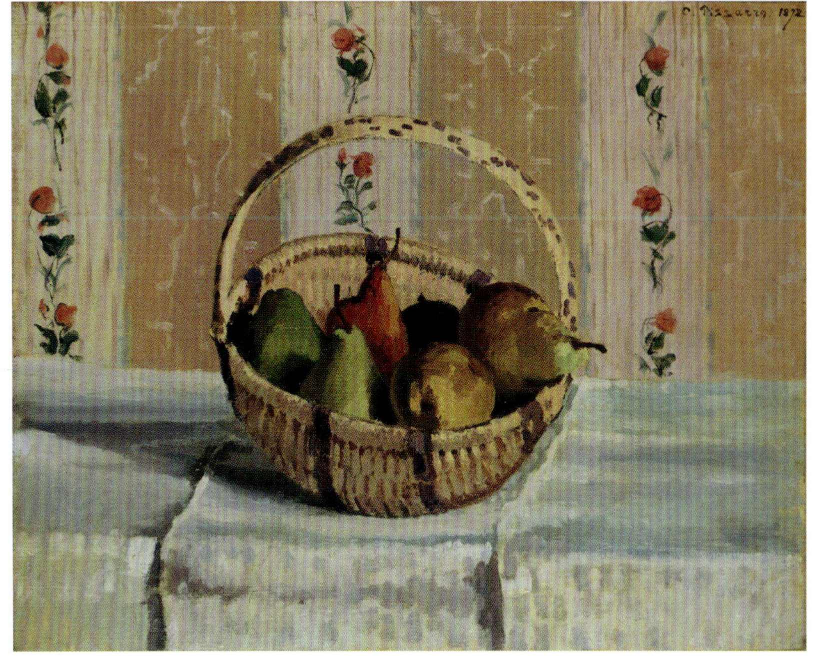

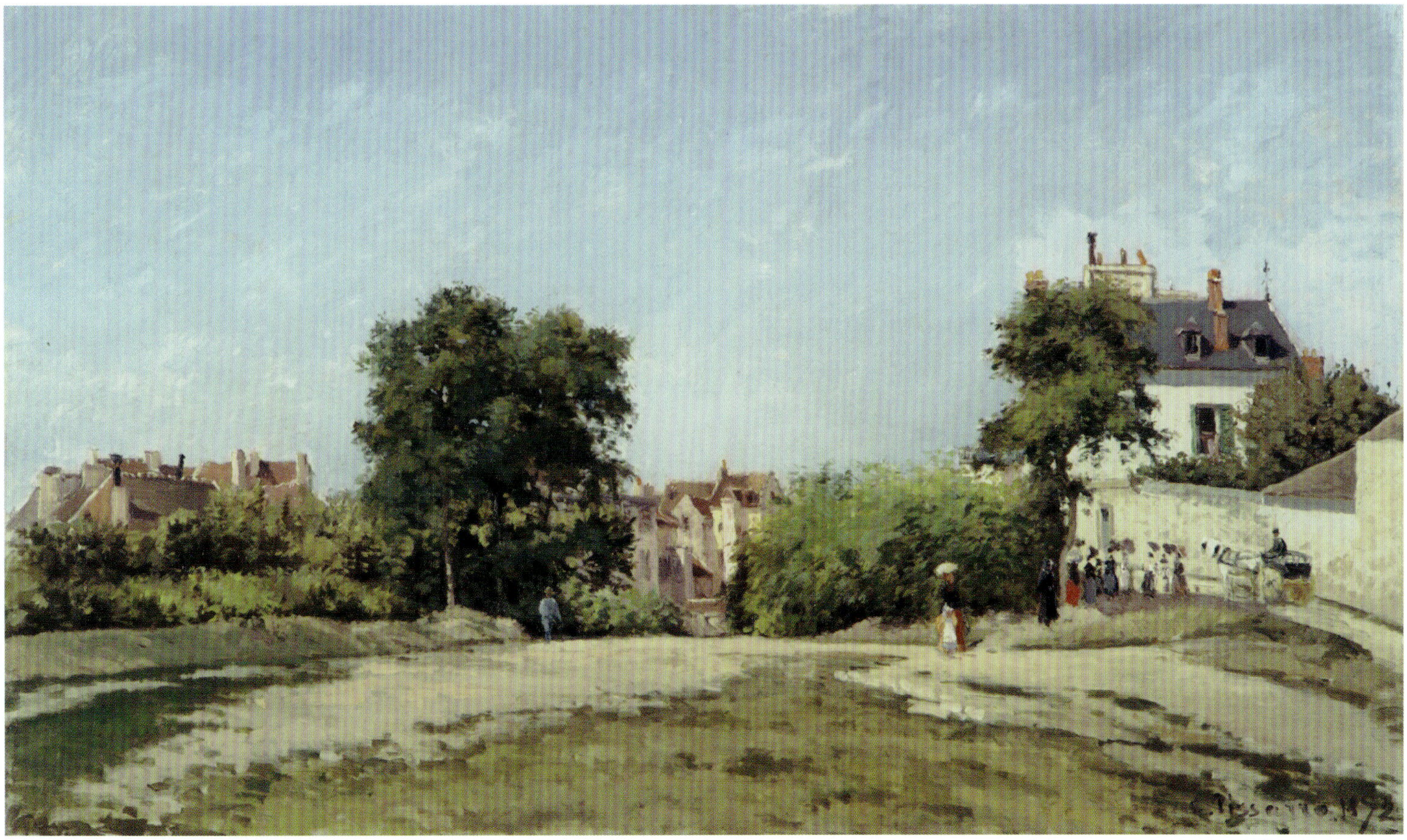

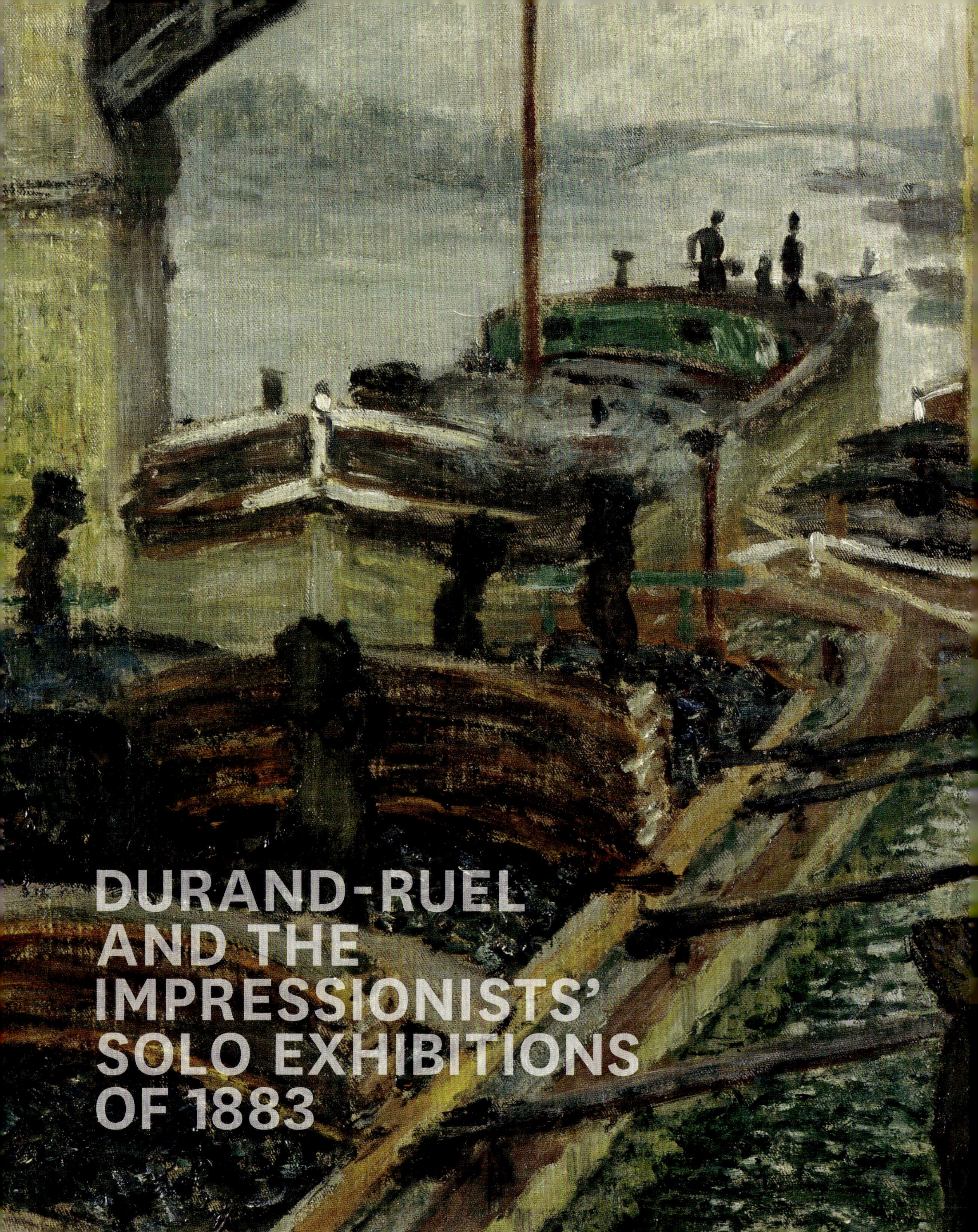

DURAND-RUEL AND THE IMPRESSIONISTS' SOLO EXHIBITIONS OF 1883

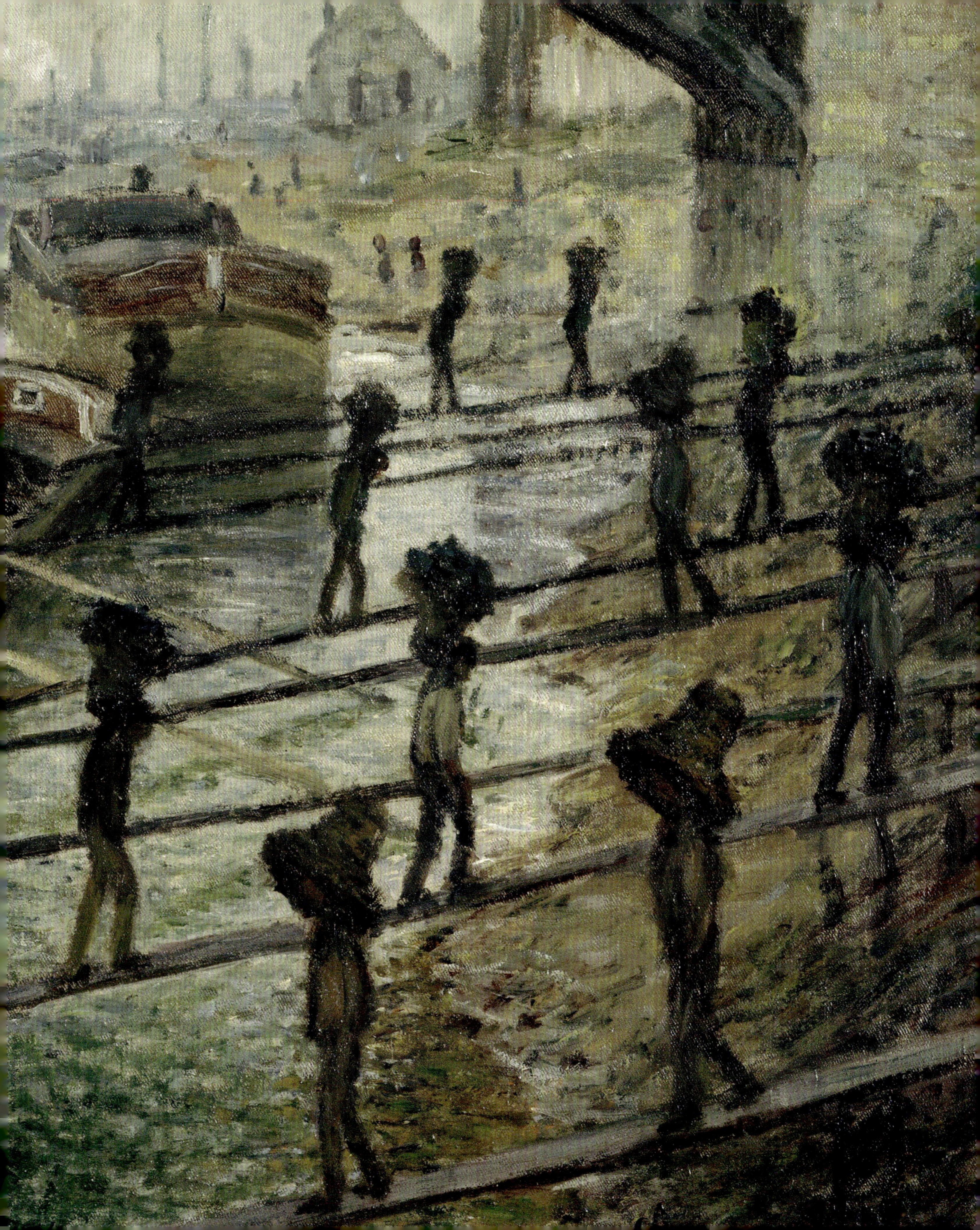

Durand-Ruel and the Impressionists' Solo Exhibitions of 1883

Sylvie Patry

'It is not enough to create [masterpieces]. They must be put on display'[1]

You think I am not showing your pictures enough . . . They are all I am showing; they are all I have concerned myself with for some years now; I have put into them all my heart, all my time and all my fortune, and that of my family.
Durand-Ruel to Monet[2]

'After M. Boudin, M. Monet; after M. Monet, M. Renoir. These three meals have been served to us one after the other in a very short space of time, and a particularly strong stomach is needed to effortlessly digest this peculiar food for which the general economy is not made'.[3] The names of Pissarro and Sisley would be added to these three names listed by the *Courrier de l'art* in April 1883. Between February and June, from the first to the 25th of each month[4] in his new premises near La Madeleine Durand-Ruel devoted a solo exhibition to each of these five painters; he had been buying their works since the early 1870s but had never exhibited them on their own. At a time when the regulations of the Salon and the Musée du Luxembourg did not allow more than one or two works by an artist to be shown together at once, the solo exhibition[5] was neither the ordinary 'food' of the diet of art nor the artistic accolade we recognise today. 'An artist holds an exhibition of his works once during his lifetime ... but that must be all, and I think it would be better to do it after his death',[6] believed Gauguin. The 1883 series appears to have been a first in the history of exhibitions, in the experience of the dealer and in those of the painters, midway through their careers: 'Some claim the Impressionists are making concessions, others that it is the public that has become accustomed to their painting and begun to understand them ... The exhibition by Claude Monet ... will be of great importance for the movement and will demonstrate support for the new school',[7] noted the *Journal des arts*. The importance afforded to Durand-Ruel and these exhibitions in the emerging Impressionist market cannot be over-emphasised, despite the mixed reception they received. After having returned to the purchase of Impressionist works in 1881 and with new collectors on his books,[8] Durand-Ruel was again faced with a serious crisis. He kept up his intense activity in terms of exhibitions regardless, showing the painters in London in 1882 and 1883, and for the first time in the United States, Germany and Holland in 1883. Durand-Ruel 'makes considerable efforts', but 'perhaps a little too much as a dealer',[9] concluded Pissarro, highlighting the dealer's growing role. Even Van Gogh's expression 'Impressionists of the *g[ran]*[d] *B[oulevar]*[d]',[10] coined in 1888 referring to Monet, Renoir, Pissarro and Sisley and the elegant location of their gallery, conveys the evolution and challenges linked to the 'spaces of the avant-garde' identified by Martha Ward.[11] With this in mind, the 1883 exhibitions are often considered a milestone in the 'historical and commercial construction of modernism', based on showcasing the artist through the development of a biographical discourse, as analysed by Robert Jensen[12] in particular. With the aid of the gallery's archives, sometimes unpublished letters and newspapers, this essay aims to return to the genesis, staging and outcome of these events, which have never been studied as a whole,[13] by examining whether, within the context of a movement built on the idea of independence, they sealed a new alliance between Impressionism and the market.

Launching a new type of exhibition

The exhibition initiative started by Durand-Ruel in late 1882 was part of what the press noted as a 'new fashion that is becoming more widespread',[14] particularly in private circles, and among artistic societies and certain dealers. In the eyes of contemporaries, this type of exhibition, which had appeared in France in the late eighteenth century, had commercial overtones: there was the example of the role played by the Association des Artistes and the dealer Francis Petit in the Scheffer and Court exhibitions (1859);[15] the exhibitions of Delacroix and Manet (1864) put up by Martinet;[16] and the Carolus-Duran (1874) and Doré (1877) exhibitions at the Cercle de l'Union Artistique. In the 1880s, 88 monographic exhibitions were staged in Paris, compared with 35 in the previous decade.[17]

The Impressionists were part of this boom: Renoir in June 1879, Monet in June–July 1880, and Sisley in November 1881,[18] all enjoyed their first solo exhibitions held at the premises of the newspaper *La Vie moderne*, founded by the publisher and collector of Impressionism, Georges Charpentier. Edmond Renoir, brother of the painter, underlined the novelty of these exhibitions, of which he was in charge, and, with a cutting remark, made it clear that if the collector 'would like information, he should obtain it through an official, impartial and scrupulous intermediary and not from a dealer keen to sell'.[19] The newspaper took 15% of the sales.[20] With 18 works (including 14 that had recently been painted), the Monet exhibition[21] illustrates this innovative combination that blended monographic works, intimate spaces, the championing of Impressionism and the management of critics. The artist contributed to his own promotion by reproducing some of his works in the press. Critical success was genuine and this exhibition even 'determined the career' of the young Signac,[22] although despite several offers[23] it seems only one picture was sold – to Marguerite Charpentier.[24] Monet succeeded in having his exhibition run extended.[25] He even wanted to stage another at the premises of *La Vie moderne* or *L'Art*,[26] a sign of the growing interest in initiating exhibitions shown by the press. Durand-Ruel also supported this movement by lending about 15 Impressionist works to *L'Événement*[27] in 1879, and by sending paintings by Boudin, Manet, Sisley and Pissarro to the periodical *Gil Blas* in the same year,[28] as well as 18 paintings by Sisley for a monographic presentation at *Le Gaulois* in late 1881.[29] The 1883 series was therefore only one element of his multi-faceted business, which saw Durand-Ruel exhibit Impressionist paintings in theatres and at the Cercle des Arts Libéraux in 1881, with 42 works, including *The Ballet Scene from Meyerbeer's Opera 'Robert le Diable'* by Degas (see fig. 82) and *Luncheon of the Boating Party* by Renoir (see fig. 33).[30] Faced with the emergence of new competitors, the solo exhibitions of 1883 can also be understood as an attempt by the gallery owner to assert his role in the field.

Although Durand-Ruel was not the first to organise monographic exhibitions for the Impressionists, he demonstrated a methodical approach to a type of exhibition with which he had little experience – apart from some studio pre-sale exhibitions and displays, and with the notable exception of the exhibitions by Rousseau in 1867, Whistler in 1873 and Daumier in 1878. Instigated by Whistler himself and friends of Daumier, these events, which were among the first solo exhibitions to be held in a French gallery, were failures.[31] On the other hand, the group exhibition by the Impressionists in the spring of 1882 set a decisive precedent. For the first time, Durand-Ruel was directly involved in assembling the displays of work by Renoir, Monet, Pissarro and Sisley from his own stock for the most part. The exhibition brought together 36 paintings by Pissarro, 35 by Monet, 27 by Sisley and 27 by Renoir.[32] It was the first time that such large numbers of paintings by the individual artists had been exhibited, with the exception of the 29 pictures by Monet shown in 1879. Already undermined by personal differences, the model of the independent group exhibition controlled by the artists made way, at the instigation of the dealer, for a juxtaposition of

FIG. 68
Pierre-Auguste Renoir
The Cup of Chocolate, about 1877–8
Oil on canvas, 100 × 81 cm
Private collection
[cat. 73]

monographic series. The harmony and coherence that resulted were hailed by the critics.

However, Durand-Ruel did have to overcome the reticence of the artists. Sisley, smarting from his failure in 1881, put forward the following argument:

> All the precedents prove that group exhibitions have been the most successful, and that in general this has not been the case with solo exhibitions. But not only would this be a series of solo exhibitions, it would also be a sort of permanent exhibition that a dealer could stage at his gallery; the painters cannot help but lay themselves open to tiring and upsetting everyone. Whether we exhibit together or in single file (in the same location), the public will always see us as *Impressionists* ... It does not seem to me that at the moment we cease being nomads, when we have a permanent, well-sited location, we should think of ushering in a new type of exhibition, or to experiment. For me, our interest and yours is less about showing great numbers of paintings than about doing what must be done to sell those we are painting.[33]

Agreeing with Sisley that a series of individual exhibitions 'could tire the public',[34] Monet recommended 'a personal exhibition here and there',[35] and, despite being 'terribly afraid'[36] like Renoir, left the decision up to the dealer:[37] 'If I do it, it is so as not to hurt Durand-Ruel, our only friend', wrote Renoir, who was equally concerned about the prospect of a solo exhibition.[38] Despite being supported by Monet and heralded by Burty, Degas would take no part.[39]

Solo exhibitions and exclusivity

'The new painting is entirely in his hands' wrote Renoir,[40] in acknowledgment of Durand-Ruel's powerful position. For the artists, selling and exhibiting were two opposing concepts; Durand-Ruel, on the other hand, gambled on the fact that the two were linked, providing he could find a suitable type of exhibition. The independent group exhibitions had undoubtedly marked the painters out as avant-garde figures, and Monet had returned to the Salon in 1880, as had Renoir between 1878 and 1883 (fig. 68), while Boudin had been awarded a medal at the Salon in 1881. But both the cooperative and official platforms were in crisis at that time[41] and this did nothing to broaden the client base of the dealer, who in any case had been forced to stop buying Impressionist works after 1875. Durand-Ruel began purchasing works again between 1880 and 1882. Despite the collapse of his backer, the Union Générale, on 2 February 1882, he added to his stock with 164 works by Boudin[42] (compared with six still noted as unsold in 1877),[43] 157 by Monet[44] (20 in 1877), 95 by Pissarro[45] (32 in 1877), 88 by Sisley[46] (46 in 1877), 87 by Renoir[47] (two in 1877), and 38 by Degas.[48] 'Did you know that from the high-speed train Durand-Ruel is taking with Sisley and Monet, who are steaming away with their pictures, he will soon have 400 pictures he will not be able to get rid of?',[49] warned Gauguin, echoing Boudin's admission: 'Here I am forced to produce and support my important celebrity'.[50] What could be a more appropriate way of showcasing such quantities of works than a monographic exhibition?

The dealer intended to establish a monopoly, in keeping with a method he had already tried and tested with Rousseau, combining bulk purchasing with a personal exhibition in 1867.[51] Boudin, who had refused an offer of the same kind from Hagerman in 1869,[52] described a visit from Durand-Ruel in 1881: '"I'll take them ... and this one and this one." "Right", I said. "All of them?" "Yes, all of them!" ... he asked me to work only for him'.[53] In late 1881, Boudin wrote: 'Here I am being completely monopolised by Durand-Ruel. Yes! He has bought up all my pictures scattered among the dealers.

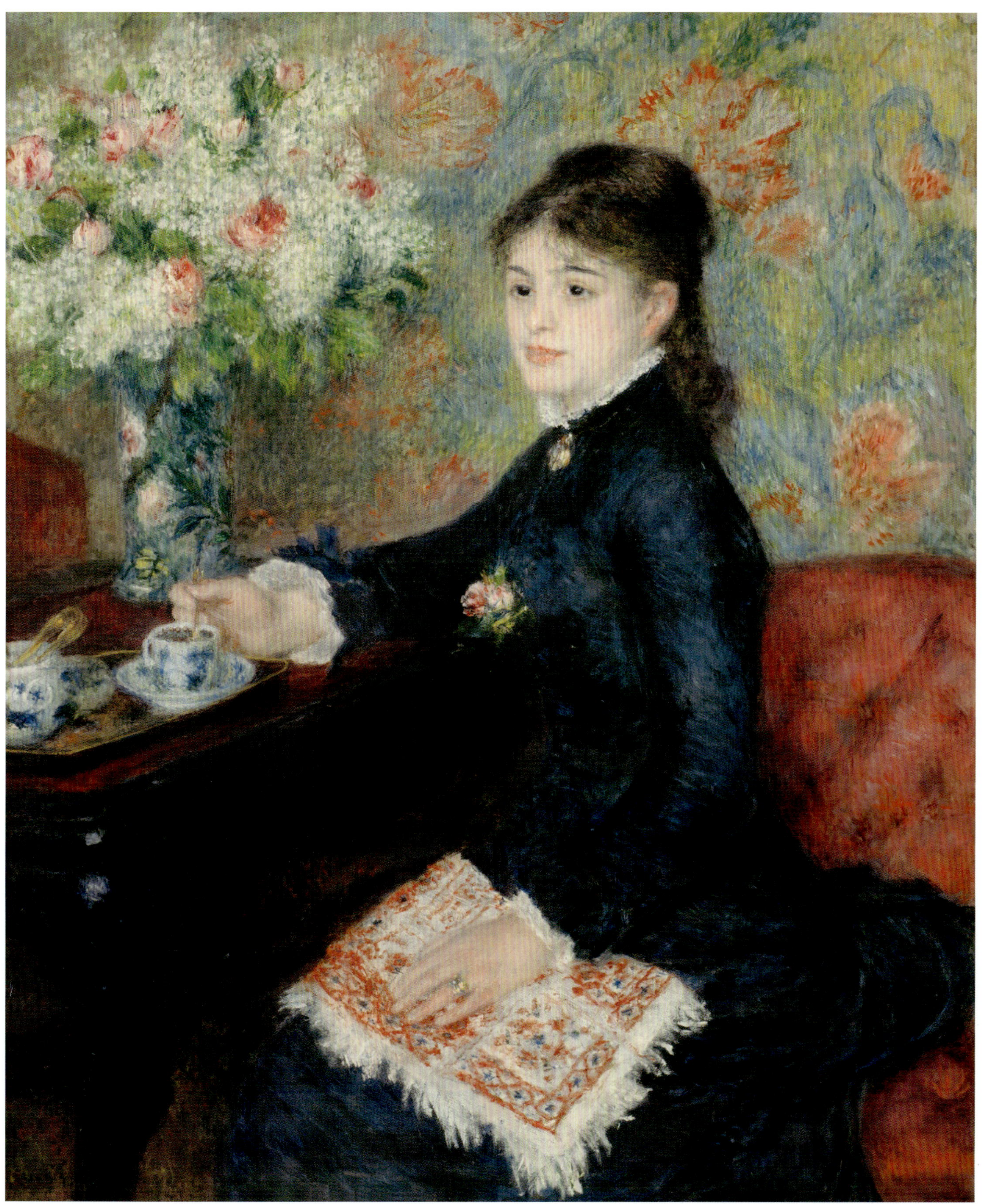

FIG. 69
Claude Monet
Windmill and Boats near Zaandam, Holland, 1871
Oil on canvas, 48 × 75.5 cm
Ny Carlsberg Glyptotek, Copenhagen
[cat. 33]

He has forbidden me from painting any for the collectors and especially for his colleagues. In spite of myself, I'm becoming very important: they can't get enough of Boudin'.[54] Although he satisfied Boudin, who continued nonetheless to sell to other merchants, such as Detrimont, Durand-Ruel's 'monopolising' created plenty of reservations and tensions among Monet, Sisley and Pissarro.

Monopolistic buying and monographic exhibitions went hand in hand with increased competition among the dealers. Legrand, an unsuccessful pioneer of Impressionism in America in 1878, could be seen as a serious competitor until 1883, while the discreet Portier, employed by Durand-Ruel in 1882, played a central role in the Impressionist exhibitions of 1879 and 1882 and remained a regular purchaser. However, a new type of competition began to take shape with Georges Petit. The son of a dealer and also an imaginative entrepreneur, Petit challenged Durand-Ruel in his areas of expertise, such as the sale of Barbizon School paintings at high prices and the purchase of Impressionist works. Like Pissarro, Monet, from whom Durand-Ruel had not bought anything since 1874, turned to Petit in 1878,[55] but the dealer did not buy his first picture from Monet until 1880 – a still life for 500 francs.[56] Transactions were then limited to rare purchases, including a *Snow Effect at Vétheuil* for 300 francs in about 1880. This picture was never received by Petit[57] and Durand-Ruel later purchased it at public auction but not 'in my name so that the public thinks it has been sold to a collector. This will have a better effect'.[58] Although the prices paid by Durand-Ruel were often lower than those paid by Petit (between 150 and 300 francs for a landscape by Sisley, Pissarro or Monet), his payments were regular: Monet, for example, received 24,700 francs from him in 1882.[59] In fact, it was from Durand-Ruel that Petit made his major purchases of Impressionist pictures; the rivals came to a secret agreement[60] before 'savage warfare'[61] broke out again in 1884 and another front opened up with Theo van Gogh.[62] So it was that in July–August 1883, Petit, finally 'converted', as Durand-Ruel described it, and bought 46 works by Monet, Sisley and Pissarro from him for 33,300 francs.[63]

Competition also played a role in the exhibitions. Like Durand-Ruel before him, Petit focused on the quality of the spaces. In 1882, he opened a gallery in rue de Sèze, which, according to Blanche, became 'a popular, central spot for the rich'.[64] That same year he attracted the Société des Aquarellistes (Society of Watercolour Painters), who had abandoned Durand-Ruel, thus depriving him of income that allowed him to pay the rent for rue Laffitte.[65] The 'luxury of the room' at Petit's gallery also appealed to Renoir and Monet, to the extent that they questioned their participation in the 1883 monographic exhibitions.[66] A stone's throw from rue de Sèze, Durand-Ruel rented new premises at 9 boulevard de la Madeleine in 1882. This four-roomed[67] mezzanine[68] apartment was 'small and intimate',[69] according to Monet, but 'quite large'[70] in Boudin's words. It was elegantly furnished by the dealer: its walls were hung with 'red cloth',[71] again reported by Boudin ('with that awful official red', complained Pissarro).[72] There were tables, chairs (also upholstered in red), thick rugs, plants and flowers (100 francs were spent on them per exhibition), as well as sculptures and decoration made from *carton pierre*, a type of papier-mâché, and a statue of Cleopatra on a gilded plinth.[73] 'It is a little dark during the day, but at night the gas brightens it up to very good effect',[74] noted Boudin, even if one journalist regretted that Monet's paintings 'in a back room, in total darkness, had completely passed [him] by'.[75] He was presumably unaware that it was the artist himself who had demanded the blinds![76]

However, Durand-Ruel's efforts were nothing compared to Petit's chic style, another sign of their differing views. At boulevard de la Madeleine – unlike at the shows staged by the press or abroad – Durand-

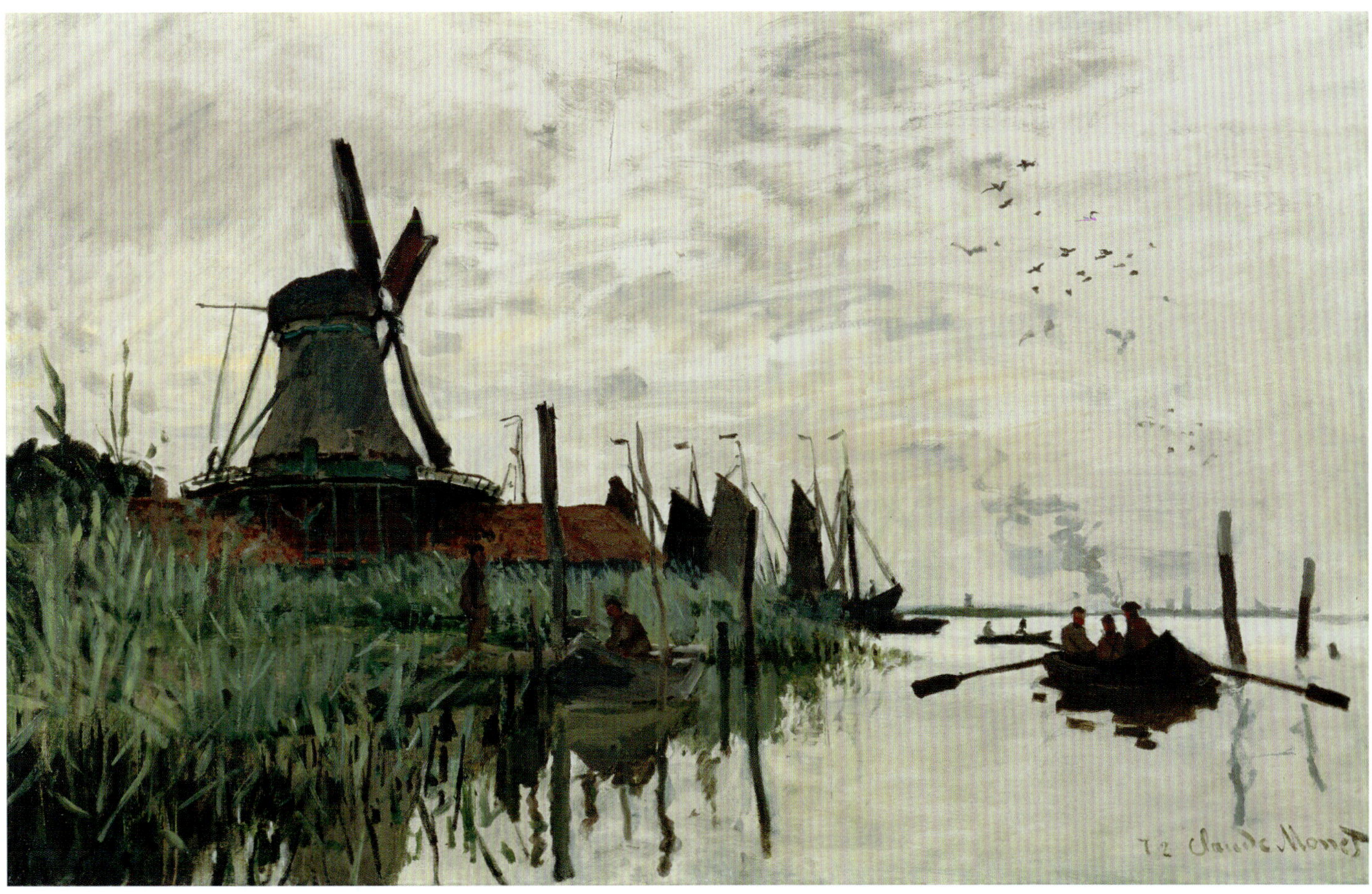

Ruel gambled on presenting the image of a school of painting, or a 'church', to use the term in vogue at that time, risking the monotony and marginalisation of which Sisley was so afraid. At his 'international exhibitions' set up in 1882, Petit instead focused on a conservative eclecticism: from 1885 onwards, on the condition – which ultimately went unfulfilled – that 'not one single picture belonging [to Durand-Ruel] would appear',[77] he mixed established and Impressionist artists, to whom he would not grant solo exhibitions until the late 1880s.[78] Durand-Ruel therefore retained his painters until 1885, when Monet judged that 'it would not be bad in the eyes of the public and the collectors if we did not appear to be entirely under your protection and in your hands'.[79] The 1883 exhibitions seemed to prove him right, seeing a convergence of the attempt to create a monopoly with the controlling of the circulation of works. But rather than it appearing as if Durand-Ruel had taken over, the preparation, as well as the staging of these exhibitions, instead indicated a collaboration between the dealer and his painters.

'Protection' or freedom?

In response to the concerns about image alluded to by Monet, Durand-Ruel would later recall having 'taken care to clearly show that these exhibitions were in the best interest of the painters, to borrow pictures by each of them from all the main collectors who owned their works'.[80] The catalogues[81] are dotted with the names of long-standing collectors, such as Faure (fig. 69), Duret, Ephrussi, Charpentier and Deudon (fig. 70), some of whom – De Bellio, Chocquet and Caillebotte – seldom bought from the gallery.[82] The names of more recent collectors, such as Gauguin, Berard and Clapisson, are also listed, as well as those who were more local, such as Serveau de Mantes or 'Père Paul' Graff, an innkeeper and chef from Pourville, all of whom lent splendid works by Monet. This strategy was so successful that the press, pretending to believe that the exhibition had been organised by 'admirers',[83] praised 'the lucky hand of whoever purchased this wonderful gem',[84] probably a view of Varengeville (fig. 72), a certain M. du Balan. This name was merely a front used by the dealer, among many other 'fantasies' noted by Boudin in his catalogue,[85]

FIG. 70
Pierre-Auguste Renoir
The Dancer, 1874
Oil on canvas, 142.5 × 94.5 cm
National Gallery of Art, Washington, DC
[cat. 70]

DURAND-RUEL AND THE IMPRESSIONISTS' SOLO EXHIBITIONS OF 1883

opposite names such as Lafon, Moreau, Smith, De Rivière, Richard, Charpentier, Goldschmidt, Hayes, Dreyfus, Fould, Kahn and Kann. This artifice, which was aimed at removing the shadow of the dealer while bestowing credit and respectability on the painters, varied from one artist to the next. The list of 70 works by Pissarro makes no mention of Gauguin, Murer, De Bellio, Duret or Faure, despite the fact that they had lent a dozen works; 25 of the 46 works identified[86] belonged to the dealer. Fifty-three of the 70 paintings by Renoir appear in the catalogue alongside the name of their owner (10 for Durand-Ruel). The exhibitions were therefore not a simple showcase of the gallery's stock aimed merely at offloading works; the painters played an active part in selecting the works, as revealed by Monet, Pissarro and Renoir's letters in particular. Monet, keen to show pictures that had 'never been seen by the public',[87] contacted the collectors directly (see fig. 105).[88] Pissarro interceded in the loan of a Sisley and was paid by Durand-Ruel for his 'assistance', which could, in some cases, go as far as restoration, something Renoir did with a Sisley.[89] Not all requests were successful (fig. 73) and some works were (already!) difficult to locate, as described by Boudin: 'Some views of Antwerp in 1870 have been brought back . . . but as I don't know where my most successful pictures are, I had to be content with Durand's stock'.[90] The artists also took part in the hanging process, as requested by the dealer[91] and in accordance with their wishes. 'For an exhibition to be staged correctly, we must be the ones to take care of it . . . I have left plenty of space between the pictures. I am satisfied with my arrangement. Durand gave me complete freedom; I have two rooms with white frames, which is very good indeed',[92] said Pissarro, despite Durand-Ruel having initially refused to use the white frames, probably because of their association with the independent exhibitions, for fear of turning away collectors.

Depending on the circumstances, the involvement of the artists or following adjustments by the dealer, the exhibitions varied in size from 300 works for Boudin (including 150 'studies, pastels and watercolours')[93] to 55–60 for Sisley, according to the press (or almost 80, according to the archives),[94] with 56 for Monet and 70 for both Pissarro and Renoir, for whom works not included in the catalogue must be added, such as *Charles and Georges Durand-Ruel* (see fig. 22). An examination of the works, which cannot always be identified from the catalogues, archives or press reports, suggests that the artists tried to demonstrate their range of expertise by varying techniques (oils, watercolours, pastels, etc.) and genres, with the exceptions of Sisley and Boudin, who limited themselves to landscapes.[95] Figures, which had attracted attention in 1882, were once again present in Pissarro's works (almost all of which belonged to the dealer, fig. 71); they also vividly dominated Renoir's work (*Marie-Thérèse and Jeanne Durand-Ruel*, see fig. 24 and *Luncheon of the Boating Party*, see fig. 33). All, except Boudin and Sisley, also exhibited still lifes, deemed to be more saleable according to a tactical move introduced by Monet in 1882; Monet chose five works of this type,[96] while Durand-Ruel lent another seven under his own name. The dealer therefore supported an attempt to make the artist appear, in the words of the critic Geffroy, as much a 'master decorator' as a 'master landscape painter'[97]. This also chimed with the advice Durand-Ruel gave to Pissarro: 'We must consider varying your exhibition as much as possible; it is with diversity that we will appeal to the public'.[98] A striving for variety underscored the retrospective element of the exhibitions, in which the works ranged from the 1860s to 1883 (figs 74 and 75), something that Monet had already attempted on a smaller scale at the Impressionist exhibitions of 1876 and especially in 1879. Solo exhibitions of living artists essentially remained presentations of recent works, unlike the posthumous retrospectives that began to

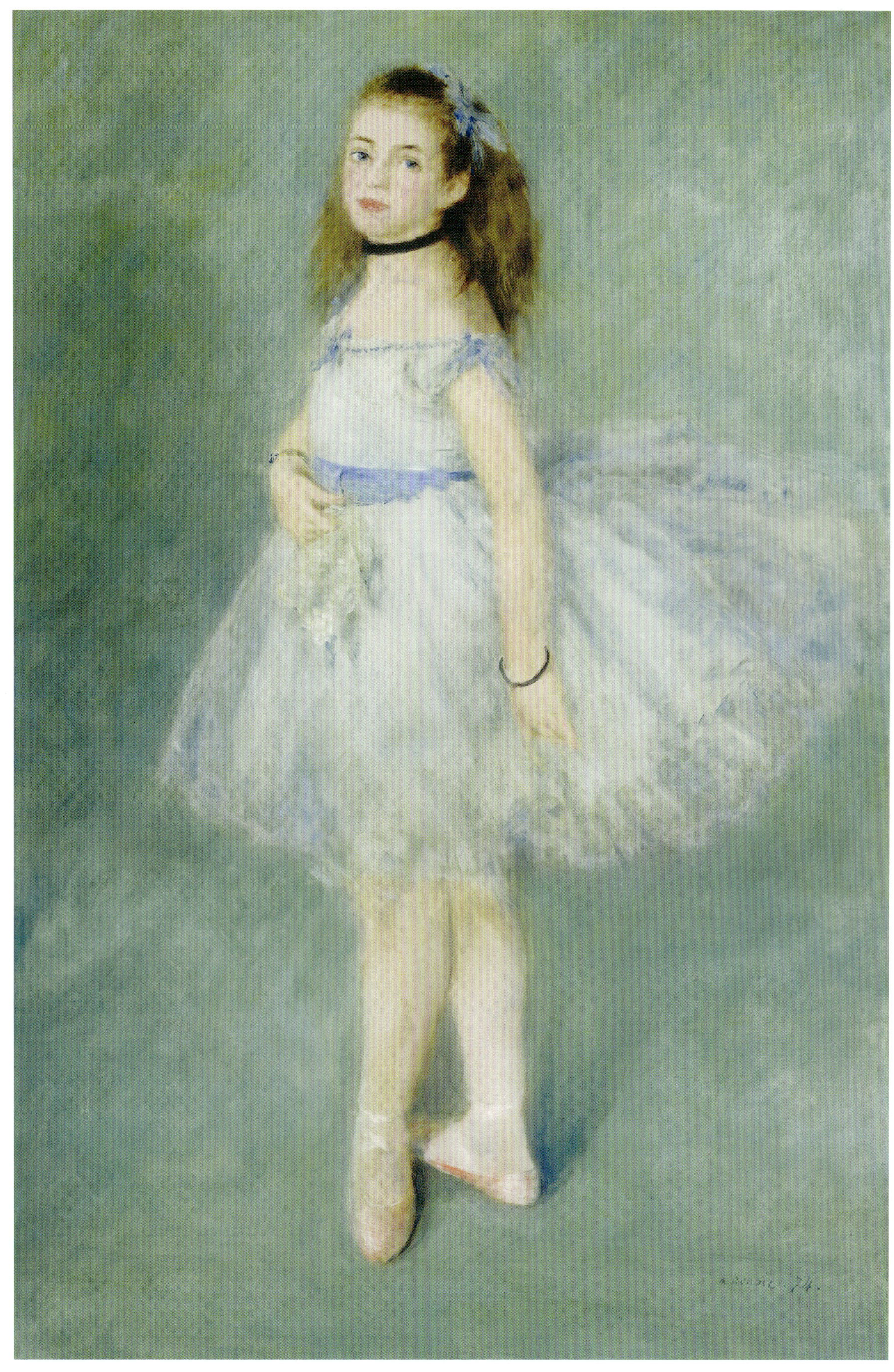

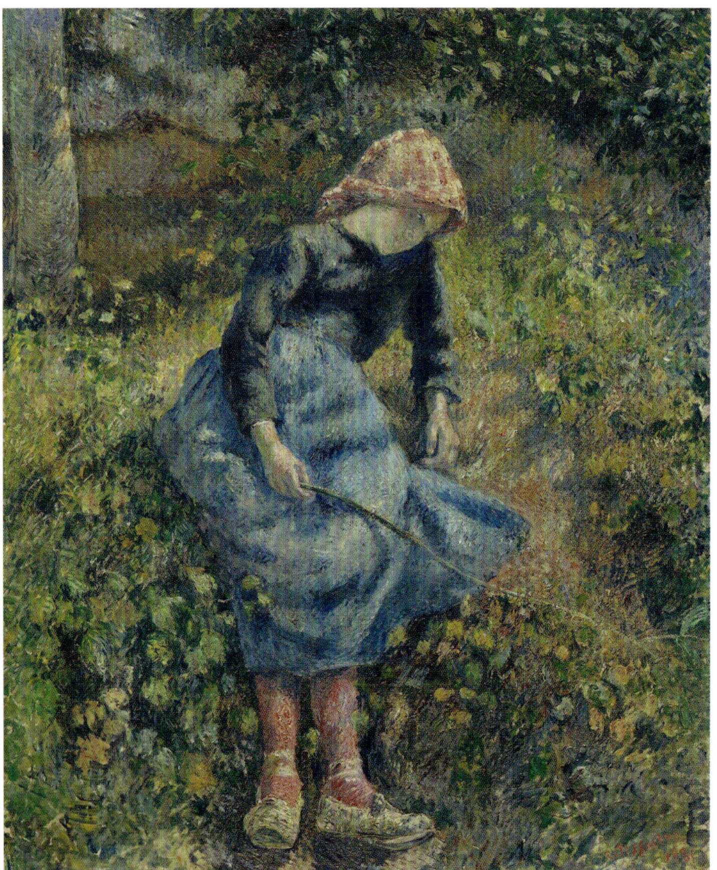

FIG. 71
Camille Pissarro
The Shepherdess, 1881
Oil on canvas, 81 × 65 cm
Musée d'Orsay, Paris

emerge at the Ecole des Beaux-Arts in particular. With the exception of the highly visible shows of Courbet (1855 and 1867) and Manet (1867) on the fringes of the Universal Exhibitions, exhibitions of paintings for public auctions[99] and presentations of works in studios, events of this kind were often reserved for artists who were already enjoying a certain amount of commercial success. The 1883 series chipped away at normal practices, benefiting painters who were still controversial.[100]

DURAND-RUEL AND THE IMPRESSIONISTS' SOLO EXHIBITIONS OF 1883

However, the 1883 exhibitions did not really retrace the careers of the artists: they illustrated an 'oeuvre' but without creating a coherent historical and visual discourse. The majority of the paintings were still recent works (40 of the 56 paintings by Monet – figs 72, 76 and 77 – and about 60 of the 70 by Renoir, for example). Some of them were even painted specifically for the exhibition: 'I have more than 50 canvases left to finish by the end of the month . . . I assure you I am extremely concerned that I alone have to fill a series of rooms usually used by a group', wrote Boudin in mid-December 1882. The same sentiment was echoed by Renoir, whose production increased between January and March,[101] and by Monet, less than 20 days before the opening, when he was painting in Etretat: 'I am sorry to be so pressed for time for my exhibition . . . I am working a lot. I am trying hard to have at least three or four new canvases'.[102] Although the issue of artists needing to produce works for an exhibition was not new, the general feeling was that the monographic format, which required a considerable number of works, increasingly bound the artist to the dealer, who was also in control of the schedule. All the more so because Durand-Ruel could appear pushy, telling Pissarro to paint 'these small compositions or small figures in gouache, on taffeta . . . You know they have been very successful and I am certain these small compositions will be the quickest and best sellers at our next exhibition'.[103] There was a certain amount of ambiguity in these events; some would have it that the Impressionists had taken their place as 'commercial painters',[104] according to the charge aimed at Boudin by Edmond Turquet, the Under Secretary of State for Fine Arts. In a sense, Turquet confirmed the warning issued by Gauguin, at the other end of the artistic spectrum: 'It is not without deep sadness that I see your exhibitions go the way of a personal showcase at a dealer's gallery . . . I only give you a few years until the public is disgusted and says you have prostituted yourself to the dealer as have the others'.[105] However, these accusations must be qualified: the speed of the Impressionists' working methods also provoked similar suspicions in the context of the independent exhibitions, as was the case with the Vétheuil canvases shown by Monet in 1879. According to Burty, the link with Durand-Ruel would conversely free the artists from the tyranny of the market: 'M. Claude Monet, among others, has achieved undeniable progress. He is no longer enslaved by hurried production due to the need to sell from day to day, the absence of official purchases at the Salons, the systematic exclusion from medals and the proscription of the Musée du Luxembourg . . . By selling at a high price, he is able to spend longer working on a canvas, to generate clearer

FIG. 72
Claude Monet
The Church at Varengeville. Morning, 1882
Oil on canvas, 60 × 73 cm
Private collection
[cat. 43]

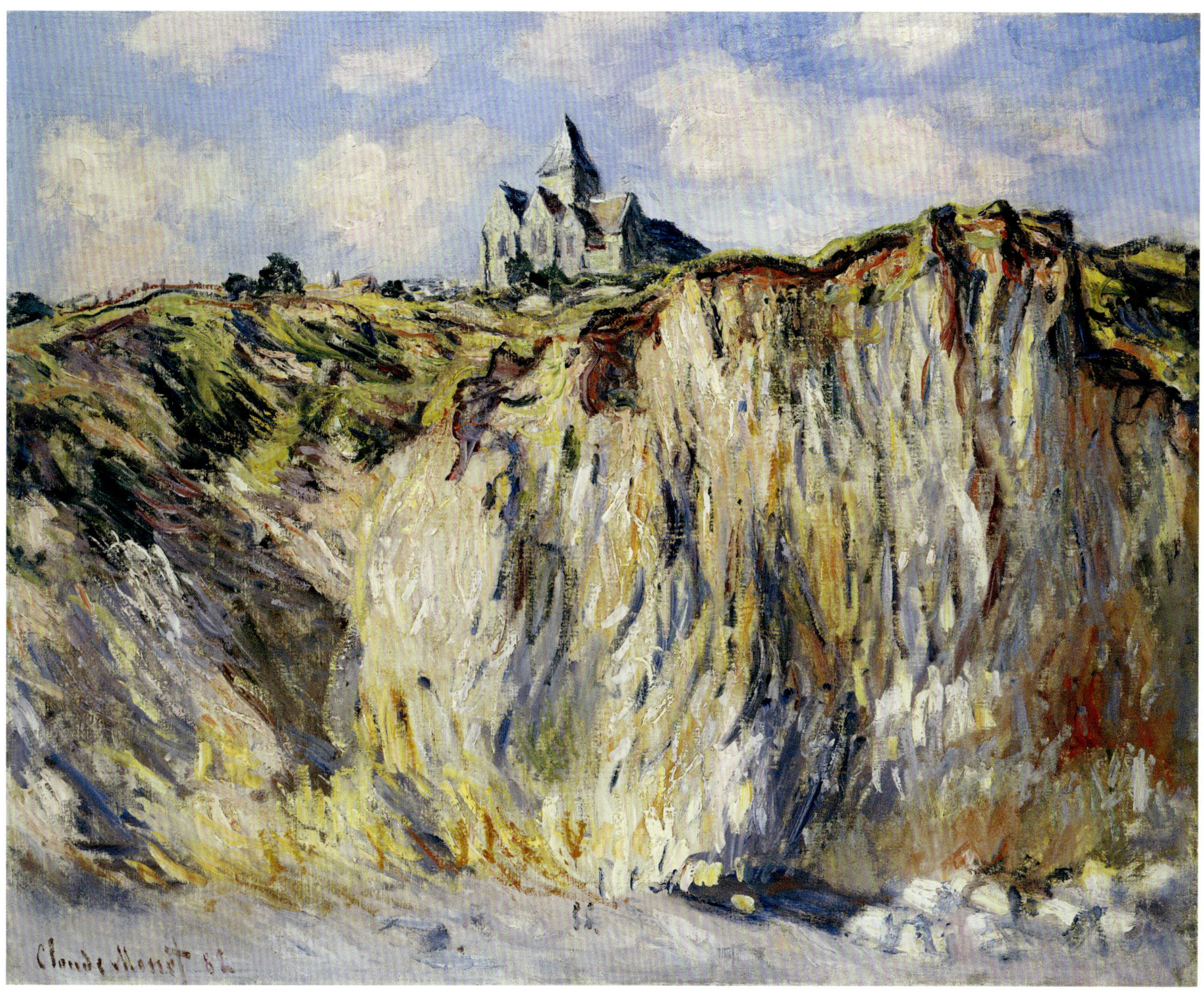

FIG. 73
Claude Monet
The Coal Carriers, about 1875
Oil on canvas, 54 × 66 cm
Musée d'Orsay, Paris
[cat. 40]

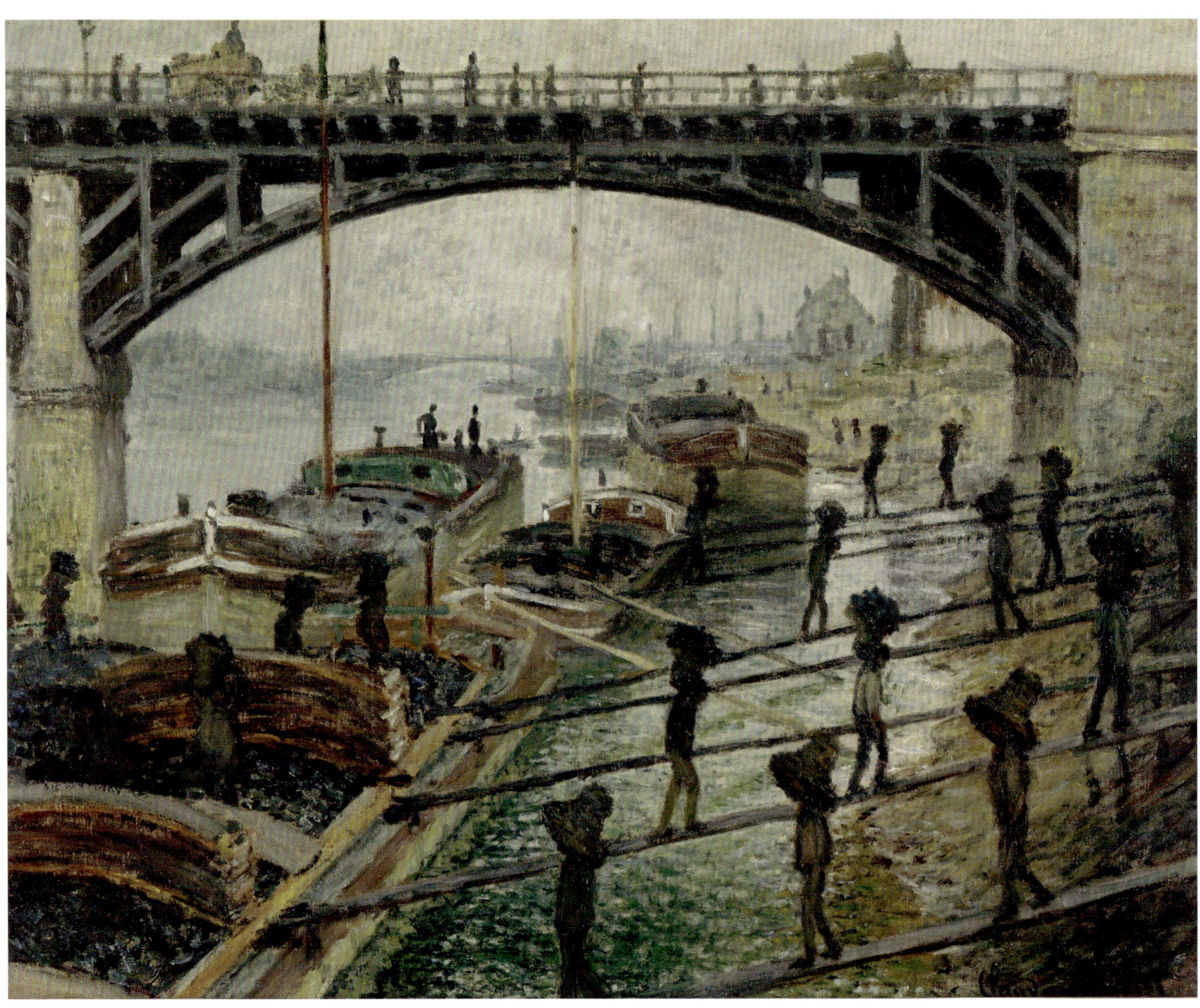

FIG. 74
Claude Monet
La Pointe de la Hève, Sainte-Adresse, 1864
Oil on canvas, 41 × 73 cm
The National Gallery, London
[cat. 29]

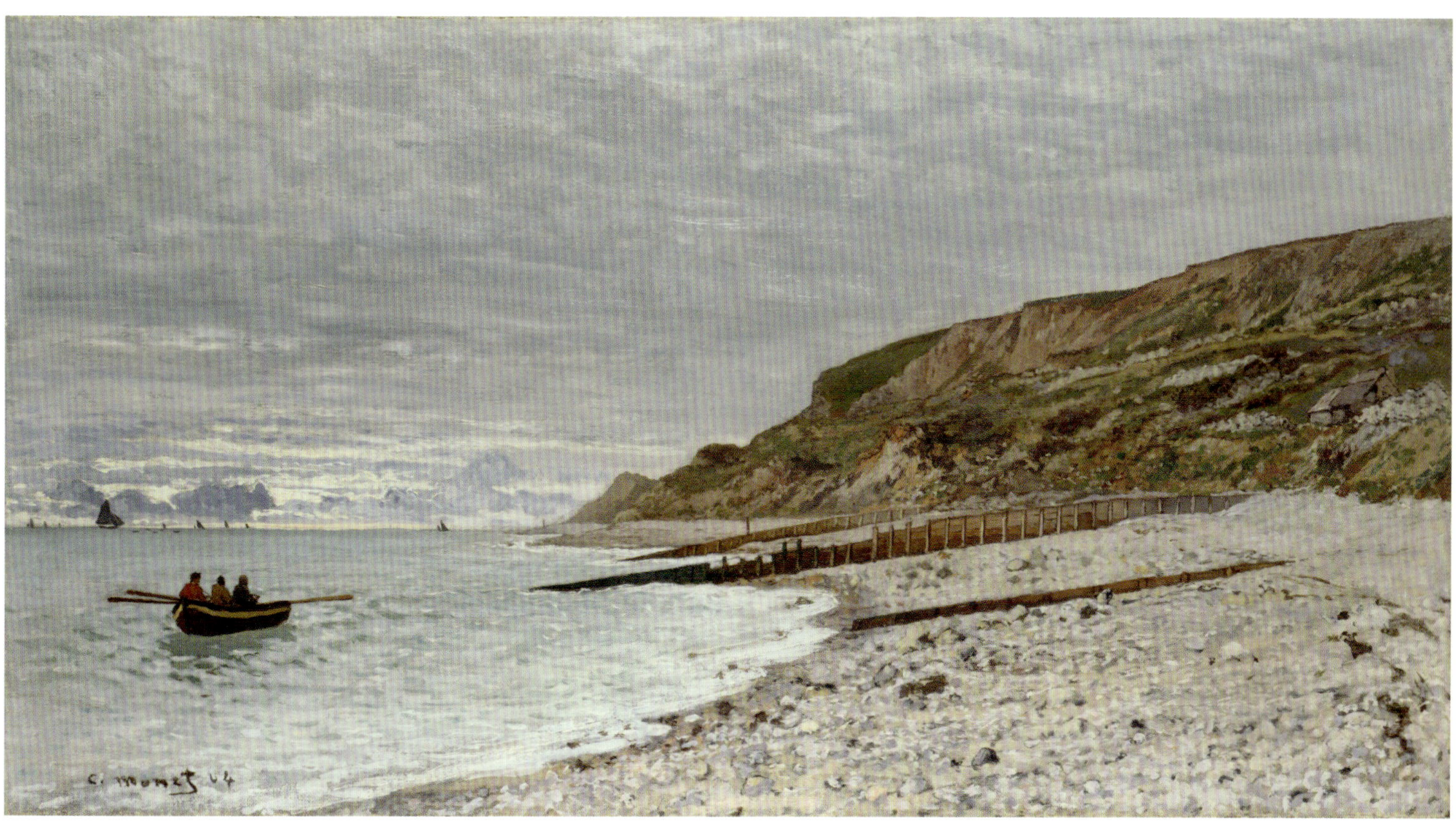

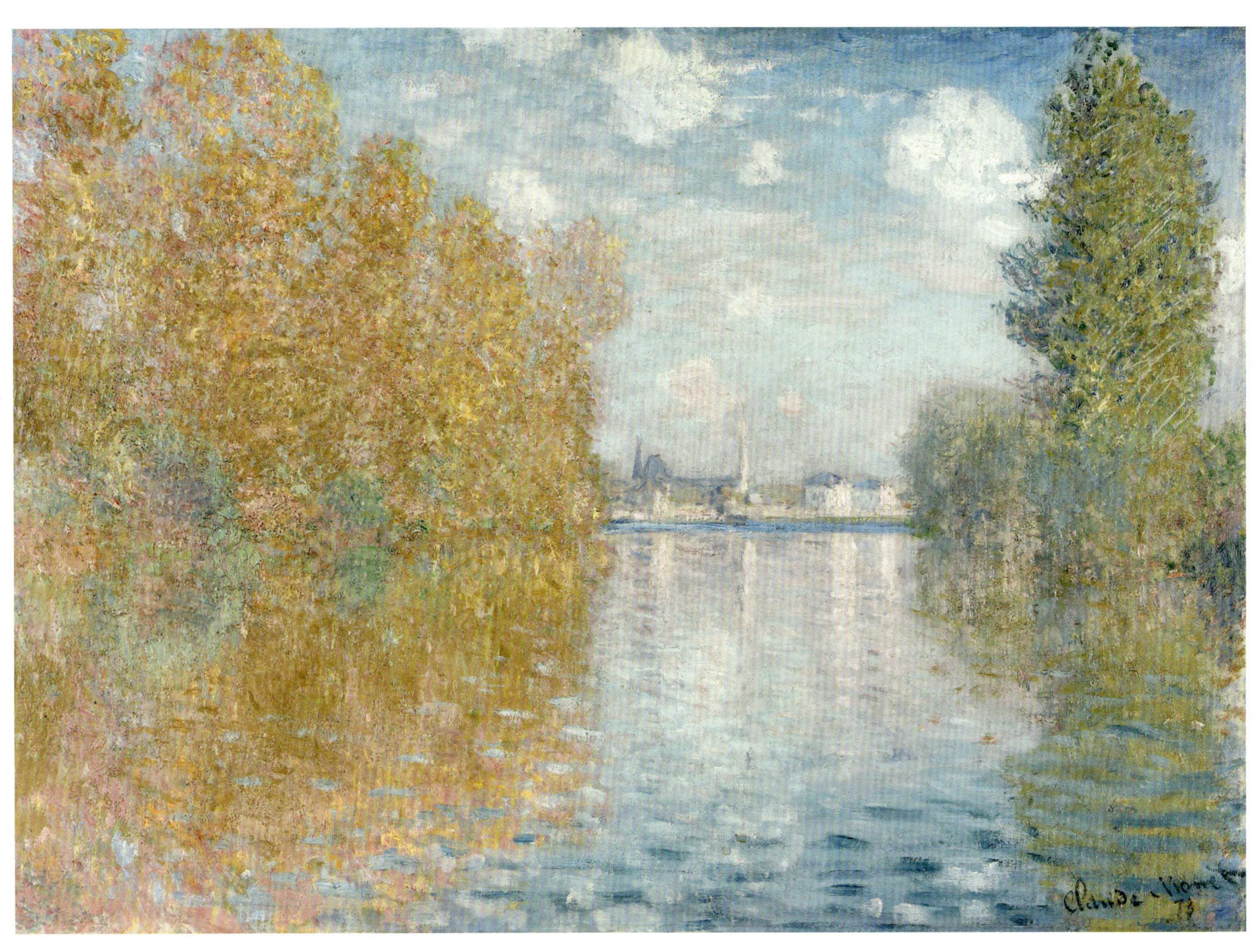

FIG. 75
Claude Monet
Autumn Effect at Argenteuil, 1873
Oil on canvas, 55 × 74.5 cm
The Samuel Courtauld Trust,
The Courtauld Gallery, London
[cat. 36]

intentions and even to rest on days when daydreaming or fatigue prevail'.[106] We have been unable to find any trace in 1883 of the gouaches or taffeta fans demanded by the dealer from Pissarro, while Monet, dissatisfied with the works painted in Etretat for the exhibition, abandoned exhibiting them in favour of pictures painted in Normandy in 1882. All except one of these 24 canvases[107] certainly belonged to Durand-Ruel, but the way they were displayed highlighted the repetition of some of the motifs, also revealing a key aesthetic that would lead to Monet's later series.

Evaluating success

In a letter to Pissarro, Monet asked: 'What has been the result of our exhibitions?'[108] Durand-Ruel's view was that a distinction should be made between immediate financial benefits and 'moral results'.[109] The undertaking rested on a new economic model for the dealer: although the rent of the premises – 3,000 francs per quarter, in addition to the 4,500 francs spent for the gallery on rue de la Paix – seems to have been offset by the 7,500 francs he received from the Banque Nationale, subtenant of rue Laffitte,[110] he invested more than 11,000 francs in fittings (including more than 4,900 francs for the rugs!),[111] a sum that was large enough to make an impression on Boudin.[112] In keeping with the model of the independent exhibitions, but going against standard practice for the gallery, an entrance fee was charged, with 'turnstile' takings of 600 francs (Boudin and Renoir) and 500 francs (Monet), but significantly less for Pissarro and Sisley, who collected 296 francs and 160 francs respectively.[113] If we suppose that an entrance fee of one franc was charged, as was the case at the Salon and other exhibitions, it would seem that attendance was low, as corroborated by accounts, compared with the 6,000 visitors to the Watercolour Painters exhibition staged by Petit in 1882, for example.[114] Revenue and expenditure seemed to balance nonetheless, with modest profits of between 40 and 100 francs depending on the exhibition. On the other hand, the total balance of sales was very poor. Only seven pictures by Boudin were sold, for a total of 3,800 francs. The clients included Gallimard,[115] the painter Roll[116] and Jules Feder, who was one of Durand-Ruel's financial backers,[117] as was Cotinaud. This dealer's relative may have purchased a Monet from the exhibition two days after it closed.[118] The Scottish collector James Duncan also acquired *The Bay of Naples* (fig. 78) for 3,000 francs at the closure of Renoir's exhibition. No sales were registered at any point during either Pissarro or Sisley's exhibitions.

The dealer chose to begin the exhibition series with Boudin, considered by Burty to be 'one of the least revolutionary',[119] whose works he had shown alongside those of more conventional painters in exhibitions in France or abroad prior to the Impressionist shows. However, the success was relative and ephemeral:[120] from 8 June, Boudin stopped delivering to the dealer, who bought nothing from him until February 1884. We should probably also not be surprised that half the paintings by Monet sold to Petit on 9 August were those that had not been sold during the 1883 exhibition; prices averaged 675 francs per picture, as did those by Pissarro and Sisley, instead of the 2,000 hoped for by Durand-Ruel.[121] According to Pissarro, this was precisely one of the reasons behind the failure in 1883, against the backdrop of a general market crisis. This was also a time when Durand-Ruel's purchases were slowing, decreasing from 89 to 42 and from 43 to 16 for Monet and Renoir, for example. 'My exhibition did nothing in terms of numbers of visitors', wrote Pissarro. 'There were one or two offers of purchase but Durand was asking too much and *stood firm on his prices* (strangely enough!). Sisley's exhibition was even worse: nothing, nothing at all'.[122] The selection of 70 pictures by Renoir was dominated by 48 portraits and figure paintings, of which only *Dance*

FIG. 76
Claude Monet
Customhouse, Varengeville, 1882
Oil on canvas, 60.3 × 81.4 cm
Philadelphia Museum of Art, Pennsylvania
[cat. 45]

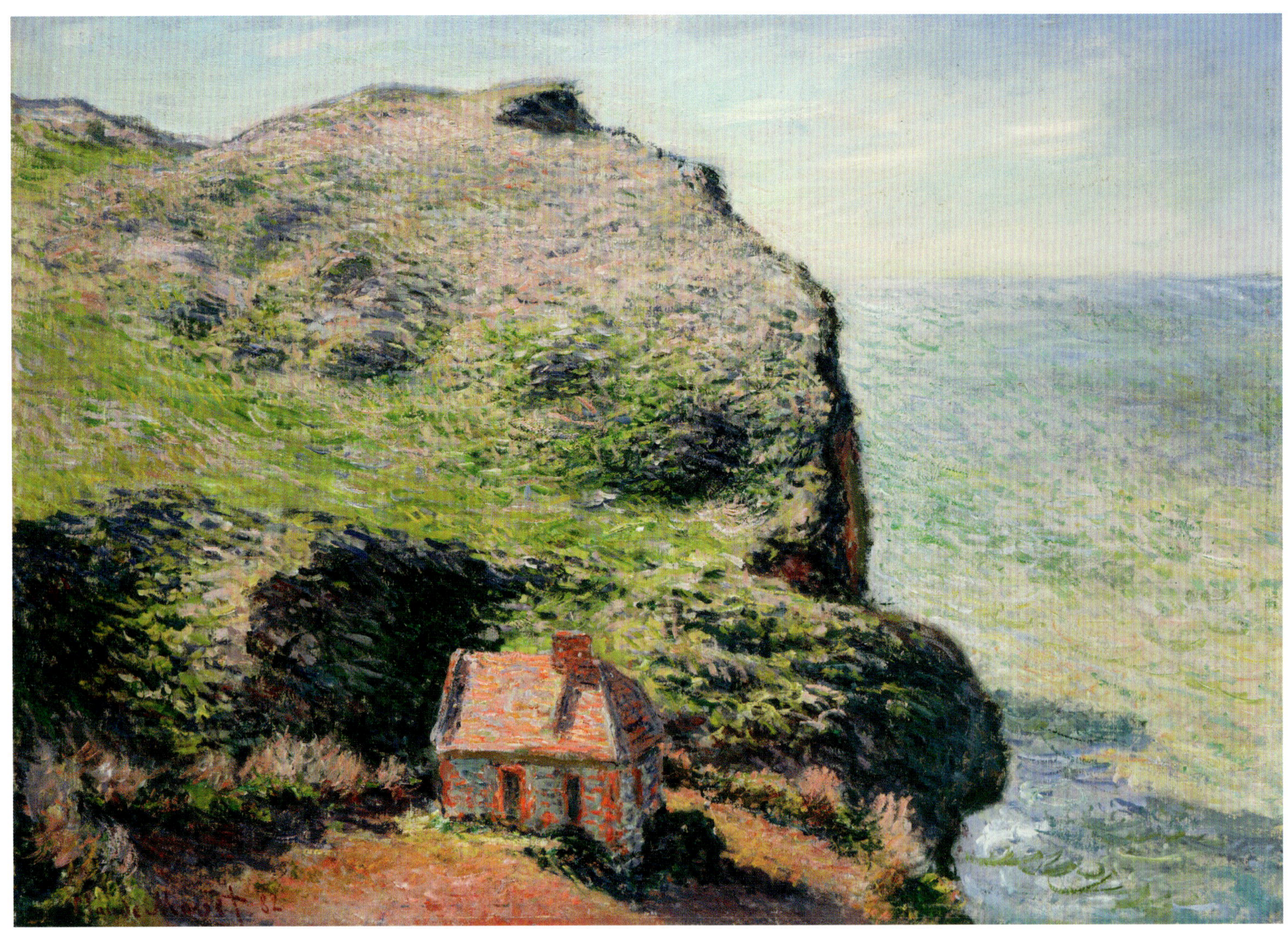

FIG. 77
Claude Monet
Road at La Cavée, Pourville, 1882
Oil on canvas, 60.3 × 81.6 cm
Museum of Fine Arts, Boston
[cat. 44]

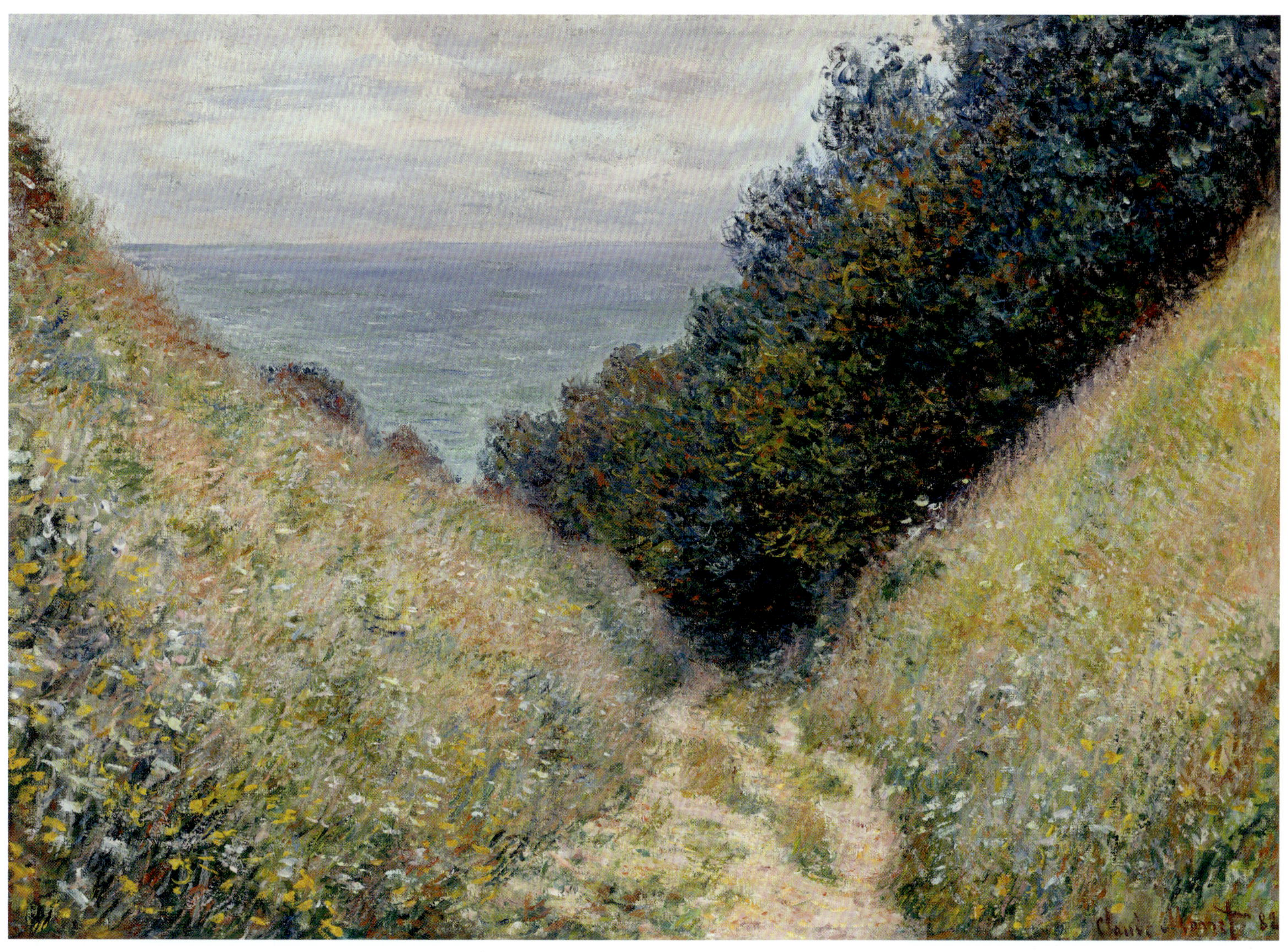

in the Country and *Dance in the City*, submitted by the artist, were listed as being for sale. If we suppose that the pictures listed as the property of the dealer belonged to his personal collection, this may lead us to wonder about bias. Some of these paintings would remain in his collection until his death, although the definition of what was and was not gallery stock remained fluid. Renoir and Durand-Ruel had therefore not really opted for a selling exhibition, even if more than half the 15 or so pictures probably from his stock were landscapes, with views of Italy and Algiers in particular, subject matter that had already captivated collectors the previous year and had even been remarked on by the press in 1883.

Durand-Ruel therefore underlined the 'moral' benefit of these events to the artists, who, including Pissarro, were 'overwhelmed by fear of the future and great discouragement'.[123] The previews, for which the gallery sent about a thousand invitations,[124] were a success: 'Lots of people . . . almost a competition of devotees, with Durand at their head. The pictures looked good in the gaslight', reported Boudin after Monet's preview.[125] Burty also confirmed that Monet 'said to us, the day after the

FIG. 78
Pierre-Auguste Renoir
The Bay of Naples, 1881
Oil on canvas, 59.7 × 81.3 cm
The Metropolitan Museum of Art, New York

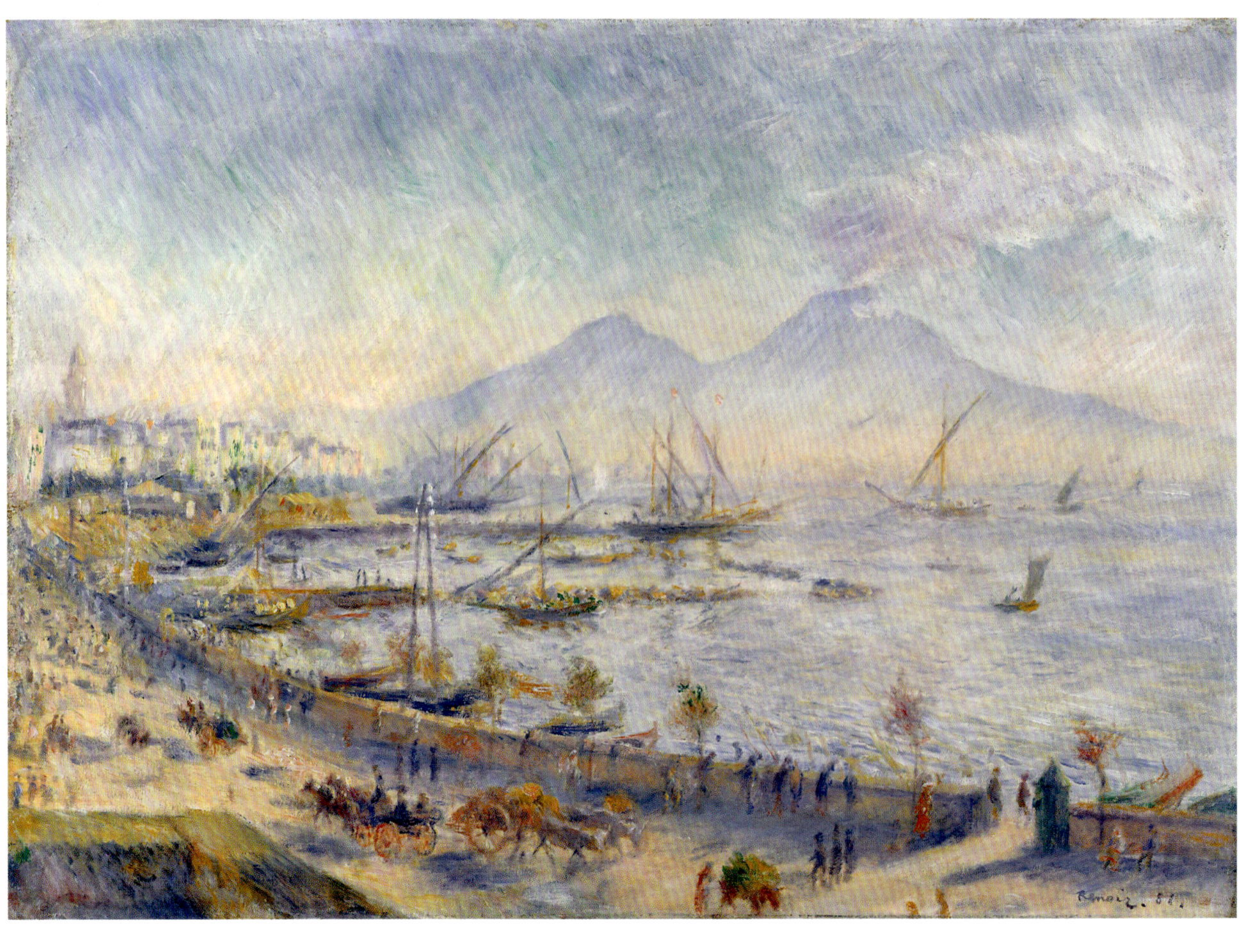

evening of the opening that had been attended by the elite of the critics and real collectors: "No one laughed at any of my canvases". How much swallowed bitterness these ingenuous words contained!'[126] This was also echoed by Pissarro: despite the simultaneous opening of the Salon, 'they flocked in . . . and we noted more than one famous person from the art world amid the throng'.[127]

Durand-Ruel invested in marketing, placing several advertisements in the press (*Courrier de l'art*, *La Justice*, *L'Europe artiste*, *Beaumarchais*, *Le Parnasse*, *La Lanterne*, etc.), and putting up posters: 'You can't spend eight days on the walls of Paris without people expecting something',[128] admitted Boudin. There were a number of press articles, particularly about Boudin, who identified 48 different ones 'in the spotlight',[129] as well as about Monet, Pissarro and Renoir, who each collected between 10 and 20; the exhibitions were also covered in the foreign press.[130] Even when they were rare, which was especially the case with Sisley, the reviews were generally favourable, praising the colours, light and sincerity of the pictures on display. Some works in particular were remarked upon, such as the *Dances* by Renoir (see figs 3 and 4), *The Côte des Boeufs at l'Hermitage* by Pissarro (National Gallery, London), *The Forge* by Sisley (Musée d'Orsay, Paris), and *The Galettes* by Monet (fig. 79), worthy, according to Geffroy, 'of the immortal brioche by Chardin'.[131] The artist himself had borrowed this picture from Graff, mounting it on a new canvas for the occasion.[132] Publications such as the *Moniteur des arts* (with Sisley on the front page),[133] the *Courrier de l'art*, *Le Journal des artistes*, the *Journal des arts*, *La Vie moderne* and *L'Intransigeant* each covered at least three of the five exhibitions, among which the texts by Fourcaud in *Le Gaulois*, by Burty in *La République* and by the young Geffroy in Clemenceau's newspaper *La Justice*, with Monet on the front page, stand out. Monet was probably the most enterprising of all the painters exhibited, acting against Durand-Ruel's advice: 'I think it would be better to allow these gentlemen to speak freely and leave them to use their initiative rather than asking them for paid articles. It is a bad principle in my opinion to beg for publicity for a talent such as yours'.[134] As was the case for his 1880 exhibition at *La Vie moderne*, the artist reproduced some of his pictures for the press, for the influential *Gazette des Beaux-Arts*[135] in particular. The painter even rewarded the critic Burty with a work.[136] For the first time, the monographic format gave rise to articles that assessed the painters' careers, particularly useful texts insofar as the exhibitions provided lists of the works in lieu of catalogues, except in the case of Renoir, who benefited from a booklet with an introduction by Duret. This critical success seemed to satisfy Durand-Ruel; in his eyes these individual exhibitions, which avoided the need to hang works next to those by artists judged to be 'compromising', rewarded the 'serious nature' of what appeared to be an act of legitimisation. He boasted to Monet: 'You have been successful among people of taste. The number of those who understand you is growing day by day. Your reputation among the masses will come on its own; that day will arrive and it is not far away. As far as I am concerned, you should not worry. I never get downhearted and even if I had a thousand of your pictures that hadn't sold I would not change my opinion'.[137]

A 'painful birth'

Such a statement legitimises the interpretation of Durand-Ruel as a visionary dealer. In the absence of immediate results, he went for long-term impact and invented a kind of '*auteur*' approach,[138] to use François Truffaut's famous word, based on the defence of a whole body of work rather than isolated examples, a feeling of closeness to the painter and a love of the

FIG. 79
Claude Monet
The Galettes, 1882
Oil on canvas, 65 × 81 cm
Private collection
[cat. 46]

work.[139] We should not forget the revolutionary role 'the startling display'[140] of paintings by Delacroix had played for Durand-Ruel in 1855. However, the success of the years 1890–1900 colour this reading with a teleological dimension that masks the experimental and ultimately isolated character of the 1883 series, which Durand-Ruel would later describe as a 'trial'.[141] Although these exhibitions asserted his return to the nascent market for Impressionism in the early 1880s, it would be mistaken to claim that they tipped the painters over into a dealer system controlled by him, as Gauguin feared they would. In fact, they compensated for the renewed decrease in his purchases in 1883 and only temporarily strengthened his links with the artists, who would also deal with Portier, Van Gogh and Petit the following year. In this context, Durand-Ruel planned to create a new society of artists, returning to a model tested throughout the nineteenth century outside the official, or purely dealer-based, systems.[142] Pissarro, like Monet, would refuse this formula, for which Renoir may have already begun to draw up statutes.[143]

Eventually, the dealer decided to explore avenues other than exhibitions and gallery spaces, leading him to move out of the premises on boulevard de la Madeleine in late January 1884, emptying them of 150 Impressionist pictures:[144] 'I am resolved to have nothing further to do with exhibitions of any kind', he wrote to Monet. 'They have all cost me an enormous amount of money and effort, bringing me nothing but trouble and blame in return. I believe the best exhibitions are those held in the collectors' apartment. Since I have been bringing many people to rue de Rome, it has been a revelation for most of them, who have never seen your pictures look so good'.[145] The dealer's impatience to finally see delivery of all the decorative panels he had commissioned from Monet for the doors of his *grand salon* (see figs 26–32) may not have been unrelated to the role given to the new apartment on the first floor of 35, rue de Rome, which he moved into in January 1884.[146] Believing that 'real artists no longer make mistakes by doing exhibitions',[147] Durand-Ruel seems not to have organised any further shows in rue Laffitte either in 1885 or 1886, embarking instead on a major new project in New York in 1886. It was almost ten years before he staged monographic exhibitions again for the Impressionists (and then only after Theo van Gogh and Petit),[148] motivated by the development of series in Monet's work or at the instigation of his critic friends, such as Arsène Alexandre in 1892. Alexandre would remember: 'I managed to have the idea of a comprehensive exhibition to repair the failure of that of La Madeleine approved by Durand-Ruel . . . The public and the artists came in unforeseen numbers'.[149] They certainly did to Monet's *Poplars* exhibition in February (see figs 11–14) as well as to the Pissarro retrospective in 1892. Thus, during the successful early 1890s, which saw Degas accept one of the extremely rare solo exhibitions of his career in 1892, the Durand-Ruel Gallery organised almost 65 monographic shows, playing its part in a genre that would include more than 300 examples in Paris over the course of the decade (compared with fewer than 100 in the previous decade).[150] After the vicissitudes of 1883, these successes bear witness to the 'painful birth' of the solo exhibition, to paraphrase the title of a volume by Francis Haskell,[151] and subsequently emphasise the slow and problematic emergence of methods of disseminating artworks that are taken for granted today. Durand-Ruel played an innovative role in a process that did indeed require 'a particularly strong stomach'.

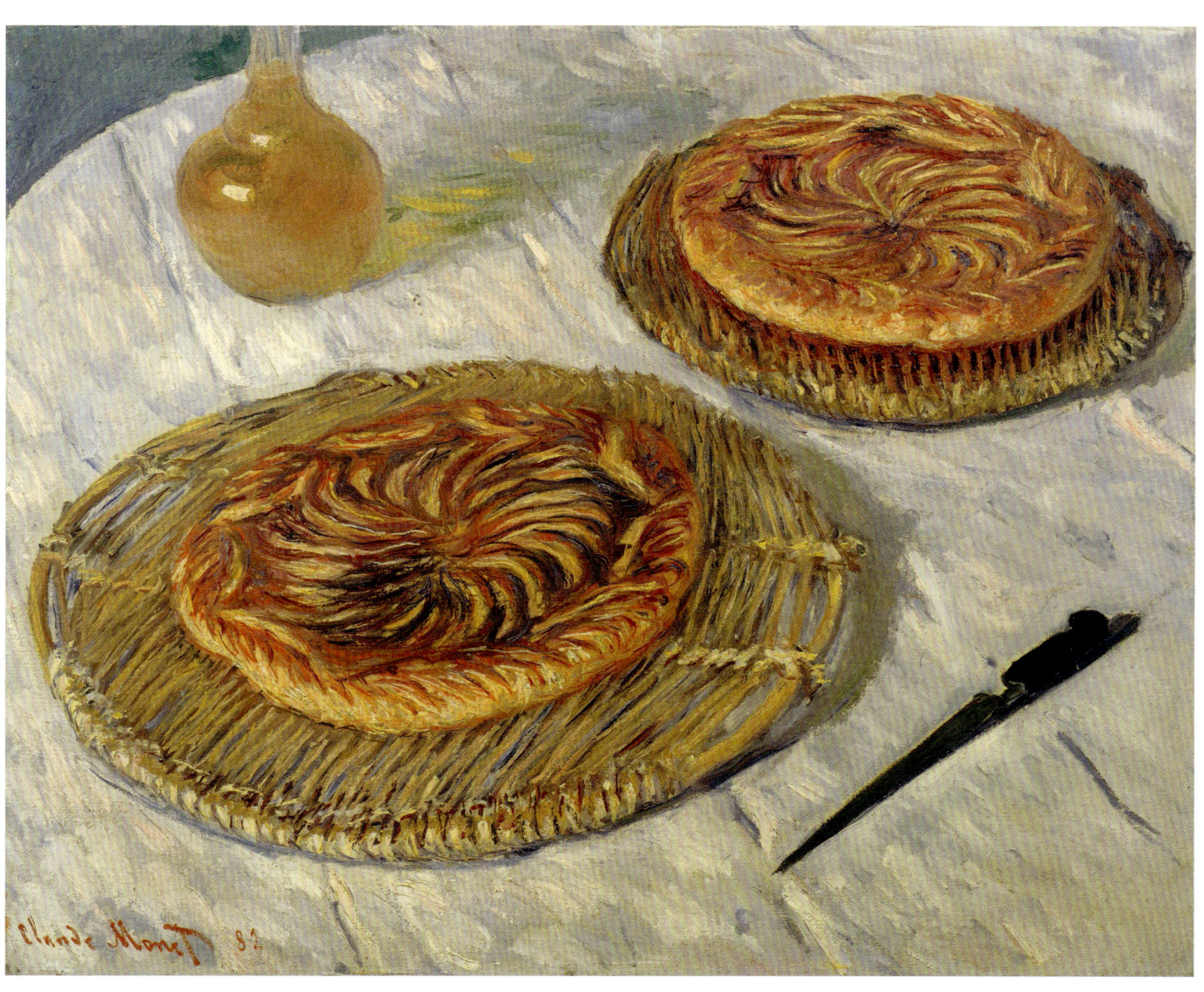
Claude Monet 82

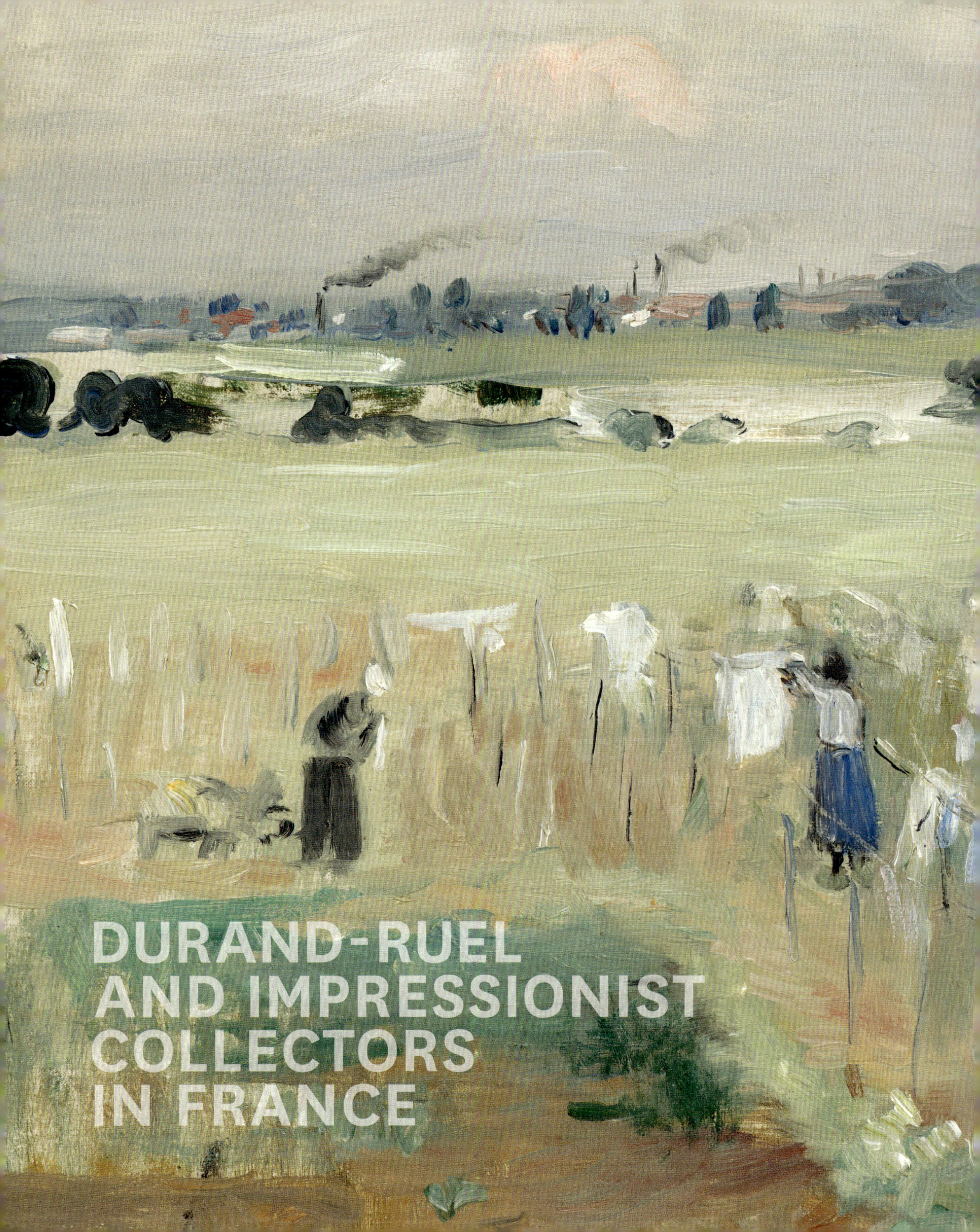

DURAND-RUEL AND IMPRESSIONIST COLLECTORS IN FRANCE

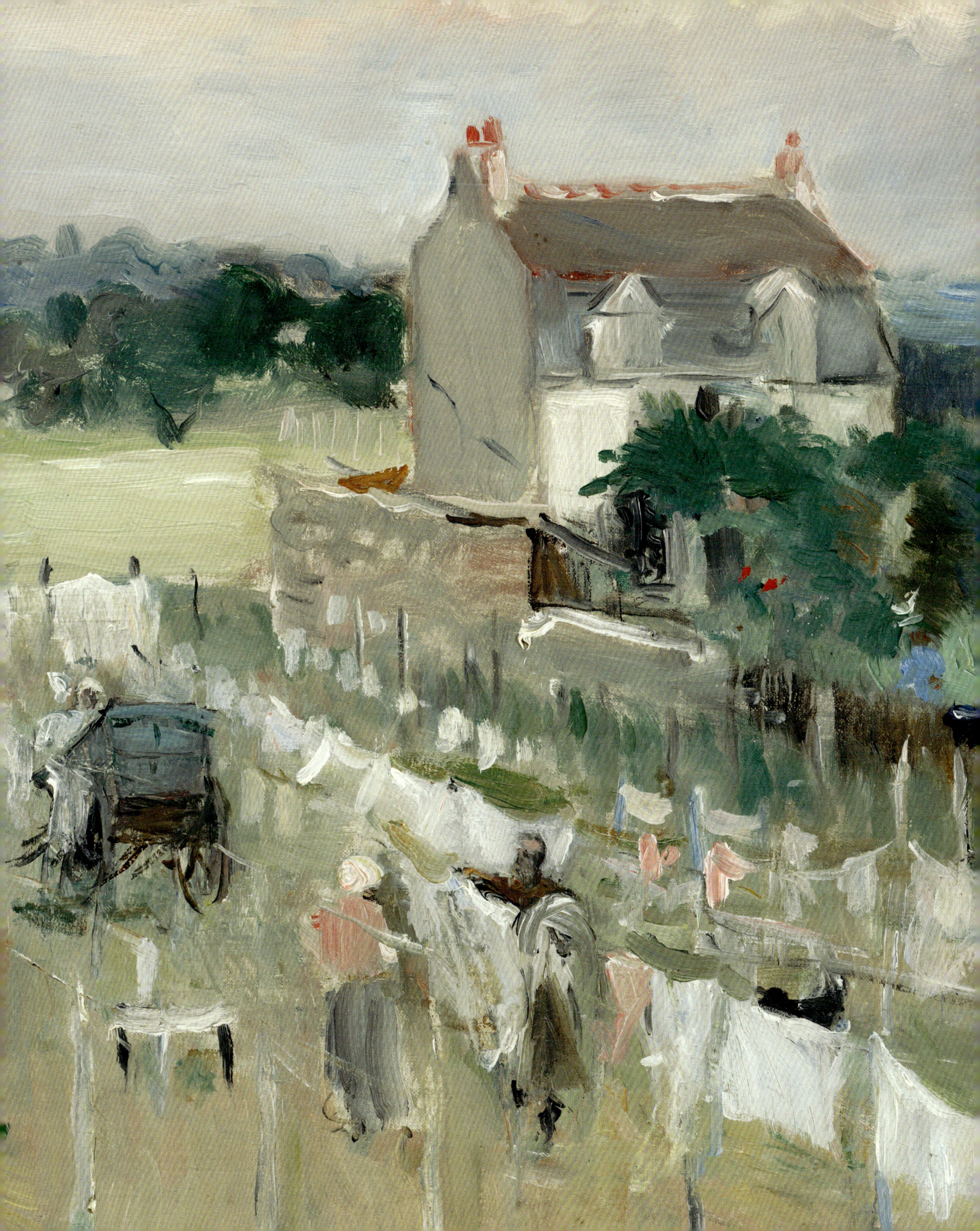

Durand-Ruel and Impressionist Collectors in France

Anne Distel

The 1874 exhibition

The spring of 1874 saw the opening of the first exhibition by the artists who came to be known as 'The Impressionists'. They decided to exhibit their works outside the official Salon, from which they were now regularly excluded by a jury hostile to their artistic choices. Without the approval of this jury they were also banned from the system of public and private commissions and purchases, passed on by particular dealers, on which artists depended at that time. However, an embryonic distinct commercial network of collectors and dealers already existed around this small group, which included Degas, Monet, Berthe Morisot (fig. 83), Camille Pissarro, Renoir and Sisley, to which Manet, who was tolerated by the Salon, should also be added.

Durand-Ruel initially made contact with Monet and Pissarro in 1871 in London, where they had taken refuge during the Franco-Prussian War. On his return to Paris the by now well-established art dealer purchased a number of works from Manet, Monet, Degas, Sisley, Pissarro and Renoir during the first six months of 1872, as well as from Berthe Morisot and Eva Gonzalès in July and August of the same year. The purchase price for these artists ranged from 100 to 1,500 francs per work. These were not large sums for the artists, but they were windfalls nevertheless; prior to this, they had depended on serendipitous sales and purchases from small dealers, who hardly benefited from the reputable status enjoyed by Durand-Ruel. Overall, Durand-Ruel paid what were not insignificant sums and he was the only dealer at that time who was able and willing to consider investments of that kind. Emile Zola, while writing *L'Oeuvre*, published in 1886, would call this Durand-Ruel's 'breakthrough on behalf of the Impressionists'.[1] In 1872 the group had been neither founded nor named, but Durand-Ruel, making a choice based on conviction, sensed the vitality shown by this new generation of artists. Despite this, the dealer did not abandon the trade in prestigious artists for which he was known; he continued to sell works by Corot, Delacroix and the 1830 School, while supporting Courbet and Puvis de Chavannes, who still surprised despite their notoriety. He operated amid a multitude of other small Parisian dealers, including Pierre-Firmin Martin (Père Martin), all of whom created healthy competition and more opportunities for exhibitions and contact with the public.

Returning to the situation as it was in 1874, the exhibition cited the following lenders: Doctor Paul Gachet for Cézanne and Guillaumin – he knew the artists personally and would later play host to Vincent van Gogh in Auvers-sur-Oise; the painters Edouard Brandon and Henri Rouart (both of whom were taking part in the exhibition); the opera singer Jean-Baptiste Faure; and M. Mulbacher [sic], a carriage manufacturer, for works by Degas.[2] Paintings by Berthe Morisot were lent by 'M. Manet', either the painter or his brother Eugène, Morisot's husband. Durand-Ruel was listed as the owner of two landscapes by Sisley (fig. 80), linking his name to the exhibition that had been organised on neutral ground, in the former studios of the photographer Nadar. Another dealer, 'M. Martin, dealer in pictures, rue Laffitte, 52' (Père Martin), supplied a Parisian

FIG. 80
Alfred Sisley
Ile de la Loge or *The Flood*, 1872
Oil on canvas, 45 × 60 cm
Ny Carlsberg Glyptotek,
Copenhagen
[cat. 88]

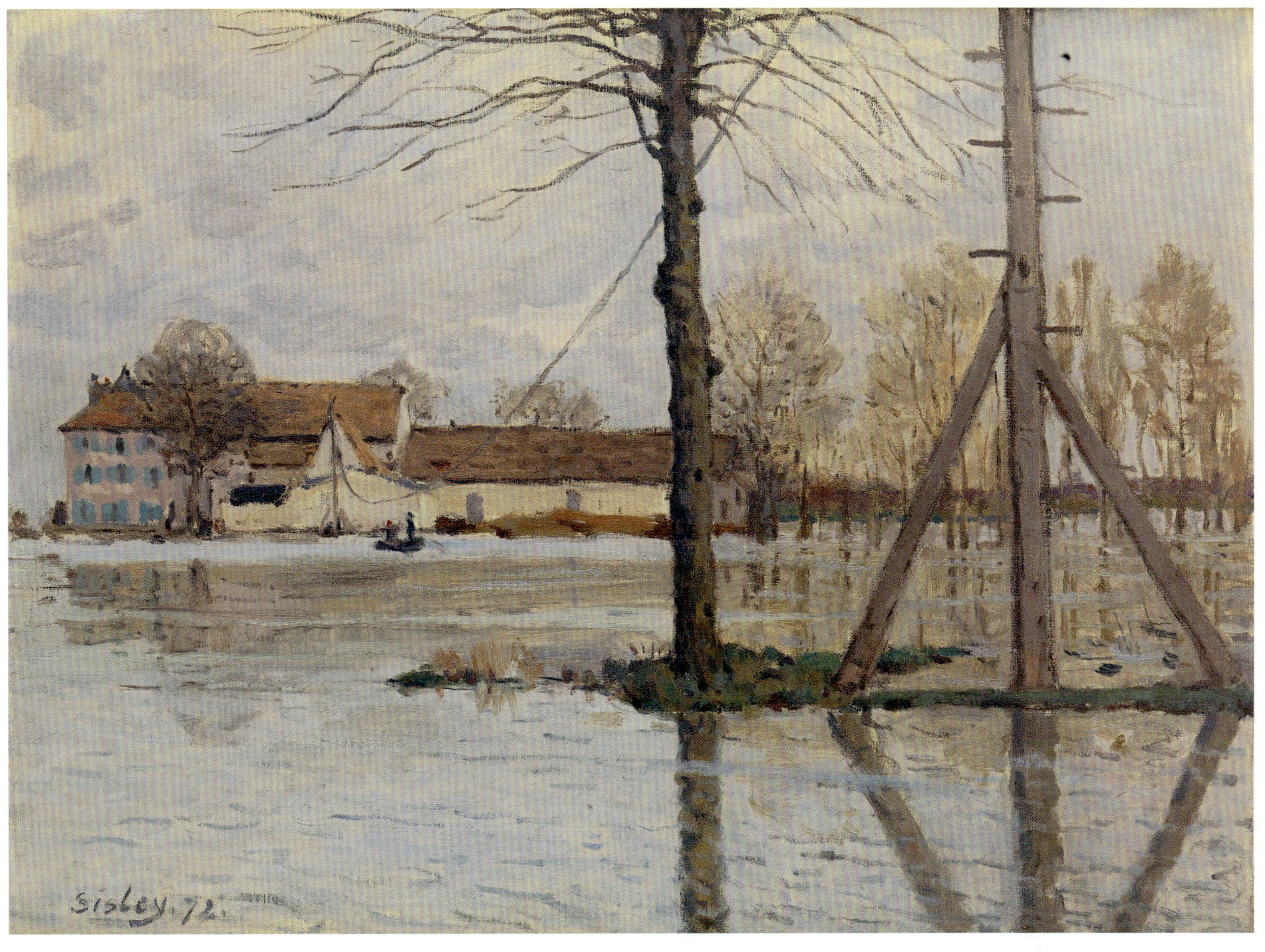

address for the painters E. Béliard and A.-F. Cals, another form of publicity. The Société Anonyme des Artistes Peintres, Sculpteurs, Graveurs, the cooperative to which the exhibiting artists belonged, was also responsible for selling works on display, as demonstrated by an annotated catalogue showing the asking prices; these were officially authorised by the signature of the secretary of the cooperative's board, the enameller Alfred Meyer.[3] In addition to a painting by Louis Latouche (250 francs), the cooperative also seems to have sold a canvas by Renoir, *The Harvesters* (to M. Hartmann, the music publisher), now in a private collection in Switzerland; a landscape by Sisley, *The Seine at Port-Marly*, which cannot be easily identified; and even Monet's *Impression, Sunrise* (Musée Marmottan Monet, Paris). These last two works were sold for 1,000 francs each but the names of their buyers have not been recorded. The reality, as reflected in Monet's account books, was more complex: Monet notes that his *Impression* was sold 'to M. Hoschedé p. Durand' for 800 francs, revealing that Durand-Ruel acted as the intermediary between the artist and Ernest Hoschedé (fig. 81), heir to a prosperous Parisian textile business, who was, alongside Jean-Baptiste Faure (fig. 82), one of the dealer's rare clients for his 'young' painters in 1873.[4]

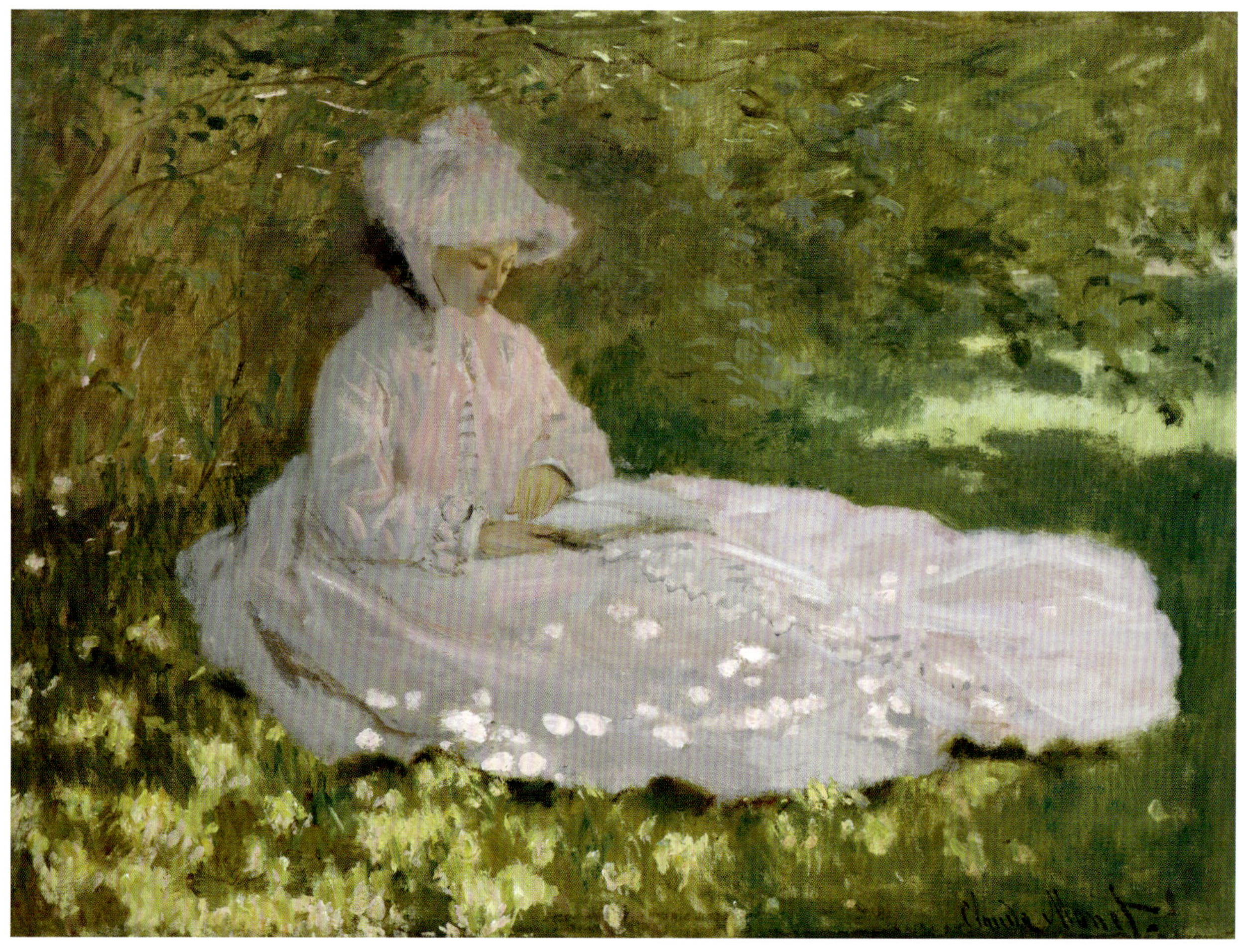

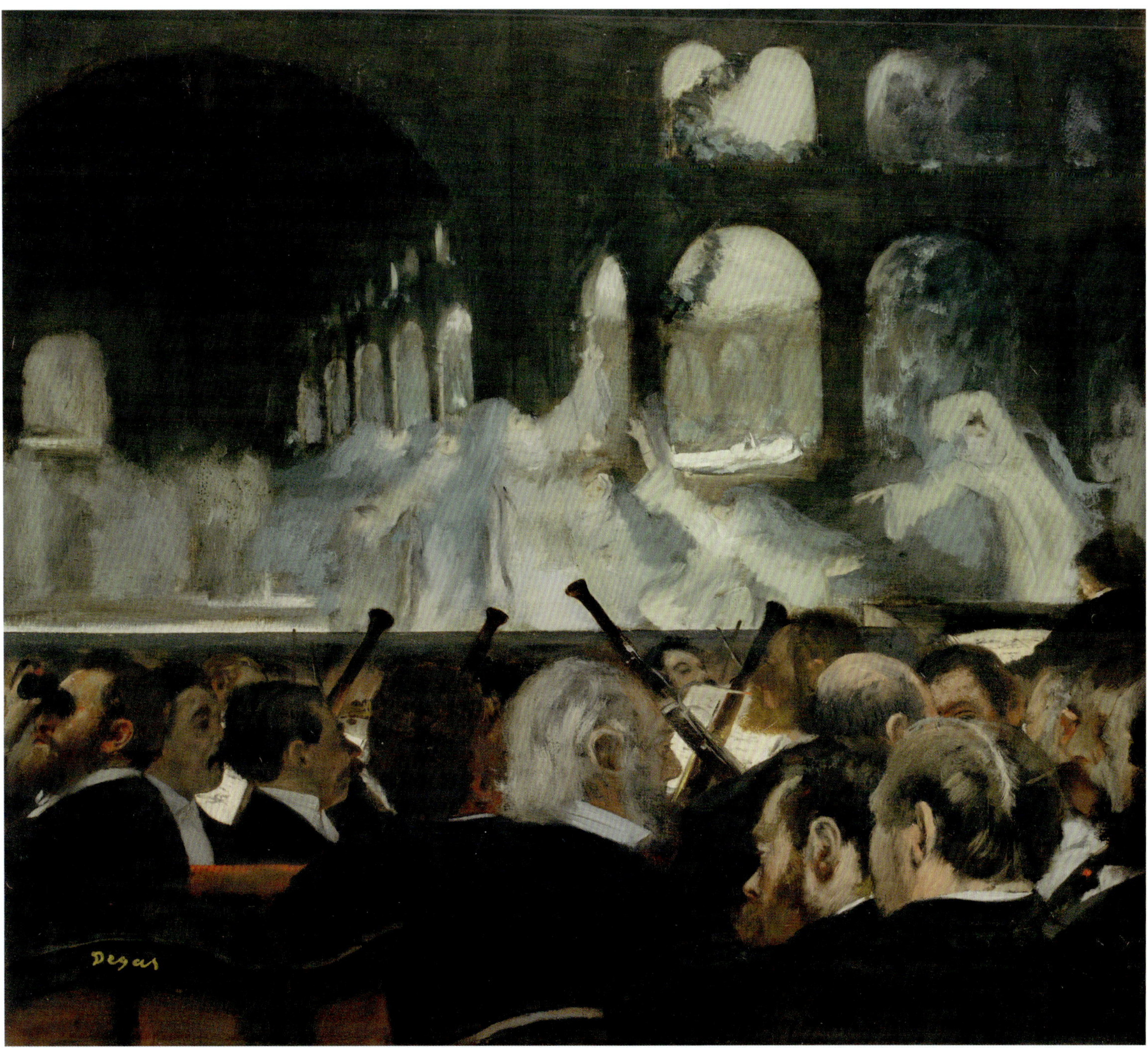

FIG. 81
Claude Monet
Springtime, or *Woman reading*, 1872
Oil on canvas, 50 × 65.5 cm
The Walters Art Museum, Baltimore
[cat. 34]

FIG. 82
Edgar Degas
The Ballet Scene from Meyerbeer's Opera 'Robert le Diable', 1876
Oil on canvas, 76.6 × 81.3 cm
Victoria and Albert Museum, London
[cat. 13]

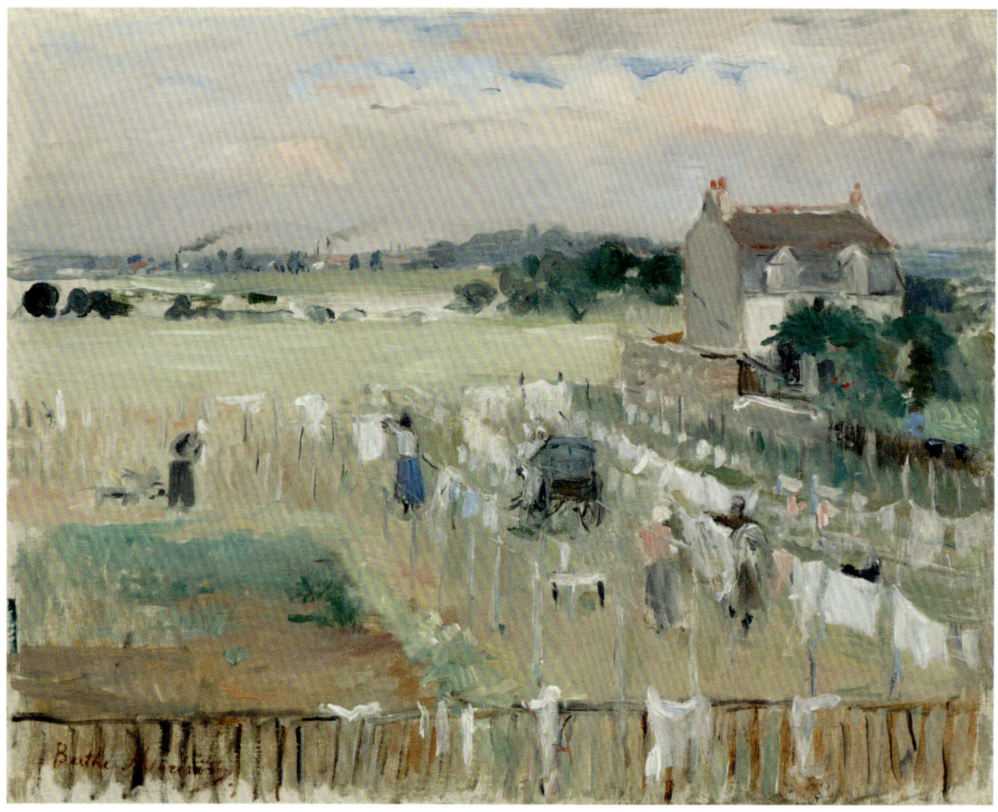

Théodore Duret, *Les Peintres impressionnistes*, May 1878

The names of other collectors and dealers are recorded in the catalogues produced in 1876 and 1877 for the group's second and third exhibitions.[5] This led the critic Théodore Duret, himself a collector (and a client of Durand-Ruel), to draw up a list of the collectors of these artists in his *Peintres impressionnistes*, published in May 1878: 'M.M. d'Auriac [sic], Étienne Baudry, de Belio [sic] (figs 83 and 84), Charpentier, Choquet [sic], Deudon, Dollfus, Faure, Murer, de Rasty'. If we interpret the first name on this list as a misspelling of Count Doria, it provides us with the key players in the new generation of Impressionist collectors. This was also the first time a critic had publicly associated a group of private collectors, with independent tastes, with the genesis of an artistic movement. Duret mentions neither Caillebotte nor Rouart, painters who were exhibiting with the group but were also their patrons. The history of art has not forgotten Henri Rouart, thanks to the financial success of the sales of his collections (1912), the portraits of himself and his family by Degas, and the pen of Paul Valéry.[6] As for Gustave Caillebotte (fig. 85), his collection, bequeathed to the State in 1894 and now at the Musée d'Orsay, Paris, has long eclipsed his skill as a painter. The omission of the name of Ernest Hoschedé is more significant; he was already reduced to bankruptcy by his excessive enthusiasm for the new painting, and the judicial sale of his collection that took place 5–6 June 1878 represented a genuine catastrophe for the painters and dealers. Duret's brief, dated list, published and circulated by Durand-Ruel, who sold the critic's pamphlet, provided the other collectors with visibility. They were indispensable to the survival of the Impressionists, who they knew personally and to whom they were often extremely close.[7] Many of these collectors also bought at auction.[8]

A number were clients of Durand-Ruel, but others were not. With limited means, Victor Chocquet, a modest customs official; Murer, the pseudonym of Eugène Meunier, a *pâtissier* who ran a hotel in Rouen and was a failed painter and man of letters; and his friend Doctor Gachet, all purchased from the artists or at auction at low prices. Durand-Ruel's books also make no mention before the 1880s of Georges Charpentier, the publisher of 'Naturalist' authors such as Zola, although his name does appear on many occasions among buyers at auction at the Hôtel Drouot. He rapidly developed a close friendship with Renoir, from whom he commissioned portraits, and with Monet, buying directly from both

FIG. 83
Berthe Morisot
Hanging the Laundry out to Dry, 1875
Oil on canvas, 33 × 40.6 cm
National Gallery of Art, Washington, DC
[cat. 59]

FIG. 84
Claude Monet
The Train in the Snow, 1875
Oil on canvas, 59 × 78 cm
Musée Marmottan Monet, Paris
[cat. 39]

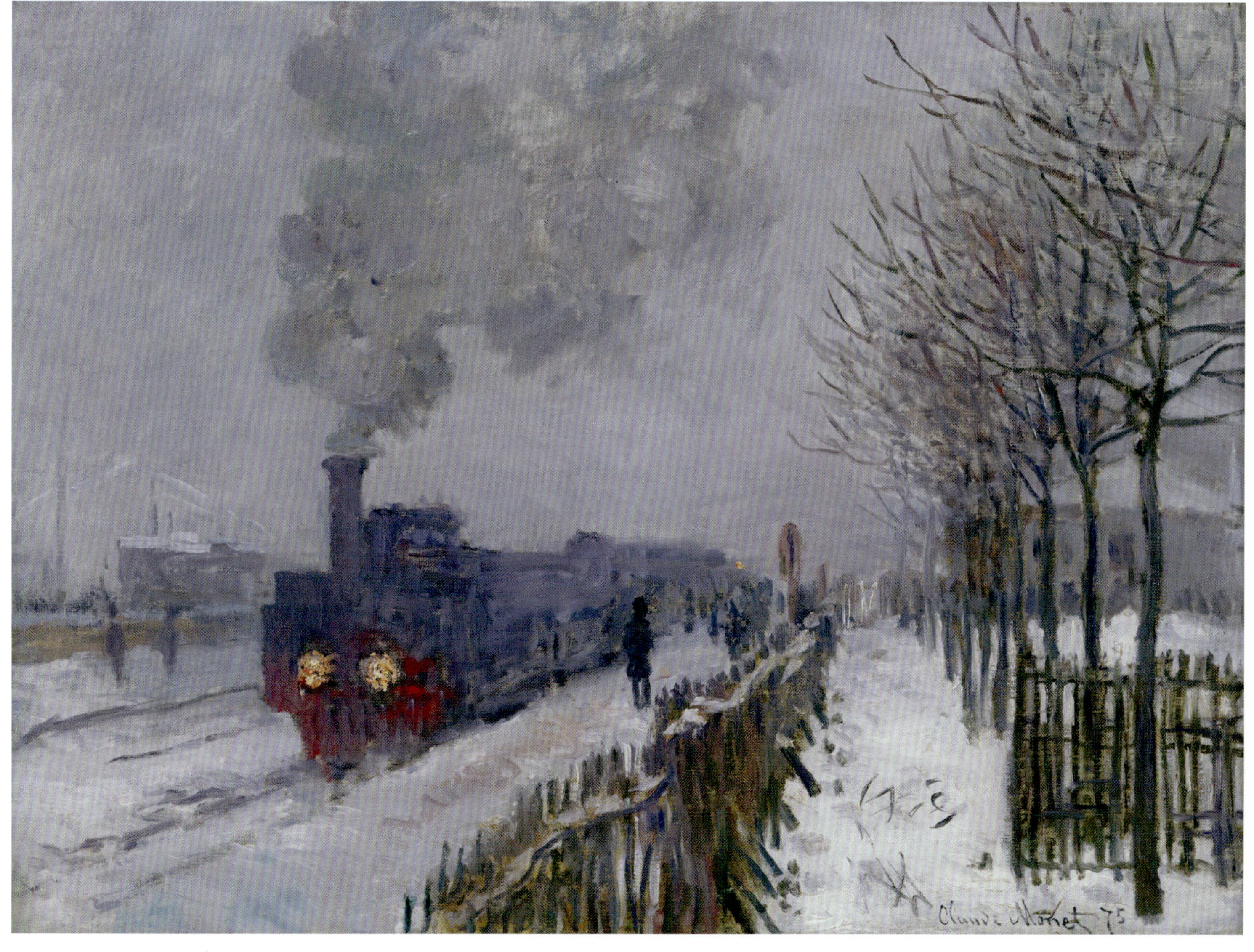

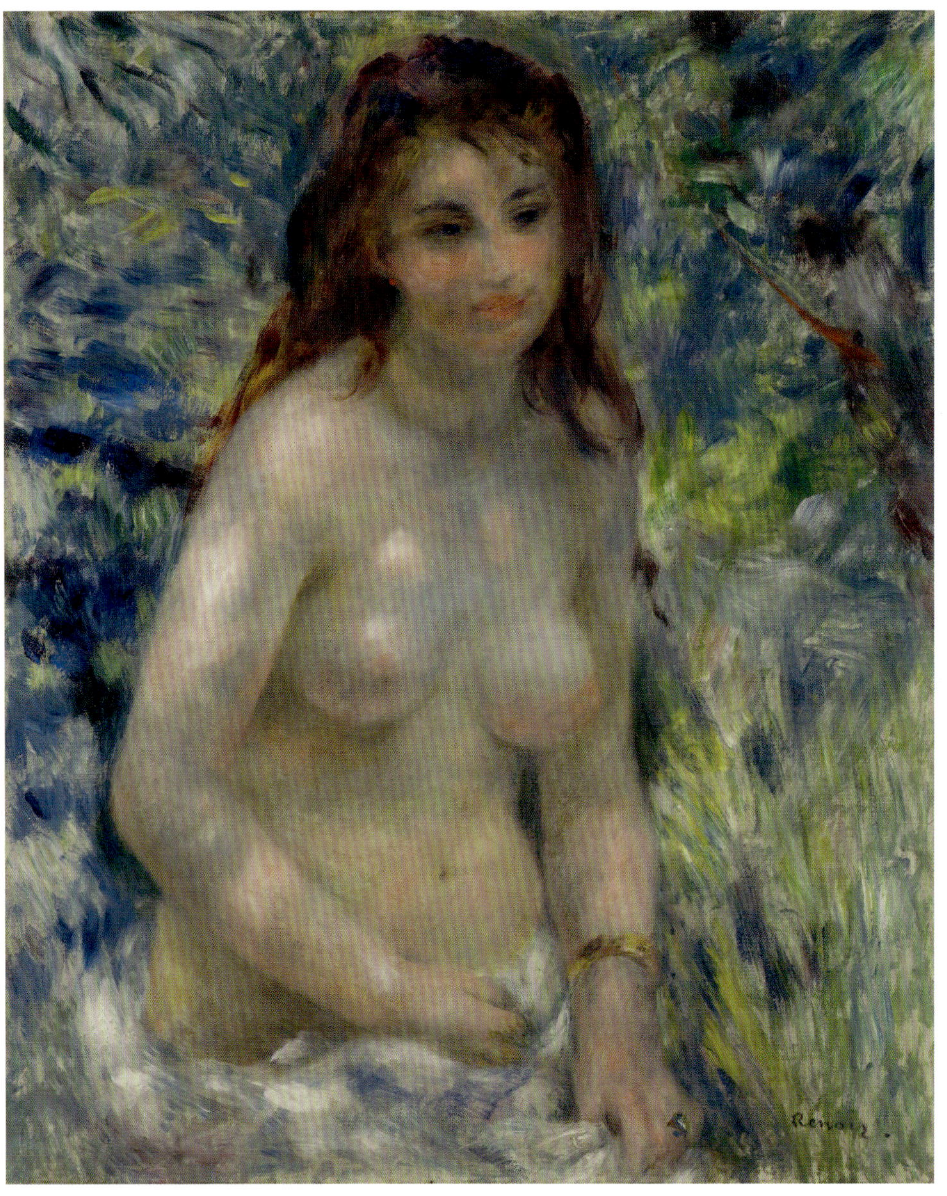

artists. A well-known figure among Paris's intellectual and artistic circles – his wife would hold salon get-togethers – Charpentier did much for the movement's reputation, even loaning the premises of his review, *La Vie moderne*, for short exhibitions. Jean Dollfus, heir to a dynasty of textile industrialists, was also a regular at public auctions, where he bought art from earlier periods and *japonaiseries,* as well as contemporary works. However, paintings by Renoir, including the portrait of Claude Monet at his easel (Musée d'Orsay, Paris) were purchased directly from the artist. Dollfus is known to have been a client of Père Martin but he does not seem to have bought from Durand-Ruel.

The following figures were all clients of Durand-Ruel, although they did not buy from him exclusively. Count Armand Doria, aristocrat, landowner and scholar, adopted an eclectic approach: although it is likely he purchased the famous *Hanged Man's House* (see fig. 127) directly from Cézanne at the end of the 1874 exhibition, it was from Durand-Ruel (who noted his address for the first time in 1873) that he bought three works by Renoir in 1876, at low prices. Doria, passionate about the 1830 School and Corot, was a frequent visitor to the gallery and must have been tempted. But thanks to his protégé, the painter A.-F. Cals, he was also in direct contact with the artists who took part in the 1874 exhibition and with Père Martin, whose insight and modesty he appreciated.

Georges De Bellio, 'a Romanian gentleman', as Théodore Duret described him, took up residence in Paris. An unpretentious man of independent means

FIG. 85
Pierre-Auguste Renoir
Study: Torso, Sunlight Effect, 1875–6
Oil on canvas, 81 × 65 cm
Musée d'Orsay, Paris
[cat. 72]

who practised homoeopathy, he began his collection at the sale of Delacroix's studio. Although he purchased a Pissarro and a *Still Life with Melon* by Renoir from Durand-Ruel in November 1874 and 1876 respectively, the bulk of his collection came from the artists themselves, who knew how to appeal to his generosity (fig. 84). It was he who convinced his compatriot Constantin De Rasty to buy works by the Impressionists.

Charles Deudon, a friend from school[9] and also a friend of Duret, the painter Bonnat and the Ephrussi brothers, was an artistic dandy and a man of independent means. He bought paintings from the artists he knew: Monet (from 1877) and Manet, from whom he acquired *Plum Brandy* (National Gallery of Art, Washington) in 1881 (plus several other works at the sale of Manet's studio). However, he did not hesitate to pay full price at the Durand-Ruel Gallery for an important Renoir, *The Dancer* (see fig. 70), on 17 May 1878.

The opera singer Jean-Baptiste Faure, a talented baritone acclaimed across Europe and a favourite of Meyerbeer, Gounod and Verdi, is a slightly different case: he too purchased from Durand-Ruel and the artists, but on a much larger scale, priding himself on owning a 'gallery' in the princely tradition. Having already begun to purchase paintings by Manet both from Durand-Ruel and directly from the artist, he disposed of his first collection, including works by Corot, Delacroix, Dupré, Millet, Roybet, Ribot, Rousseau and Troyon, at a public auction on 7 June 1873. Durand-Ruel, who had been selling him works since 1870, acted as the expert for the sale, although he also purchased a number of works himself. In addition to Manet, Faure was interested in Monet, Sisley, Pissarro and Degas. He was undoubtedly a speculator, who would also succeed in selling on his pictures when a new generation of collectors emerged during the last decade of the century.

While all these collectors could be considered winning players in the gamble on the Impressionists, Ernest Hoschedé seems to have been the biggest loser.[10] Like Faure, he attempted to sell on his works in order to target young promising artists, but he did so too quickly in a market that was still too limited. In order to finance his purchases, he got himself heavily into debt. A client of Durand-Ruel, he also became his debtor after declaring bankruptcy on 24 August 1877. The judicial sale of his collection on 6 June 1878 liquidated, at a loss, the hundred or so works by Manet and the Impressionists he had accumulated over several years. Durand-Ruel (who was not the expert at this sale) only bought a single Pissarro, probably due to lack of funds and a plentiful stock, allowing other dealers, such as Diot and Petit, to purchase at very low prices. The main beneficiaries of this sale were all the collectors just mentioned, who were able to acquire exceptional works at prices lower than those demanded by Durand-Ruel and the other dealers. It is noticeable that after 1870 the majority of Durand-Ruel's clients were members of the active bourgeoisie with independent means, contrasting sharply with the multitude of titled names who made up the bulk of his clientele in the 1860s, which was similar to that of a Parisian trader in luxuries.

After 1870, Durand-Ruel was not alone in founding his hopes on the Impressionists. His books reveal transactions with dealers or brokers about whom we still know little: Martin (mentioned above); Alphonse Legrand, involved in the 1876 and 1877 exhibitions (fig. 86); Victor Poupin; M. and Mme Latouche; Hagerman; Hourquebie, etc., but it is clear that none of these had the same commercial importance as Durand-Ruel, who worked with London and Brussels. Driven by Durand-Ruel, this shuffling of works could only benefit the painters. However, until 1880, apart from the transactions just mentioned, resales of Impressionist works were few and far between.

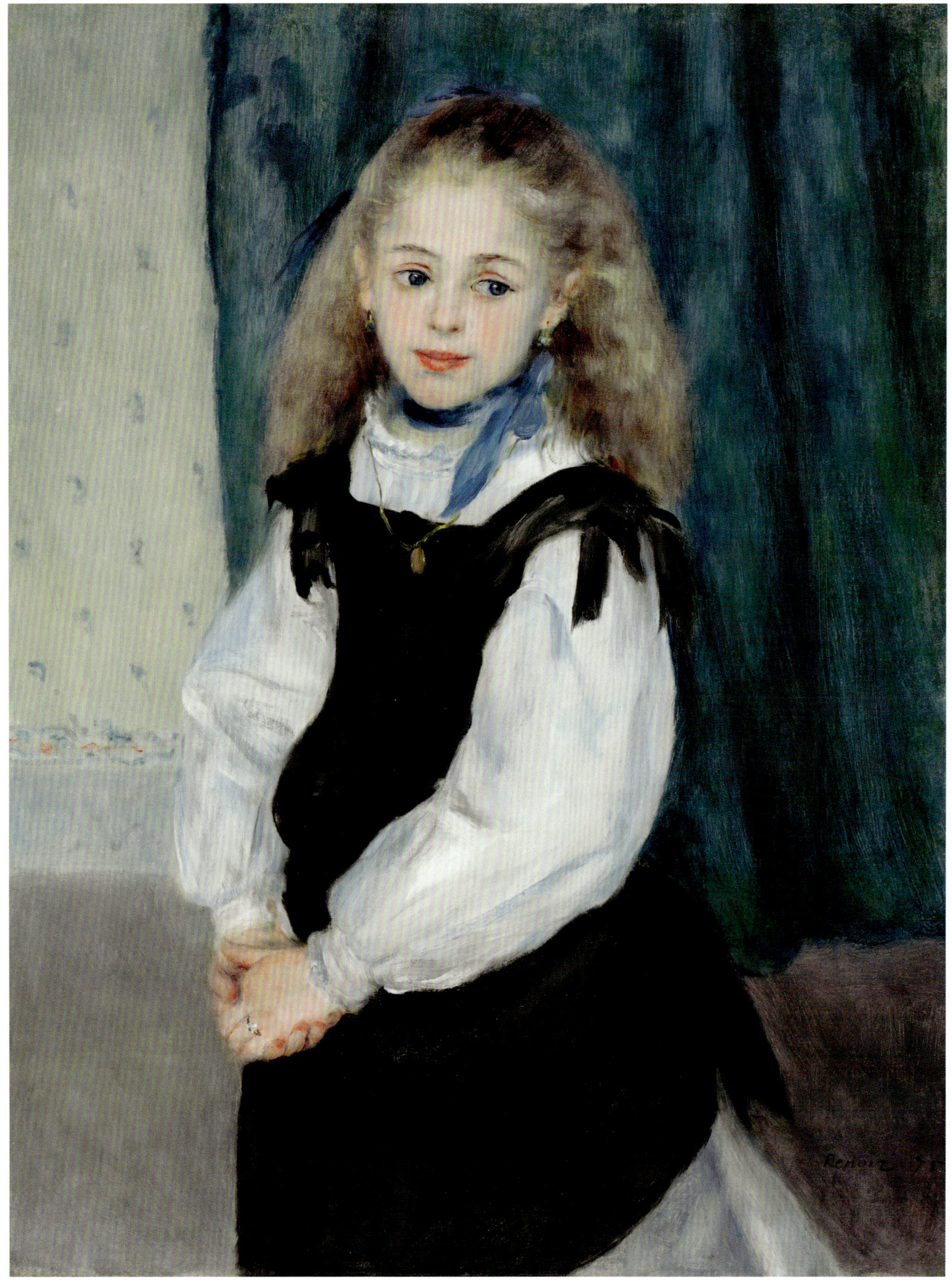

FIG. 86
Pierre-Auguste Renoir
Portrait of Mademoiselle Legrand, 1875
Oil on canvas, 81.3 × 59.7 cm
Philadelphia Museum of Art, Pennsylvania
[cat. 71]

FIG. 87
Edouard Manet
The Fife Player, 1866
Oil on canvas, 160 × 97 cm
Musée d'Orsay, Paris

The 1880s: crisis and consolidation

The early 1880s was a difficult time for Durand-Ruel, who was bound by his financial obligations to his lenders and caught up in the bankruptcy of his backer Jules Feder, as demonstrated by long lists of works marked as collateral in his books and then later re-inventoried. Nonetheless, the dealer was able to continue his Impressionist purchases, which he paid for with regular advances, even markedly increasing his base prices. The solo exhibitions he organised for the artists were their showcase and revived interest among the collectors.

He retained long-standing clients, such as the financiers Ernest May, linked to Degas, and the brothers Henri and Albert Hecht (friends of Manet, also linked to Degas).[11] He also recruited new ones: Charles Hayem, known as a collector of Gustave Moreau in particular;[12] Paul Berard, who also commissioned portraits from Renoir; a certain Paul Gauguin, not quite a painter yet; Léon Clapisson;[13] the surprising 'Abbé' Paul Gaugain;[14] and Paul Gallimard, son of a collector and father of the future founder of the *Nouvelle Revue Française*.[15] All these collectors also knew the painters and bought from them directly, even if, as carefully noted by Emile Zola, they 'prefer to transact with a dealer in pictures because they expect to pay less. They do not dare to bargain with an artist; they always expect the artist to overestimate and steal from them'.[16] Or they waited for windfalls, such as the sale of Manet's studio in February 1884, at which prices remained low; the purchases made on this occasion by Durand-Ruel (expert at the auction) were on behalf of clients, Charles Edward Haviland,[17] Henri Rouart and the painter Degas.

An unmistakable sign of Durand-Ruel's success was the emergence of competitors among the other dealers dominating the Paris market. Georges Petit (1856–1920), who profited from the legacy of his father, also a reputed dealer, coaxed the artists by inviting them to prestigious international exhibitions held at his luxurious premises on rue de Sèze. Theo van Gogh, brother of the painter

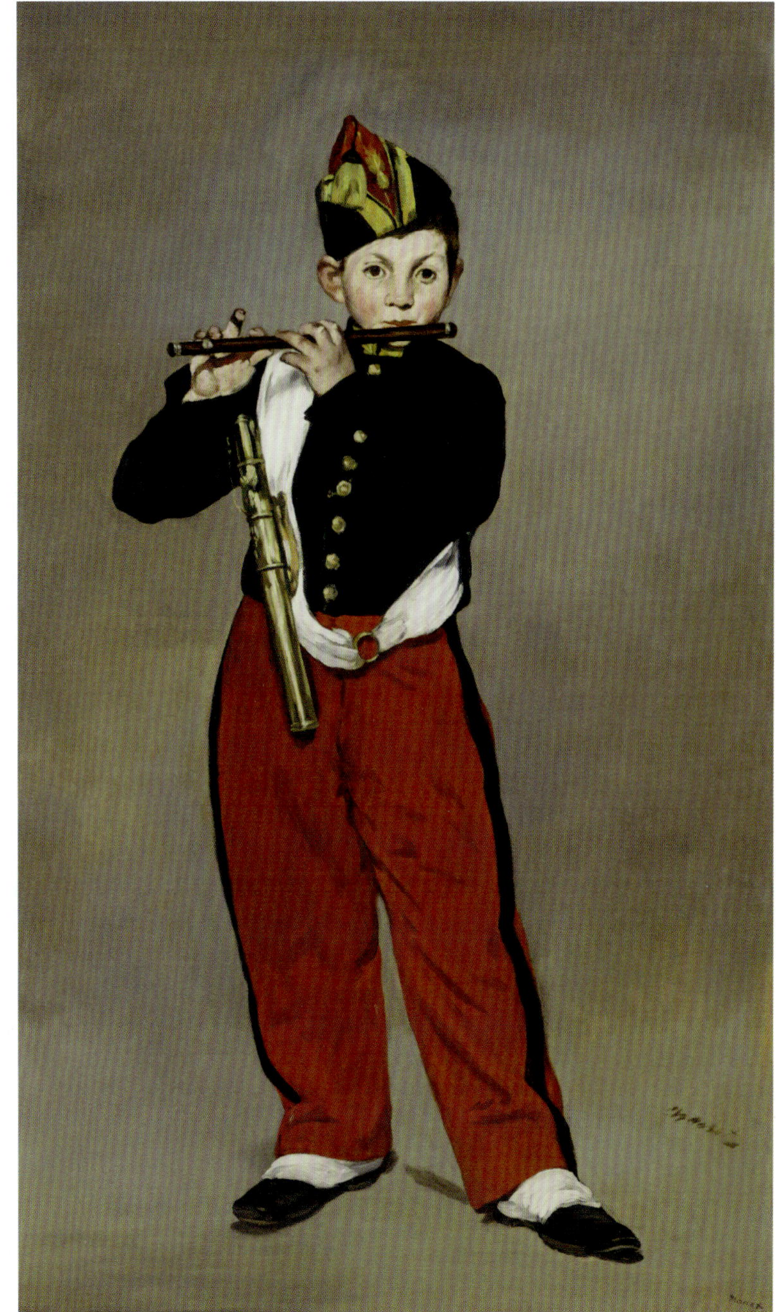

FIG. 88
Alfred Sisley
The Watering Place at Marly-le-Roi, probably 1875
Oil on canvas, 49.5 × 65.4 cm
The National Gallery, London
[cat. 92]

and an employee of Boussod & Valadon, a well-established firm, also courted Monet, Renoir, Sisley and Pissarro from 1884;[18] the response from the artists was decidedly positive from 1887 until Theo's death in 1891. Even Alphonse Portier, a small dealer on rue Lepic, who staged the fourth Impressionism exhibition in 1879, must also be taken into account.

1890–1914: towards the triumph of Impressionism

Genuine competition did increase in the final decade of the century. On the one hand, Paul Durand-Ruel's position was strengthened: Degas, Monet and Renoir were selling well and American collectors were highly receptive; the dealer's financial situation had improved and, in 1893, he reformed the family company as 'Durand-Ruel and Sons' to take advantage of a stock that was increasing in value. Less short of money, he was able to intervene to bolster prices at public auctions at a time when earlier collections were being dispersed following the deaths of their owners. But, on the other hand, pressure from his competitors became greater. Georges Petit was supported by his assistant Isidore Montaignac, who later set up on his own. Alexandre Bernheim Jeune, on the instigation of his two sons, Joseph-Josse and Gaston Bernheim Jeune, and his nephew Jos Hessel, turned his attention back to Impressionism. The appointment of Félix Fénéon at the Galerie Bernheim Jeune in 1906 also saw the arrival of works by the Neo-Impressionists, who had been neglected by Durand-Ruel. Finally, in around 1895, newcomer Ambroise Vollard became increasingly important; by 'discovering' and showing Cézanne, Gauguin and Van Gogh, he played a part in refocusing collectors' tastes.

With bases on both sides of the Atlantic and activity across Europe that extended as far as Moscow and St Petersburg, the Maison Durand-Ruel presided over the formation of new collections. In France, the most remarkable of these belonged to Count Isaac de Camondo, Etienne Moreau-Nélaton, Antonin Personnaz and Raymond Koechlin; through donations and bequests, these collections would go on to form the bulk of the Impressionist collections at the Louvre, now at the Musée d'Orsay (fig. 87). Another collector, François Depeaux, an industrialist from Rouen,[19] (fig. 88), similarly intended to give works to the museum in his own city but was unfortunately only able to partially fulfil his wishes: *Dance at Bougival* by Renoir (see fig. 5), which Durand-Ruel had agreed to sell him in January 1894, anticipating that it would eventually take its place in one of France's greatest museums, was offered at public auction in 1906 and sold to Depeaux's brother-in-law, Edmond Decap, also a client of Durand-Ruel.[20] By selling to the Havemeyers and the Potter Palmers in America, and to the Shchukins and Morosovs in Russia, Durand-Ruel was also responsible for the origins of the Impressionist collections of the greatest American and Russian museums.

One of the most prominent Impressionist collectors of the early twentieth century, Alexandre Berthier, Prince de Wagram, made his first large-scale purchases from Durand-Ruel in 1905. A military man following family tradition, he believed in escaping the monotony of his circumstances by collecting frantically, thanks to his large fortune, and became a dealer himself. A bad payer (he asked Durand-Ruel if he could pay in two years and owed him more than 600,000 francs in early 1908) and a poor speculator, he was mired in a lawsuit with Bernheim Jeune and was forced to resell quickly; his collection had already been widely dispersed before his death at the front in 1918.

This new generation of collectors, with fewer personal links to the artists, directly benefited from the legacy of Durand-Ruel's first clients. A study of the dealer's books dating from the early 1890s makes it clear

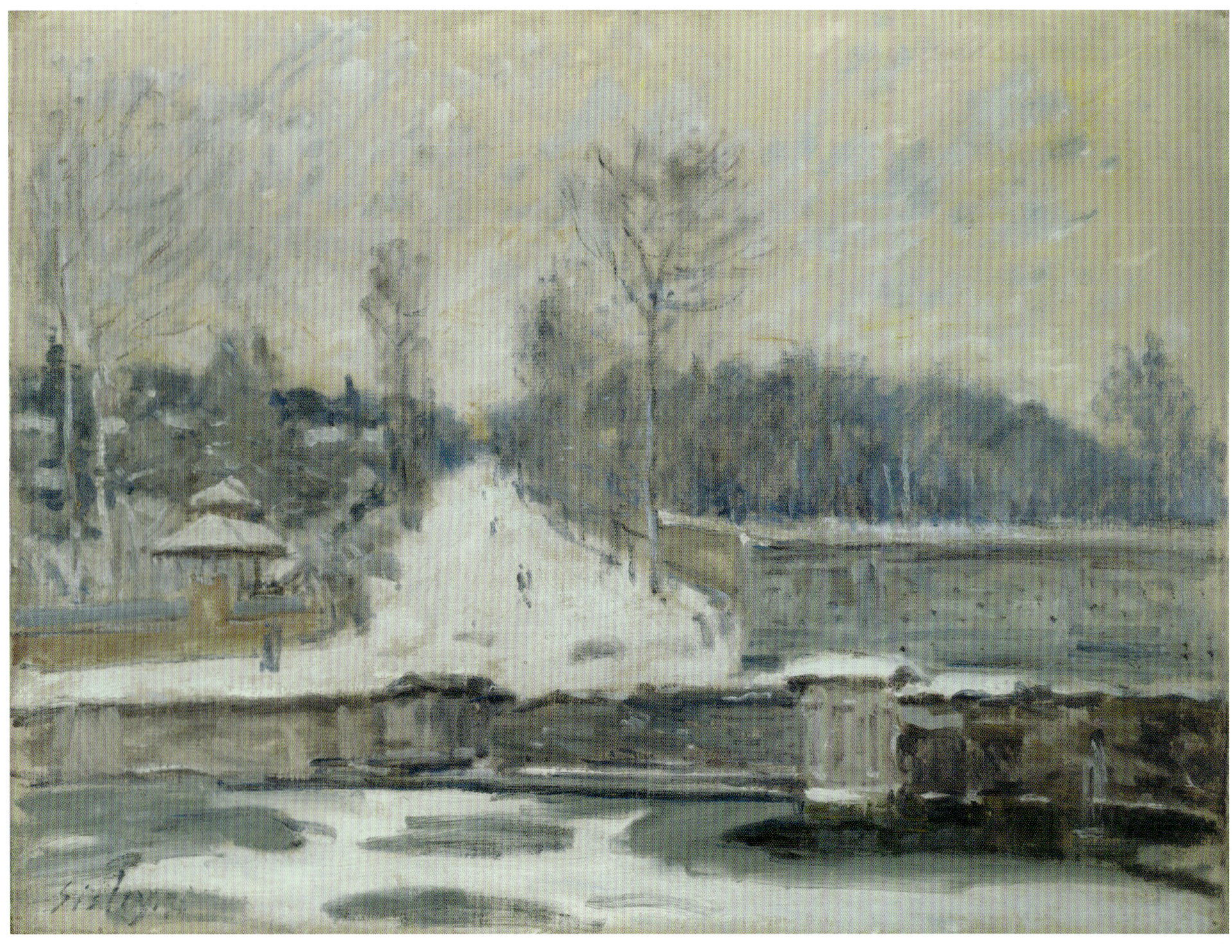

that he purchased works at many public salerooms to replenish his stock. The most important of these sales were those of Ernest May (June 1890); Théodore Duret (March 1894); Léon Clapisson (April 1894), which had been organised by him after a series of private purchases from his former client; Emmanuel Chabrier (March 1896, supplemented by a private transaction with Chabrier's widow the following year); Henri Vever (February 1897); Count Doria (May 1899); Victor Chocquet's widow (July 1899); the 'Abbé' Paul Gaugain (May 1901), which he had in reality purchased in bulk before the auction; Paul Berard (May 1905); and finally, Georges Charpentier (April 1907), where he bought *Portrait of Mme Charpentier and Her Children* for the Metropolitan Museum of Art in New York.

Several collections were the subject of private negotiations between dealer and owner whenever the latter preferred discretion, which Durand-Ruel, in the best traditions of a well-established family-run business, was able to guarantee, in addition to market prices. Robert de Bonnières (1894, 1897); the Prince de Polignac (1897); the partner of Edmond Maître (1898 and 1899); Georges May (1898); and Louis Flornoy, a collector from Nantes, who resold *La Loge* (London, Courtauld Institute Galleries) and *After the Luncheon* (see fig. 110) in 1899, all dealt with Durand-Ruel. So did the Swiss painter Auguste de Molins (1899), who had exhibited with the Impressionists in 1874, and the widow of collector Edward Bérend, who was close to Manet and Signac.[21] Some negotiations must have been hard-fought: Jean-Baptiste Faure, who began to rid himself of his Manet paintings in 1892, sold *Déjeuner sur l'herbe* (Musée d'Orsay, Paris) to Durand-Ruel for the first time in late August 1895, only to buy it back again two weeks later. He then made up his mind to sell it back to him once again on 22 December 1898, before it became part of the Etienne Moreau-Nélaton collection in 1900. The bulk of his collection was then ceded to Durand-Ruel in 1906–7, firstly by the singer himself and then by his widow in 1919.

Paul Durand-Ruel and his sons supported the careers of the Impressionists and of several generations of collectors. Modern dealers, like the art they championed, would play a full part in what Paul Signac described in 1899 as the 'apotheosis of Impressionism'.[22]

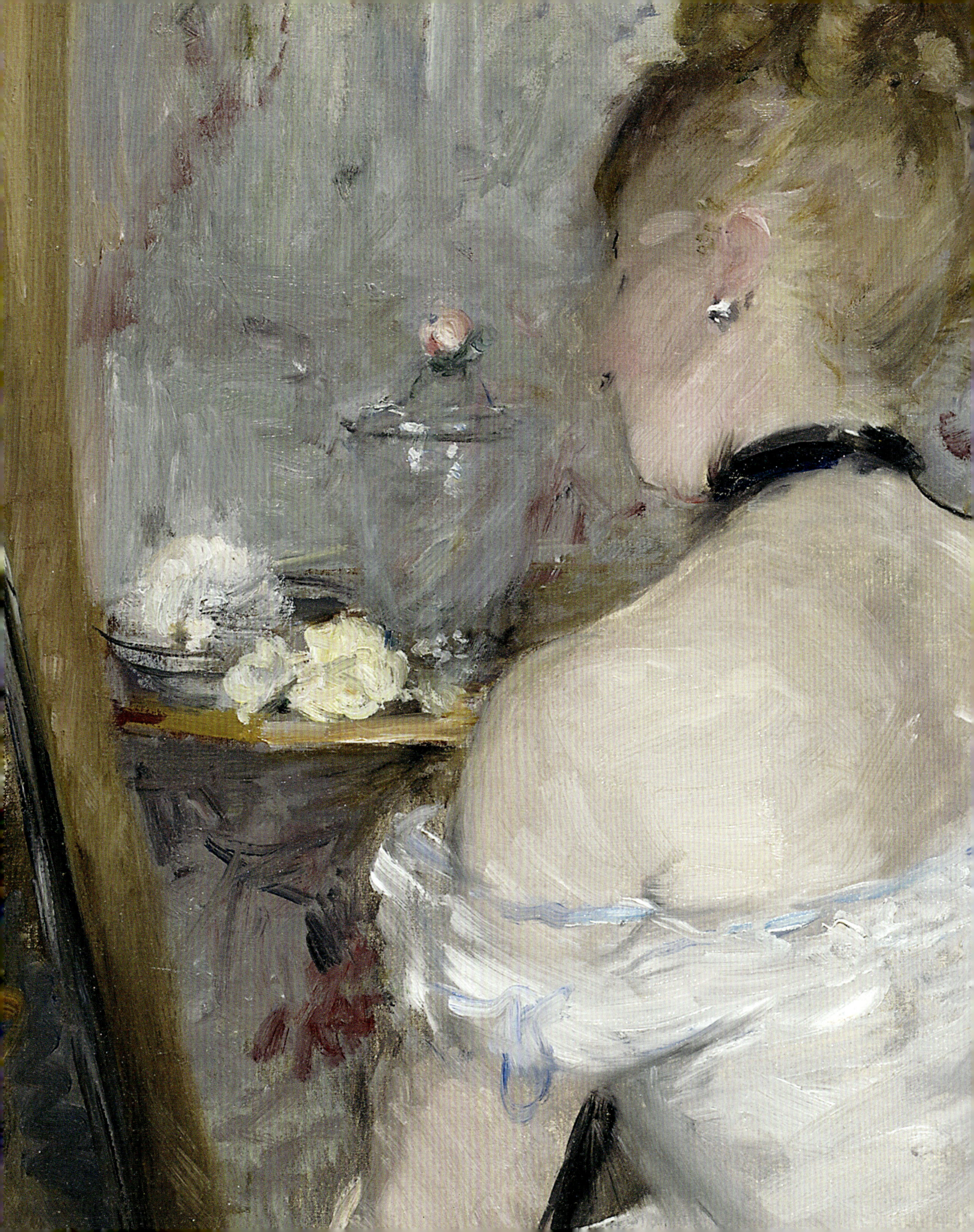

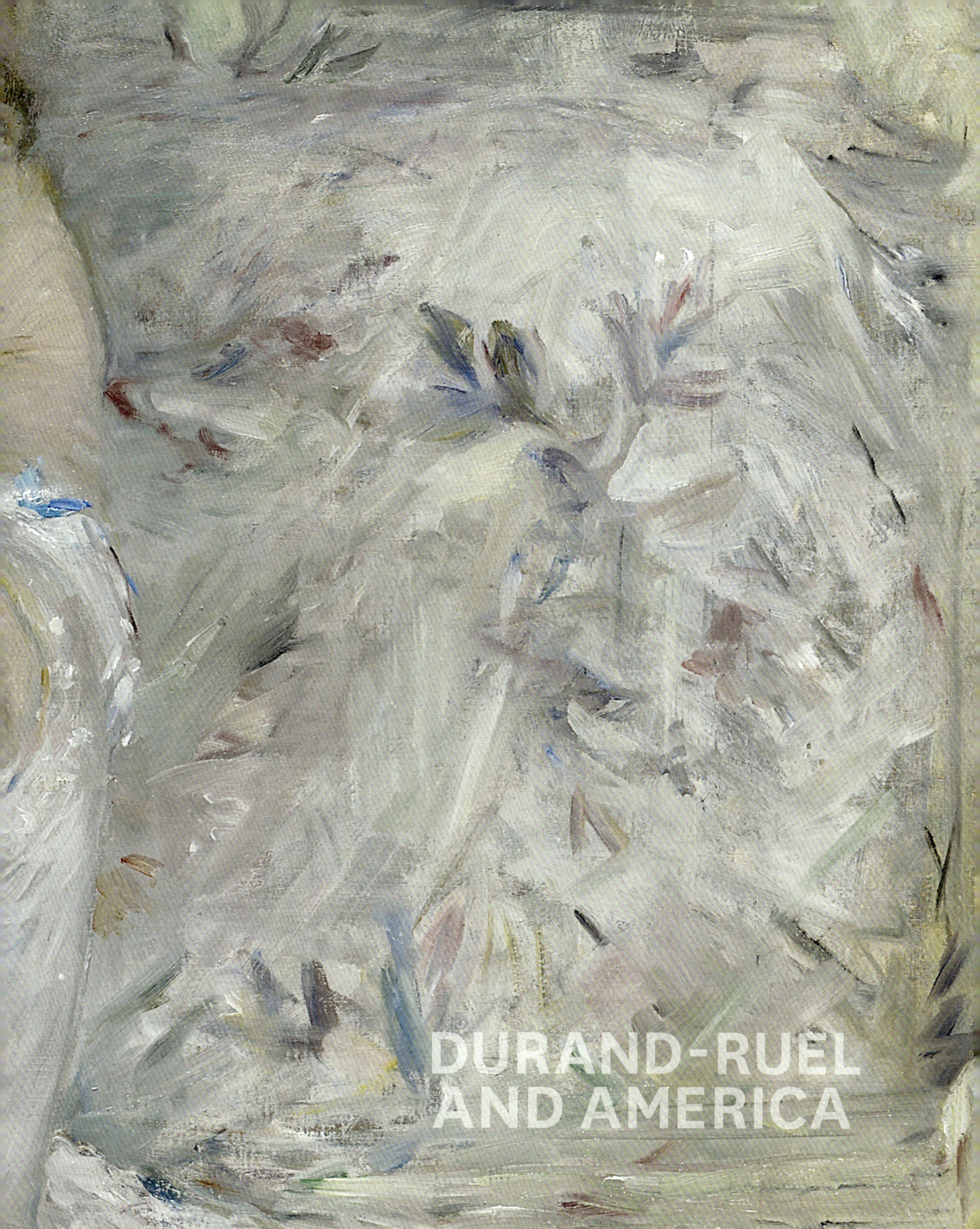
DURAND-RUEL
AND AMERICA

Durand-Ruel and America

Jennifer A. Thompson

'Do not think the Americans are savages. On the contrary, they are less ignorant, less close-minded than our French collectors.'[1]

In 1887, a dozen years after closing his London branch, Paul Durand-Ruel opened a gallery in New York City. American collectors, artists and dealers had been regular visitors to the rue de la Paix and the rue Laffitte in Paris from the mid-1860s and helped establish the firm's reputation as a reliable purveyor of paintings of the School of 1830. The exhibitions and auctions organised by Durand-Ruel in the United States in the 1880s met with varying levels of success, but they convinced him that America was a promising market for modern French painting. The foreign enterprise soon flourished and was instrumental in the development of American collections of Impressionism, despite high tariffs on imported artwork and the distance – a ten-day trans-atlantic crossing – from Paris. In the dealer's mind, the venture rescued him: 'Without America, I would have been lost, ruined, after having bought so many Monets and Renoirs. The two exhibitions there in 1886 saved me. The American public bought moderately, it is true, but thanks to that public Monet and Renoir were enabled to live and after that the French public followed suit.'[2]

American visitors to the rue Laffitte

Clients from New York, Philadelphia, Cincinnati and Boston appear in the Parisian gallery's earliest account books, where their purchases and addresses are carefully noted. Among them were dealers Samuel P. Avery, William Schaus, George Lucas, Michael Knoedler, Martin Kennard and Henry W. Derby, all of whom acquired stock from the gallery. The first recorded American collector is Levi Parsons Morton, a banker and distinguished Congressman, ambassador and Vice-President.[3] On 13 September 1865, Morton made his first acquisitions – paintings by Hugues Merle, Joseph-Urbain Melin and Leon Caille – from Durand-Ruel.[4] Although the 60-odd paintings that the New Yorker assembled from the gallery and other dealers could not be considered among the most adventurous in America, Morton would prove helpful to Durand-Ruel in the 1880s.[5]

Following Morton, a string of Philadelphia clients appear in the books, beginning with Adolph E. Borie, an importer of goods from Mexico and Asia who was briefly Secretary of the Navy under President Ulysses S. Grant. Borie made his first visit on 12 November 1866 and acquired more than 35 paintings from the gallery over the next six years. At his death in 1880, his collection numbered 115 works, including four remarkable Delacroix paintings, three Rousseaus, four Millets, a Fantin-Latour and a Boudin.[6] In his *Memoirs*, Durand-Ruel described Borie fondly, noting the boldness of the Philadelphian's taste and regretting that he had not opened a gallery in America in the 1870s as Borie suggested.[7]

In addition to his purchases, Borie encouraged colleagues to visit Durand-Ruel. Henry Probasco, a Cincinnati hardware merchant, arrived in the gallery in 1867 bearing a letter of introduction from Borie, and Philadelphians William P. Wilstach, J. Gillingham Fell and Henry Gibson all made substantial purchases between 1867 and 1872.[8] These merchants, distillers and railway men, along with others such as William H. Herriman, an American living in Rome, were dedicated collectors who would readily pay 20,000 to 30,000 francs ($4,000 to $6,000) for works by Decamps, Millet or Delacroix. By 1869 Durand-Ruel was so well-regarded among Americans that a business journal reported: 'This gentleman is universally known for his great capacity of appreciating paintings of all schools, ancient and modern, and chiefly to Americans for his fascinating manners and straight forwardness in his dealings.'[9]

FIG. 89
Camille Pissarro
Flood at Pontoise, 1873
Oil on canvas, 45.5 × 55.5 cm
Private collection

Few collectors displayed an interest in Impressionism in the 1870s. George Lucas, a Paris-based art agent from Baltimore, bought a snow scene by Pissarro from Père Martin in 1870, 11 months before Durand-Ruel met the artist in London.[10] Five years later, Henry Clay Angell, a Boston ophthalmologist, may have been the first American to purchase an Impressionist painting from Durand-Ruel when he acquired Pissarro's *Flood at Pontoise* (fig. 89) with the assistance of artist J. Foxcroft Cole.[11] Angell was followed by 22-year-old Louisine Elder (later Mrs H.O. Havemeyer) who, in the company of Mary Cassatt, purchased a Degas pastel and a Monet landscape from an unidentified Paris shop in 1877.[12] Cassatt herself (fig. 90) began to accumulate Impressionist paintings in 1878 and encouraged her family members to do the same.[13]

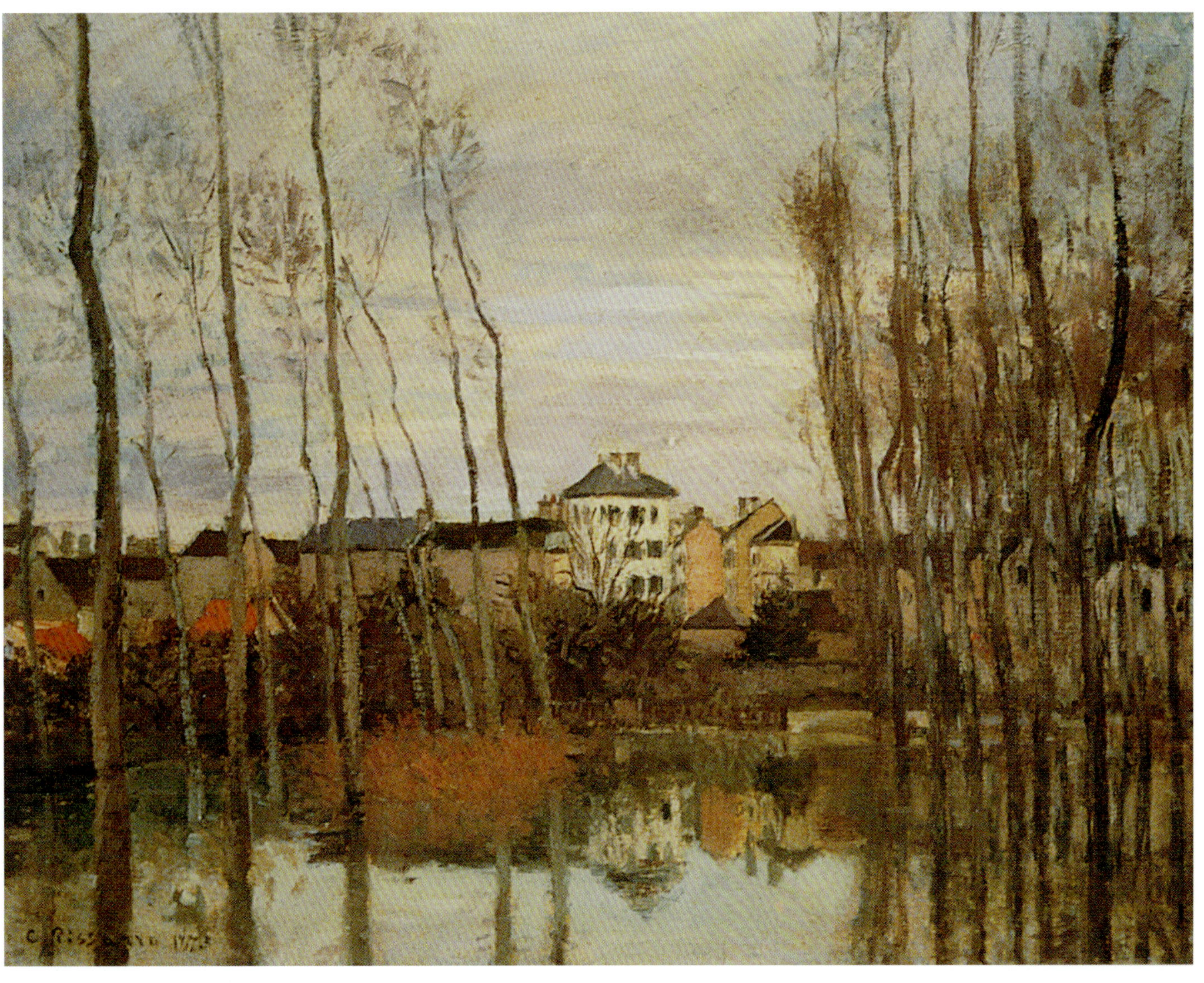

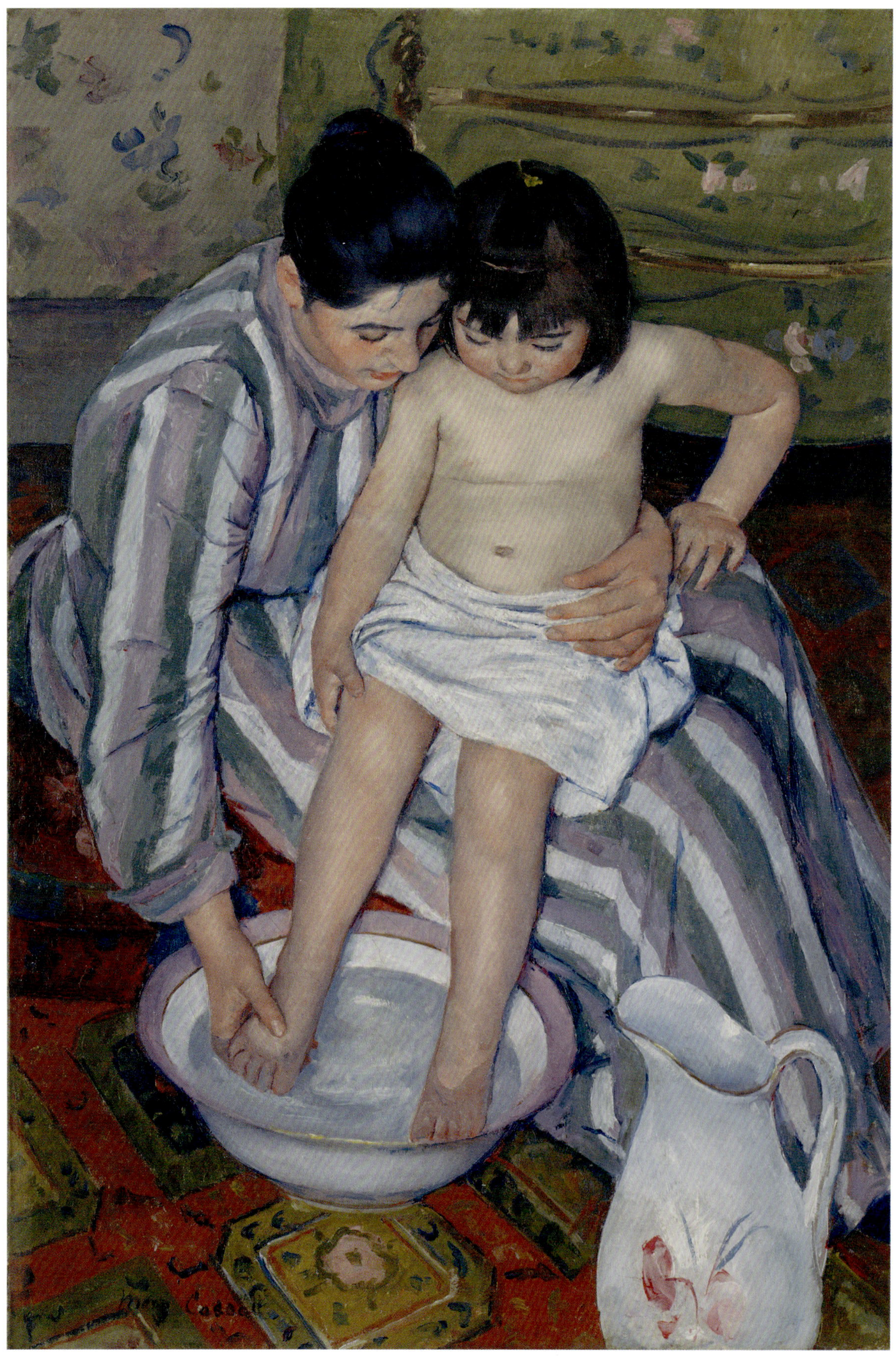

FIG. 90
Mary Cassatt
The Child's Bath, 1893
Oil on canvas, 100.3 × 66.1 cm
The Art Institute of Chicago, Illinois
[cat. 4]

In November 1880 she began helping her brother Alexander, then First Vice-President of the Pennsylvania Railroad, acquire paintings for his home outside Philadelphia.[14] Within months she had obtained a Degas (fig. 92), Monet and Pissarro for him.[15] Katherine Cassatt warned her son that the pictures might look 'eccentric,'[16] but they must have appealed to the railway executive and his wife, since in spring 1883 they made repeated visits to the Durand-Ruel Gallery, buying canvases by Monet, Cassatt and Renoir.[17] A few years later, Alexander's collection contained over 30 Impressionist works. In Philadelphia, where the Cassatts entertained lavishly, the paintings attracted admirers. Among them was Frank Thomson, who later succeeded Cassatt as Vice-President of the Pennsylvania Railroad.[18] At Thomson's request, Mary Cassatt began looking for Monets for him in spring 1884.[19] Soon after, Thomson and his daughter Anne bought works by Monet (see fig. 12), Renoir, Pissarro, Sisley, Degas and Cassatt directly from the gallery. Their independent purchases exasperated Cassatt, who wrote in September 1886 that Thomson had acquired a Monet from Durand-Ruel for 3,000 francs, a price she regarded as extraordinary.[20] Cassatt's loyalty to Durand-Ruel, her occasional dealer in this period, was tempered by her desire to find the best and most reasonably priced Impressionist paintings for American collectors.[21]

Another artist, J. Alden Weir, bought modern paintings in Paris for Erwin Davis, a businessman with interests in mining and finance. In 1880 Weir acquired Bastien-Lepage's *Joan of Arc* (Metropolitan Museum of Art, New York) from the Salon, and the following year he purchased several paintings from Durand-Ruel for Davis: two works by Georges Michel, a Degas and two Manets (fig. 91).[22] From 1882 onward, Davis made his own purchases of Degas's, Monets and Pissarros from the gallery.[23] The adventurous spirit of these American clients and the enthusiastic support of their artist-agents encouraged Durand-Ruel in the early 1880s when, faced with financial trouble in France, he resolved to 'revolutionise the New World simultaneously with the Old.'[24]

Ventures in the New World

In 1883 Durand-Ruel sent a significant group of paintings to an exhibition in Boston honouring the centenary of the signing of the Treaty of Paris. Edward King, an American writer who was in charge of the French section, approached the gallery for loans, probably at the encouragement of Levi Parsons Morton, an early client.[25] On 19 May 1883, Morton, United States Minister to France and honorary exhibition commissioner, hosted a banquet for French and American officials at which he urged the French government to participate and announced that a special act of Congress would admit all goods duty-free.[26] Durand-Ruel is not recorded among the banquet attendees, but two weeks later he shipped 80 pictures to Liverpool for forwarding to Boston.[27] Despite assurance that no import duty would be levied, the dealer sent his stock early so that it would arrive before the tariff on imported art rose on 1 July.[28] In June, Durand-Ruel asked the New York publishing firm Root & Tinker to supervise the unpacking and hanging of his paintings and to represent him in the event of sales.[29]

When the American Exhibition of the Products, Arts, and Manufactures of Foreign Nations opened on 3 September, 43 nations were represented. The French section included ladies' jewellery, furs, chocolates, wines, machinery and geological specimens. Unacknowledged in the exhibition catalogue, Durand-Ruel was responsible for most of the art loans, though Siegfried Bing sent porcelains and medals, Auguste Rodin lent a bronze bust, and paintings by artists such as Raffaëlli and Edouard Sain were submitted independently or by other dealers.[30] Durand-Ruel showed a broad selection of works by John Lewis Brown, Léon Lhermitte, Georges

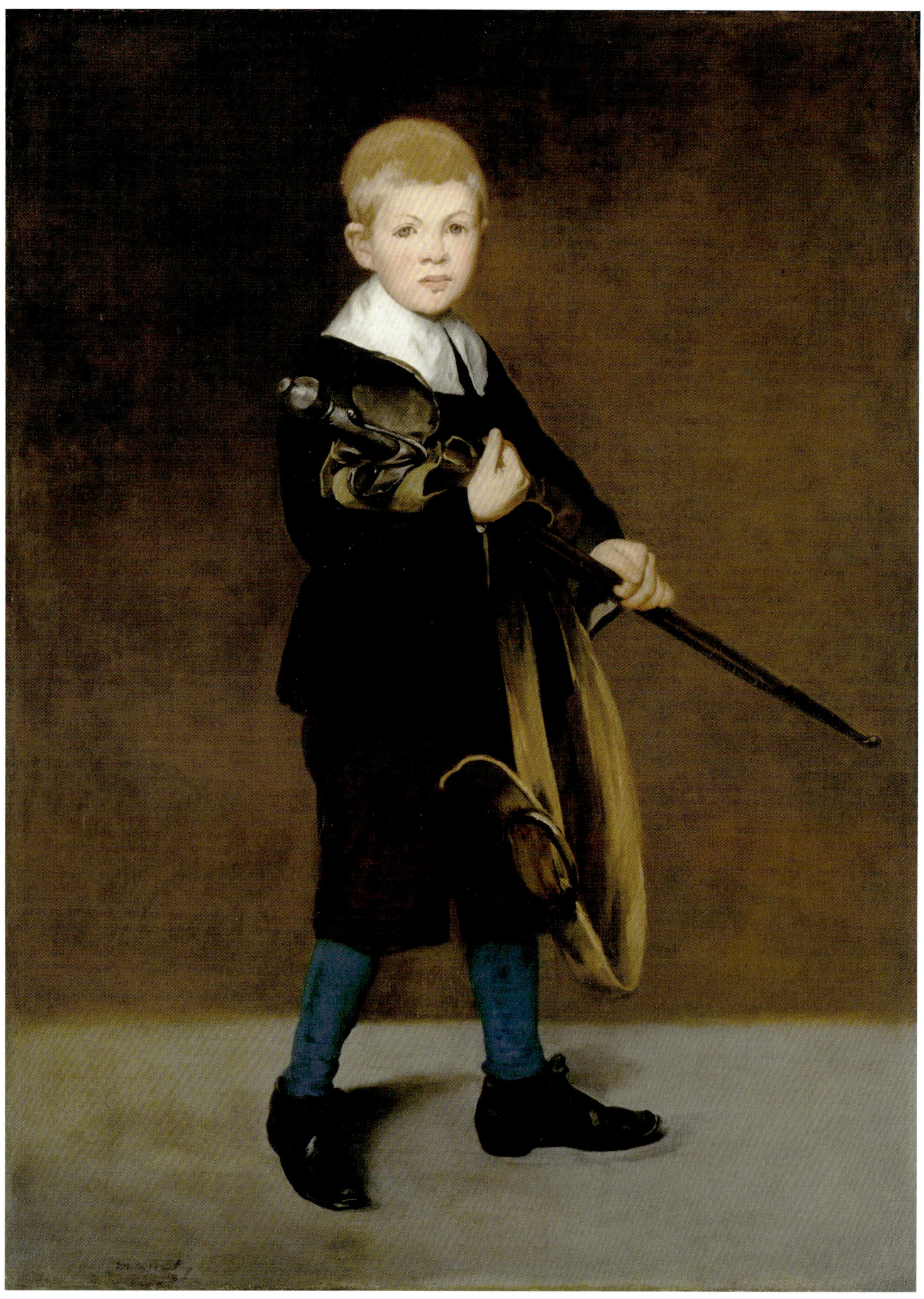

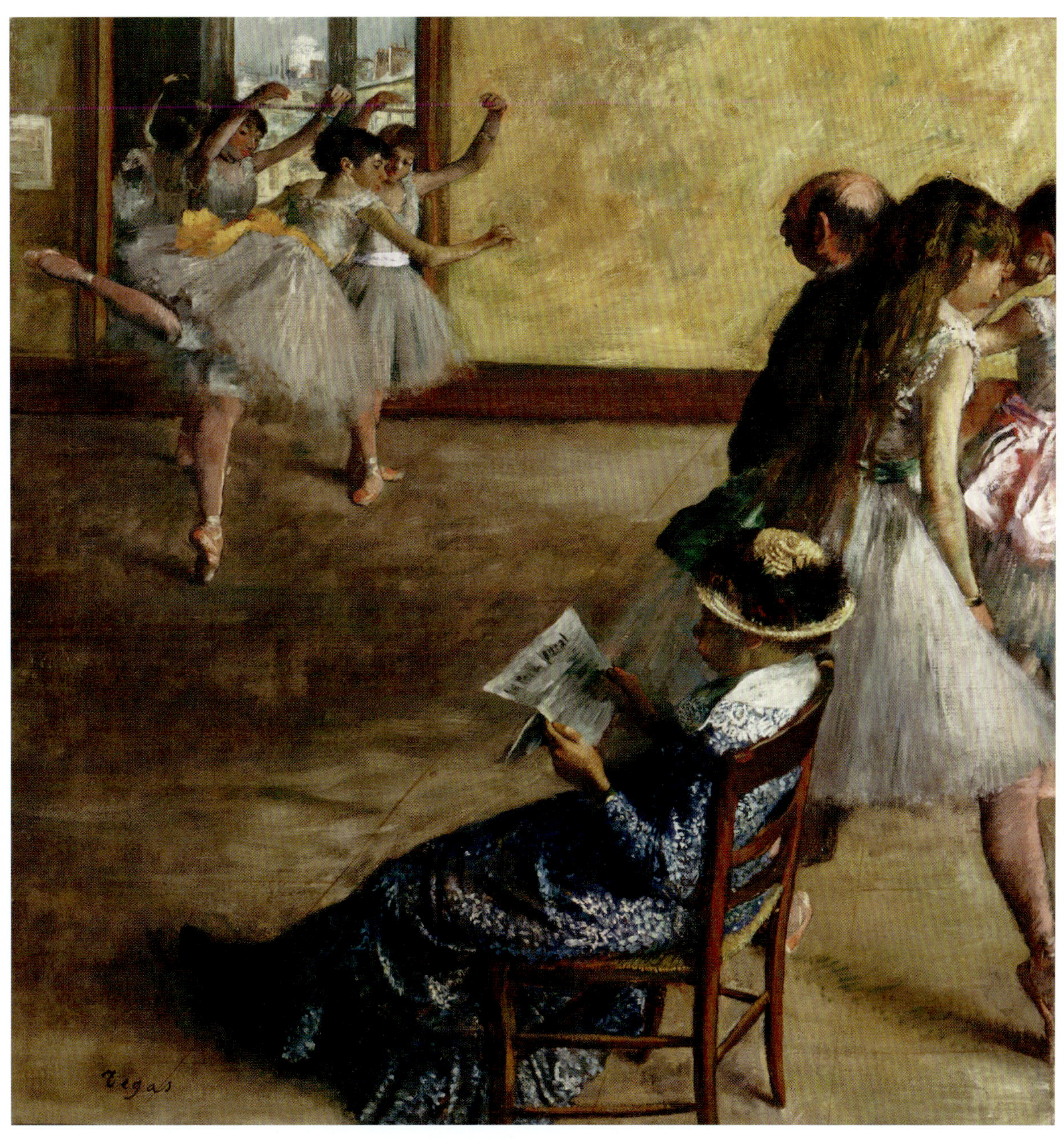

FIG. 91
Edouard Manet
Boy with a Sword, 1861
Oil on canvas, 131.1 × 93.4 cm
The Metropolitan Museum of Art, New York
[cat. 20]

FIG. 92
Edgar Degas
The Ballet Class, about 1880
Oil on canvas, 82.2 × 76.8 cm
Philadelphia Museum of Art, Pennsylvania
[cat. 17]

FIG. 93
Edouard Manet
The Dead Christ with Angels, 1864
Oil on canvas, 179.4 × 149.9 cm
The Metropolitan Museum of Art, New York

Haguette, and others, as well as Boudin, Courbet, Manet, Monet, Pissarro, Renoir and Sisley. Although the Impressionists accounted for only 20% of the loans, they were represented by significant canvases such as Manet's *Dead Christ with Angels* (fig. 93), Renoir's *A Box at the Theatre* (The Sterling and Francine Clark Art Institute, Williamstown) and Monet's recent landscapes, and were avidly discussed by newspapers across the country. *The Art Amateur* bemoaned the trade show quality of the event but acknowledged: 'The modern pictures in the art gallery form the best part of the exhibition. A collection of works by some of the French impressionists is particularly interesting as showing that these young men are not without talent, although their conceit of themselves is certainly excessive.'[31] A less agreeable review noted: 'Here is a man, named Pisarro [sic], who has had the nightmare and mistaken it for a colour inspiration; and here is Renoir, who shrieks himself into notice by a lewd picture of fast French oarsmen breakfasting with women of the *demi monde* at Asnieres or some other equally disreputable place ... Monet has some pictures that justify the feeling that there is but a narrow line – perhaps only an imaginary line – between madness and the genius of the French impressionists.'[32] A Chicago critic offered Durand-Ruel some hope for the future by defending Renoir's *Luncheon of the Boating Party* (see fig. 33) as 'like a page from Zola – it is brilliant.'[33] Boston collectors were apparently unmoved by the gallery's loans, and these returned to Paris unsold in spring 1884.

A year later, James F. Sutton, an American art promoter with a keen eye for new opportunities, visited Durand-Ruel in Paris and proposed an Impressionist exhibition at the American Art Association, a New York gallery and auction venue for which Sutton was a director. By June 1885, Monet had learned of the venture and in July wrote to Durand-Ruel about his most recent paintings, adding, 'I confess that certain of these pictures I would regret to see sent to the land of the Yankees.'[34] The dealer successfully assuaged Monet's concerns and secured the support of many other artists by asking them to personally select paintings for New York.[35]

In September 1885 Durand-Ruel wrote to the French Ministry of Fine Arts, seeking their support for the exhibition and asking to be appointed an official delegate of the government to assure the enterprise of 'a decisive victory.' He explained that the art market in France was stagnant, her artists faced competition from Italian, Spanish and German painters, and the New York exhibition was not for his personal benefit or vanity: 'I have always placed my time, my activity, my fortune in the service of artists. It is a passion that has cost me dearly, but I do not regret it.'[36] The Ministry evaluated the proposal, acknowledging that Durand-Ruel's presentation of modern French painting would be a real service to artists, but in mid-October they determined that the venture was primarily a private, commercial one and declined to offer support.[37]

Despite this setback, plans for the exhibition proceeded, though it was moved from February to April 1886. In late March, Durand-Ruel and his son Charles arrived in New York, having shipped 43 crates of pictures valued at $81,799.[38] Two-thirds of the works came from Durand-Ruel stock, but the remainder was on deposit from collectors such as Jean-Baptiste Faure and artists like Caillebotte, Guillaumin, Morisot, Seurat and Signac. On 10 April, the American Art Association at 6 East 23rd Street opened an exhibition of 289 paintings, pastels and watercolours, including 40 Monets (see fig. 75), 41 Pissarros, 35 Renoirs (see figs 5, 24, 33 and 94), 20 Degas's, 15 Manets (see figs 21, 53 and 87), 14 Sisleys (see fig. 80), 14 Seurats, 10 Caillebottes, eight Morisots (fig. 95), six Signacs (see fig. 132), and work by Henry Lerolle, Jean Paul Laurens, Victor Huguet and others. The source of the collection was not noted in the

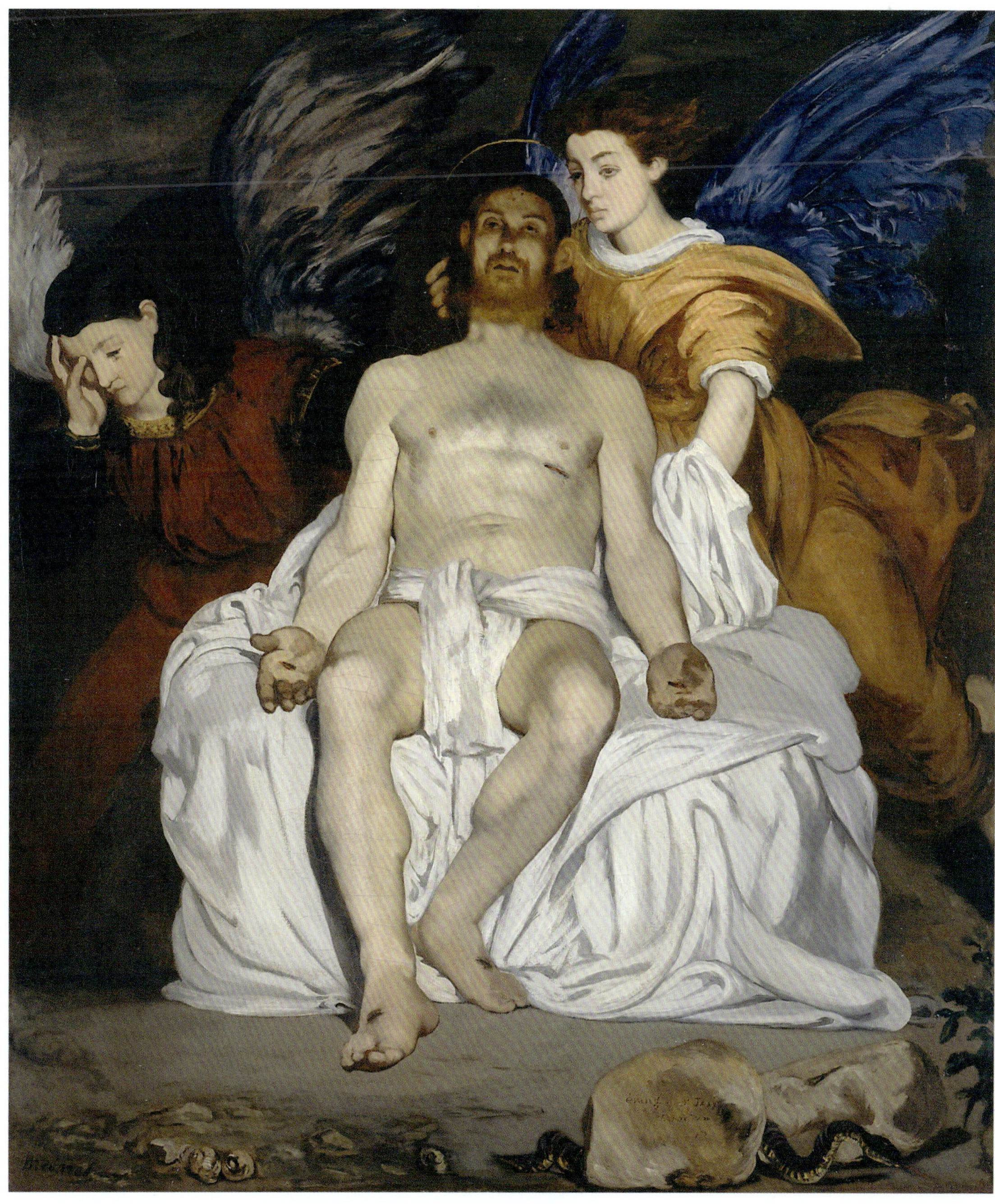

exhibition catalogue, but it was widely acknowledged in the press that the paintings belonged to Durand-Ruel. After two weeks, the exhibition moved to the National Academy of Design and reopened on 25 May for a month.[39] Between venues, 21 paintings were added: eight Monets and Renoirs that had recently been exhibited with Les XX in Brussels, and 13 lent by American collectors Alexander Cassatt (fig. 92), Erwin Davis (fig. 91), H.O. Havemeyer and an anonymous lender.

The exhibition attracted a great deal of interest, with critics alternating between ridicule and curiosity at its 'strange and unholy splendour.'[40] Manet was generally praised while Seurat's 'monstrous' *Bathers at Asnières* (see fig. 131) bore some of the most fervent criticism. The *Brooklyn Eagle* conceded bitingly that 'There are a few good pictures, but they are the ones that are not impressionistic, and the mass of contributions look amazingly as if painted in a lunatic asylum.'[41] One journal pointed out, perhaps at Durand-Ruel's request, that it was 'a fuller demonstration of the aims and daring of a certain revolutionary set than has ever been made in Europe.'[42]

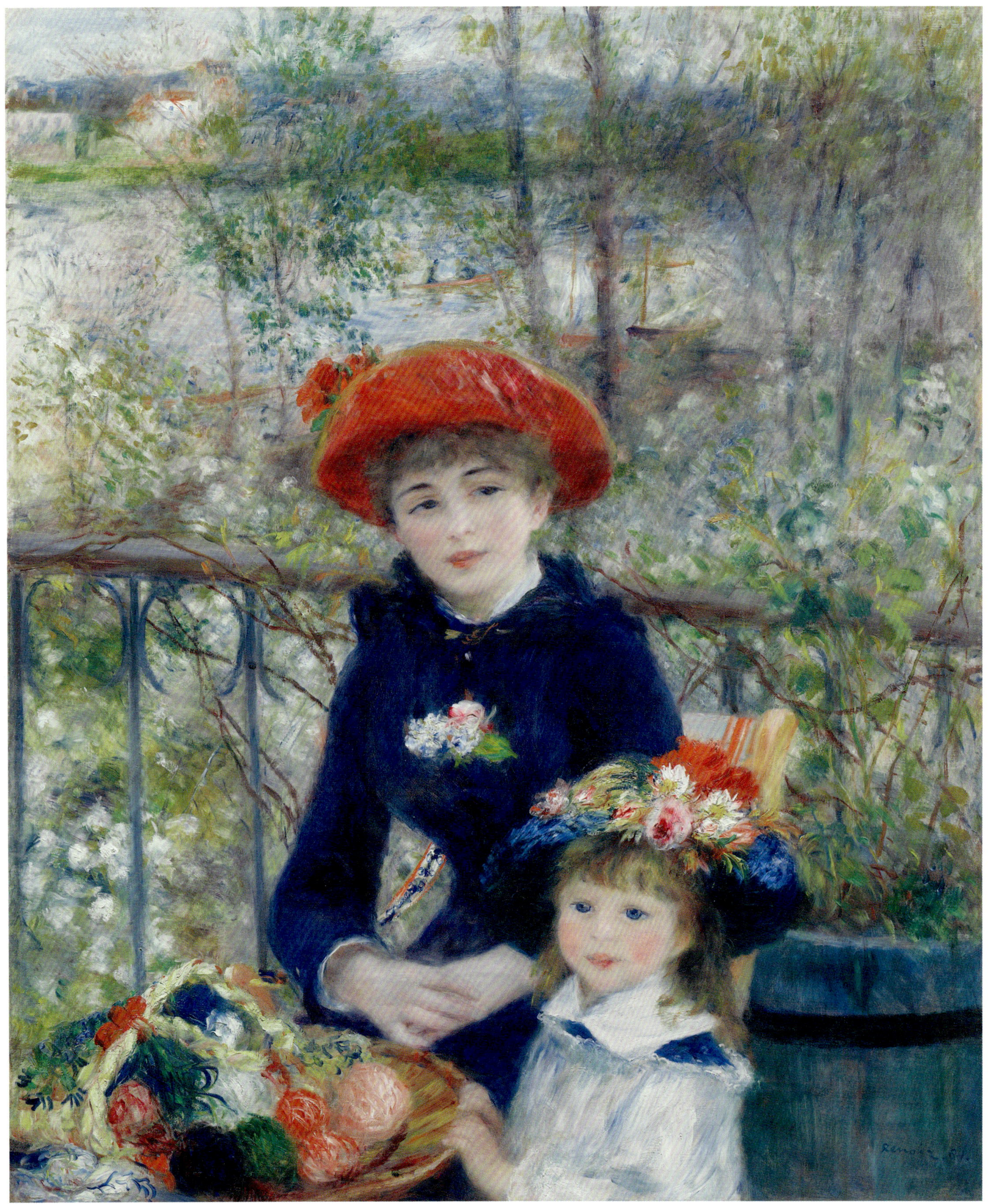

FIG. 94
Pierre-Auguste Renoir
Two Sisters (On the Terrace), 1881
Oil on canvas, 100.4 × 80.9 cm
The Art Institute of Chicago, Illinois
[cat. 75]

FIG. 95
Berthe Morisot
Woman at her Toilette, about 1875–80
Oil on canvas, 60.3 × 80.4 cm
The Art Institute of Chicago, Illinois
[cat. 60]

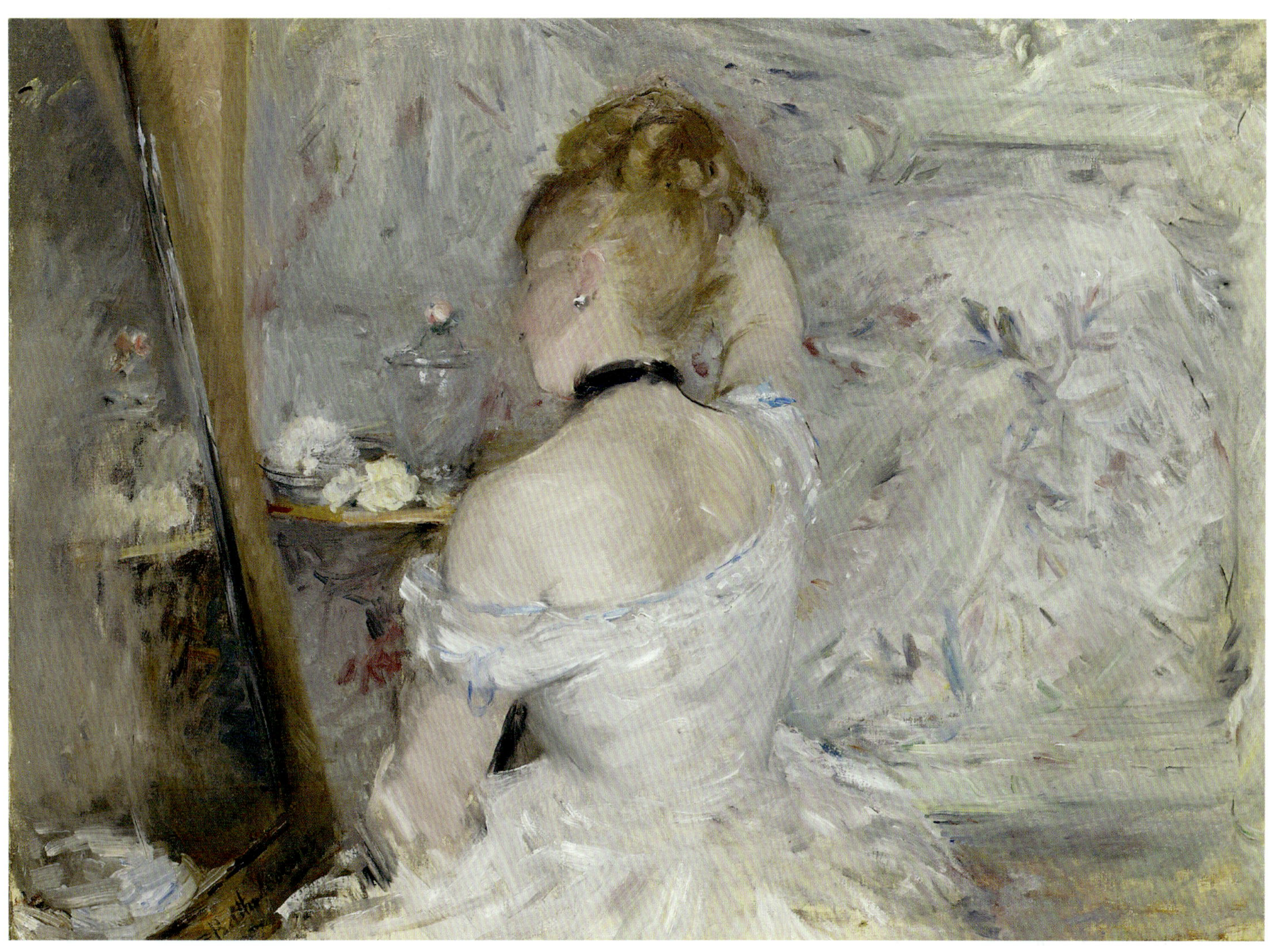

Paul and Charles Durand-Ruel remained in the United States during the exhibition and used the opportunity to strengthen relationships with collectors. They called on William Rockefeller, and Paul travelled to Washington, DC for a few days in mid-May.[43] He may have gone to Philadelphia to convince Alexander Cassatt to lend seven works to the National Academy venue, and it is likely he visited Henry Probasco in Cincinnati.[44]

By the end of the exhibition, 49 paintings by Monet, Renoir, Brown, Boudin, Lerolle and others sold for a reported sum of $40,000.[45] Erwin Davis (see fig. 75) and the Havemeyers (see fig. 53) were among the buyers, as were William Merritt Chase (fig. 95), Cyrus Lawrence, George Seney, William Loring Andrews, Albert Spencer, Desmond Fitzgerald and William H. Fuller. The largest number of works – 14 Monets and two Renoirs – was purchased by an elusive A.W. Kingman.[46]

Back in Paris in July, Durand-Ruel reported to Pissarro that he 'did not make a fortune with miraculous luck nor did he engage in sharp practice and have to decamp. He is very glad that he went to New York himself, and he has great hopes in possible developments there.'[47] Within weeks, Durand-Ruel began assembling works for a second New York exhibition.[48] To Fantin-Latour, he wrote: 'I had a lot of success with paintings that took twenty years to be appreciated in Paris. I sold Monets, Renoirs, Browns and many others, but I also had a whole series of theirs to show. That's what I would like to do with you, if you give me the means. I am sure that your work would cause a very great sensation.'[49] Though Fantin-Latour declined, Durand-Ruel was able to convince Puvis de Chavannes to participate.[50] The dealer relied on loans from the Scottish merchant James Duncan, an unidentified lender named Schnall and Suzanne Manet.[51] Nearly 300 paintings were sent to America in late October, but the exhibition was postponed until May the following year.[52] The firm ran into considerable trouble with United States Customs, which required a hefty 30% tariff on imported art. In the spring Durand-Ruel and Sutton had successfully argued that the paintings were being imported for the educational purpose of an exhibition, allowing them in tax-free. American dealers objected vociferously to this arrangement since Durand-Ruel did not have to pay duty on unsold works that were shipped back to Paris.[53] After months of negotiation, he was able to obtain a bond for the works on deposit to him, but he was forced to pay tariff on those from his stock.[54]

In March 1887 Durand-Ruel returned to New York and within a month opened a gallery in temporary quarters at 28 West 23rd Street, where he began to hold exhibitions.[55] According to a New York art journal, he was braving 'the bandit-terrors of our customs-house and tariff.'[56] One of his first actions was to place 127 paintings in an auction at Moore's Art Galleries in early May.[57] In selling works from his stock, he was adapting a practice set in the 1850s and 1860s by dealers Ernest Gambart and Alfred Cadart, who had organised large exhibitions in America followed by auctions.[58] At Durand-Ruel's sale, the *New York Times* noted that few buyers were present and 'bidding was at times sluggish', but their published auction results suggest that 47 paintings sold for between $255 and $2,400.[59] In truth, most paintings were bought in; only 35 sold for a total of $9,870.[60]

On 25 May, Durand-Ruel's delayed exhibition opened at the National Academy of Design. Boudin, Manet, Monet, Pissarro, Renoir and Sisley represented the modern French school with 45 paintings, or about 20% of the 223 works shown. The bulk of the exhibition was devoted to artists from the School of 1830 and contemporary painters like Pierre Damoye, Jean-Jacques Henner and Adolphe Monticelli. The catalogue stated that the works were 'brought to this country from Paris for exhibition only' and included biographical sketches of Delacroix and Puvis. Not surprisingly, these artists were

FIG. 96
Alfred Sisley
View of Saint-Mammès, about 1881
Oil on canvas, 54 × 74 cm
Carnegie Museum of Art, Pittsburgh
[cat. 93]

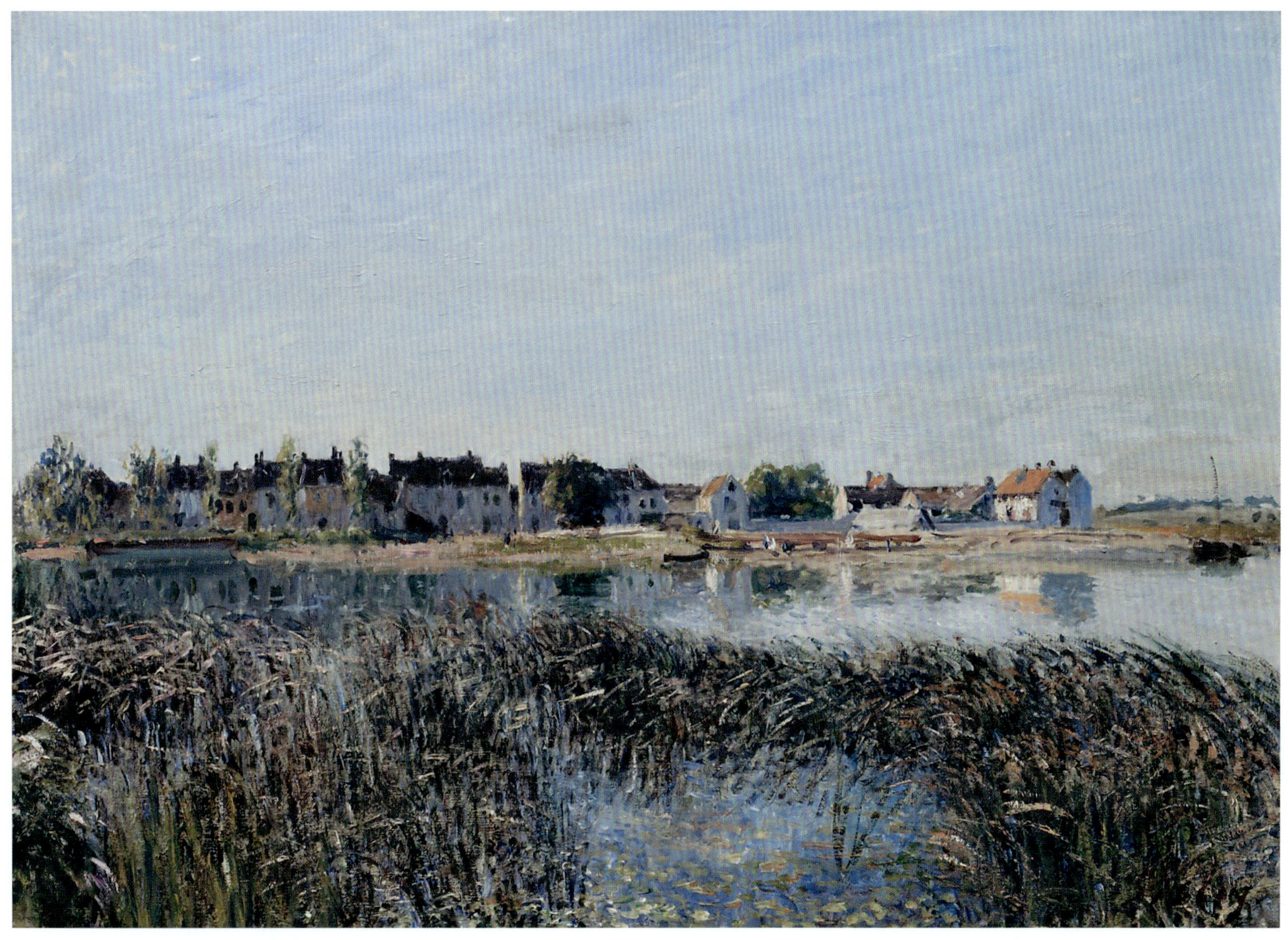

FIG. 97
The Copley Society exhibition of Claude Monet paintings, Boston, 1905
Photograph
Archives of American Art, Smithsonian Institution, Washington, DC

frequently mentioned in the press. Delacroix's massive *Death of Sardanapalus* (see fig. 20) was heralded as 'theatrical and magnificent', while Puvis's 10 works (see fig. 7) were a revelation to Americans. Critics recognised that the exhibition was intended to please a variety of tastes and was less coherent overall than the previous one. The Impressionists received little notice, though one prescient writer remarked, 'It cannot be long before the wonderful accuracy and beauty of their landscapes will be recognised.'[61]

Following the exhibition, the 140-odd works on deposit from Duncan and others returned to Paris, but the gallery stock stayed in the country.[62] Determined to make the American enterprise successful despite uneven sales and tepid response, Durand-Ruel returned to New York in November 1887.[63] During this trip, the gallery moved into more spacious rooms at 297 Fifth Avenue, and offered works at auction with limited success in November 1887 and February 1888.[64] Sales to collectors slowly followed; Pissarro's *Woman at a Well*, exhibited at the National Academy of Design in 1887, sold in February 1888 to William Loring Andrews, a trustee of the Metropolitan Museum of Art.[65] Catholina Lambert, a silk manufacturer, acquired a Monet in April, and Erwin Davis purchased a dozen Pissarros in April and May 1888 (see fig. 67).[66] A new client, Philadelphia lawyer John G. Johnson, acquired 10 works that year, beginning with a Monet in February and followed by Pissarro, Corot, Millet, Manet (see fig. 21), and five Puvis's.[67] With cautious optimism, Durand-Ruel turned the American business over to his sons.

Durand-Ruel & Sons

To a large extent, making the New York branch profitable was the responsibility of Joseph, Charles and Georges Durand-Ruel, and correspondingly, the American operations were known as Durand-Ruel & Sons by 1893.[68] Paul Durand-Ruel made regular transatlantic trips until 1898.[69] In his absence, he was ably represented by his sons according to Alfred Trumble, who wrote: 'They, like him, regard art with a personal as well as a commercial eye ... they combine a thoroughly American energy, rapidity of ideas and execution.'[70] From 1886 to 1892, Charles played a central role in American affairs, and his death the latter year was a terrible blow, not least in New York where he was well liked.[71] Thereafter, Joseph and Georges divided their time between New York and Paris, ensuring that one family member was in the country at nearly all times.

In America and France, the gallery faced competition as other dealers began to realise profits in Impressionism. In 1888 Boussod, Valadon & Co. established a gallery in New York at 303 Fifth Avenue where they sold works by Monet, Degas and others to some of the same collectors.[72] James Sutton, Durand-Ruel's former collaborator, began working with Isidore Montaignac in Paris to acquire Monet paintings (see fig. 14), and Knoedler and Alphonse Legrand attempted a partnership in 1886 to sell Impressionist works in New York.[73] In response to these challenges, the Durand-Ruel Gallery developed a particularly nimble business in America, utilising temporary exhibitions, loans and travel to great advantage. Despite market fluctuations, the branch thrived and had a reliable client base by the early 1890s, when works by Monet were increasingly regarded as acceptable furnishings for a wealthy American banker or industrialist's home.[74]

Impressionist paintings were a permanent feature in the New York gallery, but the firm soon diversified its offerings. The first monographic show in America was devoted to the sculptor Antoine-Louis Barye in 1893, followed by Puvis in 1894 and Monet, John La Farge, Manet and Cassatt in 1895. By September 1889, the gallery had moved to 315 Fifth Avenue. It began showing work by Rembrandt, Rubens, Hals, de Hooch and others, and in 1890 produced its first printed catalogue.[75] The gamble was a profitable one – the Dutch exhibition was widely and favourably covered in the press, and sugar magnate H.O. Havemeyer bought two of the Rembrandts.[76] Havemeyer's wife, Louisine, was an early collector of the Impressionists, and the couple acquired works by Manet (see fig. 53), Degas and Désiré François Laugée from the 1886 exhibition, but they did not begin to collect paintings in earnest until the end of the decade.[77] Havemeyer's interests were wide-ranging; early in his marriage he acquired hundreds of Japanese tea jars before turning his attention to ceramics, glass, textiles and metalwork. In July 1889 the Havemeyers purchased 20 Barbizon and Old Master works from Durand-Ruel in Paris for over 800,000 francs.[78] Due to Louisine's persuasion and the advice of Mary Cassatt, Havemeyer came to embrace more modern painting such as Courbet nudes (see fig. 25), Degas pastels, Manet portraits and Monet landscapes. By the early twentieth century, the couple had assembled the largest Impressionist collection in America, over half of which was acquired through Durand-Ruel. One of the more unusual ways Havemeyer and Durand-Ruel were linked was through an elegant mansion at 389 Fifth Avenue, originally built for tobacco manufacturer Pierre Lorillard. Havemeyer bought the property in November 1893 and leased it to Durand-Ruel the following March for $25,000 a year. The building's first-floor ballroom, regarded as one of the finest in the city, was converted into galleries, and the basement housed a Western Union Telegraph office, a convenient fellow-tenant for Durand-Ruel's transatlantic business.[79]

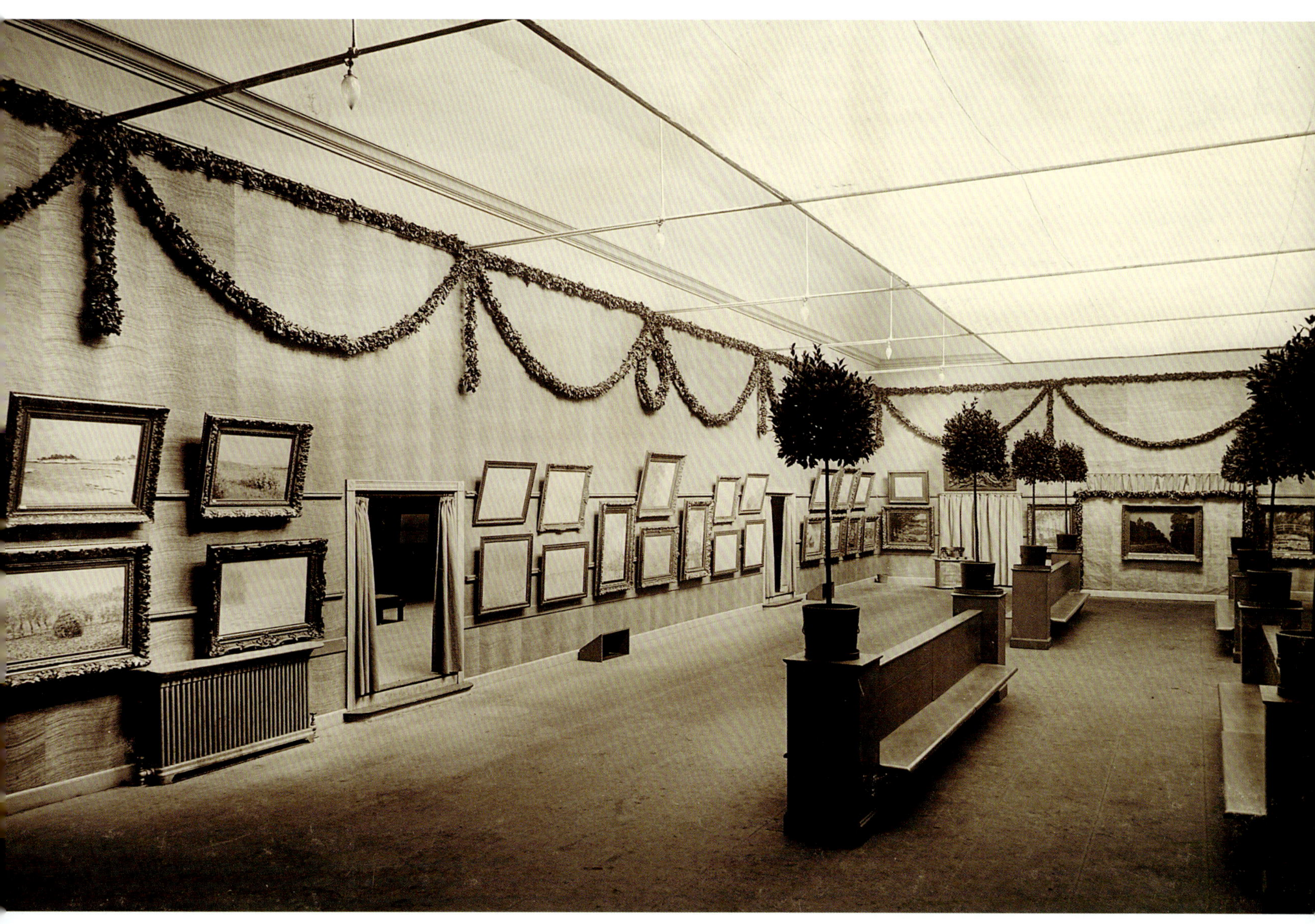

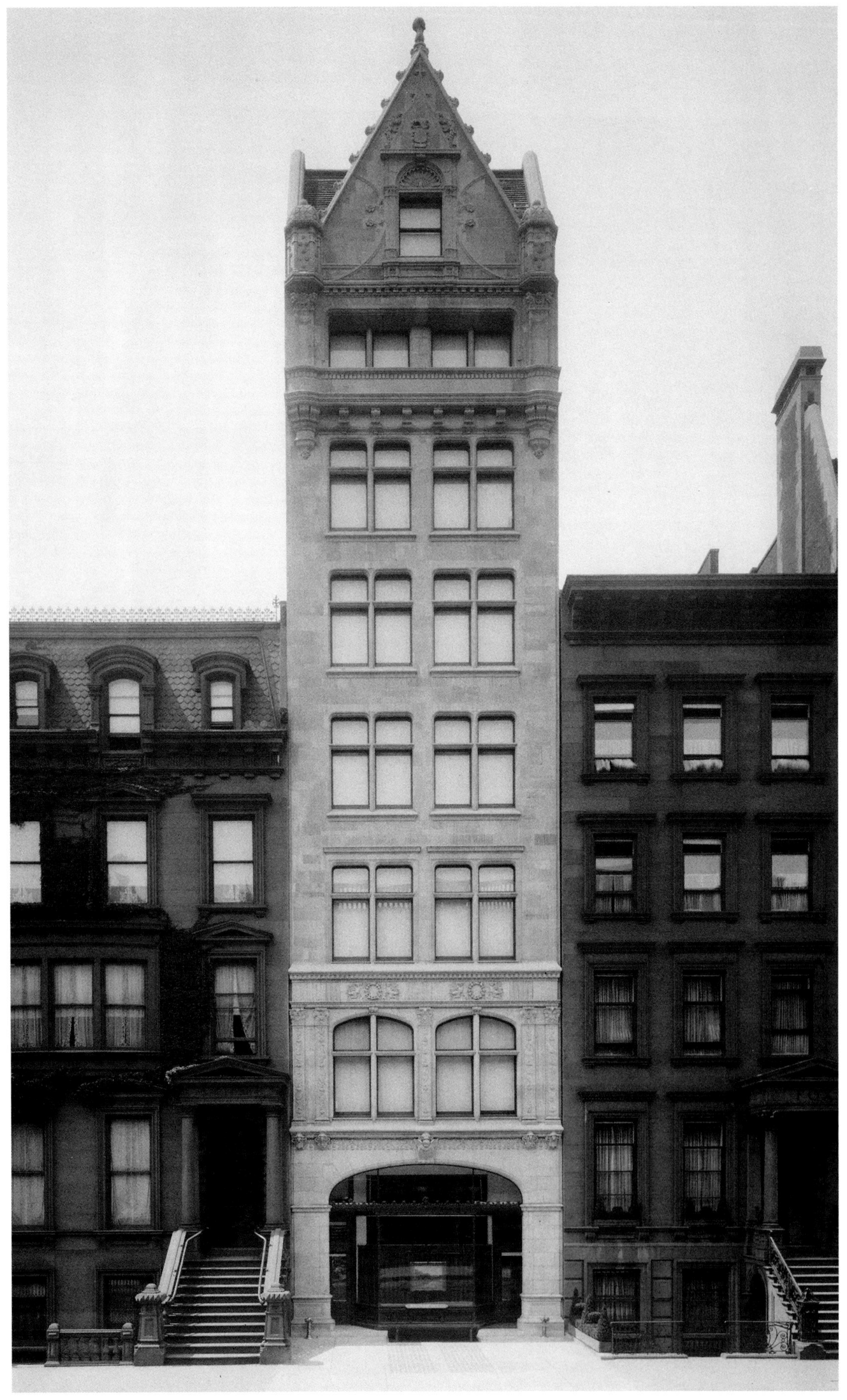

FIG. 98
Wurtz Bros
Durand-Ruel Gallery at
12 East 57th Street, New York
Silver gelatin print
Museum of the City of New York

In 1888 the firm began organising short-term exhibitions in art galleries and hotel rooms outside New York City. Usually featuring two dozen Old Master and Barbizon paintings with the occasional canvas by Degas or Monet, these displays proved an effective means of attracting new clients. In Chicago they exhibited at Thurber's Art Gallery, the Palmer House Hotel and the Art Institute of Chicago, enterprises that enabled them to develop close relationships with Bertha and Potter Palmer, Charles L. Hutchinson, Martin Ryerson, Charles Yerkes and Sara Hallowell, the curator responsible for the rich displays of French art at the Chicago Interstate Industrial and World's Columbian Expositions.[80] The Carnegie International, an annual exhibition of recent work by American and European artists, drew many dealers, Durand-Ruel among them, to Pittsburgh.[81] The gallery regularly presented paintings by Corot, Daubigny, Diaz, Turner and Van Dyck at Gillespie's Gallery and in rented rooms in the Carnegie Building and the Henry Hotel.[82] In addition, they faithfully lent paintings by Monet (see fig. 75), Renoir, Sisley (fig. 96), Pissarro (see fig. 119) and Cassatt to the International, occasionally selling them to the Carnegie Museum and local collectors like Henry Clay Frick or David Watson. On a more modest scale, the firm sent paintings to exhibitions in St. Louis and Omaha[83] and to commercial art galleries in Philadelphia and Boston.[84] Durand-Ruel's westernmost venture occurred in Denver where Russell Spaulding, a representative of the New York branch, exhibited 20 paintings in a parlour of Brown's Hotel in November 1897.[85]

These activities, conveniently situated on major railway lines, were accompanied by frequent visits of the dealer and his sons. Durand-Ruel made regular calls in Pittsburgh,[86] Cleveland[87] and Chicago, where he attended the Columbian Exposition in its final days and dined with local collectors the following year.[88] Joseph and Georges were visitors to these cities and to Minneapolis, where they advised collector James J. Hill on the hanging of his picture gallery.[89] Despite the westward expansion of the firm's interests, the family does not seem to have seriously entertained opening a second American gallery, instead using social calls and temporary exhibitions as a means of cultivating clients.[90]

By 1905, the American branch had assisted in the formation of impressive Impressionist collections and through exhibitions introduced thousands of Americans to modern French painting. The New York gallery, in new quarters at 5 West 36th Street, organised shows that year on Monet, Sisley, Jongkind, Boudin and American artist Henry C. Lee, and aided the Copley Society of Boston in the organisation of an important Monet exhibition in which three-quarters of the 95 loans had once belonged to the gallery (fig. 97).[91] Simultaneously, large portions of the American stock appeared in exhibitions organised by the gallery in Philadelphia and Toledo, and individual loans were made to the Worcester Art Museum and the Art Association of New Orleans.[92] Durand-Ruel reflected in his *Memoirs* six years later: 'As our American operations kept growing, we were able to gradually emerge from the financial uncertainty against which I had struggled so long, to pay back all the money lent me by friends, and to supervise the business with a sense of serenity.'[93] That serenity, buoyed by new clients like Dr Albert C. Barnes of Philadelphia, was manifest in 1913 when the family bought property at 12 East 57th Street and commissioned the architectural firm Carrère and Hastings to construct an eight-storey gallery and residence (fig. 98). The firm continued to lead the American market for French Impressionism until February 1950, when changing economic circumstances forced the third generation of the Durand-Ruel family to shut the New York gallery, bringing to an end nearly a century of activity in America.

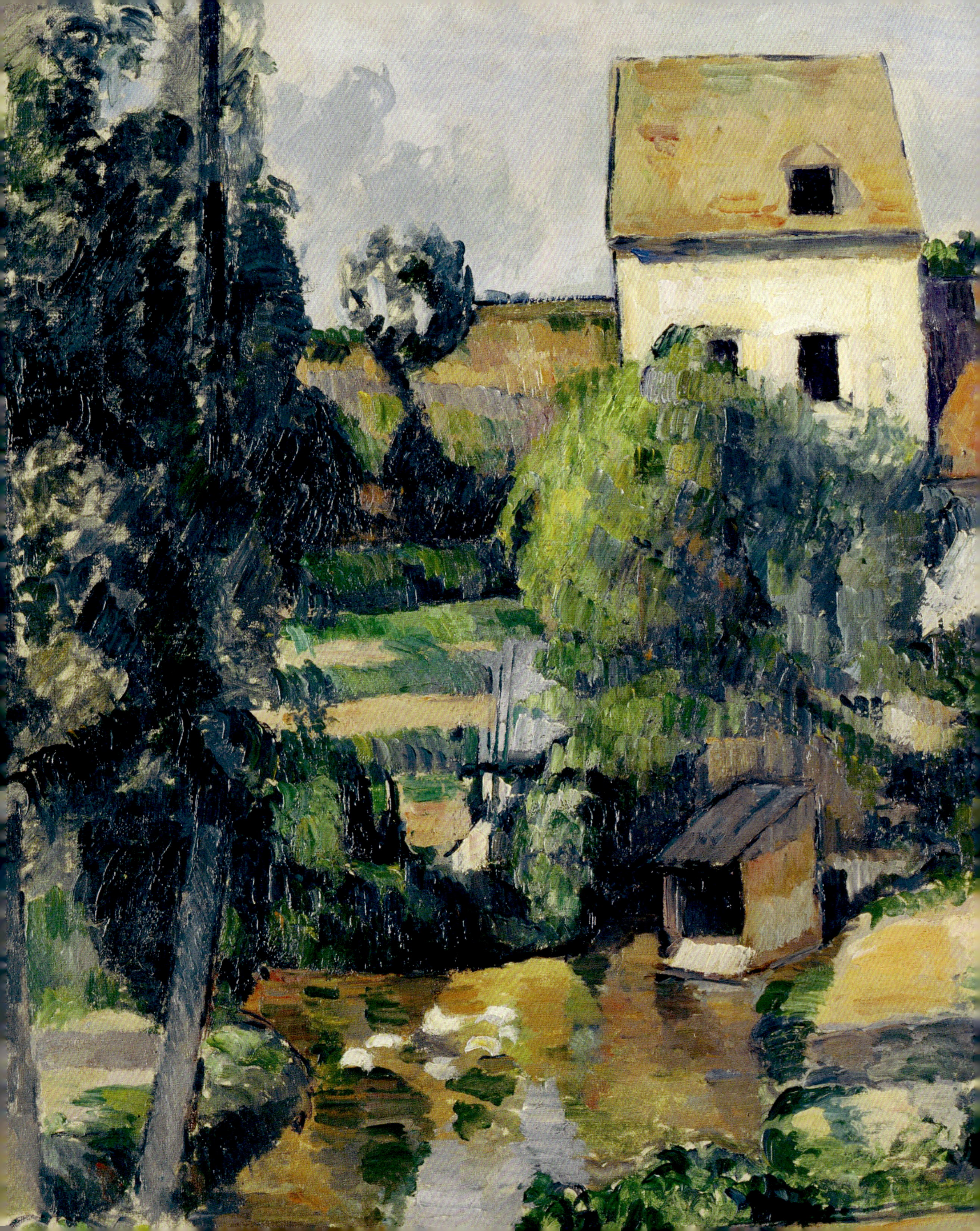

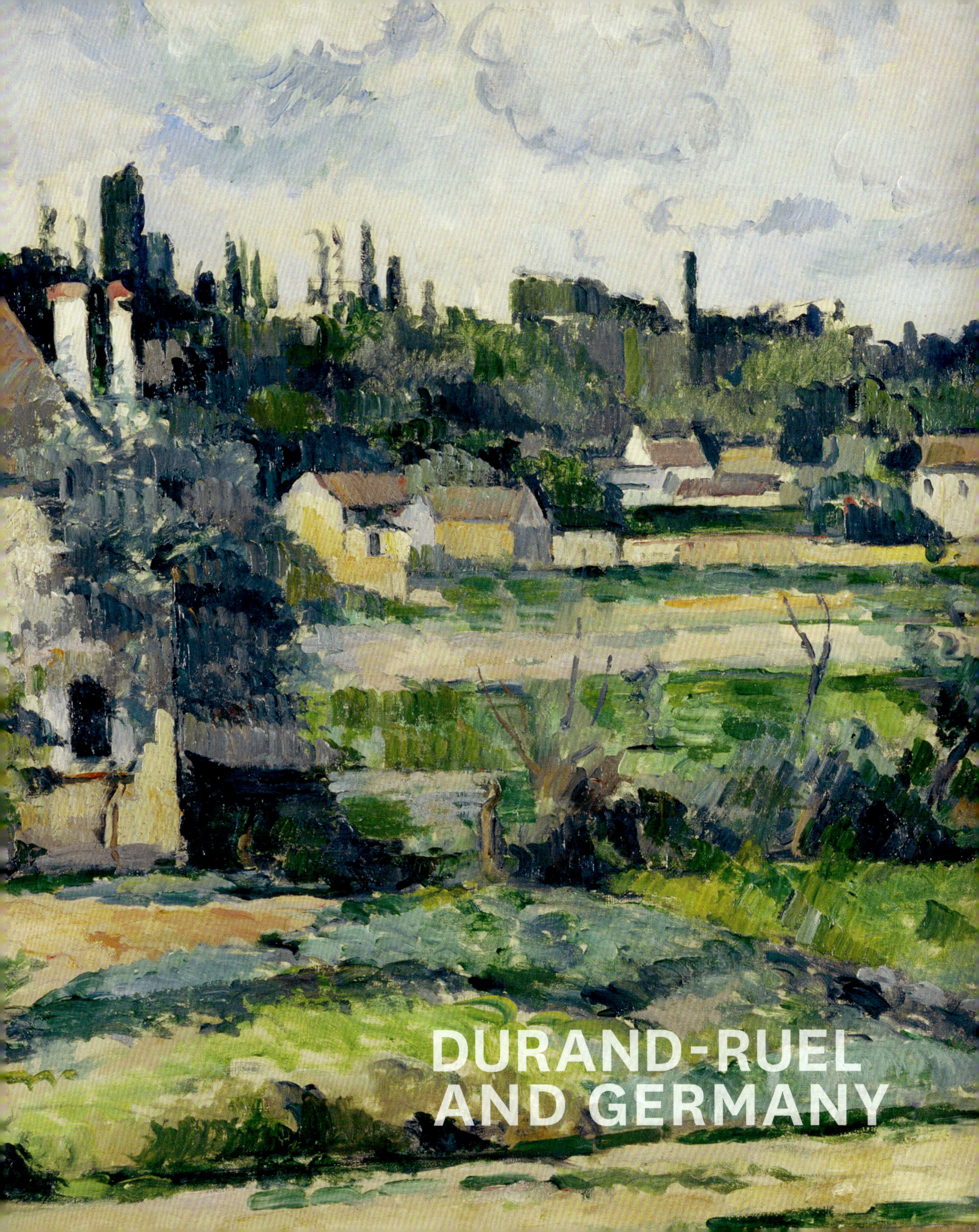
DURAND-RUEL
AND GERMANY

Durand-Ruel and Germany

Dorothee Hansen

'The role that was once played in the life of the artist by the priest, the prince and the patrician, as protector, employer, and intellectual guide is nowadays played by the art dealer,' wrote Alfred Lichtwark (1852–1914), Director of the Hamburger Kunsthalle in 1901. 'All that museums have found impossible in the last two decades has been achieved by art dealers, both here and in France.' He respectfully added that 'one single dealer, Durand-Ruel is alone responsible for creating a great, original school, that of Manet-Monet. That is something that has never happened in the whole history of the world.'[1]

Lichtwark's tribute aptly defines Paul Durand-Ruel's exceptional importance. Only a few years after the French dealer had made a breakthrough with Impressionist pictures in New York, he began to expand into Germany, where he quickly opened up the second biggest sales market for the new French painting and also paved the way for its entry into museums.

First business contacts with Germany

Durand-Ruel established preliminary contacts with the German art market as early as 1867. His first customer was the Berlin auctioneer and art-dealer Rudolph Lepke (1845–1904), who had opened a gallery in 1869[2] and regularly purchased pictures from him. At a time when relations between France and Germany were marked by great political tension, culminating in the Franco-Prussian War of 1870–1, the Berlin dealer bought a total of 29 paintings from his French colleague – predominantly by Salon artists like Alfred Stevens, Auguste Toulmouche or Alexandre Calame, but also by artists of the Barbizon School such as Jean-Baptiste-Camille Corot, Théodore Rousseau or Constant Troyon.[3] However, his purchases from Durand-Ruel ceased in 1873.

Ten years later Durand-Ruel established contact with the Berlin art dealer Fritz Gurlitt (1854–1893). Since 1880, Gurlitt had been running a gallery offering an extensive programme ranging from Old Masters to modern arts and crafts.[4] In October 1883, with the support of Durand-Ruel, he mounted the first exhibition of Impressionists in Germany. The starting point for the show was the collection of Carl and Felicie Bernstein, who had lived in Berlin since 1878.[5] During a trip to Paris in the summer of 1882, the couple had followed the advice of Carl's cousin Charles Ephrussi and purchased some 10 pictures by Manet, Monet, Sisley and Pissarro. At the end of September 1883 Durand-Ruel sent 24 pictures to Gurlitt in Berlin.[6] The most significant work was Manet's painting *The Railway* (National Gallery of Art, Washington, DC, RW 207) which was also the most highly priced at 15,000 francs. In addition there were pictures by Degas, Monet, Cassatt, Morisot, Pissarro, Sisley, Renoir and Boudin, with prices ranging from 1,000 to 4,000 francs.[7]

Carl Bernstein seems to have conceived a plan to exhibit his pictures publicly as early as 1883,[8] but just how it happened that the exhibition was organised at Gurlitt's and who exactly took the initiative must remain open questions. However it came about, the project admirably suited Paul Durand-Ruel's foreign activities, which were increasing at that time, and the extensive, sometimes very critical press coverage drew attention to the French painters.[9] It now ranks as a milestone in the reception of French Impressionism. However, no pictures were sold and this remained the only collaboration between Durand-Ruel and Gurlitt.

Emil Heilbut – a middleman in Hamburg

After the mid-1880s, Durand-Ruel concentrated on his successful activities in New York. From his strengthened position he turned with renewed intensity towards the German market around 1890. At first, his significant middleman was the art critic Emil Heilbut (1861–1921),

FIG. 99
Claude Monet
Road at La Cavée, Pourville, 1882
Oil on canvas, 73 × 60 cm
Private collection

also known by the pseudonym Hermann Helferich. A native of Hamburg, he was a nephew of the Paris Salon painter Ferdinand Heilbuth (1826–1889), who introduced him to the Parisian art world.[10] From that time, Heilbut was enthusiastic about the work of the Impressionists and he was one of the first to introduce them to Germany when, in 1889, he gave a series of lectures on French art at the Grand Ducal Saxon School of Art in Weimar. For visual material during the lectures he used three pictures by Monet. Two of these he had bought from Durand-Ruel[11] (fig. 99), and they mark the beginning of a fruitful business relationship.

As a critic, Heilbut published the first text in German on Claude Monet in 1890.[12] But what was crucial for Durand-Ruel was Heilbut's contacts with the important Hamburg collectors Erdwin Amsinck (1826–1897)[13] and Eduard L. Behrens (1824–1895),[14] whom he advised on their purchases.[15] The Barbizon School formed the focus of French painting in the Behrens and Amsinck collections. Behrens especially had built up this aspect of his collection after 1890 with Heilbut's support. In January of that year, Durand-Ruel sent Heilbut a seascape by Jules Dupré, and by February the picture had been sold to Eduard Behrens for the handsome sum of 18,000 francs.[16] There followed further deliveries of paintings to Heilbut and also directly to Behrens, to whom Durand-Ruel now personally submitted offers by letter.[17] However, Heilbut's ambition was to bring more progressive art to Germany. As early as 1891 he tried, without success, to negotiate the sale of a Degas to Behrens. But the work that Durand-Ruel had sent for viewing to Hamburg returned in March 1892 to Paris.[18] It was not until shortly after the death of her husband in 1897 that Anthonie Amsinck bought two pictures by Degas from Durand-Ruel.[19]

Heilbut also acted as go-between for Hamburg art lovers with other Parisian dealers such as Goupil or Boussod & Valadon. In a letter to Amsinck of 1889 he

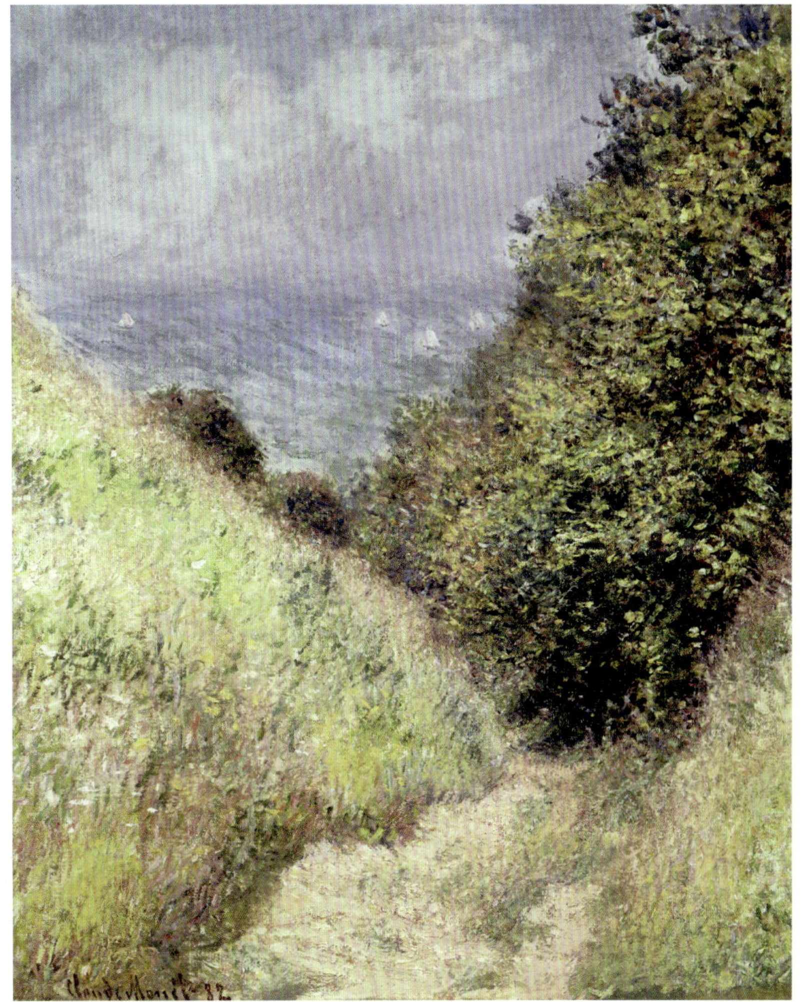

compares their business methods: 'I have always found Durand-Ruel to be expensive, in other matters also. But he is always very well informed about the real value of his pictures and, if they are good, is not prepared to let them go cheaply. That is in contrast to Goupil, who prefers to take account of the purchase price, so that as soon as he has purchased something cheaply one can also expect to buy cheaply from him.'[20] He describes Durand-Ruel's dealership as 'together with Goupil the oldest and biggest house in this field. As it does not bother with publicity, it is not well known abroad. But it has a richer stock of pictures than Goupil.'[21]

Heilbut and Durand-Ruel soon developed further plans. In October 1892, Durand-Ruel wrote that he wished to come to Hamburg to exhibit some of Millet's pictures in a hotel. If Heilbut could bring along some interested collectors, he would share 10% of the sales premium.[22] 'We must combine our efforts to increase our German business significantly', he wrote.[23] But no written contract was offered, for 'between honest men, one's word is more sacred than the most solemn treaties'.[24]

The 1895 exhibition in the Hamburger Kunsthalle

We do not know whether Durand-Ruel carried out his plan and brought some of Millet's pictures to Hamburg in 1892. However, Alfred Lichtwark purchased Millet's *Narcissi and Violets* (fig. 100) from him in that year. He could actually have bought the picture in Paris in June, for he was a regular visitor to Durand-Ruel's gallery from this time. By the following year he seems to have got to know Durand-Ruel better. The art dealer invited Lichtwark to visit his private collection, which made a great impression: 'It is a really modern collection, lots of Monet, a few celebrated Manets, Degas, ... Pissarro, Sisley and especially Renoir ... At the present time, one can only get acquainted with all these artists in this collection'.[25]

Lichtwark's comments bear witness to his enthusiasm for Impressionist painting. He had already seen the Berlin exhibition at Gurlitt's in 1883 and had even published two reviews about it, in which he showed a certain amount of scepticism, it is true, but at the same time expressed his hopes for new stimuli for art in Germany.[26] Meanwhile, he had further developed his taste and he began increasingly to promote the cause of French painting. In March 1895 he asked Durand-Ruel for several pictures by Puvis de Chavannes as loans for the great art exhibition of the Hamburg art society (Kunstverein) which was shown in the Kunsthalle. As no painting by this artist was available, Durand-Ruel offered Impressionist pictures – or was this perhaps a deliberate strategic move? From 14 March to 27 April, paintings from Durand-Ruel's gallery could be seen at the Kunsthalle, including three pictures each by Boudin, Courbet, Monet and Sisley, four pictures each by Renoir and Pissarro, plus further Impressionist paintings from other lenders.[27] In the context of the whole exhibition, which included 690 works, this was a small selection, but it was the first significant presentation of Impressionist painting in Germany since the exhibition at Gurlitt's 13 years previously, and what is more, it took place in a celebrated museum.

New contacts with Berlin 1896

During 1896, in addition to his activities in Hamburg, Durand-Ruel clinched new business deals in Berlin, where the liveliest German art market was developing.[28] What is striking is that he did not initially approach Berlin art dealers. More crucial to his access to the Berlin art market were his contacts with the painter Max Liebermann (1847–1935) and Hugo von Tschudi (1851–1911), who had directed the Berlin National Gallery since 1896. Both were friends of Lichtwark and also knew the Bernstein collection. In June 1896, Liebermann and

FIG. 100
Jean-François Millet
Narcissi and Violets, about 1867
Pastel on paper, 40 × 50 cm
Hamburger Kunsthalle, Hamburg

Tschudi journeyed to Paris where they visited Durand-Ruel's gallery. Liebermann later described viewing Manet's painting *In the Conservatory* (fig. 102) as an 'awakening' for Tschudi: 'In Durand-Ruel's gallery he saw Manet's work for the first time in all its originality. Manet's genius opened up a new world for him'.[29]

It was at that time that Tschudi's decision to create a collection of recent French painting at the National Gallery grew to fruition.[30] In August that year he purchased Manet's painting from Durand-Ruel for 22,000 francs. To raise the cash he sought out four patrons, Eduard Arnhold, Ernst and Robert von Mendelssohn and Hugo Oppenheim.[31] The well-to-do art lovers were from now on 'infected' with the new French art. As Tschudi convinced them about Impressionism, he automatically won new clients for Durand-Ruel, who saw his chance and sent 12 paintings to be viewed at the National Gallery in October 1896: seven pictures by Monet, three by Degas, one Pissarro and a picture by Max Liebermann.[32] Tschudi bought two works by Monet (fig. 101) and Degas for the National Gallery,[33] and another picture found a buyer, for Eduard Arnhold (1849–1925) paid 10,000 francs for Monet's *Rocks near Pourville at Ebb Tide*.[34] In the following years, advised by

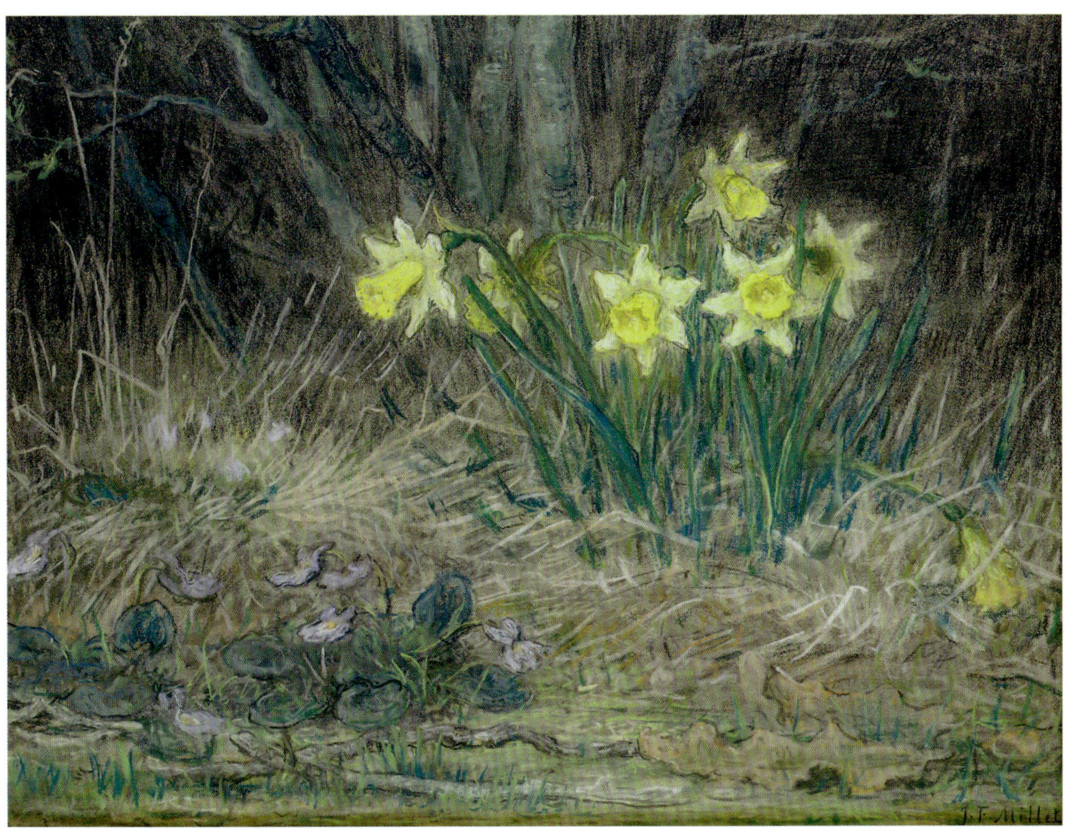

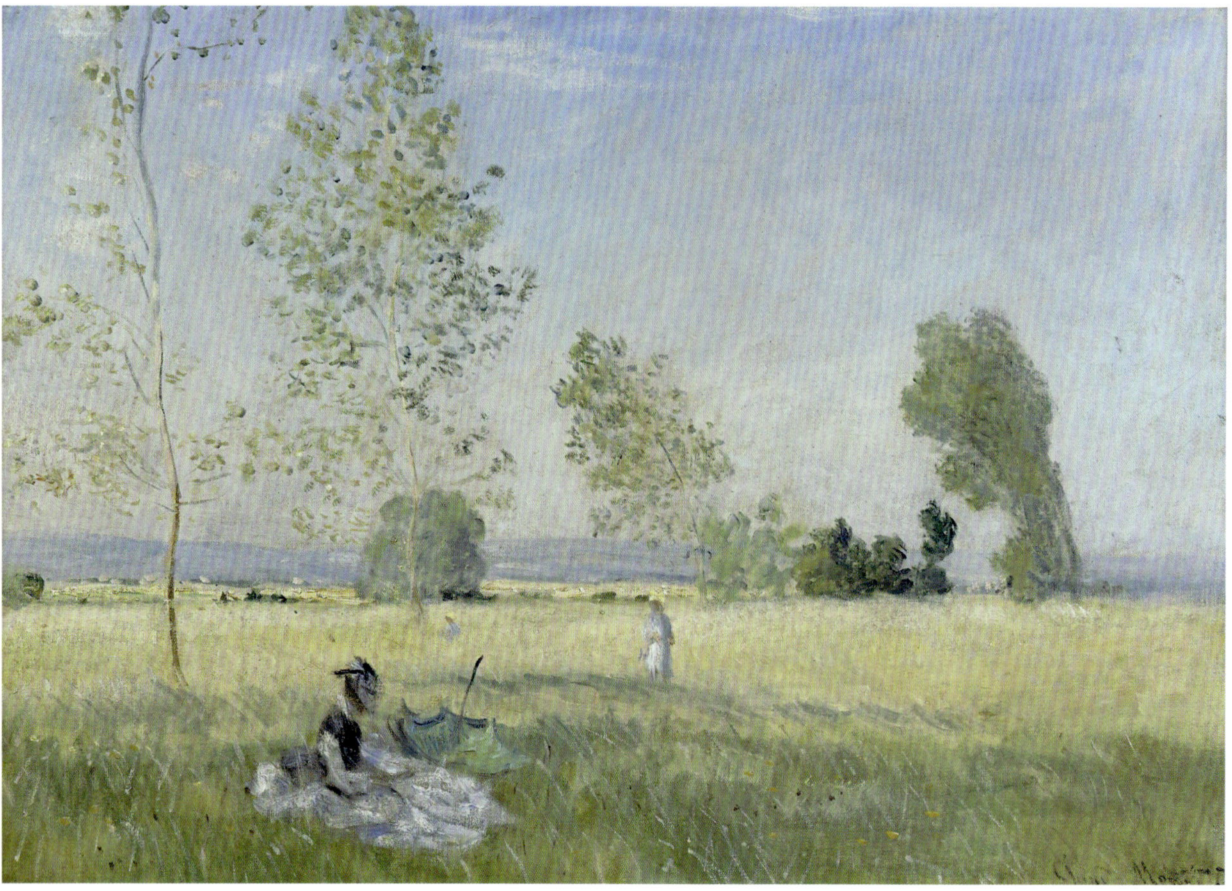

Tschudi, he built up one of the most significant collections of French painting in Germany.[35]

Durand-Ruel continued to be Tschudi's key point of contact for extending the collection of French Impressionists and their predecessors. At the very beginning of 1897 he procured Millet's *November Evening* for him for 55,000 francs – a considerable sum, but in France Millet was also one of the painters most marketed by dealers.[36] On the other hand, for Sisley's *Snow at Louveciennes* and Cézanne's *Mill on the Couleuvre near Pontoise* (fig. 103) Tschudi paid his Paris dealer only 7,000 francs in total.[37] At the International Art Exhibition in Dresden in spring 1897, he also bought Monet's *Houses at Argenteuil* and Pissarro's *Court House at Pontoise*, which had likewise been supplied by Durand-Ruel.[38] But after this brilliant start, Tschudi ran into criticism from the highest level. Kaiser Wilhelm II, who represented the most conservative taste in art, obstructed the further rapid development of the Berlin Impressionist collection in the following years, and it was not until the turn of the century that Tschudi could once more start to build.[39]

'A well-placed picture produces offspring',[40] Max Liebermann would say, and that was certainly true for Tschudi's new purchases. Liebermann himself was, together with the museum director, the most significant advocate of the Impressionists in Berlin, and his own painting also increasingly bore witness to the reception of the French artists.[41] What is more, he began to build up his own collection. So he was not only an important propagator for Durand-Ruel but also his direct customer. In December 1896 Liebermann bought a picture by Courbet from him; in May 1897 he bought Degas' pastel *At Rest*; in October he acquired Manet's *Madame Manet in the Garden at Bellevue*; and in December, Courbet's *Still Life with Apples*.[42]

Liebermann acted in some ways as a middleman for Durand-Ruel, for example recommending pictures by Manet and Degas to the Lübeck collector Max Linde (1862–1940). On 8 May 1897 he wrote to Linde: 'At the moment I'm acting as host to a wonderful Manet, a young woman in black, a life-size, knee-length portrait set in leafy surroundings. Durand-Ruel from Paris, who was here until yesterday, has entrusted me with the

FIG. 101
Claude Monet
Spring, 1874
Oil on canvas, 57 × 80 cm
Nationalgalerie, Staatliche Museen zu Berlin

FIG. 102
Edouard Manet
In the Conservatory, 1878–9
Oil on canvas, 115 × 150 cm
Nationalgalerie, Staatliche Museen zu Berlin

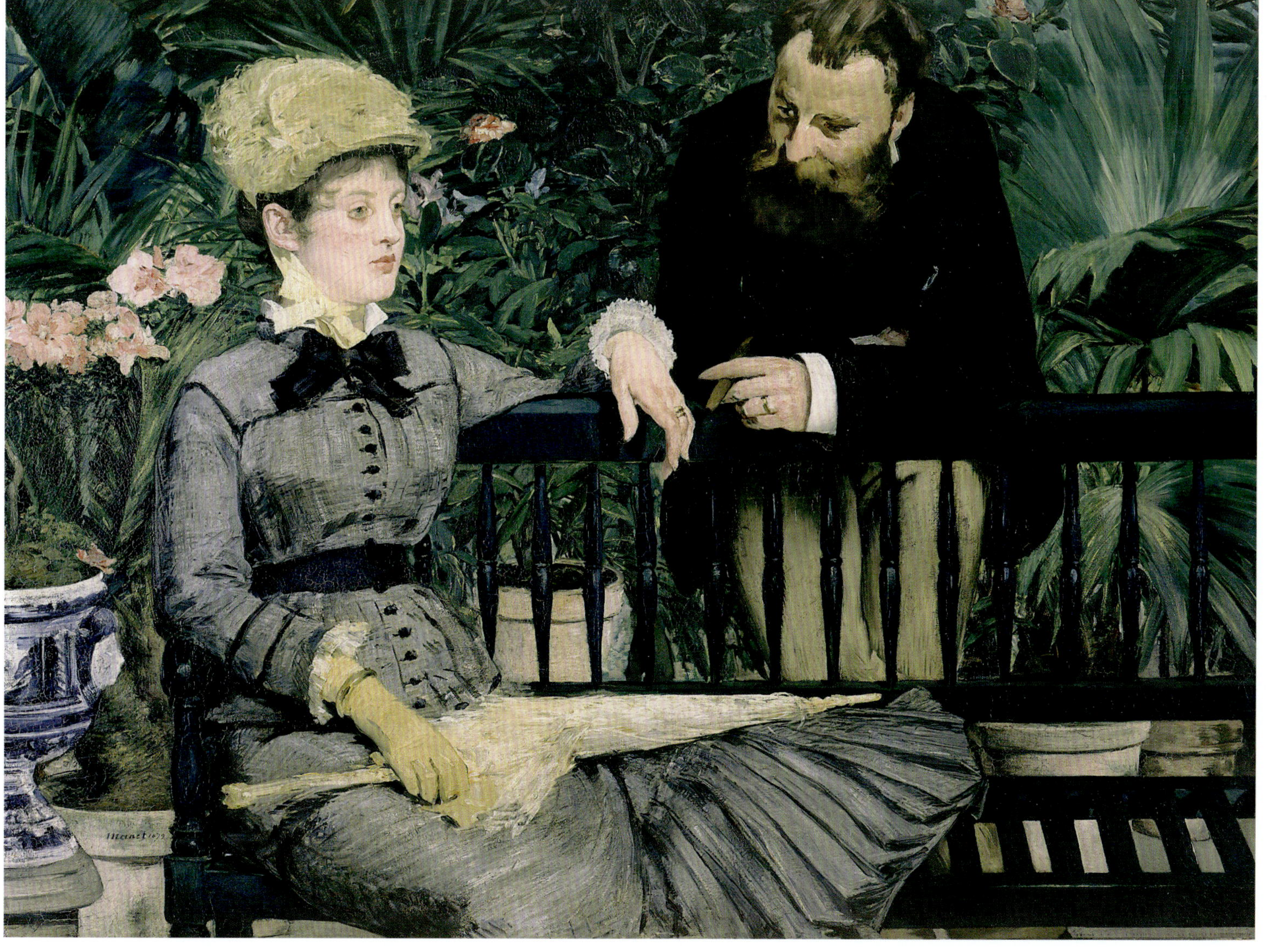

FIG. 103
Paul Cézanne
The Mill on the Couleuvre near Pontoise, about 1881
Oil on canvas, 73.5 × 91.5 cm
Nationalgalerie, Staatliche Museen zu Berlin
[cat. 6]

FIG. 104
Max Liebermann
Break Time in the Amsterdam Orphanage, 1881/2
Oil on canvas, 79 × 108 cm
Städelsches Kunstinstitut, Frankfurt am Main

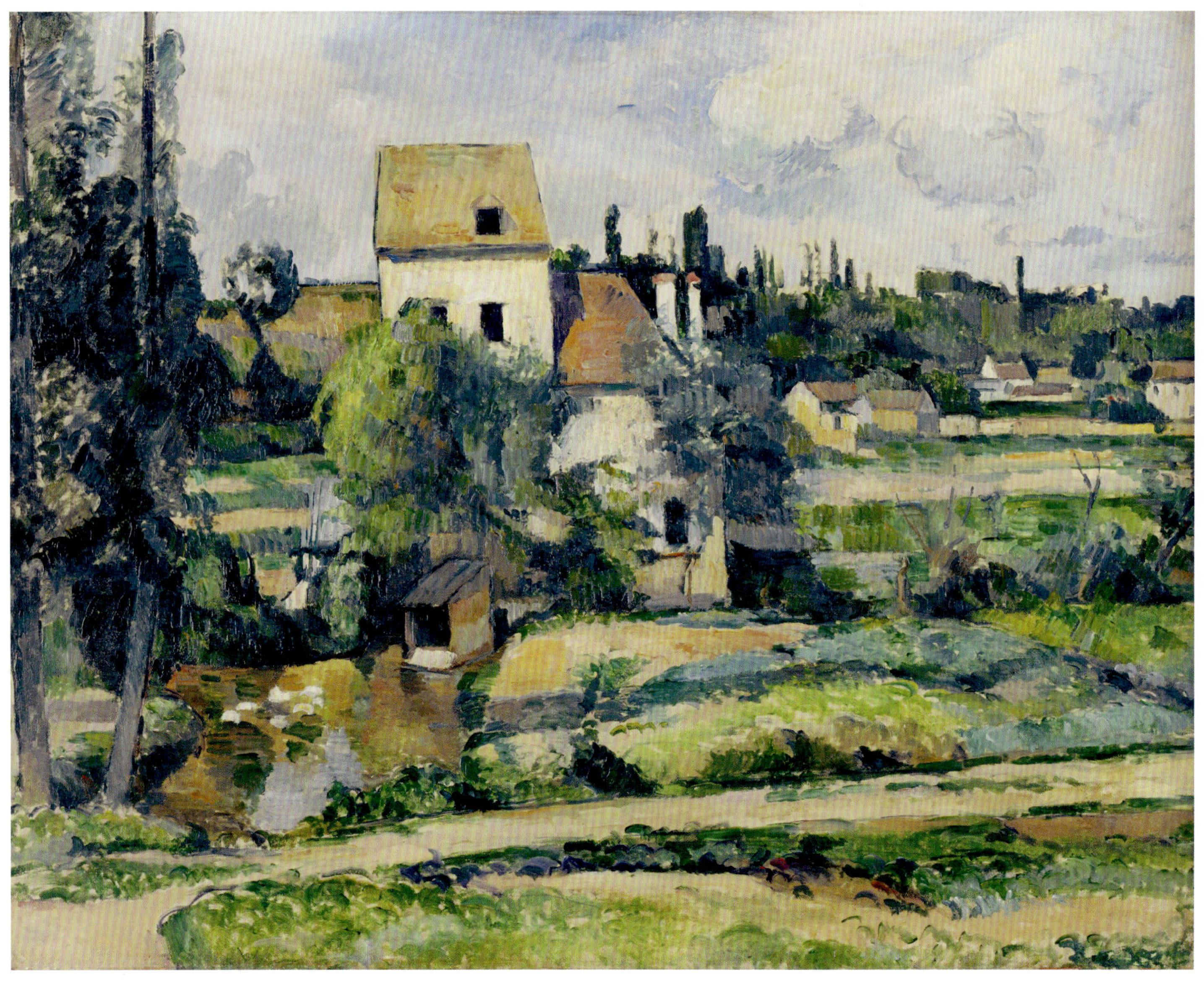

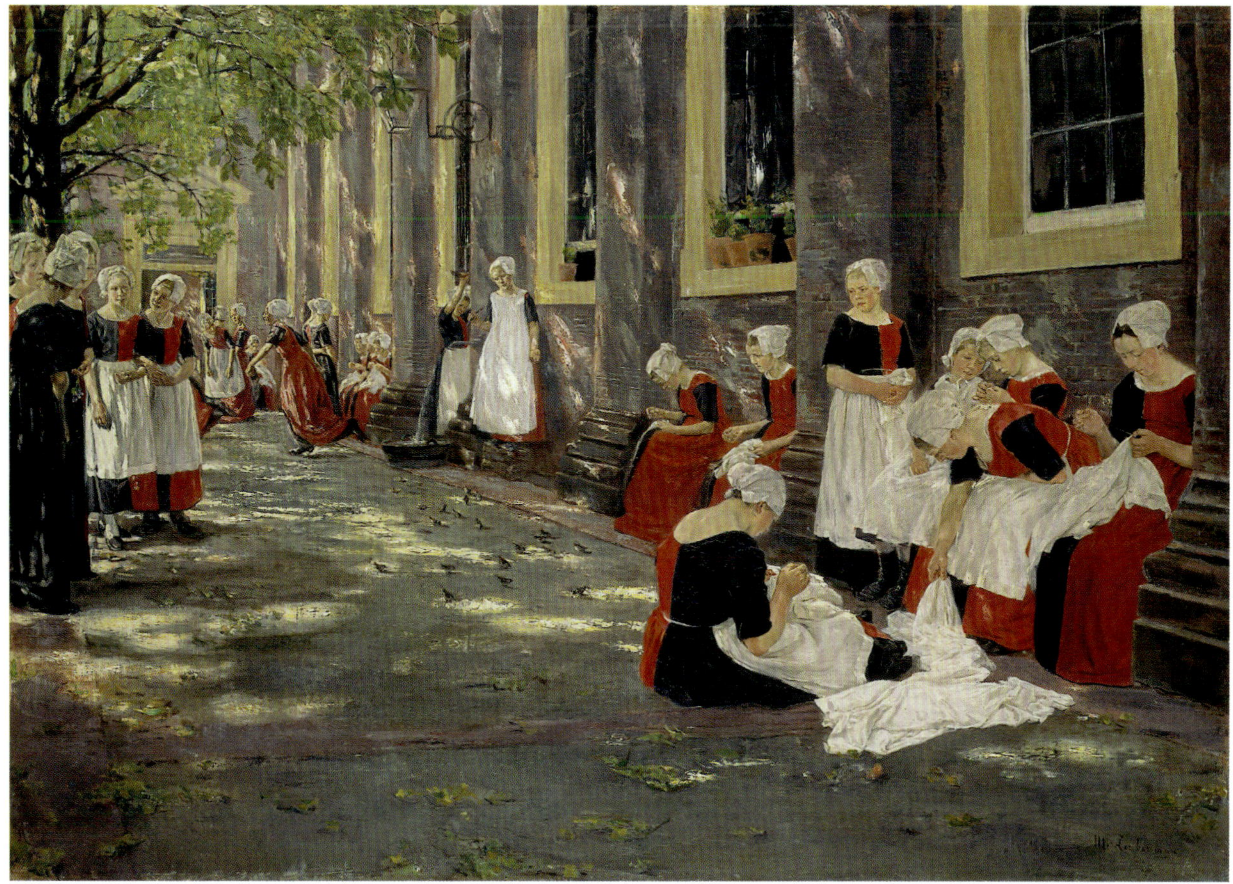

picture. The selling price is 8,000 francs and I'd love to find a buyer for it, as it is a quite marvellous painting.'[43] Liebermann must also have influenced his brother Georg (1844–1926), who bought two pictures by Courbet and one by Sisley from Durand-Ruel in 1897.[44]

Durand-Ruel knew how to flatter Max Liebermann by including his important painting *Break Time in the Amsterdam Orphanage* (fig. 104) as part of his delivery of pictures to the National Gallery in October 1896.[45] And Liebermann, for his part, used this as publicity. He wrote excitedly to Richard Graul, Director of the Leipzig Museum of Applied Arts, delighting in his 'brilliant deal': 'Durand-Ruel, who brought a wagon-load of Degas and Claude Monet for Tschudi also had one of my pictures from 1882, for which he asked the trifle of 20,000 francs, whereas the Monets cost 5,000–7,000.'[46] Whereas Durand-Ruel had bought this picture by Liebermann from Faure's collection in Paris, he himself bought two smaller pictures with similar subjects from the painter in the following year.[47] Thus Liebermann proved to be a key figure for Durand-Ruel in his conquest of the Berlin art market. He was an artist and also a collector; he was a middleman to museum directors like Tschudi and Lichtwark, to private collectors and critics; and last but not least, he expressed his own views as a writer on art, publishing an essay on Edgar Degas in the luxuriously produced journal *Pan*, which was illustrated by half-tone engravings 'by permission of Mr Durand-Ruel, Paris'. The art dealer could not have wished for better publicity.[48]

'Mouth-watering elite exhibitions'

Whereas Durand-Ruel had focused above all on Hamburg in the first half of the 1890s, Berlin took centre stage after 1896. He had now established numerous contacts there without being dependent on his earlier link with Heilbut. Therefore he was not prepared to pay Heilbut commission for sales, writing: 'My list for Berlin was already just about complete and I personally added even more to it during my stay in Berlin.'[49] He now planned to intensify his conquest of the German market by making personal presentations in hotels.

Durand-Ruel had already spoken about this idea in 1892 with reference to Hamburg,[50] and the plan for a tour to include stops in Hamburg and Berlin was also conceived at that time. But it was not until the end of 1896 that the plan was carried out. In Hamburg he gained a new partner in Moritz Meyer, whom he had known since 1893.[51] He was neither collector nor art dealer, but an agent and 'commissioner'.[52] In addition, Durand-Ruel's son Georges and his business partner Charles Destrée were sent to Hamburg to prepare the exhibition in the exclusive Hôtel de l'Europe on the Alsterdamm (now Ballindamm).[53]

From 5 to 8 December 1896, 38 pictures could be viewed there, most of which were subsequently exhibited in Berlin.[54] Shown alongside some Dutch seventeenth-century paintings and high-priced pictures by Corot, Troyon and Millet, were some magnificent Impressionist landscapes, still lifes, landscapes and figure paintings by Monet, Pissarro, Degas and Renoir.[55] Durand-Ruel could now sell a whole string of pictures to Hamburg collectors such as Eduard Behrens. Most important, however, was Lichtwark's purchase of Claude Monet's still life *Pears and Grapes* for the Hamburger Kunsthalle (fig. 105). Just a few months after the purchase by the Berlin National Gallery, Durand-Ruel had succeeded in placing an Impressionist work in another German museum.[56]

When the pictures were eventually exhibited in Berlin, Durand-Ruel's sales successes were significantly greater there than in Hamburg, as the network established by Tschudi and Liebermann proved most effective. The well-to-do Berlin bankers Julius von Bleichröder (1828–1907) and Franz von Mendelssohn (1865–1935), who later supported Tschudi when he was making purchases, bought several expensive pictures,[57] and it was with their support that Tschudi bought Millet's painting *November Evening* for the National Gallery[58] (fig. 106).

From now on Durand-Ruel concentrated on Berlin as his sales outlet. As early as the spring of 1897 he tried to build on his success and in April–May he organised his biggest exhibition to date in Germany. The place he

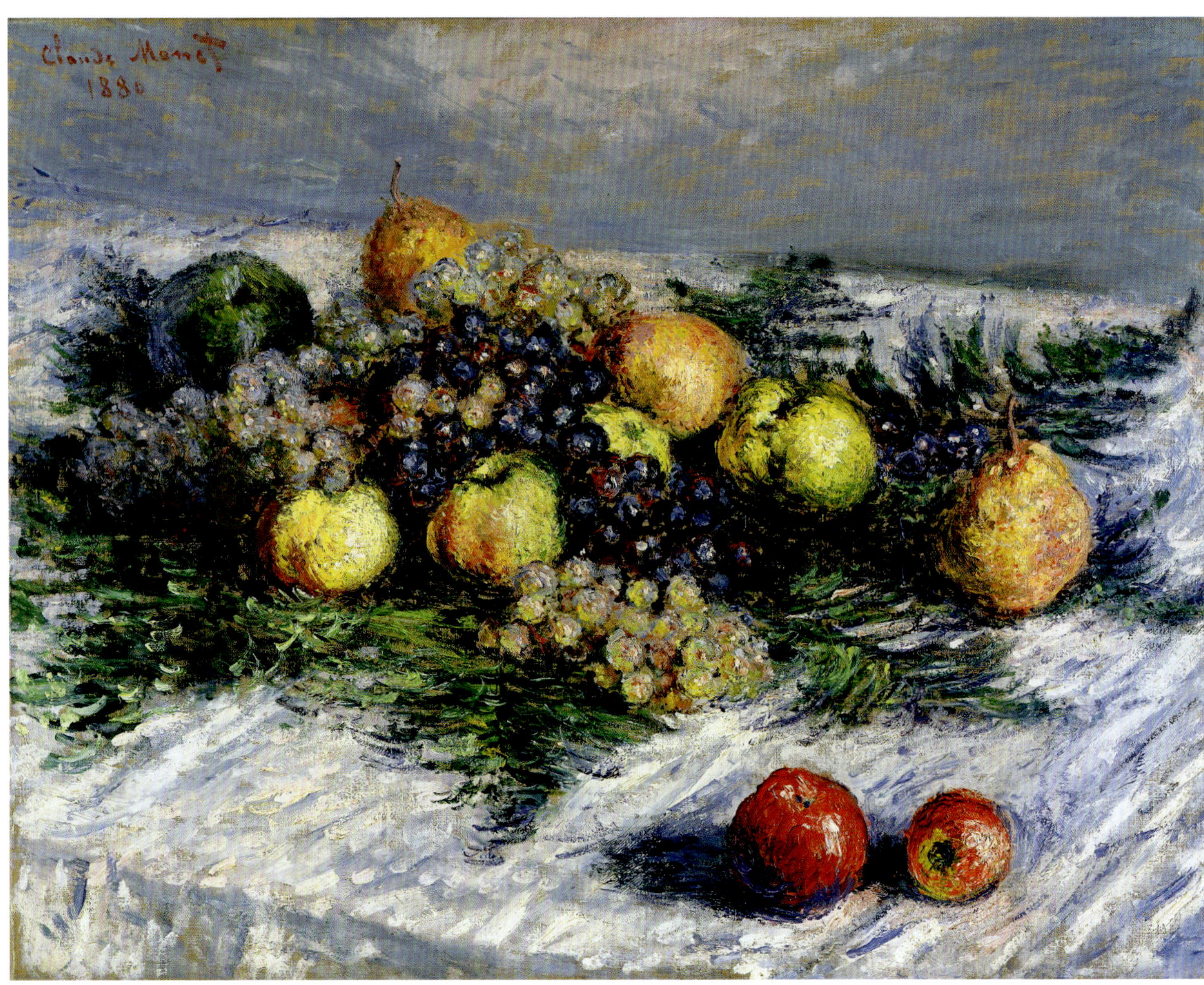

FIG. 105
Claude Monet
Pears and Grapes, 1880
Oil on canvas, 64 × 81 cm
Hamburger Kunsthalle, Hamburg
[cat. 42]

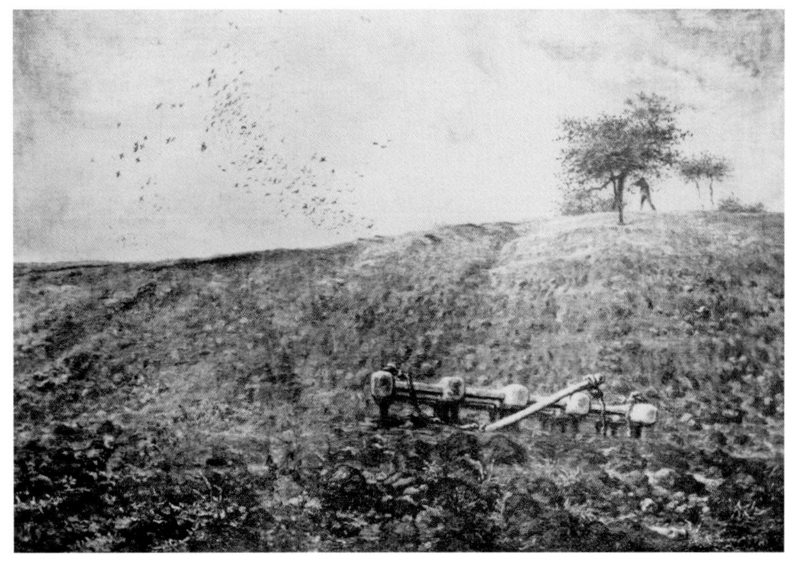

FIG. 106
Jean-François Millet
November Evening, 1870
(lost painting)
Oil on canvas, 97 × 144 cm
Nationalgalerie, Staatliche
Museen zu Berlin

chose for this event demonstrated his aspirations and underlined the quality of his pictures. The exhibition took place in the Grand Hotel Kaiserhof, the most exclusive establishment of the capital. The art critic Julius Elias (1861–1927) described Durand-Ruel's hotel presentations as 'mouth-watering elite exhibitions', saying, 'They were the first of their kind.'[59] It is true that there were no sales on this occasion, but the exhibition, which was subsequently shown in Hamburg,[60] had illustrious visitors like the editors of the journal *Pan*, founded in 1895.[61] Members of this group included museum directors such as Alfred Lichtwark, Richard Graul, Karl Woermann and Woldemar von Seidlitz, but also poets and art writers such as Julius Meier-Graefe (at the beginning), Otto Julius Bierbaum, Eberhard Freiherr von Bodenhausen and Harry Graf Kessler. Their meeting in Berlin was an important platform for exchanges about the most recent developments in the art world. Kessler noted in his diary for 2 May 1897: '*Pan* meeting. Afterwards, Bodenhausen, Liebermann, Lichtwark and Seidlitz and myself had breakfast at the Durand-Ruel exhibition'.[62] So Durand-Ruel's network was increasingly consolidated in Germany through the *Pan* editors and he also obtained a mouthpiece. As early as 1897 the journal published an essay by Seidlitz on Degas in which Durand-Ruel was explicitly mentioned.[63]

Although the expenditure on packing, transport, insurance, hotels and travel must have been considerable, Durand-Ruel did not allow himself to be deflected. In any case, gaining access to the Kaiserhof was excellent publicity. During 1897 he sold further pictures to his Berlin and Hamburg collectors and he added new customers, such as Julius Stern (1858–1914),[64] Director of the National Bank in Berlin, and the independent scholar Hans Weidenbusch in Wiesbaden.[65] Thinking that perhaps the spring date of the exhibition had been unfavourable, Durand-Ruel fixed his next exhibition for the pre-Christmas period. In December 1897 he again sent Georges to the Kaiserhof, with 29 paintings, including some by Corot, Degas, Renoir, Pissarro and Sisley. It was there that Max Liebermann himself bought a Courbet and his brother Georg bought a Sisley and a Courbet.[66] A notice of the exhibition in the *National-Zeitung* bears witness to the high regard 'the much-cited art-dealer Durand-Ruel' enjoyed in Berlin at the time: 'The artistic significance of a great number of these pictures makes this small exhibition into a big event in our artistic life'.[67] It is not obvious from the business records that there was a second showing in Hamburg, but Lichtwark ordered two pictures by Degas and a Monet to be displayed at the Kunsthalle. In addition, Durand-Ruel sent him two pictures by Courbet.[68] Lichtwark clearly wanted to win over the board of his museum to the idea of a purchase, but he was sadly unsuccessful.[69] However, he did act as middleman in the sale of a *Winter Landscape* by Monet to the Hamburg senator Gottfried Holthusen (1848–1920).[70]

In November 1898 Durand-Ruel launched his fourth and last hotel exhibition in Hamburg and Berlin. The show of 31 pictures opened at the Hamburger Hof on the Jungfernstieg and then moved to the Berlin Kaiserhof. It was there that Tschudi bought a Monet and Max Linde a Renoir.[71] But the outlay for such tours proved too high in the long run, so from 1898 Durand-Ruel began to look around for an art dealer with whom he could work as a partner.

The search for a suitable partner

At the end of September 1898, Lichtwark reported on the dynamically expanding Berlin art market, saying that 'Durand-Ruel from Paris is going to establish a branch here.'[72] Obviously that was a rumour, but it was the case that Durand-Ruel was sounding out the possibility of working with German art dealers. His co-operation with the newly founded gallery of Bruno and Paul Cassirer was the starting point.

The Berlin art writer Julius Meier-Graefe (1867–1935) established the first contact. Like Bruno Cassirer, he had been a member of the *Pan* editorial board, and since 1895 he had lived mainly in Paris where he got to know Durand-Ruel.[73] In August 1898 he approached the Paris dealer with a request for pictures by Edgar Degas to exhibit at the Cassirer gallery. Joseph Durand-Ruel resisted at first, saying that he had insufficient works by the artist available, adding: 'Nevertheless, as my brother plans to go to Berlin during the coming month, he would be happy to establish links with Messieurs Cassirer.'[74] Meier-Graefe's negotiation was successful, and Durand-Ruel sent 27 pictures by Degas and two works by Max Liebermann in addition to Berlin,[75] where they were shown from 1 November to 1 December in the Cassirers' select new premises. Designed by Henry van de Velde, these offered an elegant setting for the inaugural exhibition dedicated to Degas, Liebermann and the sculptor Constantin Meunier.[76]

The choice of artists was trend-setting. The Cassirers staked out their central area of interest in painting and sculpture as German and French Impressionism. By their choice of artists and price level, the young Berlin newcomers were targeting the high end of the market. The Cassirers themselves purchased five pictures by Degas for a total outlay of 74,000 francs – a clever move that was certainly aimed at winning over the respected French art dealer. But for the time being, Meier-Graefe acted as middleman. Durand-Ruel sent him the contract and the list of pictures for the exhibition and issued instructions for insurance and transport.[77]

Just a few weeks later Durand-Ruel delivered 38 pictures for an Impressionist exhibition at the Berlin art salon of Reiner and Keller, which took place 24 November–15 December.[78] At the beginning of 1899 the pictures moved on to the Ernst Arnold Gallery in Dresden, where Ludwig Gutbier, the son of the proprietor, organised a large Impressionist exhibition which brought together German, French and other European artists in March 1899.[79] But the dedicated Dresden art dealer could not sell any of Durand-Ruel's pictures. The market for modern art had become focused on Berlin.

Collaboration with the Cassirer art gallery

By the start of 1899, Durand-Ruel had made his assessment of the German art market. He now decided that in future he would work with the young Berlin art dealers Bruno (1872–1941) and Paul (1871–1926) Cassirer. The two cousins came from a wealthy family of entrepreneurs of Jewish origin and were financially independent – a good basis for founding the business.[80] By December 1898 they had already begun preparing the second exhibition together. In January 1899, Durand-Ruel sent a total of

26 pictures by Monet, four by Degas and two by Manet to them in Berlin. This was the brilliant start to a whole sequence of high-class exhibitions of French painting that were shown in the Cassirer gallery in the following years. Although the German Kaiser rejected French painting and even asked Hugo von Tschudi in 1899 to hang the recently acquired Impressionist paintings in a less prominent room of the National Gallery, nevertheless the response of the critics to exhibitions in the Cassirer art gallery was, on the whole, very positive.[81] In the spring of 1899 the Cassirers promptly sold three pictures by Monet and two by Degas that Durand-Ruel had sent them.[82]

From now on Durand-Ruel regularly sent large consignments of pictures to the Cassirer gallery. A particular high point of this collaboration was the exhibition of Manet, Degas, Puvis de Chavannes and Max Slevogt in October to December 1899, in which Durand-Ruel participated by contributing 13 pictures by Puvis, ten by Degas and eight by Manet, including his masterpiece *Le Déjeuner sur l'herbe*.[83] The critics celebrated the ambitious show and acknowledged Degas and Manet in particular as masters and pioneers of the Impressionist movement.[84] It was the excellent collaboration with art criticism that underpinned the future success of the Cassirer gallery. An important factor in this success was the foundation of the journal *Kunst und Künstler*, published by Bruno Cassirer from 1902 after he had parted company with his cousin. Emil Heilbut was engaged as editor-in-chief,[85] and Meier-Graefe also published in the journal regularly, so the well-tried network of Durand-Ruel and the Cassirers was united in a highly effective way.

Paul Cassirer developed further activities to promote the success of French painting. In November 1901 he opened a branch at 16, Neuer Jungfernstieg in Hamburg, to which Durand-Ruel delivered just 30 pictures. In this way he could use Cassirer to provide a service to his Hamburg clients.[86] Bruno and Paul Cassirer won a further platform for their artists, together with those of Durand-Ruel, when they became business managers of the Berlin Secession.[87] As early as March 1901, 11 pictures from Durand-Ruel were shown there, including masterpieces such as Renoir's *Lise* and Monet's *Camille* (fig. 107), which were highly praised in the press and bought a little later for the collection of Karl Ernst Osthaus in Hagen and the Kunsthalle Bremen.[88]

The exhibitions of the Berlin Secession became an important forum for German and French Impressionism in the following years. Interest was also growing in other German towns at the same time, so Durand-Ruel was asked for loans by museums and galleries throughout Germany. In 1901, 25 of his pictures were shown in the Württembergischer Kunstverein in Stuttgart, and in 1902 he sent pictures to the Glass Palace in Munich and to the Great Art Exhibition in Karlsruhe. In 1903 he even sent 20 pictures to the Great Art Exhibition in Berlin. In 1904 several groups of works went to Düsseldorf, Krefeld and Weimar; in 1906, 1910 and 1914 he sent pictures to the international art exhibitions in Bremen; in 1907 he sent batches to Krefeld, Strasbourg, Mannheim (fig. 108) and Elberfeld, and also to the Heinemann gallery in Munich.[89] With such numerous presentations the demand for Impressionist paintings in Germany increased. For the most part, Durand-Ruel dealt directly with the museum directors, but essentially the business was transacted through Cassirer.

Success and protest

Following the private collectors, more German museums now began to buy Impressionist pictures and almost always Durand-Ruel or his partner Paul Cassirer was involved. The demand received a significant boost after 1905. In that year, Paul Cassirer presented parts of Paul Durand-Ruel's private collection in his Berlin gallery,

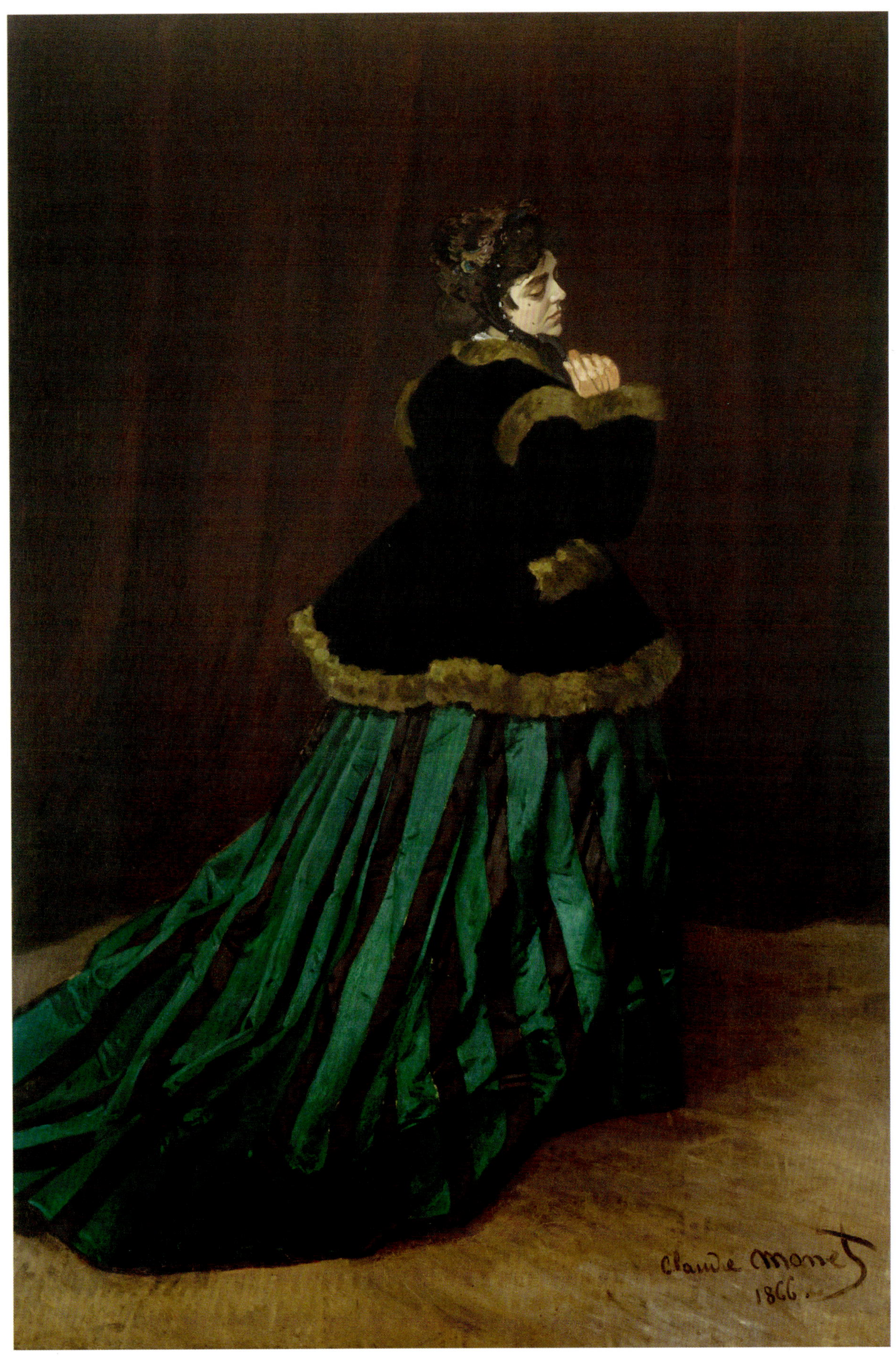
Claude Monet
1866.

FIG. 107
Claude Monet
Camille, 1866
Oil on canvas, 231 × 151 cm
Kunsthalle Bremen

FIG. 108
Pierre-Auguste Renoir
Still Life with Peonies and Poppies, 1872
Oil on canvas, 66.5 × 82.5 cm
Kunsthalle Mannheim
[cat. 69]

paying homage to the Parisian art dealer's commitment to winning over the public to Impressionist painting.[90] The previous year's publication of Meier-Graefe's *Entwicklungsgeschichte der modernen Kunst (Modern Art)*, which introduced the Impressionists into the art-historical canon, must also have increased interest among museums.[91] From now on Director Gustav Pauli systematically bought modern French works from Durand-Ruel for the Kunsthalle Bremen. In 1905 he bought a Courbet; in 1906 Monet's early masterpiece *Camille*; in 1908 Manet's *Portrait of the Poet Zacharie Astruc* (fig. 109); and in 1910 Renoir's *Madame Choquet at the Window* and Monet's *The Garden*.[92] In 1906–7 Tschudi bought two pictures by Monet, a Renoir and a Daumier[93] from Durand-Ruel for the Berlin National Gallery. The Elberfeld city museum obtained a landscape by Sisley in 1907;[94] the Hamburger Kunsthalle extended its collection in 1907 and 1910 with two

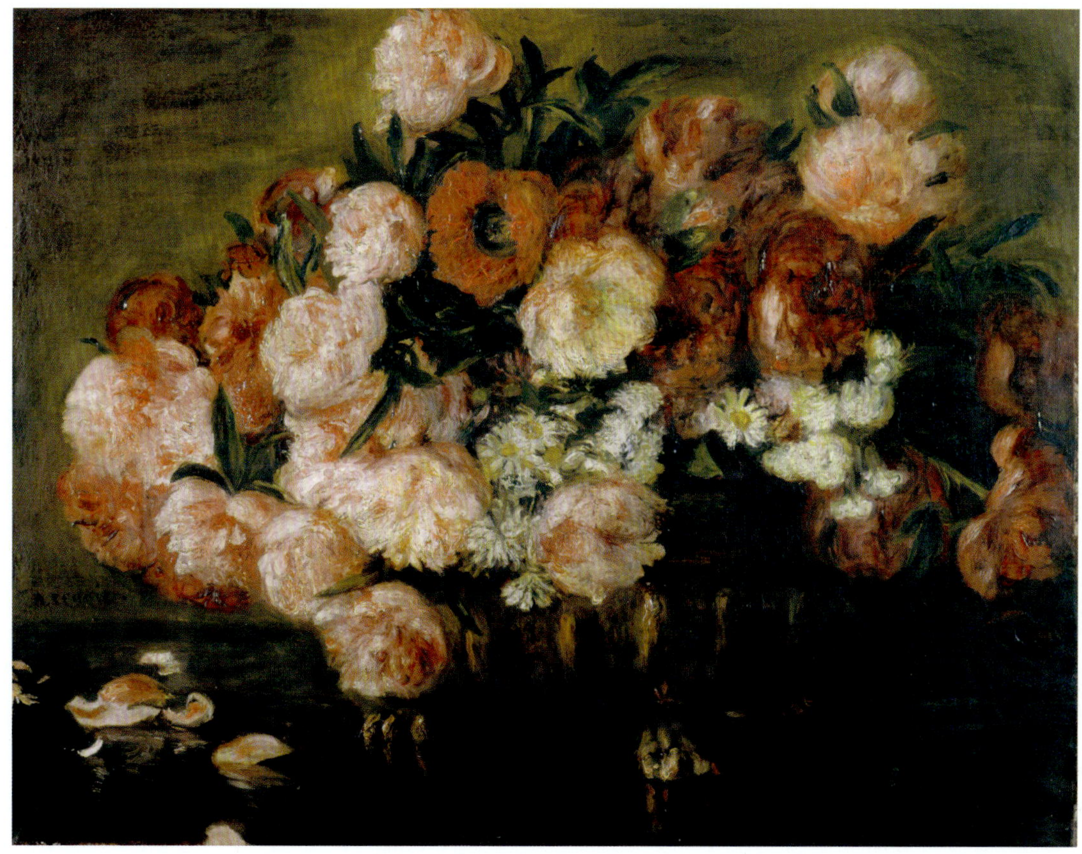

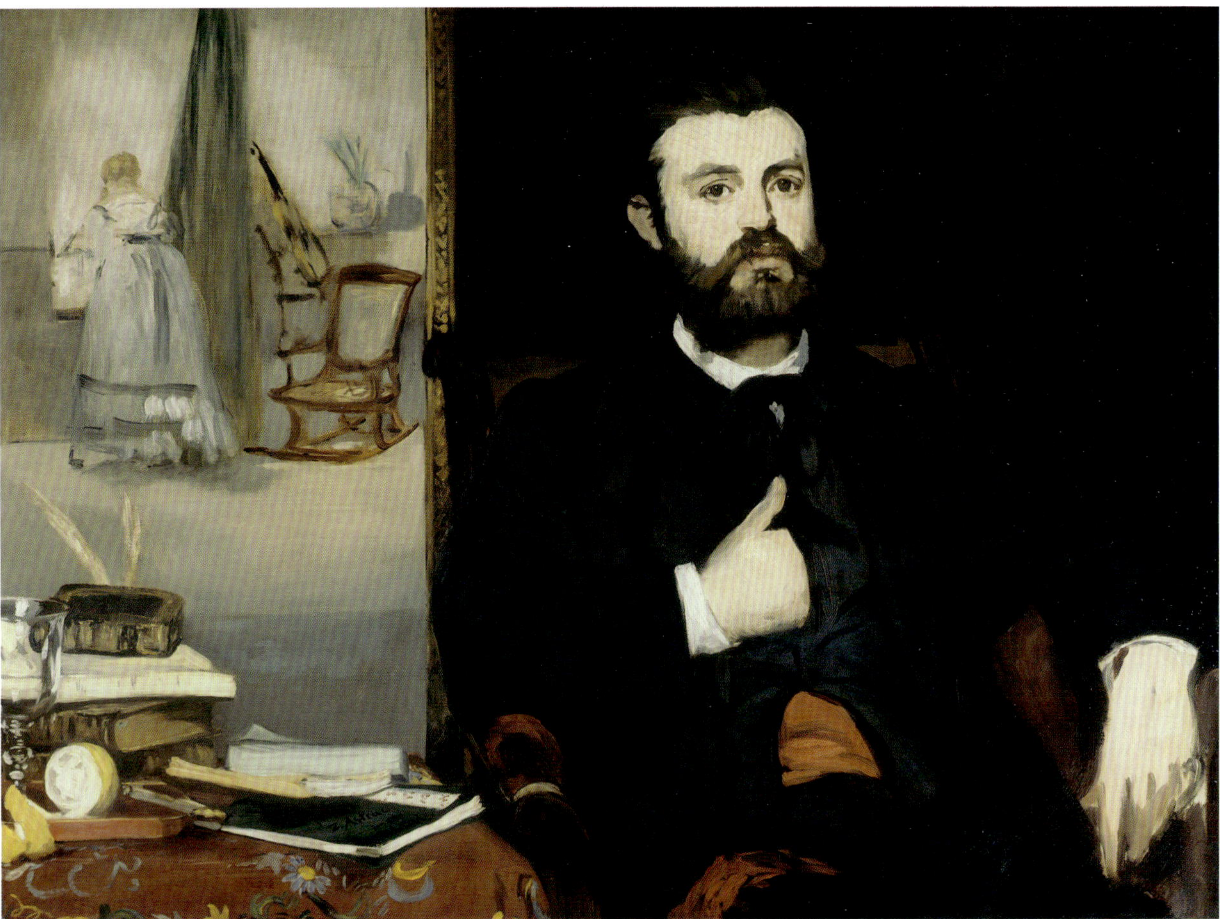

pictures by Manet;[95] and the Städel Museum of Frankfurt bought important works by Monet and Renoir in 1910[96] (fig. 110).

These successes soon provoked opposition. Already by the end of 1904 the painter Fritz von Uhde was complaining that he felt 'threatened by an art dealer plot, at the head of which stands Cassirer in Berlin as enforcer for the Parisian group Durand-Ruel'.[97] What was at first an isolated voice intensified in 1911 to an artists' dispute, which sent shockwaves through the art scene throughout Germany. The trigger was the purchase of Van Gogh's painting *Field with Poppies* for the Kunsthalle Bremen. The opponents of the purchase declaimed against a supposed flooding of the German market with poor-quality French pictures that had been bought at too high a price. But under the surface lay the real concern for the home market as well as powerful political resentment against the French 'traditional enemy'.[98] On the other hand, progressive museum staff and artists supported the director of the Kunsthalle Bremen in the battle for international modern art,[99] which was further pursued in the following years. The best evidence for this is the Sonderbund-Ausstellung (League of West German Art Lover and Artists exhibition) in Cologne in 1912.[100] Van Gogh, Cézanne and Gauguin were represented here with a broad selection of paintings and were honoured as 'Fathers of the Moderns'. The younger generation of artists was represented by the painters of Die Brücke and Der Blaue Reiter, among others.

Around that time, Paul Durand-Ruel's achievements were celebrated in Germany in various important essays. In 1912, Julius Elias wrote in the journal *Kunst und Künstler*: 'No French art dealer and art expert enjoys today such unshakeable trust as Paul Durand-Ruel'.[101] The previous year, an essay on Durand-Ruel by Arsène Alexandre had appeared in the journal *Pan*.[102] In 1913, Meier-Graefe published an article summing up Durand-Ruel's decisive role in French art dealing for the German art market in a detailed analysis of markets and prices.[103] 'The Parisian art market is international', he wrote. 'America and Germany have long had a greater significance for the Parisian dealers than Paris.'

FIG. 109
Edouard Manet
Portrait of the Poet Zacharie Astruc, 1866
Oil on canvas, 90.5 × 116 cm
Kunsthalle Bremen

FIG. 110
Pierre-Auguste Renoir
After the Luncheon, 1879
Oil on canvas, 100.5 × 81.3 cm
Städelsches Kunstinstitut, Frankfurt am Main

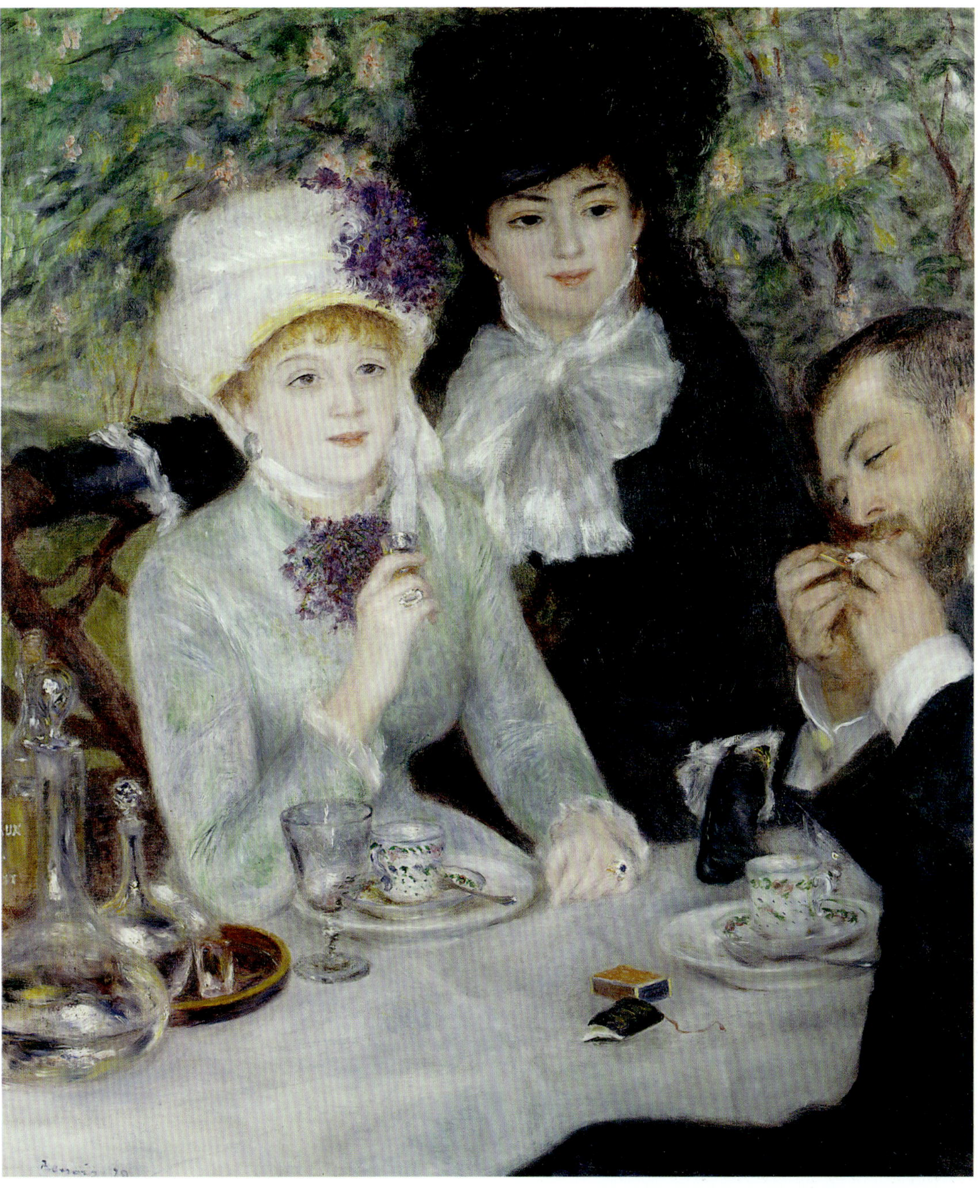

DURAND-RUEL'S CONQUEST OF LONDON

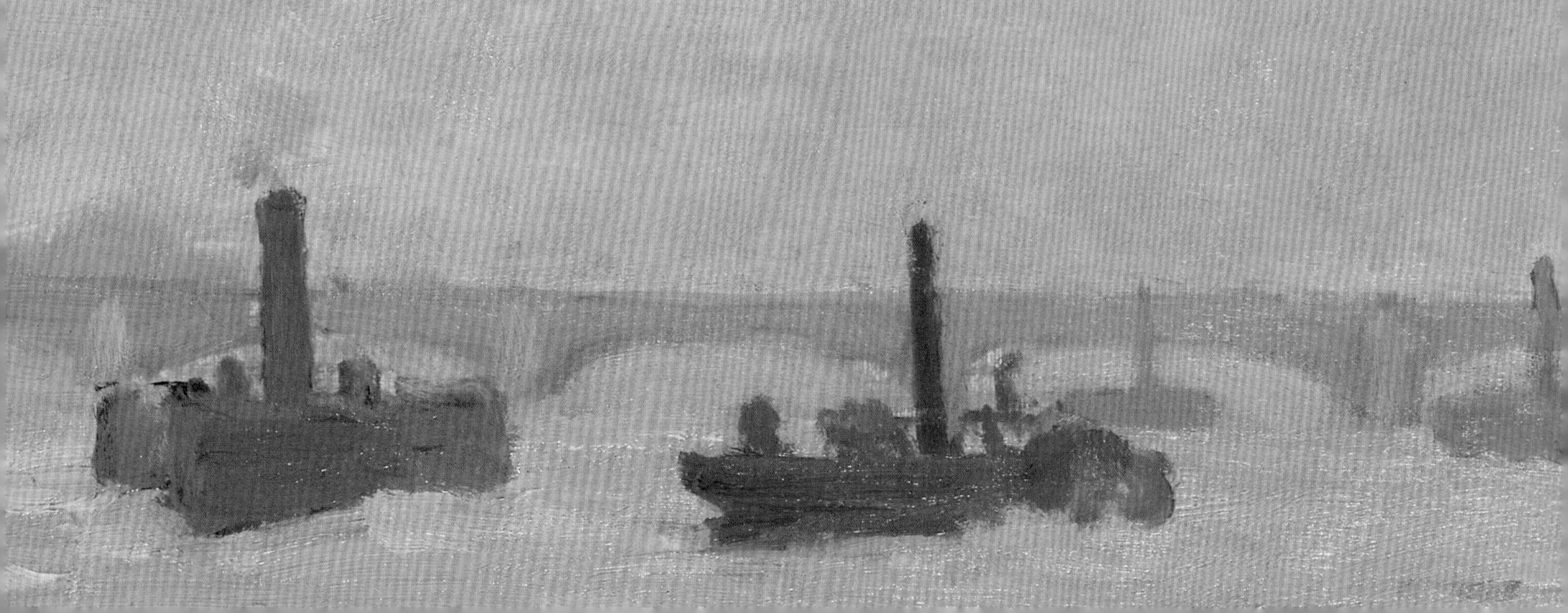

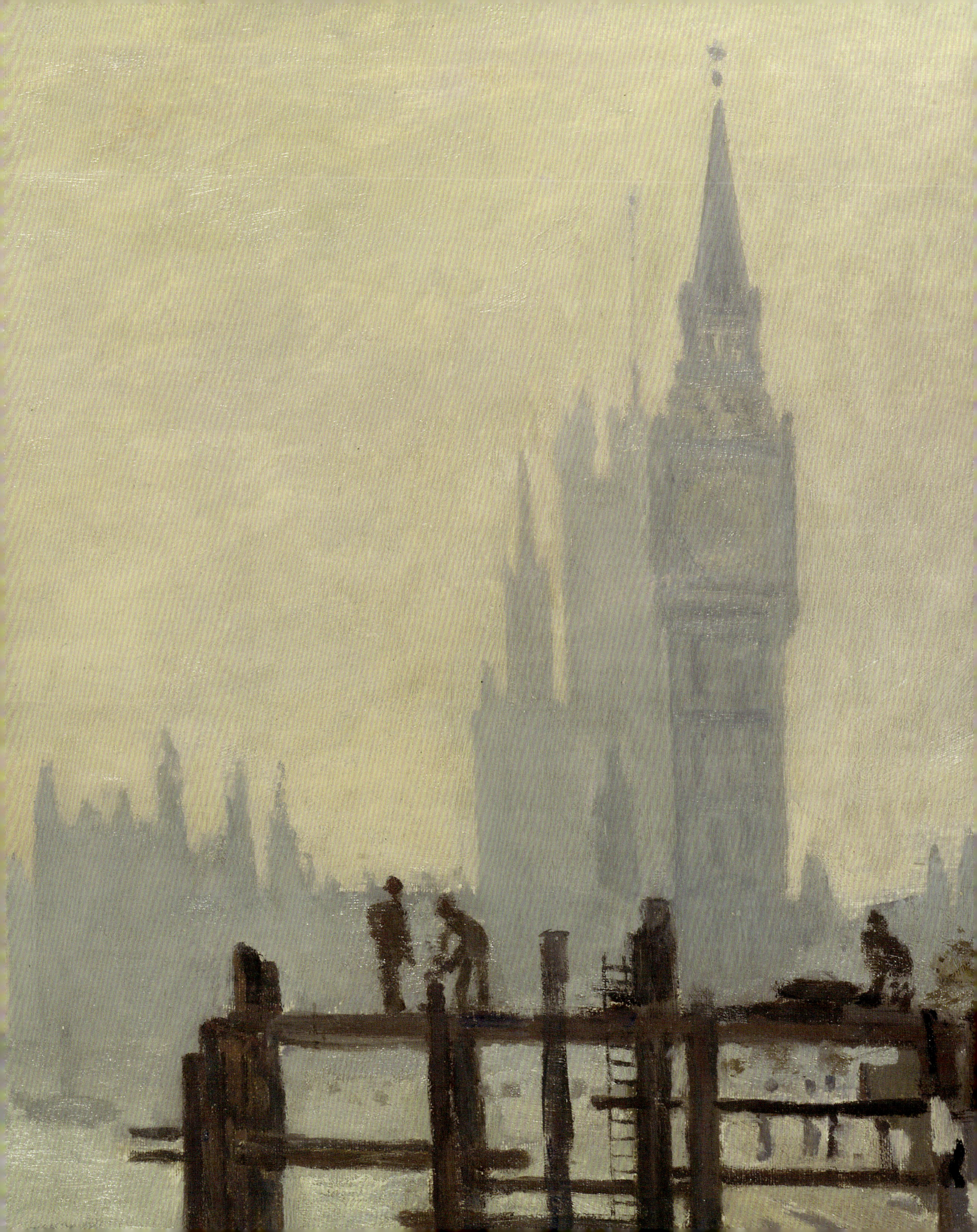

Durand-Ruel's Conquest of London

Anne Robbins

'He may not succeed, but he has come formidably armed'[1]

Visiting the landmark exhibition in the Grafton Galleries in London in 1905, an unprecedented – and unmatched – gathering of Impressionist masterpieces, a critic enthused: 'Thanks of all art-lovers are due to M. Durand-Ruel for providing Londoners with a magnificent opportunity of studying the pictures in whom for the last thirty years he has taken so courageous an interest'[2] (figs 111 and 112). The London public had every reason to be grateful, for in the previous three decades Paul Durand-Ruel, a French dealer from Paris, had – on their own territory – deployed extraordinary energy in discovering, introducing and promoting the work of the Impressionists. The 'conquest' of London was carried out in stages. It was brought about first of all by exterior circumstances – when the dealer, taking refuge from Paris during the Franco-Prussian War, set up shop in London. During the 1880s, and with the later Grafton Galleries adventure, it became part of Durand-Ruel's carefully considered strategy to win England over to his cause, and, in the words of Monet, to 'deal London a decisive blow'.[3]

'On the streets of London, where the storm had driven us'[4]

In July 1870 France declared war on Prussia. Within weeks, Durand-Ruel had diligently organised his departure from the rue Laffitte gallery in Paris, where he had settled only months earlier. Having planned the transfer of his pictures and his business to London, he left France on 8 September 1870.[5] His intention was to receive the shipment once he had arrived, then to review options about to how to resume his operations.[6] The consignment, consisting of more than 50 cases, comprised some 35 crates of pictures from the gallery stock, and some 20 more containing works entrusted to the dealer by private collectors: Laurent-Richard's alone filled 15 cases, and other pictures belonged to Verdier, Goldschmidt and the singer Jean-Baptiste Faure. The baritone's Hamlet costume also formed part of the shipment,[7] as it was needed for his operatic role at Covent Garden.[8] Faure and Durand-Ruel soon became neighbours, both living on Brompton Crescent, Knightsbridge, where the dealer started to rent 'a small house with a garden'.[9]

The London art scene Durand-Ruel encountered upon his arrival was a bustling one; an ever-growing number of galleries dotted the streets of the West End and the area south of Piccadilly, around the Royal Academy, which had moved to Burlington House three years earlier. Along with its long-established print market, London's picture trade was in full expansion. Increasingly luxurious, lavishly appointed galleries lined the streets of St James's – between jewellers and other shops specialising in luxury goods[10] – organising rapidly changing exhibitions for an elite clientele. This milieu was hardly terra incognita for Durand-Ruel; when he took over the gallery from his father, the young man had inherited a pool of British contacts with whom he had done business in the 1850s and 1860s – clients, but also dealers. The gallery's archives record a large number of transactions with England: pictures shipped to exhibitions, paintings or photographs sold to fellow dealers (occasionally bought from them too) or print publishers,[11] and pictures placed on deposit at London galleries. Thus, from the rue de la Paix office, the expediting of pictures to England (mostly conventional and saleable mid nineteenth-century genre scenes) formed part of the daily routine. In the years leading up to the Franco-Prussian War Durand-Ruel himself made repeated trips to England, visiting clients and dealers (mostly those specialising in French art).[12] The Mayfair-based Agnew, McLean and Wallis were his most regular contacts,[13] and there was occasional communication with Ernest Gambart. The Belgian Gambart was the

FIG. 111
Grafton Gallery, London, 1905
Silver gelatin print
Archives Durand-Ruel

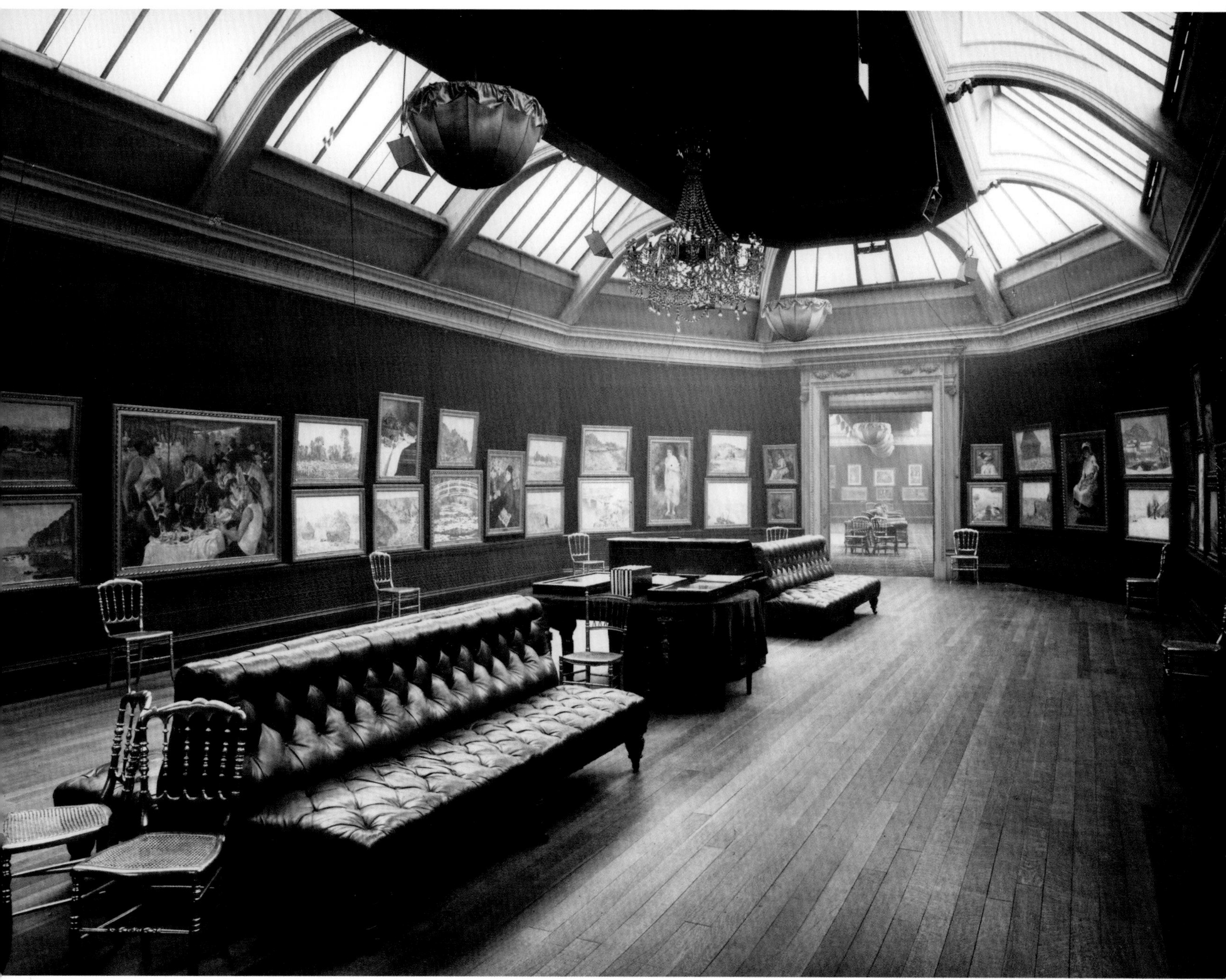

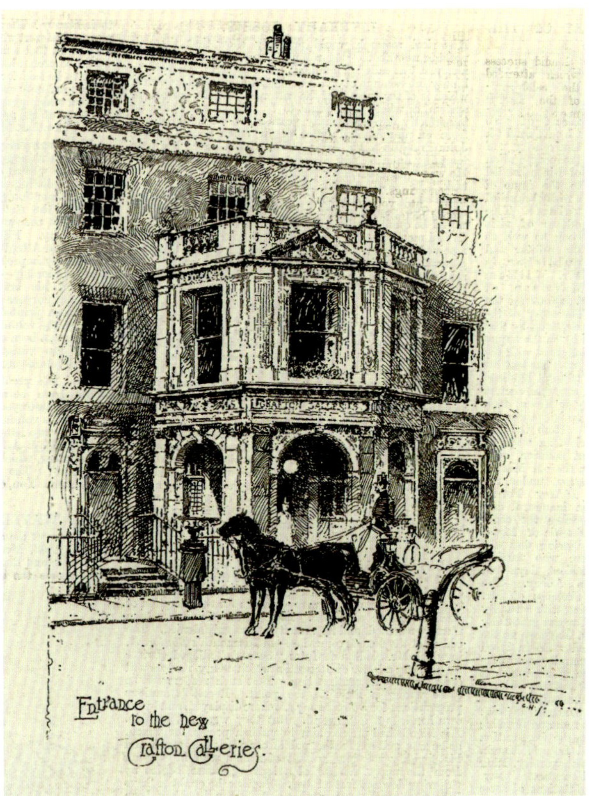

FIG. 112
Entrance to the new Grafton Galleries, opened in February 1893 at 8, Grafton Street, Mayfair, London. Drawing, published in *Illustrated London News*, 25 February 1893, p. 248

founder of the French Gallery in Pall Mall, which since 1861 had been managed by his employee Henry Wallis. When the war forced Durand-Ruel to take refuge abroad, his substantial shipment was addressed to Wallis,[14] who handled the pictures on arrival at the London customs. It was Wallis who found temporary premises[15] for the works at 7 Haymarket, in the commercial gallery of Thomas McLean – a dealer and printer who was himself a contact of Durand-Ruel. The French dealer's 'determination to go to England'[16] was not the result of a chance decision. London, far from being a random destination for his exile, was the one that offered the most business potential, and his name was already well known on the Mayfair streets that were lined with art galleries.

Durand-Ruel could also rely on a network of French artists already installed in the capital, such as the painter Alphonse Legros, resident in London since 1863, or Daubigny and Bonvin, who had fled the war and were both struggling to make a living.[17] For them, Durand-Ruel's presence in London was a gift. On 15 October Daubigny encountered the dealer,[18] who by 2 November had commissioned 'three paintings based on [his] studies of Villerville' from him. Eager to buy new pictures, Durand-Ruel visited Bonvin the day after the artist's arrival in London,[19] immediately providing these artists with providential, unhoped-for support.

Durand-Ruel's 'active solicitude'[20]

Durand-Ruel's French contacts in London generated new ones. In January 1871 Bonvin jotted down a list of artists exiled in London, which gives an idea of the wide range of painters in this French community:[21] Daubigny, but also Jean-Léon Gérôme (1824–1904), one of the most officially acclaimed artists of his time, who specialised in widely successful Orientalist genre painting and historical scenes; the lesser-known Ferdinand Heilbuth (1826–1889), a French painter of German descent; and Julien de La Rochenoire (1825–1899), a friend of Daubigny and Manet, who, like Bonvin himself, wandered as far south as Dulwich to visit its 'jewel of a museum'[22] in the autumn of 1870. His name appears in Dulwich Picture Gallery's visitors' book for 25 November, next to Alphonse Legros's and Monet's.[23] Monet also featured on Bonvin's list. The young artist, who arrived in London in the autumn,[24] was painting along the Thames when his easel 'caught the eye' of Daubigny.[25] The artists lived near each other,[26] and Daubigny introduced Monet to Durand-Ruel soon afterwards – allegedly, the day after the two painters' supposed encounter by the river;[27] in any event by January 1871.[28] The dealer was aware of Monet through his works shown at the Salon, but they had not met. Years later Monet recalled this decisive moment – the opening act of five decades of dealings with Paul Durand-Ruel:

FIG. 113
Claude Monet
The Thames below Westminster, about 1871
Oil on canvas, 47 × 73 cm
The National Gallery, London
[cat. 31]

> Several Frenchmen gathered in the Café Royal [in London] and we didn't know how to earn any money. One day Daubigny asks me what I am doing. I tell him, some little landscapes in the park [fig. 114] He tells me, 'But how wonderful. You are not going to sell this. I am going to introduce you to a dealer.' And he goes to find Durand, who had set up a shop in London to sell paintings during the war. Ever since then we have been in touch.[29]

Another regular visitor to that meeting place of refugees from Paris, the French-owned and managed Café Royal on Regent Street[30] was Camille Pissarro,[31] remembered Monet, who also credited Daubigny for introducing Pissarro to Durand-Ruel: '[Daubigny], who is filled with unbridled enthusiasm, swears to help us, Pissarro and me. "I'm going to send you a dealer", he said, and Durand did indeed arrive shortly afterwards'. However, a letter of 21 January 1871 from Durand-Ruel to Pissarro suggests the dealer encountered Pissarro's paintings before meeting him in the flesh. 'The painting you have brought me is charming and I am sorry that I was not at the gallery to compliment you myself... Your friend Monet asked me for your address. He didn't know

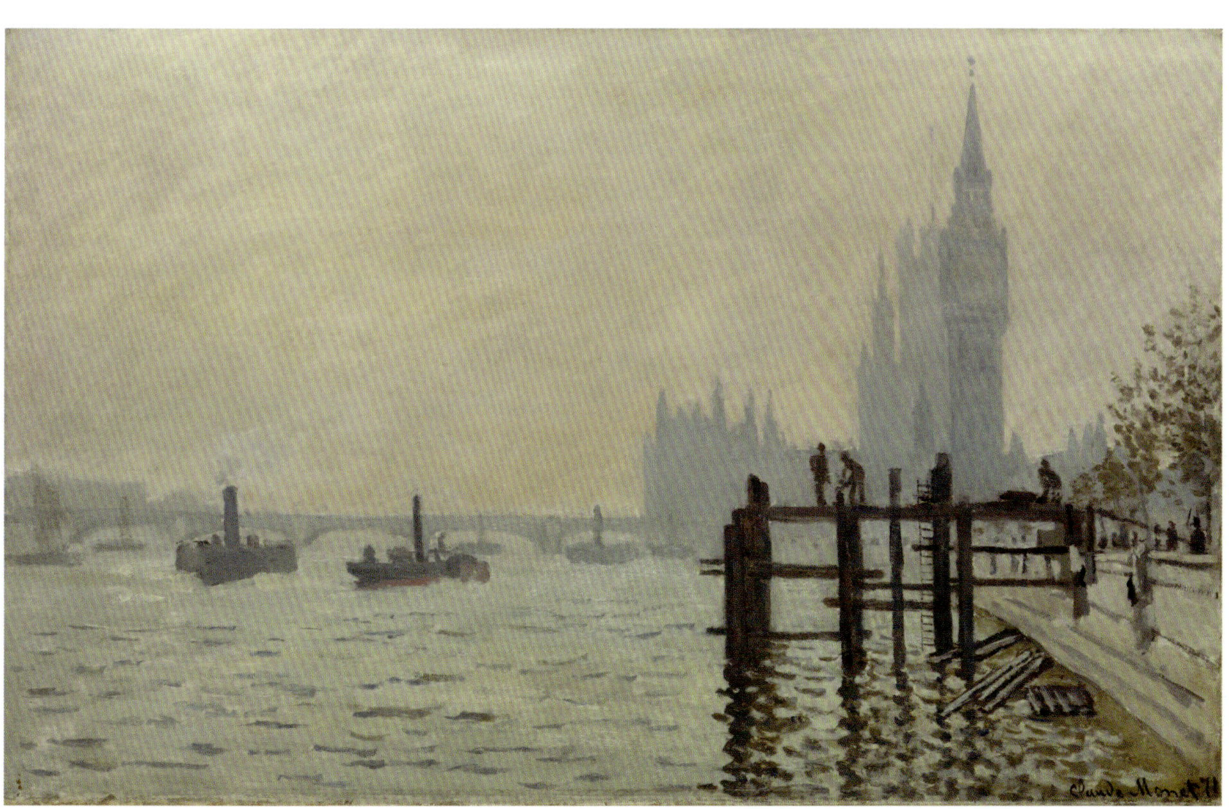

FIG. 114
Claude Monet
Green Park, London, 1870 or 1871
Oil on canvas, 34.3 × 72.5 cm
Philadelphia Museum of Art, Pennsylvania [cat. 30]

you were in England'[32] This note also suggests Monet and Pissarro had not yet come across each other in London, and that Durand-Ruel brought them together. Pissarro was struggling with difficult circumstances: 'Apart from Durand-Ruel, who bought two small pictures, my painting is not getting a single bite; this is following me everywhere.'[33] It was opportune that the dealer bought four pictures from him while in London[34] (including fig. 58), his first ever purchases from the artist. These were all recent canvases painted there, since unlike Monet, Pissarro had not brought any existing pictures to England. 'Please be so kind as to send me others as soon as you are able to. I must try to sell many of them for you here', Durand-Ruel wrote to the latter in 1874.[35]

A 'German Gallery' of French art

Durand-Ruel was soon able to show his stock and new acquisitions in London. By 29 October an 'Exhibition of High-Class French Paintings at T. McLean's New Gallery, 7 Haymarket' was ready to open, with the following notice: 'M. Durand-Ruel of Paris, having removed most of his pictures to London ... [they] will be on view during the next few days'. One was admitted 'on presentation of a visiting card.'[36]

Meanwhile, Durand-Ruel was making plans to open his own gallery, a rented space at 168 New Bond Street:[37] the German Gallery. The venue derived its name from a series of exhibitions of modern German artists it had hosted in the 1850s;[38] it had later been taken on by Gambart,[39] who staged shows of British and French art there.[40] The space – available for hire – was not affiliated to any dealer or school, though it remained known as the 'German Gallery'. The 'fairly spacious'[41] gallery consisted of two rooms, one of which was on the first floor.[42] Described as 'gaunt and staring' – before Durand-Ruel took over and turned it into a 'home of culture, skill and refinement'[43] – it at least benefited from an advantageous location, in London's exclusive Mayfair. The choice of this particular site[44] was part of Durand-Ruel's reasoned strategy of expansion, which required a careful positioning of his business among his London competitors, so as to attract his own clientele. As a dealer in French art, Durand-Ruel infringed on the market of other, more established galleries with the same 'niche' (at a time when galleries tended towards increasing national specialisation):[45] most notably the French Gallery, Gambart's establishment, by then run by Wallis. Durand-Ruel ended up organising 10 exhibitions in the German Gallery, starting with two shows in 1870–1, during his time in London. After the family's return to Paris in September 1871, the dealer kept the premises open, as the London outpost of the Paris head office, in 1872 mounting three exhibitions there, each comprising between 120 and 140 pictures. From 1873 a pace of two shows a year was set: one in the spring, when the Royal Academy's exhibition attracted a crowd of potential buyers; the second in the autumn, or off-season, when the art-deprived London public could be catered for by private galleries.[46]

In order to cultivate his own clientele in a competitive London market, Durand-Ruel set up an 'imaginary committee' composed of French painters whose reputations were already established – including in England – and whose work formed most of Durand-Ruel's London stock: Corot, Millet, Dupré, Diaz, and the London-based Daubigny, Bonvin and Legros; then Fromentin. This ingenious scheme of a made-up committee of French artists conferred undeniable allure and respectability on the New Bond Street gallery and its exhibitions. Its name, the Society of French Artists, may have been modelled on the existing Society of British Artists,[47] on whose reputation Durand-Ruel may have wanted to capitalise: 'You will see that I have placed my gallery under your patronage and that of your friends' he

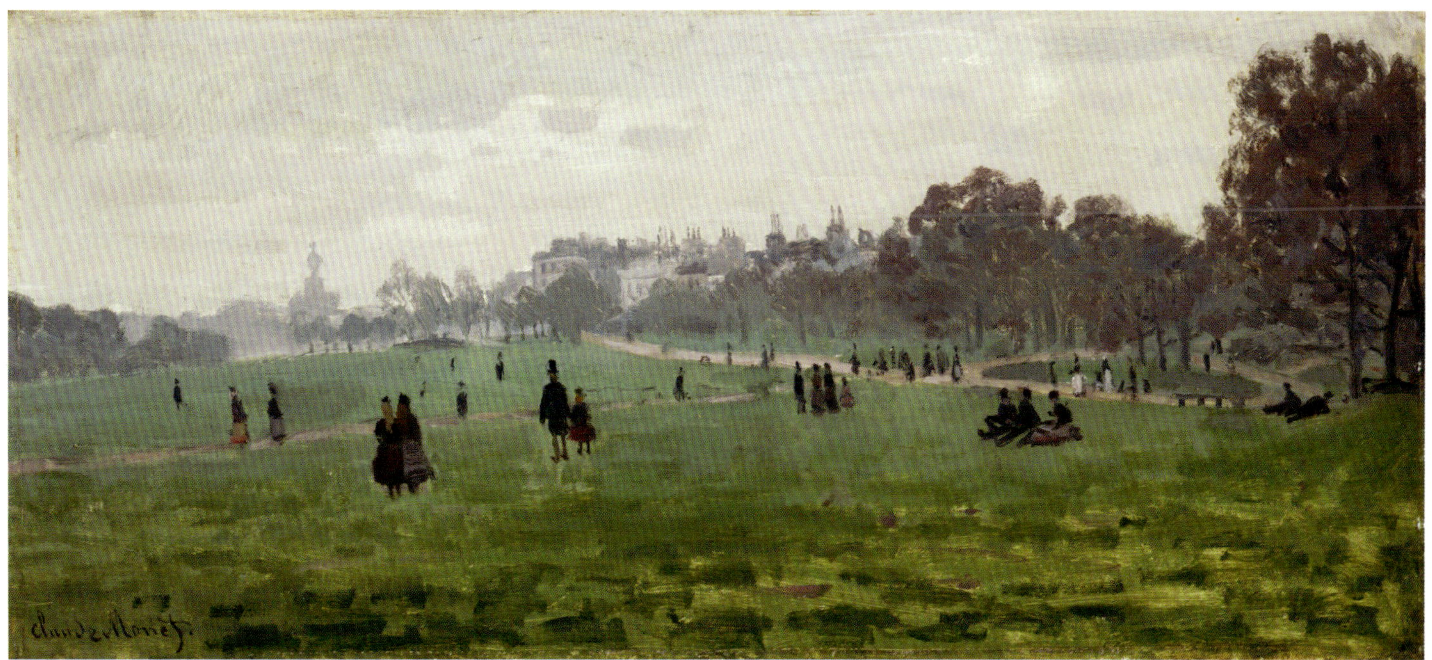

wrote to Fromentin, 'to give my exhibition an artistic cachet and to distract from the business side.'[48] The exhibitions were not solely of pictures contributed by the Society of French Artists: 'Many of the works bear the names of men who have long since passed away', wrote a reviewer of the first exhibition in February 1871.[49] No-one was fooled. A number of the pictures in these shows were indeed on loan – rather than selected from Durand-Ruel's own stock – and borrowed from private collections rather than from the artists themselves.[50]

As Durand-Ruel stated, his intention was to highlight the 'artistic cachet' of his London exhibitions: the introduction of an entrance fee (one shilling) from the second exhibition reinforced their exclusive character, and every show was accompanied by a catalogue.[51] Emphasis was placed on the gallery's aesthetic mission as a venue for the display of French art, rather than retail. Unsurprisingly the moniker 'German Gallery' soon proved incongruous,[52] and by the second exhibition in April 1871 the name had been dropped, to prevent confusion about the gallery's identity.

Durand-Ruel's efforts to take over and control the market for French art in London were not limited to his own New Bond Street gallery. When preparations were in progress for the International Exhibition, which was to open in South Kensington, the dealer ensured he was on the organising committee of its French section.[53] This was meant to serve his own interests, but also those of French art. 'There is no time to lose', he wrote in January 1871, 'otherwise, France will be horribly represented in such an important exhibition'.[54] With the Paris Commune preventing the expedition of pictures from France, a shortage of art was expected and pictures had to be borrowed locally.[55] Monet loaned two pictures,[56] including *Meditation* (see fig. 57), and Pissarro two snow scenes, one of which may have been *Fox Hill, Upper Norwood* (fig. 115).[57] All three works had been painted shortly before in London; both Pissarros were singled out in the press.[58] A substantial group of pictures from Durand-Ruel's London stock also joined the vast exhibition: David's *Death of Marat*, Regnault's *Summary Execution under the Moorish Kings of Granada,*[59] together with works by Corot, Rousseau, Courbet and some 1830 School painters; Delacroix's *Interior of a Dominican Convent in Madrid*[60] (see fig. 37) was also on view.

Some of these pictures had already been seen in the first exhibition of Durand-Ruel's Society of French Artists, notably David's *Marat*, and the large Regnault, whose display acquired particular poignancy after the painter's death at the front in January 1871, when the painting was 'shift[ed] to a much apter position than that which it formerly occupied.'[61] Pictures kept being added and removed; this constant movement, reflecting the gallery's intense activities, would also have kept the interest of the clients alive, while maximising Durand-Ruel's chances to sell.

The exhibitions Durand-Ruel organised in his New Bond Street gallery were of mixed nineteenth-century French art, 'representing … the present condition and

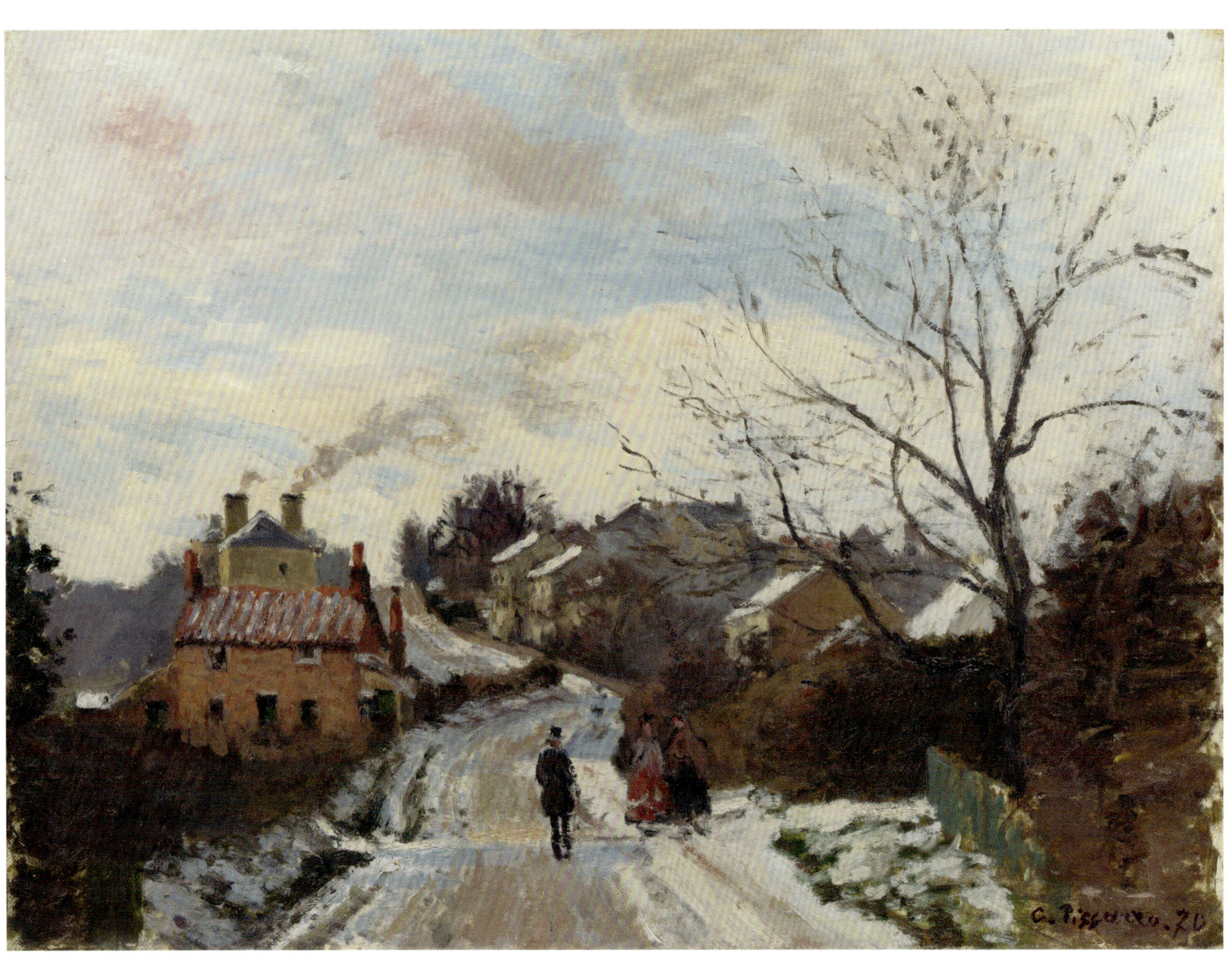
C. Pissarro. 70

FIG. 115
Camille Pissarro
Fox Hill, Upper Norwood, 1870
Oil on canvas, 35.3 × 45.7 cm
The National Gallery, London
[cat. 61]

aims of landscape and figure-painting in France'; the pictures were 'of cabinet size', consisting, from the very first show in 1870, largely of sketches and studies[62] by those artists on the Society committee, including Corot, Daubigny, Dupré, Diaz and Millet. There were exceptions such as the Regnault; and the displays were not solely of contemporary paintings but included, most notably in the first exhibitions, works by 'historic' academic artists from France, such as David and Ingres.[63] Pictures by Greuze, Chardin and Boilly were also shown.[64]

'Paris celebrities'

To get his exhibitions noticed, Durand-Ruel applied a strategy of maximum contrasts: next to the small, sketchier and cheaper paintings likely to find a buyer were displayed striking and often large canvases – 'Paris celebrities', as one reviewer put it[65] – iconic French pictures such as David's *Marat*[66] in 1871 or, in 1874, Millet's *Angelus*, which the dealer had acquired two years earlier at a record price.[67] The most famous of these was no doubt Delacroix's *Death of Sardanapalus* (see fig. 20), which Durand-Ruel sent to the New Bond Street gallery in 1873.[68] (Delacroix's work had already been shown extensively in the first five exhibitions of the Society.) Durand-Ruel's recent and sensational acquisition of *Sardanapalus* had even been reported in the British press.[69] The exhibition catalogue reproduced a quotation from Byron, and a lithograph of the picture could be purchased from the gallery.[70] A context was also being proposed for the painting, which hung next[71] to Fantin-Latour's *Homage to Delacroix* of 1864.[72] Fantin-Latour's tribute to the Romantic master showed some of the artists also represented in Durand-Ruel's exhibition – Manet for one, who featured in the New Bond Street show, with no less a statement than *The Balcony*[73] hanging in the same room – and affirmed the link between Delacroix and the younger generation of painters indebted to him.

Durand-Ruel had pioneered the idea of using a large 'manifesto painting' by Fantin-Latour (who was a fixture of the New Bond Street gallery, with 68 paintings in total exhibited in the Society shows) to introduce an exceptional painting, or group of paintings, two years earlier in his third London exhibition. There he showed, for the first time, seven paintings by Manet next to Fantin-Latour's group portrait *Manet's studio at Batignolles, Paris* of 1870 (Musée d'Orsay),[74] a vibrant homage to a painter whose reputation in England was mostly negative.[75] The same exhibition also contained a refined touch: pottery by Laurent Bouvier,[76] whose ceramic work can be seen in the vase on the table to the left of Manet in Fantin-Latour's painting.

A French gallery of British art?

Following the display of pottery by Laurent Bouvier, the following year Charles Cazin's ceramics were shown.[77] The artists, both French, embraced the Arts and Crafts aesthetic, and their work probably gave the New Bond Street exhibitions an unexpected 'English' look. An intriguing feature in Durand-Ruel's fiercely French exhibitions was their British art component, starting in early 1872 when nine British pictures – including five drawings by Edward Burne-Jones[78] – were introduced into the third of Durand-Ruel's shows. By then the dealer had returned permanently to Paris,[79] having appointed Charles Deschamps as the new Secretary of the Society of French Artists.[80] In the dealer's absence, Deschamps was in charge of managing the space. As the nephew of dealer Ernest Gambart, and a friend of the painter Alma-Tadema and the ageing Pre-Raphaelites,[81] the young man arrived with both a network of contacts – which no doubt facilitated business with British and British-based artists such as Edwards and Whistler[82]

FIG. 116
Charles-François Daubigny
St Paul's from the Surrey Side, 1871–3
Oil on canvas, 44.5 × 81 cm
The National Gallery, London
[cat. 10]

(and collectors) – and his own taste, giving the gallery a subtle new orientation. Gambart and Deschamps are portrayed in Alma-Tadema's large painting *A Picture Gallery in Roman Times* of 1874, where it is believed Paul Durand-Ruel also features (to the right, seated in profile).[83] Deschamps showed a few paintings by Alma-Tadema and his wife too in Durand-Ruel's Society exhibitions;[84] as well as pictures by Whistler[85] and the Francophile Edwin Edwards.

The introduction of non-French paintings into these shows was probably aimed at widening the audience for them, and encouraging visitors to draw parallels between the French and the English schools, often compared by critics. This also created another level of contrasts, in keeping with Durand-Ruel's strategy of opposing large and small pictures, old and recent, expensive and cheap, famous and unknown – all enhancing each other. Variety in subject matter was also sought, with views of Paris and its surroundings contrasted with pictures of London by Edwards or Daubigny[86] (fig. 116).[87] Recent works by Monet and Pissarro, executed during their London exile, were also shown: Pissarro's *Sydenham* (see fig. 58) in early 1872;[88] Monet's *Green Park* (fig. 114), displayed later that year alongside the artist's earlier, more finished Paris picture *Saint-Germain l'Auxerrois*;[89] and Monet's *Thames below Westminster*[90] (fig. 113) exhibited in the New Bond Street gallery in the spring of 1873.

Monet and Pissarro

In 1871, Durand-Ruel started to show the work of these two artists, his fellow refugees in London. There, as he recalled, he began by 'slipping'[91] into his mixed shows of French art two London pictures by Pissarro, including *View in Upper Norwood* (possibly fig. 115), and a view of Trouville harbour by Monet.[92] These went unnoticed, blending in seamlessly with other landscapes by Barbizon or Society of French Artists painters displayed on the walls. Yet only two years later, the Monets in the sixth Society exhibition – which included *The Thames below Westminster* (fig. 113) – and the Sisleys were acknowledged as forming a school of painting distinct from its predecessors, its young French exponents described as 'defiant and uncompromising'.[93]

This shift can be explained by the increasing number of works by the painters later called Impressionists being introduced in the Society exhibitions of 1872 and 1873, which reached a peak in the summer of 1872 with 18 paintings out of a total of 128. By then Durand-Ruel had returned permanently to Paris, where he embarked on actively buying, at a quick pace and in large numbers, the works of these young artists and of Manet.[94] The new purchases were immediately sent to London for exhibition. Displays there mirrored the dealer's activities in Paris, with 14 Manets shown in 1872, instantly following the dealer's block-purchase of the artist's studio contents.[95] Among these, selected to convey the variety of the artist's production, were *The Reader* (see fig. 52), *The Salmon* (see fig. 53), *The Fife Player* (see fig. 87) and the 'peculiarly effective' *Moonlight at the Port of Boulogne* (see fig. 54). One critic commented: 'Consummate knowledge is apparent here, notwithstanding the roughness of the painting'.[96] It was also on the walls of Durand-Ruel's London gallery that, as early as 1872, Degas's and Sisley's work was exhibited for the first time in Britain,[97] as well as Renoir's in the next show,[98] and Morisot's the following year.[99] Monet had introduced Renoir to Durand-Ruel shortly before, and the first Renoir on display in London – *The Pont des Arts, Paris,* 1868 – was also the first picture the dealer had acquired from the artist, in March 1872. The Sisleys on display also reflected the dealer's recent purchases.[100]

Despite Durand-Ruel's attempts to adjust his exhibitions to the local clientele, only a handful of the 83 'modern' pictures exhibited in the 10 German Gallery

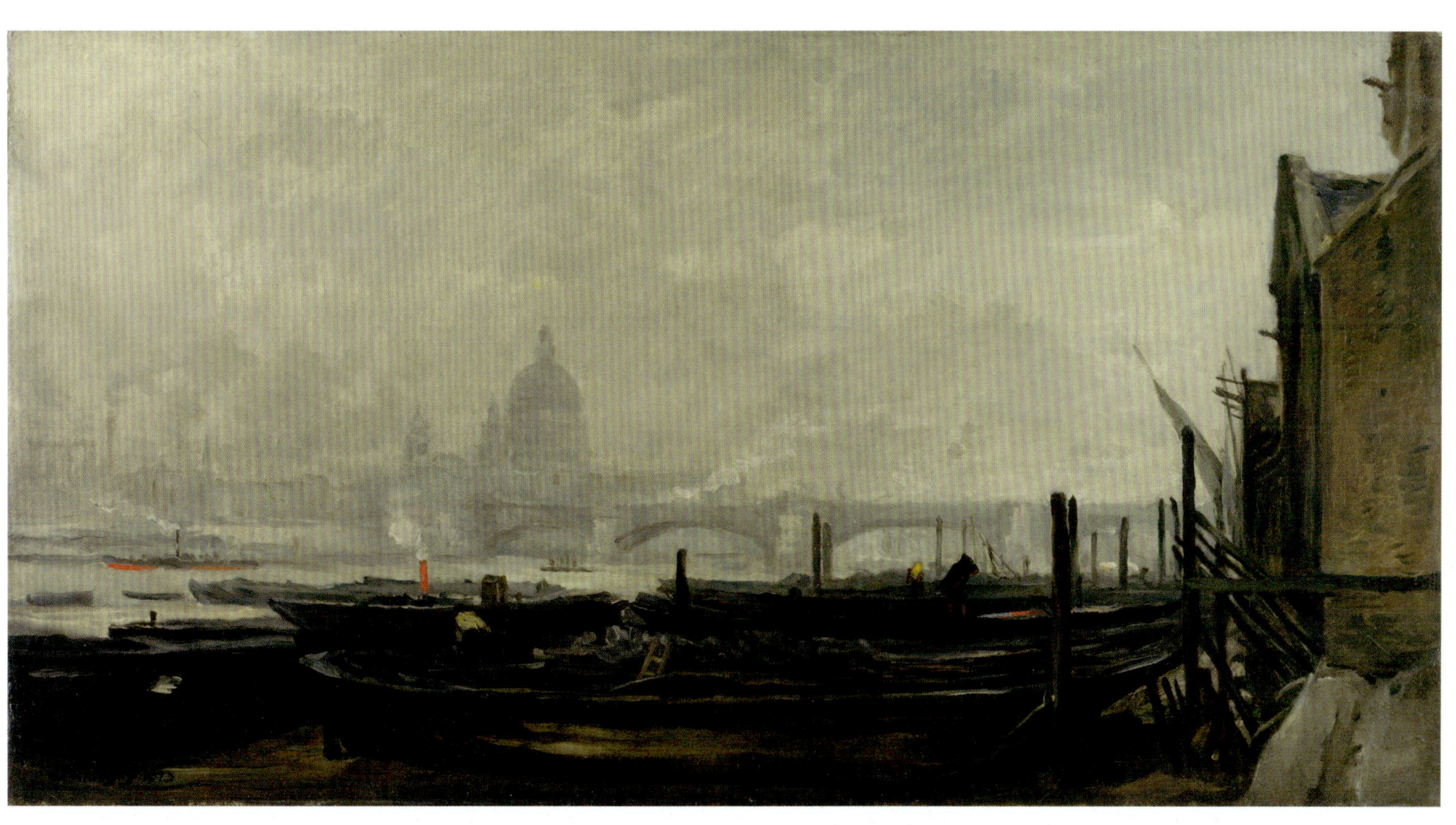

FIG. 117
Edouard Manet
Eva Gonzalès, 1870
Oil on canvas, 191.1 × 133.4 cm
The National Gallery, London
[cat. 26]

exhibitions found buyers. In 1873 a defiantly industrial-looking painting, Monet's *Factory*, was 'slipped' into a display of more rural pre-Impressionist landscapes.[101] The picture was probably intended for England's mercantile collectors, but these showed no interest in buying images of modernity, and the prevalent taste was for dark Barbizon paintings. Likewise, the Degas pictures selected for the sixth exhibition in the spring of the same year were all of horses: images designed to appeal to the English predilection for sporting subjects. These actually sold, but to a Frenchman – Faure, the London-based baritone, and a regular client of Durand-Ruel's.[102] Among the soon-to-be-called Impressionist pictures shown in the Society exhibitions, those by Degas were considered the least disconcerting; featuring figures, they probably appealed to a Victorian sensibility. The artist stood out as the leader of the group, and his pictures tended to sell better:[103] the first sale of a modern painting from these shows was a Degas, *The Dance Foyer of the Opera at rue Le Peletier* (see fig. 62) acquired by Louis Huth in December 1872.[104] Huth, the son of a German banker, and director of an insurance company, was a great collector of Whistler, who may have taken him to the New Bond Street gallery.[105] Another buyer at the London branch of the Durand-Ruel gallery was Captain Henry Hill of Brighton, Quartermaster in the 1st Sussex Rifle Volunteers,[106] who in 1874 purchased the first of seven Degas's he was to acquire from Durand-Ruel in London in the next two years.[107]

These sales, albeit scarce, were the first transactions of these types of 'new' pictures made by any dealer in Britain; Durand-Ruel's London exhibitions had given these artists the first opportunity to show their work outside of the Salon, and to enter the commercial gallery system. In November 1874[108] financial difficulties forced Durand-Ruel to withdraw from the Society, and its directorship was handed over to Deschamps, who organised two more shows under its banner.[109] After four years and well over 1,000 pictures shown in the German Gallery, one critic wrote that 'the exhibitions of the society of French Artists [had] made for themselves a unique place in the London Art-season'.[110] What is more, a distinctive new school of French painting had emerged, heralded that same year in Paris with the first Impressionist exhibition. These were young artists 'determined ... not [to] allow themselves the least attempt at ideal pathos or dignity', as Sidney Colvin observed as early as 1872.[111] By the eighth exhibition in 1874, Durand-Ruel had made his reputation as the dealer of the new group: a Frenchman influenced by contemporary French modes in art, representing 'the more daring and eccentric of these.'[112]

Britain's first Impressionist show

It was not until the early 1880s that Durand-Ruel resumed his exhibitions in Britain, with three isolated shows in London, held in the space of existing art galleries after the dealer had given up his New Bond Street *pied-à-terre*. The closing of the gallery, after Deschamps's own exhibition in 1876,[113] ended the possibility of Impressionist paintings being seen in London, where other dealers had yet to embrace the cause of the 'new painting'. Meanwhile, in the early 1880s, back in Paris Durand-Ruel had invested heavily in these avant-garde painters, turning them into the gallery's special field. The dealer returned to London specifically to promote and sell Impressionist pictures rather than mixed French paintings, and his exhibitions in 1882 and 1883 were the first explicitly Impressionist shows in Britain.

The most important was the second,[114] with 65 works displayed in the gallery of Charles William Dowdeswell at 133 New Bond Street[115] – a stone's throw from the German Gallery. This show had been preceded the previous summer by a 'little exhibition' of about ten pictures, 'in a small room near St James's street,'[116]

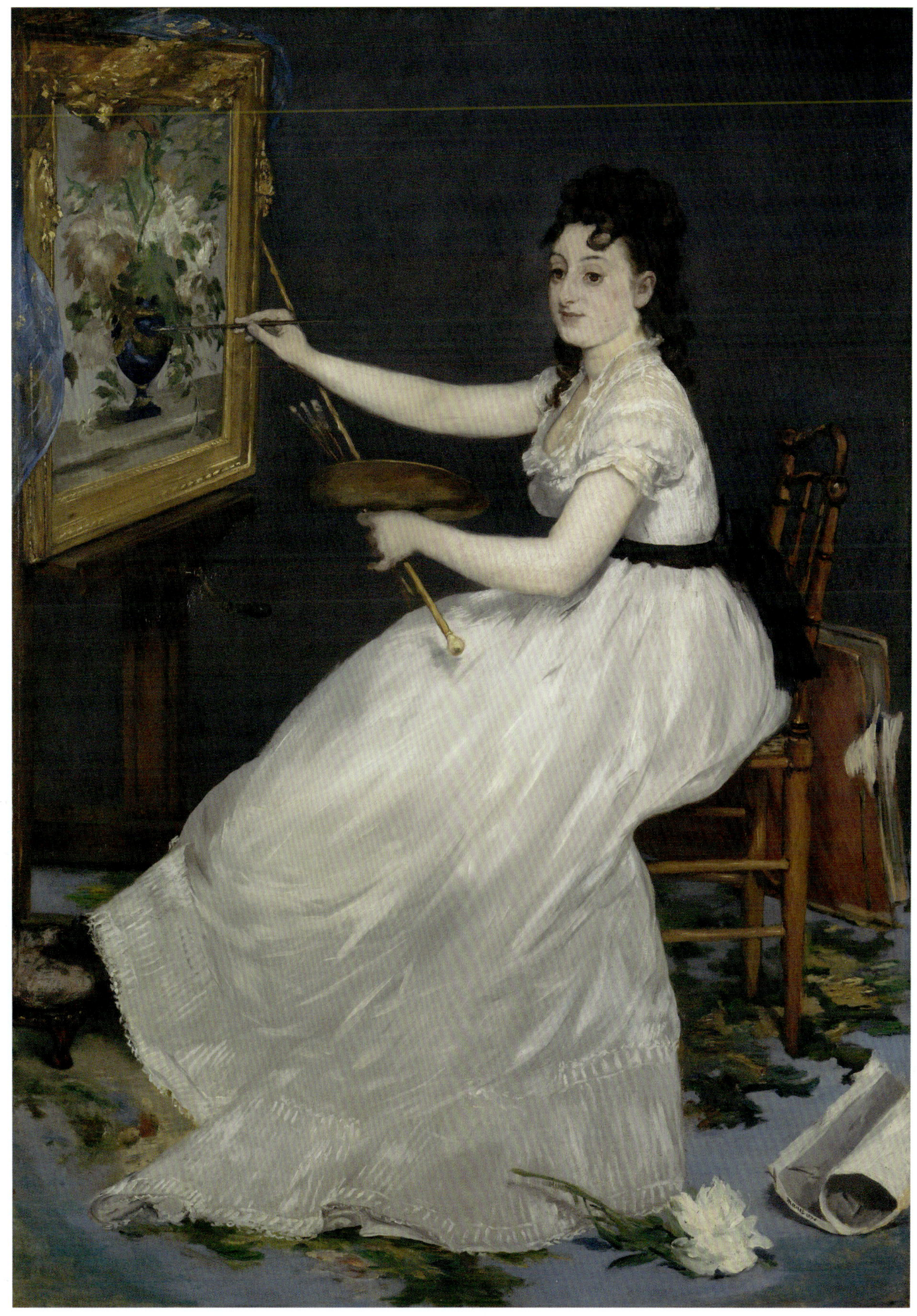

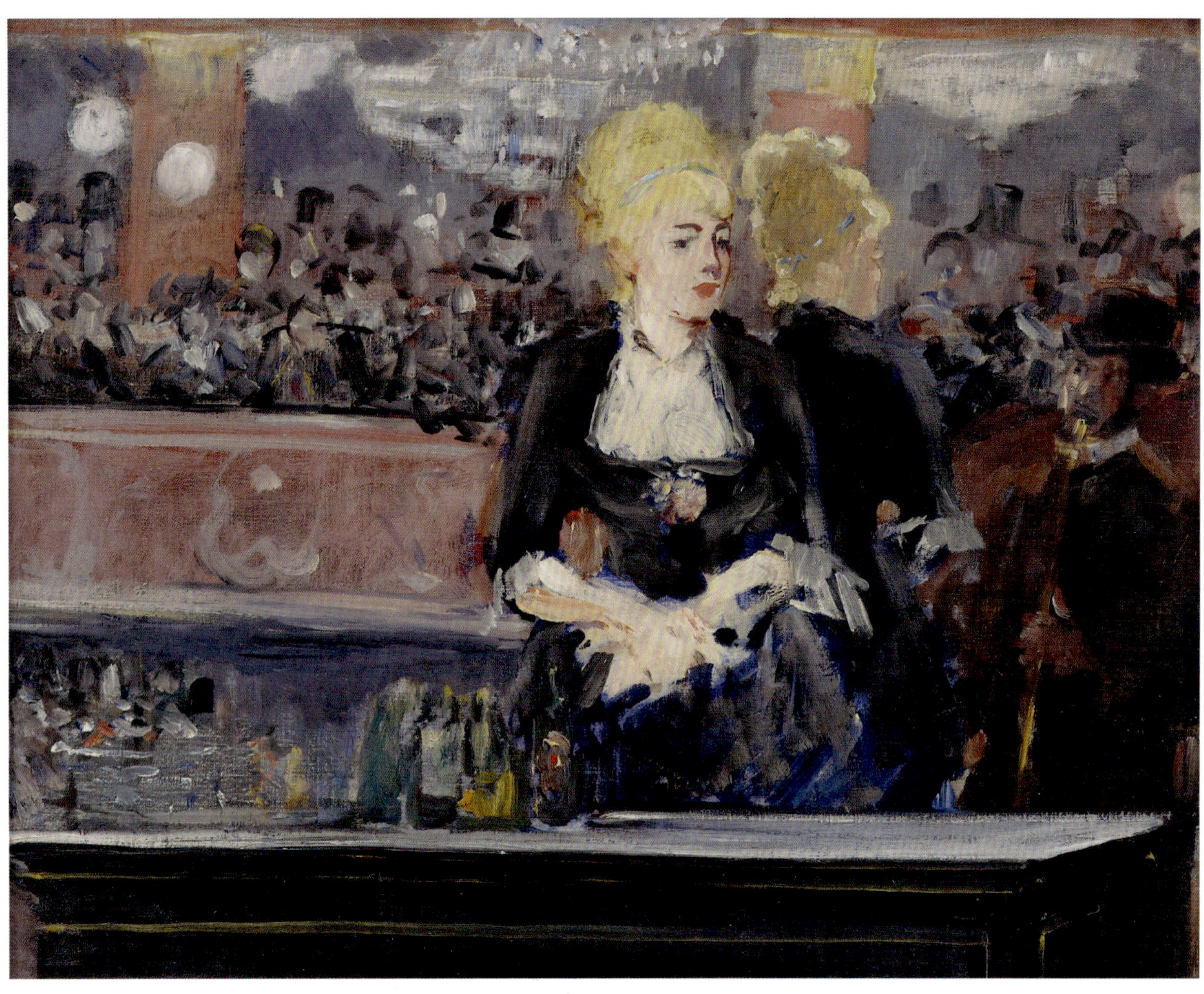

FIG. 118
Edouard Manet
Bar at the Folies-Bergère, 1881
Oil on canvas, 47 × 56 cm
Private collection
[cat. 27]

a prelude to the 1883 exhibition, yet 'scarcely representative.'[117] In May 1884 another modest display followed, in Piccadilly's Dudley Gallery, London's famous Egyptian Hall,[118] which included five Monets; one of these, *Autumn Effect at Argenteuil* (see fig. 75), featured in all three shows.[119] Thus, for three summers in a row Durand-Ruel re-established his presence in London, at a time of great commercial crisis for his organisation. Impressionism did not sell, and in January 1882 the bank that had been backing him in Paris had gone bankrupt. To an extent Durand-Ruel's new venture in London was again brought about by circumstances: this time not war, but severe financial setbacks, and the pressure to turn the tide.

In 1883, the dealer was organising in Paris a series of monographic shows devoted to each of the Impressionists, stressing their individuality. Yet the exhibition at Dowdeswell's in the same year aimed to present these artists as a coherent, cohesive group, reinforcing their collective identity – something London had not yet had a chance to see and assess. The show comprised pictures by Cassatt, Morisot, Degas, Monet, Sisley, Renoir and Pissarro. Works by Boudin and John Lewis Brown (a French painter of Scottish descent), both on the fringes of Impressionism, were also part of the exhibition,[120] as well as three Manets, including the *Pont de l'Europe*, at £400 one of the two most expensive pictures for sale.[121] Prices were indicated in the catalogue, whose preface, attempting to give a definition of Impressionism, referred to an article by Frederick Wedmore published earlier that year – then the first significant piece written about Impressionism in English.[122] It also quoted Théodore Duret, inserting an untranslated paragraph from the latter's foreword to the catalogue of the recently closed Renoir one-man show at Durand-Ruel's Paris gallery.[123] On the occasion of the Dowdeswell exhibition, the official-sounding 'Société des Impressionnistes' was chosen to enhance the title of the show, which was intended for the enlightened connoisseur. The names of the pictures were also printed in French. These were challenging works, largely recent: Pissarro's pictures of peasants, and Monet's Normandy paintings executed a few months earlier, such as *Road at La Cavée, Pourville*[124] (see fig. 77), surrounding the aggressively modern Manet *Pont de l'Europe.*[125] Degas's images of horses and dancers cemented his position as leader of the new school and Renoir, a relative newcomer,[126] was a revelation for the London public: 'After Degas [he is] really the strongest of the school', exclaimed a reviewer, who also deplored the absence of Renoir's *Dance at Bougival.*[127] The large canvas (see fig. 5) was added to the show at a later date,[128] where it was no doubt given pride of place, and a high price tag.[129]

The exhibition, forcefully asserting the importance of the new school of painting, was largely ridiculed, the pictures deemed too sketchy, too bright.[130] It proved a commercial failure[131] (not even the Manets sold, despite reports of the painter's death 10 days after its opening).[132] With the subsequent show in 1884 it marked the start of period of inactivity in London, when the promotion and sale of Impressionist paintings was taken over by other firms: Goupil, who organised the first Monet one-man show in Britain;[133] Alexander Reid in Glasgow; and new exhibition societies such as the New English Art Club[134] or the International Society of Sculptors, Painters and Gravers,[135] which occasionally borrowed works from the Durand-Ruel Gallery in Paris.[136] The most motivated collectors of Impressionism would travel to France for their purchases, and from the mid-1880s Durand-Ruel had successfully transferred his efforts to the American front: 'Monet is more familiar in American backwood towns than here', resented the critic D.S. MacColl in his review[137] of an exhibition of 51 paintings[138] held at the Hanover gallery in 1901.[139] This show, organised by Durand-Ruel, left Monet unimpressed ('For me, it did not have the desired effect at all').[140] Not a single picture

FIG. 119
Camille Pissarro
Pont Boieldieu, Rouen, Rainy Weather, 1896
Oil on canvas, 73.6 × 91.4 cm
Art Gallery of Ontario, Toronto
[cat. 68]

sold. But it may have renewed Durand-Ruel's interest in the British art market, prompting him, undeterred, to prepare his last great assault on London – this time carefully plotted.

The Grafton Galleries, 1905

Durand-Ruel's project of a much larger exhibition in London was debated with Monet in an exchange of letters throughout the year 1904. 'Staging an exhibition by several painters would, in my opinion, be unwise to start with', warns Monet, 'those that I have seen in London have done more harm than good, and, because of the number and quantity of exhibiting artists, have baffled the public that knows very little about us'.[141] In January 1905, an exhibition of colossal proportions opened in London: a staggering 315[142] paintings shipped and displayed by Durand-Ruel in Mayfair's Grafton Galleries,[143] round the corner from the now familiar New Bond Street.[144] All the pictures selected were (with the exception of Boudin and Manet), 'canvases painted only by [members of] the group', and both their quality and calibre was astounding, with a majority of these actually coming from Durand-Ruel's own private collection.[145]

'An exhibition of unusual magnitude and completeness'[146] and an exceptional event on every account, the show took place in a venue matching its scale. The Grafton Galleries, a place of entertainment and leisure, was a series of rooms that could be hired separately or as a whole[147] for exhibitions, concerts and dances; the Music Room, the largest of them, had a recess that could accommodate an orchestra. The venue was under French management: M. Benoist, its owner, treasurer and manager was also its caterer and chef. A large restaurant in the basement and a club on the upper floors made it 'one of the most beautiful places to dine in London'.[148] Dealers or art societies would stage their shows in its monumental rooms. Even before Durand-Ruel's 1905 exhibition, modern continental painting had been seen there: the Galleries' inaugural exhibition 12 years earlier included the Degas's highly controversial *L'Absinthe*,[149] and in 1903 Durand-Ruel himself had sent some pictures to an exhibition of French art.[150]

The show was meant to impress. From the entrance vestibule visitors descended a few steps to enter the so-called Octagon, where Durand-Ruel chose to display Boudin's work as a prologue to Impressionism, together with a few Renoirs, whose *Two Sisters* (see fig. 94) hung among an assortment of Monets and Pissarros (fig. 119). The Octagon led into the vast Music Room, its curved stage blocked off with a false wall adorned with more pictures, Pissarros and Renoirs. This gallery was dominated by Manets, with large canvases such as *Eva Gonzalès* (fig. 117) anchoring the display, alternating with smaller ones (*Bar at the Folies-Bergère*, fig. 118). There a door opened into two adjoining rooms: the Long Gallery devoted largely to Renoir, with his great *Luncheon of the Boating Party* (see fig. 33) from Durand-Ruel's private collection, as its centrepiece. Opposite, Renoir's *Dancer* (see fig. 70) and his *Girl with Cat* (see fig. 35) were interspersed with pictures by Monet and a few Pissarros. Finally, in the End Gallery, works by Pissarro hung on one side of the room, pictures by Sisley on the other in a display that comprised *February Morning at Moret-sur-Loing* (fig. 120) and *View of the Thames* (fig. 121). The show culminated with Degas, at the far end of this gallery, starting with *Miss La La* (fig. 123) and a group of ironing women, ballet dancers and horse-racing scenes (including the fine *At the Races, before the Start* (fig. 124) forming the vista from the Music Room).

The carefully curated exhibition was a retrospective of Impressionism of the sort no-one had ever attempted. Organised largely as a series of monographic displays in a single show, it started with Boudin, presented as anticipating Impressionism and among all artists on display

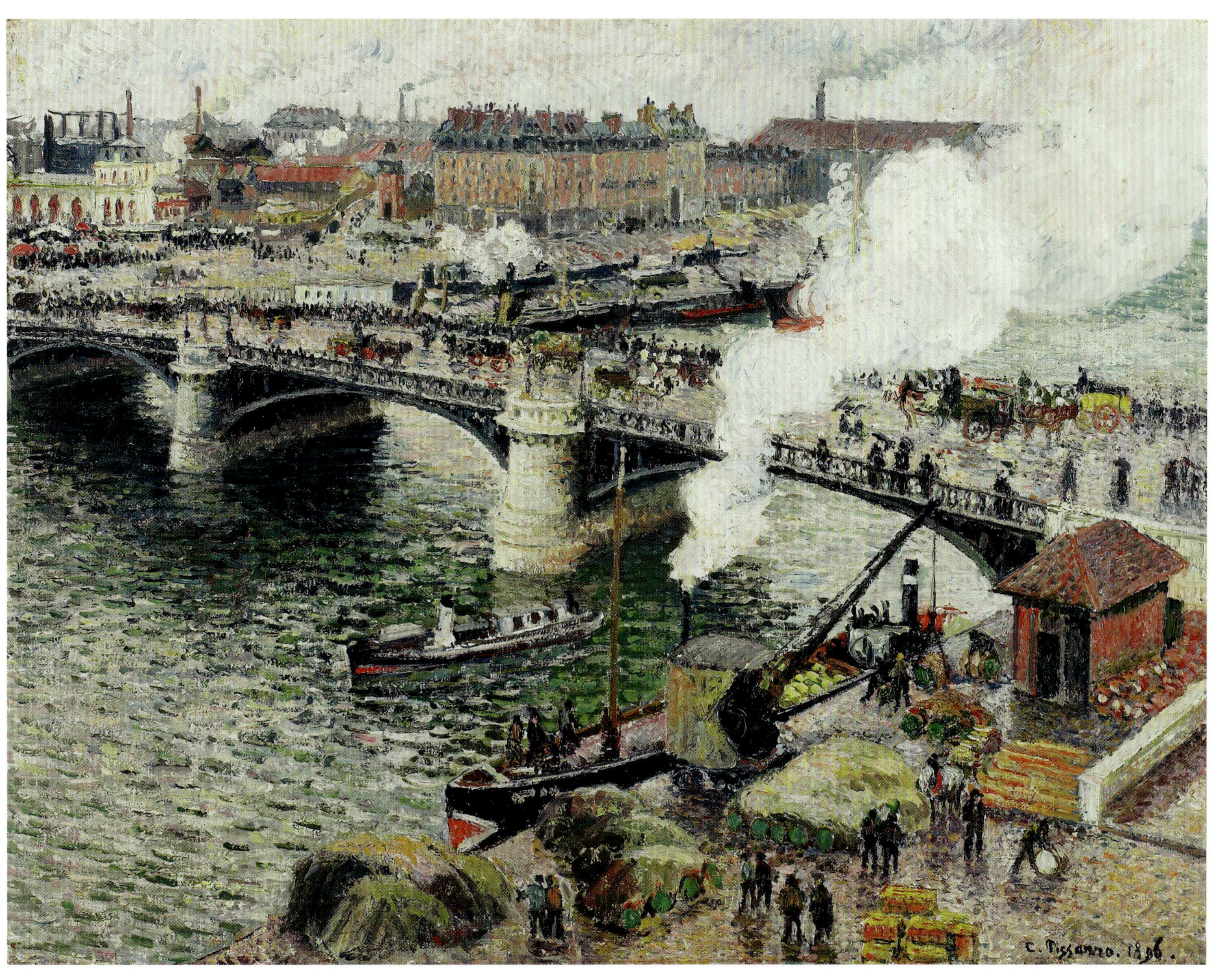
C. Pissarro. 1896.

FIG. 120
Alfred Sisley
A February Morning at Moret-sur-Loing, 1881
Oil on canvas, 50 × 65 cm
Private collection

FIG. 121
Alfred Sisley
View of the Thames: Charing Cross Bridge, 1874
Oil on canvas, 33 × 46 cm
The Andrew Brownsword Arts Foundation
[cat. 91]

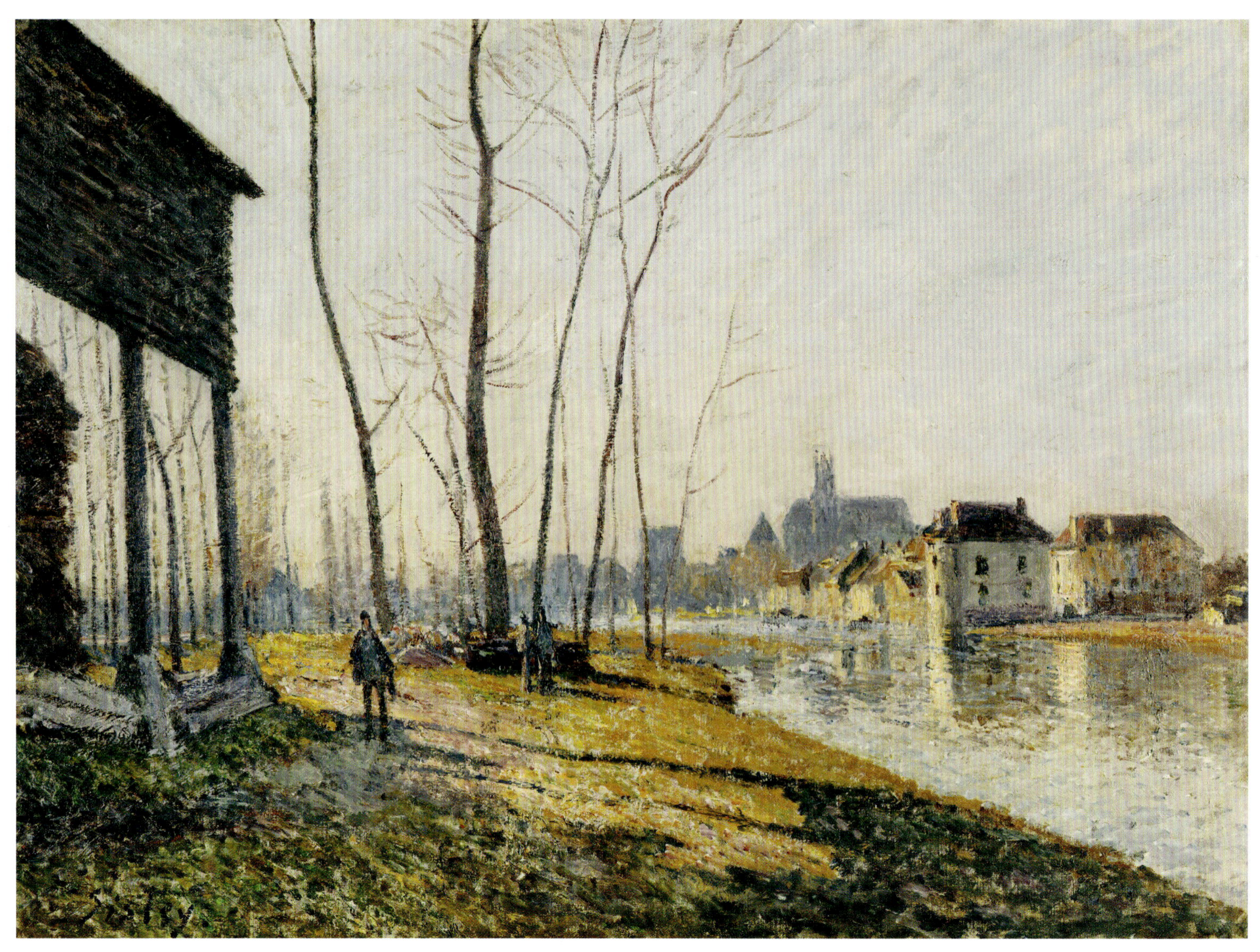

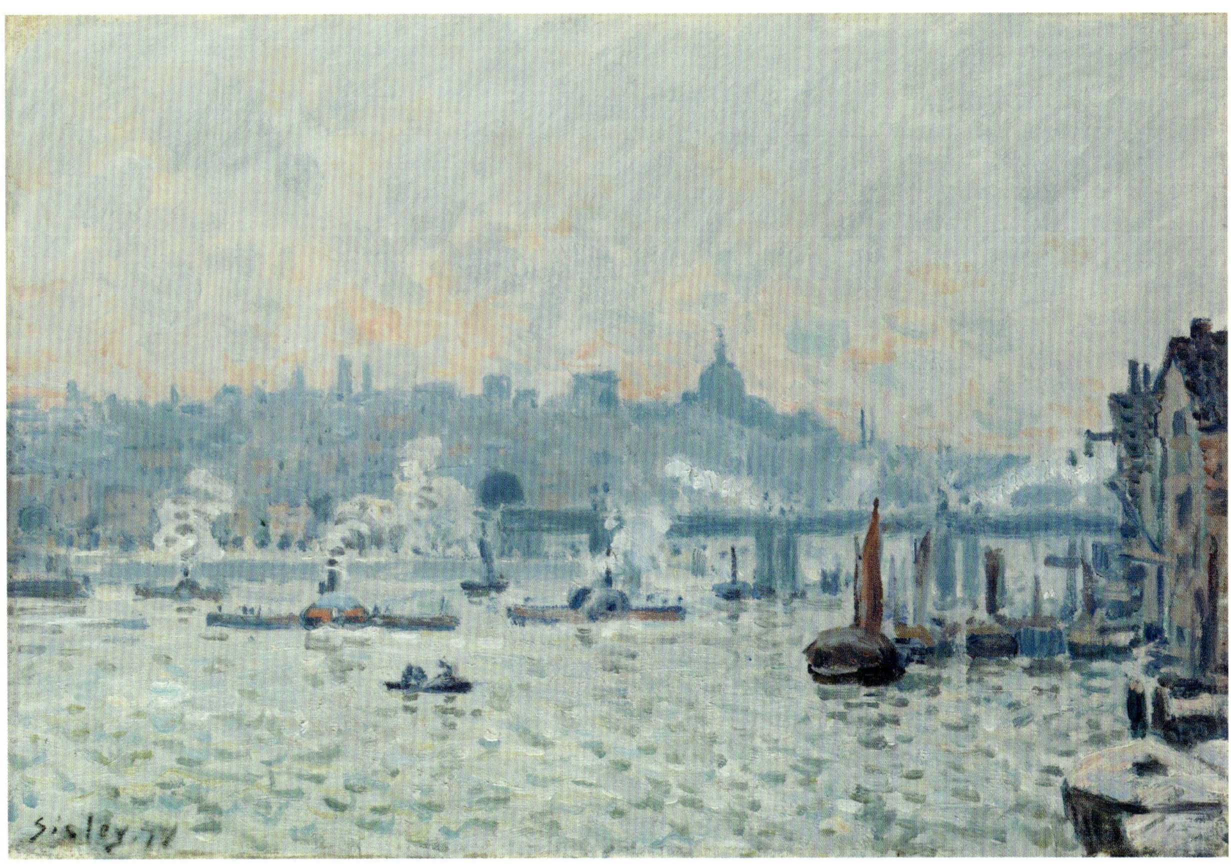

the least provocative. Pictures by Manet, the arch-priest for the group, followed: 'a persistent record of a certain ugly aspect of life.'[151] His *Music in the Tuileries Gardens* (fig. 122) adjoined a Cézanne landscape – two modern manifestos side by side. The well-orchestrated crescendo grew towards Degas's recent works, daring pastels executed, in some cases, a few months earlier.

Among the 55 Monets, not one of the painter's Thames series pictures was included, despite their likely popularity with the London public. The painter had specifically asked Durand-Ruel not to display any of his 'Londres', as he was planning to exhibit them in a separate show[152] (prompted by the success of Durand-Ruel's exhibition of Monet's London pictures in Paris).[153] The project never materialised, but despite the absence of Monet's London views the exhibition was considered exhaustive – 'by far the most representative exhibition of the kind that London has ever seen' – providing visitors with a chance to judge and understand Impressionism. 'Now, through the good services of Messrs. Durand-Ruel and Sons, at the Grafton Galleries, London has its first opportunity of studying their works', wrote the critic Everard Meynell.[154] In some quarters, resistance remained as the term 'Impressionism' retained its connotation of ridicule; visitors also complained about the timing of the show, inconveniently scheduled in the winter.[155] But from the point of view of its attendance the exhibition was a great success, attracting huge crowds, including art students and visitors of note – royalty such as Princess Louise, Duchess of Argyll, and the statesman and politician Joseph Chamberlain.[156] Over 11,000 people saw it, 'a larger number than had visited any two exhibitions in the same galleries for many years past'.[157] On Saturday 5 March alone, 2,927 people visited, walking through galleries that could hold 500 guests at a time.

However, only a feeble total of 13 sales from the exhibition was recorded, almost exclusively to foreign collectors: the celebrity photographer Baron de Meyer bought a Monet and a Morisot;[158] the American expatriate painter Romaine Brooks purchased a Degas;[159] the latter's *Miss La La* was acquired by Toronto millionaire Cawthra Mulock; the French soprano Blanche Marchesi bought two pastels of dancers by the same artist.[160]

FIG. 122
Edouard Manet
Music in the Tuileries Gardens, 1862
Oil on canvas, 76.2 × 118.1 cm
The National Gallery, London
[cat. 22]

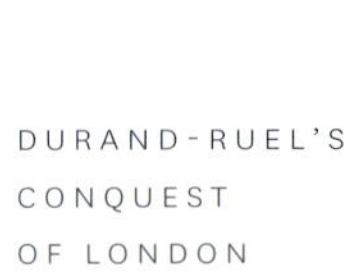

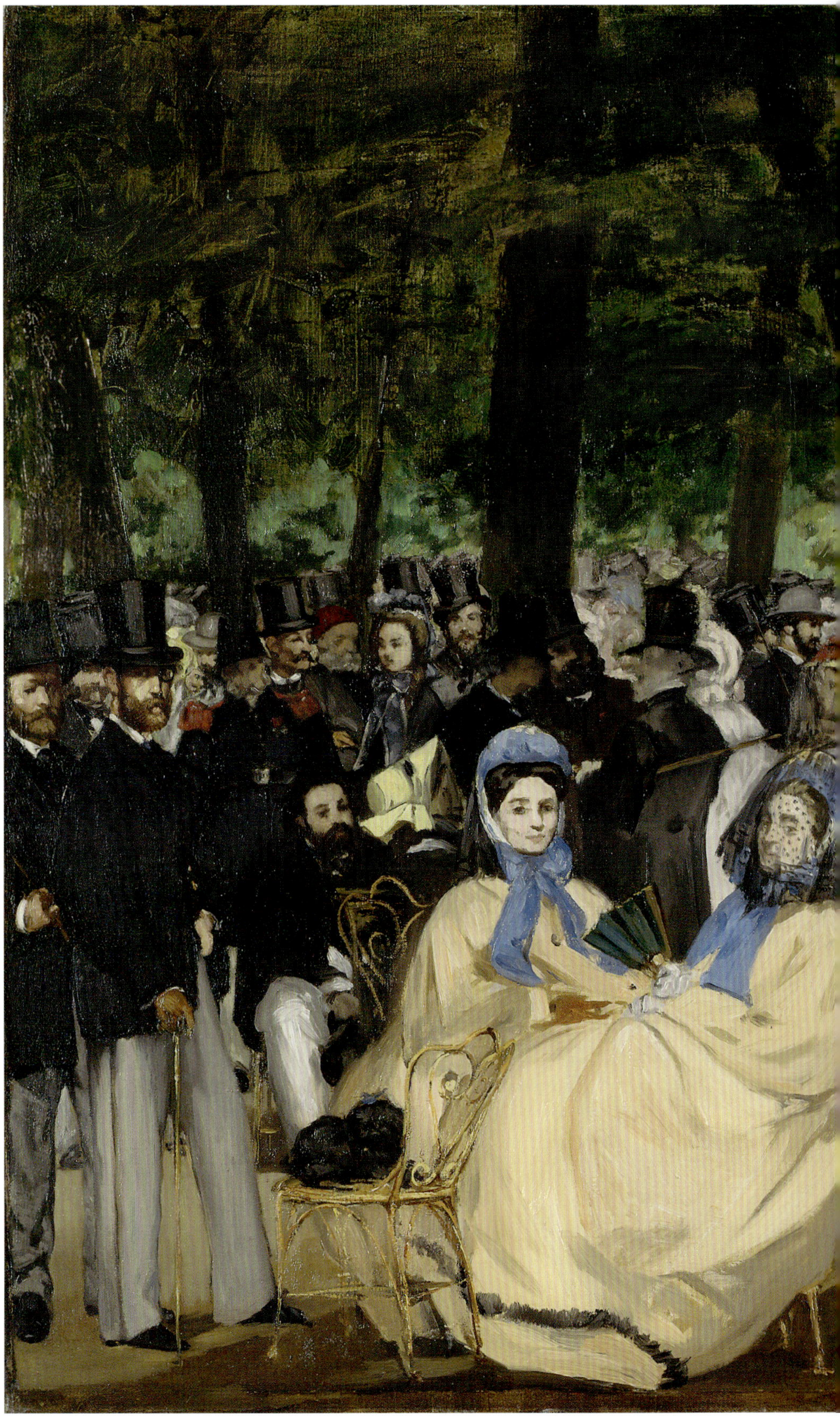

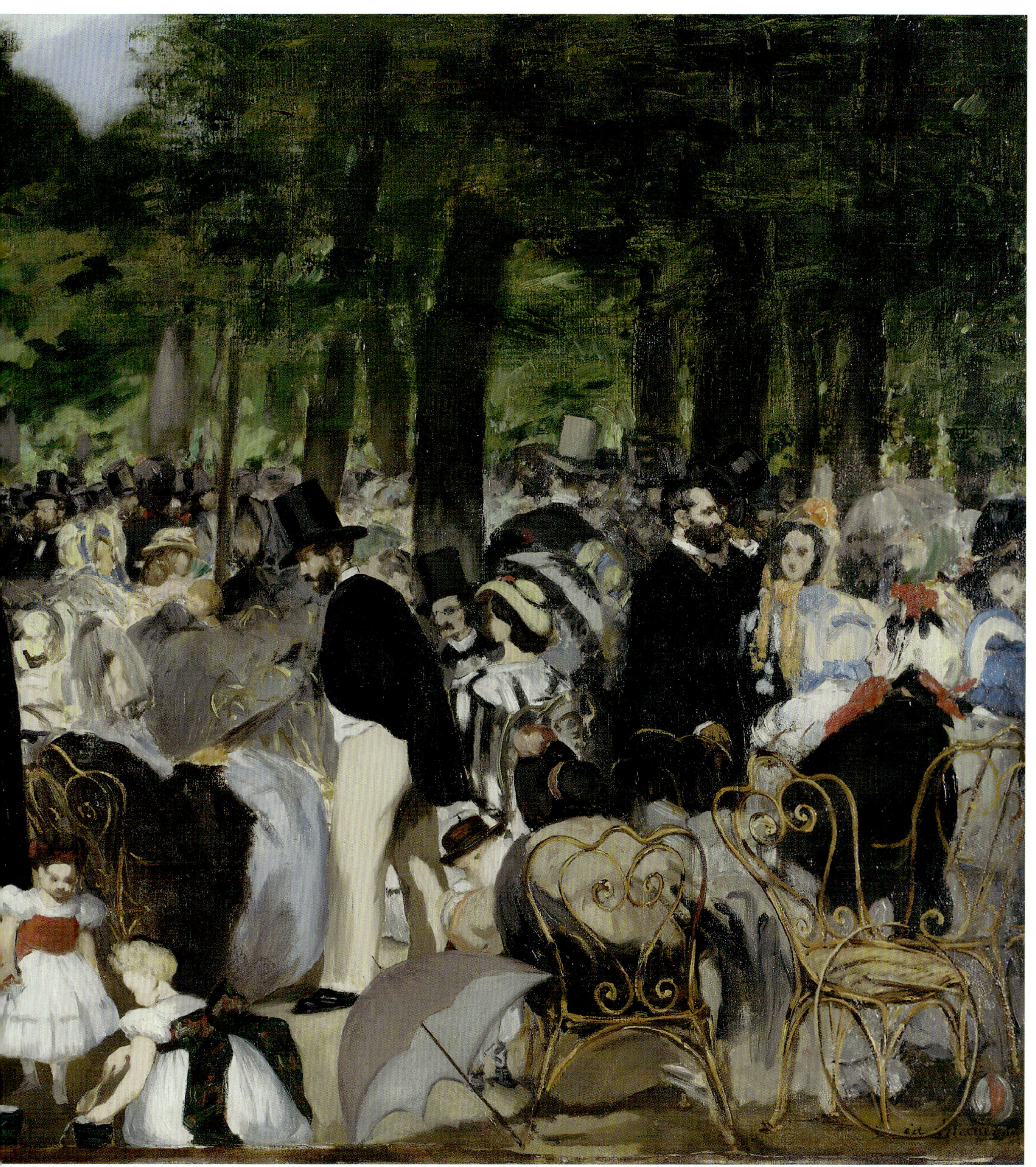

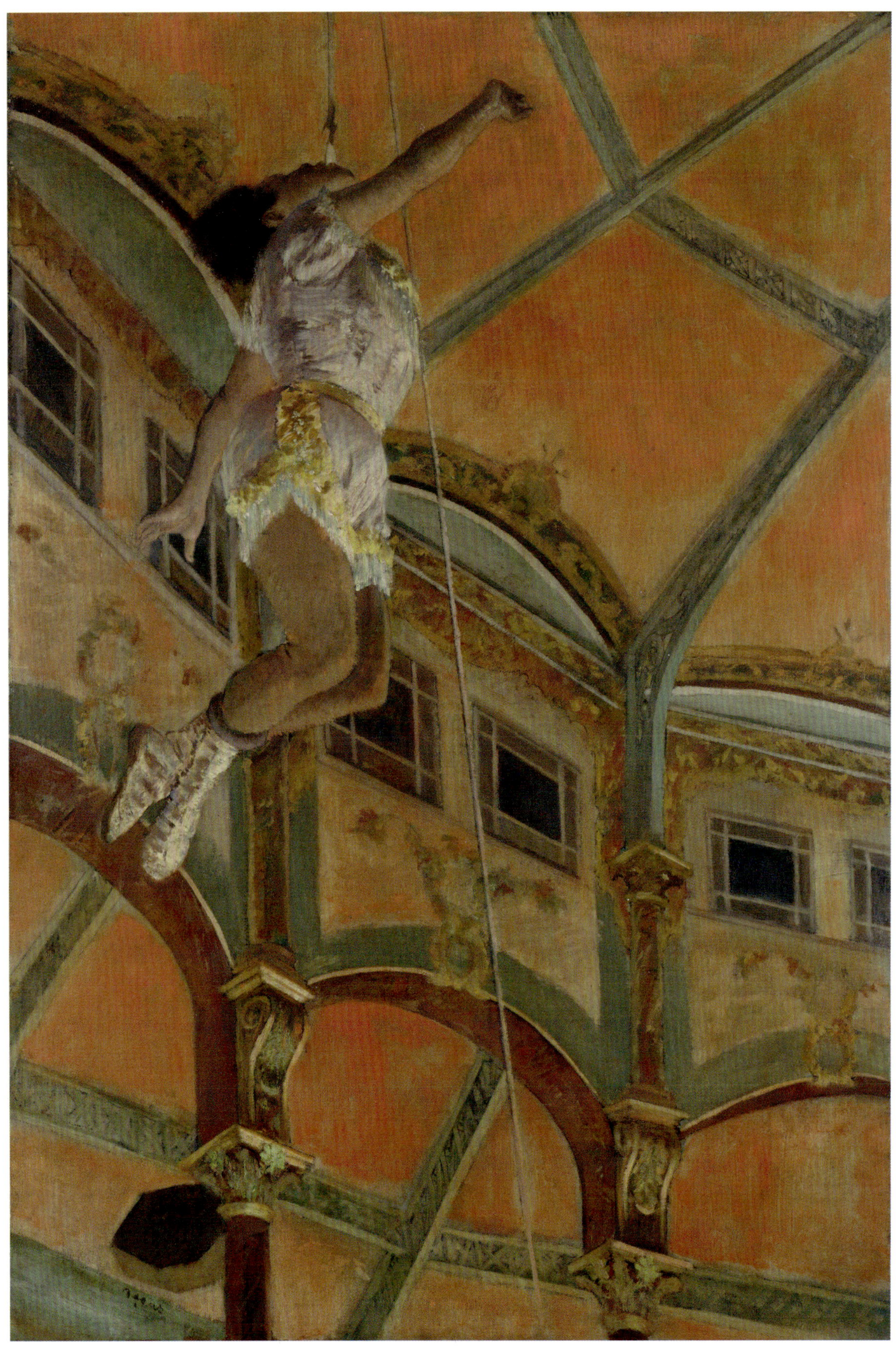

FIG. 123
Edgar Degas
Miss La La at the Cirque Fernando, 1879
Oil on canvas, 117.2 × 77.5 cm
The National Gallery, London
[cat. 16]

FIG. 124
Edgar Degas
At the Races, before the Start, about 1878–90
Oil on canvas, 40 × 89.8 cm
Virginia Museum of Fine Arts, Richmond
[cat. 15]

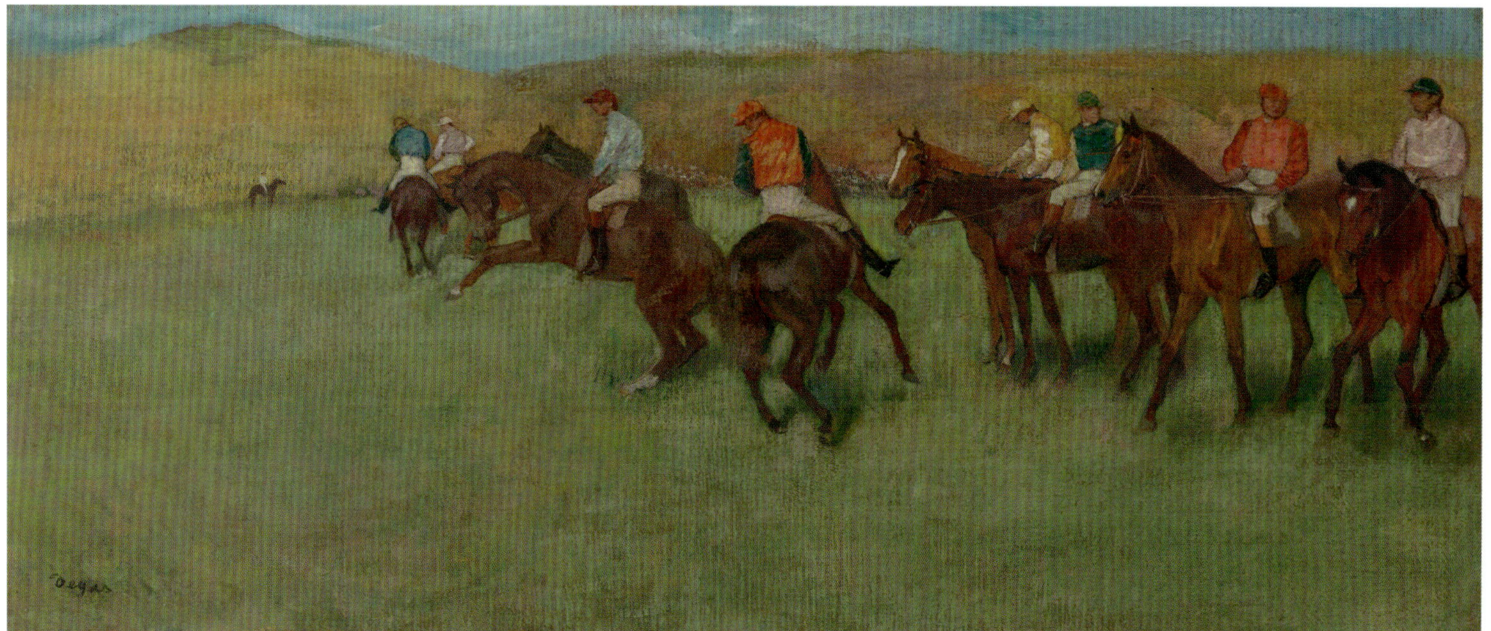

A Pissarro, *Boulevard Montmartre, Morning, Cloudy Weather*, was purchased by the National Gallery of Victoria, Melbourne (see fig. 165); two Scots were also among the Grafton buyers, A.B. Hepburn and Sir Hugh Shaw Stewart (both acquiring Monet landscapes)[161] as well as two Irishmen, George Moore and Hugh Lane. The latter, an Anglo-Irish collector and dealer of note, acquired Manet's *Music* and Monet's *Lavacourt under Snow* (see fig. 1), as well as Pissarro's *Spring at Louveciennes*,[162] which was not on display on the Grafton Galleries walls. Likewise, the exhibition prompted a few further sales in the following months, such as Manet's *Eva Gonzalès*, also purchased by Lane. But the long-standing campaign of derision directed at the work of the Impressionists, revived in the press during the course of the exhibition, seems to have deterred less-motivated collectors from buying, and the show failed to make the pictures popular with the public. In any case, despite the publication of an exhibition catalogue and of an illustrated album reproducing the highlights of the show,[163] a large part of the exhibits, coming from the dealer's private collection, were actually not for sale. As one critic put it: 'Among the unrivalled series of works now on view at the Grafton Galleries are not a few paintings which M. Durand-Ruel could never be tempted to let pass out of his possession'.[164]

Durand-Ruel's enterprise in London was thus not entirely entrepreneurial, and hardly proved a commercial success, but it was a triumph in every other way: the result and culmination of his 30 years of dogged attempts to impose himself, despite barely any sales at all, as the sole merchant of Impressionism in Britain, and the incomparably efficient promoter of this particular avant-garde.

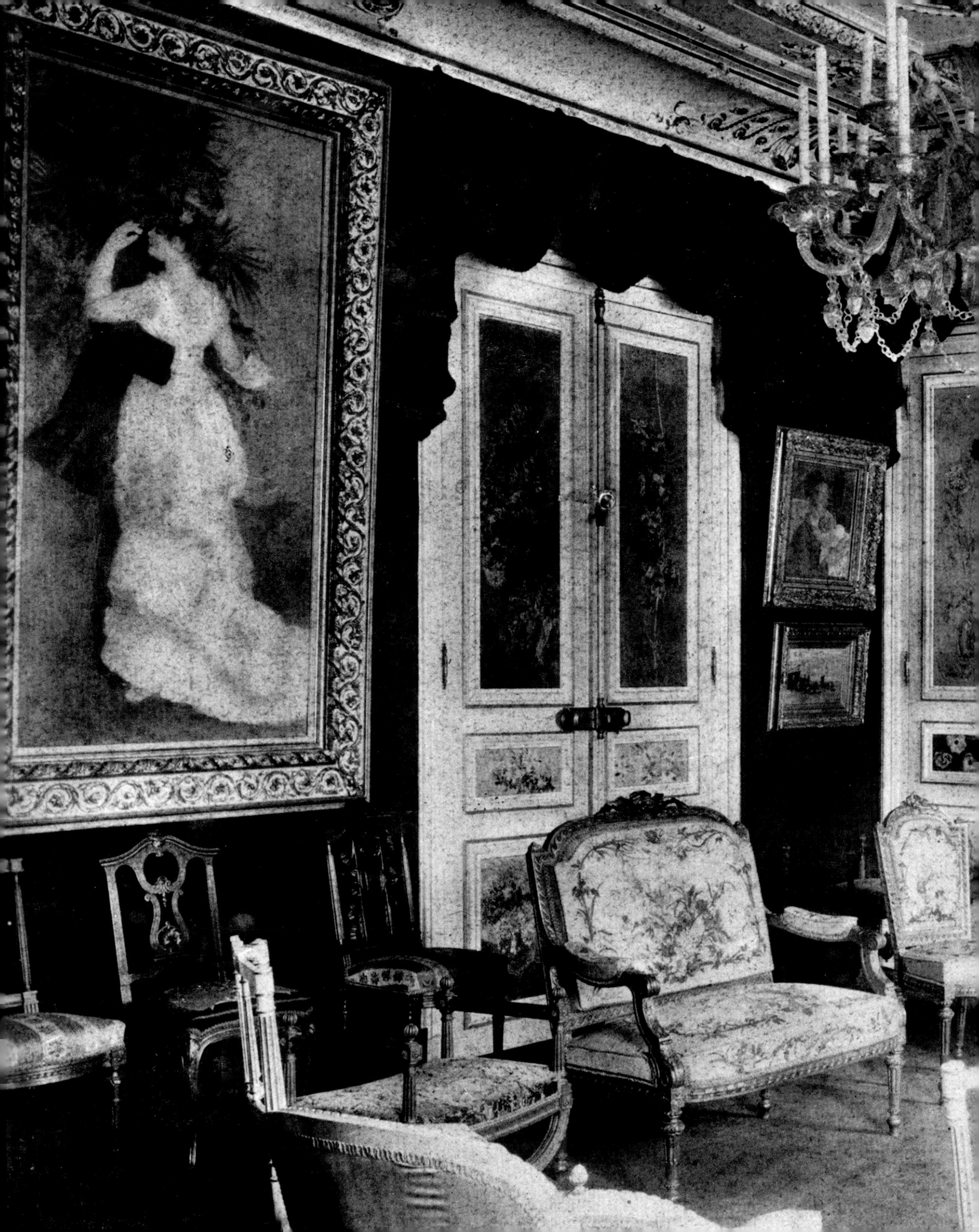

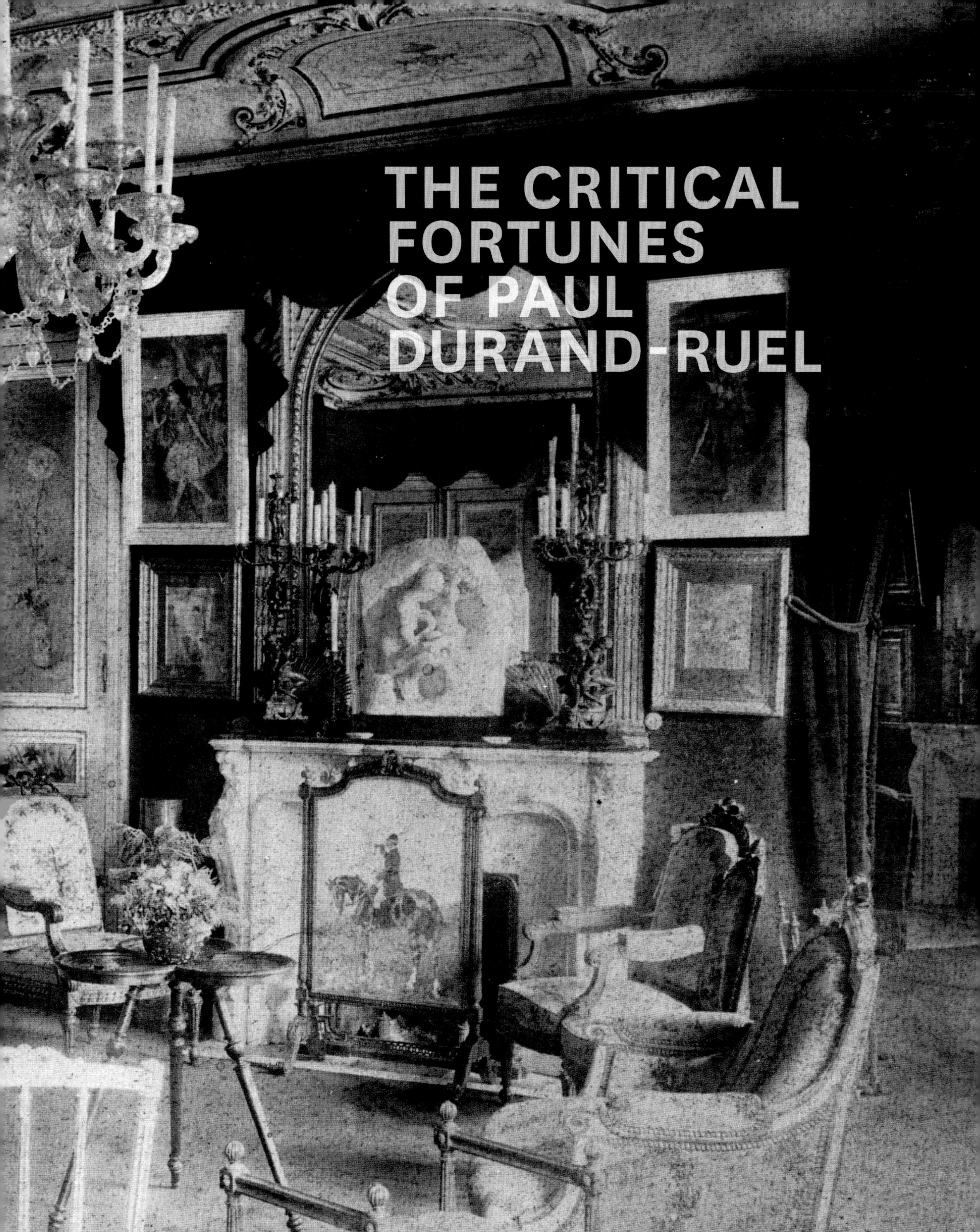

THE CRITICAL FORTUNES OF PAUL DURAND-RUEL

The Critical Fortunes of Paul Durand-Ruel

Joseph J. Rishel

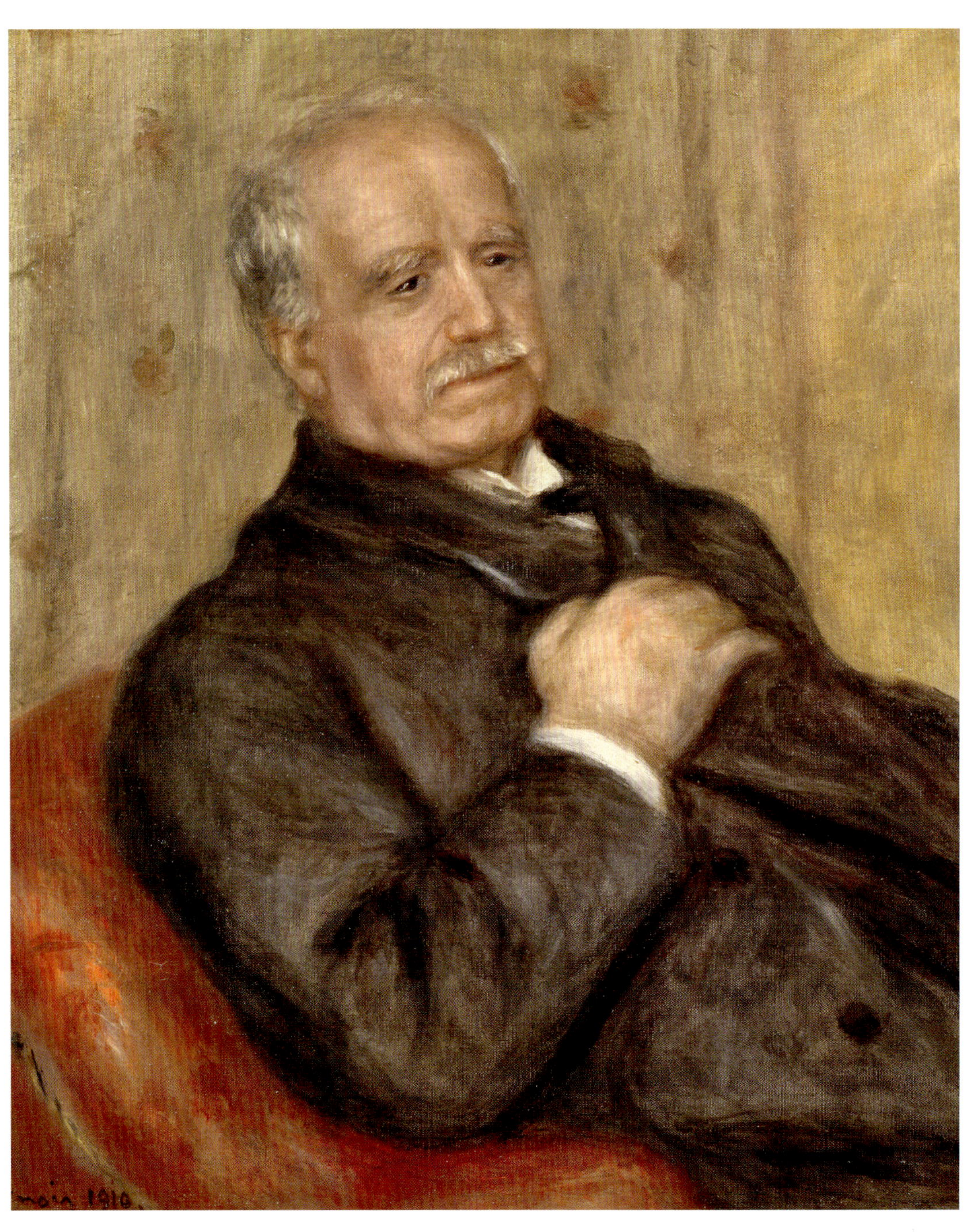

FIG. 125
Pierre-Auguste Renoir
Paul Durand-Ruel, 1910
Oil on canvas, 65 × 54 cm
Private collection
[cat. 83]

FIG. 126
Paul Cézanne
Ambroise Vollard, 1899
Oil on canvas, 100 × 81 cm
Petit Palais, Musée des Beaux-Arts
de la Ville de Paris

On his death in 1922 at the age of 90, Paul Durand-Ruel's fame as one of the greatest art dealers of his time was assured. It is startling to reconfirm today how many of the business practices he either set in place or invented are still in common use, and the degree to which the vastness of his enterprise in terms of stock and sales compares to early twenty-first-century international businesses. Perhaps the most resounding statement in praise of Durand-Ruel's achievements is John Rewald's tribute published in 1943 in connection with an exhibition in the company's New York gallery marking the 140th anniversary of the founding of the organisation by Paul Durand-Ruel's grandfather.[1]

> No name of a non-artist is more closely bound up with the history of Impressionism than that of Paul Durand-Ruel. This man was more than the dealer of the Impressionists – he was their defender and friend, among the first to understand their revolutionary art, and for many years the only one with courage enough to invest up to his last cent in their paintings, a gesture which often brought him near bankruptcy.[2]

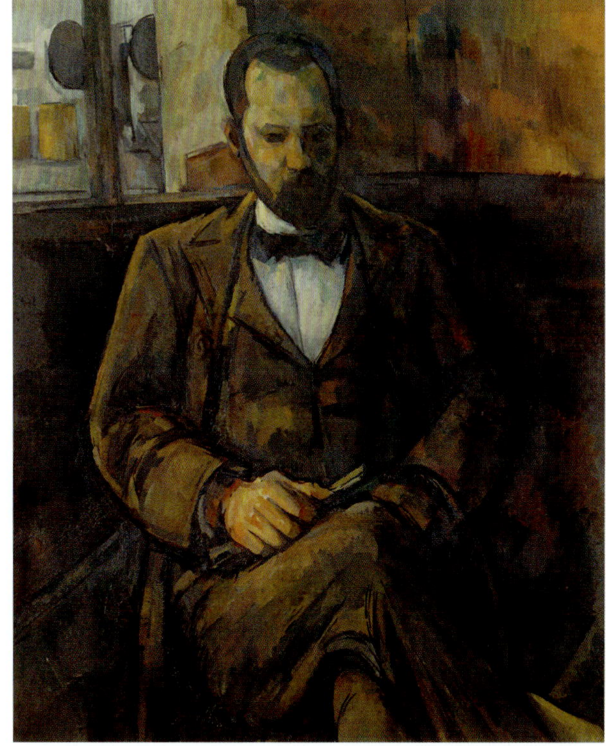

Three years later, near the conclusion of his monumental *History of Impressionism* (the first of three editions commissioned by the Museum of Modern Art), Rewald opened and closed the issue of Durand-Ruel's aesthetic and commercial boundaries by confronting on the same page Renoir's portrait of Paul Durand-Ruel of 1910 (fig. 125) with that of Ambroise Vollard by Cézanne of 1899 (fig. 126).[3] This was an encounter between two artists – friends of the same generation and already well on their way to becoming the principal touchstones of past and future in the Modernist canon – portraying two dealers who defined the passage into the twentieth century.

More than a generation apart (Durand-Ruel was born in 1831, Vollard in 1866), these dealers and their preferences provide us with a rich field of value discriminations to question.[4] It would seem that there could hardly have been two more different people in the same trade: Durand-Ruel, an accomplished businessman with a closely knit family who supported and joined him in his international enterprises; Vollard, a mysterious loner, rough mannered and secretive in his business dealings. But such characterisations can make for shallow distinctions when in fact so many of the differences in taste were generational. We discuss here a handful of examples to demonstrate Durand-Ruel's participation in avant-garde art, albeit never with the same embrace and loyalty that he gave to 'his own' artists.

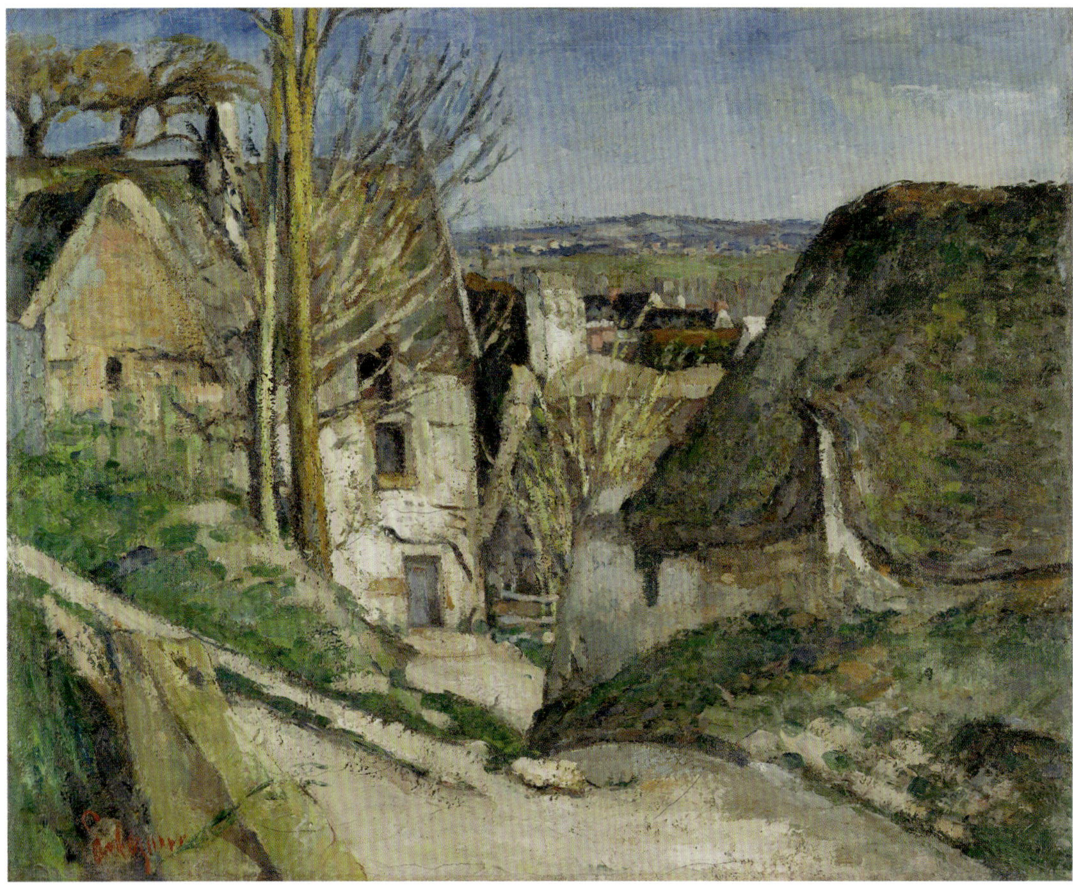

Paul Cézanne

Pissarro, the oldest and wisest of Durand-Ruel's inner circle, was also the one most likely to press him to move forward and consider less familiar artists. Perhaps the most important of the new relationships that resulted was the complicated one with Paul Cézanne. What Durand-Ruel knew of Cézanne before the early seventies is far from clear,[5] but it is interesting to note that much later in life, when preparing his *Memoirs*, he went out of his way to remind us of his early encounter with Cézanne's *The Hanged Man's House* (Musee d'Orsay, Paris) (fig. 127) at the first Impressionist exhibition in 1874:

> Cézanne had only three pictures, including one titled La Maison du pendu (The Hanged Man's House), perhaps the most remarkable piece he had ever painted … It was bought by my friend Mr. Chocquet, one of the few people whose eyes were opened by the new school I showed in my galleries. In his posthumous estate sale [in 1899], I bought this same painting on behalf of Mr. Camondo for 6,200 francs.[6]

Pissarro introduced the work of Cézanne to the young Ambroise Vollard in 1894, and the following year Vollard gathered together approximately 150 pictures, which he showed in his modest space at 39 rue Laffitte in November and December in what proved to be the beginning of public recognition of the artist – who until then was only known by those few who visited the Père Tanguy's modest artists' supply shop or by certain collectors, such as Victor Chocquet on the rue de Rivoli.[7]

Perhaps inspired by Vollard's audacious act, Durand-Ruel made his biggest single acquisition of Cézanne in the 1899 Chocquet estate sale, when he bought 18 paintings[8] (fig. 128), including such masterpieces as *Mardi-Gras* of 1888 (Pushkin State Museum of Fine Arts, Moscow), which he sold to the Russian collector Sergei Shchukin.[9] While Vollard should be celebrated as one of the first dealers to aggressively champion Cézanne (something he would continue to do well into the twentieth century with Albert Barnes of Philadelphia as one of his principal clients), Durand-Ruel's role was hardly inconsequential. It possibly peaked with his sale in

FIG. 127
Paul Cézanne
The Hanged Man's House, Auvers-sur-Oise, 1873
Oil on canvas, 55 × 66 cm
Musée d'Orsay, Paris

FIG. 128
Paul Cézanne
Still Life with a Dessert, 1877 or 1879
Oil on canvas, 59 × 72.9 cm
Philadelphia Museum of Art, Pennsylvania
[cat. 5]

1897 of *The Mill on the Couleuvre near Pontoise* (see fig. 103) to Hugo von Tschudi at the Berlin Museum, making it the first work by Cézanne to be purchased for a public museum. The Metropolitan Museum of Art followed when it acquired *View of the Domaine Saint-Joseph* through Vollard in 1913.[10]

Perhaps one of the most telling surviving documents of Durand-Ruel's loyalty to his inner group – and his hesitation towards Cézanne – is a candid 1908 letter to Renoir.[11]

> The Cézannes are from the Chocquet collection and some are from our collection on the rue de Rome. Although remarkable, they are, in my opinion, and in the opinion of all real connoisseurs, quite dull next to the Monets and your paintings. We have terribly overrated the reputation of this excellent and conscientious painter. And those fools, who pretend that only three artists, Cézanne, Gauguin and Van Gogh, are great masters, have unfortunately mystified the public, especially in Germany and in Russia, by taking advantage of the ignorance of amateurs ... All of this is a shame and is most detrimental to our dealings.[12]

That said, Durand-Ruel included 10 Cézanne paintings in the 1905 Grafton show in London, his grand declaration of what he and his gallery stood for.[13]

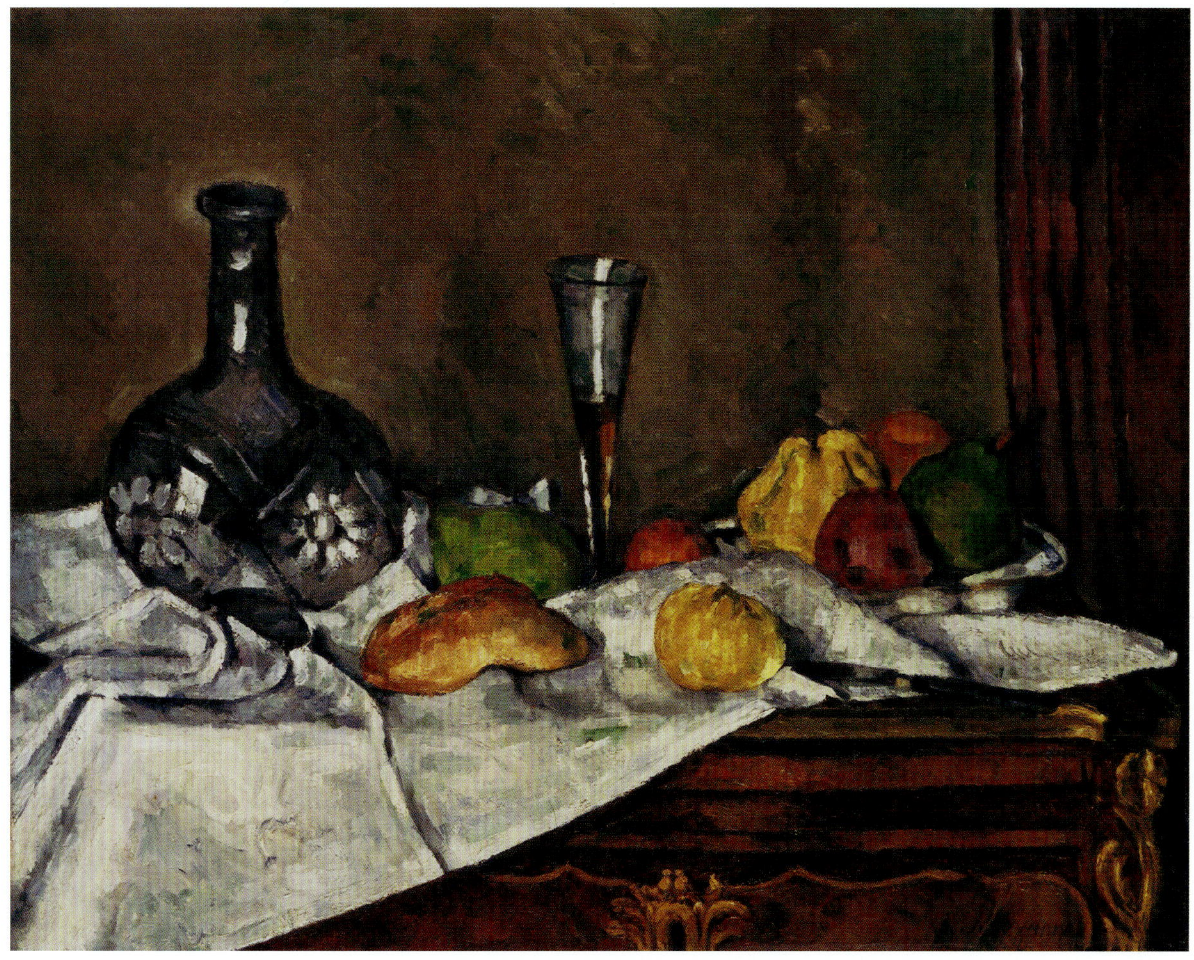

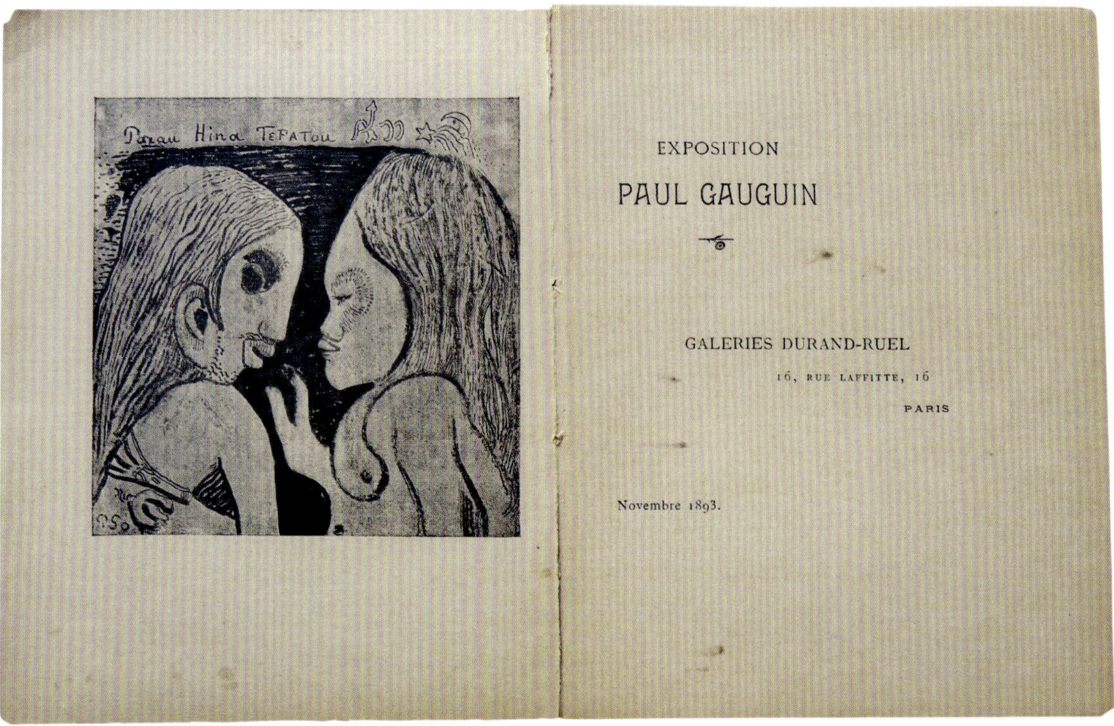

Paul Gauguin

Gauguin and Durand-Ruel started out with a mutually productive relationship, which began when Gauguin the young banker and budding artist came to buy a Monet marine and two Renoirs from the gallery on 27 April 1881. That same year Durand-Ruel, encouraged by Degas, bought four landscapes from the young painter.[14] These exchanges occurred even as Gauguin, encouraged by Pissarro, was working hard at his art-making and entered a marble bust of his son in the fourth Impressionist exhibition in 1879.[15] All of this ended in 1882, in the crash of the Union Générale, which liberated Gauguin into the bold and independent if impoverished life of a painter, and nearly destroyed the overextended Durand-Ruel.[16]

Dealer and artist did not reconnect until Gauguin returned from Tahiti in 1893, when Durand-Ruel agreed to give him a one-man show from 9 to 25 November 1893.[17] The exhibition contained 41 new Tahitian paintings – including such masterworks as *Hina Tefatou* (*The Moon and the Earth*, Museum of Modern Art, New York) and *Manao tupapau* (*Spirit of the Dead Watching*, fig. 130), three paintings from Brittany, a ceramic and several sculptures.[18] A catalogue was prepared with an essay by the poet Charles Morice and a handsome frontispiece by Gauguin, *Parau Hina Tefatou* (*Words of Hina and Fatu*, fig. 129).

Reactions to the exhibition were numerous and varied considerably, from praise to ridicule. Gauguin kept several articles in his *Cahier pour Aline*, including critical reviews.[19] In December, he wrote to his wife that most importantly his exhibition had been a great success, even provoking 'passion' and 'jealousy', though he would write in the same month that it was a financial let-down.[20] Eleven paintings sold, two to Degas.[21] Durand-Ruel retained six on deposit.[22] But as time evolved the dealer found it impossible to either sell Gauguin's work or to support him financially, even having to refuse the artist's offer to sell him 35 paintings for 21,000 francs in January 1895.[23] As he told Gauguin, it was impossible considering his affairs.[24] Gauguin returned to Tahiti soon after and moved to the isolated Marquesas Islands, where he would live out his short life. It was at this point that Vollard entered the scene, able to offer financial sustenance and eager to promote Gauguin's work, including his lifetime achievement *Where do we come from? What are we? Where are we going?* (Museum of Fine Arts, Boston), which stands at the threshold of the new century.

FIG. 129
Paul Gauguin
Parau Hina Tefatou from the frontispiece of the catalogue of the 1893 exhibition at the Durand-Ruel Gallery
19 × 29 cm (when opened)
Archives Durand-Ruel

FIG. 130
Paul Gauguin
Spirit of the Dead Watching (*Manao tupapau*), 1892
Oil on canvas, 116 × 135 cm
Albright-Knox Art Gallery, Buffalo, New York

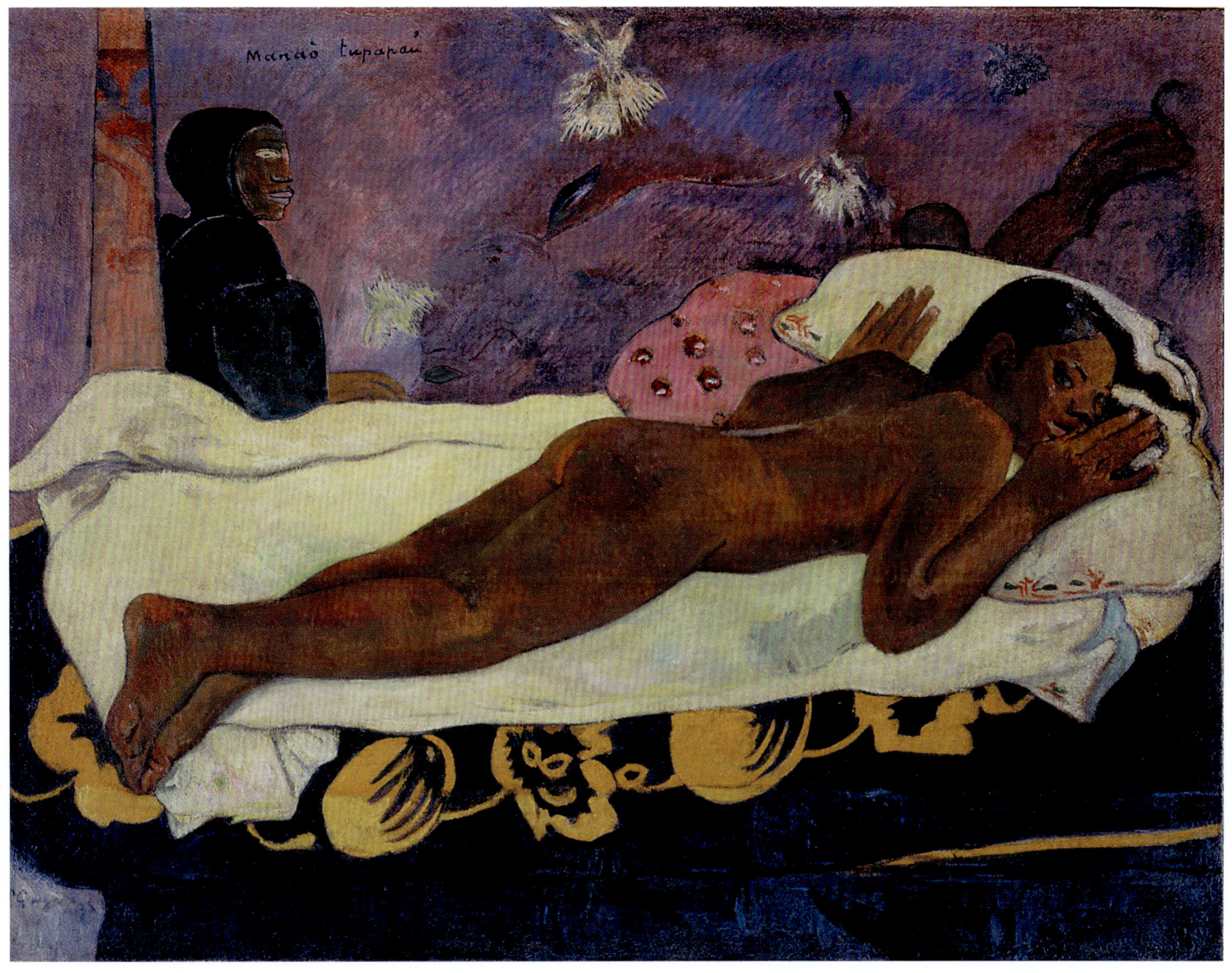

FIG. 131
Georges Seurat
Bathers at Asnières, 1884
Oil on canvas, 201 × 300 cm
The National Gallery, London

FIG. 132
Paul Signac
The Coal Crane, Clichy, 1884
Oil on canvas, 59 × 91 cm
Glasgow Museums: Art Gallery and Museums, Kelvingrove

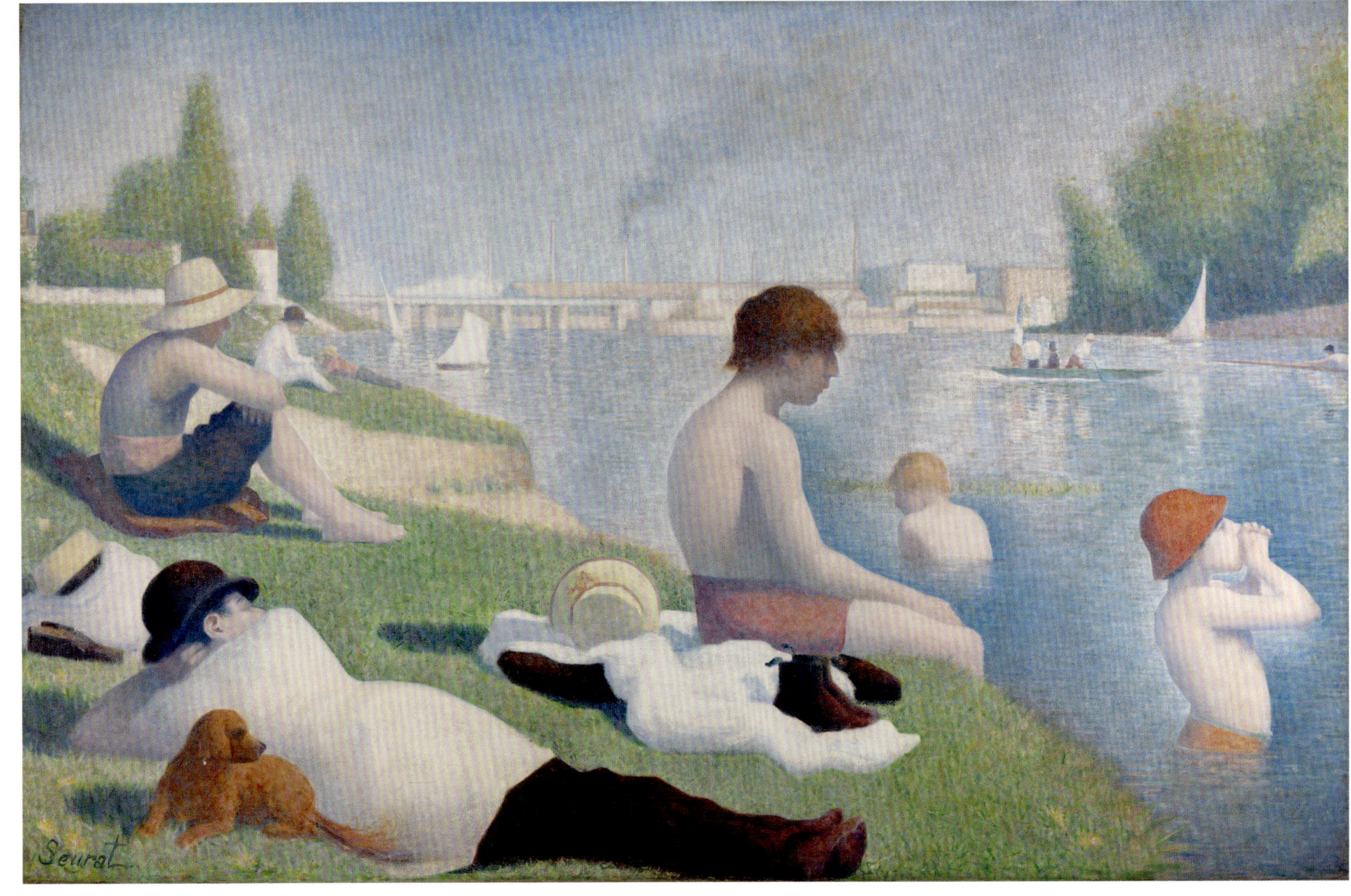

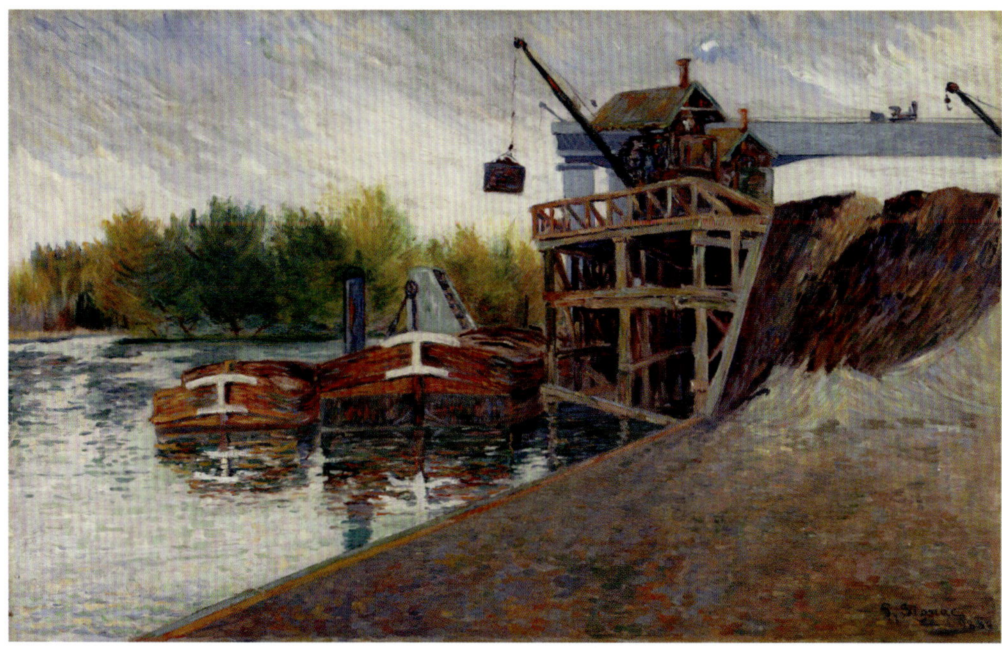

Seurat, Pissarro and Neo-Impressionism

If Durand-Ruel's step back from Gauguin seems abrupt with – one can only assume – full knowledge that he was leaving the field to Vollard, his relationship with Neo-Impressionism, the other major movement challenging received values, was more tempered and complicated.

The eighth and final Impressionist exhibition, opening in May 1886, brought it all to an end when, through pressure from Pissarro and with Degas's support, nine works by Seurat and 18 by Signac were included. This proved to be too much for Renoir and Monet, who departed from the group, bringing to an end the union formed in 1874. Seurat's *Grande Jatte* (Art Institute of Chicago) provided the primary cause of the fissure between Impressionist artists and opened up a new, more varied field of exploration, one of the most critical shifts in art history.

What is sometimes overlooked is that in the same month Durand-Ruel's exhibition at the American Art Galleries in New York included Seurat's *Bathers at Asnières* (fig. 131), the artist's first large declaration of his new vision, as well as a large preparatory canvas for the *Grande Jatte* and a group of 12 preparatory drawings.[25] These were joined with six paintings by Signac (fig. 132) and drew harsh criticism in the press.[26]

Pissarro fell under the spell of Seurat, somewhat to the discomfort of Durand-Ruel, who was quick to realise that the pleasures of seemingly spontaneous painting were in jeopardy with Pissarro's new manner, whose evolution he had witnessed as early as 1885. It was certainly Pissarro's persistence that initiated the inclusion of his new art in the New York show, but there is sufficient evidence that Durand-Ruel was following his own good sense of both the importance of this new, seemingly experimental pointillist style, and its financial possibilities. In January 1886 Pissarro wrote to his son Lucien that Durand-Ruel had just been to see Signac and was shortly on his way to see Guillaumin and Seurat.[27] Pissarro himself was fully aware of the perils of his own convictions, writing to Lucien in 1886, 'Durand likes many paintings, but not the [style of] execution. His son, the one who went to New York with him, saw them but has not said a word to me. Durand prefers the old execution, however he grants that my recent paintings have more light – in short, he isn't very keen.'[28] By 1890 Pissarro could admit that the new style was too restricting, even if it served as a vehicle for some of his most wonderful canvases.[29] Yet they were no less effective in the market: for example, Durand-Ruel bought the charming *Railroad to Dieppe* (fig. 133) from the artist in 1886 and sold it to Erwin Davis two years later.[30] The dealer seems never to have completely abandoned his interest in pointillism. In 1899, he gave Maximilien Luce, another Belgian deeply affected by Seurat and his resolution, a one-man show at rue Laffitte. In the same year, he held a group show featuring works by Luce, Bonnard and Signac.[31]

FIG. 133
Camille Pissarro
Railroad to Dieppe, 1886
Oil on canvas, 54 × 64 cm
Philadelphia Museum of Art,
Pennsylvania

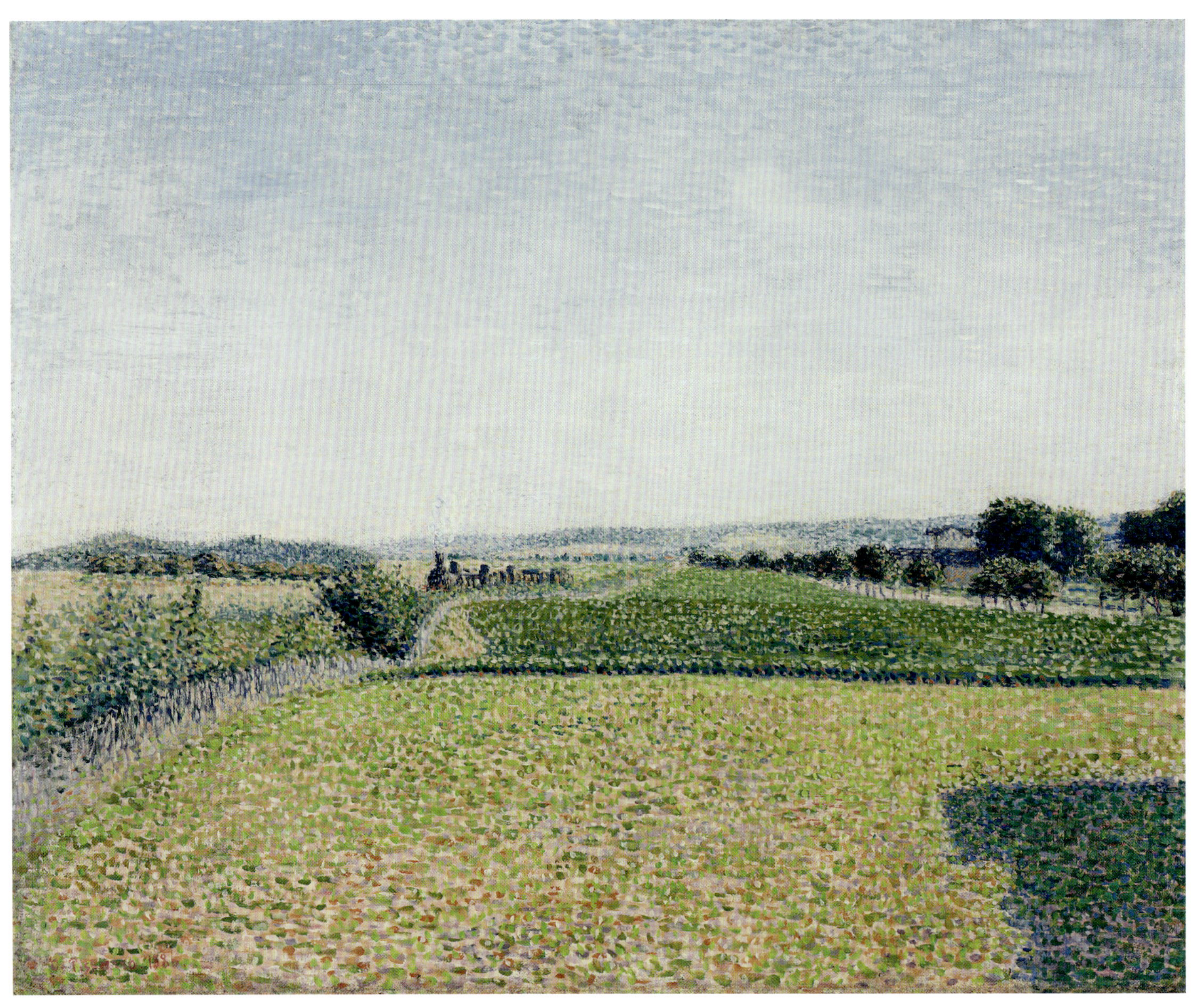

Theo and Vincent van Gogh

Theo van Gogh was in complete despair following the death of his brother in July 1890. One thing that kept him going was his urgent desire to find a means to bring Vincent the recognition he deserved.[32] On 27 August 1890, Theo mentioned in a letter to the poet-critic Albert Aurier that he had approached Durand-Ruel to organise an exhibition. In September, he could report to Paul Gachet:

> As to the exhibition, I've seen Durand-Ruel, the father, who came to my apartment and found the drawings and the paintings very interesting, as he put it. But when I spoke of an exhibition, he said that the public had always held him responsible whenever some people complained; he therefore put off his decision until he had seen the canvases [stored] at Tanguy's. He promised to call me for the following week, but he has not come back.[33]

It was a project destined to fail, for Theo would be dead four months later.[34] As with Gauguin, the field was open for Vollard. By the late 1890s Vollard also had to withdraw his promotion of Van Gogh, and the sales continued to be sporadic.[35]

However, more than aesthetic values were involved in Durand-Ruel's decision to abandon a Van Gogh exhibition, as suggested in a letter to Pissarro in October 1890:

> What makes you think that I am less interested in your work than before? You are dead wrong. It is true that I am busier now than before, but I have not changed my mind, and I am just as ardent a partisan of your work as ever. The only obstacle to our dealings was this unfortunate Van Gogh who is coming to a miserable end. He put a wrench in our plans, and I never understood your weakness for him. As he is now fading out of the picture, you may absolutely count on me.[36]

The Van Gogh in question is of course Theo, who was indeed emerging as a major competitor. He bought 14 Monet paintings in 1887,[37] a move clearly seen by Durand-Ruel as an invasive attack on his core group, and Theo was in correspondence with Pissarro concerning purchases from him beginning in January 1888.[38] It seems likely that Durand-Ruel's letter was provoked by one from Pissarro to Theo on 7 October 1890, agreeing to his proposition to buy five of his canvases for 2,500 francs:

> I think it will be good to do a second exhibition; I am in the middle of preparing several canvases. I will try to do my best. I hope you will believe that what you say about my latest paintings gives me strength; I was really beginning to worry, and you know how much that affects our work.[39]

Conclusion

The contrast of style and content between Durand-Ruel and Vollard was of course not confined to the artists represented by each dealer. Historian Daniel Halévy tartly sums up the enigma in his memoirs: 'Finally there was Vollard; Vollard, youth; Vollard, the future ... these dealers are a strange breed. ... Vollard was Renoir, Cézanne, Picasso. Durand-Ruel was in step with Maufra, Guillaumin ...'[40] As cynically biased against Durand-Ruel as this may be, it does remind us of the great diversity of his taste and enterprise.[41]

Let us close with the thoughts of fellow dealer Daniel-Henry Kahnweiler in his 1961 interview with Francis Crémieux: 'But above all there were two great art dealers, whom I respect very much and whom I think of as my masters, Durand-Ruel and Vollard.'[42] Durand-Ruel did stay loyal to the Impressionists, who of course produced the advanced art of his generation. Our brief survey here looks at how well he fared with his personal and professional engagement with some of the principal players of the next generation, whose revolts were no less radical than those of the heroes of 1830 or 1874.

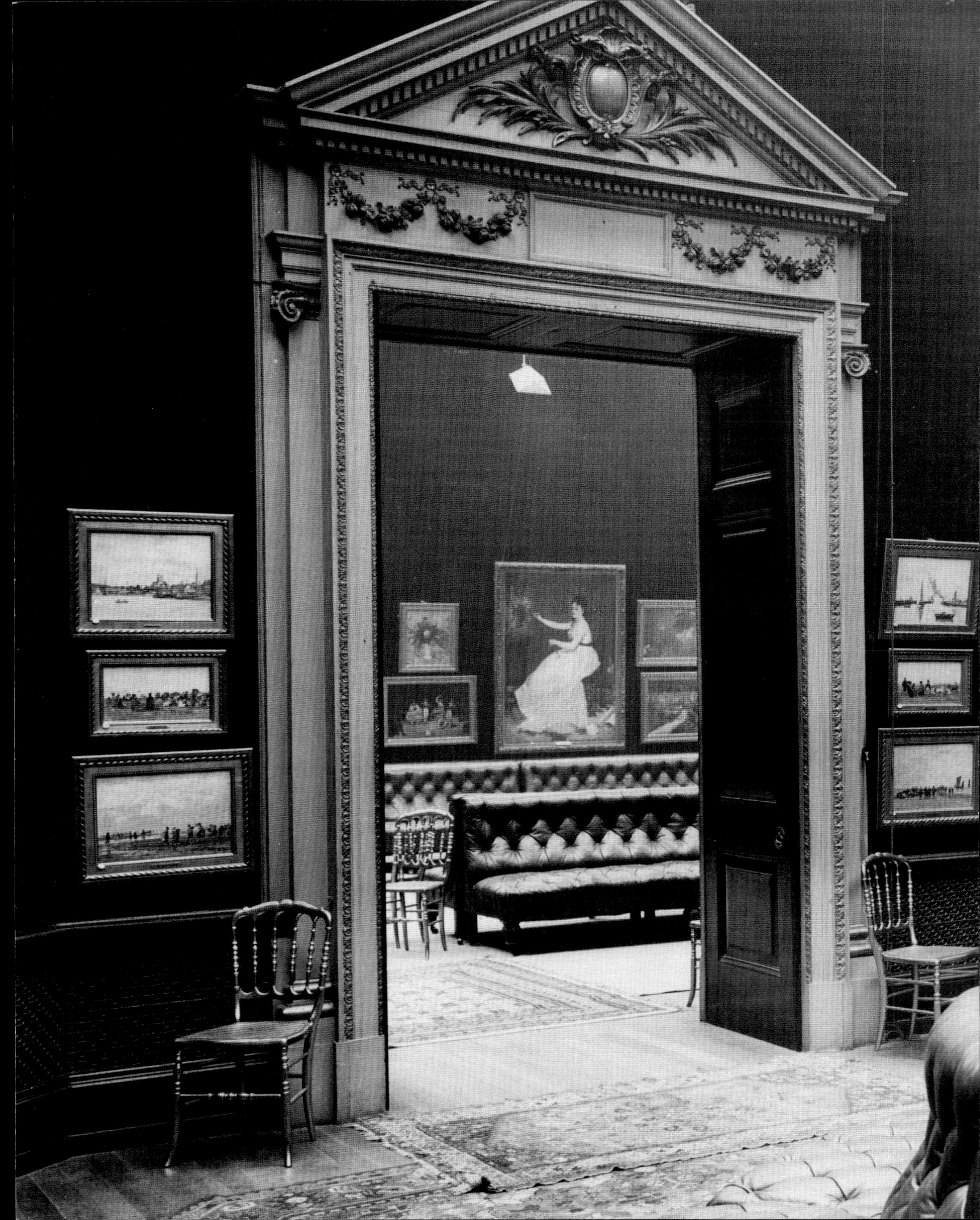

CHRONOLOGY
(1869–1905)

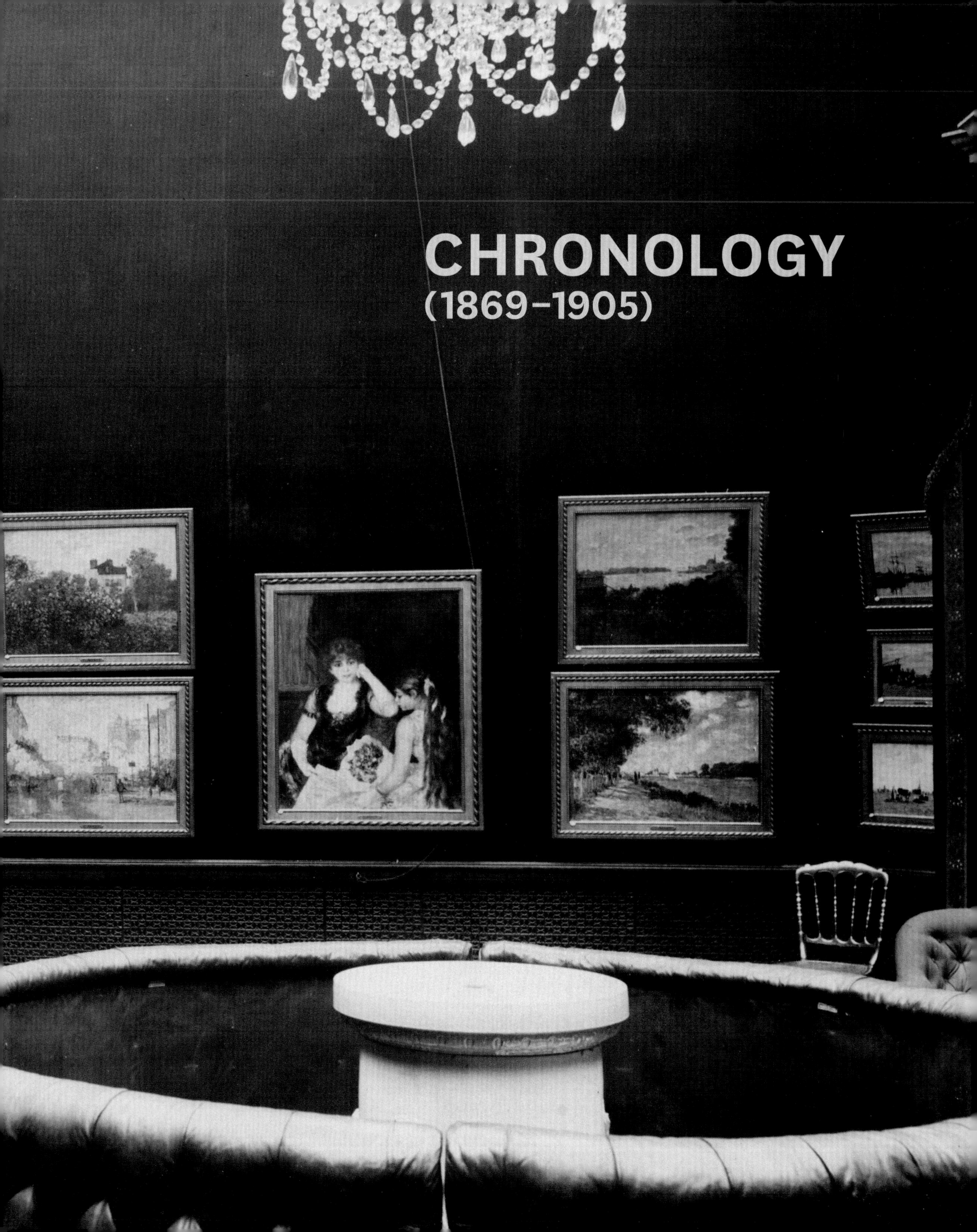

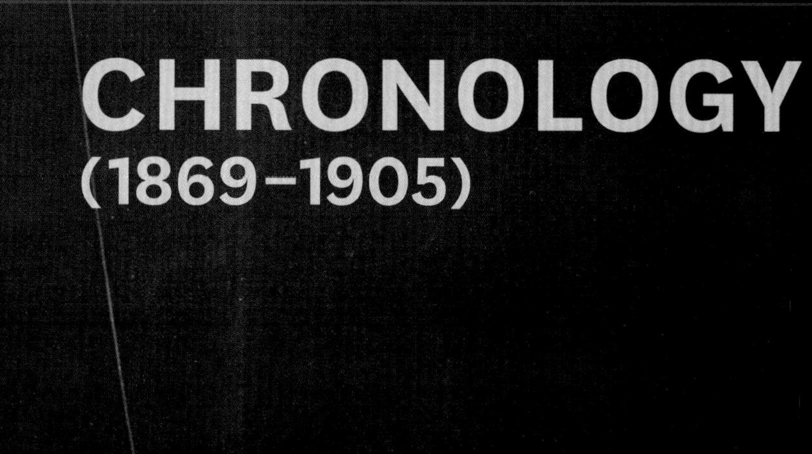

Chronology (1869–1905)

Paul Durand-Ruel and the Impressionists

Isabelle Gaëtan and Monique Nonne

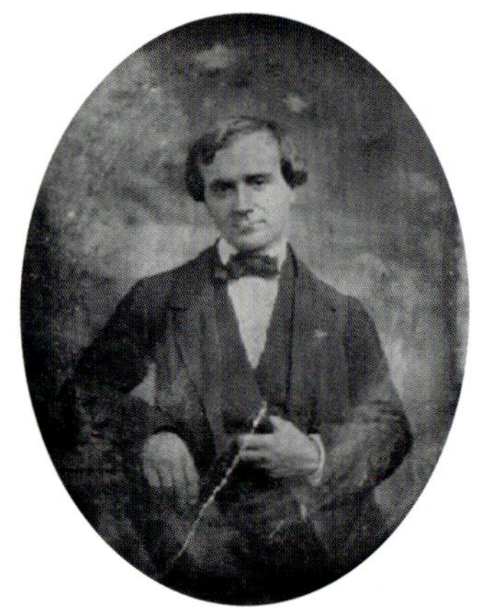

FIG. 134
Paul Durand-Ruel at the age of nineteen, 1850
Daguerrotype
Archives Durand-Ruel

This chronology focuses on the relationship between Paul Durand-Ruel and the Impressionists. The full extent of the gallery's activity could not be retraced in its entirety. The work is based on the analysis of the correspondence between the artists and Durand-Ruel in particular. Some of these sources remain unpublished; they are rich in material for Monet and Pissarro, yet more incomplete for Sisley. In the cases of Degas and Renoir, the letters deal predominantly with requests for money for the period covered by the chronology. We have provided only the main chronological references for the periods before 1869 and after 1905.

Unless otherwise mentioned, exhibition information has been taken from the corresponding catalogues. Exhibitions were held at the Galerie Durand-Ruel in Paris unless otherwise stated. The sources used are quoted in square brackets and have been abbreviated.

We have only indicated the current location of those works belonging to public collections. When the work in question belongs to a known private collection, we have included a reference to the artist's catalogue raisonné.

Before 1869

1831

31 October Birth of Paul Marie Joseph Durand, 174, rue Saint-Jacques in Paris, son of Jean Marie Fortuné Durand (5 October 1800–18 March 1865) and Marie Ferdinande Ruel (10 February 1795–26 February 1870) [AP, V3E/N823 and 5Mi 1/368], married on 11 October 1825 [ADR]. His parents begin using the trading name Durand-Ruel for their business in 1838.

1839

Opening of a shop at 103, rue Neuve-des-Petits-Champs, Paris. Durand-Ruel is listed as a stationer and art dealer in the *Almanach du commerce*.

1843–4

Opening of the gallery at 82, rue Neuve-des-Petits-Champs.

1845

The gallery publishes the finest works from its stock in a collection of engravings, *Spécimens les plus brillants de l'école moderne* (fig. 135). This includes works by Dauzats, Decamps, de Dreux, Delacroix, Dupré, Johannot, Gavarni, Jadin, Marilhat, Robert-Fleury and Roqueplan, among others.

1851

Durand-Ruel (fig. 134) is admitted to the Ecole Militaire de Saint-Cyr (no. 142 of 241 students admitted) but is forced to abandon his military career for health reasons. He resigns for 'the duty of remaining with my parents and helping them out' [Durand-Ruel [1939], p. 155].

1855

Durand-Ruel admires the work of Delacroix at the Universal Exhibition in Paris (see fig. 20); this revelation lies at the source of his vocation as a dealer [Durand-Ruel [1939], pp. 158–9].

About 1856

'To build on our relationships and to make myself aware of what was happening outside Paris, I also travelled to Lyon, Bordeaux, Belgium, Holland and England, as well as to Berlin and Hamburg, taking pictures with me.' [Durand-Ruel [1939], p. 162].

1857

1 July Durand-Ruel rents premises at 1, rue de la Paix (fig. 136), on the corner of rue des Capucines, for an annual rent of 7,500 francs [AN, MC/ET/I/1140].

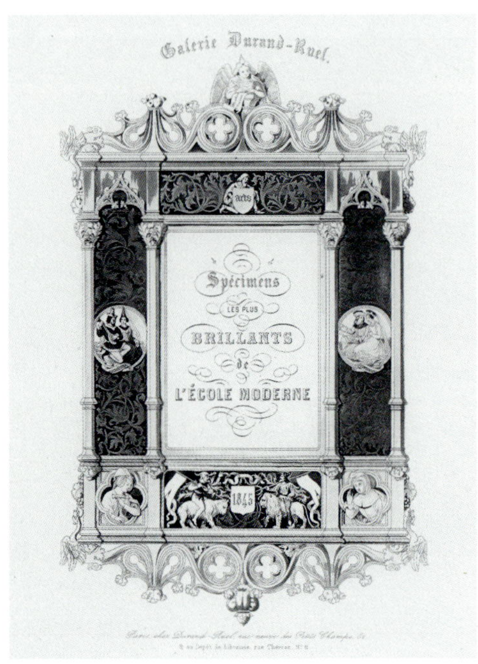

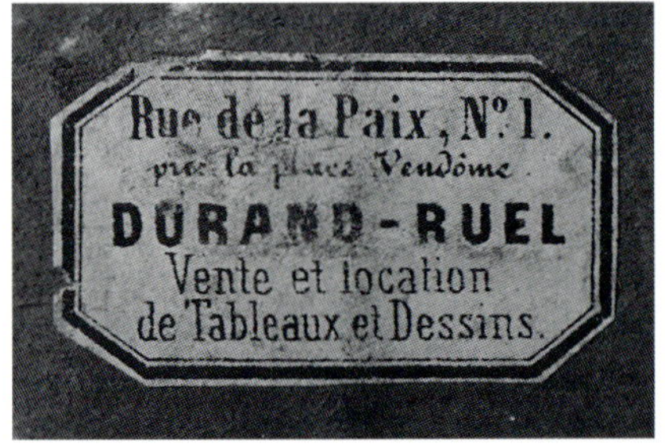

FIG. 135 (*left*)
Title page of *Galerie Durand-Ruel. Spécimens les plus brillants de l'école moderne*,
Galerie Durand-Ruel, 1845
Etching
Musée d'Orsay, Paris

FIG. 136 (*above*)
Galerie Durand-Ruel label
Printed on paper, 7.3 × 4.2 cm
Archives Durand-Ruel

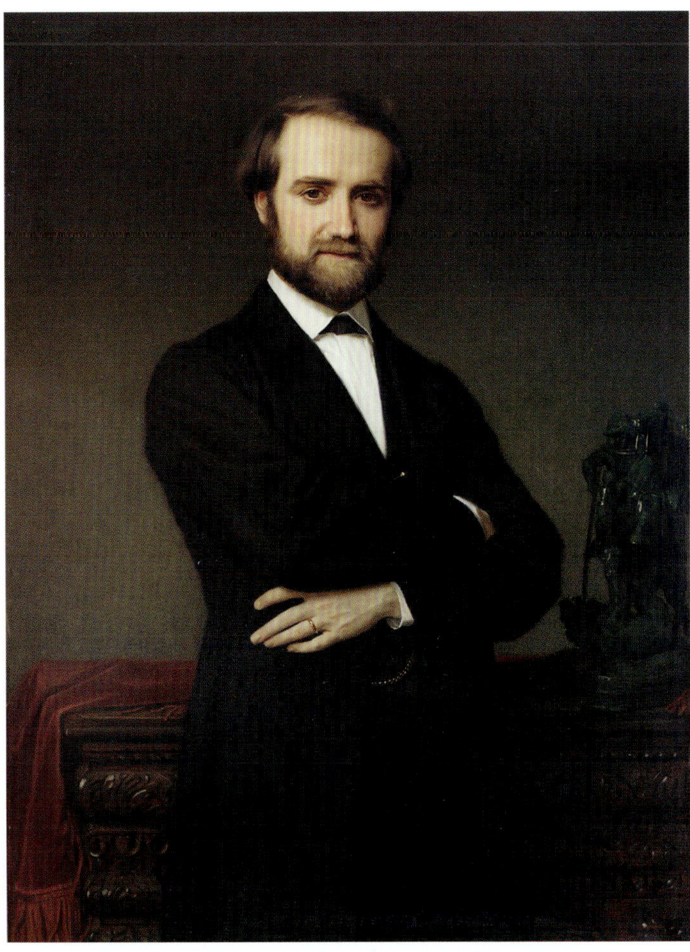

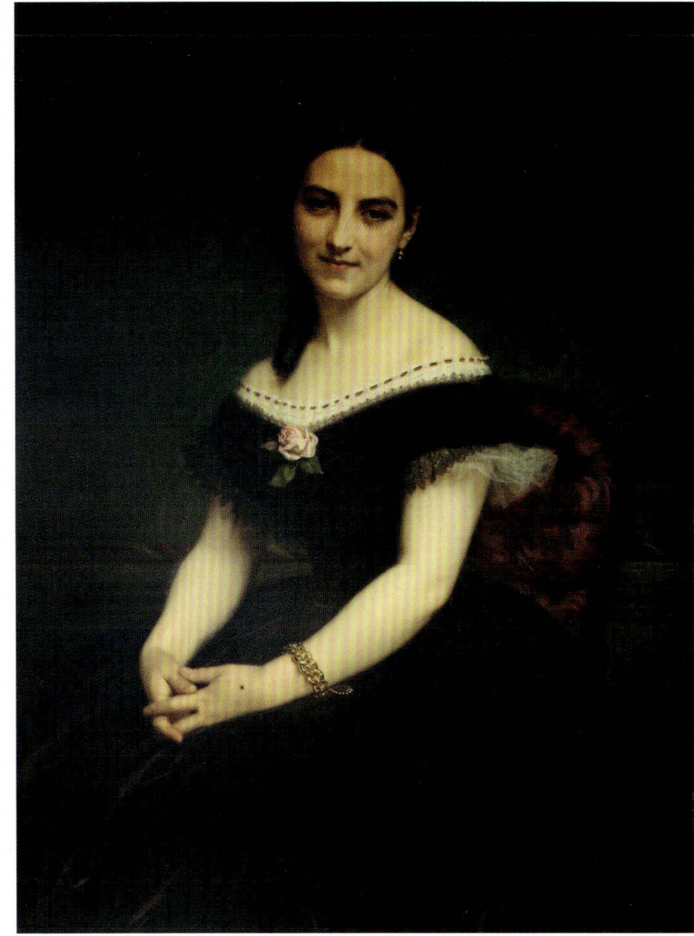

FIG. 137
Hugues Merle
Paul Durand-Ruel, 1866
Oil on canvas, 113 × 81.5 cm
Archives Durand-Ruel

FIG. 138
Hugues Merle
Madame Paul Durand-Ruel née Eva Lafon, 1865
Oil on canvas, 113 × 81.5 cm
Archives Durand-Ruel

1858

He is listed only as an art dealer in the *Almanach du commerce*.

1862

4 January Marriage, in Paris's 2nd *arrondissement*, of Paul Durand-Ruel (fig. 137) and Jeanne Marie Eva Lafon (fig. 138), born in Périgueux on 14 November 1841 [AP, V4E 124]. The marriage contract is dated 2 and 4 January [AN, MC/ET/I/1189].
25 November Birth of their first child, Joseph Marie Pierre, at 1, rue de la Paix [AP, V4E 122].

1863

30 March Durand-Ruel acts as the expert at an auction of modern paintings for the first time; the auctioneer is Boussaton [Lugt 27221; CAC, no. 20, p. 177].

1865

9 January Birth of Charles Marie Paul, their second son [AP, V4E 148].
19 March Death of Jean Marie Fortuné, at 1, rue de la Paix [AP, V4E 155].

1866

2 August Birth of Georges Marie Jean Hugues, at 1, rue de la Paix [AP, V4E 158].

1868

31 August Birth of their first daughter, Marie Thérèse (fig. 140) s48, at 1, rue de la Paix [AP, V4E 176].

1869–1905

1869

15 January Publication of the first issue of *Revue internationale de l'art et de la curiosité*, a monthly review founded by Durand-Ruel to report on current events in the art world and to promote his artists. The dealer entrusts the running of the review to the writer Ernest Feydeau. The war halts publication and the final issue is published on 15 August 1870 [Kelly, this book].
27 March Durand-Ruel is about to return from St Petersburg, where he has negotiated the sale of the collection of the Countess Gregoire Koucheleff and visited the Hermitage [*American Register*, no. 51, p. 3, quoted in Fidell-Beaufort 2000, p. 105, note 22].
1 July 'Abandoning my beautiful shop on rue de la Paix was a great mistake'. [Durand-Ruel [1939], p. 174]. Durand-Ruel sublets his gallery at 1, rue de la Paix to Marnyhac for 13,950 francs, as well as the adjoining premises and the apartment, 'two shops and their annexes, three cellars, and several rooms on the mezzanine', which he had occupied with his family since 1857 [AP, D1P4 836 (1862); AN, MC/ET/I/1140 and MC/ET/I/1237]. He moves his business to larger premises at 16, rue Laffitte / 11, rue Le Peletier comprising 'on the ground floor, storage, a small shop with a room and a second shop'; a storeroom in the basement; three offices and three shops on the first floor. The lease is renewed on 1 July 1879. The annual rent comes to 30,000 francs [AP, D1P4 636 (1876), D1P4 601 (1876), D31U3 348 (1438)].

FIG. 139
Pierre-Auguste Renoir
Jeanne Durand-Ruel, 1876
Oil on canvas, 114 × 74 cm
The Barnes Foundation, Merion, Pennsylvania

FIG. 140
Pierre-Auguste Renoir
Marie-Thérèse Durand-Ruel sewing, 1882
Oil on canvas, 64.9 × 54 cm
Sterling and Francine Clark Art Institute, Williamstown, Massachusetts

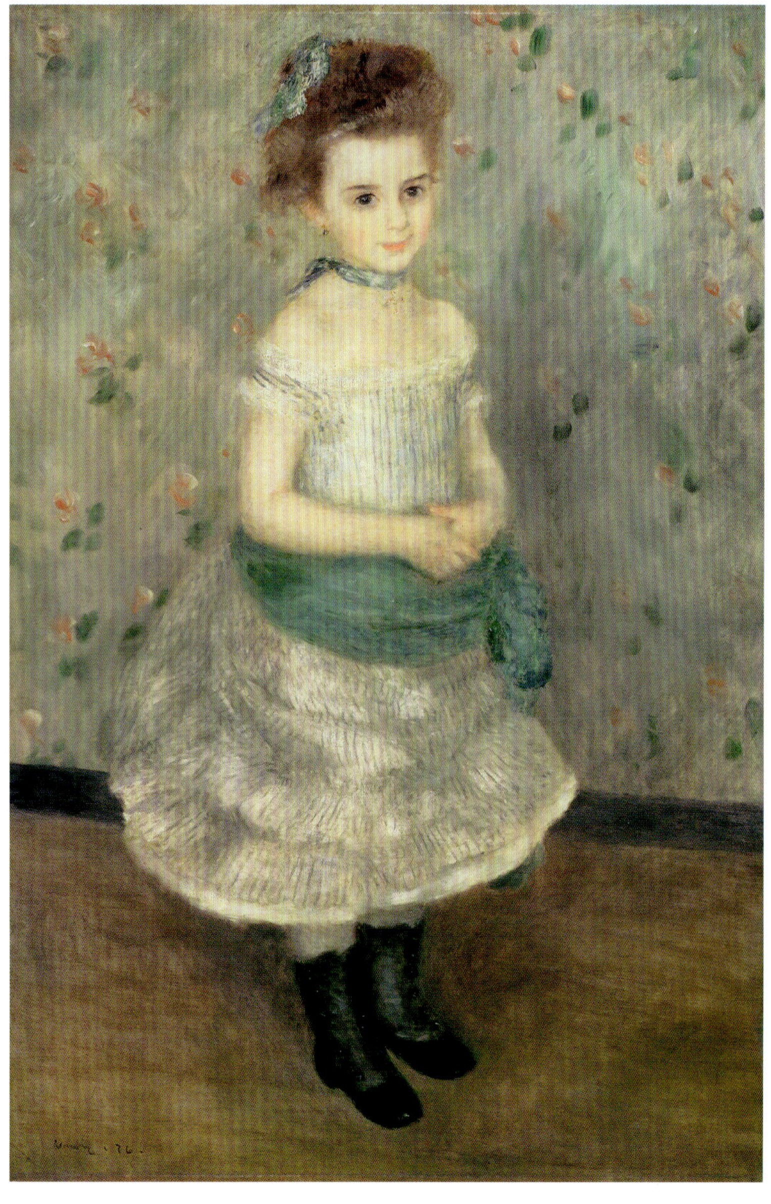

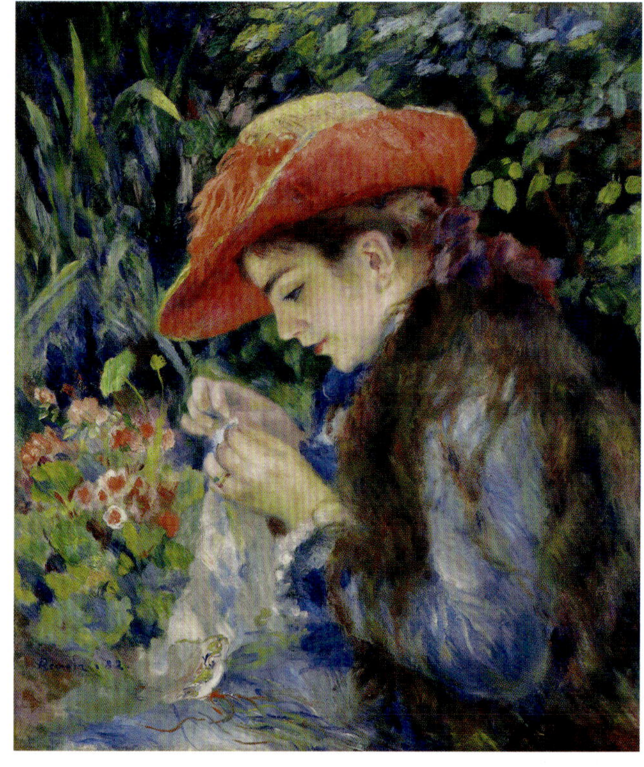

1870

26 February Death of his mother, Marie Ferdinande Ruel, who lived at 24, rue du Marché-Saint-Honoré [AP, V4E 98].
7 March Sale of the collection of the businessman Charles Edwards, assembled by Durand-Ruel, as security against funds for purchasing works: 'As I had provided all the pictures, I thought it best not to run the sale myself as an expert'. The sale does not reap the expected benefits. Durand-Ruel buys back 14 works for 232,000 francs [AP, D42E3 53; Durand-Ruel [1939], pp. 165, 170; Venturi 1939, I, p. 14; Zarobell, this book; Kelly, this book].
1 April Signing of a lease for an apartment located on the third floor of 7, rue Lafayette: three bedrooms, living room, small living room, dining room and kitchen [AP, D1P4 596 1862].
April Durand-Ruel exhibits approximately 20 canvases by Jules Dupré dating from the previous decade [Anonymous 1870a].
27 May Birth of his fifth child, Jeanne Marie Aimée Durand (fig. 139), at 7, rue Lafayette [AP, V4E 1063].
30 May First in a series of art lectures held on Monday and Thursday evenings in the gallery's premises. Alfred Sensier and Philippe Burty are among the speakers [Anonymous 1870b].
19 July Outbreak of war between France and Germany. Napoleon III surrenders at Sedan on 2 September. On 4 September, the Third Republic is proclaimed. The German army soon lays siege to Paris.
Summer Durand-Ruel sends his family 'to the Périgord, to Les Balans, property owned by [his] parents-in-law'. [Durand-Ruel [1939], p. 175].
8 September 'Departure of M. D. R. to London' [ADR, daybook]. He is 'determined to go to England and to send [his] pictures there' to continue to work, support his family and help his friends [Durand-Ruel [1939], p. 176]. Henry Wallis, Director of the French Gallery, takes care of the transportation of his pictures and those of other collectors. He stores them at the Thomas McLean Gallery, at 7 Haymarket [Robbins, this book].
29 October Durand-Ruel exhibits a group of works brought from France at the McLean Gallery until early December [House 1978, p. 637]. The public is able to see them on presentation of a 'visiting card' [Maas 1975, p. 223; Robbins, this book].
10 December Opening of the first exhibition of the Society of French Artists [House 1978, p. 637], founded and directed by Durand-Ruel, at the German Gallery, 168 New Bond Street, London, which he has just rented: 'Right to enjoyment of the rental of the largest part of a house in London ... twelve thousand five hundred francs in annual rent' [AP, D32U3 348 1429].

1870 or 1871

In London, Durand-Ruel rents 'a small house with a garden on Brompton Crescent, near the South Kensington Museum'. His wife and four of his children join him there [Durand-Ruel [1939], p. 177].
December 1870 or January 1871 Daubigny introduces Monet to the dealer, who later recalls: 'I immediately bought the paintings he had just painted in London from him' [Durand-Ruel [1939], p. 179; House 1978, pp. 637–8 and note 18].

1871

21 January Durand-Ruel writes to Pissarro to ask him the price of a picture: 'Please be so kind as to send me others as soon as you are able to' [Durand-Ruel and Durand-Ruel 2014, p. 175]. It is likely he purchases two pictures, listed in the October 1872 stock book as 'bought from Pissarro in 1870 [*sic*]' for 400 francs [ADR stock; House 1978, p. 638 and note 17].
6 March The first annual exhibition of the Society of French Artists continues in London with around 80 additional works, including one by Monet and two by Pissarro, as listed in the catalogue published for this second hanging [House 1978, p. 637]. The society's secretary is Arthur A. Hutton, former secretary of the French Gallery [Robbins, this book].
18 March Proclamation of the Paris Commune. The insurrection lasts for two months.
20 March After a stay of several days in Paris (having returned on 17 March), 'M. DR takes seven pictures by Dupré, one by Merle, seven by Corot, one by Diaz [etc.] to London' [ADR, daybook].
6 April Durand-Ruel travels between London and Brussels [*Correspondence Fromentin* [1995], II, no. 1064, p. 1670].
27 April Opening at the German Gallery in London of the 'Second Annual Exhibition of The Society of French Artists', which includes works by Millet, Corot, Rousseau and Diaz, among others. [House 1978, p. 637]. Durand-Ruel also exhibits the Laurent-Richard Collection (71 works), which he has helped to assemble and at the sale of which he will act as expert on 7 April 1873 in Paris.
1 May Opening of the International Exhibition in South Kensington, London (Fine Arts Department, East Galleries). Durand-Ruel, one of the organisers of the French section, lends 17 pictures by Corot, Cabanel, Courbet, Delacroix, Diaz, Merle and Rousseau, among others. Monet and Pissarro also send works [exh. cat. London 1871c; House 1978, p. 637].
June Durand-Ruel spends several days in Paris [*Correspondence Fromentin* [1995], II, no. 1071, p. 1679]. His initial purchases from Pissarro and Monet are noted in the stock book: Pissarro, untitled, 200 francs; Pissarro, *Snow Effect*, 200 francs; Monet, *Trouville*, 325 francs; Monet [*Trouville*], 300 francs.
September 'We stayed in our house until September' [Durand-Ruel [1939], p. 178].
30 September On returning to Paris, Durand-Ruel sends pictures to London [ADR, daybook].
27 November At the age of 30, Jeanne Marie Eva Lafon, Paul Durand-Ruel's wife, dies as a result of an embolism [AP, V4E 3482, DQ7 12344, 27 August 1872, no. 980]. The dealer is left alone with five children, of whom the eldest is nine. He never remarries.

1872

January The purchase from Manet of two pictures, deposited by the artist with Arthur Stevens, for 800 francs each: *The Salmon* (fig. 53) and *Moonlight at the Port of Boulogne* (fig. 54). The two canvases are sold on 6 January for 6,000 francs to M. de Villars, who sells them very quickly. On the same day, Durand-Ruel buys *Boy with a Sword* by Manet (fig. 91) from the dealer Febvre for 1,500 francs, as well as '*Paysage, le chasseur*' by Millet for 20,000 francs [ADR, daybook]. That same month, he buys a further 23 canvases from Manet for 35,000 francs [Durand-Ruel and Durand-Ruel 2011]. Publication, with Léon Techener, of Alfred

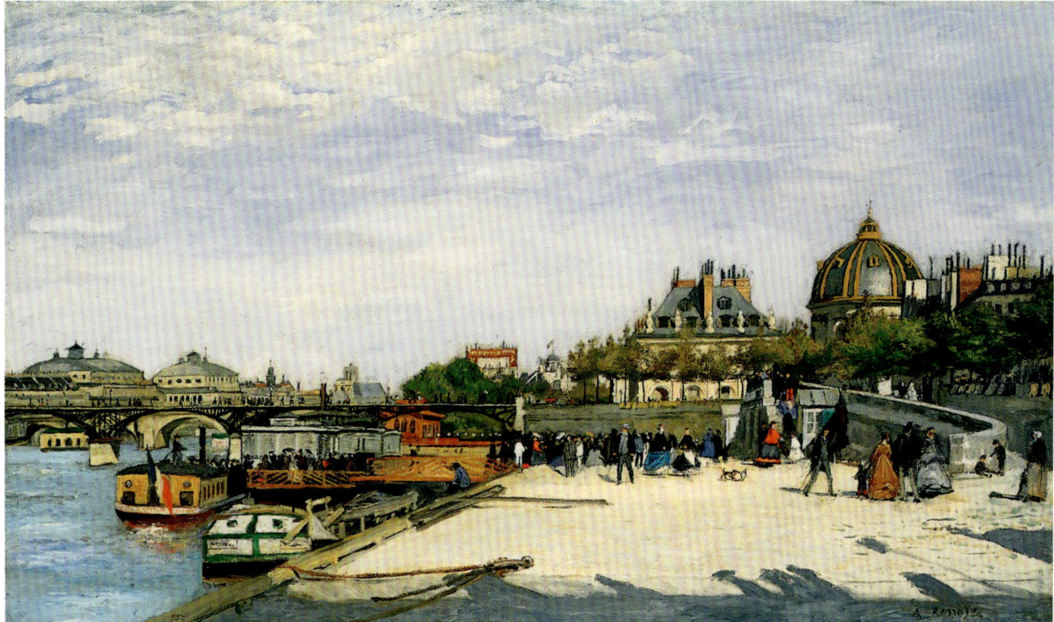

FIG. 141
Pierre-Auguste Renoir
The Pont des Arts, Paris, 1867
Oil on canvas, 60.9 × 100.3 cm
The Norton Simon Foundation, Pasadena, California

Sensier's *Souvenirs sur Théodore Rousseau*, which had appeared in an abridged version in serial form in *Revue de l'art et de la curiosité* in 1870–1.
First purchases from Degas: *The Dancing Class* (Metropolitan Museum of Art, New York), without a list price [stock 943], sells for 1,000 francs on 16 January to Premsel [ADR, daybook]; *The Ballet from 'Robert le Diable'* (Metropolitan Museum of Art, New York), 1,500 francs [stock 978].
3 February Purchase of Millet's *The Angelus* from Emile Gavet for 30,000 francs [ADR, daybook; stock 993; Kelly, this book].
[28 February] Opening at the German Gallery in London of the 'Third Exhibition of The Society of French Artists' with works by Manet, Fantin-Latour, Pissarro, Corot and Daubigny. Charles W. Deschamps, nephew of the art dealer Ernest Gambart, becomes secretary of the society [Maas 1975, p. 233; Robbins, this book].
5 March Sensier writes to Millet: 'Durand is exhibiting ten or twelve of your pictures, including *Oedipus*, *The Angelus*, *Death and the Woodcutter*, *November*, etc., etc. They have all been much admired' [*Correspondence Millet* [2005], II, no. 1360–a598, p. 318]. Durand-Ruel puts Millet's works on permanent display between February and April [exh. cat. Paris 1975, p. 30].
12 March Purchase of his first picture by Sisley, *Snow Effect*, from the dealer Latouche for 200 francs [ADR, daybook; stock 1106].
March Purchase of his first picture by Renoir, *The Pont des Arts* (1867, Norton Simon Museum, Pasadena, fig. 141), for 200 francs [stock 1868–1873, no 1131]. It is Monet who introduces his friend to the dealer [Fénéon 1970, p. 351].
23 March Initial purchases from Sisley: three pictures at 200 francs each, *The Way to Church*, *The Iron Bridge* and *The Seine at Billancourt* [ADR, daybook: stock 1173 to 1175].
6 April Purchase of 26 pictures by Courbet from the artist for a total of 54,300 francs [ADR, daybook].
15 May In partnership with M. Edwards, who would be due a third of the profits, Durand-Ruel purchases the collection of Alfred Sensier comprising 133 pictures for 245,210 francs, and 28 drawings for 28,450 francs, including 23 by Rousseau, 34 by Millet, 22 by Diaz and eight by Corot, etc. [Durand-Ruel [1939], pp. 184–5; ADR, daybook, 1872].
23 May Purchase from Renoir of a picture of flowers (*Still Life with Peonies and Poppies*, fig. 108) for 300 francs [ADR, daybook].
Summer 'Summer [Fourth] Exhibition of the Society of French Artists', London, German Gallery, with works by Boudin, Fantin, Manet, Puvis, Sisley, Monet and Degas, shown for the first time in an exhibition staged in Great Britain [Korn 2004, p. 193; Robbins, this book]. Durand-Ruel also sends *The Angelus* by Millet.
Early July Berthe Morisot asks Manet to show one of her landscapes of Cherbourg to Durand-Ruel [exh. cat. Washington, Fort Worth and South Hadley 1987–8, p. 50].
8 July Durand-Ruel sells *The Angelus* by Millet to Gauchez for 38,000 francs [stock 993].
10 July Purchase of a canvas from Berthe Morisot, *The Jetty*, for 300 francs (*Entrance to the Port of Boulogne*, Musée Léon-Alègre, Bagnols-sur-Cèze) [ADR, daybook, noted on 9 July 1872; stock 1765], and of three watercolours for 100 francs each [ADR, stock].
13 July On the recommendation of Alfred Stevens, Durand-Ruel sends 24 works to the president of the triennial Brussels Salon, including one work by Pissarro, one by Monet, one by Sisley, three by Manet, one by Courbet and one by Millet [AMRBAB, FSTB, 1872, 18].
10 August Hourquebie installs himself at the Hôtel de la Poste in Brussels, where he represents Durand-Ruel. He has 54 paintings with him [ADR, daybook; Hourquebie to Stiénon, Secretary of the Brussels Salon, AMRBAB, FSTB, 1872, 18].
15 August–15 October Triennial exhibition of Fine Arts in Brussels. The works sent by Durand-Ruel comprise three by Manet, including *Le Combat des navires américains Kearsarge* [sic] *et Alabama* (fig. 21), valued at 20,000 francs, one by Monet, and works by Corot, Millet and Courbet, etc. [exh. cat. Paris and Ghent 1997, p. 174].
20 August Purchase of 11 works from Fantin-Latour, for a total of 2,300 francs [stock 1855 to 1865].
1 September Three-year lease for premises located at 4, rue du Persil in Brussels [Durand-Ruel to Everard, Paris, 3 November 1874, ADR], for an annual rent of 7,000 francs [AP, D32U3 348, file 1429]. The premises are the former shop of the photographer Louis-Joseph Ghémar, who had died in May. Hourquebie will manage the branch until 1873.
2 September Durand-Ruel asks that the works rejected by the Brussels Salon (Colin, La Rochenoire, Tassaert, Monet, Pissarro and Sisley) be returned to M. Hourquebie [Durand-Ruel to M. Stiénon, Secretary of the Triennial Brussels Salon, AMRBAB, FSTB, 1872, 18].
3 September The dealer sends 58 pictures to Brussels, including one by Degas, one by Pissarro and two by Manet [ADR, daybook].
Winter 'Winter [Fifth] Exhibition of the Society of French Artists', German Gallery, London. Works by Boudin, Fantin, Monet, including *Green Park, London* (fig. 114), Renoir, Manet, Pissarro, Degas and Sisley are exhibited. First sale of an Impressionist picture by the Society: a Degas not included in the catalogue, *The Dance Foyer* (fig. 62).

FIG. 142
James Abbott McNeill Whistler
Arrangement in Grey and Black No. 1, also called *Portrait of the Artist's Mother*, 1871
Oil on canvas, 144 × 163 cm
Musée d'Orsay, Paris

FIG. 143
The Death of Sardanapalus by Eugène Delacroix, etching by Amédée-Paul Greux, published in *Galerie Durand-Ruel. Recueil d'estampes gravées à l'eau-forte*, 1875
Bibliothèque du Musée d'Orsay, Paris

1873

January Durand-Ruel exhibits seven paintings and drawings by Whistler, including *Arrangement in Grey and Black no. 1*, or *Portrait of the Artist's Mother* (fig. 142). The exhibition is a commercial failure and Whistler waits nine years before exhibiting in Paris again [Lacambre 1994, pp. 44–5]. First delivery of a series of instalments published every month: *Galerie Durand-Ruel. Recueil d'estampes gravées à l'eau-forte*, with a preface by Armand Silvestre. Publication continues until June 1875. Courbet, Delacroix, Millet and the 1830 School are well represented, but Degas (two), Manet (seven), Monet (three), Pissarro (five), Sisley (two) are also included, all from Durand-Ruel's stock.

February Rejected by the official section of the International Exhibition in Vienna, Courbet entrusts Durand-Ruel with sending 11 canvases to the Austrian capital for exhibition at the premises of the Österreichischer Kunstverein. Due to lack of space, only six works are exhibited, including *The Artist's Studio* (MO), among the 152 paintings in the exhibition [Huemer 2012, p. 4 and note 27].

26 February Purchase of 26 pictures from Courbet, for sums ranging between 500 and 4,000 francs, for a total of 40,000 francs [ADR, daybook].

21 March Durand-Ruel purchases *The Death of Sardanapalus* by Delacroix for 96,000 francs (figs 20 and 143) at the Wilson sale [ADR, daybook].

Spring 'Summer [Sixth] Exhibition of the Society of French Artists', German Gallery, London. Durand-Ruel exhibits *The Death of Sardanapalus* as well as Degas, Fantin, Manet (*The Balcony*, fig. 55), Whistler, Monet, Pissarro, Sisley and others.

Spring (?) The dealer rents a gallery on Elisabethstrasse and sends an employee to look after the 'Vienna branch'. Visitors can see works by Courbet, Monet, Pissarro, Boudin, Sisley and others. It is a failure and the works return to Paris in early 1874 [ADR, daybook, 23 February 1873–26 January 1874; Durand-Ruel [1939], p. 197; AN, LH/870/7, Huemer 2012, p. 2].

1 May Opening of the International Exhibition in Vienna. Twenty works belonging to Durand-Ruel are listed in the catalogue, including Corot, Delacroix, Manet (*The Reader*, fig. 52) and Millet (*The Sower*, Museum of Fine Arts, Boston).

May Several days after the opening of the exhibition, the Vienna Stock Exchange collapses, leading to a severe financial crisis that spreads to Europe and the United States in the following months. Durand-Ruel begins to experience the consequences in late 1874 and is forced to slow down his activities in the years that follow.

Autumn Delacroix's *Sardanapalus* is exhibited in the galleries of the Kunstverein in Vienna. From 18 July, Durand-Ruel sends 100 lithographs and 45 photographs of the picture to the Vienna branch [ADR, daybook; Huemer 2012, p. 2].

18 October Because business is not good and Hourquebie is ill, the dealer wants to wind up operations in Brussels and give over his lease for rue du Persil to the Belgian dealer Everard, based in London [Durand-Ruel to Mme Ghémar, 18 October 1873, ADR]. He nevertheless retains the lease for the room opening out onto the street and its adjoining bedroom until its expiry [Durand-Ruel to Everard, 3 November 1873, ADR].

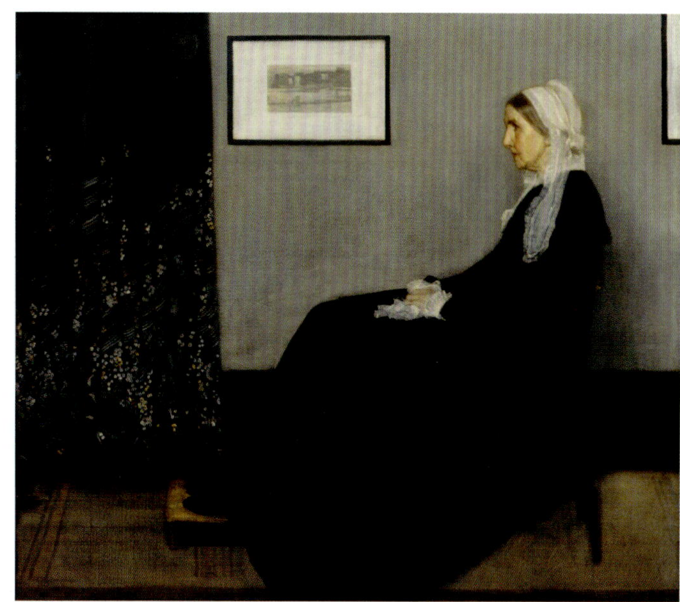

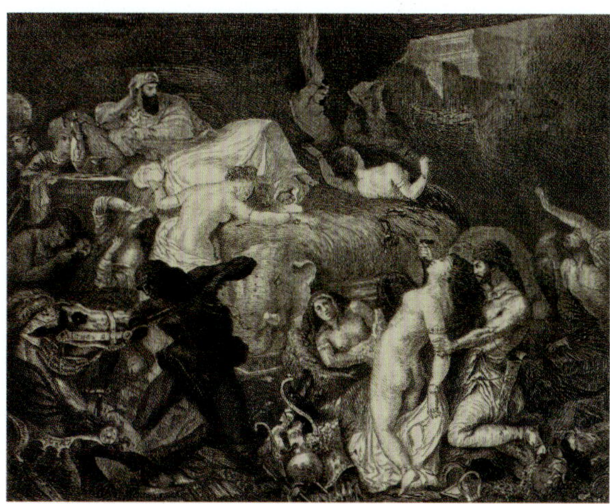

31 October Durand-Ruel writes an article for the front page of *Le Figaro* in which he states: 'Business at the moment is delayed by nothing more than the fear of falling again into the hands of republicans, and we all aspire, both as Frenchmen and as tradesmen, to the return of the hereditary monarchy, which is the only institution that can bring an end to our difficulties.'
8 November Opening of the 'Seventh Exhibition of the Society of French Artists', German Gallery, London. Works by Pissarro, Fantin, Manet, Degas, Monet, Whistler, Sisley and others are exhibited [Robbins, this book].

1874

1 April–15 May Loan of two Sisleys to the first Impressionist exhibition.
27 April Opening of the 'Eighth Exhibition of the Society of French Artists', German Gallery, London. Works by Corot, Courbet, Daubigny (fig. 116), Manet (one), Pissarro (four), Fantin (two), Monet (three), Sisley (three) and Morisot (one) are exhibited [Flint 1984, p. 34].
11 July Founding of the *Société générale des arts*, a limited stock partnership with the name 'Durand-Ruel & Cie' registered at the gallery's address. Company share capital is set at 1,500,000 francs, represented by 3,000 shares of 500 francs. Two thousand shares are allocated to Durand-Ruel, who has the right, as manager of the business, to an annual salary of 18,000 francs. On 6 October 1874, the share subscription statement gives the names of the associates of Durand-Ruel (150 shares) for the remaining thousand shares as Charles-Anatole Berlencourt (498) and Camondo & Cie (150) [AP, D31U3 348, file 1429].
November 'Ninth Exhibition of the Society of French Artists', German Gallery, London. Works by Fantin, Renoir, Sisley, Pissarro and Monet are included, as well as 13 canvases by Millet (nos. 126–38), including *The Angelus*. After the exhibition, Durand-Ruel withdraws to make way for Deschamps [Pickvance 1963, p. 258, note 20].

1875

Durand-Ruel gives up his *pied-à-terre* in Brussels, the lease for which expires on 1 September. He ceases purchasing Impressionist pictures almost entirely until 1880 [Durand-Ruel Godfroy 1992, pp. 45–7].
24 March Sale of paintings and watercolours by Monet, Morisot, Renoir and Sisley at the Hôtel Drouot. The auctioneer is Charles Pillet; the expert is Durand-Ruel. Durand-Ruel purchases four works by Monet, two by Renoir and 12 by Sisley for an average of 170 francs per picture [AP, D46E 3 65].
14 October The dissolution of the *Société générale des arts* is pronounced at a meeting of the shareholders. Durand-Ruel notes that the company has incurred significant losses due, among other things, to 'the Mosler bankruptcy, that of several art dealers ... and the financial crisis that reigns in Europe and the United States'. More than half the company's capital is absorbed by losses [AP, D31 U3 364, file 741].

1876

The dealer rents an apartment on the second floor of 11, rue Treilhard, in the 9th *arrondissement*: two bedrooms with fireplaces with a large room, two bedrooms with fireplaces, a dining room, living room, lavatories and a small room [AP, D1P4 1148 (1862) and (1876)]. Durand-Ruel commissions the portrait of his daughter Jeanne from Renoir (fig. 139).
30 March Opening of the *2e Exposition de peinture, Paris, Société anonyme des artistes peintres, sculpteurs, graveurs, etc.*' at 11, rue Le Peletier. Durand-Ruel leases three rooms to the Impressionists, who assemble approximately 250 works [Zola [1991], p. 313].
15 May Durand-Ruel rents rooms for the '*Exposition libre des œuvres d'art refusées au Salon de 1876*', which exhibits work by 75 artists. [[Anonymous] 1876].

1877

February At a rent of 30,000 francs, Durand-Ruel sublets the premises at 11, rue Le Peletier for one year to the Foyer-Davenne upholstery business [AP, D1P4 636 (1876)], which has been evicted due to the building of the avenue de l'Opéra. The Impressionists set out to find a space for their forthcoming group exhibition. 'Durand-Ruel's premises have been rented for the whole year to an upholsterer evicted for the avenue de l'Opéra' [Caillebotte to Pissarro, 24 January 1877, BnF, Est., Arch. Pissarro microfilm].

1878

17 April Opening of the Daumier exhibition at the Durand-Ruel Gallery, with 244 works in the catalogue (paintings, drawings and lithographs). It is a commercial failure and the deficit amounts to 9,150 francs [Melot 1988, p. 5].
8 July–10 October On the fringes of the '*Décennale*' at the Universal Exhibition, open to works painted in the last ten years, Durand-Ruel pays tribute to earlier works by organising an *Exposition rétrospective de tableaux et dessins de maîtres modernes*, in which he shows more than 382 works, including 88 by Corot, 30 by Courbet, 34 by Delacroix (including no. 141, *The Death of Sardanapalus*, which belongs to M. Frémyn, his notary and associate, a front man on this occasion) and 61 by Millet (including no. 235, *The Angelus*, which belongs to M. Wilson).

1879

As a reaction to government policy, Durand-Ruel organises a sale in support of free Christian schools [Assouline 2002, p. 200]. He demonstrates in support of these and is arrested by the police [Durand-Ruel and Durand-Ruel, this book].
1 January Durand-Ruel sublets premises located at the corner of 16, rue Laffitte (fig. 144) and 11, rue Le Peletier to the Society of Watercolour Painters for 16,000 francs [AP, D1P4 636 1876].
10 May He sells *Sardanapalus* to James Duncan for the sum of 52,500 francs [ADR, daybook; Watson 2011, p. 106; Durand-Ruel [1939], p. 198].
Late 1879–May 1880 Durand-Ruel lends his support to the preparation for an exhibition in Algiers and serves as an intermediary between artists and lenders, including the Musée du Louvre, which sends the *Arab Horsemen* by Fromentin [ADR, daybook]. The paintings section, comprising almost 500 works, contains many works sent by Durand-Ruel, including two Courbets and one Boudin. The inauguration takes place on 15 January 1880 (Alger 1880; written communication L. Houssais, 26 June 2014).

1880

1 February Founding of a general trading partnership with regard to M. Durand-Ruel and a limited partnership with regard to Messieurs Balensi, Feder, Jenty, the Count d'Auberjeon, Saint-Léger and Pellorce, who bring 100,000 francs to the business for a 5% annual return. The

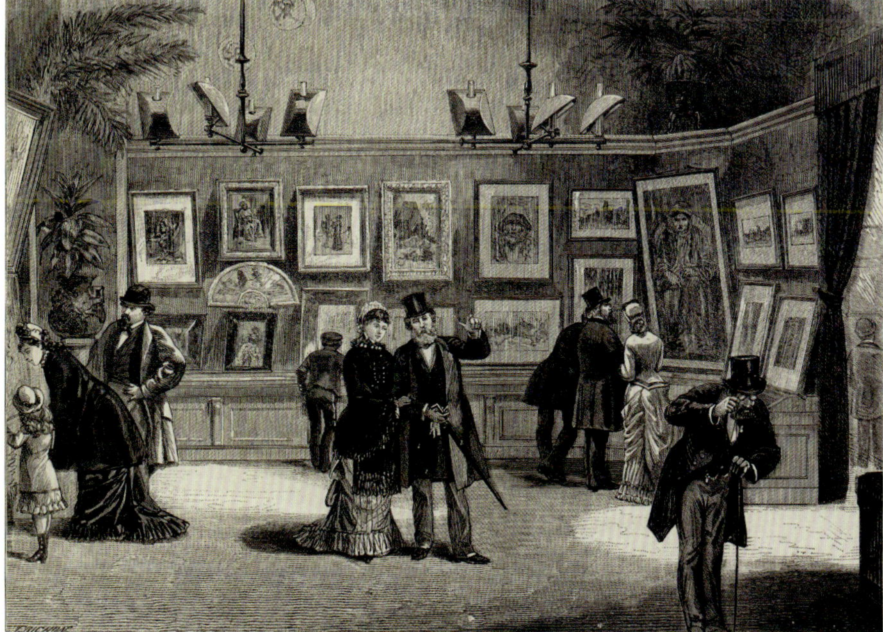

FIG. 144
Exhibition of watercolour artists, Durand-Ruel Gallery, 1879. Engraving by Auguste Trichon, published in *L'Univers illustré*, 26 April 1879
Engraving
Bibliothèque Nationale de France, Paris

articles are filed on 27 February [AP, D31U3 440, dossier 37]. Durand-Ruel is solely responsible as far as third parties are concerned. He enjoys a monthly payment of 1,500 francs to meet his needs; money earned as an expert at public auctions remains his. The company is later dissolved on 1 December 1881 [AP, D31U3 4116, file 1310].
26 February Resumption of the purchase of works from Boudin (two pictures for 200 francs each) [ADR, daybook, 2 February–30 November 1880].
25 March Resumption of the purchase of works from Sisley, to whom he pays an advance of 500 francs on pictures to be delivered [ADR, daybook, 2 February– 30 November 1880].
19 June Durand-Ruel presents a picture by Georges Michel, *Landscape with a Ploughed Field and a Village*, to the Metropolitan Museum of Art in New York.
August He sends 92 pictures, including three by Boudin and two by Jongkind, to an exhibition in Trouville, 'an unfortunate attempt', according to Boudin [ADR, daybook, Boudin to Martin, 11 August 1880, Paris, INHA-Doucet, Ms. 212].
18 September Works by Courbet, Boudin, Sisley, Monet, Pissarro, Eva Gonzalès and Manet (*The Spanish Ballet* and *Bullfight*) are sent to the 'Fine Arts' section at the *Exposition industrielle, des beaux-arts et scolaire*, in Oran (Algeria), at which 233 pictures are exhibited [ADR, daybook].
Late 1880–early 1881 Thanks to advances granted by the banker Jules Feder, Durand-Ruel is able to resume his buying policy and the Impressionists begin to feel that their future is more secure.
26 October Resumption of relations with Monet: Durand-Ruel purchases two landscapes for 250 francs each from the frame-maker Dubourg [ADR, daybook; stocks 557 and 558]. On 17 February 1881, he buys 15 canvases directly from the painter for a total price of 4,500 francs, of which 4,000 francs are paid immediately, followed in April by 24 canvases at 300 francs each. In May, Monet writes in his notebook: 'Sold to M. Durand-Ruel, 22 canvases at 300 francs'; in June he receives 3,000 francs [Wildenstein 1996, I, pp. 117–19].
27 November Purchases two pictures by Renoir from Dubourg: *Fisherman's Children* (Barnes Foundation, Philadelphia), for 2,500 francs [stock 611], and *A Box at the Theatre* (Clark Art Institute, Williamstown) for 1,500 francs [ADR, daybook].
Late December Purchases four paintings, one gouache and one watercolour from Pissarro. Durand-Ruel offers to take 'everything I am going to paint' [*Correspondence Pissarro* [1980–1991], no. 84; Buffévent 2005, p. 170].
Purchases 36 canvases from Sisley, followed by another 45 in 1881. Durand-Ruel reaches an agreement with the artist, who agrees to give him everything he produces [Durand-Ruel Godfroy 1992, pp. 46–7].

1881

6 January Purchases *Girl with a Cat* (fig. 35) from Renoir for 2,500 francs. The artist sells 49 canvases to the dealer in 1881 for between 150 and 700 francs each, allowing him to travel first to Algeria and then to Italy [Durand-Ruel Godfroy 2009, p. 275].
January Durand-Ruel moves into the third floor of 35, rue de Rome: on the left, antechamber, two rooms with fireplaces, hall leading to the dark room, room with fireplace, room with fireplace, small salon, large salon, dining room, room with a fireplace, room, dark room; through the corridor on the right, room with a fireplace, servants' dining room, kitchen. The lease, for three, six or nine years, comes to 7,600 francs [AP, D1P4 973 1876].
Purchases works from Degas for a total of 9,000 francs in 1881 and 14,650 francs in 1882 [Tinterow 1988, p. 371].
February Durand-Ruel visits Boudin in his studio and purchases 'all' his works. He asks the artist to work only for him [Patry, this book].
24 February The dealer organises the sale, at which he also acts as expert, of the collection of the financier Charles Edwards, which he assembled as collateral against loans. Thanks to money from Feder, he is able to purchase 18 pictures from Corot, Delacroix, Rousseau, Dupré and Ribot for a total of 285,510 francs. Manet's *Boy with a Sword* (fig. 91), is sold to him for 9,100 francs and Delacroix's *Convulsionists of Tangier* (Minneapolis Institute of Arts) for 95,000 francs [Durand-Ruel [1939], p. 210; AP, D43E3 69].
16 March Durand-Ruel makes his first purchases from Gauguin: *Landscape*, *Village Church* and *Corner of the Garden* for 1,500 francs. In turn, Gauguin purchases works for his own collection, including a seascape by Manet on 25 March [exh. cat. Paris 1989, p. 36].
9 April Mary Cassatt buys a Monet (W 174) for her brother Alexander, followed by a Degas on 18 June (fig. 92). The same year, Durand-Ruel purchases a painting from the artist: *Two Girls in a Loge* (private collection, DB 62).
15 August While on holiday in Sainte-Adresse, Durand-Ruel asks Monet, who is experiencing a crisis of confidence in his work, to visit him in Le Havre [sales cat. Paris 2006a, no. 58].
30 November Founding of a general partnership with regard to M. Durand-Ruel and a limited partnership with regard to Messieurs Balensi, Feder, Jenty, d'Auberjon, Lallou, Pellorce, Cotinaud, Quisard, Marieton and Fontaine, who provide 500,000 francs of sponsorship. The registered address is 1, rue de la Paix. To meet his needs, M. Durand-Ruel has the right to 1,500 francs per month, and any additional expenses he incurs [AP, D31U3 502, file 1310].

1882

January Durand-Ruel sublets the premises on rue Le Peletier, previously occupied by the Society of Watercolour Painters, to the Banque Nationale for 17 years [AP, D1P4 636, 1876].

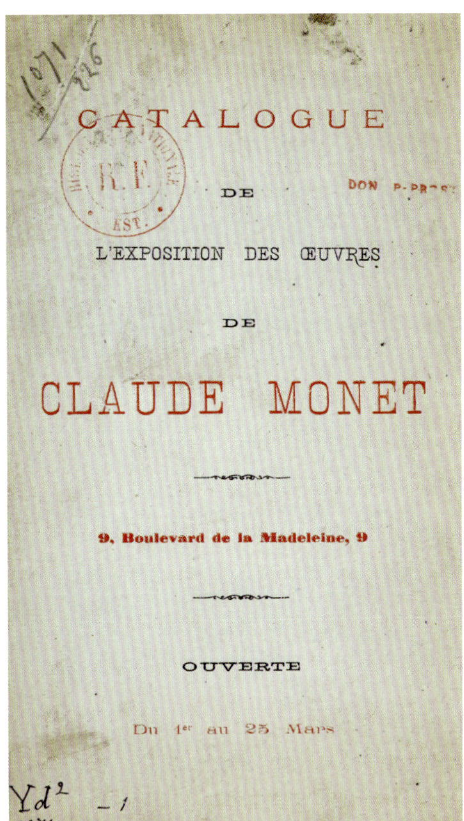

CATALOGUE

DE

L'EXPOSITION DES ŒUVRES

DE

CLAUDE MONET

9, Boulevard de la Madeleine, 9

OUVERTE

Du 1er au 25 Mars

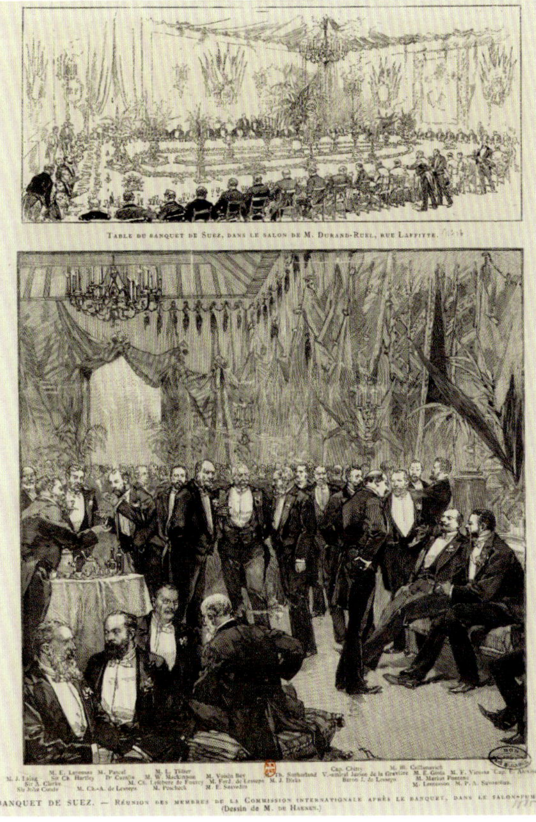

FIG. 145
Catalogue from *Exposition des oeuvres de Claude Monet*, Galerie Durand-Ruel, 9, boulevard de la Madeleine, 1–25 March 1883
Bibliothèque Nationale de France, Paris

FIG. 146
Suez banquet held at rue Laffitte, 11 February 1885, *Le Monde illustré*, 21 February 1885, p. 132
Bibliothèque Nationale de France, Paris

The Union Générale, the bank run by Jules Feder, ceases payments. On 2 February, its bankruptcy leads to the collapse of the Stock Exchange. Feder is ruined and Durand-Ruel is forced to pay back the advances granted to him by the banker. Clients become increasingly rare and the dealer is no longer able to send as much money to the artists as he had the previous year.
The company founded in 1881 is amicably dissolved [Assouline 2002, p. 210].
31 January 'Like you, I am in great difficulty thanks to the terrible crisis that has broken out at the Stock Exchange' [Durand-Ruel to Monet, in sales cat. Paris 2006a, no. 59].
March? 'Business is bad. All these financial events have almost cleaned everyone out and painting is feeling the effects' [Manet to Morisot, in *Correspondence Morisot* [1950], p. 102].
1 March Opening of the seventh '*Exposition des artistes indépendants*' in the rooms of the Panorama de Reichshoffen at 250, rue Saint-Honoré. 'For Durand and even for us, this exhibition is a necessity' [*Correspondence Pissarro* [1980–1991], no. 98]. Thanks to the purchases of recent months, the dealer has a considerable stock and lends a great number of pictures: 'Durand-Ruel is up to his neck in the affair and has had to work the press' [Manet to Morisot, in *Correspondence Morisot* [1950], p. 104; Patry, this book].
22 April Purchases 16 pictures from Monet for the sum of 6,000 francs and seven pictures for 400 francs each on 25 April [Monet's account statement dated 26 April 1882, in sales cat. Paris 2006a, no. 60].
April–July The collector Léon Clapisson buys the most important pieces in his Impressionist collection from Durand-Ruel, leading Pissarro to describe him as the dealer's 'front man' [Distel 1997a, p. 80; Distel 1997b]. From 1891 onwards, Durand-Ruel purchases part of the collection for twice the price paid by Clapisson (50,000 francs) and acts as the expert at the auction that sees the dispersal of the collection on 28 April 1894 [Distel 1997a, p. 83].
26 May Durand-Ruel confirms his commission of Monet to paint door panels with flowers and fruits for the dining room of his apartment at 35, rue de Rome [sales cat. Paris 2006a, no. 60]. The artist takes three years to complete them (figs 26–32).
12 June Degas invites Durand-Ruel to his house-warming (*Correspondence Degas–Durand-Ruel* [1989], no. D).
22 June 'Durand ... wants to have me paint his entire family and ... has retained me for the month of August' [Renoir to Berard, quoted in exh. cat. Ottawa, Chicago and Fort Worth 1997–8, p. 190 and p. 311, note 7].
July Durand-Ruel organises an exhibition in London, at White's Gallery, 13, King Street, St James's, which includes works by Cassatt, Degas, Monet, Renoir and Sisley [Robbins, this book].
August Durand-Ruel finds a small house with a garden in Dieppe that is perfect for his family holidays. There Renoir paints a portrait of five of the dealer's children: Joseph on his own, Marie-Thérèse and Jeanne together, and Charles and Georges together (figs 24, 22 and 23). He also depicts Marie-Thérèse as she is sewing (fig. 140). But he records that Durand-Ruel is not satisfied with these light-filled canvases and is afraid that he will lose his business: 'Do not say anything more to me about portraits in the sunshine' [Renoir to Berard, quoted in exh. cat. Ottawa, Chicago and Fort Worth 1997–8, p. 190 and p. 311, note 4].
End of the year At 9, boulevard de la Madeleine, Durand-Ruel rents an elegantly fitted-out four-room apartment on the mezzanine, where, from February to June 1883, he organises five solo exhibitions of works by Boudin, Monet (fig. 145), Renoir, Pissarro and Sisley. He gives up this space in February 1884 [Patry, this book].
The dealer pays 24,700 francs to Monet, who, in 1882, has an income of 31,241 francs [Wildenstein 1996, p. 184].

1883

19 May 'I was in Holland when your first letter arrived' [Durand-Ruel to Pissarro, BnF, Est., Arch. Pissarro microfilm].
[20] April–July Durand-Ruel sends 82 pictures to London, to the Dowdeswell & Dowdeswell Gallery, 133 New Bond Street, for an exhibition entitled 'Paintings, Drawings and Pastels by Members of "*La Société des Impressionnistes*"', which comprises works by Cassatt, Degas, Manet, Monet, Pissarro, Sisley, Morisot and Renoir, including *Dance at Bougival* [exh. cat. New York 2012, p. 206]. The exhibition attracts the attention of the British press [Robbins, this book].
30 May Durand-Ruel sends 80 canvases to the Foreign Exhibition in Boston: Boudin, Courbet, Renoir, Monet and Sisley are represented with three pictures each, Pissarro with six and Manet with two.
8 July? 'At last [Durand-Ruel] is a little less stretched; he seems very satisfied with the way the exhibition of our works in Rotterdam has turned out'. [*Correspondence Pissarro* [1980–1991] no. 167.

3 September The 'American Exhibition of the Products, Arts and Manufacturers of Foreign Nations' opens in Boston before closing its doors on 13 January of the following year [Thompson, this book]. For Durand-Ruel, this is a test. He takes advantage of the occasion to show the Impressionists without having to pay customs duties [Pissarro to Monet, 12 June 1883, in *Correspondence Pissarro* [1980–1991], no. 158].
6 September Monet updates Durand-Ruel as to the progress of his work on the dining room panels commissioned from him: 'I think I have succeeded in understanding the way I should paint your dining room panels' [Venturi 1939, I, no. 73, p. 261].
October The first Impressionist exhibition in Germany. In late September, Durand-Ruel sends 24 pictures to Gurlitt in Berlin, including *The Railway* by Manet (National Gallery of Art, Washington), valued at 15,000 francs, and works by Degas, Monet, Cassatt, Morisot, Pissarro, Sisley, Renoir and Boudin [Hansen, this book].
17 October 'Here I am back from my short trip to Holland where I spent a week in the company of my second son' [Durand-Ruel to Pissarro, BnF, Est., Arch. Pissarro microfilm].
October Durand-Ruel plans to visit his son, who is in Rouen, and also to call on Pissarro [Durand-Ruel to Pissarro, BnF, Est., Arch. Pissarro microfilm].

1884

1 January Durand-Ruel moves into the first floor of 35, rue de Rome, into an apartment identical to the one on the third floor he also occupied [AP, D1P4 973 (1876)].
He consolidates his financial position by obtaining an 'amiable liquidation (Luckily, my creditors were all my friends). I owed millions. It took me ten years, from 1884 to 1894, to pay them' [Fénéon 1970, p. 352].
7 February After Manet's studio sale on 4 February, Duret regrets: 'Not a single dealer, except Durand, was present'. The dealer, who had acted as the expert alongside Petit, purchased, among other works, *The Music Lesson* (Museum of Fine Arts, Boston, 4,400 francs), *Hamlet* (Folkwang Museum, Essen, 3,500 francs) and *Corner of a Café-Concert* (National Gallery, London, 2,500 francs) [Duret to Monet, MO, ODO 2007-1-27; AP, D48E3 72].
[10 March] '[Durand-Ruel] was in Holland the other week ... It seems he is going to a lot of trouble. On his return from Holland, he's going to set out for London because business is so bad in Paris' [Monet to Alice Hoschedé, Bordighera, WL 441].
Spring The dealer organises an exhibition in London at the Dudley Gallery, Egyptian Hall, Piccadilly, with 24 works, including 12 by Sisley [Durand-Ruel Godfroy 1992, p. 51] and five by Monet, including *Autumn Effect at Argenteuil* (fig. 75) [Robbins, this book].
20 June Durand-Ruel returns from Holland [Durand-Ruel to Monet, in sales cat. Paris 2006a, no. 64].

1885

11 February A banquet takes place in 'M. Durand-Ruel's *salons*', bringing together the members of the International Commission for the Definitive Improvement of the Suez Canal (fig. 146), at the instigation of Ferdinand de Lesseps [[Anonymous] 1884].
1 April Monet tells Durand-Ruel he is coming to Paris the following day [WL 559]. He plans to bring him the panels for rue de Rome in the morning.
27 May The dealer decides to send his son to Brussels with some pictures [Durand-Ruel to Monet, in sales cat. Paris 2006a, no. 65].
30 May 'Would you like to come to rue de Rome for lunch this Thursday at noon? Renoir and Monet will also be there, as well as Mirbeau, who would like to see you' [Durand-Ruel to Pissarro, BnF, Est., Arch. Pissarro microfilm].
June Durand-Ruel exhibits Degas, Renoir, Monet, Sisley and Pissarro 'in his bedroom' at the Hôtel du Grand Miroir in Brussels [[Anonymous] 1885].
18 June He returns from Brussels – 'Our pictures made a great impression there' – although he does not sell anything. His son travels to Antwerp to see some collectors [Durand-Ruel to Monet, in sales cat. Paris 2006a, no. 65].
17 July Durand-Ruel sends a company employee, Charles Casburn, to Holland with pictures by Monet and Renoir: 'He is going to try to drum up trade over there as we are going to do everywhere' [Durand-Ruel to Monet, in sales cat. Paris 2006a, no. 66].
24 July The dealer, who steps up his efforts in Holland, boasts to Monet that this country is 'so rich and so important as to have you and our other friends accepted' [sales cat. Paris 2006a, no. 66].
14 August He sets out for Antwerp and Rotterdam [Durand-Ruel to Monet, in sales cat. Paris 2006a, no. 66].
16 September 'I am spending more time than ever on my plan to travel to and exhibit in America' [Durand-Ruel to Pissarro, BnF, Est., Arch. Pissarro microfilm].
18 September Durand-Ruel writes to Edmond Turquet, Under Secretary of State for Public Instruction and Fine Arts, to explain his plans to exhibit French art in New York and to ask for the patronage of his ministry [AN, F/21/4054/B].
October 'I met Pissarro at Durand-Ruel's' [Seurat to Fénéon, 20 June 1890, in exh. cat. Paris 1991b, p. 383].
26 October He complains of the 'rage of Petit, Goupil and the other dealers ... They are seeking to damage me by any means' [Durand-Ruel to Monet, 26 October, in sales cat. Paris 2006a, no. 66]. He warns Monet against Petit and is saddened to see Sisley and Pissarro attempt to 'negotiate alone' [Durand-Ruel to Monet, 14 December, in sales cat. Paris 2006a, no. 66].
5 November Durand-Ruel publishes an article on the front page of *L'Événement* about a picture by Daubigny belonging to Georges Petit that he believes to be a fake. The rivalry between the two dealers thereby intensifies.
10 December Monet writes to Durand-Ruel that he, Pissarro and Sisley wish to revoke the moral contract that binds them to the dealer in order to exhibit at Petit's gallery [WL 638].
23 December Publication in serial form of *L'Oeuvre* (The Masterpiece) by Zola, which borrows some of Durand-Ruel's traits for the character of the dealer Naudet. In his preparatory notes, the writer describes Durand-Ruel at length and mentions his 'breakthrough on behalf of the Impressionists' [Zola [1986], p. 244].

1886

January On the advice of Pissarro, Durand-Ruel visits the studio of Signac [*Correspondence Pissarro* [1980–1991], no. 306].
15 January 'I am working with a fervour you cannot imagine to recruit new collectors and to stir up the others. I am gaining ground every day despite the hostility of my dear colleagues and we will eventually triumph' [Durand-Ruel to Monet, MO, ODO 2007-1-17, fig. 147).
6 February Opening of the Les XX exhibition in Brussels, to which Durand-Ruel sends five pictures by Monet from his collection. Renoir agrees to lend the two *Dance* panels (figs 3 and 4) and *Young Woman on a Bench* (private collection), which he has placed on

FIG. 147
Letter from Paul Durand-Ruel to Claude Monet, 15 January 1886
Musée d'Orsay, Paris

deposit with the dealer. At the closure of the exhibition on 14 March, these eight canvases join the exhibition in New York [Thompson, this book].
8 February Durand-Ruel purchases *Saint-Mammès, Loing Canal* from Sisley for 200 francs. From this date, having purchased 400 pictures by Sisley since 1872, he definitively ceases buying directly from the painter. The two men nevertheless remain in contact until 1891 [Durand-Ruel Godfroy 1992, p. 46].
11 March 'I am sending you 200 francs this evening, before I leave. My son Joseph is staying here. He will pass on my news' [Durand-Ruel to Pissarro, BnF, Est., Arch. Pissarro microfilm].
25 March Durand-Ruel and his son Charles (fig. 148) arrive in New York aboard the S.S. *Amérique*. They are accompanied by 43 cases containing works of art worth $81,799, two-thirds of which belong to Durand-Ruel's stock, while the remaining third belongs to collectors or artists [Thompson, this book].
10 April Opening at the American Art Galleries, New York, of the exhibition 'Works in Oil and Pastel by the Impressionists of Paris', which includes 289 works. Closing on 25 April, from 25 May it is exhibited at the National Academy of Design, with 21 extra pictures, 13 of which belong to American collectors [Thompson, this book].
Mid-May Durand-Ruel travels to Washington [Thompson, this book].
25 June Closure of the exhibition in New York. Durand-Ruel has sold 49 pictures by Monet, Renoir, Pissarro, Boudin, etc., for a total of $40,000 [Thompson, this book].
30 June 'My father will leave on 10 July [on board the] Champagne from New York. He will therefore not arrive in Paris until the 20th' [Joseph Durand-Ruel to Pissarro, BnF, Est., Arch. Pissarro microfilm].
October Durand-Ruel sends almost 300 works to New York but encounters difficulties with American customs [Thompson, this book].
27 October He lends a picture by Manet, *The Bullfight* (AIC), and one by Monet, *Mail Post at Etretat* (location unknown), as well as a Montenard (location unknown), for the exhibition of French art organised at the Union League Club in New York in honour of the French delegation for the inauguration of the Statue of Liberty.
2 November Durand-Ruel asks Pissarro for a text about his work: 'It is to send to my sons who have been in New York for two weeks already and have asked me to send your biography and notes to help with a better understanding of your works and those of your friends'. He too was soon due to set off: 'I am keen to get over there, where I can see a bright future' [BnF, Est., Arch. Pissarro microfilm].
4 November Pissarro, who has begun to focus on Neo-Impressionism, replies: 'What do you intend to use to support these new doctrines? You have nothing by me, nor by Seurat, Signac or even Dubois-Pillet . . . that has anything to do with these doctrines . . . This will be confusing; these ideas cannot be seriously applied to earlier painting' [*Correspondence Pissarro* [1980–1991], no. 357].

1887

26 February Durand-Ruel, who has sublet rue de la Paix, writes to Monet: 'In addition to the expense, I was disgusted by the display of pictures that only serves to harm those things that are good. I am going to reopen my galleries on rue Laffitte and I will try to be more useful to my painters there than in my shop' [sales cat. Paris 2006a, no. 70; AP, D1P4 837 (1876)].
14 March Durand-Ruel arrives in New York on board *La Champagne* [ancestry.com].
April He opens a Gallery at 28 West 23rd Street [Thompson, this book].
5–6 May At the art sale staged at the Moore's Art Galleries in New York, of the 127 works on display, 35 sell for a sum of $9,870, some to front men [ADR; Thompson, this book].
25 May Opening in New York, at the National Academy of Design, of the exhibition 'Celebrated Paintings by Great French Masters', which closes on 30 June: 223 works are exhibited [Thompson, this book].
Summer After the exhibition, works lent by collectors return to France, but those in Durand-Ruel's stock remain in New York [Thompson, this book].
14 September After he has been back in France for two months, Durand-Ruel writes to Monet saying he has been in the South of France and Holland. He has work done on rue Laffitte and moves back in [sales cat. Paris 2006a, no. 70; AP, D1P4 837 (1876)].
5 November Durand-Ruel leaves Paris yet again for New York, where he arrives on 14 November on board *La Bourgogne*. During this visit, the gallery moves to 297 Fifth Avenue [Thompson, this book].

1888

February Monet tries to involve his friends in his refusal to exhibit at the Durand-Ruel Gallery. Only Rodin follows suit. Morisot, Renoir, Whistler, Boudin, Caillebotte, Pissarro, Sisley, Lépine and Brown take part in the exhibition that opens on 25 May.

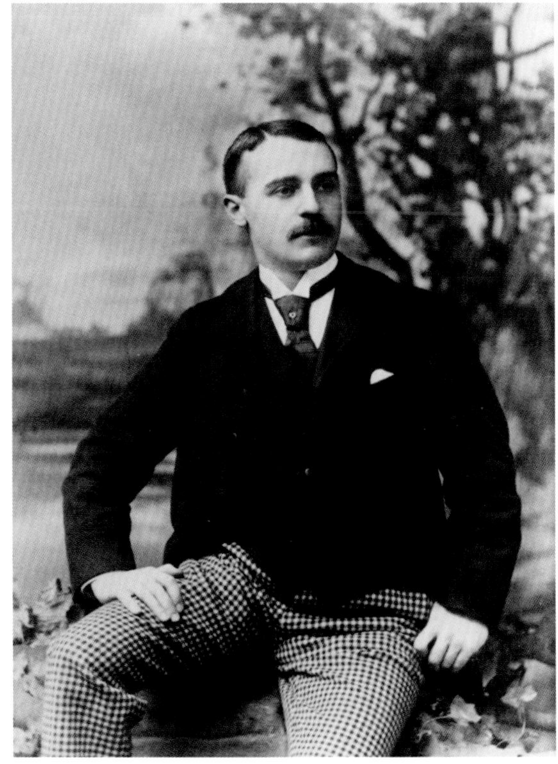

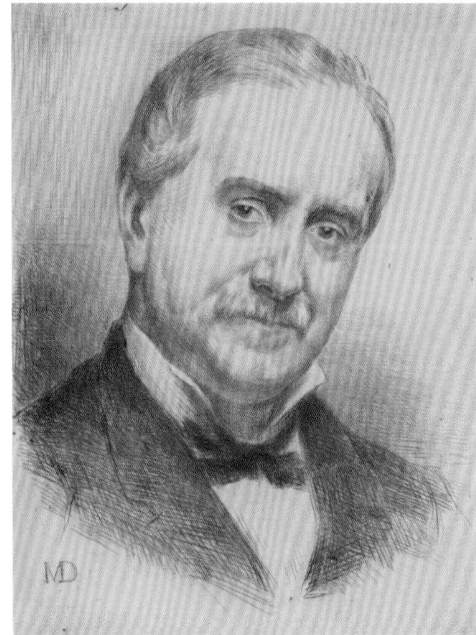

FIG. 148
Charles Durand-Ruel, about 1886
Silver gelatin print
Archives Durand-Ruel

FIG. 149
Marcellin Desboutin
Portrait of Paul Durand-Ruel, 1882
Drypoint etching, 19.7 × 14.7 cm
Paris, bibliothèque de l'INHA, collections Jacques Doucet

21–23 February Sale 'Manet, Monet, Boudin and others' at the American Art Galleries in New York. Durand-Ruel owns several of the works sold [*The Sun*, 16 February; *New York Times*, 17 February].
3–11 March Return to France of 'Durand-Ruel [who] is not satisfied with his business in America' [Charles Durand-Ruel to Duncan, 24 February, ADR; *Correspondence Pissarro* [1980–1991], no. 492].
10 March Opening, before the First Chamber of the Civil Court of the Seine, of the trial relating to *The Death of Marat* by David (Musée National du Château, Versailles) [CAC, no. 10, 10 March, p. 77]. In April 1885, Durand-Ruel and Brame sell a version of the picture presented as an original at the exhibition *Portraits du siècle* (Ecole des Beaux-Arts, Paris) to M. Terme. M. David-Chassagnolle, grandson of David, had claimed ownership of the only original picture and, at that time, demands a change in the catalogue attribution, along with a payment of 1,000 francs in damages. His widow brings an action against M. Terme, who calls Durand-Ruel as guarantor. The Court of Cassation finds in favour of Durand-Ruel on 2 January 1892 [CAC, no. 1, 2 January 1892, p. 3].
30 March Boudin delivers 41 of the 44 pictures that Charles has purchased from him [exh. cat. Honfleur 1988, p. 191].
6 April Resumption of purchases from Pissarro. Despite this the painter enters into business with Theo van Gogh in September, leading to strained relations with Durand-Ruel [Durand-Ruel Snollaerts 2005, I, p. 26].
Early April Durand-Ruel wants to re-establish relations with Monet, who would 'always be happy to do business with [him] again', but declines his exhibition proposal [WL 865 and 868].
May Exhibition of approximately 20 paintings from the Durand-Ruel collection at Thurber's Art Gallery in Chicago [*Chicago Daily Tribune*, 20 May]. William Wallace Kimball purchases a Corot, probably *Bathing Nymphs and Child* (AIC).
8 May Durand-Ruel informs Whistler of his intention to open an exhibition in his galleries of 150 of the best works by Monet, Renoir, Sisley, Rodin and others. He asks him for works and the names of collectors for loans [8 May 1888, GUW 00978 (2013-05-17)].
25 May–25 June Group 'international' exhibition bringing together 120 pictures by Boudin, Brown, Caillebotte, Lépine, Morisot, Pissarro, Renoir, Sisley and Whistler.
4 June Following tensions between Monet and Durand-Ruel, Theo van Gogh successfully exhibits 10 canvases depicting Antibes, purchased from Monet, at the Boussod & Valadon Gallery. This new competition annoys Durand-Ruel [WL 898 and 899].
11 September Van Gogh praises the visionary qualities of Durand-Ruel: 'From another point of view you'll be doing something like Durand-Ruel, who in the past, before other people recognised Claude Monet's individuality, bought paintings from him. And Durand-Ruel didn't earn from it either; at one point he had quantities of those paintings without being able to dispose of them. But after all, what he did will always remain well done, and today he can always say to himself that he won his cause' [*Correspondence Van Gogh* [2009], no. 680].
24 September Monet is very disconcerted, because 'while wanting to be nice to [Durand-Ruel] and to sell [him] paintings again' he wants to maintain good relations with Theo van Gogh (at Boussod & Valadon, formerly at Goupil): 'What would have become of me without firstly M. Petit and the Maison Goupil?' [WL 903].
Late October–mid-November Second exhibition of French painting organised by Durand-Ruel at Thurber's Art Gallery in Chicago [*Chicago Daily Tribune*, 14 October and 18 November].
23 December Pissarro agrees to take part in the *Exposition des peintres-graveurs* planned by Durand-Ruel for the coming January [*Correspondence Pissarro* [1980–1991], no. 511].
26 December Marcellin Desboutin, who takes part in the *Exposition des peintres-graveurs*, informs Durand-Ruel that the copper for his portrait has been lost and suggests having him pose for another plate [Venturi 1939, II, p. 72, fig. 149].

1889

23 January Opening of the first *Exposition des peintres-graveurs*. The exhibitions are held at the gallery until 1893. Charles Durand-Ruel visits collections in New York in the company of Duret [Duret to Monet, MO, Monet archive, ODO 2007-1-35].
29 March Pissarro delays replying to a request from Durand-Ruel on behalf of a buyer because he has 'had to do a lot of research to gather the collection of prints you asked for. I selected the rarest proofs and artist proofs, which explains the somewhat high prices of some pieces' [*Correspondence Pissarro* [1980–1991], no. 524].
May First purchases by Bertha and Potter Palmer: a collection of prints, followed in September by *On the Stage*, a pastel by Degas (AIC) and a canvas by Renoir (D 1046) [Jensen 2012].
1 May Monet asks Durand-Ruel to lend canvases for his exhibition with Rodin

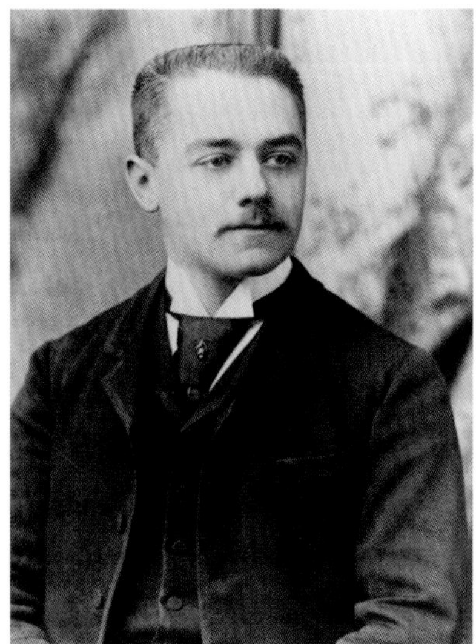

FIG. 150
Portrait of Georges Durand-Ruel, 1882
Silver gelatin print
Archives Durand-Ruel

FIG. 151
The second Durand-Ruel Gallery (1889–94), New York, 315 Fifth Avenue
Silver gelatin print
Archives Durand-Ruel

at Petit's gallery during the Universal Exhibition. 'This exhibition may be somewhat successful and for [Durand-Ruel] it will be a chance to sell'. Durand-Ruel's refusal surprises Monet [WL 969 and 990].
June Durand-Ruel sends 55 pictures to the press pavilion opposite the Fine Arts Palace at the Universal Exhibition [Durand-Ruel Godfroy 1992, p. 55, and 61 note 82].
7 August Monet asks Durand-Ruel to participate in the public subscription to acquire Manet's *Olympia* for the State. He donates 200 francs [WL 1002 and 1010].
September The New York Gallery is established in new premises at 315 Fifth Avenue (*The Art Amateur*, no. 4, pp. 87–8).
21 October First mention of a purchase by the 'Abbé' Gaugain: Boudin, *The Beach at Berck*, and Lépine, *The Pont des Arts*, for 1,300 francs [stock 2509 and 2305]. The priest becomes a regular client of the gallery [Distel 2010, p. 252 and notes 16 and 17].
25 November Durand-Ruel arrives in New York with Georges (figs 150 and 151).

1890

Durand-Ruel commissions Renoir to paint panels to decorate the doors of his salon. Two of these are completed, *Girl with a Basket of Fish* and *Girl with a Basket of Oranges* (National Gallery of Art, Washington).
30 January Charles wants to buy Rodin's marble *The Young Mother at the Grotto* 'for the house', and 'if it hadn't been a question of money, [he] would very much have liked to ... purchase the three pieces [Rodin] showed him'. He hopes to see him with his father, 'who is about to return from New York', and invites Rodin to participate in their forthcoming *Exposition des peintres-graveurs*. On 17 February, the marble is installed in rue de Rome. Durand-Ruel finds it 'wonderful' [Charles Durand-Ruel to Rodin, AMR].
February Joseph organises an exhibition in Chicago, at the Palmer House Hotel, room 348. Works by Watteau, Van Loo, Lorrain, Teniers, Corot, Daubigny, Diaz, Delacroix, Rousseau, Dupré and Degas are included [*Chicago Tribune*, 26 February, p. 8].
12 February Rodin purchases a pastel portrait of a child by Renoir for 1,000 francs [invoice Durand-Ruel, 12 February, AMR].
6–26 March *Exposition des peintres-graveurs*, at which the State purchases engravings through the intermediary of Burty, including two by Pissarro (*View of Pontoise* and *Meadow and Mill*), with the intention of founding a collection of prints at the Musée du Luxembourg [Distel 1984].
May Boudin exhibits 13 paintings, watercolours and pastels at the Chase's Gallery in Boston with the support of Durand-Ruel [exh. cat. Honfleur 1988, p. 192].
4 June Durand-Ruel has just returned from Florence [Durand-Ruel to Monet,

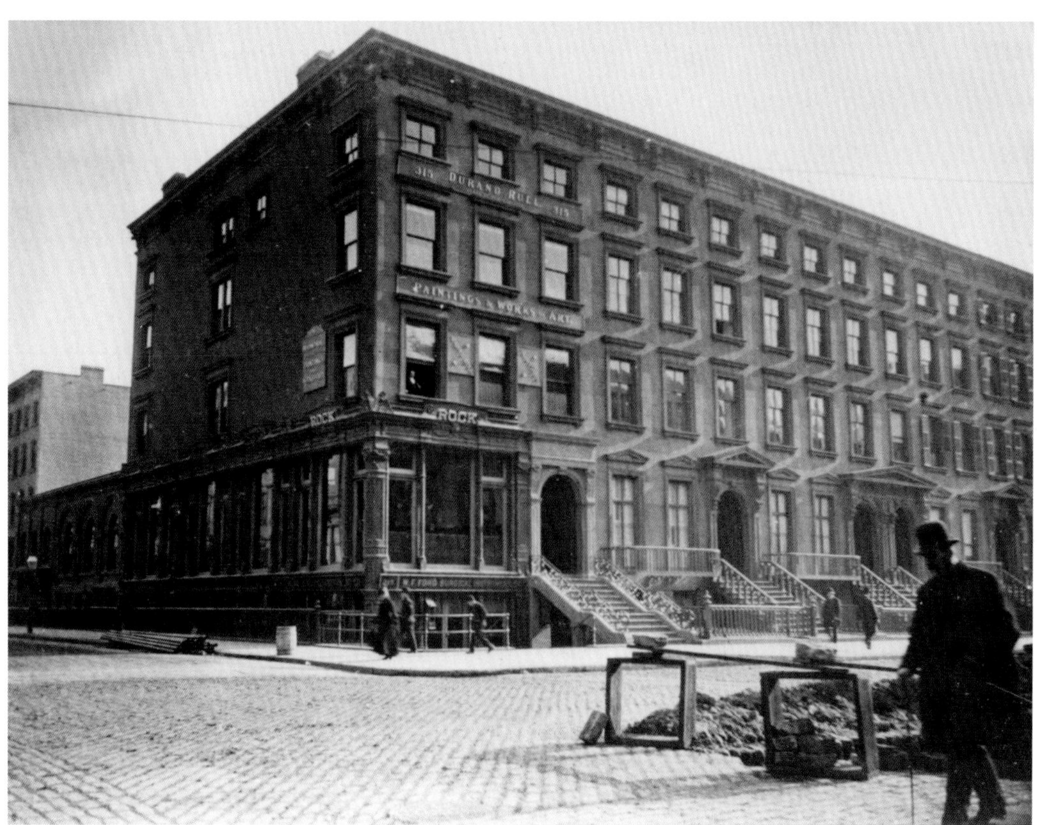

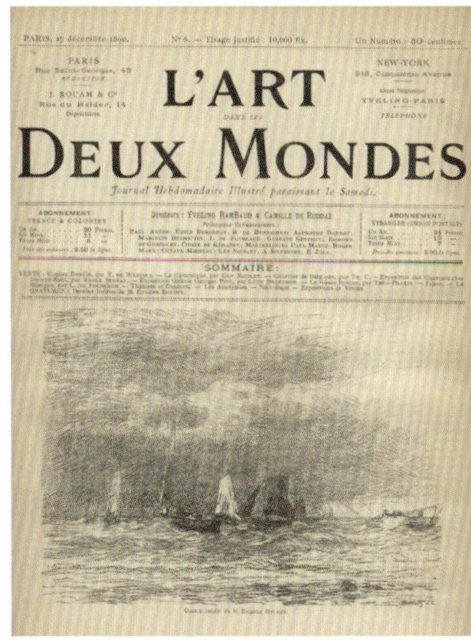

PARIS, 27 décembre 1890. N° 6. — Tirage justifié : 10,000 Ex. Un Numéro : 50 centimes

PARIS
Rue Saint-Georges, 48
RÉDACTION

J. ROUAM & Cie
Rue du Helder, 14
Dépositaires

L'ART
DANS LES
DEUX MONDES

Journal Hebdomadaire Illustré paraissant le Samedi.

NEW-YORK
315, Cinquième Avenue

YVELING-PARIS
TÉLÉPHONE

ABONNEMENT
FRANCE & COLONIES

DIRECTEURS : YVELING RAMBAUD & CAMILLE DE ROUDAZ

ABONNEMENT
ÉTRANGER (UNION POSTALE)

SOMMAIRE :

FIG. 152
L'Art dans les deux mondes,
vol. 6, 27 December 1890
Newspaper print
Archives Durand-Ruel

in sales cat. Paris 2006a, no. 72].
At the Ernest May sale, where Georges Petit acts as the expert, Durand-Ruel acquires nine pictures for 11,750 francs: one by Manet (*The Guitar Player*, RW 122, Hill-Stead Museum, Farmington, Conn., 3,000 francs); three by Monet (W 189, 1,500 francs; W 539, 1,950 francs; W 402, 2,100 francs), and five by Pissarro (PDRS 195, 1,400 francs; PDRS 316, 200 francs; PDRS 295, 800 francs; PDRS 492, 700 francs; PDRS 437, 100 francs). He pushes up the prices of Pissarro's pictures [Lugt 49193; Durand-Ruel to Pissarro, 4 June, in Venturi 1939, II, p. 253].
29 July Death of Van Gogh. His brother Theo tries in vain to have his work exhibited by Durand-Ruel [exh. cat. Amsterdam and Paris 1999–2000, p. 56].
3 September–18 October. Durand-Ruel New York lends French paintings to the Interstate Industrial Exhibition in Chicago [Jensen 2007, p. 229].
September–October Durand-Ruel lends at least two pictures by Pissarro to the annual exhibition in Saint Louis (nos. 71 and 72).
22 November Publication of the first issue of *L'Art dans les deux mondes*, a new review founded by Durand-Ruel, which is published every Saturday until 11 July 1891 for a total of 34 issues (fig. 152).
25 November Mirbeau, who does not wish to 'play the dealers' game' and wants to preserve his independence, resigns from *L'Art dans les deux mondes*. He reverses his decision shortly afterwards when Monet asks him for an article. The painter takes charge of the illustrations [*Correspondence Mirbeau* [2009], II pp. 309–11; Monet to Durand-Ruel, WL 1085].
3 December Durand-Ruel lends some pictures from his collection (including one by Delacroix and one by Corot) to the exhibition of painting and engraving at the Union League Club in Brooklyn [ADM, no. 8, 10 January 1891, p. 86].
December Durand-Ruel exhibits 99 paintings and pastels by Boudin. He purchases 52 works from him [exh. cat. Honfleur 1988, p. 193].

1891

Durand-Ruel starts to photograph the works that pass through the gallery. [Durand-Ruel and Durand-Ruel, this book]. Mary Cassatt asks Durand-Ruel if Miss Paget [Vernon Lee], the famous American writer, can come to admire his personal collection of works by Degas [Venturi 1939, II, p. 114]. Sisley breaks off relations with Durand-Ruel, who, according to the artist 'acts as a modern speculator, with angelic sweetness' [13 April 1891, *Correspondence Pissarro* [1980–1991], no. 653].
17 January Purchase of '20 superb antique paintings ... by the Chicago museum through the intermediary of Durand-Ruel' [ADM, no. 9, 17 January, p. 99].
8 February Durand-Ruel lends *Old Chelsea Bridge* by Pissarro and five pictures by Sisley to the Les XX exhibition in Brussels.
13 February Durand-Ruel lends works to the first Monet exhibition at the Union League Club in New York [*New York Times*, 13 February; Zafran 2007, p. 94].
23 February Gauguin sale at the Hôtel Drouot auction house. At the request of Mirbeau, Durand-Ruel acts as the expert [*Correspondence Mirbeau* [2009], II, pp. 335–6].
March 'Monet–Sisley' exhibition in New York [Rewald 1956, p. 460].
9–17 March Boudin exhibition [ADM, no. 7, 3 January, p. 79].
11 March Foundation of the Société des peintres-graveurs at a general meeting hosted by Durand-Ruel [Buhot to Boudin, BnF, Est., 4-Z-7].
17–28 March The exhibition *The Impressionists of Paris [Claude Monet Camille Pissarro Alfred Sisley] from the galleries of Durand-Ruel Paris and New York* at the Eastman Chase Gallery in Boston is highly praised by the critics.
19–22 March Exhibition of Burty's collection of Japanese and Chinese art objects. The sale also takes place at the gallery 23–28 March [ADM, no. 18, 21 March, p. 219].
20 March–27 April Salon des Indépendants, after which Henry Lerolle introduces Maurice Denis to Durand-Ruel [Bona 2012, p. 379].
April Berthe Morisot is disappointed by her first monographic exhibition at Durand-Ruel's, and in particular by the way a portrait of her daughter is displayed [Stuckey-Scott 1987, p. 148].
4–30 April Exhibitions of works by Cassatt and Pissarro at the same time as that of the *peintres-graveurs*. The latter is visited by the President, as well as M. Bourgeois, Minister for Public Instruction and M. Larroumet, Director of the Ecole des Beaux-Arts. The State acquires several engravings [Fénéon 1970, I pp. 184–6; ADM, no. 22, 18 April, p. 267, no. 25, 9 May p. 301].
May Joseph offers James Hill (Minneapolis) a plan for the hanging of his collection in his home [O'Sullivan 1991, p. 52, no. 33].
4 May Opening of the *Exposition d'œuvres récentes de Cl. Monet*, in which 15 of the 22 canvases on display depict haystacks. The preface to the catalogue is written by Geffroy.
1 or 4 June–13 or 15 July Durand-Ruel organises the first exhibition of works by American painters in Paris. The preface to the catalogue is written by Theodore Stanton.
July The Palmers from Chicago, and their agent, Sara Hallowell, visit the Paris gallery. They purchase six works by Monet [exh. cat. Pittsburgh 1997, p. 329].
4 July Durand-Ruel shows recent works by Renoir and nine canvases by Courbet [ADM, no. 33, 4 July, p. 83].
19–20 October In order to purchase his house at Giverny, Monet asks Durand-Ruel for an advance of 20,000 francs against the 29,000 francs for the canvases he is preparing to deliver to the dealer [WL 1122 and 1123].
5 December Purchase by the Musée des Beaux-Arts in Lyon of *Head of a Woman* by Ribot for 4,500 francs [Lyon, AM, 78wp5].

1892

25 January Durand-Ruel, back from 'a long trip' invites Rodin to dinner on 1 February. Puvis de Chavannes and 'some friends' will also attend [AMR].
1–20 February Pissarro exhibition, including 50 paintings and 21 gouaches. The preface to the catalogue is written by Lecomte. Durand-Ruel purchases 10 unsold canvases from the artist for between 500 and 1,100 francs [Durand-Ruel Snollaerts 2005, p. 31].
29 February–10 March Exhibition of Monet's *Poplars*. The painter, satisfied by the results of his exhibition, confirms to

FIG. 153
View of an exhibition of prints by Utamaro and Hiroshige, Paris, Durand-Ruel Gallery, 22 January–20 February 1893
Bibliothèque Nationale de France, Paris

FIG. 154
Paul Durand-Ruel, two of his sons, his daughters and their husbands, 1894
Silver gelatin print
Archives Durand-Ruel

Durand-Ruel that he wishes to keep his independence and does not want to reserve his entire production for a single dealer [WL 1138].
10 March–10 April The Salon de la Rose-Croix exhibits 200 works at Durand-Ruel's by 69 artists. The galleries are filled with flowers for the opening and receive 11,000 visitors on the first day [*Le Figaro*, 11 March, p. 1].
23 April Publication of Georges Lecomte's book *L'Art impressionniste d'après la collection privée de M. Durand-Ruel*, published by Durand-Ruel. Fénéon finds it 'luxurious in literature and appearance' [Fénéon 1970, I, p. 216].
7–20 May Renoir retrospective with 110 works. Lenders include Caillebotte, Gallimard, Chabrier, Blanche, Berard, Ephrussi and De Bellio. The preface to the catalogue is written by Arsène Alexandre.
8 May Rodin dines at Durand-Ruel's with the Palmers from Chicago [Durand-Ruel to Rodin, 3 and 4 May, AMR].
June A series of *Poplars* by Monet is exhibited in New York.
13 June The Goncourts visit the rue de Rome. 'An instance of the curious dwelling of a picture dealer in the nineteenth century is provided by Durand-Ruel's home. It is an enormous apartment on the rue de Rome, full of paintings by Renoir, Monet, Degas, etc., in which there is a bedroom with a crucifix by the bed and a dining room with a table set for eighteen, where each dinner guest has a graduated array of six drinking glasses. Geffroy tells me that the table is set in this manner every day for Impressionist painting'. [Goncourt [1989], III, p. 723; trans. Assouline [2004], p. 228.]
29 June Pissarro asks Durand-Ruel to advance him the 2 or 3,000 francs he needs to purchase his house at Eragny. Durand-Ruel accepts [*Correspondence Pissarro* [1980–1991], no. 797].
21 July Durand-Ruel, in Switzerland and Savoy for three weeks with his daughters, congratulates Rodin on receiving the Légion d'Honneur [Interlaken, AMR].
September–October The exhibition of 25 pastel and watercolour landscapes by Degas is the first of two such exhibitions to take place during the artist's lifetime. Durand-Ruel invites Roujon, Director of the Beaux-Arts, to the event [exh. cat. Paris, Ottawa and New York 1988–9, pp. 488, 502].
18 September Charles dies of peritonitis at the age of 27, shortly after his sixth visit to America [AP, V4E6155; Durand-Ruel [1939], p. 215].
5 October Durand-Ruel sends *The Bather* and *The Dance* (fig. 5) by Renoir to the *Exposicion Internacional de Bellas Artes* in Madrid. *The Dance* is praised by critics [Distel 2014].
28 October Durand-Ruel and his daughters are expected at Giverny (fig. 155) on 30 October. Monet is happy to see him but has nothing to show him: 'I have been entirely lazy this year ... You are going to scold me, which will be the right thing to do and will give me courage' [WL 1167].

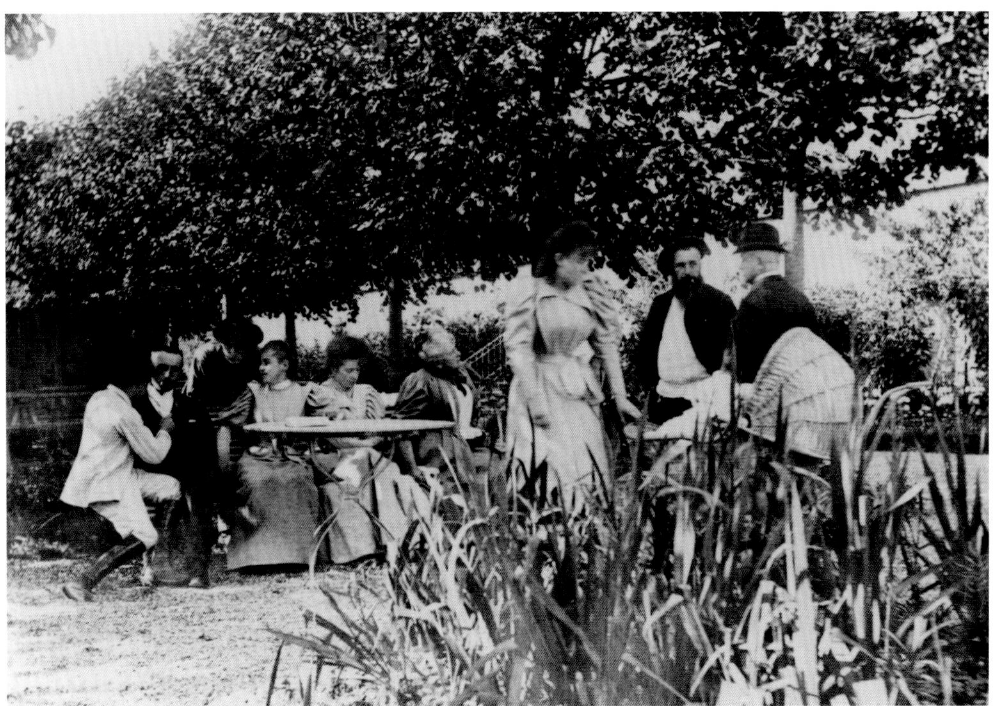

FIG. 155
Claude Monet, his family and Paul Durand-Ruel in Giverny, June 1893
Photograph taken by Joseph Durand-Ruel
Archives Durand-Ruel

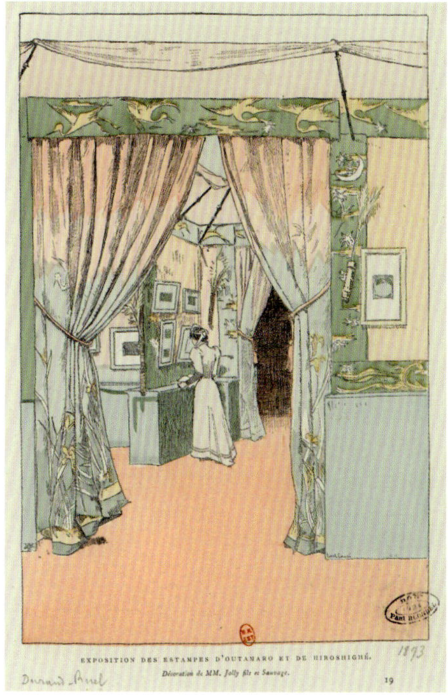

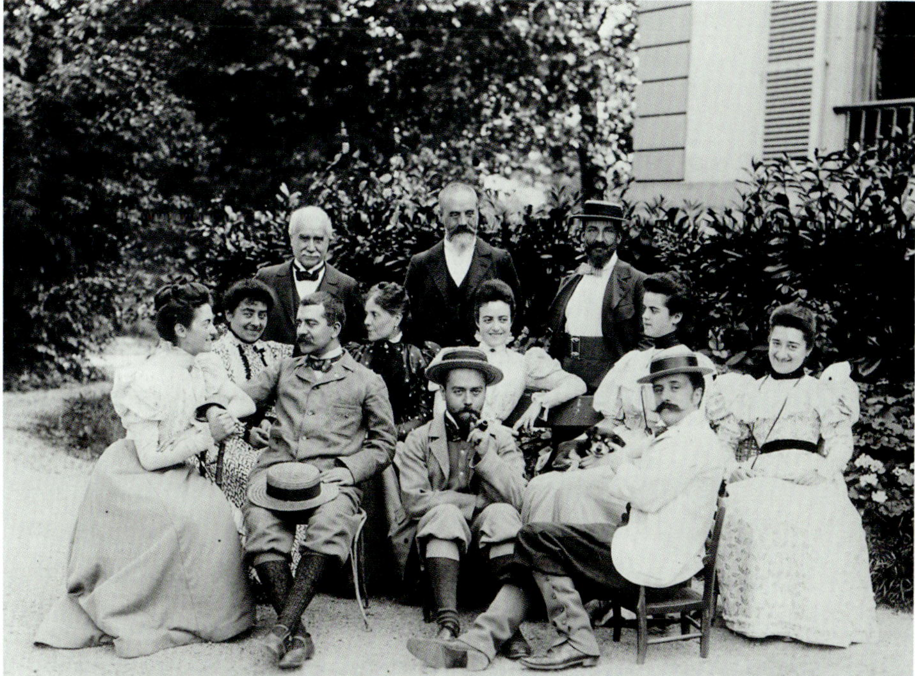

13 November Durand-Ruel visits Pissarro. 'The *Gardens* . . . were very successful. He almost took everthing'. On 16 November, the painter sends Durand-Ruel a list of the 19 selected canvases with their prices (28,100 francs in total) [Pissarro to Mirbeau, 14 November, in *Correspondence Pissarro* [1980–1991], no. 827; Pissarro to Durand-Ruel, 16 November, ibid., no. 828].
27 November Pissarro refuses to agree to a monopoly with Durand-Ruel but agrees to triple his prices for collectors [*Correspondence Pissarro* [1980–1991], no. 837].
21 December Monet delivers four canvases to Durand-Ruel and four others for the Palmers (WL 1173).
1892 is the year that sees the greatest number of works by Pissarro (42) purchased by the dealer [Durand-Ruel Snollaerts 2005, p. 32].

1893

January Exhibition of bronzes by Barye in New York [*New York Times*, 23 January].
1 February Monet visits the exhibition of prints by Hiroshige and Utamaro (fig. 153) held at Durand-Ruel's gallery, 22 January–20 February. He meets Pissarro there. The galleries are decorated pink and pistachio green [Wildenstein 1996, p. 289].
15–30 March Exhibition of recent works by Pissarro. The preface to the catalogue is written by Lecomte.
20 March Isaac de Camondo acquires his first Impressionist work from Durand-Ruel (Degas, *Café-concert at Les Ambassadeurs*, MO). Later that year he purchases works by Monet, Manet, Sisley and Degas for 64,500 francs, then, the following year, *Horses before the Stands* by Degas (fig. 61) and *The Fife Player* by Manet (fig. 87) [notebook of Isaac de Camondo, documentation of the Département des Objets d'Art at the Louvre].
23 May Marriage in Paris of the eldest of the Durand-Ruel daughters, Marie-Thérèse, to Félix André Aude. Degas and Puvis are witnesses [AP, V4E8691]. Monet is unable to attend [WL 1213 and 1214].
5 September Marriage in Paris of Durand-Ruel's second daughter, Jeanne, to Albert Edouard Louis Dureau. Degas and Puvis are again witnesses [AP, V4E8692]. Boudin regrets that he is unable to attend [Boudin to Durand-Ruel, 27 August, in Venturi 1939, II, p. 89, (fig. 154)].
8 September Paul Durand-Ruel and his sons Joseph and Georges found a general partnership, 'Durand-Ruel et fils', 'with the aim of exploiting the business assets of pictures and works of art at 16, rue Laffitte in Paris and New York 315 Fifth Avenue', for a duration of five years from 5 September. It is registered on 18 September [AP, D32U3 716].
23 October Durand-Ruel arrives in New York, then visits the 'World Columbian Exposition' in Chicago, which takes place 1 May–30 October. It features 11 canvases by Monet, Pissarro and Degas [ancestry.com; Kysela 1964].
4 November Exhibition of recent works by Paul Gauguin, 'at the request of Degas', with 44 pictures and two sculptures. The preface to the catalogue is written by Charles Morice [exh. cat. Paris, Ottawa and New York 1988–9, p. 489; Rishel, this book].
November–December Mary Cassatt exhibition. André Mellerio writes the preface to the catalogue, which includes 98 paintings, pastels and engravings.

1894

2 January François Depeaux, the collector from Rouen who begins purchasing Impressionist works in 1893, buys *Dance at Bougival* (fig. 5) from Durand-Ruel, who eventually sells him 65 canvases [Lespinasse 2010, p. 131].
14 January Durand-Ruel leaves New York for Paris [*The Chicago Tribune*, 14 January, p. 11].
20 January–10 February Guillaumin exhibition of 106 paintings and pastels.
11 February Redon asks Durand-Ruel to lend him a room in his gallery and offers him a higher percentage on sales in return [11 February, copy MO, Berson archive]. The exhibition takes place 29 March–14 April. The preface to the catalogue is written by Mellerio. One hundred and twenty-four works are exhibited.
March The New York gallery moves to 389 Fifth Avenue. The lease costs $25,000 a year. The expense of renovating the premises, which belong to Havemeyer, prevents Durand-Ruel from opening a branch in Chicago [Weitzenhoffer 1986, p. 125].
1 March Cassatt asks Durand-Ruel for 5,000 francs to purchase a property in the Oise [ADR].
3–21 March Pissarro exhibition with 98 paintings, watercolours, gouaches and pastels. The financial returns are mediocre [Durand-Ruel Snollaerts 2005, p. 35].
19 March Duret sale at the Galerie Petit, with 30 Impressionist lots out of a total of 42. Durand-Ruel is one of the experts. He purchases three works by Degas, three by Manet (RW 111, 164, 179), three by Monet (W 433, 172, 528), two by Renoir, two by Pissarro, one by Sisley, and on behalf of Duret, who buys *Young Girl in a Ball Gown* by Morisot for the State, for a total of 62,250 francs [Lugt 52368; AP, D48E3 79; Lille and Martigny 2002, pp. 194 and 196].
5 April Dinner at Renoir's with Mallarmé. Berthe Morisot and Régnier are also invited [*Correspondence Mallarmé* [1965–1985], VI, p. 248].
7 April–27 May Durand-Ruel discovers Albert André at the Salon des Indépendants and becomes his dealer.
24–25 April Durand-Ruel is the expert at the sale of Millet's widow's estate [CAC, no. 18, 5 May, p. 138].

FIG. 156
Henri de Toulouse-Lautrec
Paul Durand-Ruel in his gallery, rue Laffitte
Drawing, 20 × 12.5 cm
Archives Durand-Ruel

29 April Durand-Ruel visits Monet, who offers him a price of 15,000 francs for each of his *Cathedrals*, putting him in competition with Valadon, Joyant and the collector Camondo. Durand-Ruel, Valadon and Montaignac come to an agreement. Monet criticises this 'syndicate of dealers' [Wildenstein 1996, I, pp. 298–9].
Late April–12 May Durand-Ruel exhibits 40 pictures by Manet [CAC, no. 17, 28 April, p. 130].
5–12 May Exhibition of lithographs by Toulouse-Lautrec (fig. 156).
23 May Durand-Ruel suggests to Roujon that the State purchase Millet's *Winter* and *Summer*, which are due to be included in a sale the following day at which he is the expert. The suggestion is not acted upon [23 April, AMN 029 53 Roujon].
June Posthumous exhibition of Caillebotte. Monet and Renoir help to select works [exh. cat. Paris and Chicago 1994–5, p. 29].
2 June The sale of the estate of Tanguy's widow is a failure. Only two of the 101 lots sell for more than 450 francs. Durand-Ruel buys two works by Pissarro (for 410 francs), one pastel by Renoir (190 francs), two drawings by Cassatt (20 and 21 francs) and one work by Puvis de Chavannes (120 francs) [Lugt 52690; AP, D48E3 79].
29 September Durand-Ruel writes to Pissarro: 'I have just returned from the South of France and am about to depart for New York' [BnF, Est., R 10958].
October Durand-Ruel again exhibits landscapes by Degas and six works by Puvis de Chavannes [*Le Siècle*, 5 October; Brown-Price 2010, p. 457].
5 October Durand-Ruel returns four canvases painted in Knokke-le-Zoute to Pissarro. He argues the artist's prices are too high in light of the 'terrible state of affairs for eighteen months': 'It seems to me that you were not at ease working in a new country and that you did not put the qualities you usually possess into these works. I much prefer your earlier pictures' [BnF, Est., R 10958].
6 October Durand-Ruel and Joseph depart for New York, where they disembark on 13 October [ancestry.com; Wildenstein 1996, p. 301].
2–3 December Durand-Ruel dines in Chicago with the collectors Arthur J. Eddy and John A. Lynch [Eddy to Whistler, 5 December, GUL E8, GUW 01020 (2014-05-14)].
14 December Signac admires 'early Manets' at Durand-Ruel's [GBA, July–September 1949, p. 112].
15-31 December 'M. Puvis de Chavannes: Loan Exhibition of Paintings, Pastels and Decorations' is shown in New York, with 32 works [Brown-Price 2010, p. 457].

1895

Durand-Ruel exhibits works at the Gillespie's Galleries in Pittsburgh. He does the same in 1896, 1897, 1901, 1902 and 1905 [Pittsburgh 2007, pp. 58, 350–51, note 24].
5 or 6 January Durand-Ruel returns to Paris [Georges Durand-Ruel to Rodin, 5 December 1894, AMR].
12–27 January First Monet retrospective at the New York gallery, with 40 or 48 canvases. A reduced version of 27 pictures is exhibited in Boston, at the St Botolph Club 4–16 February. Seven pictures come from private collections and 20 from Durand-Ruel's own collection [*New York Times*, 14 January, p. 4; *The Collector*, VI, 15 January, p. 90].
26 February–16 March The first annual exhibition of Orientalist painters is staged at the gallery. The shows continue there until 1900.

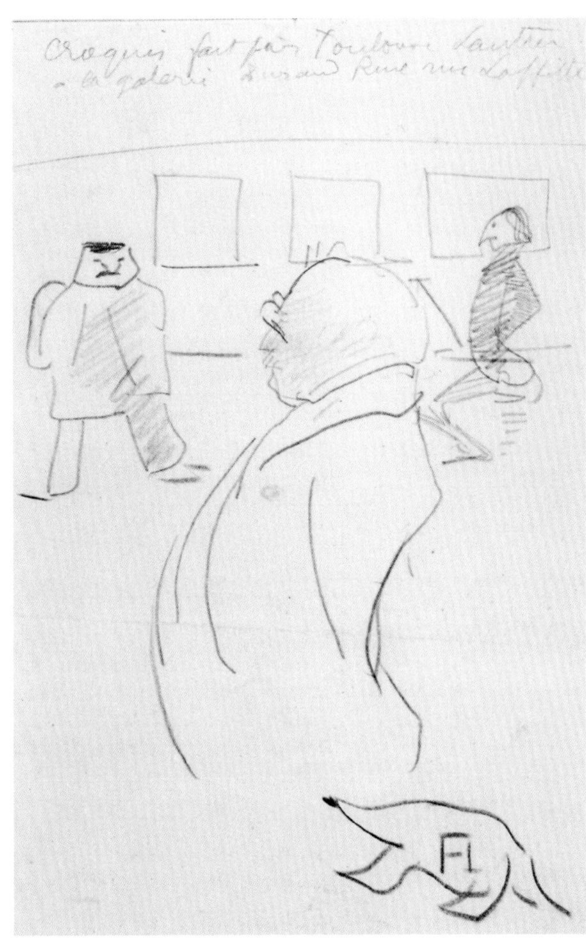

March Durand-Ruel lends 20 canvases by Monet to the Art Institute of Chicago [*Daily Inter Ocean*, 24 February, p. 23].
6 March Durand-Ruel attends the funeral of Berthe Morisot in Passy [Geffroy to Monet, MO, Monet archive, ODO 2007-1-90].
14 March–27 April At the request of Lichtwark, Director at the Hamburg Museum, Durand-Ruel sends canvases by Boudin, Monet, Sisley, Courbet, Renoir and Pissarro to the Kunstverein exhibition [Hansen, this book].
22 March Second exhibition at the Photo-Club in Paris, entitled *Exposition d'art photographique*.
April Extensive retrospective of Mary Cassatt in New York, with 54 works.

FIG. 157
Joseph Durand-Ruel at the time of his engagement, August 1896
Photo taken by Studio Reutlinger
Silver gelatin print
Archives Durand-Ruel

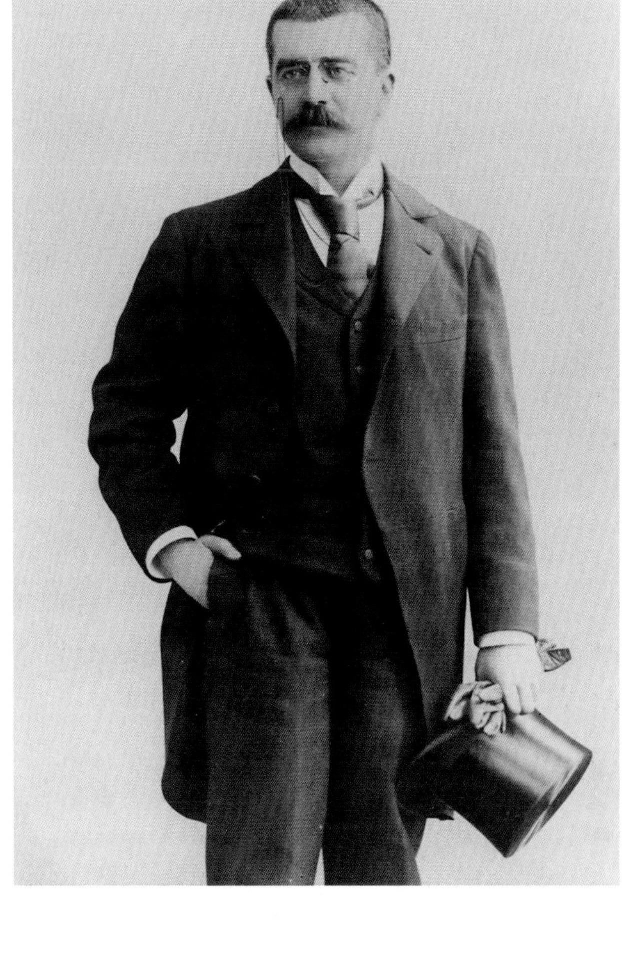

10–31 May Exhibition of recent works by Monet, including 20 *Cathedrals*, which are received enthusiastically by Pissarro, Cézanne and Clemenceau.
1 July Christening of Jean Renoir, to whom Georges is godfather [Mérigeau 2012, p. 31].
23 November Monet complains to Durand-Ruel: 'Since my exhibition, everything has been done to prevent the sale of the aforementioned Cathedrals'. The dealer responds that these are works that the painter does not want to sell [WL 1320 to 21; Durand-Ruel to Monet, 24 November, in sales cat. Paris 2006a, no. 77].
30 December Durand-Ruel arrives in New York [ancestry.com].

1896

January 'At Durand-Ruel's to see some Monets' [Proust [1976–1993], II, p. 7].
6–22 January First Bonnard exhibition at the Durand-Ruel Gallery.
March Maufra exhibition. Durand-Ruel, his main buyer, goes on to organise several exhibitions for the artist.
2–21 March Posthumous exhibition of Berthe Morisot. Julie Manet, Mallarmé, Renoir and Degas actively participate in organising it. Mallarmé writes the preface to the catalogue, which includes almost 380 entries. Julie gives the painting *Tea* to pay for the rental of the gallery (Fondation Madelon, Vaduz) [Stuckey-Scott 1987, p. 177, note 2].
16 March Durand-Ruel returns from New York [ADR, letter from Joseph Durand-Ruel to Flandrin's widow, 17 March].
26 March Chabrier sale, which includes 17 Impressionist lots out of a total of 38. Durand-Ruel is the expert. He acquires almost all the Impressionist lots, as well as three pictures by Manet (RW 266, 316, 376) for a total of 27,210 francs [Lugt 54240; AP, D48E3 80].
15 April–9 May Exhibition of recent works by Pissarro. The preface to the catalogue is written by Arsène Alexandre.
15–30 April Exhibition of watercolours by René Binet. The artist begins to exhibit regularly at the Durand-Ruel Gallery [CAC, no. 16, 18 April, p. 151].
25 April Presidential decree legalising the surname 'Durand-Ruel'.
19 May First purchase from Maurice Denis. The work is *Easter Morning*, which Durand-Ruel has seen in Lerolle's collection [MMD, ms. 6960 and 6962; Lyon 1994, p. 218].
28 May–20 June Exhibition of 42 canvases by Renoir [exh. cat. London, Paris and Boston 1985–8, p. 389].
June The painter Max Liebermann and Hugo von Tschudi, Director of the Nationalgalerie, Berlin, visit the gallery [Hansen, this book].
July Exhibition of three recent panels by Puvis de Chavannes painted for the Boston Library: *Philosophy*, *Chemistry* and *Physics*. The reduced versions are exhibited in January 1897 [CAC, no. 3, 16 January, p. 22; Lobstein 2014, p. 362].
8 August Tschudi purchases *In the Conservatory* by Manet for the Nationalgalerie, Berlin (22,000 francs, fig. 102). This is the first direct purchase from Durand-Ruel by a European Museum [Hansen, this book].
23 September Joseph marries Jenny Lefebure (fig. 157). Degas and Puvis are witnesses [AP, V4E 8829]. Despite being invited to the wedding on this occasion, Pissarro does not attend [Durand-Ruel Snollaerts 2005, p. 40].
October Durand-Ruel sends 12 canvases to the Nationalgalerie in Berlin: seven by Monet, three by Degas, one by Pissarro and one by Libermann [Hansen, this book].
10 October Joseph arrives in New York on board *La Touraine* [ancestry.com].
5 November–1 January 1897 First annual exhibition at the Carnegie Institute in Pittsburgh. Durand-Ruel lends one work by Degas, four by Monet, two by Puvis and one by Zorn [*Pittsburgh Times*, 21 November, p. 7].
14–21 November Exhibition of paintings from the Durand-Ruel collection at the Carnegie Hotel in Pittsburgh, including works by Corot, Diaz, Millet, Delacroix, Puvis, Monet and Frans Hals [*Pittsburgh Bulletin*, 14 November, p. 12, 21 November, p. 12].
28 November 'Saw paintings by Degas and Manet at Durand-Ruel's' [Gide 1996, p. 240].
2 December Signac visits the Manet exhibition at the Durand-Ruel Gallery [Cachin 2000, p. 369].
5–8 December Georges and Destrée are in Hamburg for the exhibition of 38 works at the Hôtel de l'Europe [Hansen, this book].
Late 1896 Durand-Ruel, who has sent pictures, including works by Monet, to Reims, Berlin and St Petersburg, would also like to send some to Stockholm [Durand-Ruel to Monet, in sales cat. Paris 2006a, no. 78].

1897

1–2 February The Vever sale at Petit's gallery is a success. Durand-Ruel buys two works by Corot, *Ludus Pro Patria* by Puvis (22,500 francs), three by Monet, two by Degas, three by Renoir, seven by Sisley, two by Pissarro, one by Boudin, one by Brown, six by Lebourg, one by Théodore Rousseau and one watercolour by Daumier for a total of 155,310 francs [Lugt 54974; AP, D48E3 81].
16 February–13 March Chassériau retrospective [CAC, no. 5, 30 January, p. 42, no. 8, 20 February, p. 69].
March–April *Views of Rouen by Pissarro* exhibition in New York. Of the 37 entries in the catalogue, 22 are earlier works by the painter with a variety of subject matter.
Spring Durand-Ruel sends 11 canvases to the Internationale Kunstausstellung in Dresden [Hansen, this book]. At the end of the exhibition, Tschudi purchases Pissarro's *Bourgeois House at L'Hermitage*,

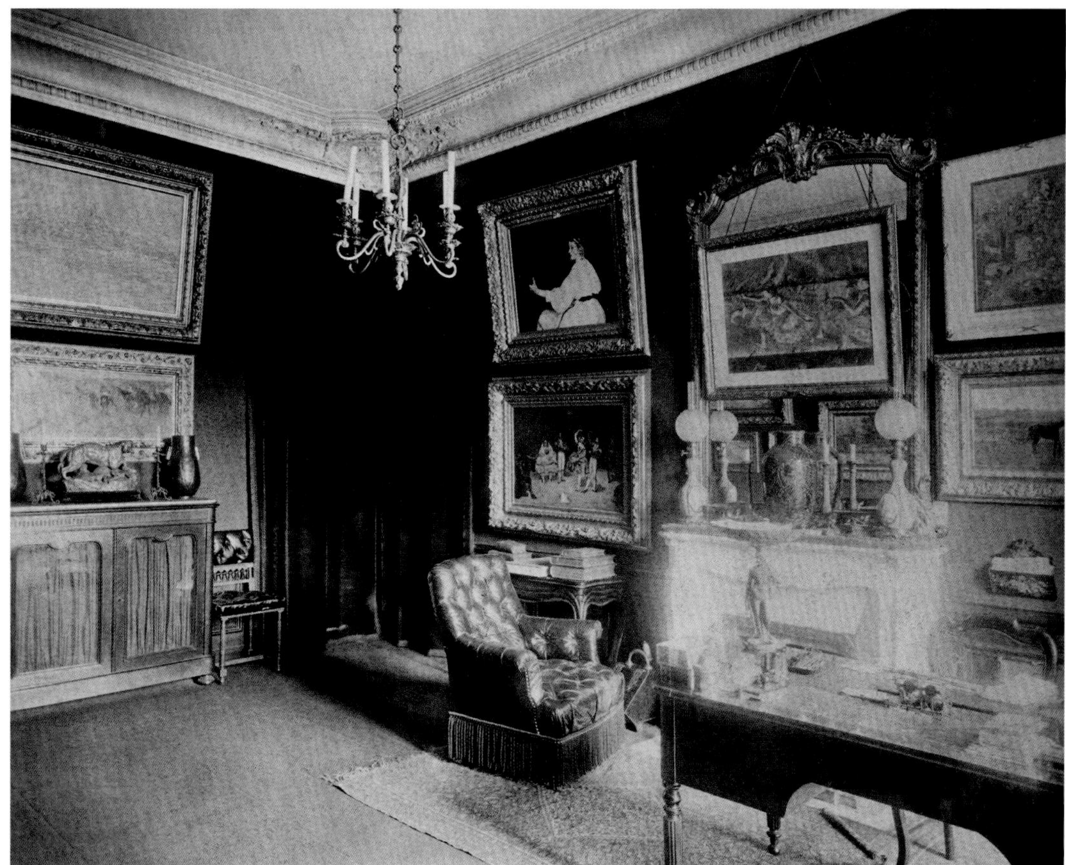

FIG. 158
Office of Paul Durand-Ruel,
35, rue de Rome, Paris, 1889–1912
Photograph
Archives Durand-Ruel

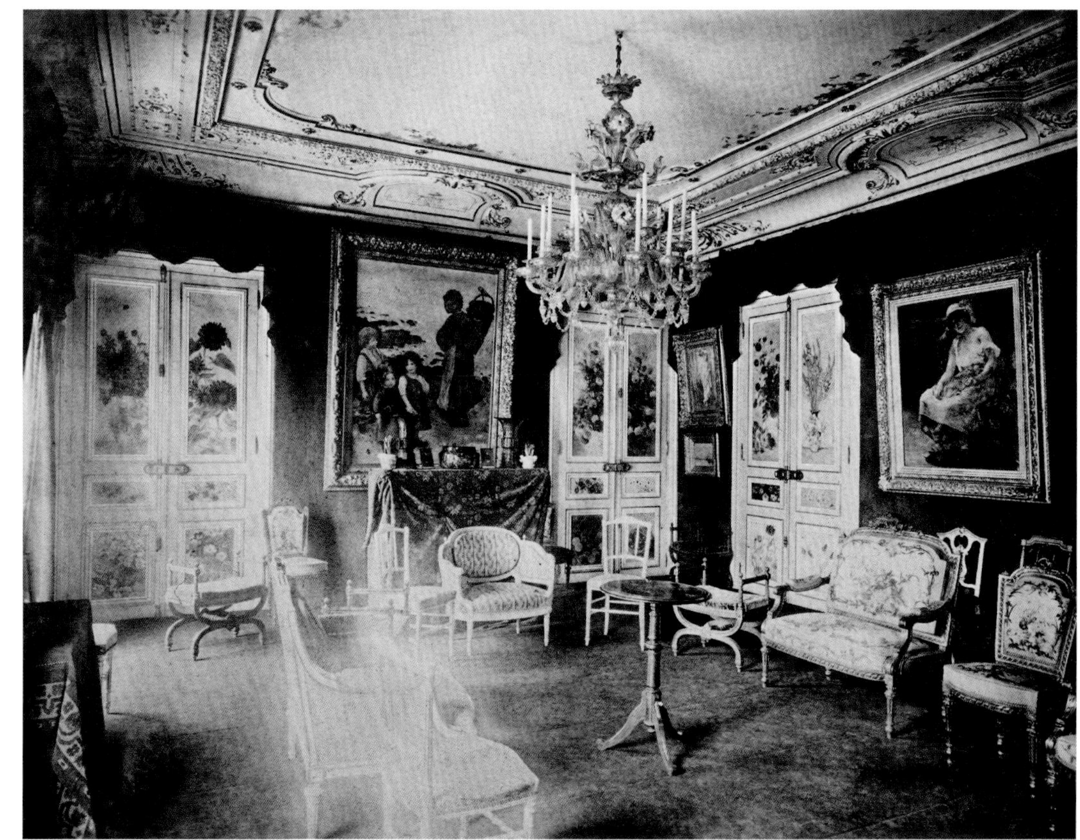

FIG. 159
Large salon of Paul Durand-Ruel,
35, rue de Rome, Paris 1889–1912
Photograph
Archives Durand-Ruel

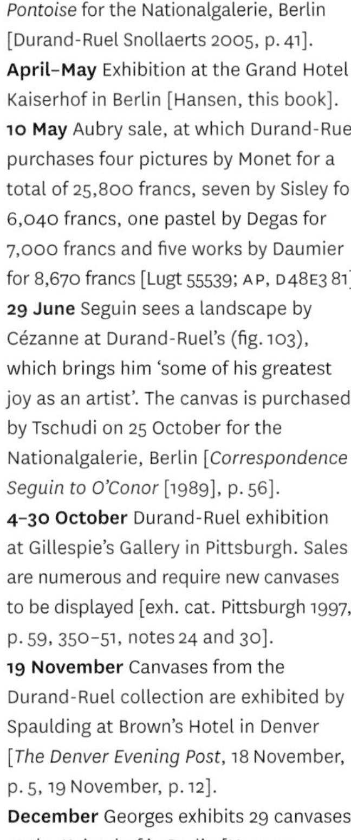

Pontoise for the Nationalgalerie, Berlin [Durand-Ruel Snollaerts 2005, p. 41].
April–May Exhibition at the Grand Hotel Kaiserhof in Berlin [Hansen, this book].
10 May Aubry sale, at which Durand-Ruel purchases four pictures by Monet for a total of 25,800 francs, seven by Sisley for 6,040 francs, one pastel by Degas for 7,000 francs and five works by Daumier for 8,670 francs [Lugt 55539; AP, D48E3 81].
29 June Seguin sees a landscape by Cézanne at Durand-Ruel's (fig. 103), which brings him 'some of his greatest joy as an artist'. The canvas is purchased by Tschudi on 25 October for the Nationalgalerie, Berlin [*Correspondence Seguin to O'Conor* [1989], p. 56].
4–30 October Durand-Ruel exhibition at Gillespie's Gallery in Pittsburgh. Sales are numerous and require new canvases to be displayed [exh. cat. Pittsburgh 1997, p. 59, 350–51, notes 24 and 30].
19 November Canvases from the Durand-Ruel collection are exhibited by Spaulding at Brown's Hotel in Denver [*The Denver Evening Post*, 18 November, p. 5, 19 November, p. 12].
December Georges exhibits 29 canvases at the Kaiserhof in Berlin [Hansen, this book].

1898

The apartment on rue de Rome (figs 158, 159, 160) is open to visitors daily from 2pm, then later on Tuesdays only from 1901 [Durand-Ruel Godfroy 2000, p. 89].
15 January Durand-Ruel's last visit to America. He returns to Paris on 1 April [ADR].

FIG. 160
Small salon of Paul Durand-Ruel,
35, rue de Rome, Paris, 1889–1912
Photograph
Archives Durand-Ruel

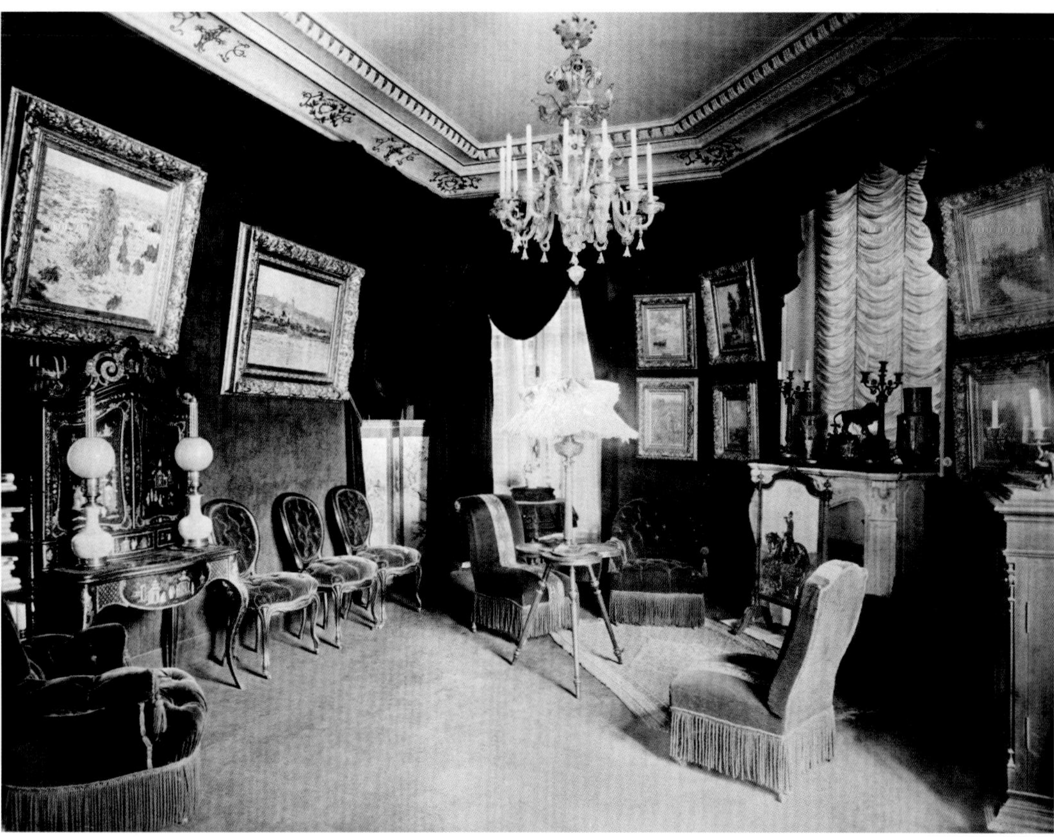

26 March–9 April Durand-Ruel exhibits works by Gustave Loiseau. The artist has been under contract since 1897 and the dealer purchases the majority of his production [CAC, no. 13, 26 March, p. 112; exh. cat. Pont-Aven 2001, pp. 31–3].
30 March–16 April First exhibition in New York of the Group of The Ten. Formed in December 1897 by Benson, Decamp, Dewing, Willard, Metcalf, Reid, Simmons, Tarbelle, Hassam, Weir and Twachtman, the group goes on to exhibit regularly at Durand-Ruel's gallery [Gerdts 1984, p. 171; *New York Times*, 30 March].
1 April Monet writes to Durand-Ruel that 'it is not without sorrow, and also with a little disappointment that [he has] seen the visits to which [he had] long been accustomed become less frequent, not to say cease, and which, by ceasing had caused [him] to feel abandoned.' [WL 1405].
27 April Signac visits the Guillaumin exhibition at the Durand-Ruel Gallery [Cachin 2000, p. 370].
May–June Exhibition of recent works by Pissarro, Renoir, Monet, Sisley and Puvis, with one room dedicated to each artist [*Correspondence Pissarro* [1980–1991], no. 1552; exh. cat. London, Paris and Boston 1985–8, p. 390; exh. cat. London, Paris and Baltimore 1992–3, p. 288].
15 May Opening of the exhibition of the International Society of Sculptors, Painters and Gravers at the Prince's Skating Ring in London, to which Durand-Ruel lends canvases by Degas, Monet and Manet, including *The Execution of Maximilian*, thanks to the intervention of Whistler [Howard to Whistler, 11 April, GUL 146, GUW 02306; Ludovici to Whistler, 11–17, 16 and 19 April, Library of Congress, PWC2/18/18, GUW 807; GUL 141, GUW 2301; GUL 142, GUW 2302; Lavery to Whistler, 21 April, GUL 143, GUW 2303 (2014-05-17)].
12 August Durand-Ruel attends the funeral of Boudin in Paris [Manœuvre 1998, p. 196].
28 August 'I am reproached for always setting prices that are too high and yet my claims have never been exaggerated.' [Durand-Ruel to Pissarro, BnF, Est., R 10958].
3 September Opening of the Rembrandt exhibition in Amsterdam, to which Durand-Ruel lends works. Abraham Bredius, Director of the Mauritshuis in The Hague, purchases *David Playing the Harp for Saul* from the dealer and deposits it at the museum [CAC, no. 23, 11 June, p. 202, no. 37, 26 November, p. 334].
11 October Pierre Shchukin (brother of Sergei) purchases *Female Nude (Anna)* by Renoir. On 17 April 1899, he purchases *Maternal Caress* by Cassatt and then a *Landscape at Sainte-Adresse* by Monet [Durand-Ruel Godfroy 1999, p. 33 and note 23].
November Final exhibitions at the hotels in Berlin and Hamburg [Hansen, this book].
1 November–1 December Durand-Ruel sends 27 works by Degas for the *Ausstellung von Werken von Max Liebermann, H. G. E. Degas und Constantin Meunier* exhibition at the Cassirer Gallery in Berlin. This exhibition marks the start of relations with Cassirer [Hansen, this book].
10 November First purchase by Sergei Shchukin: *Pyramids at Port-Coton, Rough Sea* by Monet (Pushkin Museum of Fine Arts, Moscow, fig. 161). He goes on to purchase 14 works before 1904 [Durand-Ruel Godfroy 1999, pp. 33, 37, note 24].
4 December Signac admires *Camille* by Monet (fig. 107) at Durand-Ruel's gallery [Cachin 2000, p. 370].

1899

January Durand-Ruel sends 26 works by Monet, four by Degas and two by Manet on deposit to Cassirer, who purchases three by Monet and two by Degas [Hansen, this book].
24 January *View of Saint-Mammès* by Sisley is acquired by the Carnegie Museum of Art in Pittsburgh (fig. 96). This is the first picture to be purchased from Durand-Ruel by an American museum.
28 January Following the request from Redon, Durand-Ruel 'asks nothing more than to serve [the] interest [of Denis] and of talented young artists'. He advises them: 'The more you restrict yourselves in number, the more you will gain in interest'. Durand-Ruel asks for 10% commission on sales [Durand-Ruel to Denis, 28 January, MMD, Ms. 3645].
February–20 March Durand-Ruel, who wants to acquire the collection of Charles Deudon, asks Renoir to intervene. Despite the painter's visits to the collector, the sale does not take place. Durand-Ruel's sole purchase is Renoir's *Dancer* from Deudon's cousin Eugène (fig. 70).
27 February–15 March First Sisley exhibition in New York, with 28 canvases.
10–31 March A collective exhibition of Post-Impressionist artists includes 199 works by 28 exhibitors: Redon, all the Nabis and some Neo-Impressionists (Luce, Cross, Signac, Van Rysselberghe),

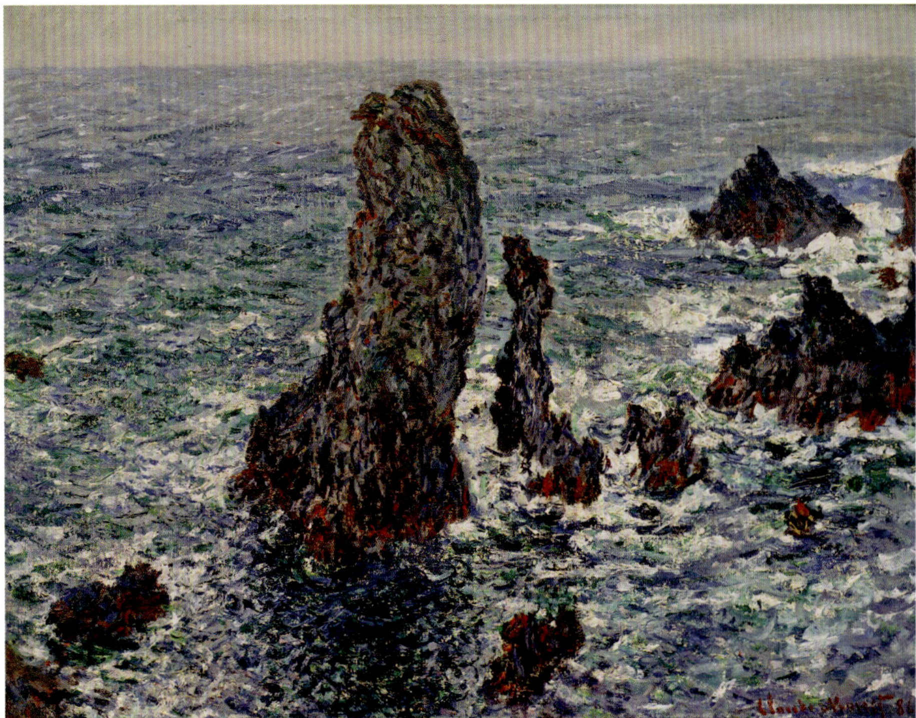

FIG. 161
Claude Monet
Pyramids at Port-Coton, Rough Sea, 1886
Oil on canvas, 65 × 81 cm
Pushkin State Museum, Moscow

as well as Charpentier and Minne. The preface to the catalogue is written by Mellerio.
20–21 March Boudin's studio sale. Durand-Ruel is one of the experts [CAC, no. 12, 25 March, p. 111].
10–22 April Exhibition of works by Monet, Pissarro, Renoir and Sisley. Twenty-six works by Corot are also exhibited in room five, until 29 April. Signac writes: 'When you enter Durand's gallery you would think you were at the Louvre', but he notes in his journal: 'Corot has painted pictures; with the exception of Renoir, the other works are studies' [Signac to Bardur, 26 April, copy MO, Berson archive; Rewald 1953, p. 54].
26 April At the Desfossés sale, Durand-Ruel acquires all the works by Pissarro, *The Coal Carriers* by Monet (fig. 73), two works by Corot, two seascapes by Boudin and one by Daumier, for a total of 66,200 francs [Lugt 57153; AP, D48E3 83].
1 May Sisley's studio sale, followed by another organised by the artists with the proceeds going to the painter's widow and children. At the second sale, Durand-Ruel purchases one work by Morisot, one pastel by Degas and, jointly with Bernheim-Jeune, one Monet and one Pissarro [Lugt 57151; AP, D48E3 83].
4–5 May Sale of the Count Doria's collection, at which Durand-Ruel purchases one work by Degas, two works by Morisot and four by Renoir for a total of 48,200 francs, plus *Melting Snow, Fontainebleau* by Cézanne for Monet for 6,750 francs [Lugt 57195; AP, D48E3 83].
19 June–July *Tableaux esquisses et dessins de Puvis de Chavannes* exhibition of 103 works.
1–4 July Sale of Chocquet's widow's estate, at which Durand-Ruel purchases 15 of the 34 canvases by Cézanne (fig. 128), three of 11 by Monet, three of five by Manet and two by Courbet [Lugt 57430; Rewald 1969, pp. 33–96; Rishel, this book].
5 August A gas explosion occurs in the basement of the New York gallery. There are no injuries [*New York Daily Tribune*, 6 August, p. 12].
30 September Prorogation for ten years of the Durand-Ruel & Sons general partnership [AP, D31U3 860 (898)].
October Durand-Ruel lends 13 works by Puvis, 10 by Degas and eight by Monet to an exhibition at the Cassirer Gallery [Hansen, this book].
16–31 October Luce exhibition [CAC, no. 32, 21 October, p. 296].
6 November Monet reserves seven *Water Lilies* (between 6,000 to 7,000 francs each) and 11 views of the Thames (at 6,000 francs each) for Durand-Ruel (WL 1474).
11 November–4 December Raffaëlli exhibition in New York then at the St Botolph Club in Boston from the 9 December [*The Pittsburgh Bulletin*, 11 November, p. 12].

1900

January Exhibition of the American Art Association of Paris, with 92 works included in the catalogue. The association goes on to exhibit regularly at the Durand-Ruel Gallery.
20 January Durand-Ruel warns Roger Marx, following the refusal by Monet, Renoir, Pissarro and Degas to take part in the centennial Universal Exhibition, that he would not be able to lend their works, deeming it 'inadmissible that the Fine Arts administration should assume the right to exhibit pictures by artists without their consent and despite their formal defence'. The artists reverse their decision and Durand-Ruel sends their pictures, nonetheless stating on 30 March: 'It would have been interesting to show a complete overview of this artistic movement so considerable that collectors and artists from every country rightly concern themselves with it, and it seems to me that the measures taken are too insignificant to achieve this result'. However, the Impressionists are well represented [Durand-Ruel to Roger Marx, INHA, Aut 1285].
Late March–20 April 'For several days, M. [Joseph] Durand-Ruel has opened the doors to his private home at [35] rue de Rome, to display the decorations carried out in his *salon*, dining room and study. The dining room was commissioned from M. André; the other two rooms from M. D'Espagnat'. Visits take place on Tuesdays and Fridays [CAC, no. 13, 31 March, p. 118]
21 April Moreau-Nélaton purchases Manet's *Déjeuner sur l'herbe* for 55,000 francs (MO) [Paris 1991, p. 104].
1 May Opening of the centennial exhibition of French art at the Grand Palais des Champs-Elysées. The Impressionists are grouped together in one room. *Dancer* by Renoir is lent by Mme Joseph Durand-Ruel (fig. 70); Manet's *Bullfight* (RW 109) and Renoir's *La Loge* (Courtauld Institute, London) by the dealer's daughter, Mme Aude; Manet's *Eva Gonzalès* by Georges (fig. 117); Manet's *Steamboat Leaving Boulogne* (AIC) and Pissarro's *Sunset at Val-Hermé* [*sic*] (PDRS 621) by his daughter, Jeanne Dureau. Durand-Ruel lends *Vigilance* (P 145) and *The Fisherman's Family* (P 327) by Puvis de Chavannes.
10–26 May Exhibition of earlier and recent works by Redon [CAC, no. 19, 12 May, p. 188].
22 November–15 December Exhibition of recent works by Monet, including the first *Water Lilies*.

1901

January Durand-Ruel exhibits 37 paintings at the Hanover Gallery in London in the *Exhibition of Pictures by French Impressionists, Monet, Sisley, Pissarro, Renoir and other Masters*.

FIG. 162
Pablo Picasso
Sebastià Junyer i Vidal visits Durand-Ruel, 1902
Pen and ink and coloured pencil on paper, 22 × 16 cm
Museu Picasso de Barcelona, gift of Sebastià Junyer i Vidal, 1966

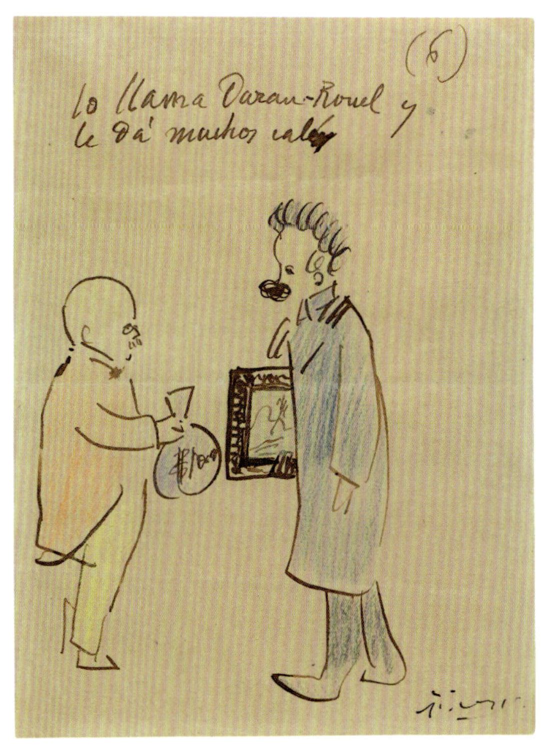

Monet, who visits the exhibition with Sargent, writes it had 'a pitiful effect. It will do little to raise our profile in this country' [Monet to Alice Hoschedé, 26 January, WL 1588]. Works by Degas are hung in New York [exh. cat. Atlanta and Minneapolis 2001, pp. 67–8].
14 January–2 February Exhibition of recent works by Pissarro, which the gallery organises independently. There are 48 catalogue entries [Durand-Ruel Snollaerts 2005, p. 47].
25 January Renoir asks Durand-Ruel to send *Woman playing a Guitar* to the museum in Lyon (fig. 15). The acquisition is approved by the municipal council on 7 September [Lyon, AM, 1400 WP 4].
11 February At the Feydeau sale, Durand-Ruel purchases *The Bridge at Argenteuil* by Sisley for 10,000 francs; *The Sainte-Catherine Bank in Rouen in the Mist* by Pissarro for 10,000 francs; two pictures by Renoir for 10,800 francs; five seascapes by Boudin for 16,710 francs and *The Port* by Isabey for 10,500 francs [Lugt 58792; AP, D48E3 85].
March Durand-Ruel lends 11 pictures to the Secession in Berlin [Hansen, this book].
23 March Durand-Ruel has some pictures stolen. Renoir informs him that Fauché has some canvases to show him and asks if he has recovered the remainder of the stolen pictures [Grasse, 23 March, *Correspondence Renoir–Durand-Ruel* [1995], I, p. 151].
30 April Durand-Ruel leaves for London for several days [Georges Durand-Ruel to Pissarro, BnF, Est., Arch. Pissarro microfilm].
After 2 May On his return from London, Durand-Ruel writes to Pissarro: 'You know how I feel towards you and you also know what I have done to have your works appreciated in the way they deserve. I have neglected neither effort nor money in this task and you will never know, nor will Monet or Renoir, how much you have cost me. I am now beginning to reap the fruits of my labour; to achieve success we must be more restrained than ever and an absolute understanding must exist between us... I ask you not to deliver anything before I have seen it. I will speak to you frankly as usual and as it should always be between us' [Durand-Ruel Snollaerts 2005, p. 47].
6 May Sale of Abbé Gaugain's collection. Durand-Ruel, who is the expert, purchases two works by Monet, two by Sisley and one by Renoir for 33,300 francs. For him, 'it is essential that public sales reach big figures, whether or not the prices are fabricated. This is the only way we will achieve great success' [Lugt 59125; Durand-Ruel to Renoir, Paris, 4 May, *Correspondence Renoir–Durand-Ruel* [1995], I, p. 157].
14 May Pissarro informs Durand-Ruel that he wishes to 'take back complete freedom for the sale of [his] works', and sends Bernheim-Jeune the list of works brought back from Moret. On 17 May, he sends the list of nine pictures (of the 20 painted), which he reserves for the dealer and asks him if he agrees with the increase in price of 500 francs [*Correspondence Pissarro* [1980–1991], nos. 1818 and 1819]. Although he did not choose the works in the painter's studio himself in the usual way, the dealer accepts and purchases the small group of paintings for 24,000 francs [Durand-Ruel Snollaerts 2005, p. 47].
12 October Durand-Ruel is unable to visit Denis's decoration of the Church of Sainte Marguerite in Le Vésinet 'at the same time as their mutual friends Moreau-Nélaton, Lerolle and others' [MDD, Ms. 3643].
November Durand-Ruel delivers 30 canvases to the branch that Cassirer has just opened in Hamburg [Hansen, this book].
5 November Pissarro asks Durand-Ruel to wait 'until Friday, for them to dry' for the six pictures he lists with prices (21,000 francs in total) [5 November, *Correspondence Pissarro* [1980–1991], no. 1859].
24–26 November Monet had sold three canvases to Durand-Ruel in April for 20,000 francs. He negotiates for nine others, which he agrees to sell at 60,000 francs: 'You know I am always willing to give you the advantage; there are some paintings I could have sold to others at a much higher price but [I] did not.' [WL 1646 and 1647].
?–31 December Ker-Xavier Roussel exhibition [CAC, no. 40, 21 December, p. 328].

1902

11–25 February Exhibition of 37 works by Monet in New York.
15 February–1 May Sisley exhibition [exh. cat. London, Paris and Baltimore 1992–3, p. 300].
14–31 May Toulouse-Lautrec exhibition. The preface to the catalogue is written by Arsène Alexandre.
?–21 June Exhibition of 40 works by Renoir [CAC, no. 24, 21 June p. 196].
1 July The museum in Lyon plans to purchase three works by Monet sent by Durand-Ruel: *White Frost at Giverny* (9,000 francs), *Spring: The Banks of the River* (9,000 francs) and *Rough Sea at Etretat* (15,000 francs). After attempting to negotiate for *White Frost at Giverny* and *Rough Sea* for 20,000 francs, the museum eventually acquires *Spring* and *Rough Sea* [Lyon, MBA, minutes of the advisory and monitoring committee of the museums of the city of Lyon].
October Picasso makes a caricature of the dealer in Paris [exh. cat. New York 1980, p. 47] (fig. 162).

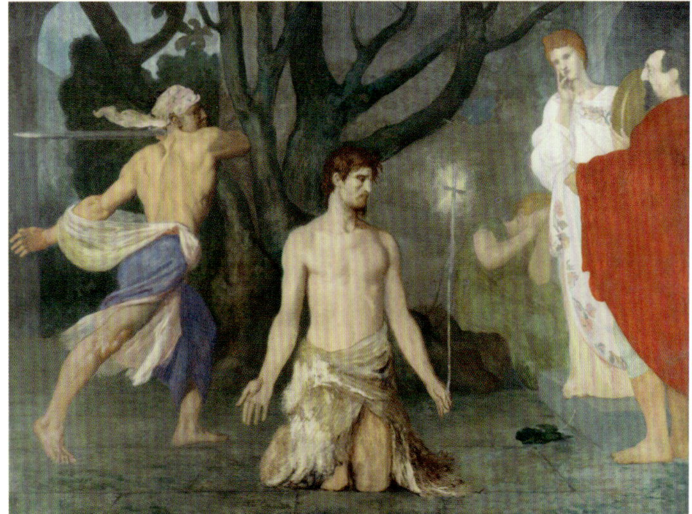

FIG. 163
Pierre-Cécile Puvis de Chavannes
The Beheading of Saint John the Baptist, about 1869
Oil on canvas, 243.5 × 318.4 cm
The National Gallery, London

1903

January–February Sixteenth exhibition of the Vienna Secession, devoted to French Impressionism. Durand-Ruel contributes several loans. The Belvedere purchases Monet's *The Chef (Père Paul)*, the first Impressionist work to enter an Austrian Museum [exh. cat. Vienna 1998–9, p. 215].
18 January Pissarro refuses the prices offered by Durand-Ruel following his own offer – 2,000 francs for the 30 size canvases and 1,500 for the 25 size canvases [*Correspondence Pissarro* [1980–1991], no. 1997] – and no sales take place between the dealer and the painter that year [Durand-Ruel Snollaerts 2005, p. 50].
27 January For 30,000 francs, instead of the 50,000 asked by the dealer, the Louvre acquires a portrait of a man by Goya (*Portrait of Don Evaristo Perez de Castro*) [AMN, P6, 7 March 1903].
10 June Franz Marc writes to his parents: 'The private gallery of Durand-Ruel, an enormous collection of Impressionists [Manet, Renoir, Monet, Pissarro, Boudin] has been decisive for me.' [Jansen 2007, p. 17].
5 November Monet asks Durand-Ruel what he intends to do with his views of London, 'being unable to continue saying indefinitely that these canvases are promised to you.' [WL 1699].
28 November–12 December Exhibition of 40 works by Pissarro in New York.
16 December Durand-Ruel offers *The Hills at Morgat* by Maufra to the State. He would like the work to be exhibited at the Musée du Luxembourg [Durand-Ruel to Bénédite, 16 December, AMN, file L8 1900–1907]. The work is finally acquired by the State for 800 francs and deposited at the Musée Fabre, Montpellier, in April 1904 [AN, F21/4245, F21/4909/B, F21/2275].

1904

The New York gallery moves to 5 West 36th Street.
25 February–29 March Durand-Ruel lends 17 canvases to the *Exposition des peintres impressionnistes* exhibition at La Libre Esthétique in Brussels: eight by Monet, three by Sisley, one by Pissarro and five by Renoir.
7–30 April Posthumous retrospective of Pissarro, with 178 works (paintings, gouaches, drawings and engravings). Mirbeau writes the preface to the catalogue, which is illustrated with the painter's work.
9 May–4 June *Monet: Vues de la Tamise à Londres* exhibition. The preface to the catalogue is written by Mirbeau. The exhibition is a great success and is extended until 7 June. Proust visits on 7 June [Proust [1976–1993], XXI, no. 449]. The plan to exhibit the series in London does not come to fruition [WL 1748 and 1785].
11 May and 7 June Monet sells 24 views of London to Durand-Ruel for 252,000 francs [Wildenstein 1996, p. 364].
11 October First purchase by Hugh Lane (*The Beheading of Saint John the Baptist* by Puvis de Chavannes), which marks the beginning of his relationship with Durand-Ruel (fig. 163).
14 October Monet and his family meet up with Durand-Ruel in Madrid. They visit museums, churches and academies together [Wildenstein 1996, p. 367].

1905

January–February *Pictures by Boudin, Cézanne, Degas, Manet, Monet, Morisot, Pissarro, Renoir, Sisley* at the Grafton Galleries in London. This is the largest exhibition of Impressionist works organised by Durand-Ruel. Three hundred and fifteen works are exhibited, including 196 from Durand-Ruel's private collections (fig. 164).
4 March–11 April 'Loan Collection of Paintings by Claude Monet and Eleven Sculptures by Auguste Rodin' exhibition at the Copley Society in Boston. Durand-Ruel lends 11 works and intervenes in other loans.
16 March The National Gallery in Melbourne purchases *Boulevard Montmartre, Morning, Cloudy Weather* by Pissarro (fig. 165), which had been exhibited at the Grafton Galleries [Durand-Ruel Godfroy 1999, p. 35 and note 41].
12 April–1 May Exhibition of works by Monet, Boudin, Cassatt, Sisley, Pissarro, Jongkind, Renoir and others at the Robert M. Lindsay Galleries in Philadelphia. The canvases come from the stock kept in New York. For the press, this is one of the most important collections recently exhibited in Philadelphia [*Philadelphia Inquirer*, 16 April].
8 June Durand-Ruel submits two works by Degas (one pastel, *Dancers*, 32,000 francs, and *Head of a Child*, 6,000 francs) to the committee at the museum in Lyon, which is interested in the works but finds them too expensive [Lyon, MBA, minutes of the advisory and monitoring committee of the museums of the city of Lyon].
27 December Through the intermediary of M. Hébrard, who introduces him to Durand-Ruel, the Prince de Wagram purchases six pictures for a total of 125,000 francs: *Dance Rehearsal* by Degas, *Cliffs at Pourville, Morning* by Monet, as well as *La Mère Paul* and *River at Pourville*, *La Grenouillière* and *Leaving the Conservatory* by Renoir [invoice Durand-Ruel & Fils, AN, Wagram archive, AP173BIS340-18; Distel 1985, p. 42].

After 1905

About 1910

Durand-Ruel begins writing his memoirs, which are partially published in 1939. [Durand-Ruel [1939], p. 164].

1911

November Publication by Arsène Alexandre of an article in honour of the dealer in the review *Pan*.

1913

30 June Durand-Ruel retires from the gallery. A new company is formed by Joseph and Georges [AP, D31U3 1475 (1165)].

1918

24 July Georges marries Margaret Tierney in Brantôme, in the Dordogne [Civil Registry of Brantôme].

1920

15 April Félix Fénéon publishes an interview with Durand-Ruel in *Le Bulletin de la vie artistique* [Fénéon 1970, I, pp. 347–52].
20 July Durand-Ruel is made a Knight of the Légion d'Honneur [AN, LH/870/7].

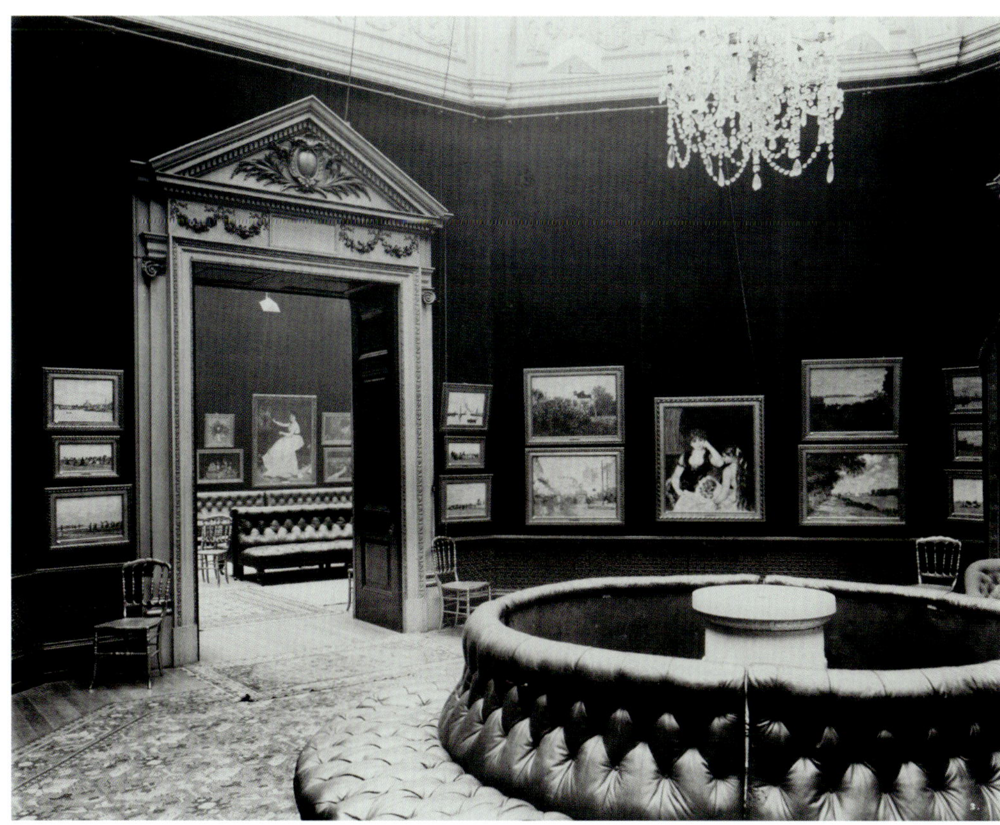

FIG. 164
View of a room of the exhibition *Pictures by Boudin, Cézanne, Degas, Manet, Monet, Morisot, Pissarro, Renoir, Sisley. Exhibited by Messrs. Durand-Ruel & Sons of Paris* at the Grafton Galleries in London in January and February 1905
Photo by Bedford Lemere & Co.
Photographic print
Musée d'Orsay, Paris

FIG. 165
Camille Pissarro
Boulevard Montmartre, Morning, Cloudy Weather, 1897
Oil on canvas, 73 × 92 cm
National Gallery of Victoria, Melbourne

1922

5 February Durand-Ruel dies at his home, 35, rue de Rome [Civil Registry of the 8th *arrondissement*].

In 1924, the gallery moves to 39, avenue de Friedland after the record sale of *Luncheon of the Boating Party* by Renoir (fig. 33). The New York gallery closes on January 1950 as does the Paris gallery in 1974 with the exhibition *1874–1974. Hommage à Paul Durand-Ruel. Cent ans d'impressionnisme*.

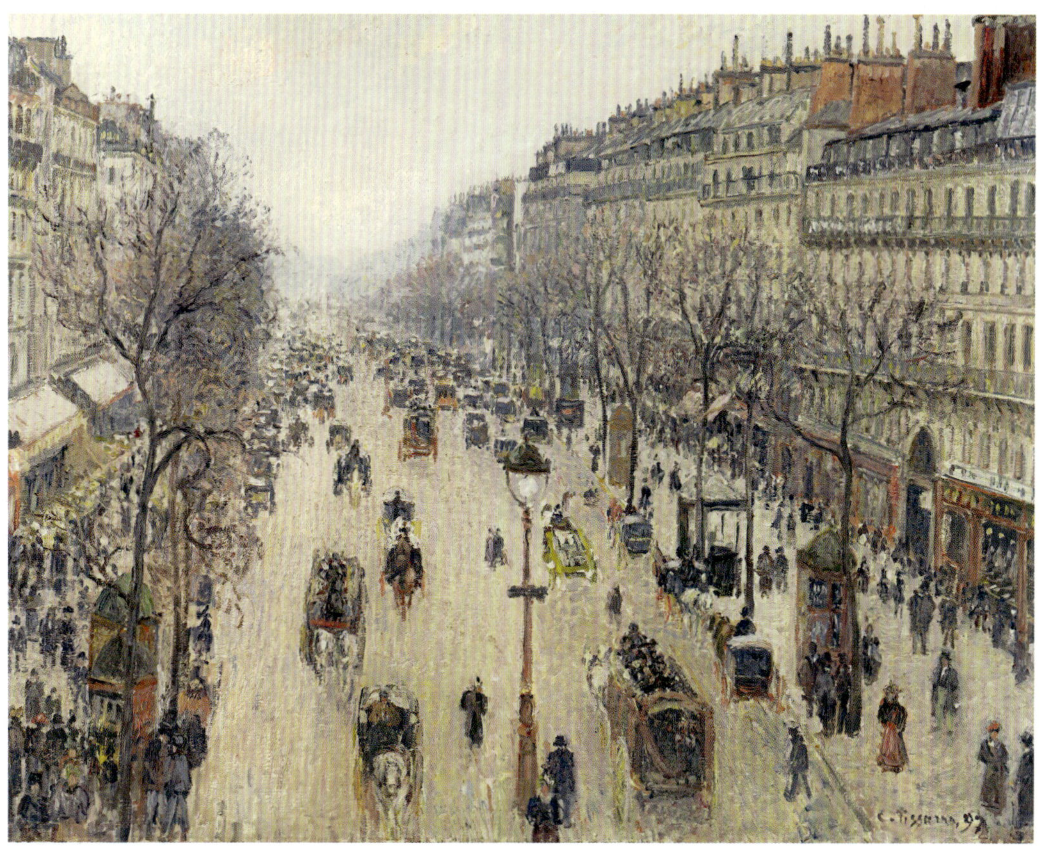

This chronology has been compiled in collaboration with Sylvie Patry and Jennifer A. Thompson, with assistance from Anne Robbins, Léa Saint-Raymond and Marie-Claire Rodriguez.

The authors would like to thank Flavie and Paul-Louis Durand-Ruel, Nienke Bakker, Annabelle Mathias, Anne Distel, Laurent Houssais and Michèle van Kalck, as well as their interns: Hélène Fernandez, Franck Joubin, Flore de Ladoucette, Clémence Laurent, Camille Richer and Coline Zellal.

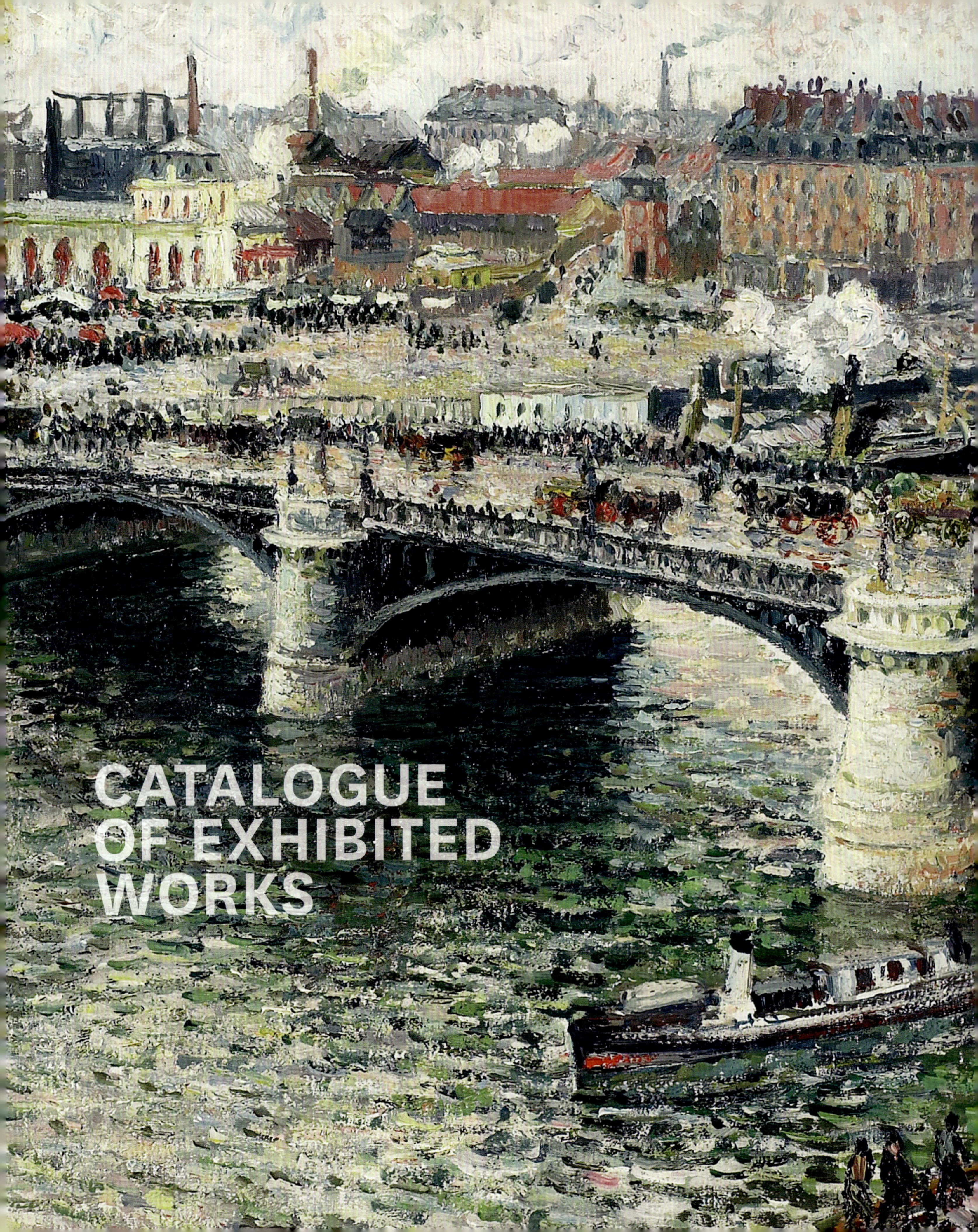

CATALOGUE OF EXHIBITED WORKS

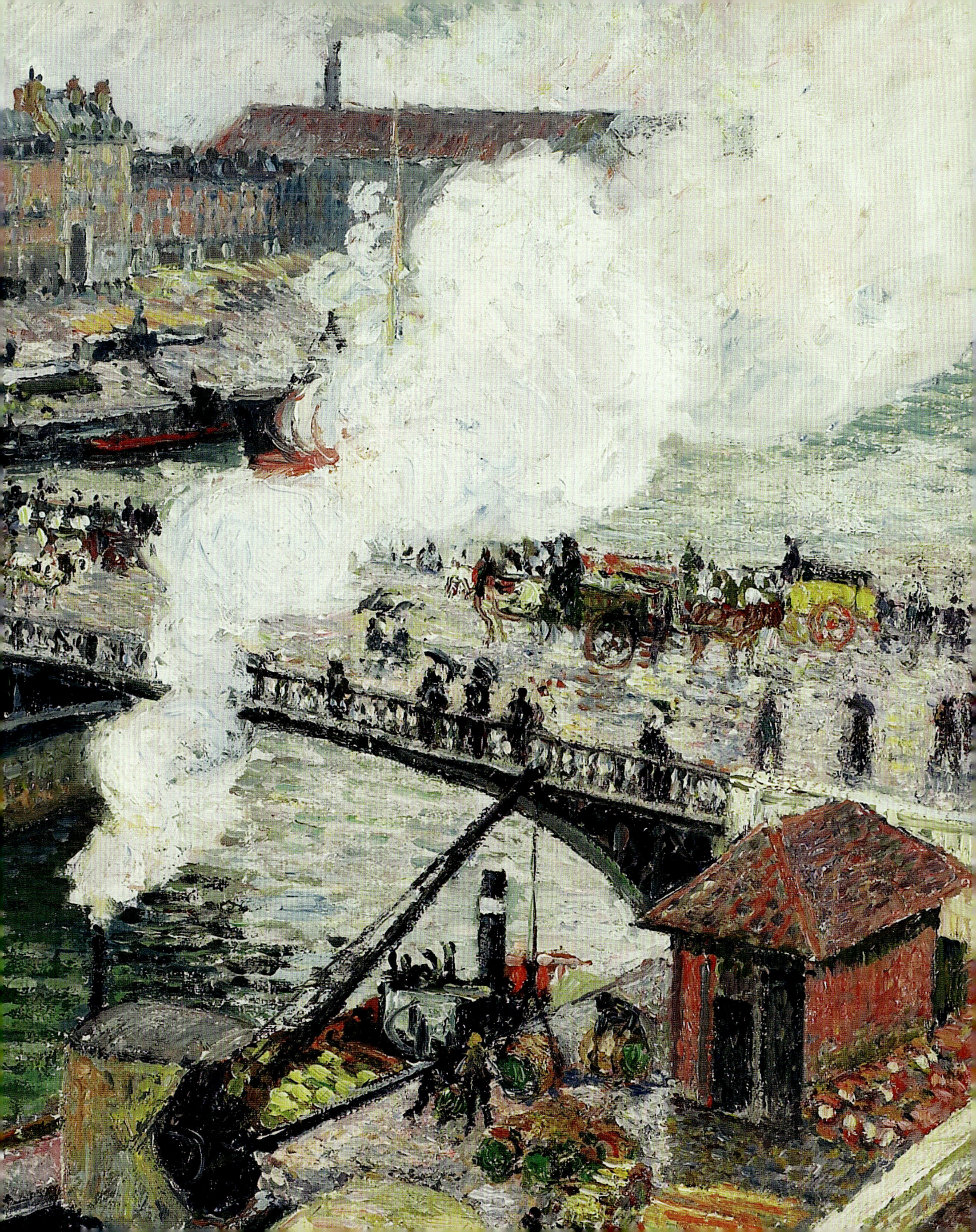

Catalogue of Exhibited Works

Works are listed in alphabetical order by artist.
Dimensions are given in centimetres, height followed by width.
Full references to the catalogues raisonnés can be found in the Select Bibliography, p. 286.
Exhibitions listed relate only to those organised by the Galerie Durand-Ruel prior to 1905. This information has been abridged. Full references can be found in the list of exhibitions, pp. 293–5.
Unless otherwise stated, the works are exhibited in London and Philadelphia.

Contributors

FB	François Blanchetière
FDR	Flavie Durand-Ruel
PLDR	Paul-Louis Durand-Ruel
CDRS	Claire Durand-Ruel Snollaerts
IG	Isabelle Gaëtan
SH	Sarah Herring
SK	Simon Kelly
MN	Monique Nonne
SP	Sylvie Patry
CR	Christopher Riopelle
JR	Joseph J. Rishel
AR	Anne Robbins
NS	Naina Saligram
JAT	Jennifer A. Thompson

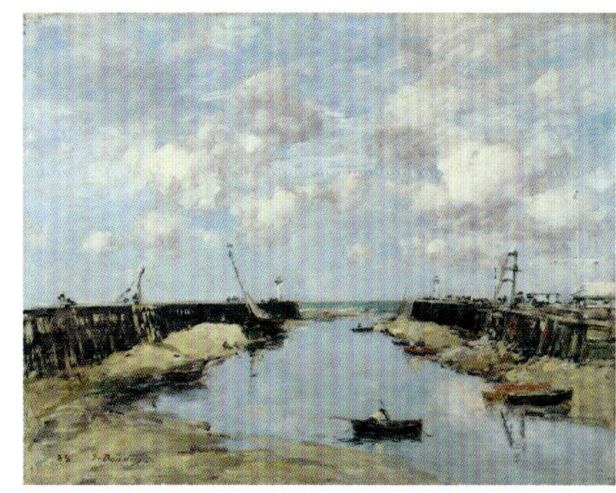

Antoine-Louis Barye

(Paris 1795–Paris 1875)

CAT. 1

Walking Lion (Lion marchant)

about 1840

Bronze, H. 24.1; L. 43.2; D. 10.3 cm
Philadelphia Museum of Art, Pennsylvania:
The W.P. Wilstach Collection, bequest of
Anna H. Wilstach, W1893-1-161

EXHIBITED IN PHILADELPHIA

CAT. 2

Walking Tiger (Tigre marchant)

1841

Bronze, H. 21; W. 42.5; D. 10.2 cm
Philadelphia Museum of Art, Pennsylvania:
The W.P. Wilstach Collection, bequest of
Anna H. Wilstach, W1893-1-158

EXHIBITED IN PHILADELPHIA

Durand-Ruel was particularly fond of Barye; he recalled in his *Memoirs*[1] that the artist had already been a regular visitor to the gallery when his father was still in charge. An 1845 engraving by Daubigny shows one of the spacious salons that was home to 'tables decorated with beautiful bronzes by Barye',[2] as the dealer went on to recollect. Significantly, it was with a sculptural group – *Arab Rider Killing a Lion* – at his side that Durand-Ruel had himself portrayed by Hugues Merle in 1866 (see fig. 137). He continued to sell 'magnificent watercolours, pictures and a number of beautiful bronzes'[3] by the artist between 1860 and 1870;[4] four watercolours were reproduced in the *Recueil d'estampes* (1873–5). Durand-Ruel also owned sculptures by Barye as part of his personal collection.

Although the archives do not allow us to precisely identify the examples that passed through the dealer's hands, the bronzes on display here were among the subjects sold by the gallery[5] and are representative of the sculptor's art. In addition to the peaceful or walking animals he tended to favour – *Walking Lion* was probably one of the most widely circulated – Barye also created works imbued with violence and cruelty: fighting or hunting that he imagined even though his only experience of wild animals came from the Jardin des Plantes zoo.

The examples shown here provide an illustration of the taste typical of French collectors of the time, combining Barbizon School paintings with sculptures by Barye; this taste was also widespread in the United States, thanks to exhibitions organised by Durand-Ruel in New York[6] and Pittsburgh,[7] which was mirrored by some of his American clients, such as Wilstach, Elkins and Johnson in Philadelphia.[8] IG-SP

1 Durand-Ruel [1939], p. 150.
2 Ibid., p. 153.
3 Ibid., p. 164.
4 When the new company, Durand-Ruel & Co., was founded in November 1881, in addition to paintings, its objective continued to be 'the trade in bronzes, objets d'art and curiosities' (see the Chronology in this book).
5 Mr Herman purchased a version of the *Walking Lion* and the *Walking Tiger* on 5 March 1868 (ADR, daybook, 1867–9) then the *Horse Surprised by a Lion* on 15 April 1869. Mr Fraissinet purchased a *Panther of Tunis* on 10 December 1868 (ADR, daybook, 1867–9).
6 Durand-Ruel held a Barye exhibition in his New York gallery in 1893 (see the Chronology in this book).
7 An exhibition of paintings by the Barbizon School and bronzes by Barye was organised at the Henry Hotel in Pittsburgh by Edwin C. Holston, the representative of Durand-Ruel's New York gallery, 27 November–10 December 1898 (*The Pittsburgh Post*, 27 November, p. 23; *Pittsburgh Bulletin*, 3 December, p. 12).
8 See the essay by Jennifer A. Thompson in this book.

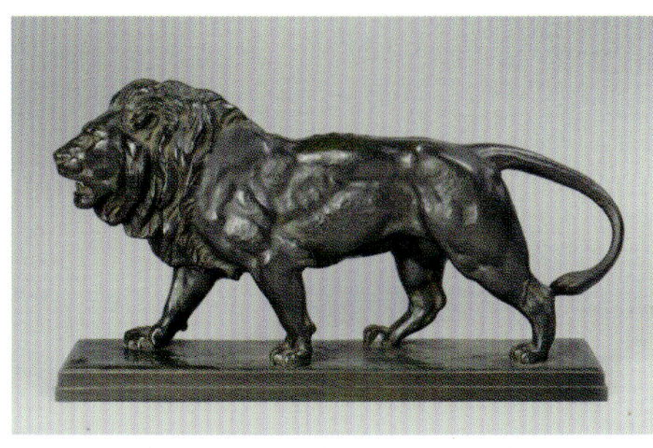

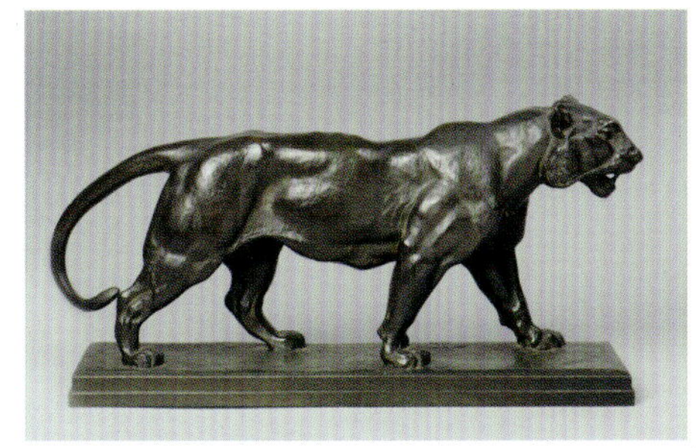

Eugène Boudin

(Honfleur 1824–Deauville 1898)

CAT. 3 [FIG. 2]

The Entrance to Trouville Harbour (L'entrée du port de Trouville)

1888

Oil on mahogany, 32.4 × 40.9 cm
The National Gallery, London. Presented by the National Art Collections Fund, 1906. NG 2078
Schmidt 2250
DR exhibition: London 1905

This harbour scene was acquired for 300 francs in 1889 from the artist by the Le Havre collector Pieter van der Velde.[1] In 1905 the French Impressionist Fund Committee in London, headed by Frank Rutter of *The Times*, purchased it from Van der Velde for £120 and the following year presented it via the National Art Collections Fund to the National Gallery. These simple statements mask a complicated story. The Committee had hoped to buy Monet's *Lavacourt under Snow* (cat. 41), displayed in the Grafton Galleries exhibition, but was warned 'that Boudin was the furthest limit to which the National Gallery was prepared to go.'[2] The ostensible reason was that Monet was living, Boudin dead. More important, certain trustees opposed including radicals like Monet in the national collection. Nor did they wish to associate with the organiser of the Grafton exhibition, Durand-Ruel. The Boudin was unobjectionable and it would be 1917 – when Monet was still not dead – before *Lavacourt* became the first Monet to enter the National Gallery, in the bequest of Hugh Lane.[3] CR

1 Rodolphe Walter, 'Pieter van der Velde, un amateur éclairé', *Gazette des beaux-arts* LXXII, October 1968, p. 204.
2 Frank Rutter, *Since I was Twenty-five*, London 1927, p. 257.
3 On this story, see also Prettejohn 1994.

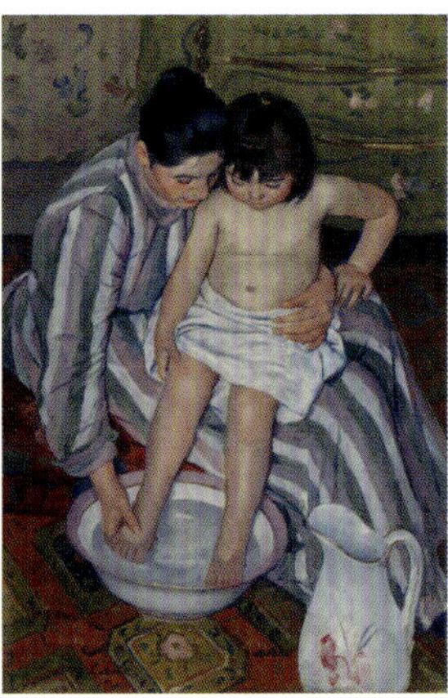

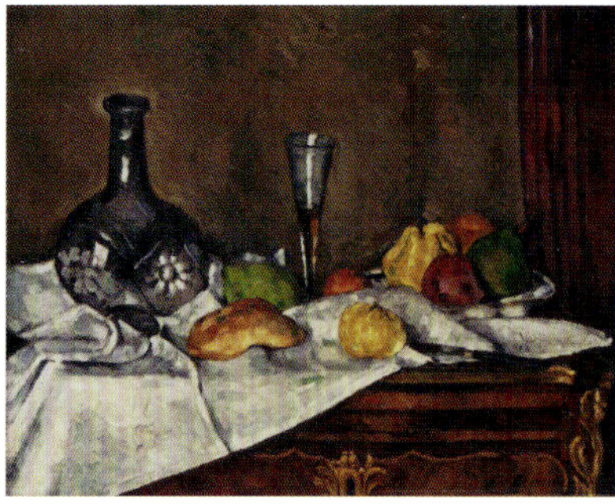

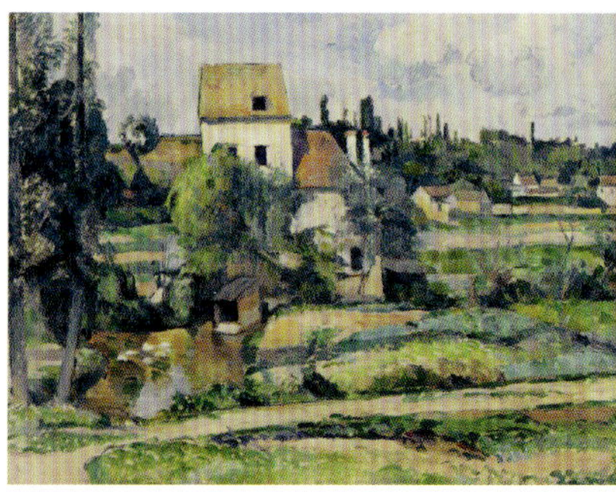

Mary Cassatt

(Allegheny City, Pennsylvania 1844–Château de Beaufresne, near Paris 1926)

CAT. 4 [FIG. 90]

The Child's Bath (La Toilette de l'enfant)

1893

Oil on canvas, 100.3 × 66.1 cm
The Art Institute of Chicago, Illinois: Robert A. Waller Fund, 1910.2
B 205
DR exhibitions: Paris 1893, no. 1 (*'La Toilette de l'Enfant'*); New York, 1895b, no. 21 (*'La Toilette'*); New York 1898, n.n.; New York 1903, no. 6 (*'La Toilette'*)

On 14 November 1893 Cassatt wrote to Harris Whittemore, 'I painted three pictures of naked babies this summer' and expressed a hope that when her friend saw them at Durand-Ruel's gallery, he would select one for his collection.[1] The Connecticut industrialist would, in fact, acquire this intimate mother and child scene from the New York gallery on 17 January 1894, selling it back to Durand-Ruel on 4 February 1899. The artist did not regularly exhibit or sell her works to Durand-Ruel until the 1890s, when he began organising monographic exhibitions for her in Paris and New York. Though Cassatt was recognised as an Impressionist in France, she was not as widely shown or collected in the United States, and the Durand-Ruel exhibitions did much to change this situation. The firm bought *The Child's Bath* from the artist on 24 November 1893, exhibiting it in their galleries and sending it to exhibitions in Pittsburgh (1897–8); Philadelphia (1898); Omaha (1898); Boston (1898 and 1909); Cincinnati (1900); and Worcester (1901 and 1905) as part of their commitment to fostering an appreciation of modern French painting throughout the country. In 1910, the Art Institute of Chicago purchased the painting from the Durand-Ruel Gallery, recognising it as more than just an undressed baby; its unusual overhead perspective and skilful interplay of materials – skin, cloth, water and ceramic – offer a rich sensory experience. JAT

1 Mary Cassatt to Harris Whittemore, letter cited in exh. cat. Chicago, Boston and Washington 1998–9, p. 151.

Paul Cézanne

(Aix-en-Provence 1839–Aix-en-Provence 1906)

CAT. 5 [FIG. 128]

Still Life with a Dessert (Nature morte au dessert)

1877 or 1879

Oil on canvas, 59 × 72.9 cm
Philadelphia Museum of Art, Pennsylvania: The Mr and Mrs Carroll S. Tyson, Jr., Collection, 1963-116-5
R 337
DR exhibition: London 1905, no. 39 (*'Dessert'*)
EXHIBITED IN PHILADELPHIA

Durand-Ruel bought this painting in July 1899 for 3,500 francs from the estate sale of Augustine Chocquet, the widow of Victor Chocquet, an early champion and public advocate for the Impressionists who had died eight years earlier. Chocquet owned over 30 Cézannes, described by Pissarro as 'first class'.[1] Durand-Ruel bought 18, including this still life. It is likely that Chocquet had commissioned Cézanne to depict the objects in his apartment at 198, rue de Rivoli. The eighteenth-century ormolu commode, elegant champagne flute and crystal carafe are a departure from the artist's usual repertory of modern stoneware and more common objects for his still lifes. Durand-Ruel's Chocquet purchases were his largest gesture towards Cézanne, an artist about whom he felt ambiguous. Durand-Ruel kept this picture in his private collection, and in 1905 it was one of ten Cézanne canvases that he exhibited at Grafton Galleries in London. JR

1 Pissarro to Lucien, 1 June 1899, in *Correspondence Pissarro* [1890–1991], no. 1639.

CAT. 6 [FIG. 103]

The Mill on the Couleuvre near Pontoise (Le Moulin sur la Couleuvre à Pontoise)

About 1881

Oil on canvas, 73.5 × 91.5 cm
Nationalgalerie, Staatliche Museen zu Berlin, 1897 Inv. no. A I 606
R 483
EXHIBITED IN LONDON

In 1883 the Berlin dealer Fritz Gurlitt held an exhibition of modern French paintings from the collection of Carl and Felicie Bernstein, which he supplemented with 24 Impressionist paintings lent by Durand-Ruel, underscoring the dealer's ambition to find an international market for his artists, as he was doing in America at the same time. Durand-Ruel's greatest coup in Germany, however, was the sale he made to the Austrian/Swiss scholar Hugo von Tschudi, who was introduced to him by Max Liebermann in 1896, the year he took on the directorship of the Berlin Nationalgalerie, which previously had only shown German art. Tschudi bought 10 major advanced French works from Durand-Ruel including Monet's *Spring* (fig. 101). The Cézanne *Mill* was purchased in 1897, making this noble and serene picture the first Cézanne to enter a public collection. All works were purchased with private funds. Despite his care and diplomacy, Tschudi's cosmopolitan outlook and boldness cost him his job in 1907. JR

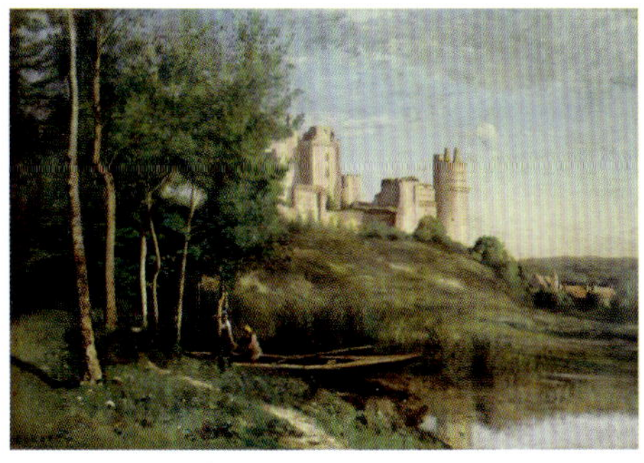

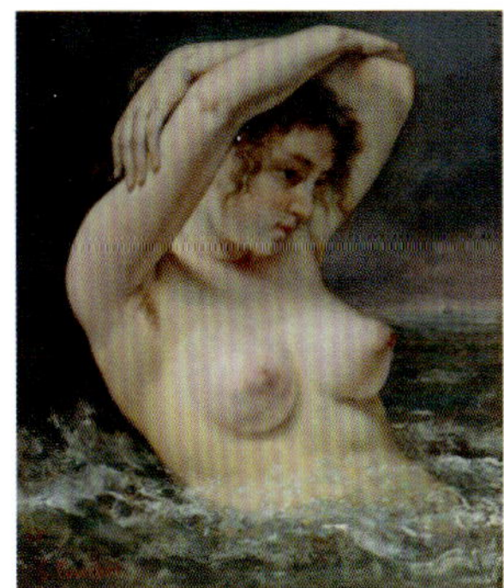

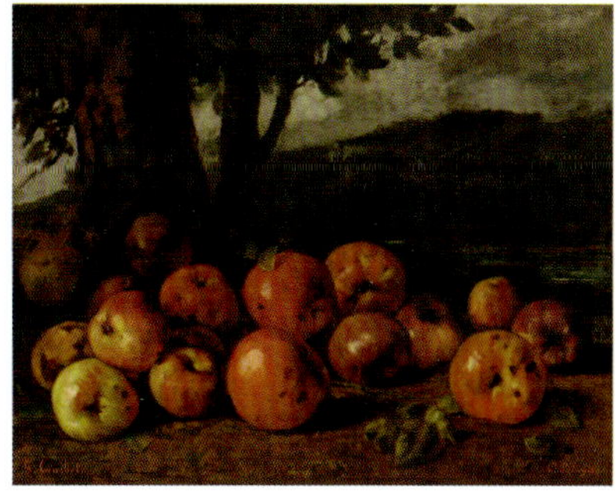

Jean-Baptiste-Camille Corot

(Paris 1796–Paris 1875)

CAT. 7 [FIG. 40]

Ruins of the Château of Pierrefonds (Les Ruines du château de Pierrefonds)

About 1840–5, re-worked about 1866–7

Oil on canvas, 74.5 × 106.4 cm
Cincinnati Art Museum, Illinois, gift of Emilie L. Heine in memory of Mr and Mrs John Hauck, 1940.965
Robaut 475

Corot here painted the turrets and keep of the fourteenth-century Château de Pierrefonds (some 60 miles to the north-east of Paris) that had fallen into ruin by the early nineteenth century. He first worked on the picture in the early 1840s, carefully rendering the distant architecture in a precise, linear manner. Shortly before exhibiting the painting at the 1867 Universal Exhibition, he revised the foreground, replacing a grassy ascent with an expanse of water that is probably a memory of the lake of Pierrefonds. He also replaced a walking man with picturesque figures in a boat.

Durand-Ruel remembered that *Ruins of the Château of Pierrefonds* was one of several exhibition pictures by Corot, including, for example, *Macbeth* (Wallace Collection, London), which he acquired in the 1860s, and which were shown principally at the Paris Salon.[1] The purchase is not, however, recorded in the stock books.[2] In its re-worked state, this picture sums up Durand-Ruel's admiration for the artist's naturalistic early painting as well as his later more imaginative style. SK

1 See Durand-Ruel [1939], p. 164.
2 The stock books begin in 1864–1866.

Gustave Courbet

(Ornans 1819–La Tour de Peilz 1877)

CAT. 8 [FIG. 25]

Woman in the Waves (Femme à la vague)

1868

Oil on canvas, 65.4 × 54 cm
Lent by The Metropolitan Museum of Art, New York: H.O. Havemeyer Collection, bequest of Mrs H.O. Havemeyer, 1929, 29.100.62
F 628
Galerie Durand-Ruel. Recueil d'estampes gravées à l'eau-forte, 1874, vol. 19, no. 186, engraved by Charles Courtry (*'Une baigneuse en mer'*).

In 1873, the French Chamber of Deputies proposed to hold Courbet responsible for the cost of the Vendôme Column's reconstruction. Dreading that the State would seize his property to generate the necessary 323,091 francs and 68 centimes, Courbet endeavoured to get his major works out of France, and looked to Durand-Ruel to assemble a retrospective exhibition in Vienna, where the artist had been barred from the French pavilion at the 1873 Universal Exhibition. Courbet hoped to showcase some 60 works in different genres, including *Woman in the Waves*, and turned his canvases over to Durand-Ruel through deposit and sale to prevent their confiscation. On 26 February in a letter to Alphonse Legrand Courbet authorised the sale of this canvas to Durand-Ruel for '50,000 francs, or 45,000 in bonds'. The picture had just returned to the gallery after having been exhibited at the 1872 Brussels Salon. There, the dealer had valued the painting at 10,000 francs, so the sum mentioned in 1873 – five times higher, and more than what Durand-Ruel paid for a group of 24 pictures by Courbet the same month – is noteworthy.

Courbet's plans for a grand retrospective did not materialise as he had hoped, but in April Durand-Ruel did send the canvas to Vienna and most likely included it in a show of French masters he organised as a side event to the Universal Exhibition. In 1874, it was published in the gallery's serial *Recueil d'estampes*. When the painting re-entered Durand-Ruel's stock in January 1893, it sold almost immediately to Henry and Louisine Havemeyer. NS

CAT. 9 [FIG. 51]

Still Life with Apples (Nature morte avec pommes)

1872

Oil on canvas, 59.4 × 73.5 cm
The Mesdag Collection, The Hague
F 770

In April 1872, having recently completed a six-month prison sentence for his participation in the Commune, Courbet submitted two paintings to the Paris Salon: a reclining nude (now lost) and a recent fruit still life. The jury, led by Ernest Meissonier, refused both works. Contemporary newspaper accounts and caricatures offer contradictory descriptions of the still life, but the Mesdag picture is a probable candidate.

Courbet's rejection immediately stirred the popular press. The apples were deemed 'admirable' and the nude described by some as the best Salon submission. While Meissonier had found the red inscription backdating the still life to Courbet's time in prison dishonorable, critics widely acknowledged that the sole reason Courbet had been blackballed was his political past. Even in right-leaning and centrist periodicals, most critics argued that artistic merit, not politics, should be the determining factor for Salon entry. If the '*affaire Courbet*' called into question the integrity of the Salon system, the new rules imposed by Charles Blanc in 1872, which reduced the number of works exhibited, only exacerbated opposition. A group of 26 artists, including Pissarro, Renoir, Cézanne, and even Manet – whose *Kearsarge and Alabama* (cat. 23) had been accepted – signed a petition requesting an officially sanctioned Salon des refusés, as had taken place in 1863 and 1864. Blanc rejected the proposal, but the private market fielded its own form of Salon des refusés. Courbet's nude was displayed by the dealer Ottoz, and, according to Jules Castagnary, the still life was on view at Durand-Ruel's by 18 May 1872.[1] Despite their opposing political beliefs, Durand-Ruel had confirmed his support for Courbet earlier in the year when he purchased 26 paintings from the artist, including other still lifes dating from his captivity. By displaying Courbet's rejected Salon still life, he declared his commitment to merit and actively positioned his gallery as an alternative to the Salon. NS

1 Castagnary 1872, p. 1.

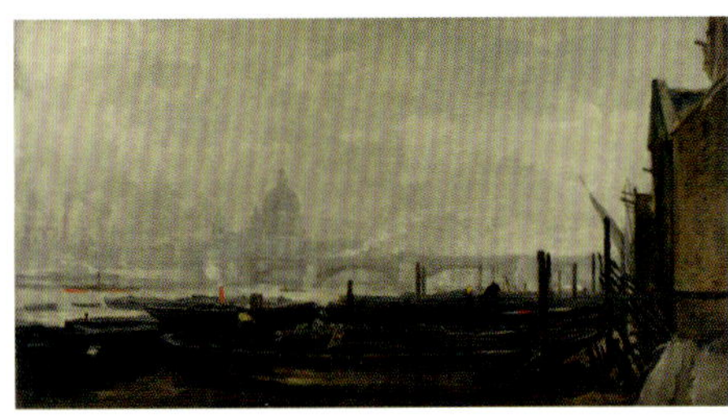

Charles-François Daubigny

(Paris 1817 – Paris 1878)

CAT. 10 [FIG. 116]

St Paul's from the Surrey Side

1871–3

Oil on canvas, 44.5 × 81 cm
The National Gallery, London, presented by friends of Mr J.C.J. Drucker, 1912
NG 2876
DR exhibition: London 1874a, no. 41
H 756

EXHIBITED IN LONDON

In October 1870 Daubigny, whose landscape paintings were regularly traded by the Durand-Ruel Gallery from the 1860s, fled to London to escape the Franco-Prussian War. A few days after his arrival he came across his dealer who had just relocated there. Not long after this, Daubigny also encountered Monet, another fellow refugee he would soon introduce to Durand-Ruel. That winter the two artists set up their easels along the Thames and painted the city. Although probably finished in the studio, this picture (together with Cat. 31, Monet's *The Thames below Westminster*) brilliantly evokes the atmosphere the painters encountered on the river banks: the bustling activity on the Thames (here observed from the south side, looking north-east towards St Paul's Cathedral, beyond Blackfriars Bridge) and the smoke rising from tugs, steamers and trains merging with the thick winter clouds. 'Fog! Visibility less than two paces', Daubigny wrote from London, moaning at having to light a candle at 11am,[1] yet mesmerised by the city's smoky vapours. Exhibited in Durand-Ruel's eighth exhibition of the Society of French Artists, the painting was praised as 'a learned and masterly study of diverse tones, and in black and rosy grey tints', with 'a rich dash of smoke . . . A masterpiece in its way'.[2] Enrolled onto the Society's committee for Durand-Ruel's first exhibition on New Bond Street, Daubigny appeared regularly in these shows (well after artist and dealer had returned to France), more often with pictures of quiet rural scenes, rather than with undeniably modern cityscapes such as this. AR

1 Moreau-Nélaton 1925, p. 102 ('Brouillard à ne pas voir à deux pas').
2 *Athenaeum*, 9 May 1874, no. 2428, p. 639, 'Exhibition of the Society of French Artists'. See also *The Era*, 31 May 1874, 'Society of French Artists'.

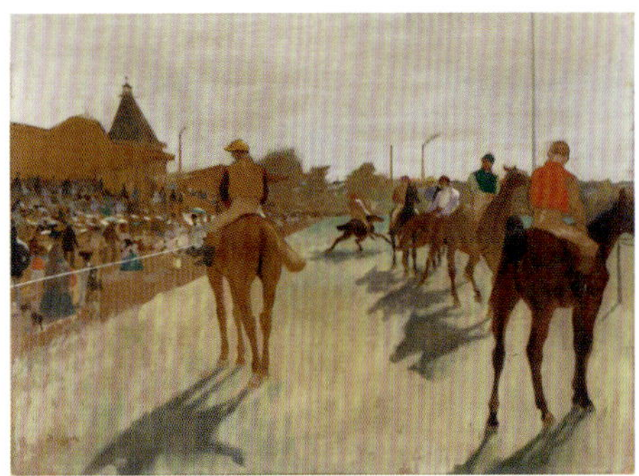

Edgar Degas

(Paris 1834 – Paris 1917)

CAT. 11 [FIG. 61]

Horses before the Stands (Le Défilé or Chevaux de course devant les tribunes)

1866–8

Oil (essence) on paper laid down on canvas, 46 × 61 cm
Musée d'Orsay, Paris, bequeathed by Count Isaac de Camondo, 1911. RF 1981
L 262

The theme of the racecourse was not new in Degas's oeuvre. However, he approached it here in an original fashion, both in terms of composition and technique, applying essence to paper laid down on canvas. It is likely that this process, which left the preparatory drawing visible, led Durand-Ruel to describe the work as an 'essence drawing' when he purchased it for 1,000 francs from Degas on 17 September 1872 (stock no. 2052, written on the frame). In the hope of selling the canvas, the dealer placed it on commission with Bowles Brothers on 8 November before sending it to Brussels on 24 May 1873 and then to London, valued at 1,500 francs. It returned to Paris on 28 January 1874, and was eventually purchased on 16 February by Jean-Baptiste Faure for 1,000 francs. Durand-Ruel bought it back from him for 10,000 francs on 2 January 1893 (stock no. 2568), before selling it on to Isaac de Camondo on 19 December that year for 30,000 francs, the highest sum paid by the collector for a work by Degas. IG

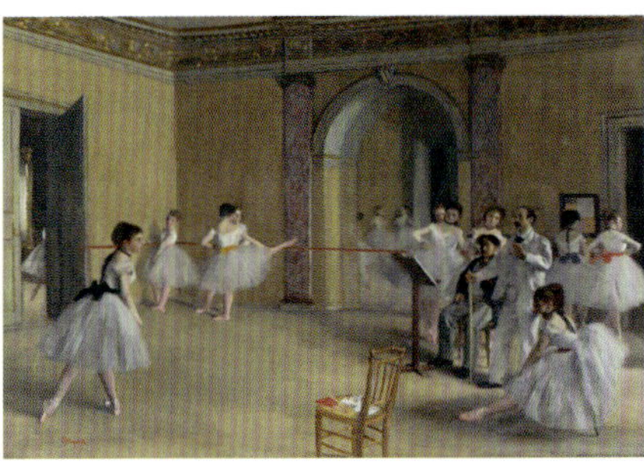

CAT. 12 [FIG. 62]

The Dance Foyer of the Opera at rue Le Peletier (Le Foyer de la danse à l'Opéra de la rue Le Peletier)

1872

Oil on canvas, 32.7 × 46.3 cm
Musée d'Orsay, Paris, bequeathed by Count Isaac de Camondo, 1911. RF 1977
L 298
DR exhibition: London 1872c, not included in catalogue
Galerie Durand-Ruel. Recueil d'estampes gravées à l'eau-forte, 1873, vol. 12, pl. 113, engraved by Martinez

Here Degas returned to a subject he had tackled the previous year in *The Dancing Class*;[1] it was to become one of his favourite themes. Durand-Ruel purchased the picture directly from the painter on 10 August 1872 for 2,500 francs (stock no. 1824). Sent to London on 29 October, the canvas featured in the fifth New Bond Street exhibition but was not included in the catalogue. Noted by the critics – Sidney Colvin celebrated 'the subtlety of exact perception and the felicitous touch in expressing it which reveal themselves in this little picture of ballet girls'[2] in an article that was full of praise – it was purchased for 4,200 francs on 7 December by the English collector Louis Huth. For this first Degas to enter a British collection, the price obtained, although slightly below the 5,000 francs hoped for by the dealer, was not insignificant for the time. By way of comparison, *The Dancing Class* was sold by Durand-Ruel on 6 February 1872, shortly after he purchased it from Degas, to the painter Brandon for 1,200 francs. IG

1 The Metropolitan Museum of Art, New York, H.O. Havemeyer Collection.
2 *Pall Mall Gazette*, 28 November 1872.

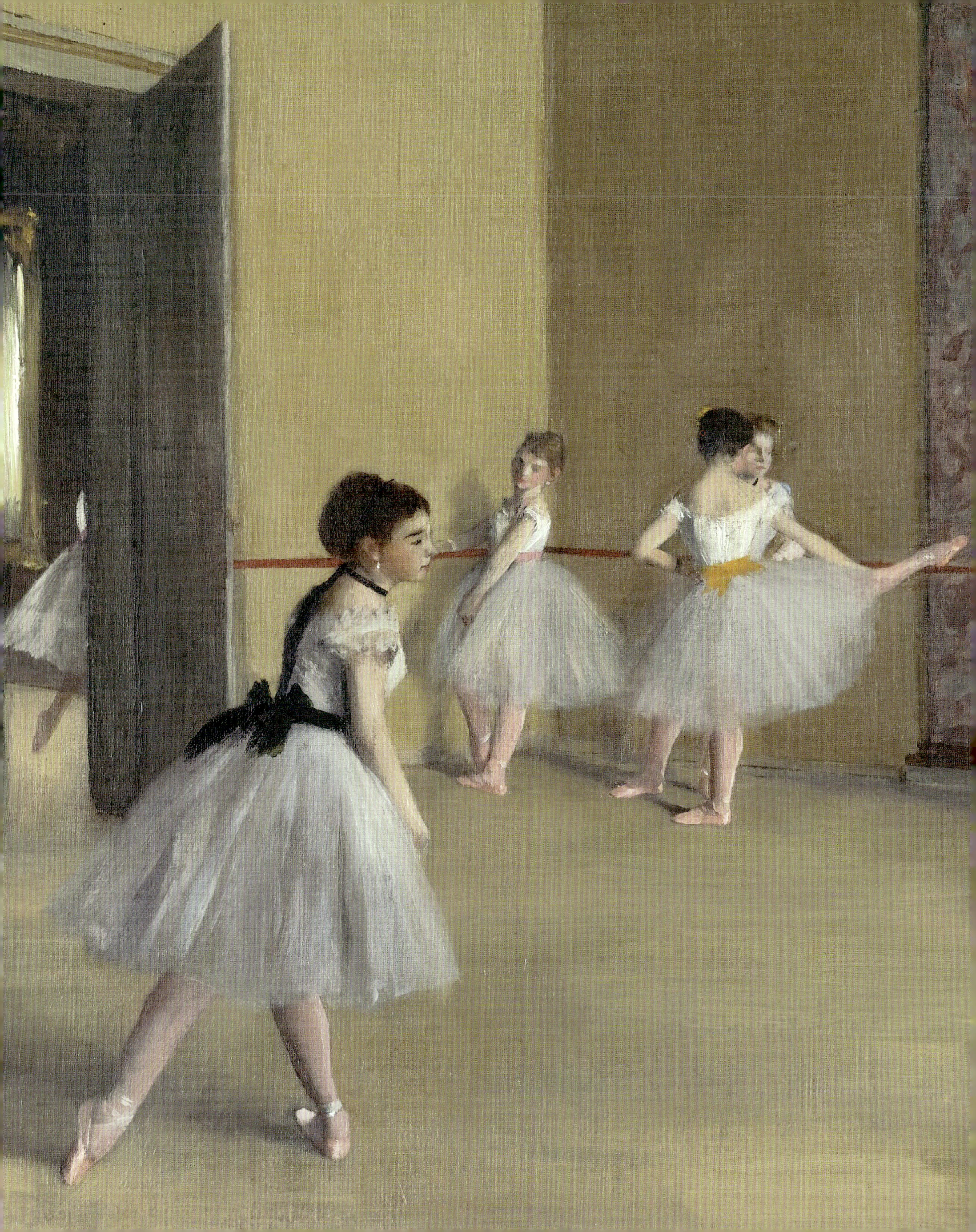

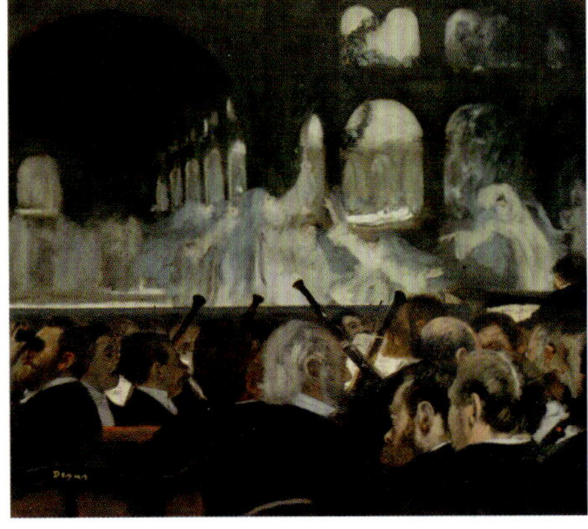
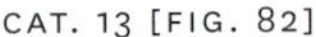

CAT. 13 [FIG. 82]

The Ballet Scene from Meyerbeer's Opera 'Robert le Diable' (Scène de ballet de l'opéra de Meyerbeer 'Robert le diable')

1876

Oil on canvas, 76.6 × 81.3 cm
Victoria and Albert Museum, London, bequeathed by Constantine Alexander Ionides, 1901. CAI.19
L 391
DR exhibition: Probably Paris 1876, no. 53 (*'Orchestre'*)

Degas likely attended an 1871 performance of Giacomo Meyerbeer's opera *Robert le Diable* (1831). His first painting on this popular romantic work (Metropolitan Museum of Art, New York) was executed immediately afterwards, showing the final act, when ghosts of nuns are brought back to life to execute an eerie dance aimed at tempting the eponymous Robert. Degas painted this version five years later, for the baritone Jean-Baptiste Faure, himself a friend and admirer of Meyerbeer. This painting is believed to have been no. 53 in the second Impressionist exhibition.[1] Deposited by Faure at Durand-Ruel's on 17 February 1881, the picture entered the dealer's stock 11 days later. On 7 June 1881 it was purchased by Constantine Ionides, an Anglo-Greek businessman who had made a fortune trading cloth between Britain and the Near East. One of the earliest Degas's to enter a British private collection, it became in 1900, with Ionides's bequest to the Victoria and Albert Museum, the first work by the artist in a public collection in Britain. AR

1 L391 is listed in exh. cat. Washington and San Francisco 1986 as no. 53 in the second Impressionist exhibition. In exh. cat. Paris, Ottawa and New York 1988–9, the painting is described as possibly exhibited in the 1876 exhibition (no. 53, *'Orchestre'*).

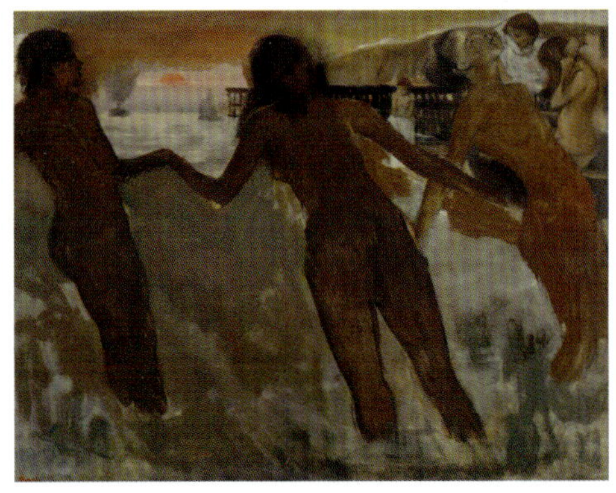

CAT. 14 [FIG. 9]

Peasant Girls bathing in the Sea at Dusk (Petites paysannes se lavant à la mer, vers le soir)

About 1869–75

Oil on canvas, 65 × 84 cm
Private collection, Ireland
L 377
DR exhibition: Probably Paris 1876, no. 56
(*'Petites Paysannes se baignant à la mer vers le soir'*)

Peasant girls enjoy the primitive thrill of an invigorating dip in the sea at dusk, their lean bodies dramatically cast into shadow by a strong backlight, like a frieze of terracotta statuettes. An unusual picture on a traditional theme – bathers in union with nature – this was almost certainly no. 56 in the catalogue of the second Impressionist exhibition. The highly unconventional effect of fading light over boisterous waves would have made it one of the most challenging works then on display on the walls of the Durand-Ruel Gallery, where this show was held. The picture appears to have attracted no comment in the press, though a number of reviews singled out Degas's paintings in general for their lack of finish. The criticism would have applied particularly well to this work, a strikingly 'new' style of painting that the dealer was ready to champion. AR

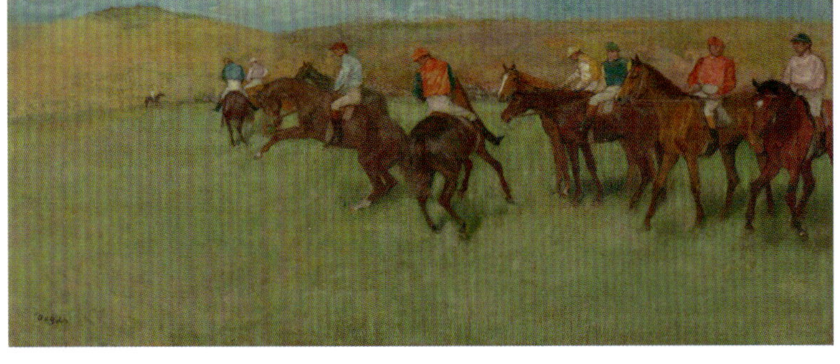

CAT. 15 [FIG. 124]

At the Races, before the Start (Aux courses, avant le départ)

About 1878–90

Oil on canvas, 40 × 89.8 cm
Virginia Museum of Fine Arts, Richmond: Collection of Mr and Mrs Paul Mellon, 1985. 85.496
L 502
DR exhibition: London 1905, no. 50

Acquired from J. Kuyper, along with Renoir's *Girl with a Cat*, on 23 May 1891, this painting was hanging in Durand-Ruel's apartment by 1892, the year it was featured in Georges Lecomte's *L'art impressionniste d'après la collection privée de M. Durand-Ruel*. It was illustrated before the first chapter on Degas and allocated a three-page-long description, suggesting the prominent place it must have held in the dealer's interior. For Lecomte, this image of frozen movement highlighted Degas's virtuosity as both draughtsman and colourist. He wrote that the jockeys' jewel-toned jerseys 'shimmer against the grass like petals', while the horses and riders, 'so vigorously drawn', maintain a sense of solidity. In London in 1905, critics also responded to Degas's draughtsmanship, some regarding the artist as a problematic Impressionist: 'The horses are drawn as finely and decisively as on a Greek bas-relief.' The picture remained with Durand-Ruel for decades, until it passed to noted London collectors Edith and Alfred Chester Beatty by 1932. NS

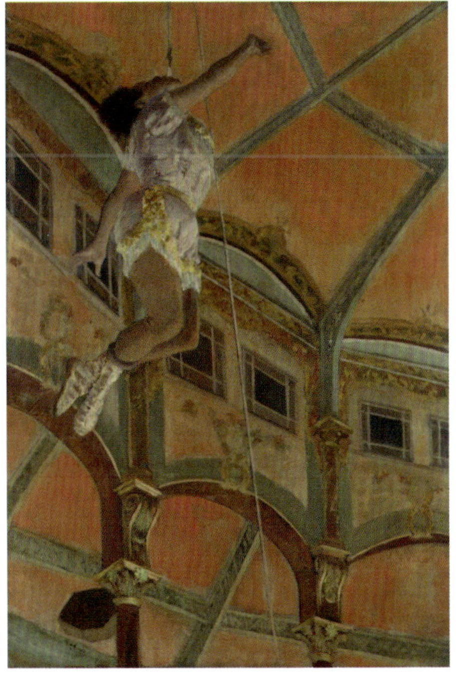

CAT. 16 [FIG. 123]

Miss La La at the Cirque Fernando

1879

Oil on canvas, 117.2 × 77.5 cm
Signed lower left: *Degas*
The National Gallery, London.
Bought with the Courtauld Fund, 1925
L 522
DR exhibition: London 1905, no. 72,
('*Miss Zaza* [sic] *at the Cirque Fernando*')

Miss La La, famous acrobat and aerialist, caused a stir in late 1870s Paris with her spectacular acts based on the strength of her jaw. Degas watched her perform in January 1879, and painted the vertiginous ascent of the gymnast to the rafters of the circus building, a rope clenched between her teeth. Decades later, on 29 November 1902, the artist deposited the painting at Durand-Ruel's and in 1905 it was one of the largest, most accomplished, and most expensive works by Degas in the Grafton Galleries exhibition.[1] On 16 March, as the show closed, the picture entered Durand-Ruel's stock and was purchased the same day by Toronto businessman, foundry owner and philanthropist Cawthra Mulock.[2] In 1905 Mulock largely financed the construction of Toronto's Royal Alexandra Theater (opened 1907), which was erected, to his specification, with a steel frame promoting his foundry's products.[3] He may therefore have found the Degas painting, dominated by the criss-cross lines of the Cirque Fernando's metallic structure, particularly inspiring. AR

1 Rutter 1933: 'the supremely decorative, slightly Japanesy *Mlle Zozo* [sic] *au Cirque Fernando*'.
2 'The large Degas, Mlle Zaza au Cirque Fernando' has, of course, found its way to America, where so many of the finer Manets and Monets and Whistlers have already gone.' (Rutter 1905).
3 Brockhouse 2008.

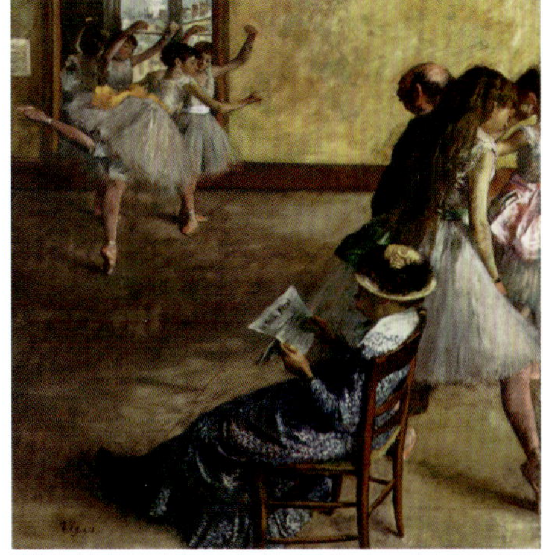

CAT. 17 [FIG. 92]

The Ballet Class (Le Foyer de la danse)

About 1880

Oil on canvas, 82.2 × 76.8 cm
Philadelphia Museum of Art, Pennsylvania: purchased with the W.P. Wilstach Fund, 1937
L 479
DR exhibition: New York 1886b, no. 299
('*Repetition of the Dance*' lent by A.J. Cassatt)

When Mary Cassatt began looking for pictures for her brother Alexander in 1880, she initially tried to acquire Degas's *Scene from the Steeplechase: The Fallen Jockey* (National Gallery of Art, Washington), a work she thought would appeal to her brother who raised thoroughbred racehorses. A year later, when it was apparent that Degas would not part with the painting, on which he continued to work, she instead sought a dance subject. Degas re-worked this canvas too, repainting the right side and adding a seated figure over a ballerina adjusting her shoe. In September 1881, Cassatt asked Durand-Ruel, who had negotiated the sale, to ship the recently finished work to Philadelphia. Alexander's reaction to it is not documented, though he later acquired a Degas pastel of jockeys from Durand-Ruel. In May 1886, Alexander lent the ballet scene to Durand-Ruel's Impressionist exhibition in New York, where it was noted as belonging to the Pennsylvania Railroad executive. JAT

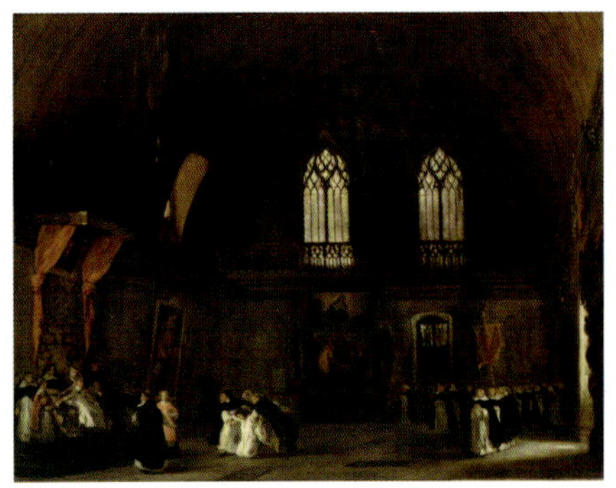

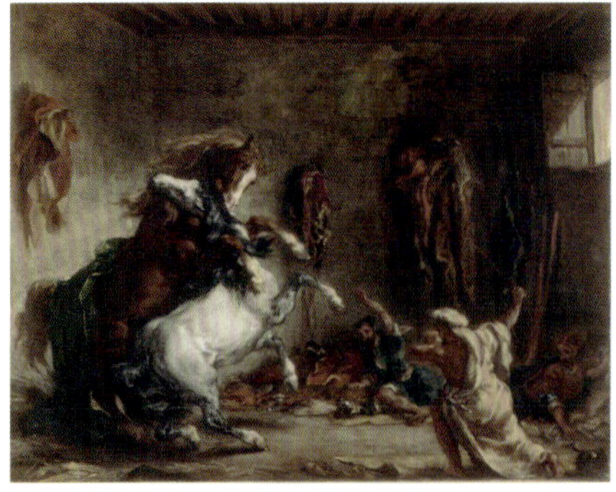

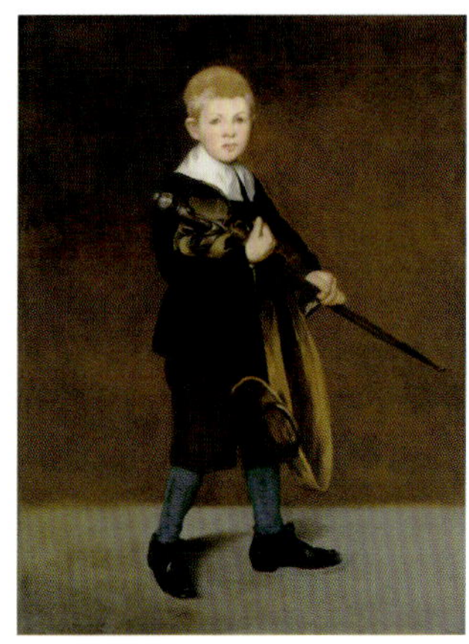

Eugène Delacroix

(Saint-Maurice-en Chalencon 1798–Paris 1863)

CAT. 18 [FIG. 37]

Interior of a Dominican Convent in Madrid (L'Amende honorable)

1831

Oil on canvas, 130.2 × 161.9 cm
Philadelphia Museum of Art, Pennsylvania: purchased with the W.P. Wilstach Fund, W1894-1-2
J 148
DR exhibitions: Paris 1872, n.n.; Paris 1873, n.n.; New York 1887, no. 72 ('*The Honorable Amend*')
Galerie Durand-Ruel. Recueil d'estampes gravées à l'eau-forte, 1873, vol. 4, pl. 37, engraved by Emile Boilvin

This 'noble picture' fascinated New York critics who lamented in 1887 that it was destined to return to Europe and the collection of Scottish merchant James Duncan.[1] Among its American admirers was John G. Johnson, who placed an emphatic checkmark beside it in his exhibition catalogue and later acquired it for the Wilstach Gallery in Philadelphia. Inspired by *Melmoth the Wanderer*, a popular 1820 Gothic tale, the canvas describes a scene, fantastically imagined in the sixteenth-century Rouen Palace of Justice, in which a monk is dragged before the Bishop of Madrid and abused for rebelling against his order. First owned by Ferdinand-Philippe, the duc d'Orléans, the painting had several owners before Durand-Ruel acquired it in partnership with Brame in 1868 and sold it on 4 November that year for 20,000 francs to William H. Herriman, a Brooklyn businessman who spent his final years in Rome. Herriman returned the canvas to Durand-Ruel prior to March 1870, when it was offered (but bought in) at the Edwards sale and exhibited at the gallery before being acquired by Duncan around 1873. JAT

1 *The Studio*, July 1887, p. 2.

CAT. 19 [FIG. 38]

Arab Horses Fighting in a Stable (Chevaux arabes se battant dans une écurie)

1860

Oil on canvas, 64.5 × 81 cm
Musée du Louvre, Paris, deposited at the Musée d'Orsay, bequeathed by Count Isaac de Camondo, 1911
DR exhibition: Paris 1872, n.n.
Galerie Durand-Ruel, Recueil d'estampes gravées à l'eau-forte, 1873, vol. 1, pl. 103, engraved by Emile Boilvin

Durand-Ruel bought this, one of Delacroix's most dramatic pictures, in February 1872. Exhibited in his Paris gallery in April that year in a room devoted to Delacroix, it was etched for the *Recueil* and sold by the end of the month to the collector John Saulnier.[1] In his *Memoirs* Durand-Ruel listed it with other important purchases and sales from that period in his life, along with Delacroix's *Assassination of the Bishop of Liège*. The dealer touchingly observed how artists such as Delacroix influenced his discovery of Impressionism, concluding: 'My passion for the School of 1830 gave me the courage to make acquisitions that colleagues and friends saw as ruinous. I will never forget the effect the landscapes which I bought in London by Monet and Pissarro had on me.'[2] JR

1 ADR, daybook, 29 April 1872.
2 Venturi [1939], II, p. 188.

Edouard Manet

(Paris 1832–Paris 1883)

CAT. 20 [FIG. 91]

Boy with a Sword (L'Enfant à l'épée)

1861

Oil on canvas, 131.1 × 93.4 cm
Lent by The Metropolitan Museum of Art, New York. Gift of Erwin Davis, 1889. Inv. 89.21.2
RW I-37
DR exhibition: New York 1886b, no. 303 ('*L'Enfant à l'épée* [*The boy with a sword*]')
Galerie Durand-Ruel, Recueil d'estampes gravées à l'eau-forte, 1873, vol. 6, no. 56, engraved by Félix Braquemond

In January 1872, Durand-Ruel saw two Manets hanging in the studio of established painter Alfred Stevens. On 8 January, he purchased *Boy with a Sword* for 1,500 francs from the dealer Alexis-Joseph Febvre. Shortly thereafter, Durand-Ruel called on Manet himself, from whom he bought 23 paintings. These purchases marked a watershed moment in Manet's career and for Durand-Ruel were a huge investment in his identity as a champion of new art. With high hopes, he sent *Boy with a Sword* to Brussels in September 1872, ambitiously priced at more than 15,000 francs.[1] In 1881 the American painter J. Alden Weir bought the picture as agent for the New York collector Erwin Davis, who lent it in 1886 to Durand-Ruel's exhibition in New York, where one critic noted: 'The pictures that form the present exhibition have been collected by Mr. Durand-Ruel, whose gallery has long been one of the chief attractions in Paris for the lovers of pictures . . . Courbet and Manet found in him one of their earliest admirers.'[2] After he failed to sell it at auction, Davis gave *Boy with a Sword* to the Metropolitan Museum of Art in 1889, making it one of the first two paintings by the artist to enter a public collection in America. JR

1 ADR, daybook, 3 September 1872. I am thankful to Sylvie Patry for pointing out the price estimate in the stock book, 1868–1873.
2 [Anonymous] 1886c, p. 246.

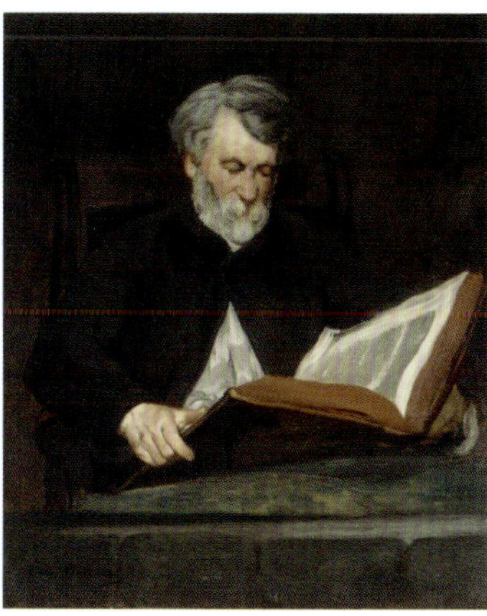

CAT. 21 [FIG. 52]

The Reader (Le Liseur)

1861

Oil on canvas, 99.7 × 81.3 cm
Saint Louis Art Museum, Missouri.
Museum purchase 254:1915
RW 35
DR exhibition: London 1872a
Galerie Durand-Ruel. Recueil d'estampes gravées à l'eau forte, 1873, vol. 1, pl. 35, engraved by Charles Courtry

This portrait of introverted absorption shows a bearded man reading a heavy volume placed on a stone ledge. The sitter was the painter Joseph Gall (1807–1888), who had a studio near Manet's. This rapidly painted work (note the abstracted form of the sitter's left hand) was regularly exhibited by Manet in the early 1860s, particularly at the Galerie Martinet, suggesting his satisfaction with the picture.[1] Durand-Ruel acquired the canvas directly from Manet for 1,000 francs in January 1872 as part of a batch of 23 paintings. The following year, he sent it to Vienna with other Manet paintings for display at the Universal Exhibition.[2] The work was sold to the opera singer Jean-Baptiste Faure on 9 February 1874 for 3,000 francs – a three-fold profit.[3] Durand-Ruel then re-purchased the painting from Faure on 13 March 1907 for 50,000 francs. It was sent to his New York office on 22 October 1909 and sold to the Saint Louis Art Museum in the late autumn of 1915 for $25,000, following considerable negotiation.[4] SK

1 It was shown, for example, at the Galerie Martinet 15–31 August 1861.
2 Vienna Universal Exhibition 1873, no. 472.
3 ADR, daybook, 9 February 1874.
4 Georges Durand-Ruel (in New York) wrote in English to Joseph Durand-Ruel (in Paris) on 26 November 1915: 'I just received a telegram from Mr. Holston [Durand-Ruel's sales manager in New York, who was negotiating with the Museum in St Louis]: "cannot get them to pay more for reader write instructions" – and I have decided to accept the offer but as I do not want such a low price to be mentioned, I telegraphed back as follows: "you can accept but we want picture sold thirty thousand we contributing five thousand as gift to museum."' Shortly after, Georges wrote again on 29 November 1915, 'I received a telegram from Mr. Holston saying that he had sold the Manet reader.' Thanks to Paul-Louis Durand-Ruel for this information, provided in an email on 25 February 2014. The invoice of the sale in the Saint Louis Art Museum archives (dated 15 November 1915) indicates a sale price of $25,000.

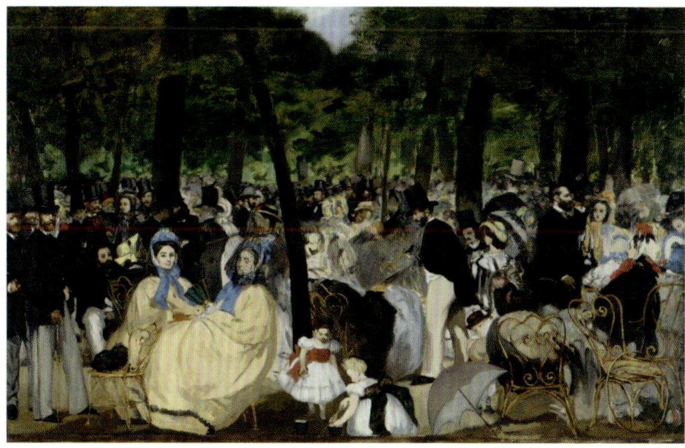

CAT. 22 [FIG. 122]

Music in the Tuileries Gardens (La Musique aux Tuileries)

1862

Oil on canvas, 76.2 × 118.1 cm
The National Gallery, London.
Sir Hugh Lane Bequest, 1917, NG 3260
DR exhibitions: Paris 1894; New York 1895c; London 1905, no. 87

A pivotal work of *Modern Painting*, *Music in the Tuileries Gardens* continues to attract the attention of scholars. Several of the people depicted are still to be identified, alongside the recognisable figures of Baudelaire, Offenbach and the artist himself. In his *Memoirs*, written much later, Paul Durand-Ruel recalls having purchased it on the occasion of his famous visit to Manet's studio in 1872. Yet this canvas it is not included in the inventory of 23 works purchased that day and it seems to have remained in the artist's possession until 1883, when it entered the collection of Jean-Baptiste Faure.[1] The singer sold it in 1898 to Durand-Ruel, who included it in the 1905 exhibition at the Grafton Galleries in London, where he gave it a prominent position. The following year, the picture was purchased by the dealer and collector Hugh Lane, with the aim of making it one of the key pieces in the Municipal Gallery of Modern Art he had founded in Dublin.[2] The fact that this work and other modern paintings belonging to Lane, including Manet's *Eva Gonzalès* (cat. 26), ended up in London instead, was for decades yet another cause for tension between Ireland and England. CR

1 Davies 1970, pp. 91–4. It is just possible that Durand-Ruel did indeed acquire the work in 1872 and that he sold it on to Faure immediately, although this purchase was not listed in the account books.
2 On Lane, see Dawson 2008.

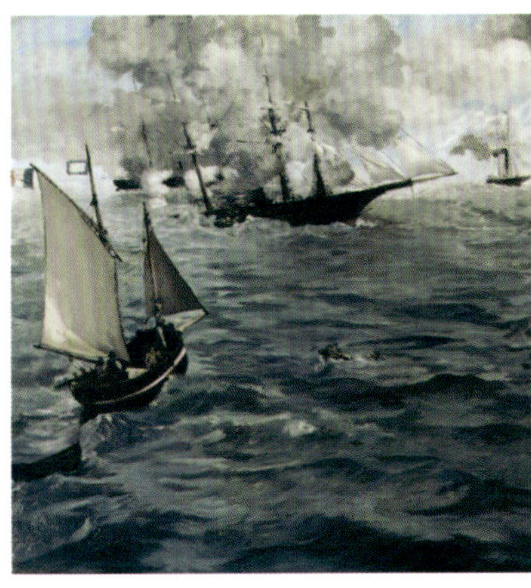

CAT. 23 [FIG. 21]

The Battle of the U.S.S. 'Kearsarge' and the C.S.S. 'Alabama' (Le Combat du 'Kearsarge' et de 'L'Alabama')

1864

Oil on canvas, 137.8 × 128.9 cm
Philadelphia Museum of Art, Pennsylvania: John G. Johnson Collection, 1917. Cat. 1027
RW 76
DR exhibitions: London 1873a (?), not in catalogue; New York 1886a and b, no. 178
Galerie Durand-Ruel. Recueil d'estampes gravées à l'eau forte, 1874, vol. 16, pl. 158, engraved by Léon Gaucherel

In June 1864, a critical battle in the American Civil War occurred near Cherbourg when the Confederate raider, the *Alabama*, was attacked and sunk by the Union warship, the *Kearsarge*. Within a month, Manet's rendering of the naval engagement was displayed in the window of Alfred Cadart's gallery in Paris. Durand-Ruel first encountered the canvas in the artist's studio in January 1872, where he purchased it for 3,000 francs. Sent to the 1872 Paris and Brussels Salons at the artist's request and etched for the *Recueil*, the painting was shown in London and owned successively by Jean-Baptiste Faure (purchased from Durand-Ruel on 17 November 1873 for 5,000 francs), Georges Charpentier (bought at Hôtel Drouot on 23 March 1878, lot 32), and Théodore Duret, all of whom left it on deposit at the gallery for long periods. In spring 1886 Durand-Ruel sent the painting to New York, where one critic commented that it was 'so grand in its treatment of the water that it makes us forget the ships.'[1] Philadelphia lawyer John G. Johnson may have admired the work then, negotiating its purchase with Charles Durand-Ruel in September 1888 for $1500. JAT

1 *The Studio*, 17 April 1886, p. 251.

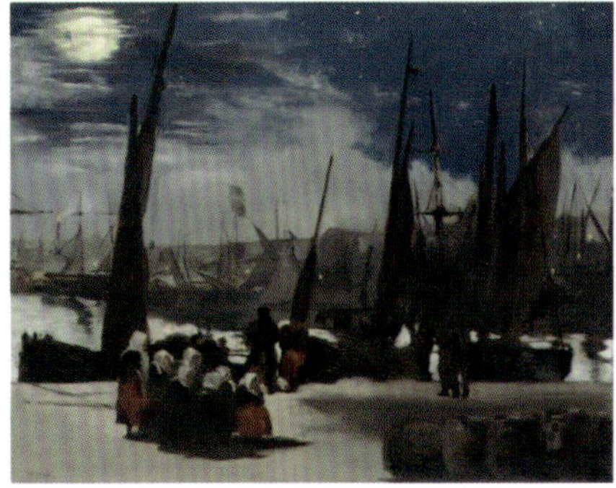

CAT. 24 [FIG. 54]

Moonlight at the Port of Boulogne (Clair de lune, or **Clair de lune sur le port de Boulogne)**

1868

Oil on canvas, 81.5 × 101 cm
Musée d'Orsay, Paris, bequeathed by Count Isaac de Camondo, 1911. RF 1993
RW 143
DR exhibition: London 1872a, no. 24
Galerie Durand-Ruel. Recueil d'estampes gravées à l'eau-forte, 1873, vol.3, pl. 30, engraved by Léon Gaucherel

Manet spent the summer of 1868 in Boulogne-sur-Mer. The stay inspired several canvases, including this *Moonlight*. Durand-Ruel recalled purchasing the work at Stevens's for 800 francs[1] (stock no. 929), while Manet included it among the 21 pictures purchased by the dealer in January 1872: the price given then was 1,000 francs.[2] Whatever the case, on 6 January 1872 the work was sold to the Baron de Villars[3] but then returned to the dealer on 9 January. It would later be purchased by Jean-Baptiste Faure for 3,000 francs, on 3 January 1873.[4] IG

1 Durand-Ruel [1939], p. 189.
2 Small notebook with list made by Manet, copied by Moreau-Nélaton, p. 131 (Paris, BnF, Estampes, Yb3-2401-8).
3 ADR, daybook, 6 January 1872. The canvas was purchased alongside a still life (cat. 25) for 6,000 francs.
4 ADR, daybook, 3 January 1873. Faure paid 500 francs in cash; the rest would later be paid by half the proceeds of the sale of four pictures he had left on deposit with the dealer.

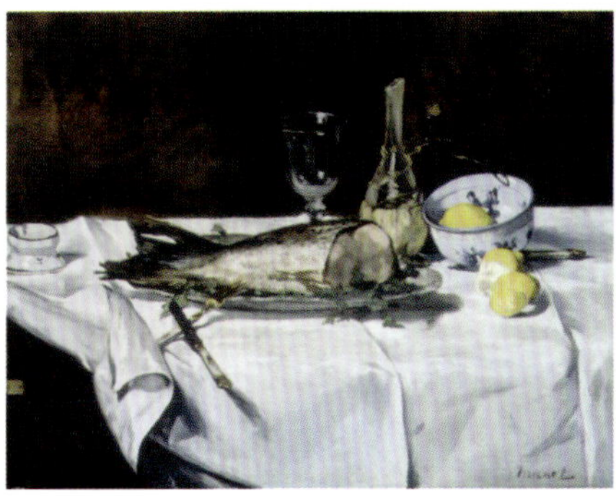

CAT. 25 [FIG. 53]

The Salmon (Le Saumon)

1869

Oil on canvas, 71.8 × 89.9 cm
Shelburne Museum, Vermont, gift of the Electra Havemeyer Webb Fund, 1960, Inc. Inv. 1972-69.16
RW I-140
DR exhibitions: London 1872a, no. 105 ('*Still Life*'); London 1872b, no. 127 ('*The Fish*'); New York, 1886a and b, no. 23 ('*Still Life*')

One of two Manets, along with *Moonlight at the Port of Boulogne* (cat. 24), that Durand-Ruel recalled seeing on the walls of Alfred Stevens's studio in early January 1872,[1] *The Salmon* initiated an immense purchase of more than 20 paintings directly from the artist. On 20 January, the dealer sent the still life with seven of his new Manet canvases to the German Gallery in London, before exhibiting the picture that summer at the Brussels Triennial (no. 490, '*Un déjeuner*'). It would return to London a second time[2] before it was purchased by Jean-Baptiste Faure for 1,500 francs in 1874. Twelve years later, Durand-Ruel included the picture in his New York exhibition and sold it for 15,000 francs to H.O. Havemeyer,[3] who debated between the *The Salmon* and *Boy with a Sword* (cat. 20). Havemeyer told his wife Louisine: 'The still life was very fine and I bought it for you, but I must confess the *Boy with the Sword* was too much for me.'[4] He may have also have been swayed to make this, his first Manet purchase, by the amiable review given by one critic: 'Manet's "Still Life" (23), again, is one of the *natures mortes* in which he was confessedly incomparable, and is one of his best and most easily understood; it contains a specimen of his capitally scaly fish, and a cut lemon, surely the most cruelly sour lemon ever painted.'[5] JR

1 Durand-Ruel [1939], p. 189.
2 ADR, daybook, 13 October 1873.
3 See New York 1993, no. 350, p. 354. Durand-Ruel purchased the painting back from Faure on 24 August 1886 for 5,000 francs.
4 Weitzenhoffer 1986, p. 44.
5 *The Nation*, 15 April 1886, p. 328.

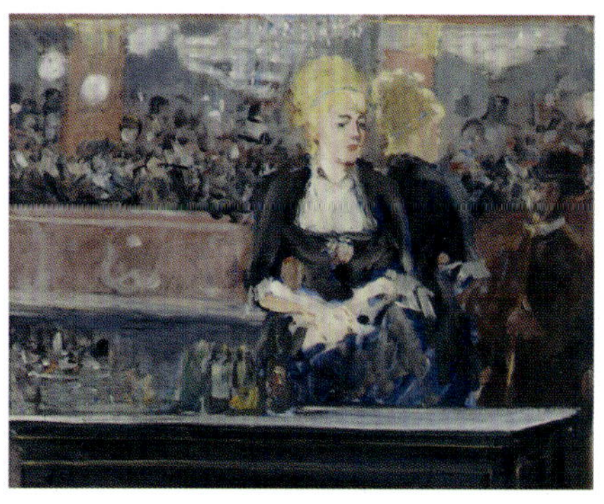

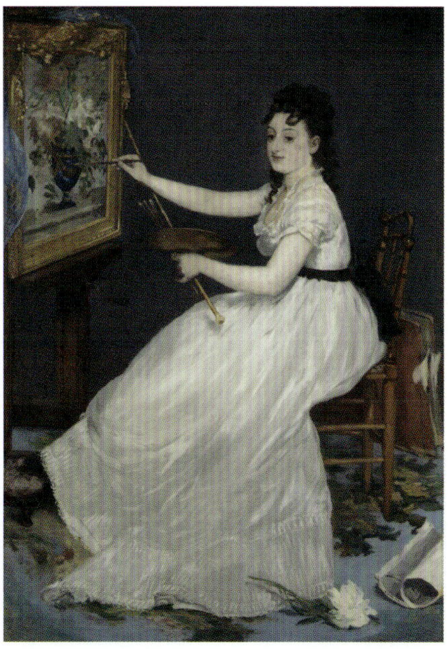

CAT. 26 [FIG. 117]

Eva Gonzalès

1870

Oil on canvas, 191.1 × 133.4 cm
The National Gallery, London, Sir Hugh Lane Bequest, 1917, NG 3259
RW 154
DR exhibition: London 1905, no. 101

Eva Gonzalès (1849–1883) entered Manet's studio as his pupil in February 1869. This portrait, in which she appears not only as a painter applying the finishing touches to a flower still life but also as a muse in her bright white dress, was completed in time to be exhibited at the Salon the following year. After the death of the late artist's husband in 1897, Durand-Ruel bought the painting from Camentron in 1899. He sent it all over Europe and lent it to the Irish collector Hugh Lane on two occasions, in 1904 and again in 1906. Lane hoped it would be bought by an Irish collector from Dublin or Belfast who would then donate it to the Municipal Gallery of Modern Art he had founded in Dublin. When no collectors came forward, Lane purchased the painting himself from Durand-Ruel in 1906, the same year as *Music in the Tuileries Gardens* (cat. 22). CR

CAT. 27 [FIG. 118]

Bar at the Folies-Bergère (Un bar aux Folies-Bergère)

1881

Oil on canvas, 47 × 56 cm
Private collection
RW 387
DR exhibition: London 1905, no. 93 (*'The Bar at the "Folies-Bergère",'* 1882)
EXHIBITED IN LONDON

Manet was represented in the Grafton Galleries exhibition by 19 pictures. Number 93 (*'Bar at the "Folies-Bergère",* 1882') was this composition sketch in oil, which Durand-Ruel acquired by 1892 from dealers Martin et Camentron. The preparatory work was a shrewd addition to the exhibition, likely to benefit from the reputation of the large Salon canvas (briefly with Durand-Ruel from 1897, and now at the Courtauld Galleries, London), acknowledged as Manet's last masterpiece. The relationship between the two works was noted in the press, but this was not always to the benefit of the smaller picture: critics may have been put off by the swift, summary brushwork – they seemed oblivious to the ease with which Manet had captured the effervescent atmosphere of the bustling crowds in the smoky music hall and to the canvas's undeniable vibrancy. For Durand-Ruel, having smaller, sketchier pictures was an efficient way of showcasing the more ambitious and expensive ones; the *Bar* hung close to Manet's *Eva Gonzalès* (cat. 26), separated by only two double-hung groups of pictures. AR

1 '"Bar at the Folies Bergères" [sic] . . . is represented . . . only by a sketch for it – a sketch not at all of the most engaging.' (Wedmore 1905).
2 Jensen 1994, p. 54.

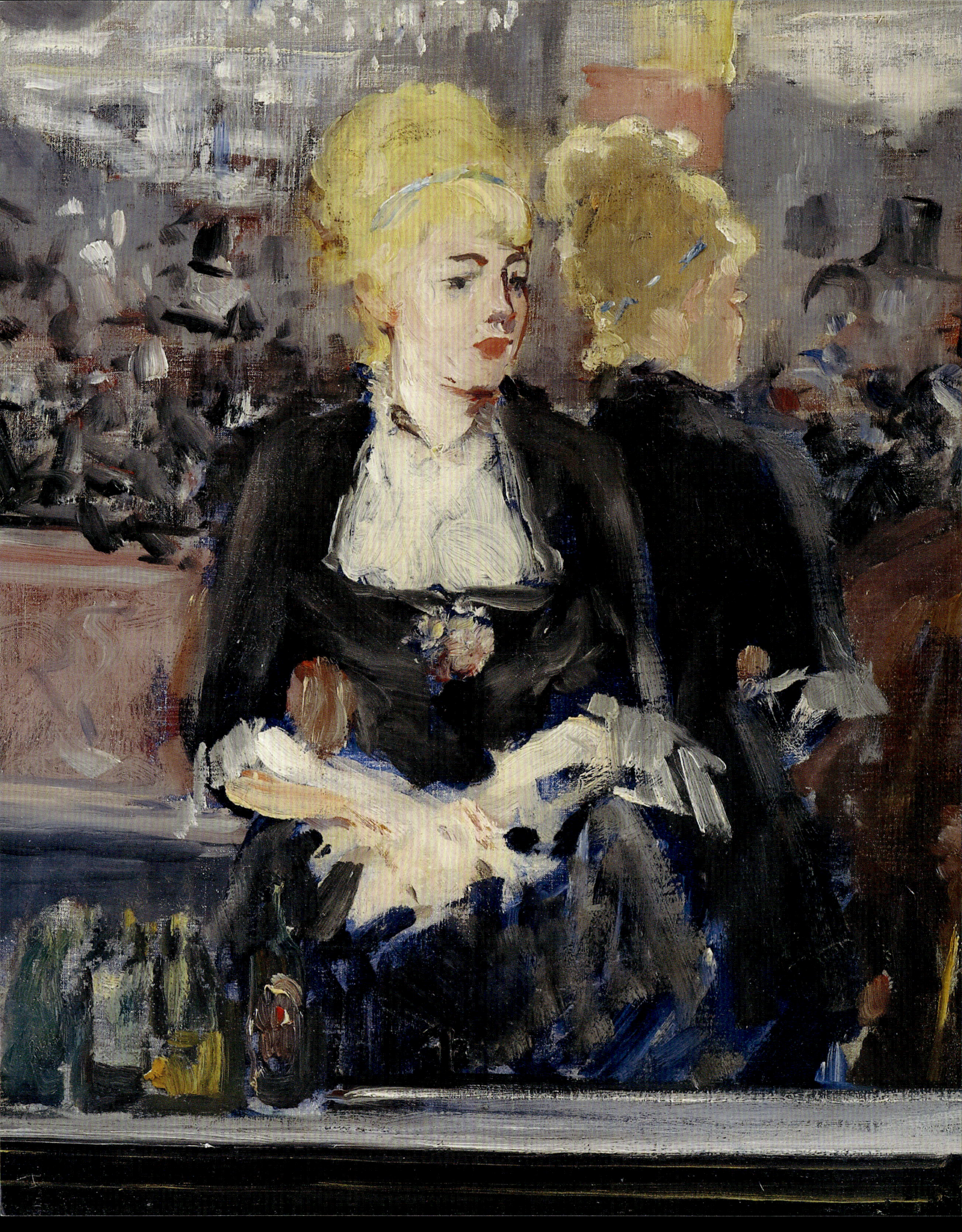

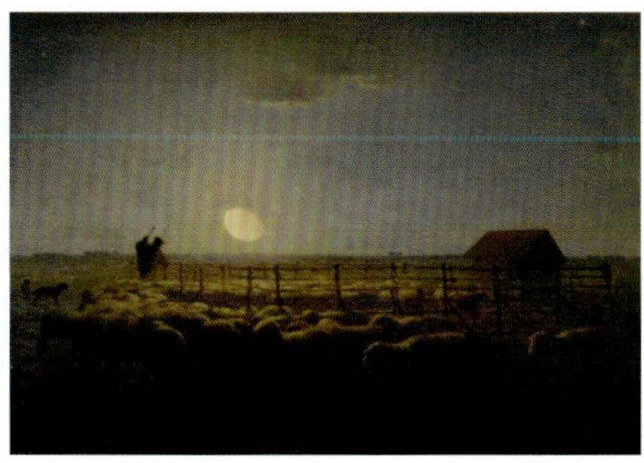

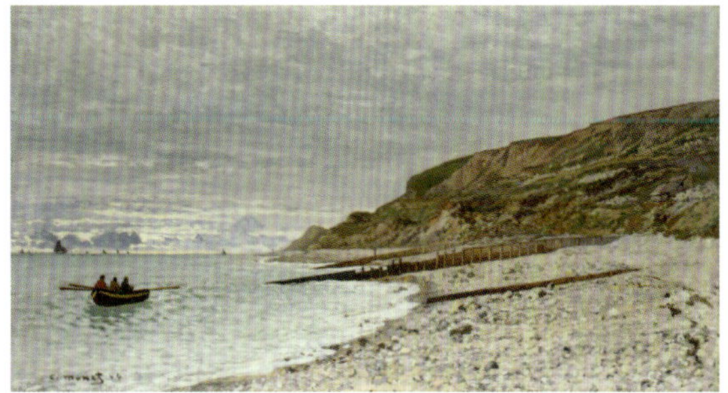

Jean-François Millet

(Gruchy 1814–Barbizon 1875)

CAT. 28 [FIG. 49]

The Sheepfold, Moonlight (La Bergerie)

About 1856–8

Oil on panel, 45.3 × 63.4 cm
The Walters Art Museum, Baltimore, Maryland, bequest of Henry Walters, 1931. Inv. 37.30
Galerie Durand-Ruel. Recueil d'estampes gravées à l'eau forte, 1873, vol. 1, pl. 40, engraved by Frédéric-Auguste Laguillermie

Millet's atmospheric nocturnal scene represents an itinerant shepherd entering his sheep into a portable pen on the plain between the villages of Barbizon and Chailly. The artist carefully depicted the waning, gibbous moon and noted: 'Oh, how I wish I could make those who see my work feel the splendours and terrors of the night! . . . they should feel the infinite'.[1] This work is the earliest and arguably most accomplished of a series of images by Millet in various media on this moonlight theme.

Durand-Ruel acquired this work at the Carlin sale in Paris on 29 April 1872 for 20,000 francs, a sale record for Millet.[2] The dealer considered this work (together with *The Angelus*) as Millet's 'masterpiece'.[3] He initially placed it with an American collector (probably John Wilson)[4] for 40,000 francs but the deal fell through. On 10 May 1872, he sold it to the prominent Millet collector, Emile Gavet, for the sum of 23,000 francs. He subsequently bought it back in March 1873.[5] SK

1 Cited in Sensier and Mantz 2005, p. 153.
2 The work was purchased for $21,000 including 5% buyer's premium.
3 'M. Durand told me he had sold your *Shepherd in the Moonlight*, which he had bought at the Carlin sale for 20,000 francs, to an American for 40,000 francs with one year of credit. He did the same with *The Angelus*, for 38,000 francs, but he added that these were Millet's two masterpieces. "They are worth twice that of the others!!"' Alfred Sensier to Jean-François Millet, Paris, 12 July 1872. Paris, Département des Arts Graphiques, Musée du Louvre.
4 This might have been John Waterloo Wilson (whose Belgian nationality was reflected in his Anglo-American name), who bought *The Angelus* in around 1872.
5 In a complicated process, Durand-Ruel bought it back from Gavet on 5 March 1873 for 31,000 francs before returning it to the collector for the same price on 11 March 1873, and then once again taking it back the same day.

Claude Monet

(Paris 1840–Giverny 1926)

CAT. 29 [FIG. 74]

La Pointe de la Hève, Sainte-Adresse

1864

Oil on canvas, 41 × 73 cm
The National Gallery, London.
Bought, 1996. NG6565
W 39
DR exhibition: Paris 1883b, no. 2 ('owned by Faure')

A study for a larger picture shown by Monet at the 1865 Salon (Kimbell Art Museum, Fort Worth), this work entered Durand-Ruel's stock in April 1872. Working at Sainte-Adresse, Normandy, in the summer of 1864, the artist painted the shingle beach, recording its variety of natural textures: gleaming pebbles, grass, sea foam and streaks of bright sunlight in the opalescent atmosphere. When the painting featured in the first monographic show Durand-Ruel devoted to Monet, in 1883, it was in the possession of singer Faure,[1] who could have owned it from 1877 (it was recorded in the dealer's ledgers, as 'Sainte-Adresse'). Two decades later Faure deposited it back at Durand-Ruel's with a number of Monets and Manets, which soon after formed part of an exhibition of pictures from the singer's collection, organised for Paris and, in Germany, Berlin, Stuttgart and Munich (Galerie Heinemann).[2] There the picture was purchased by the Neue Staatsgalerie in Munich on 11 February 1907, where it formed part of the collection until 1940. AR

1 Exh. cat. Paris 1883b, no. 2: 'owned by Faure'.
2 Heinemann archives: the picture was taken on consignment (see register of the Heinemann Gallery, stock ledger 6, LB06).

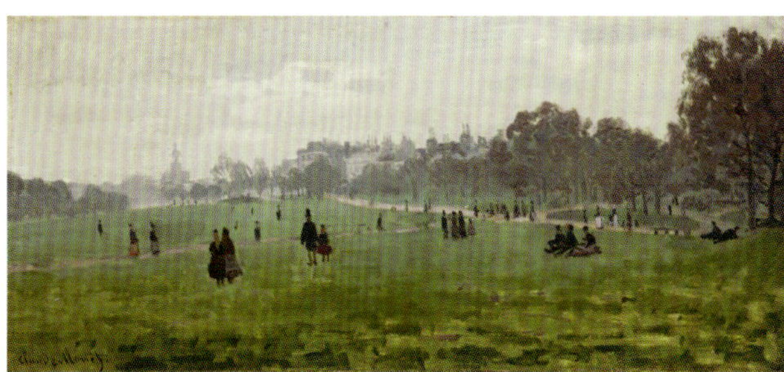

CAT. 30 [FIG. 114]

Green Park, London

1870 or 1871

Oil on canvas, 34.3 × 72.5 cm
Philadelphia Museum of Art, Pennsylvania: purchased with the W.P. Wilstach Fund, 1921. W1921-1-7
W 165
DR exhibition: London 1872c, no. 131

Monet painted this panoramic view of Green Park (like cats. 31 and 32) during the months he spent in London in 1870–1. While there he met Durand-Ruel, who was keeping his business running in spite of the war by organising exhibitions of French art. The painting, one of seven Monets the dealer purchased from the artist on 11 May 1872 (for 300 francs each) featured in the fifth of these shows, which opened on 4 November that year. Two Monets were on display: *Green Park*, with its gloomy sky, muddy grass and rapid notations of tiny dark figures hurrying through the park, alongside *Saint-Germain-l'Auxerrois* of 1867 (Nationalgalerie, Berlin[1]), an earlier, more accomplished picture showing the Gothic landmark glowing in the bright, crisp Paris sunlight. The dealer not only favoured these contrasts – early and recent work, large and small, finished and sketchy, Paris and London – but he actively sought them out as part of his commercial strategy, in the hope that this play of oppositions would enhance the respective qualities of each picture, and make them more saleable. *Green Park* was purchased in the 1880s by Alexander Cassatt of Philadelphia. AR

1 Fowle 2006, p. 142.

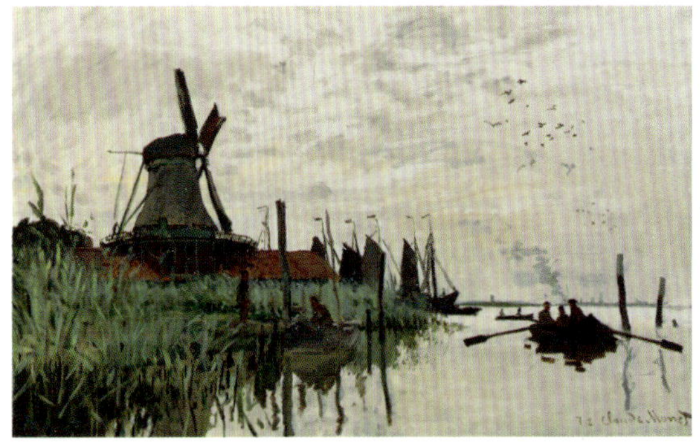

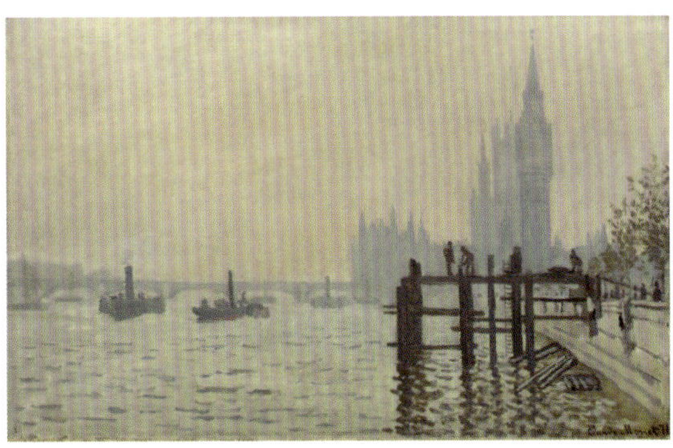

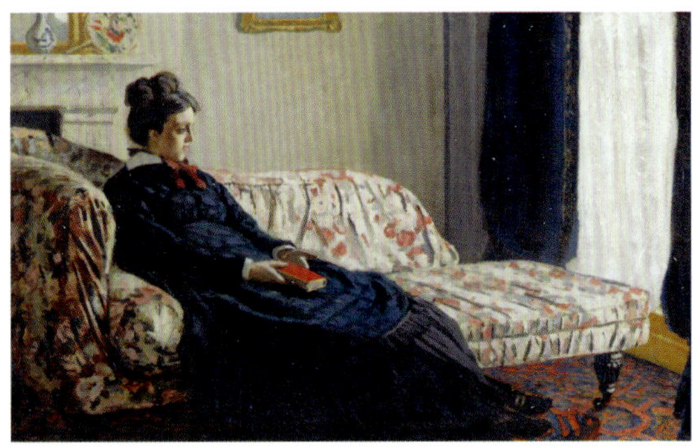

CAT. 31 [FIG. 113]

The Thames below Westminster (La Tamise en bas de Westminster)

About 1871

Oil on canvas, 47 × 73 cm
The National Gallery, London, bequeathed by Lord Astor of Hever, 1971. NG6399
W 166
DR exhibition: London 1873a, no. 114 ('The Houses of Parliament')

Late in life Durand-Ruel recalled that he 'immediately' bought the pictures Monet had painted in London.[1] In fact, while Monet produced this atmospheric view of the river Thames on a foggy London morning in the spring of 1871, it was not until 18 November 1872, back in Paris, that the dealer acquired it. The picture soon returned to London, sent by Durand-Ruel for exhibition in his New Bond Street gallery. There it hung alongside a view of Argenteuil – a more recent and equally crisp, but brighter Monet.[2] Unlike several Degas paintings also on show, the Monets failed to find a buyer and *Westminster* remained in the gallery stock until 1877, when it sold to Ernest Hoschedé. Years later, in 1906, Jean-Baptiste Faure, its next owner, left it on deposit at Durand-Ruel's, and the picture re-entered the gallery in March 1907. By then Monet had twice returned to London, painting now iconic pictures of the Houses of Parliament similarly shrouded in mist, demonstrating a life-long allegiance to the work of Turner. AR

1 Durand-Ruel [1939], p. 179: 'I immediately bought from him the pictures he had just painted in London'.
2 W200, *Voilier sur le Petit Bras de la Seine, Argenteuil*, 1872 (subsequently dated 1875), no. 120 in the sixth exhibition of the Society of French Artists, London, spring–summer 1873. (Bought by Durand-Ruel shortly before 18 February 1873, sold Sotheby's New York, 5 May 2009, lot 18.)

CAT. 32 [FIG. 57]

Meditation (Madame Monet on the Sofa) (Méditation [Madame Monet au canapé])

About 1871

Oil on canvas, 48.2 × 74.5 cm
Musée d'Orsay, Paris, bequeathed by M. and Mme Raymond Koechlin, 1931. RF 3665
W 163
DR exhibition: London 1871c, no. 1273 ('*Repos*'); in the catalogue (in French) of the French section, entitled '*Méditation*'

Monet's new wife Camille accompanied him to London in 1870; this work probably shows her in their rented house at 1 Bath Place, Kensington.[1] Sitting on a chintz-upholstered chaise longue, she looks lost in thought, her face reflecting the bleak light of a morose winter day. Of the eight surviving pictures painted by Monet during his stay, this is the only interior. In May 1871 the artist sent it with two earlier works[2] to the International Exhibition in South Kensington. Its French section included a number of loans from Durand-Ruel, who recalled how he had been approached by the organisers: with war preventing anything being sent from Paris, the pictures from his London gallery were a welcome addition. Durand-Ruel acquired the Monet two years later, probably among 25 paintings he bought on 28 February 1873, where it was recorded as '*La Lecture*'. Monet is thought to have added the red book between Camille's hands some time later, making her look pensive rather than bored. This justified the new, less Whistlerian title. AR

1 House 1978.
2 The two other Monet pictures in the International Exhibition were W154, *Entrance to the Port of Trouville* (1870, Szépművészeti Museum, Budapest), and W66, *Camille* (1866, Muzeul National de Arta al Romaniei, Bucharest), lent by M. Luquet, a reduced replica of the 1866 Salon picture now in Bremen (see fig. 107).

CAT. 33 [FIG. 69]

Windmill and Boats near Zaandam, Holland (Moulin à Zaandam)

1871

Oil on canvas, 48 × 75.5 cm
Ny Carlsberg Glyptotek, Copenhagen, bought by the Ny Carlsberg Foundation in 1986, and donated to the Glypotek the same year. MIN 3233
W 177
DR exhibition: Paris 1883b, no. 4 (lent by Faure)

In 1883 Durand-Ruel devoted one of his first one-man shows to Monet, an artist he had been supporting for over a decade. Prepared in close collaboration with the painter, the exhibition formed a retrospective of Monet's art, juxtaposing the most recent work with older pictures such as *Windmill and Boats near Zaandam*. This twilight scene was painted in the summer of 1871, which Monet spent in Holland, on his way back to Paris after his London stay. Brisk and confident, the picture served to illustrate the artist's early virtuosity, establishing him as a painter of great experience and unbroken distinction. One critic noted: 'See his two Dutch landscapes with their rain-laden skies, his sunlit or misty seascapes ... they are always exquisite.'[1] The picture was a loan to Durand-Ruel's exhibition from the famous collector and singer Jean-Baptiste Faure – at once adding to the show's prestige and enhancing Monet's credentials. Faure, a close friend of Durand-Ruel's, sold it to the gallery in 1907. AR

1 Fourcaud 1883.

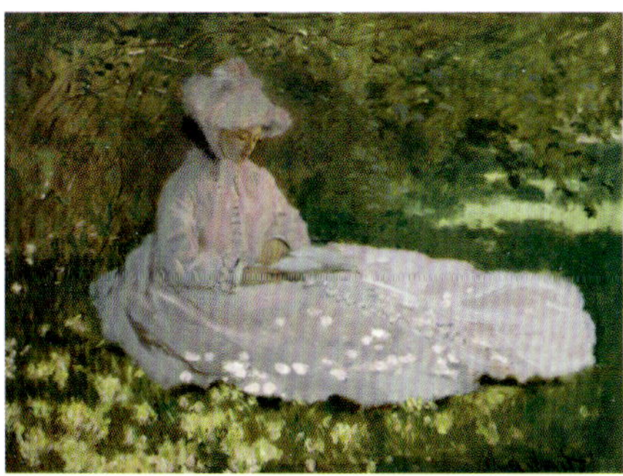

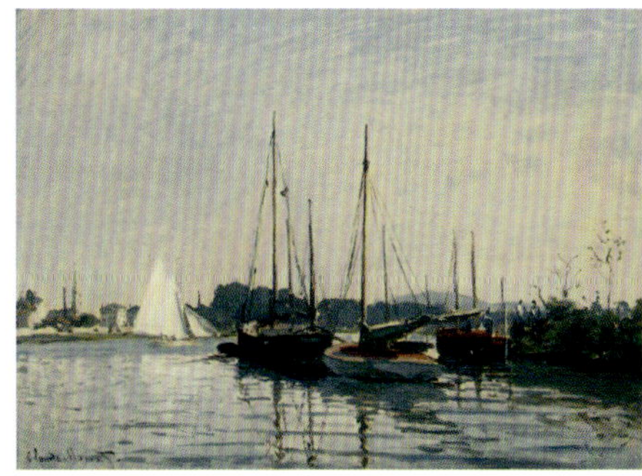

CAT. 34 [FIG. 81]

Springtime or **Woman reading (Printemps** or **Liseuse)**

About 1872

Oil on canvas, 50 × 65.5 cm
The Walters Art Museum, Baltimore, Maryland, 37.11, bequest of Henry Walters, 1931
W 205
DR exhibition: Paris 1876, no. 163 (*Le Printemps* [?])

In 1876, Monet was in dire straits. Weakened by the economic situation, Durand-Ruel imposed 'extreme restrictions'[1] on his purchases. He did, however, lease the Impressionists three rooms in his gallery. Monet exhibited 18 works in the *grand salon*, including a number of landscapes of Argenteuil, where he lived, which were lent by the famous baritone Jean-Baptiste Faure. This picture, which belonged to Mary Cassatt,[2] has been identified thanks to a description by Emile Zola in his review of the exhibition: 'We must not forget other pictures by Monet, including the portrait of a woman dressed in white, sitting in the shade of the foliage, her dress dotted with bright sequins like drops of water'.[3] MN

1 Durand-Ruel [1939], p. 201.
2 Durand-Ruel lent it to the 'Monet-Rodin' exhibition of 1889 and sold it to Walters through Lucas ([1979], II, p. 914).
3 Zola 1876, reproduced in Zola [1996], p. 279.

FIG. 166
From left to right: **Alfred Sisley**, *L'Ile Saint Denis*, 1872; **Camille Pissarro**, *Entrance to the Village of Voisins*, 1872; **Claude Monet**, *Pleasure Boats*, 1872–3
Oil on canvas, Musée d'Orsay, Paris

CAT. 35 [FIG. 8]

Pleasure Boats (Bateaux de plaisance)

1872–3

Oil on canvas, 49 × 65 cm
Musée d'Orsay, Paris, donated by Ernest May, 1923.
RF 2437
W 229

This picture was joined in a triptych (see below) by the banker Ernest May, a collector and generous museum donor, alongside *Entrance to the Village of Voisins* by Pissarro and *L'Ile Saint-Denis* by Sisley (cats 63 and 90). The pictures by Sisley and Pissarro appeared in two publications of the *Recueil gravé*, a sign of the importance Durand-Ruel placed on these early purchases, which may have taken place in April 1872 in the case of the Pissarro,[1] while *L'Ile Saint-Denis* by Sisley and the *Boats* by Monet were bought from the artists in May 1872[2] and February 1873, respectively.[3] The dealer sold these two pictures to May for 1,000 francs each in May 1882. At the sale of his collection at the Galerie Georges Petit on 4 June 1890, May bought back these three works for the modest sums of 1,850 francs (Monet, no. 47), 2,000 francs (Pissarro, no. 57) and 1,700 francs[4] (Sisley, no. 67). The pictures were shown at the Centennial of French Art at the Universal Exhibition in 1900, which officially recognised Impressionism but with a retrospective glance. These landscapes are indicative of this 'reversal' of taste – the word used by Durand-Ruel, who would later recall that 'charming studies from nature' of this type, which were not particularly popular in the 1870s, 'are now [what] collectors want most and for which they will gladly pay dearly . . . they passed almost unnoticed by all the visitors to our galleries when I exhibited them'.[5] This was not true of the painter Guillemet, who demonstrated his enthusiasm to Pissarro in 1872: 'In particular, I saw at Dur. Ruel's your light and varied paintings, spirited in a word, and I liked them. I also saw some very nice works by Monet and Sisley'.[6] Painted in 1872 in Argenteuil, where Monet had just moved, in Louveciennes and in Saint-Denis, these vibrant landscapes are characteristic of the first period of Impressionist plein-air painting, with their light palettes, open execution and modern notes, such as the pleasure boats, deliberately stripped of anything picturesque. They do not, however, exclude references to traditional landscapes, such as Hobbema's *Avenue at Middelharnis* (1689), which Pissarro may have seen at the National Gallery in London before leaving the city in late June 1871.[7] SP

1 Possibly stock 1868–73, no. 1341 with the title *Entrée de village* purchased from Herman on 20 April 1872 for 250 francs.
2 Stock 1868–73, no. 1663, *Sisley, Rivière*, for 200 francs.
3 Stock 1868–73, no. 2589 with the title *Le Bateau de plaisance* for 300 francs.
4 As the minutes of the sale have yet to be identified, these prices come from an annotated copy of the sale brought to my attention by Léa Saint-Raymond.
5 Durand-Ruel [1939], p. 195.
6 Antoine Guillemet to Camille Pissarro, 3 September 1872, in sales cat. Paris 1975, no. 79.
7 The acquisition of the picture, as part of the Peel Collection, is recorded on 5 June 1871, but the collection arrived at the museum in March and was exhibited there from 8 May (National Gallery Archive, London, Board Minutes, 5 June 1871, NG1/5). I would like to thank Alan Crookham for this information.

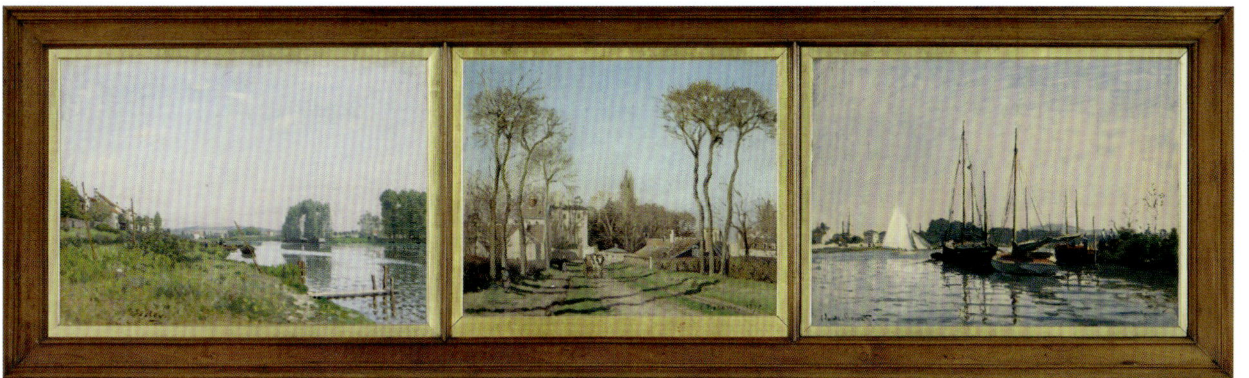

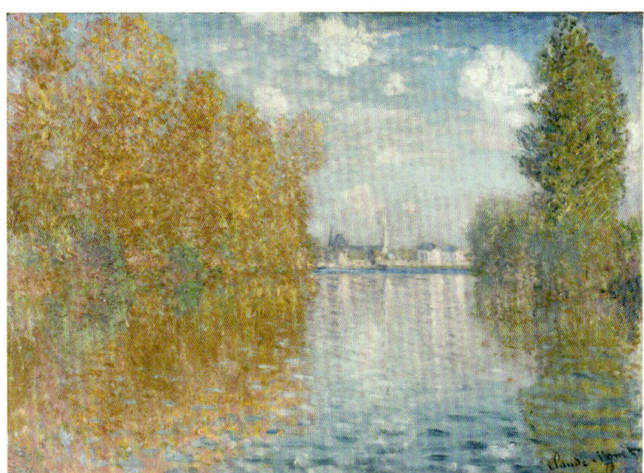

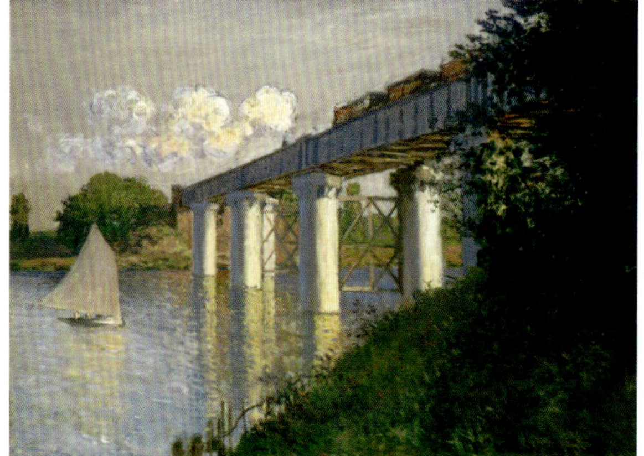

CAT. 36 [FIG. 75]

Autumn Effect at Argenteuil (Effet d'automne à Argenteuil)

1873

Oil on canvas, 55 × 74.5 cm
The Samuel Courtauld Trust, The Courtauld Gallery, London, gift of Samuel Courtauld 1932. P.1932.SC.274
W 290
DR exhibitions: Paris 1876, cat. no. 148 ('*Le Petit bras (Argenteuil)*. Owned by M. Faure.'); London 1882; Paris 1883b, no. 7 or no. 50; London 1883, no. 16 ('*Le Petit Bras à Argenteuil*'); London 1884; New York 1886a and b, no. 282 ('*Petit Bras d'Argenteuil*')

EXHIBITED IN LONDON

Possibly acquired by Faure after its completion in 1873, this picture of the river Seine and the town of Argenteuil had by 1882 entered Durand-Ruel's stock. Glowing with rich hues, the heavy mass of russet foliage framing the cooler tones of the water, the painting sums up the type of landscape Monet was preoccupied with at the time – strikingly modern (with the town's factory chimney as the focal point) and observed with a fresh sensitivity to light and atmosphere. The painting is emblematic of the dealer's initiatives in the 1880s; its extensive exhibition history reflects the story of the gallery's active foreign expansion. Durand-Ruel showed it in London three times, in the first exhibitions of explicitly Impressionist art in Britain, where it attracted much praise: 'By far the finest of Monet's pictures is the "Petit Bras à Argenteuil", extraordinary in strength and delicacy, and in colour admirable'[1] The picture also featured in Durand-Ruel's New York exhibition in 1886, where it was purchased by Erwin Davis.[2] In 1901 the canvas was back with the gallery, who sent it to the Carnegie International exhibition in Pittsburgh in 1903. AR

1 Unsigned review, *The Artist*, 1 May 1883. Also, in the *Standard*, 25 April 1883 (unsigned review): 'Claude Monet is a painter of what may be called ordinary landscape; but he manages to see it in a fresh way, and he is not afraid of strongly marked, almost violent colour. . . His "Petit Bras de la Seine à Argenteuil" (no. 16) is one of the finest and most luminous examples of his work.'
2 See the essay by Jennifer A. Thompson in this book and House 1994, p. 118.

CAT. 37 [FIG. 64]

Railroad Bridge, Argenteuil (Le Pont de chemin de fer à Argenteuil)

1873

Oil on canvas, 54.3 × 73.3 cm
Philadelphia Museum of Art, Pennsylvania: John G. Johnson Collection, 1917. Cat. 1050
W 318

CAT. 38 [FIG. 63]

The Artist's Garden in Argenteuil (A Corner of the Garden with Dahlias) (Le Jardin de l'artiste)

1873

Oil on canvas, 61 × 82.5 cm
National Gallery of Art, Washington, DC, gift of Janice H. Levin, in Honor of the 50th Anniversary of the National Gallery of Art, 1991.27.1
W 286
DR exhibitions: Paris 1889, no. 2; Berlin 1905, no. 13; London 1905, no. 149 ('*The Garden of Monet at Argenteuil*')

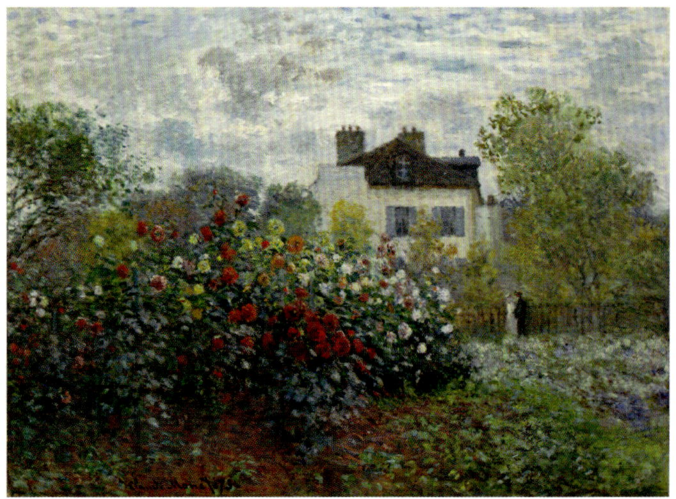

On 16 December 1873, Durand-Ruel bought three unnamed '*tableaux*' from Monet, possibly these views of Argenteuil. The growing town, 15 minutes from Paris by train, offered the artist a number of engaging subjects, from the profuse dahlias of his garden to the modern railway bridge and trains that rumbled over sailboats on the Seine. As with many of Durand-Ruel's early Impressionist purchases, these paintings took years to find buyers. *The Artist's Garden* sold to a collector named Baroux (43, boulevard Beauséjour) around 1881 and was reacquired by the gallery on 11 December 1896.[1] In August 1883 rival dealer Georges Petit bought 27 Monets from Durand-Ruel, *Railroad Bridge* among them. Four years later, Petit sold the canvas to Philadelphia lawyer John G. Johnson, for whom it was the first of many Impressionist purchases. JAT

1 Baroux purchased a Pissarro (PDRS 620) and a second Monet (perhaps W 203) from Durand-Ruel in 1881.

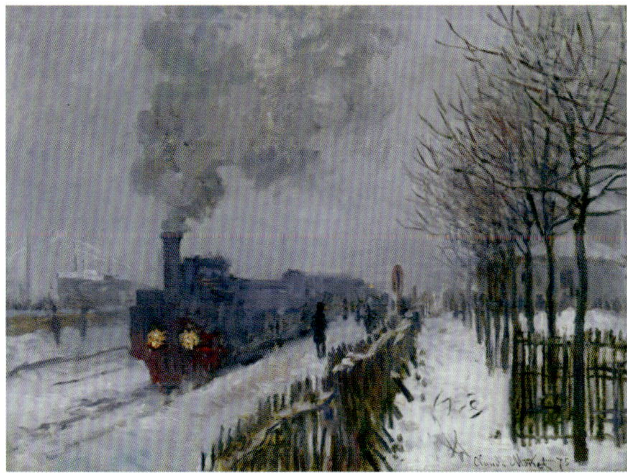

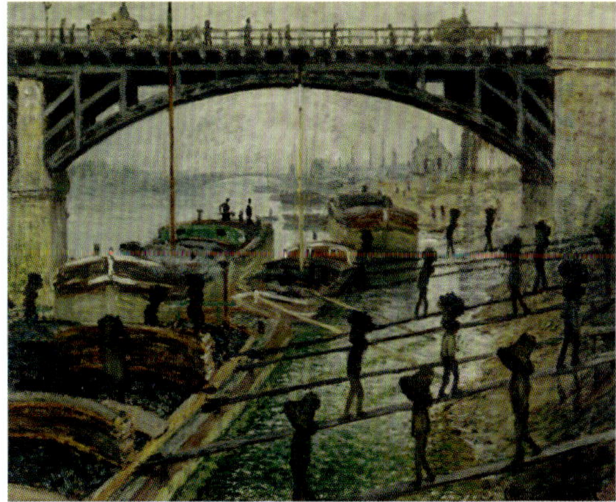

CAT. 39 [FIG. 84]

The Train in the Snow or **The Train (Le Train dans la neige,** or **Le Train)**

1875

Oil on canvas, 59 × 78 cm
Musée Marmottan Monet, Paris, bequest of Mme Donop de Monchy to the Académie des beaux-arts, 1957. Inv. 4017
W 356
DR exhibition: Paris 1883b, no. 11

EXHIBITED IN LONDON AND PHILADELPHIA

Georges de Bellio, a doctor and collector of Romanian extraction who was a loyal supporter of Monet and also the delighted owner of *Impression, Sunrise*, bought this work from the artist in November 1876. It may also have been coveted by another collector, the publisher Georges Charpentier.[1] At Monet's suggestion *The Train* (*The Train in the Snow*, deposit no. 3868) and six other pictures lent by De Bellio on 24 February (including two not in the catalogue) appeared in his first solo exhibition at the Durand-Ruel Gallery. This work, painted in Argenteuil, was mentioned by the critics,[2] including Geffroy, who praised 'the wonderful strokes that suggest the feeling of the train jolting or winding'.[3] SP

1 Monet to Charpentier, 2 July 1876, WL 91.
2 [Anonymous] 1883; Labarrière 1883.
3 Geffroy 1883, p. 2.

CAT. 40 [FIG. 73]

The Coal Carriers (Les Déchargeurs de charbon or **Les Charbonniers)**

About 1875

Oil on canvas, 54 × 66 cm
Musée d'Orsay, Paris. RF 1993-21
W 364
DR exhibition: London 1905, no. 138
(*'Unloading Coal Barges – Argenteuil'*, 1872)

Monet watched workers unloading coal for the nearby Clichy gas factory from the train that travelled from Argenteuil, where he had been living since late 1871, to Paris. 'Unusual' compared to his other work, the painter suggested to Durand-Ruel that he include it in the exhibition of his pictures in March 1883.[1] Possibly as a result of a refusal by Charles Hayem, the owner of the work at that time, or because of a choice made by the dealer, the canvas was not exhibited. Durand-Ruel purchased it for 9,000 francs on 26 April 1899 at the Victor Desfossés sale[2] (stock no. 5163). The picture then appeared in several of the dealer's exhibitions in Paris, London and New York, including at the Grafton Galleries in London in 1905. IG

1 Monet to Durand-Ruel, WL 329, 15 February 1883.
2 Information passed on by Léa de Saint-Raymond; no. 47, minutes of the Desfossés sale, AP D48E383.

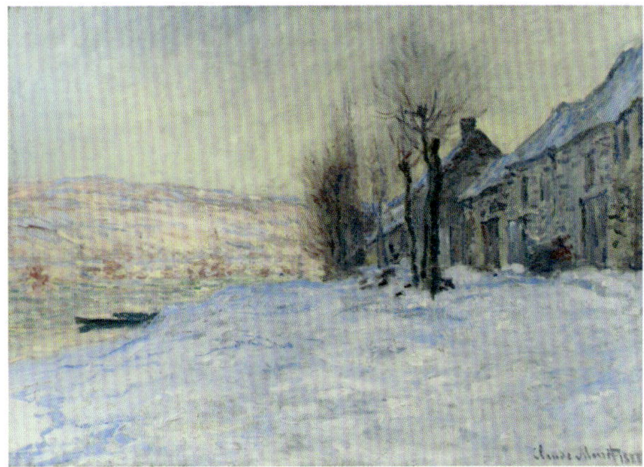

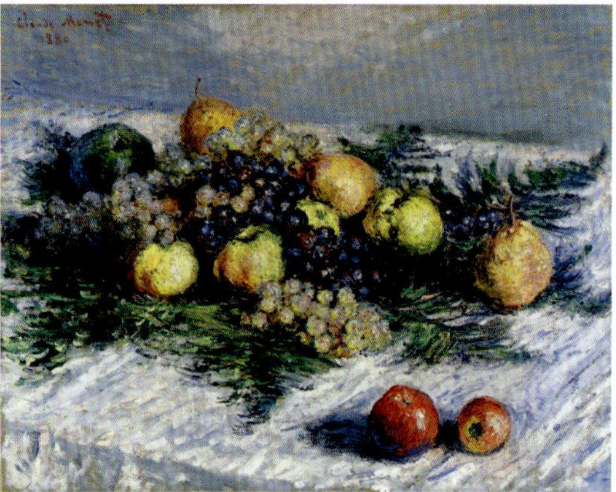

CAT. 41 [FIG. 1]

Lavacourt under Snow (Lavacourt sous la neige)

About 1878–81

Oil on canvas, 59.7 × 80.6 cm
The National Gallery, London,
Sir Hugh Lane bequest, 1917. NG3262
W 511
DR exhibition: London 1905, no. 119

The first Monet to enter a British public collection, this painting holds a special place in the 'shabby story of England's appreciation of French Impressionist painting'.[1] The canvas, probably executed in the winter of 1878–9,[2] was bought by the dealer from the artist in 1881. At the turn of the century it was sent to exhibitions from St Petersburg to Helsinki, Berlin, Dublin and London in 1905. With the exception of one Degas (cat. 13), such 'advanced' pictures had yet to enter Britain's public collections; to rectify this, a public subscription was launched and its champions proposed a gift to the National Gallery. Selected from among the 315 pictures on the Grafton Galleries walls, this painting exhibited quintessentially Impressionist qualities. Monet had excelled at depicting water in its various forms, either frost shimmering in the last of the sun's rays, or hard iridescent snow in the icy blue shade. It was too advanced: the gallery declined the gift. In April 1905 the picture was bought by collector and dealer Hugh Lane; by a twist of fate, it eventually joined the national collection as part of Lane's bequest, ten years later. AR

1 Rutter 1933.
2 Wildenstein 1996, II, p. 202, 'Painted in 1879'. Monet was staying in Vétheuil, on the other side of the river from Lavacourt.

CAT. 42 [FIG. 105]

Pears and Grapes (Nature morte avec poires et raisins)

1880

Oil on canvas, 64 × 81 cm
Hamburger Kunsthalle, Hamburg 1568
W 631
DR exhibition: Paris 1883b, no. 6, lent by Delius

EXHIBITED IN LONDON

In a letter dated October 1880, Monet describes himself as finishing two still lifes 'which will be unusual'.[1] One was this radically cropped but supremely elegant arrangement of grapes and pears spread across an immaculate table cloth. A year after the death of his wife, struggling to support his family, Monet resorted to painting still lifes – a genre likely to attract buyers. Indeed, by December 1880 Monet had sold his two pictures: 'My sales are still quite modest; however I have sold two still lifes for 1,400 francs for both.'[2] Two years later, as Durand-Ruel was making plans for a one-man show devoted to Monet, the artist remembered his two fruit still lifes, and their buyer, Theodor Delius (probably the uncle of the English composer Frederick Delius). 'If you could obtain the address of a Monsieur Delius', he wrote to the dealer, 'he has two still lifes which would be good to show.'[3] These were indeed praised by the critic Geffroy, who lauded their sense of reality.[4] At the time Monet was working on more still lifes of flower and fruit, commissioned by Durand-Ruel himself to adorn the doors of his apartment's *grand salon* (see cats. 47–52). This highly accomplished painting was with the Durand-Ruel Gallery by 1896. It was bought that same year for the Hamburger Kunsthalle by Alfred Lichtwark, its first director – a pioneering purchase for Germany, just a few months after the Berlin Nationalgalerie had acquired its first Impressionist paintings from the Durand-Ruel Gallery. AR

1 Letter to G. de Bellio, 15 October 1880. Wildenstein, 1974, I, p. 441 (201).
2 Letter to T. Duret, 9 December 1880. Wildenstein, 1974, I, p. 441 (203).
3 Letter to Durand-Ruel, 15 February 1883. Venturi, 1939, I, p. 248.
4 Gustave Geffroy, 'Chronique. Cl. Monet', *La Justice*, 15 March 1883, p. 2.

CAT. 43 [FIG. 72]

The Church at Varengeville. Morning (Eglise de Varengeville, effet du matin)

1882

Oil on canvas, 60 × 73 cm
Private collection
W 794
DR exhibitions: Paris 1883b, no. 15 (lent by du Balan); New York 1895a, no. 7

Monet visited several towns in Normandy from February to April 1882 and returned in June for the summer. Beginning in the seaside resort of Pourville, he travelled along the coast to Varengeville, where he was fascinated by a twelfth-century sailors' church perched near the cliff edge. He painted the structure at low tide when the sheer rock face created a daring perspective matched only by the artist's bold execution. Durand-Ruel bought almost all the 1882 Normandy pictures and showed them in the artist's solo exhibition the following spring. There, Gustave Geffroy praised a view of the church, most likely this one, comparing Monet to a geologist and lauding his ability to make 'some cliffs sparkle like a bunch of precious gems, while others seem to be liquid.'[1] The painting later belonged to Erwin Davis, who sold it to the New York gallery on 16 March 1893. JAT

1 Geffroy 1883. Reprinted in English in Stuckey 1985, p. 97.

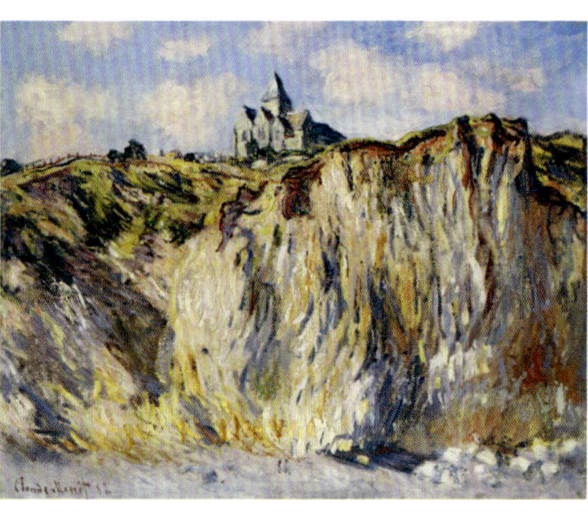

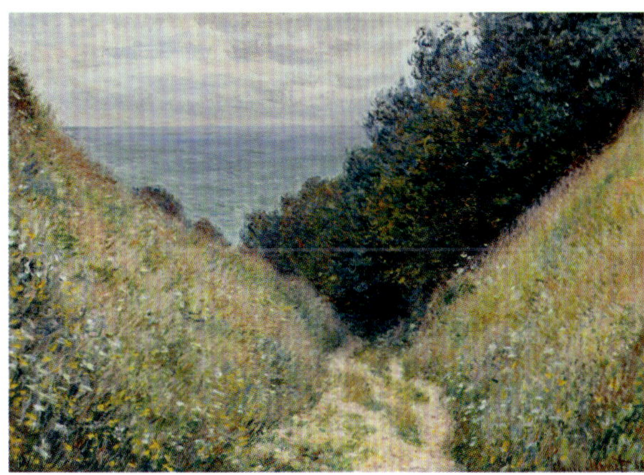

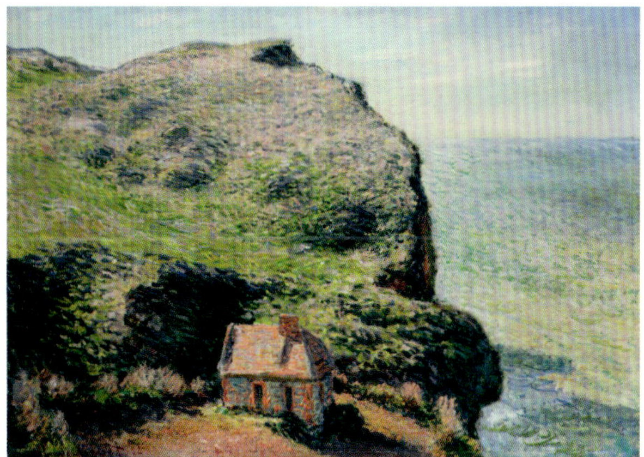

CAT. 44 [FIG. 77]

Road at La Cavée, Pourville (Chemin de La Cavée, Pourville)

1882

Oil on canvas, 60.3 × 81.6 cm
Museum of Fine Arts, Boston. Bequest of Mrs Susan Mason Loring, 1924. Inv. 24.1755
W 762
DR exhibitions: Paris 1883b, no. 24; London 1883, no. 34 (*'Chemin de la Carée'* [sic]); New York 1902, no. 13 (*'Chemin de la Cavée, Pourville'*)

At Monet's monographic exhibition in March 1883, critics commented favourably on his recent work at Pourville, with Gustave Geffroy praising the sunken path as 'a painting composed of three straight lines with two leafy, grassy slopes whose bases intersect with the sea in the background'.[1] *Road at La Cavée*, one of 25 Pourville canvases acquired from the artist by Durand-Ruel in October 1882, was sold to the Boston gallery Williams and Everett on 6 June 1888.[2] It demonstrates Monet's early popularity in New England: owned by banker Charles Fairchild, it was repurchased by Durand-Ruel in 1900 and sold in 1903 to Massachusetts judge William Caleb Loring. JAT

1 Geffroy 1883, p. 2. Reprinted in English in Stuckey 1985, p. 97.
2 In the mid-1880s, the canvas belonged to Georges Girard (8, rue d'Uzès), who resold it to Durand-Ruel on 9 March 1888. Boston Museum of Fine Arts curatorial files.

CAT. 45 [FIG. 76]

Customhouse, Varengeville (Poste de douaniers, Varengeville)

1882

Oil on canvas, 60.3 × 81.4 cm
Philadelphia Museum of Art, Pennsylvania: The William L. Elkins Collection, 1924. E1924-3-61.
W 743
DR exhibitions: Paris 1883b, no. 42; Boston 1891, no. 11

Among the 23 Normandy coast landscapes Durand-Ruel purchased from Monet in April 1882 were seven views of a customs house in Varengeville, including this picture. It was featured the next year in the solo show Durand-Ruel held for Monet, probably lent by the dealer under the pseudonym 'M. de Rivière'. In *La Justice,* Gustave Geffroy singled out the canvas for praise. He admired its luminous colour, daring perspective, and even its draughtsmanship. The inclusion of four views of this motif in 1883 suggested Monet's growing interest in displaying his work serially. Durand-Ruel exhibited *Customhouse* widely in America, in the Chicago Interstate Industrial Exhibition in 1890, and in an exhibition he co-organised with Eastman Chase in Boston the following year. Philadelphia businessman William L. Elkins purchased the painting from the New York gallery in 1892. NS

CAT. 46 [FIG. 79]

The Galettes

1882

Oil on canvas, 65 × 81 cm
Private collection
W 746
DR exhibition: Paris 1883b, no. 56 (*'La Galette'*)

On 6 October 1899, Durand-Ruel bought *The Galettes* for 3,000 francs from the dealer Knoedler & Co. in Paris. In order to depict these extremely flat objects, Monet, like Cézanne, chose an unusually elevated perspective. 'Galettes' were the speciality of the hotel-restaurant in which the artist was staying in Pourville, where the picture was painted. Durand-Ruel exhibited it in 1883 as part of his series of monographic exhibitions by the Impressionists. In the dining room of Joseph Durand-Ruel's apartment at 37, rue de Rome (which was near that of his father), the walls were covered in still lifes, including *Still Life with a Dessert* by Cézanne (cat. 5) and these *Galettes* by Monet. They were placed between door panels with a rustic theme commissioned from Albert André. The Art Nouveau furniture was by Charles Plumet and Tony Selmersheim. PLDR-FDR

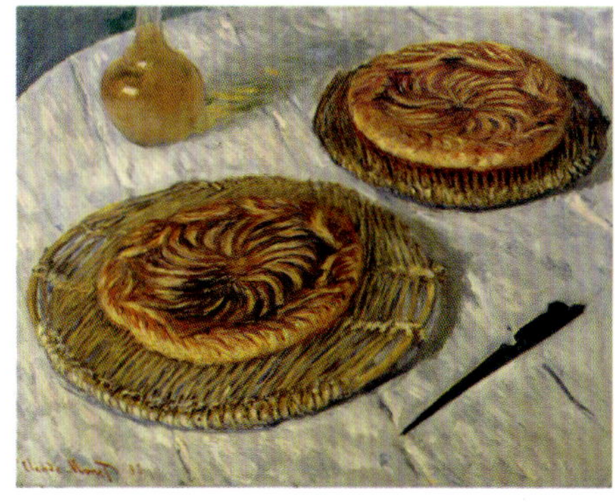

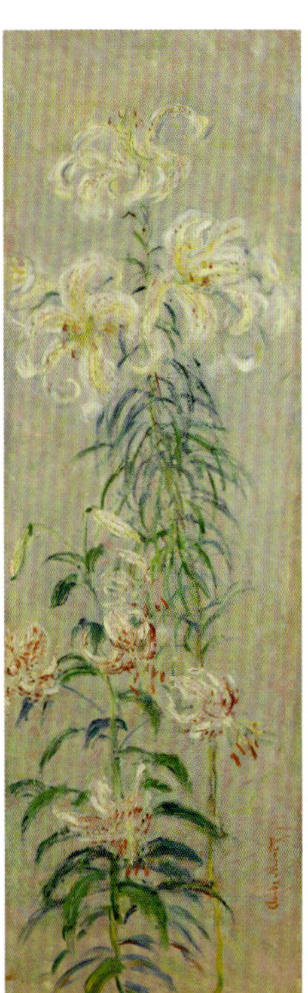

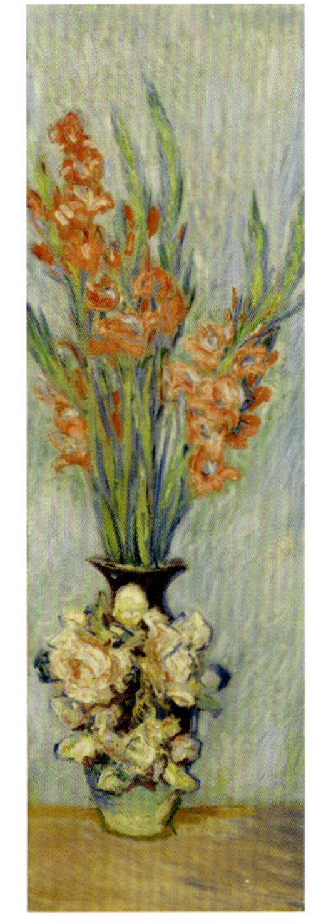

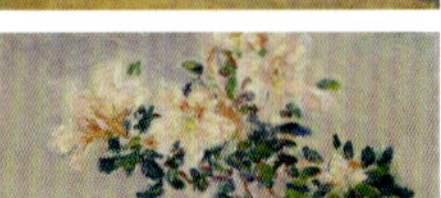

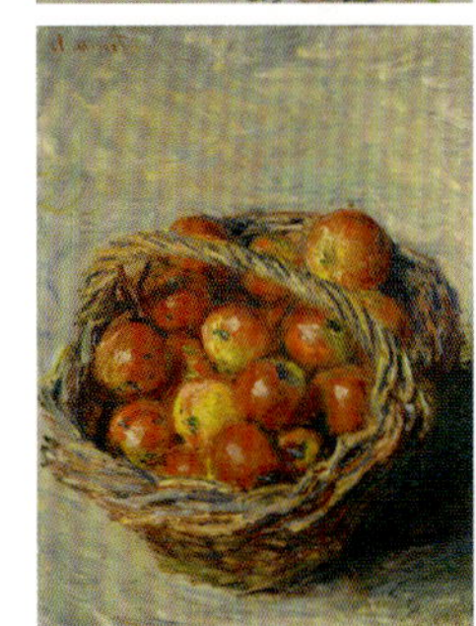

CAT. 47 [FIG. 26] *(top left)*

Japanese Lilies (Lis du Japon)

1883

Oil on canvas, door panel, 119.5 × 37 cm
Private collection
W 950

CAT. 48 [FIG. 27] *(top right)*

Gladioli (Glaïeuls)

1883

Oil on canvas, door panel, 128 × 37 cm
Private collection
W 938

CAT. 49 [FIG. 28] *(middle left)*

Chrysanthemums (Chrysanthèmes)

1883

Oil on canvas, door panel, 16.5 × 40 cm
Private collection
W 927

CAT. 50 [FIG. 29] *(middle right)*

Branches of White and Pink Azaleas (Branches d'azalées blanches et roses)

1883

Oil on canvas, door panel, 16.5 × 41 cm
Private collection
W 945

CAT. 51 [FIG. 31] *(bottom left)*

Pot of White Azaleas (Pot d'azalées blanches)

1883

Oil on canvas, door panel, 50.5 × 37 cm
Private collection
W 948

CAT. 52 [FIG. 32] *(bottom right)*

Basket of Apples (Panier de pommes)

1883

Oil on canvas, door panel, 50.5 × 37.8 cm
Private collection
W 936

In 1882, Paul Durand-Ruel commissioned portraits of his children from Renoir, and door panels on the themes of fruits and flowers from Monet. The dealer wrote to Monet on 26 May 1882: 'I am still counting on you to paint my little door panels as soon as you can . . . You can see wonderful flowers and trees at this time of year. Don't let this precious moment escape'.[1] It would take Monet three years to complete them. In March 1885, he wrote to the dealer: 'I've just spent a whole week on your panels. A week of maddening rage, restarting, scratching, puncturing my canvases'.[2] The set comprised 36 paintings on canvas, of which 30 would be mounted onto five double doors to decorate Paul Durand-Ruel's apartment. Each door followed the same pattern: the upper section was formed by two large vertical panels; two small horizontal panels lay in the centre, and two almost square panels fitted at the bottom. Each panel was treated as an individual picture. These works stood alongside other masterpieces by Renoir, Boudin, Degas, Cassatt, Puvis and Rodin. PLDR-FDR

1 Durand-Ruel to Monet, 26 May 1882, sales cat. Paris, 2006a, no. 60.
2 Monet to Durand-Ruel, 14 March 1885, ADR.

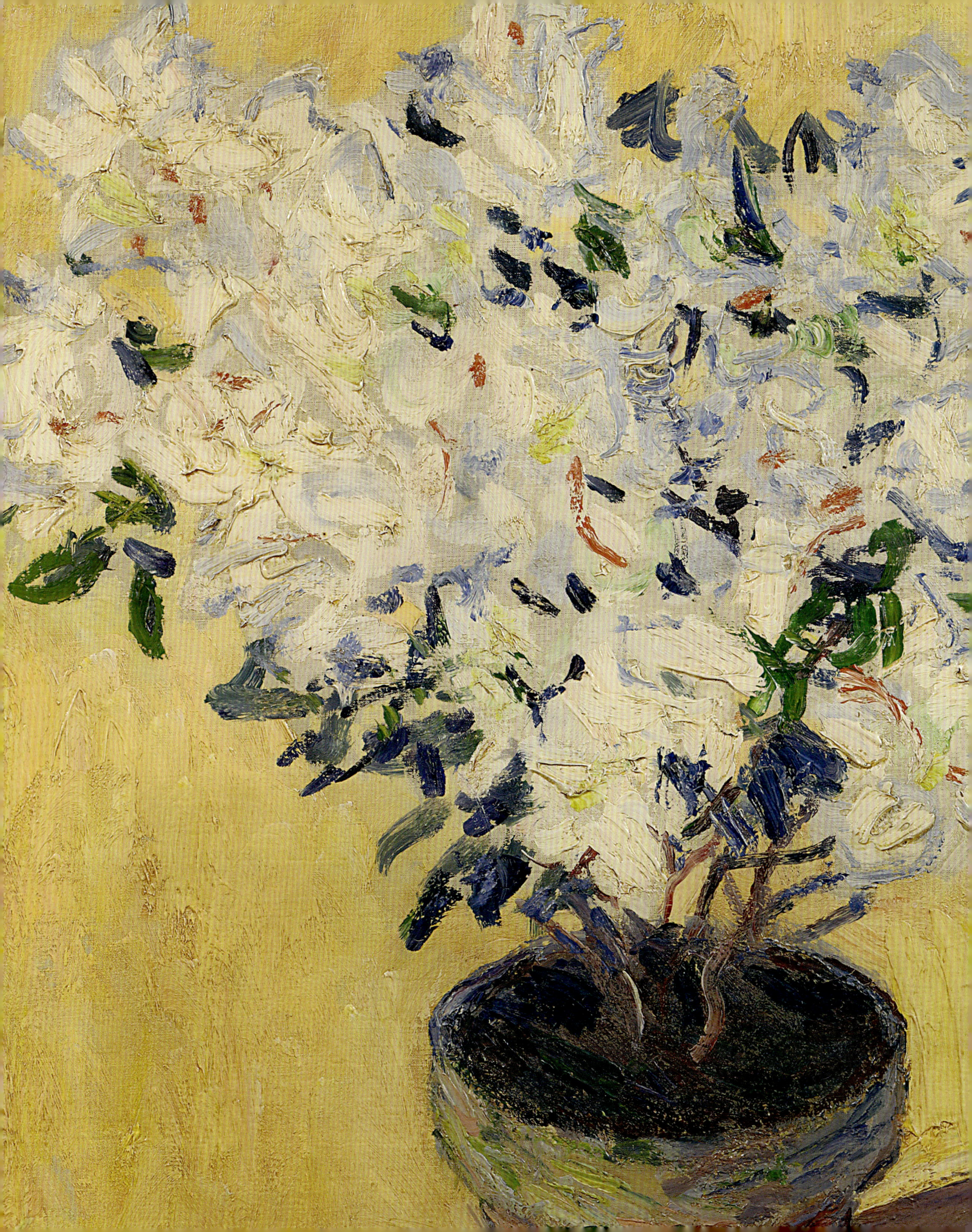

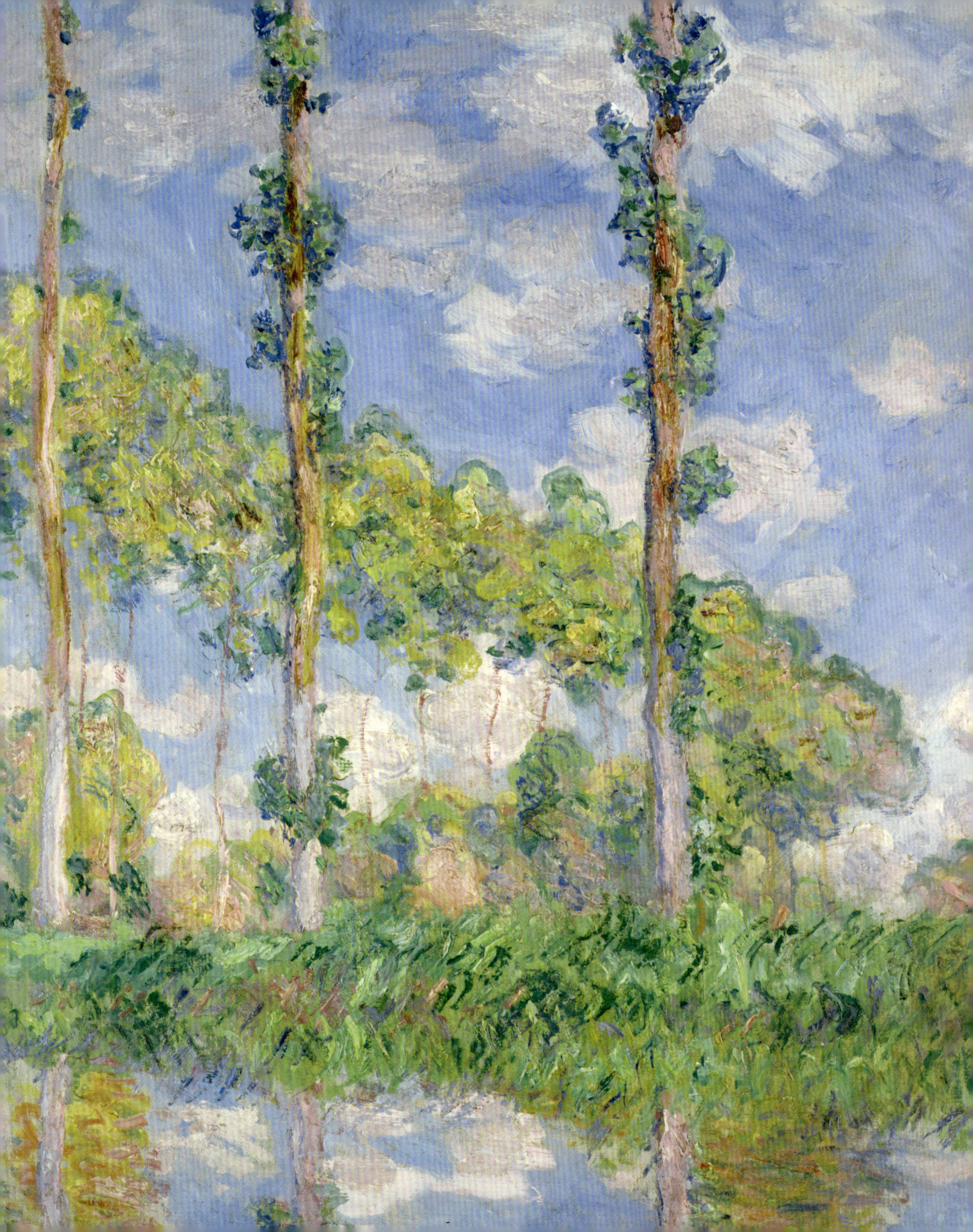

CATS 53–58

It was probably in the spring of 1891, after completing his first series of Haystacks, exhibited at the Durand-Ruel Gallery in May, that Monet began this series of Poplars. He painted 24 canvases inspired by this subject, varying the viewpoints, framing, time of day and seasons, from spring to autumn. Between 29 February and 10 March 1892, he showed 15 Poplars at the gallery, exhibiting a series in isolation for the first time.[1] Geffroy noted: 'This changing and harmonious poem develops, with nuances so closely bound together as to create the feeling of a single work of inseparable parts'.[2] The gallery space appeared to be an inherent component of the painter's artistic project that saw the pictures 'take on their true value only through the comparison and succession of the series'.[3] All the more so as it seems the group had already been dispersed even before the opening of the exhibition: Monet had sold 12 Poplars (half to Durand-Ruel) and had exhibited several at Boussod & Valadon in January.[4] This success, which had begun with the Haystacks, continued unabated, and by March the artist 'did not have a scrap of a Poplar left to sell'.[5]

The composition of the exhibition at the Durand-Ruel Gallery reflected the competition between dealers that Monet cleverly encouraged. He advised Pissarro: 'They will all want to monopolise you. Do not allow it, sell to one and then another'.[6] Monet therefore showed three Poplars from Boussod, works from his own collection and even four pictures sold to Montaignac, Sutton's representative in Paris. These included *Poplars* (cat. 58) which Durand-Ruel would have loved to buy,[7] as he shared Pissarro's admiration for this work ('it is so ornamental!').[8] In order to complete his collection, Durand-Ruel even bought back *Wind Effect* (cat. 56) from Knoedler in 1893 and never parted with it. These were not the only *Poplars* to have been appreciated by the Americans: 'We have plenty of visitors every day and many Americans in particular. You see, I was not wrong to carry out my campaign in America; it was from then on that our business began to improve',[9] Durand-Ruel wrote to Monet. *Poplars on the Bank of the Epte River* (cat. 53) was bought by the dealer and resold on 5 March 1892 to Potter Palmer,[10] who also bought *Poplars on the Bend in the Epte River, Overcast Weather* (cat. 54). More generally, the series marked a turning point in the work, career and reception of Monet: critics unanimously celebrated the decorative and poetic power of these trees magnified to the point of abstraction by the effects of rhythm, colour and light. SP

1 In 1891, there were seven other canvases in addition to the 15 Haystacks.
2 Geffroy [1980], p. 320.
3 Monet, quoted in Bijvanck 1892, p. 177.
4 *Le Journal des arts*, 15 January 1892.
5 Monet to Hamman, 17 March 1892, WL 2855.
6 Monet to Pissarro, 19 January 1892, WL 2847.
7 'I particularly liked the one that belonged to him', Durand-Ruel to Monet, 15 March 1892, in sales cat. Paris 2006a, no. 74.
8 Pissarro to Monet, W supporting documentation, no. 119.
9 15 March 1892, sales cat. Paris 2006a, no. 74.
10 New York stock number 1278 on back of picture.

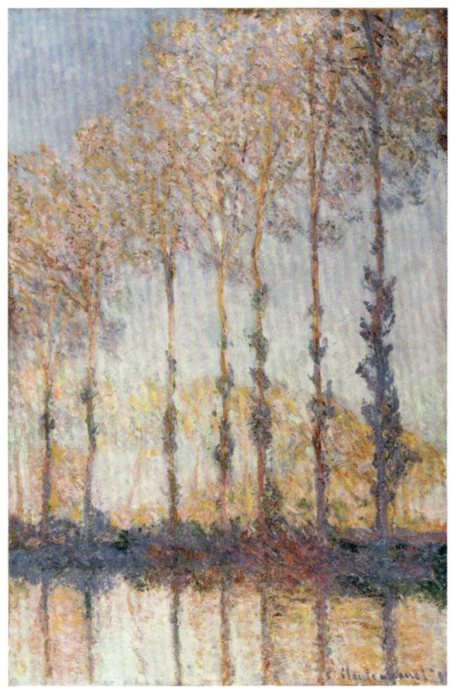

CAT. 53 [FIG. 12]

Poplars on the Bank of the Epte River (Les Peupliers, effet blanc et jaune)

1891

Oil on canvas, 100.3 × 65.2 cm
Philadelphia Museum of Art, Pennsylvania: bequest of Anne Thomson in memory of her father, Frank Thomson, and her mother, Mary Elizabeth Clarke Thomson. 1954-66-8
W 1298
DR exhibition: Probably Paris 1892b, no. 13 (*'Fin d'automne'*, lent by Boussod)

EXHIBITED IN PHILADELPHIA

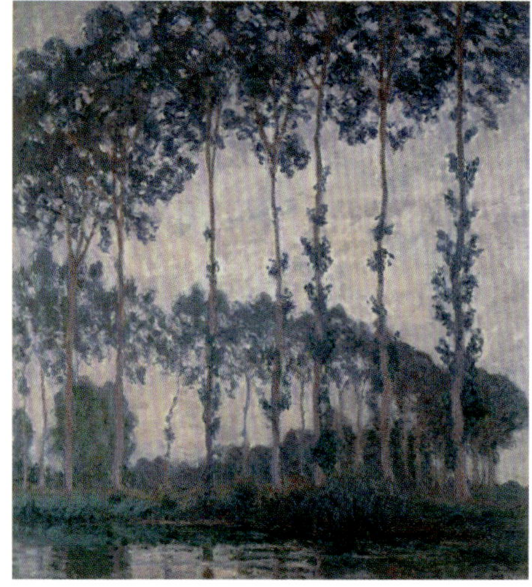

CAT. 54

Poplars on the Bend in the Epte River, Overcast Weather (Peupliers au bord de l'Epte, temps couvert)

1891

Oil on canvas, 91.5 × 81.5 cm
Ise Cultural Foundation, Tokyo
W 1299
DR exhibition: Paris 1892b, no. 5 (*'Temps couvert'*, lent by Durand-Ruel)

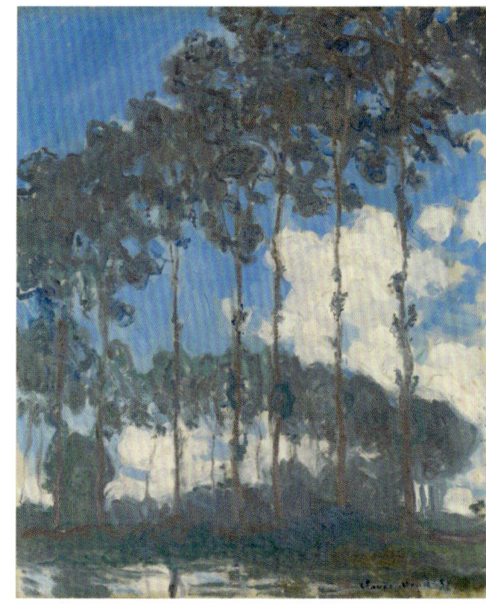

CAT. 55

Poplars on the Epte (Les Peupliers au bord de l'Epte)

1891

Oil on canvas, 92.4 × 73.7 cm
Tate, presented by the Art Fund, 1926 N04183
W 1300
DR exhibition: Probably Paris 1892b, no. 8 (*'Esquisse'*)

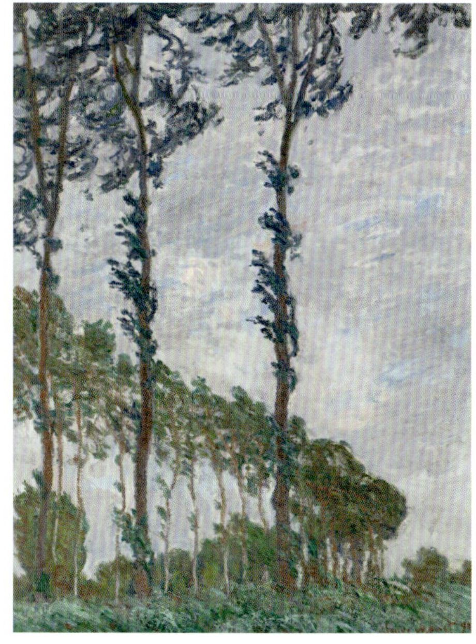

CAT. 56 [FIG. 11]

Wind Effect, Sequence of Poplars (Effet de vent, série de peupliers)

1891

Oil on canvas, 100 × 74 cm
Musée d'Orsay, Paris, accepted by the State as a gift in payment of tax, 2002. RF 2002-30
W 1302
DR exhibitions: Paris 1892b, no. 6 (*'Les Trois Arbres, temps nuageux'*, lent by Monet); New York 1895a; Boston 1895

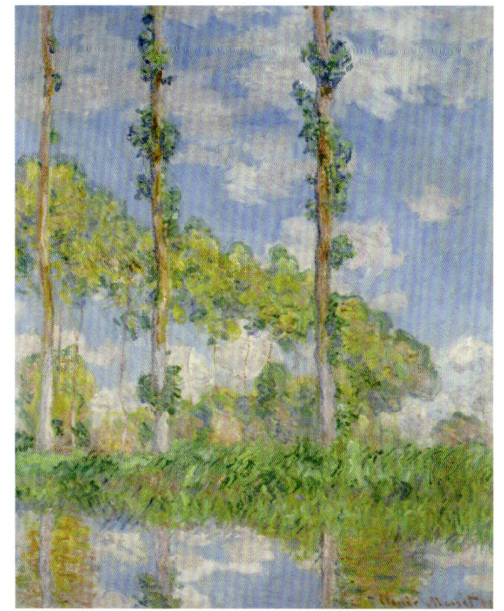

CAT. 57 [FIG. 13]

Poplars in the Sun (Les Trois Arbres, été)

1891

Oil on canvas, 93 × 73.5 cm
The National Museum of Western Art, Kojiro Matsukata Collection, Tokyo. P.1959.152
W 1305
DR exhibition: Paris 1892b, no. 11 (*'Les Trois Arbres, été'*, lent by Boussod).

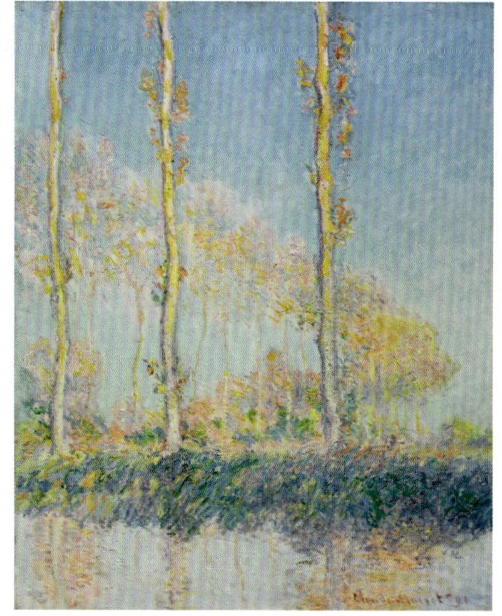

CAT. 58 [FIG. 14]

Poplars (Peupliers, trois arbres roses, automne)

1891

Oil on canvas, 93 × 74.1 cm
Philadelphia Museum of Art, Pennsylvania: The Chester Dale Collection, 1951. 951-109-1
W 1307
DR exhibition: Paris 1892b, no. 4 (*'Les Trois Arbres, automne'*, lent by Montaignac)

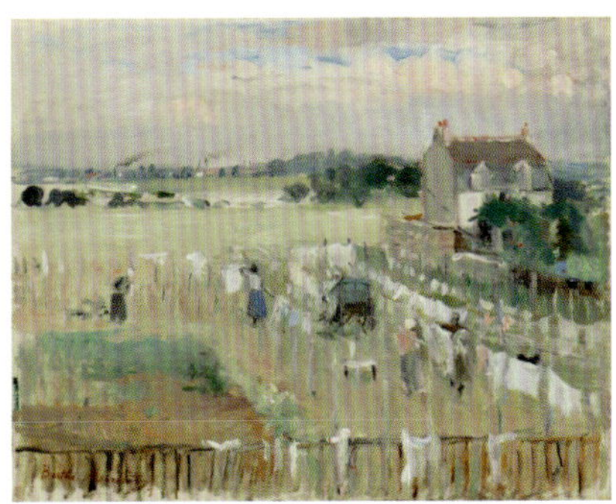

Berthe Morisot

(Bourges 1841–Paris 1895)

CAT. 59 [FIG. 83]

Hanging the Laundry out to Dry (Un percher de blanchisseuses)

1875

Oil on canvas, 33 × 40.6 cm
National Gallery of Art, Washington, DC,
Collection of Mr and Mrs Paul Mellon, 1985.
Inv. 1985.64.28
CRM 45
DR exhibitions: Paris 1876, no. 175 (*Un percher de blanchisseuse*); Paris 1896, no. 103 (*Un percher de blanchisseuses*, 1875, belonging to M.E. Denop de Mouchy [sic])

In early July 1872, Berthe Morisot asked Manet to show some of her Cherbourg seascapes to Durand-Ruel. On 10 July, the dealer bought *The Jetty* (stock 1868–1873, no. 1765) and three watercolours.[1] In April the following year, he paid 500 francs for *View of Paris from the Trocadero*.[2] Their relationship continued with Berthe's participation in exhibitions at the dealer's gallery, in 1876 for example (when *Hanging the Laundry out to Dry* was bought by the collector Georges de Bellio) as well as in London and New York. After Morisot's death, Durand-Ruel made his rue Laffitte premises available for an exhibition of the artist's work that brought together more than 360 pictures. MN

1 ADR, I would like to thank Paul-Louis Durand-Ruel. Charles Stuckey has identified 1765 with *Port Scene*, 1871, Bagnols-sur-Cèze, CMR 42; see Stuckey 1987, p. 50.
2 Santa Barbara Museum of Art; see Stuckey 1987, p. 44.

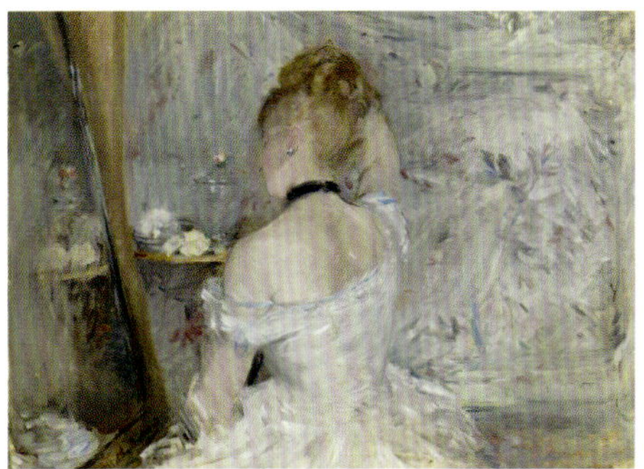

CAT. 60 [FIG. 95]

Woman at her Toilette (Femme à sa toilette, or Jeune femme de dos à sa toilette)

About 1875–80

Oil on canvas, 60.3 × 80.4 cm
The Art Institute of Chicago, Illinois,
Stickney Fund, bought 1924. Inv. 1924.127
CRM 85
DR exhibitions: New York 1886a and b, no. 141 (*The Toilette*); Paris 1896a, no. 77 (*Devant la toilette*, 1880); London 1905, no. 162 (*Before the Mirror*, 1884)

Berthe Morisot was fond of depicting women in their daily lives, going about their most private tasks. At the New York exhibition of 1886, the critics praised her style: '*Woman at her Toilette* is considered by many to be the finest picture here . . .'[1] It was probably at this event that the American painter William Merritt Chase, who was very familiar with the work of the Impressionists, bought this canvas.[2] At the sale of his collection in New York on 15 January 1896, Durand-Ruel bought the picture for 600 dollars;[3] he then sent it to Paris so that it could be exhibited at the retrospective organised by the gallery as a tribute to the artist, who had died the previous year. Her daughter, Julie Manet, played an active part in planning the exhibition, as did Degas, Monet and Renoir. On 5 March, Julie described a panel located on the right of the main gallery: '*In front of the cheval-glass*, the beautifully modelled back allows the dress to slip down; this woman, with arms that move gracefully, is styling her hair in front of the empire-style cheval-glass in which she looks at her reflection'.[4] Durand-Ruel sent the canvas to the large Impressionist exhibition at the Grafton Galleries in London before selling it for 12,000 francs to the Galerie Rosenberg on 11 January 1908.[5] MN

1 [Anonymous] 1886c, pp. 252–3.
2 Dayer Gallati 2000, p. 42 and p. 48, note 25.
3 Sales cat. New York, 1896, no. 1093.
4 Manet [1987], p. 93.
5 ADR, daybook, 11 January 1908.

Camille Pissarro

(Saint-Thomas, Danish Antilles 1830–Paris 1903)

CAT. 61 [FIG. 115]

Fox Hill, Upper Norwood

1870

Oil on canvas, 35.3 × 45.7 cm
The National Gallery, London. Presented by
Viscount and Viscountess Radcliffe, 1964. NG 6351
PDRS 180
DR exhibition: London 1871a (?), possibly no. 38 (*Pissarro, A Snow Effect*)

'The painting you have brought me is charming',[1] Durand-Ruel wrote to Pissarro in June 1871 from his New Bond Street gallery. Fleeing the Franco-Prussian War, Pissarro had arrived in London some weeks earlier, and he made contact with the dealer, who would soon begin exhibiting his works in London. This view of Fox Hill in Norwood, where the Pissarros had just begun living, could be the *Snow Effect* exhibited at the New Bond Street gallery in March 1871, or the *Effet de neige* included in the International Exhibition of May 1871.[2] One critic even boasted that Pissarro's two winter scenes displayed 'great faithfulness to nature'.[3] The presence of *Fox Hill* in these two exhibitions has been questioned in view of the picture's small size and its sketchy handling.[4] However, these characteristics do not seem to have bothered the dealer, who was exhibiting small canvases by the Barbizon School in London at the time, with which this rural and naturalistic depiction of a dirt road covered in snow on an icy winter afternoon would have blended perfectly. AR

1 Durand-Ruel to Pissarro, 21 January 1871, ADR.
2 London 1871b, possibly no. 1276, *Winter Scenery* (no. 531, *Effet de Neige* in the French catalogue), or no. 1277, *Upper Norwood* (no. 532, *Effet de neige* in the French catalogue), lent by the artist.
3 *Art Journal*, September 1871, XXXIII, p. 218.
4 This was the opinion of John House, who believed the picture to be too sketchy (House 1978, p. 638), but Kathleen Adler, in exh. cat. London 2003, p. 11, thinks it could be PDRS 180.

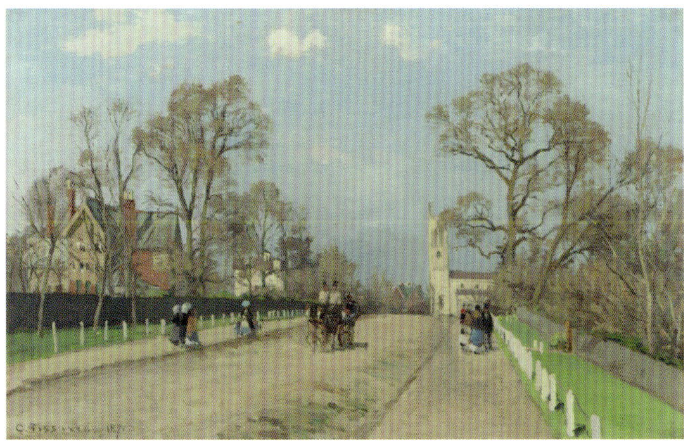

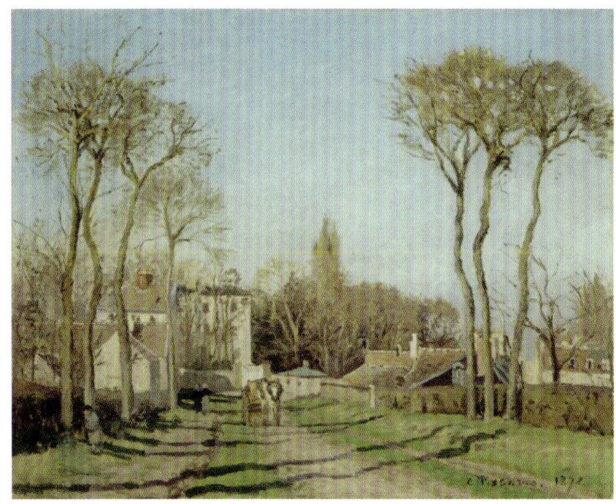

CAT. 62 [FIG. 58]

The Avenue, Sydenham

1871

Oil on canvas, 48 × 73 cm
The National Gallery, London. Bought, 1984. NG6493
PDRS 188
DR exhibitions: London 1872a, no. 113 (Pizzarro [sic], '*Sydenham*'); Paris 1892a, no. 2 ('*Eglise de Sydenham*, 1871. Appartenant à M. L'); Paris 1899, no. 39 ('*Route de Sydenham*'); Paris 1904, no. 15 ('Vue de Sydenham. M. Durand-Ruel'); London 1905, no. 202 ('*View of Sydenham*', illustrated)

As the first Pissarro Durand-Ruel purchased – presumably immediately after its completion, in April or May 1871 – this painting is a landmark of fundamental importance for the understanding of Durand-Ruel's journey as dealer and collector.[1] It remained with Durand-Ruel until the early 1920s, a token of his early meeting with Pissarro during the significant months of exile in London, and one of the finest examples of his pre-Impressionist style. It shows the peaceful and residential London suburb of Sydenham, familiar to Pissarro who had settled nearby,[2] close to the fashionable Crystal Palace. This view, with St Bartholomew's church in the distance, has not changed much.[3] Fresh, spring-like, relatively large, the picture was exhibited by Durand-Ruel on many occasions: in London in 1872,[4] and later in Paris, in monographic and group shows. Encountering it again in the 1899 Paris exhibition, Pissarro found it 'admirably well preserved . . . far superior to what I thought of this painting at the time'.[5] After showing it in the 'Exposition Centennale' of Paris's Universal Exhibition in 1900,[6] Durand-Ruel sent it back to London for the substantial Grafton Galleries show, where Pissarro was praised for his 'earnest, homely sincerity . . . The view of Sydenham, dating from the period of the Franco-Prussian war, might serve to illustrate the delicacy of his perception.'[7] It now serves to illustrate the dealer's indefatigable belief in Pissarro's painting, the certainty of his judgment and taste, and his personal attachment to a picture he lived with for half a century. AR

1 The painting, engraved by Lauzet, was illustrated in Lecomte 1892.
2 From April 1871 Pissarro and his family lived in 2 Chatham Terrace, Palace Road, off Anerley Hill (later 59 Palace Road). Kathleen Adler in London 2003, p. 8.
3 This is now Lawrie Park Avenue, London SE26.
4 Two other Pissarros were shown: no. 42, '*Winter*', and no. 111, '*Upper Norwood*'.
5 *Correspondence Pissarro* [1980–1991], no. 583.
6 Paris, Universal Exhibition, 1900, no. 519, '*Une rue à Sydenham*'.
7 *Athenaeum*, 11 February 1905, no. 4033, p. 185.

CAT. 63 [FIG. 8]

Entrance to the Village of Voisins (Entrée de village *or* Entrée du village de Voisins)

1872

Oil on canvas, 46 × 55.5 cm
Musée d'Orsay, Paris, donated by Ernest May, 1923. RF2436
PDRS 235
DR exhibition: Paris 1904, no. 17
Galerie Durand-Ruel. Recueil d'estampes gravées à l'eau-forte, 1874, vol. 13, pl. 121 (*Une route près de Voisin* [sic]), engraved by Henri-Emile Lefort.
[see cat. 35]

CAT. 64 [FIG. 65]

The Lock at Pontoise (Le Déversoir de Pontoise)

1872

Oil on canvas, 53 × 83 cm
The Cleveland Museum of Art, Ohio,
The Leonard C. Hanna, Jr. Fund 1990. Inv. 1990.7
PDRS 243

In the absence of old photographs in the Durand-Ruel Archives, the purchase of *The Lock at Pontoise* from the artist in 1872 remains a supposition. We are aware of two canvases by Pissarro depicting a lock from around that year. The first of these – entitled *L'Ecluse* – was painted in about 1868 (PDRS 129) but we do not know the date of its purchase by Durand-Ruel. Pissarro was in the habit of showing his latest work to the dealer, and a study of the relationship between the two men in the gallery's archives shows that the dealer often bought works in the same year they were painted. It is therefore highly likely that *The Lock at Pontoise* at the Cleveland Museum of Art (more accurately renamed *Le Déversoir de Pontoise* in the latest critical catalogue) is the work dated 1872. The dealer sold it a year later to Mr Tissot through his London gallery. Pissarro set up his easel on the right bank of the Oise, opposite the houses of Saint-Ouen-l'Aumône. The lock, which is not visible, is downstream of the barges. This spillway regulated the significant variations in the level of the Oise that were common at Pontoise. CDRS

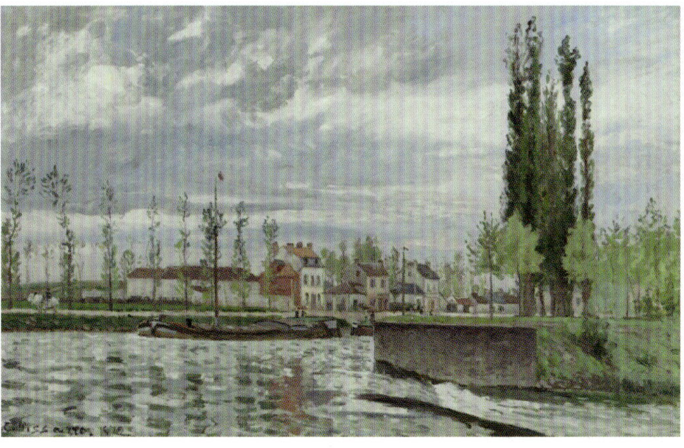

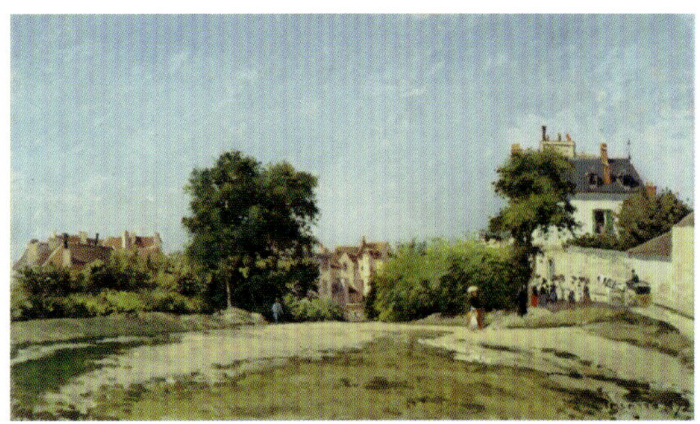

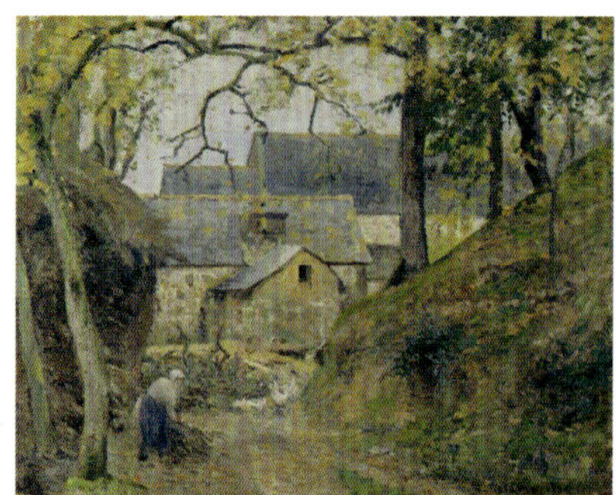

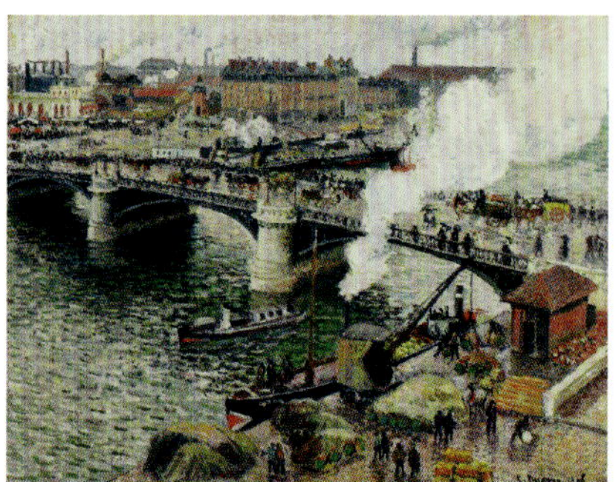

CAT. 65 [FIG. 66]

The Crossroads, Pontoise, or Square at the Old Cemetery, Pontoise (Place du Vieux-Cimetière, Pontoise)

1872

Oil on canvas, 55 × 91 cm
Carnegie Museum of Art, Pittsburgh, acquired through the generosity of the Sarah Mellon Scaife Family, 1971. Inv. 71.7
PDRS 259
Galerie Durand-Ruel. Recueil d'estampes gravées à l'eau-forte, 1875, vol. 25, pl. 245, engraved by Charles Courtry

After short stays in Pontoise between 1866 and 1868, Pissarro made it his permanent home from 1872 to 1882. This painting was bought by Durand-Ruel for 500 francs. It was the highest sum paid to the artist for a work in 1872. For his *Recueil d'estampes gravées à l'eau-forte* the dealer chose five pictures painted in 1872 by Pissarro, including this one – evidence of his high regard for the painter. CDRS

CAT. 66 [FIG. 67]

Apples and Pears in a Round Basket (Pommes et poires dans un panier rond)

1872

Oil on canvas, 45.7 × 55.2 cm
The Henry and Rose Pearlman Foundation, on long-term loan to the Princeton University Art Museum
PDRS 269
DR exhibition: Paris 1883d, no. 66
EXHIBITED IN PHILADELPHIA

The year 1872 was marked by 22 purchases from Pissarro – a significant number – for a total of 5,600 francs. Durand-Ruel paid 200 francs for this still life. In 1883, he displayed it at the painter's first monographic exhibition in his gallery. A journalist described the fruits as being 'accurate in tone and modelling'.[1] Unable to find a buyer in France, the dealer sent the picture to his brand-new New York gallery in 1888, where it was purchased by the collector Erwin Davis. When he wanted to get rid of it 10 years later, Davis offered to sell it back to Durand-Ruel without recompense. This was standard practice for the dealer, who did not hesitate to buy back works he had previously sold them from his clients in order to keep their custom. CDRS

1 Jacques 1883a.

CAT. 67 [FIG. 10]

Farm at Montfoucault (La Ferme à Montfoucault)

1874

Oil on canvas, 60 × 73.5 cm
Collection des Musées d'Art et d'Histoire de la Ville de Genève, bought 1915. Inv. 1915–33
PDRS 377
DR exhibition: Paris 1876, no. 201 (*Ferme à Montfoucault*)

Although Durand-Ruel was unable to buy any pictures from Pissarro between 1874 and 1879, he nevertheless hosted the second Impressionist exhibition. But he did not escape insulting comments: 'At Durand-Ruel's gallery, a new exhibition has opened of what are claimed to be paintings . . . Five or six lunatics, one of whom is a woman – a group of miserable individuals gripped by crazy ambition – have gathered here to exhibit their work';[1] Pissarro exhibited 12 landscapes. One of these was lent by Victor Chocquet, a collector and civil servant at the Ministry of Finance, and 11 by the artist himself, including this farm scene painted in Mayenne at the house of his friend, the painter Ludovic Piette. The critics were divided. One of them thought 'M. Pissarro has blinkers over his eyes' and had 'never been lucky enough to gaze upon the great spectacle of nature',[2] while for another, his pictures were 'strikingly truthful'.[3] The painter kept this canvas until his death. His widow, Julie, sold it to the Galerie Bernheim-Jeune in 1913. Two years later, it was bought by the Musée d'Art et d'Histoire in Geneva. CDRS

1 Wolff 1876.
2 Enault 1876.
3 Gène-Mur 1876.

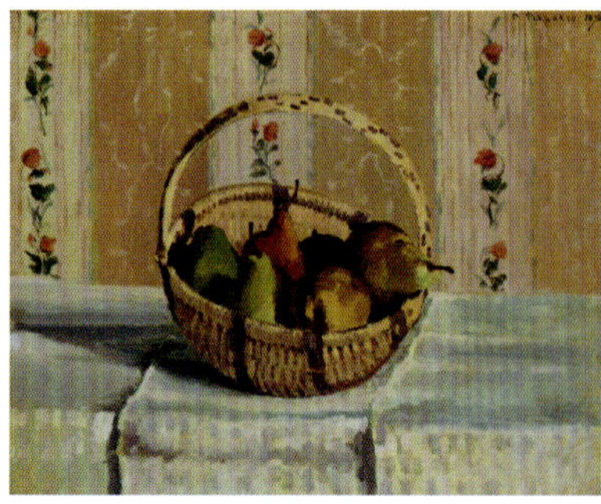

CAT. 68 [FIG. 119]

Pont Boieldieu, Rouen, Rainy Weather (Le Pont Boieldieu à Rouen, temps mouillé)

1896

Oil on canvas, 73.6 × 91.4 cm
Collection Art Gallery of Ontario, Toronto, gift of Reuben Wells Leonard Estate, 1937. Inv. 1937-2415
PDRS 1116
DR exhibitions: Paris 1896b, no. 4; London 1905, no. 199

Pissarro moved to Rouen in early 1896 to paint canvases to round off his exhibition at Durand-Ruel's, which was planned for 15 April. He knew the city well, having stayed there in 1883. *Pont Boieldieu, Rouen, Rainy Weather* was one of the 11 views of Rouen selected by the two men, 10 of which were bought by Durand-Ruel on 11 April following negotiations with Pissarro. The artist's travel expenses were reimbursed, and he had less cause for concern when it came to sales during the exhibition, as his dealer had assumed all the risk in the event of failure. In the end, Durand-Ruel did not sell *Pont Boieldieu* until 41 years later, after demonstrating unprecedented dynamism: saving neither expense nor effort, he exhibited it everywhere, in France and the United States, on a total of 24 occasions, including four at his Paris gallery and six in New York. Between 1928 and 1937, the picture criss-crossed America, travelling to New York, Toledo, Kansas City, Buffalo, San Francisco, Baltimore and Cleveland. In January–February 1933, the work was put on deposit at the Art Gallery of Toronto. The museum did not finalise its acquisition until four years later, in 1937. CDRS

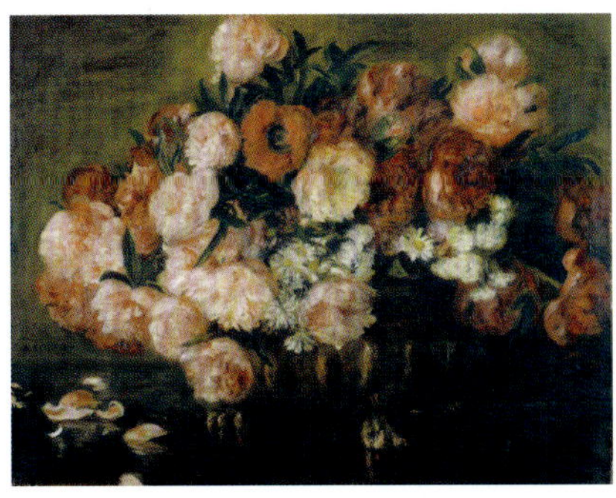

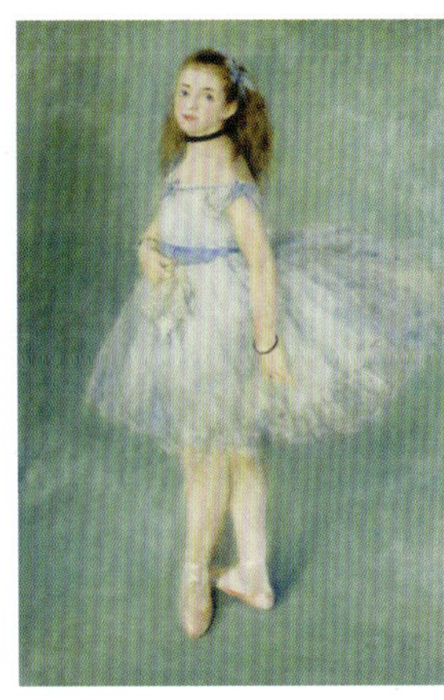

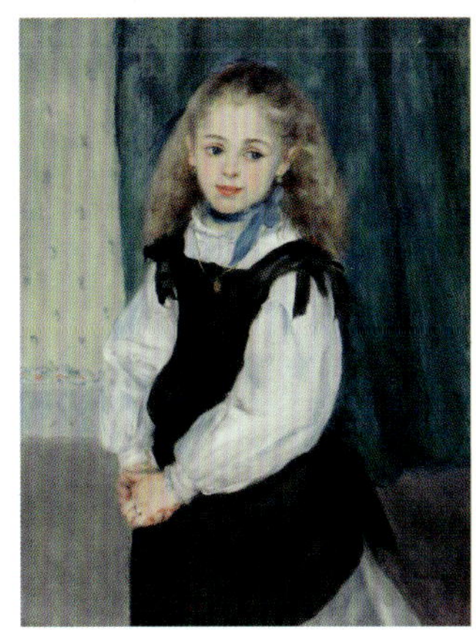

Pierre-Auguste Renoir

(Limoges 1841–Cagnes-sur-Mer 1919)

CAT. 69 [FIG. 108]

Still Life with Peonies and Poppies (Pivoines dans un vase)

1872

Oil on canvas, 66.5 × 82.5 cm
Kunsthalle Mannheim, bought 1912. M 308
D 26

EXHIBITED IN PHILADELPHIA

Durand-Ruel became interested in Renoir in 1872 and purchased two canvases from him: in March, *The Pont des Arts, Paris* (see fig. 141) for 200 francs, and on 23 May, *Pivoines et coquelicots* for 300 francs, most likely this picture. The accounts books do not allow us to accurately follow its provenance. In 1906, the dealer bought *Fleurs, les pivoines*,[1] lot 39 dated 1872, at the Depeaux sale. Three years later, Marie Held, who ran the Moderne Kunsthandlung gallery in Frankfurt and had made a name for herself dealing in Impressionist paintings in Germany, informed Fritz Wichert, Director of the Kunsthalle in Mannheim, that she had a beautiful Renoir 'you already know'.[2] Wichert exhibited this canvas at an exhibition the following December[3] but it was not until three years later, on 1 March 1912, that he acquired it for 15,000 francs. That same year, he bought works by Cézanne, Corot, Daumier, Pissarro and Liebermann for his museum, which had resolutely opened its doors to modern art.[4] MN

1 Sales cat. Paris 1906.
2 Marie Held to Fritz Wichert, Frankfurt, 19 October 1909, Mannheim, Kunsthalle archives. I would like to thank Melanie Baumgärtner.
3 Exh. cat. Mannheim 1909.
4 Rœschel 2002.

CAT. 70 [FIG. 70]

The Dancer (Danseuse)

1874

Oil on canvas, 142.5 × 94.5 cm
National Gallery of Art, Washington, DC
Widener Collection 1942. Inv. 1942 9.72
D 368
DR exhibitions: London 1874, no. 75 ('*A Ballet Dancer*'); Paris 1883c, no. 36; Paris 1899, no. 73; London 1905, no. 240 ('*The Ballet Girl*')

Here, for the first time, Renoir painted a subject that would remain unusual in his oeuvre: a ballet dancer. Almost life-size, the girl, shown in three-quarter view in her rehearsal tutu and in fifth position, stands out against a neutral background. Exhibited alongside Degas's dancers at the first Impressionist exhibition in 1874,[1] the painting appeared some months later at the ninth exhibition organised in London by Durand-Ruel.[2] It was not deposited by the artist with the dealer until 1876[3] and it was not until 17 May 1878 that it was purchased by Charles Deudon for 1,000 francs.[4] While he coveted Charles Deudon's collection, Durand-Ruel actually bought the painting from his cousin Eugène Deudon, with Renoir acting as intermediary, on 8 March 1899 for the sum of 9,000 francs.[5] Despite attractive offers,[6] the dealer kept *The Dancer* in his own collection during his lifetime. Sold to Joseph E. Widener on 11 August 1924, the picture left the same day for the United States. In March 1927, the canvas, which needed to be repaired, spent another brief stint in the New York gallery. It was to the Durand-Ruel firm that Widener turned for the restoration work.[7] IG

1 Exh. cat. New York 2012, p. 44.
2 I would like to thank Monique Nonne for telling me about this exhibition.
3 On 4 February 1875, two Renoirs were included in the 28 pictures returning from London. These were probably *La Loge* (Courtauld Institute, London) and *Dancer*, exhibited at the ninth exhibition. We may also suppose that these were the two canvases returned to Renoir on 24 February 1875 (ADR, daybook, 10 October 1874–3 August 1878).
4 According to Anne Distel (1989a, p. 64), the canvas may have been purchased by Deudon from Poupin – a business associate of Durand-Ruel – for 950 francs.
5 See Chronology, this book.
6 Exh. cat. New York 2012, pp. 51–3.
7 Durand-Ruel New York to Durand-Ruel Paris, 25 February, 24 March and 12 April 1927, ADR.

CAT. 71 [FIG. 86]

Portrait of Mademoiselle Legrand (Portrait de jeune fille)

1875

Oil on canvas, 81.3 × 59.7 cm
Philadelphia Museum of Art, Pennsylvania:
The Henry P. McIlhenny Collection in memory of Frances P. McIlhenny, 1986. 1986-26-28
D 495
DR exhibitions: Paris 1876, no. 223 ('*Portrait de jeune Fille*'); Paris 1883a, no. 7 ('*Portrait de Mlle U*' [sic])

Delphine Legrand, the timid six-year-old daughter of Alphonse Legrand, was painted twice by Renoir, commissions that helped sustain the artist in the mid 1870s when Durand-Ruel was unable to buy many paintings. Legrand assisted Durand-Ruel in the organisation of the second Impressionist exhibition and orchestrated sales for the firm in Lille and Nice prior to opening his own gallery at 22 bis rue Laffitte in 1877.[1] In 1878 he travelled to the United States, hoping to sell Impressionist paintings there, a notion he revisited with Roland Knoedler in 1886.[2] To the 1876 Impressionist exhibition in Durand-Ruel's gallery, Legrand lent a painting titled *Portrait of a young girl*, described by Zola as 'a strange and sympathetic figure with a long face, pale and barely smiling, she resembles a Spanish infanta'.[3] He was referring either to this picture or to a full-length portrait of Delphine holding a skipping rope (Barnes Foundation, Philadelphia). Legrand lent this portrait of his daughter, wearing a bold black pinafore, to Durand-Ruel in 1883 for the first Renoir monographic exhibition. From 1910 to 1933 it belonged to the dealers Bernheim-Jeune, and was jointly owned by Paul Rosenberg and Durand-Ruel at the time of its sale to Philadelphia collector Henry P. McIlhenny on 28 November 1934. JAT

1 ADR, daybook, 25 January and 4 February 1876.
2 Distel 1989b, p. 34.
3 *Lettre de Paris*, 29 April 1876 in Zola [1991], p. 315.

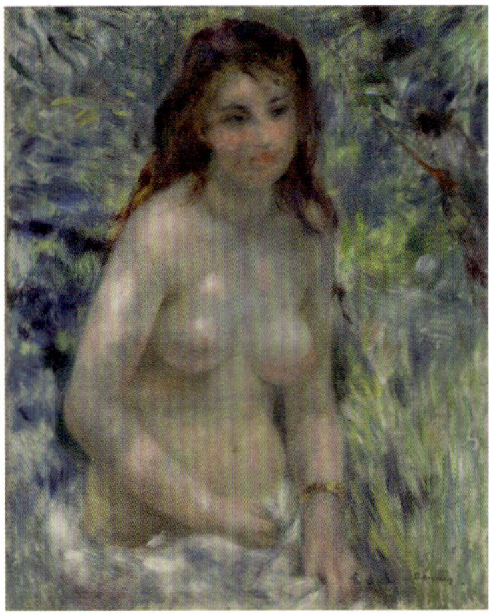

CAT. 72 [FIG. 85]

Study: Torso, Sunlight Effect (Etude. Torse, effet de soleil)

1875–6

Oil on canvas, 81 × 65 cm
Musée d'Orsay, Paris, bequeathed by Gustave Caillebotte, 1894. RF2740
D 603
DR exhibitions: Paris 1876, no. 212 (*'Etude'*); Paris 1892c, no. 11

When this painting was shown at the Durand-Ruel Gallery in the Second Impressionist exhibition of 1876 several hostile critics noted the play of colours across the model's nude body but refused to recognise what Renoir was depicting. One spoke of 'putrefaction in a corpse', another about 'the purplish tones of meat gone rank'.[1] They declined to acknowledge that Renoir had captured the dance of sunlight across flesh out of doors as light filters down through leaves overhead, and that such optical phenomena do indeed alter our perception of form. The painting was a triumph of Impressionist technique, which is surely why Durand-Ruel, the principal organiser of the 1876 exhibition, included it. He might also have suspected that it would be a red flag to opponents of the new painting, and thus a useful incitement to controversy. The painting was soon acquired by Gustave Caillebotte, a fellow painter and a leading collector of the most challenging Impressionist paintings. CR

1 Exh. cat. Washington and San Francisco 1986, no. 35, p. 184.

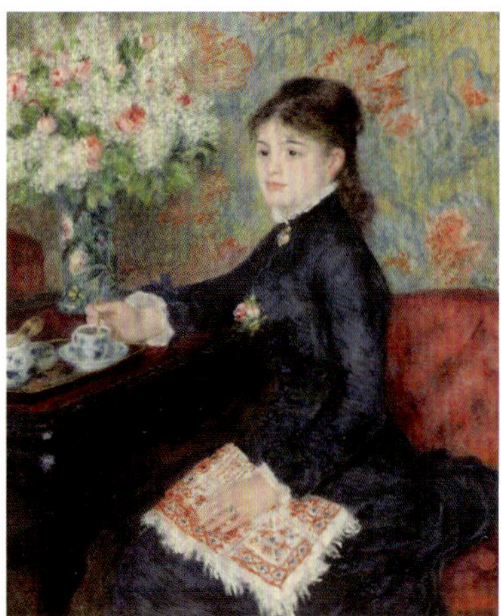

CAT. 73 [FIG. 68]

The Cup of Chocolate (La Tasse de chocolat)

About 1877–8

Oil on canvas, 100 × 81 cm
Private collection
D 272
DR exhibitions: Paris 1892c, no. 6 (*'La tasse de café'*); London 1905, no. 238 (*'Tea-Time'*)

The late 1870s was a coming of age for Renoir: his *Dance at Le Moulin de la Galette* was shown at the 1877 Impressionist exhibition; *Madame Charpentier and her Children* proved a great success at the 1879 Salon; and the ambitious *Luncheon of the Boating Party* was bought by Durand-Ruel in 1881 for Ernest Balensi and reacquired in April 1882 for the dealer's private collection. In this productive period, Renoir painted the entrancing but rarely seen *Cup of Chocolate*, which shows the artist's model Marguerite (Margot) Legrand in midnight blue in a vibrant setting, a potent demonstration of the artist's brilliant use of colour and brushwork.

Exhibited at the 1878 Salon, *The Cup of Chocolate* (sometimes known as *The Cup of Tea*) remained with the artist for nearly two decades, eventually selling to Durand-Ruel on 13 May 1897 for 2,500 francs. Renoir may have agreed to part with the canvas knowing it would be part of the dealer's renowned personal collection. The family apartment on the rue de Rome, filled with Renoirs, Monets, Degas's, Cézannes, and Rodin, was shown frequently to gallery clients. Cleveland iron magnate Alfred Atmore Pope visited in October 1898 and wrote enthusiastically to his daughter: 'Durand-Ruel took us to his own house. His collection has improved – finer much finer now he has Renoirs of such quality & quantity as one couldn't imagine.'[1]

Shown in London in 1905, the picture was pursued by museums in Mannheim and Frankfurt in 1910, but the family held on to the work, citing its vital place in their home.[2] In 1937, following the deaths of Paul Durand-Ruel and his sons, the painting was sold to Edsel Ford of Detroit. JR-JAT

1 Alfred A. Pope to Theodate Pope, 21 October 1898, Hill-Stead Museum, Farmington, CT.
2 Exh. cat. Atlanta, Seattle and Denver 1999, p. 33.

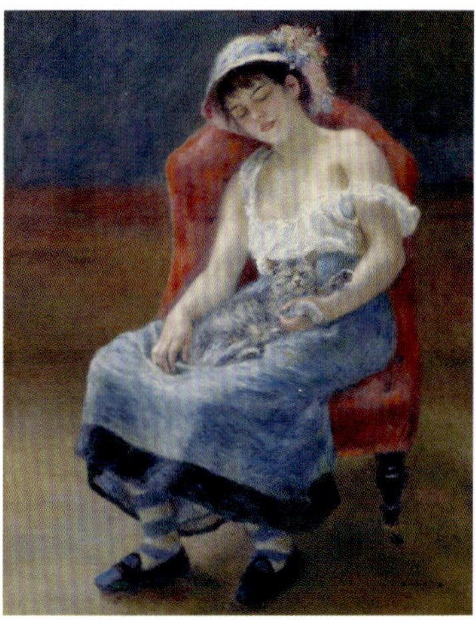

CAT. 74 [FIG. 35]

Girl with a Cat (Jeune fille endormie or **La Jeune Fille au Chat)**

1880

Oil on canvas, 120.3 × 92 cm
Sterling and Francine Clark Art Institute, Williamstown, Massachusetts, Inv. 1955 598
D 330
DR exhibitions: Paris 1883c, no. 48 (*'Jeune fille endormie*, appartenant à M. Durand-Ruel'); Paris 1892c, no. 87 (*'La femme au chat*, belonging to M. J. D.'); Paris 1899, no. 77 (*'Jeune fille dormant* 1880') and no. 79 (*'La Femme au chat* 1880'); London 1905, no. 223 (*'Sleeping Woman with a Cat'*)

Durand-Ruel assembled the works he was particularly fond of at his home at 35, rue de Rome, and *Girl with a Cat* was one of the jewels in the crown of his *grand salon*[1] (see fig. 159). After purchasing this canvas for 2,500 francs from Renoir in 1881, he sold it in 1883 before buying it back again in 1891; he then decided not to part with it and only to display it as part of an exhibition that would contribute to the painter's reputation.[2] It is also significant that he should have chosen an engraving of this picture for the frontispiece of the catalogue to the 'Monet, Pissarro, Renoir et Sisley' exhibition in 1899.

Although Durand-Ruel often hosted guests at his home and could sometimes be persuaded to negotiate on some of his pictures, he adamantly refused to give up *Girl with a Cat*. Doctor Barnes, an enthusiastic collector of Renoir's work who wanted a picture of the highest order, tried in vain to buy it in 1913, but was told: 'We will never sell [it], nor any other work from our private collection'.[3] It took all Sterling Clark's tenacity to acquire this masterpiece for his collection in New York in 1926, four years after Paul Durand-Ruel's death. MN

1 See Sarah Lees in Lees, Rand and Webber 2013, II, no. 276, pp. 662–6.
2 In particular he lent it to the Renoir exhibition at the Moderne Galerie Thannhauser, in Munich in January–February 1912, and then to the 'VI Ausstellung' exhibition at Cassirer's gallery in Berlin in February–March of the same year, no. 7.
3 I would like to thank Sylvie Patry for passing on this information. Georges Durand-Ruel to Barnes, 13 January 1913, Barnes Archives, Philadelphia, Correspondence Barnes – Durand-Ruel, AR. ABC.1913.56.

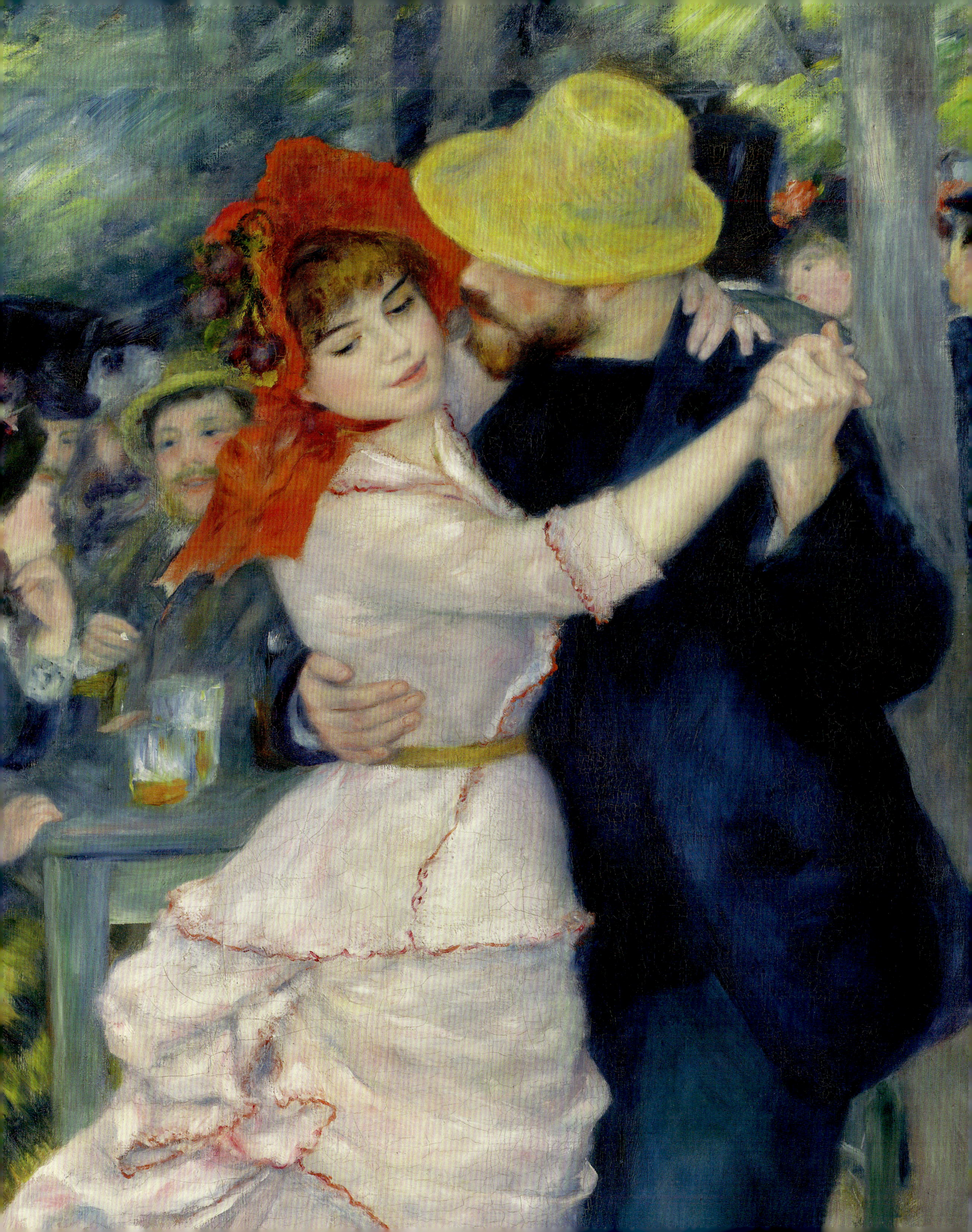

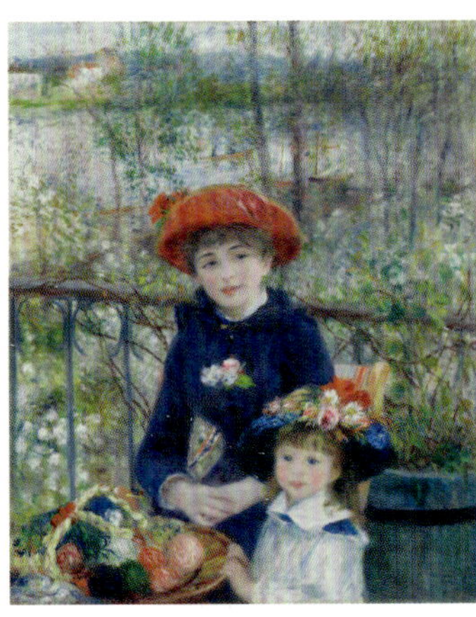

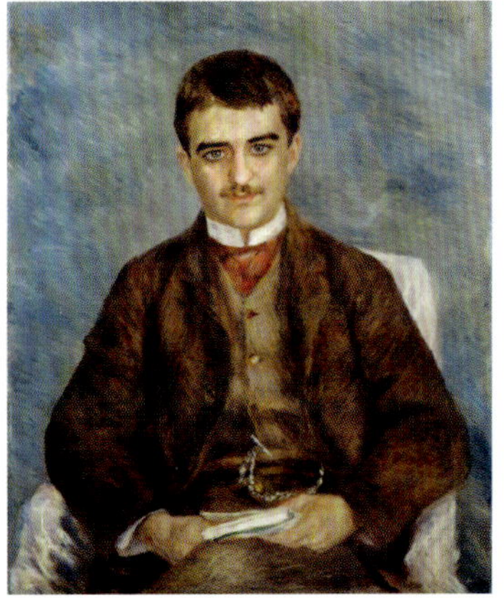

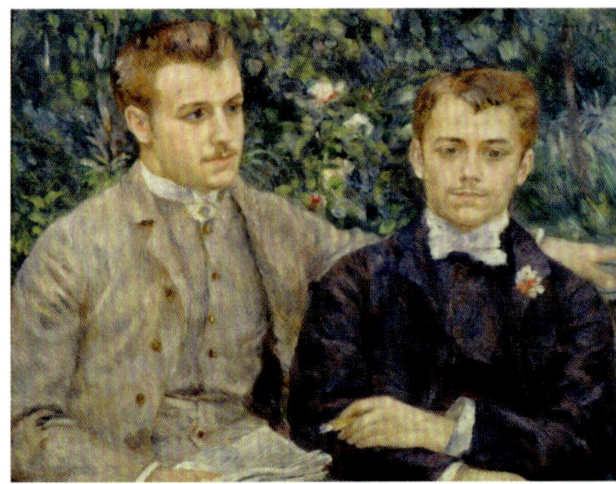

CAT. 75 [FIG. 94]

Two Sisters (On the Terrace) (Sur la terrasse)

1881

Oil on canvas, 100.4 × 80.9 cm
The Art Institute of Chicago, Illinois,
Mr and Mrs Lewis Larned
Coburn Memorial Collection, 1933. Inv.1933.455
D 254
DR exhibitions: Paris 1882, no. 138; Paris 1883c, no. 2; New York 1886a and b, no. 181; Paris 1892, no. 92; Paris 1899, no. 81; London 1905, no. 239

The terrace here, at the Restaurant Fournaise on the Ile de Chatou overlooking the Seine, is the same one Renoir depicted in his *Luncheon of the Boating Party* (see fig. 33). The artist was there in the spring of 1881 when he painted this beautiful young model, Mlle Darlaud, who has been joined in the sunshine by a fresh-faced child. The two seem not to have been related although the painting was shown in the Seventh Impressionist exhibition the following year as *Les Deux Soeurs*, a title the lender, Durand-Ruel, bestowed on it. He had purchased the painting for 1,500 francs soon after completion, on 7 July 1881. It passed to the prestigious collection of Charles Ephrussi, Editor of the *Gazette des Beaux-Arts*, but was again with Durand-Ruel by 1892, whence it travelled to important exhibitions such as a breakthrough display of Impressionist paintings at the National Academy of Design in New York in 1886, and the Grafton Galleries exhibition in London in 1905. Durand-Ruel's son Joseph sold it from the New York gallery to the Chicago collector, Mrs Lewis L. (Annie S.) Coburn, on 4 February 1925, for a handsome $100,000. CR

CAT. 76 [FIG. 23]

Joseph Durand-Ruel

1882

Oil on canvas, 81 × 65 cm
Private collection
D 1254
DR exhibition: Paris 1883c, not included in catalogue

CAT. 77 [FIG. 22]

Charles and Georges Durand-Ruel

1882

Oil on canvas, 65 × 81 cm
Private collection
D 1003
DR exhibition: Paris 1883c, not included in catalogue

CAT. 78 [FIG. 24]

The daughters of Paul Durand-Ruel, Marie-Thérèse and Jeanne

1882

Oil on canvas, 81.3 × 65.4 cm
Chrysler Museum of Art, Norfolk, Virginia, gift of Walter P. Chrysler, Jr. in memory of Thelma Chrysler Foy, 1971. Inv. 71/518
D 967
DR exhibitions: Paris 1883c, no. 5; New York 1886a and b, no. 207 ('*Portraits of the Mlles.* D.R.'); Paris 1892c, no. 1; Paris 1899, no. 86

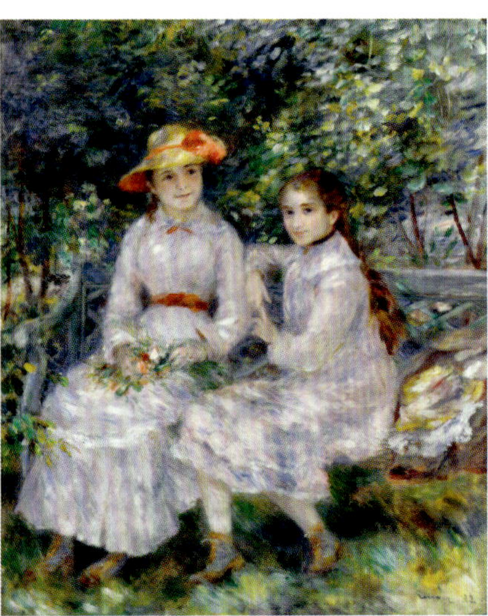

Almost ten years after they met, Durand-Ruel commissioned portraits of his children from Renoir and chose the location for the artist to work on them. He asked Monet, who was living in Pourville, 'if [he] and [his] family could find a house for the month of August either in Pourville or near Dieppe. I don't want to spend too much, yet I need plenty of room, five or six bedrooms, with eight beds… Renoir would come with me'.[1] And then again two days later: 'I'm hurrying to tell you that I have settled on a small house in Dieppe, on the rue de Rouen. There are nine beds, which is quite sufficient for us, and a little garden behind the house. Renoir will be able to paint his masterpieces far from the prying eyes of the public. We will come in early August. Renoir may be the first to arrive around 20 July if he has finished his portrait of Madame Clapisson'.[2] These three portraits, as well as a fourth, *Marie-Thérèse Sewing*, painted in Dieppe, are evidence of the respect and friendship that existed between the dealer, his family and the artist. Renoir conveyed a feeling of well-being, serenity and respectability.

Joseph (1862–1928) is sitting in an armchair, wearing a fashionable suit in warm tones that reveals a pocket watch chain. A book in his hands, he has a serious air; his direct gaze inspires confidence and radiates sincerity. As the oldest, he had his own canvas; his brothers and sisters were paired together in the other two paintings. The portrait of Charles (1865–1892) and Georges (1866–1931) is set outdoors. The two men are fashionably dressed in three-piece suits. Charles, in light grey, is wearing a locket and holding a newspaper; Georges, in a dark suit and with a cigarette in his hand, challenges the viewer with his open gaze. The two sisters, Marie (1868–1937) and Jeanne (1870–1913), are sitting on a bench, their white dresses reflecting the colours of the garden.

Paul's three sons worked alongside him from about 1883. Charles died of an illness at the age of 27. His brothers would go on to run the galleries in Paris and New York, alternating six months in France with six months in the United States. PLDR-FDR

1 Durand-Ruel to Monet, 5 July 1882, ADR.
2 Durand-Ruel to Monet, 12 July 1882, ADR.

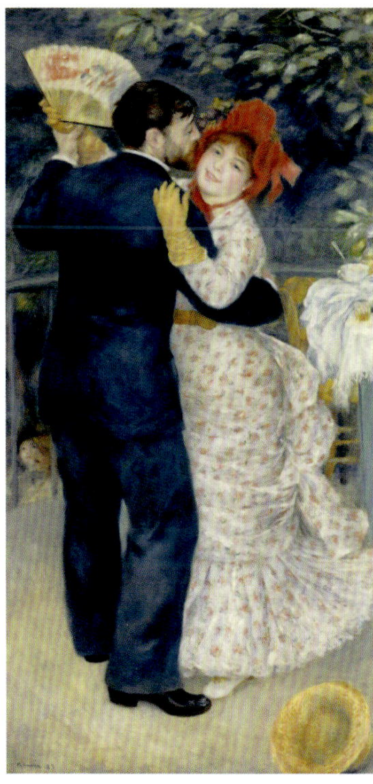

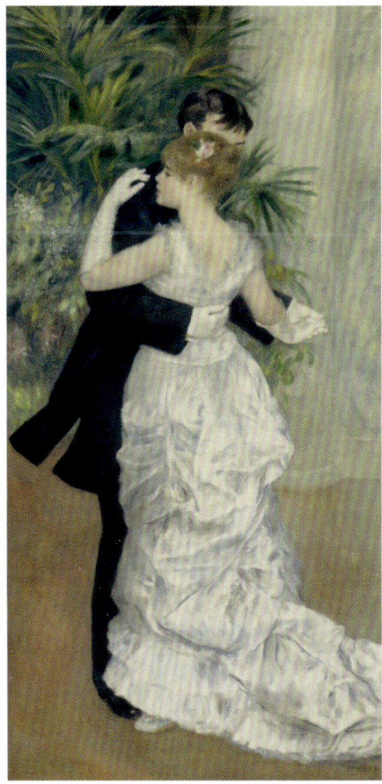

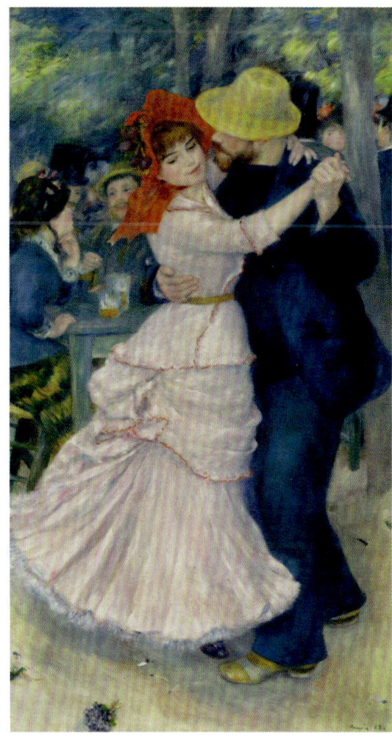

CAT. 79 [FIG. 3]

Dance in the Country (Danse à la campagne) *(left)*

1883

Oil on canvas, 180 × 89 cm
Musée d'Orsay Paris. RF 1979-64
D 999
DR exhibitions: Paris 1883c, no. 25 ('*Danseurs (Bougival)*'); New York, 1886a and b, no. 290 ('*Summer*'); Paris 1892, no. 82 ('*Danse à la campagne*'); London 1905, no. 243 ('*Dancing in the Country*')

CAT. 80 [FIG. 4]

Dance in the City (Danse à la ville) *(middle)*

1883

Oil on canvas, 180 × 90 cm
Musée d'Orsay, Paris. Accepted by the State as a gift in payment of taxes, 1978. RF 1978-13.
D 1000
DR exhibitions: Paris 1883c, no. 26 ('*Danseurs (Paris)*'); New York 1886a and b, no. 291 ('*Winter*'); Paris 1892c, no. 81 ('*Danse à la ville*'); London 1905, no. 242 ('*Dancing in Town*')

CAT. 81 [FIG. 5]

Dance at Bougival (Danse à Bougival) *(right)*

1883

Oil on canvas, 181.9 × 98.1 cm
Museum of Fine Arts, Boston, Picture Fund, 1937. Inv. 37.375
D 1001
DR exhibitions: London 1883, no. 66 ('*Danseurs à Bougival*'); New York 1886a and b, no. 204 ('*La Danse à Bougival*'); Paris 1892c, no. 83 ('*La Danse*')

On his return from Dieppe in late 1882, Renoir settled in Paris and threw himself into the ambitious composition of these three large pictures. *Dance in the Country* depicts a young couple on the terrace of a restaurant in the country. Renoir's friend, the journalist Paul Lhote, is dancing with Aline Charigot, the painter's girlfriend, who would become his wife in 1890. Lhote also appears in *Dance in the City*, in the company of the model and artist Suzanne Valadon. In *Dance at Bougival*, we find her once again; her companion is probably Alphonse Fournaise, son of the owner of the Restaurant Fournaise in Chatou.

The history of these pictures is not entirely clear. Between 1883 and 1888, Durand-Ruel was experiencing a dreadful financial crisis and resorted to a number of expedients to avoid bankruptcy. In 1883, the works were on deposit. Some evidence suggests that the sale of these three pictures to Mme Hitbrunner in 1886, registered in the Durand-Ruel Gallery account books, was in fact a pledge to secure financial loans. These canvases, alongside many others, rejoined the gallery's stock on 25 August 1891.

Although all three were painted in early 1883, they do not form a triptych. *Dance in the Country* and *Dance in the City* are a pair, but *Dance at Bougival* is slightly different in size, and was not exhibited with the others until 1892. *Dance in the Country* and *Dance in the City* decorated the *grand salon* of Paul Durand-Ruel's apartment at 35, rue de Rome, a showcase for Impressionism. Georges Lecomte described them there in 1892;[1] and they would remain in the apartment until Durand-Ruel's death in 1922. But the dealer was more than happy to send them out as part of his international exhibition campaign intended to promote Impressionism: he lent them for Renoir's monographic exhibition in Paris in 1883, for the group exhibitions of Les XX in Brussels in 1886 and 1904, in New York in 1886 and in London, at the Grafton Galleries, in 1905.

Dance at Bougival, on the other hand, never hung in Durand-Ruel's apartment. The picture took part in another international exhibition campaign organised by the dealer, including in London (at Dowdeswell & Dowdeswell) in 1883, in New York in 1886, in Paris in 1892 and in Madrid in 1892–3. It was sold to the Rouen-based collector François Depeaux in 1894 on the condition that it would become part of the collection of the Musée de Rouen. Durand-Ruel was therefore aggrieved when Depeaux sold it at auction in 1906 at the Galerie Petit.[2] Acquired at the sale by Depeaux's brother-in-law Edmond Decap, the picture was later sold to the Boston Museum in 1937. PLDR-FDR

1 Lecomte 1892, p. 147ff.
2 Durand-Ruel to Depeaux, 10 February 1906, ADR.

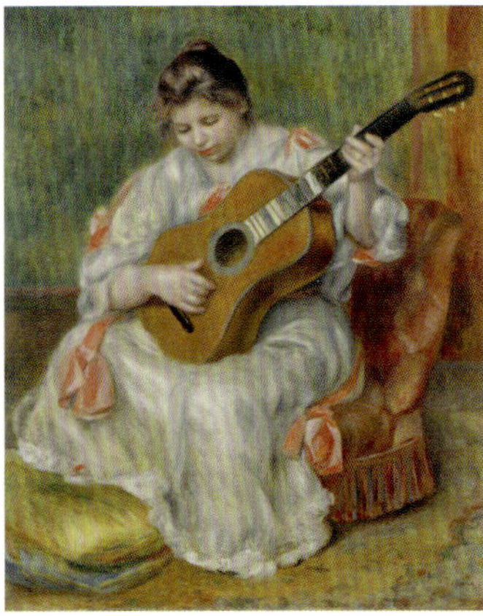

CAT. 82 [FIG. 15]

Woman playing a Guitar (Femme à la guitare)

1896–7

Oil on canvas, 81 × 65 cm
Musée des Beaux-Arts, Lyon, bought 1901. B 624
D 2231

An example of Renoir's investigations in around 1900, which reveal his taste for scenes staged in his studio rendered with a delicate palette, *Woman playing a Guitar* is recognised as the first Impressionist picture to have been bought by a French museum from Durand-Ruel. In truth, the dealer served first and foremost as an intermediary for the work, which Renoir asked him to send to Lyon on 25 January 1901,[1] and which he then committed to delivering himself.[2] On 5 February, the museum board rejected the picture, stating that it was 'not immune to certain criticisms'. It voted again on 19 March, when the mayor argued for a 'commitment to this artist whose picture has been chosen from several others to be submitted to the museums' board. The canvas is one that, both in terms of subject matter and workmanship, is not inclined to shock the eyes of those not yet used to the art produced by the new school. Its price is modest'.[3] The sum of 4,000 francs was the same as that paid by the Musée du Luxembourg in 1892 for *Young Girls at the Piano* by Renoir (Musée d'Orsay, Paris); it was well below the 20,000 francs paid in 1902 by the Lyon museums to Durand-Ruel for two landscapes by Monet, *Spring* and *Rough Sea at Etretat*. SP

1 Renoir to Durand-Ruel, 25 January 1901, *Correspondence Renoir–Durand-Ruel* [1995], p. 142.
2 Renoir to Durand-Ruel, 1 August 1910, Lyon, municipal archives, 1400 WP 4.
3 Minutes of the Board of Lyon's Museums [Advisory and Monitoring Committee of the Museums of the City of Lyon from 1 April 1897], register 1878–1905, Musée des Beaux-Arts, Lyon, documentation; meetings of 5 February and 19 March 1901.

CAT. 83 [FIG. 125]

Paul Durand-Ruel

1910

Oil on canvas, 65 × 54 cm
Private collection
D 3399

Between 1879 and 1888, Paul Durand-Ruel asked Renoir to paint portraits of his children but he did not feel the need to commission one of himself. It was not until 1910, when his success was assured and he had handed over responsibility for the business to his sons, that he asked his friend Renoir to paint him. The letters exchanged between the artist and his dealer make no mention of this portrait, which was probably painted during Renoir's stay in Paris between 15 June and 22 October 1910. Renoir focuses on the dealer's face in particular; uncharacteristically, he does not add any decorative elements. The face is handled extremely carefully and reflects the friendship that existed between the two men after 40 years of unbroken and mutual loyalty. PLDR-FDR

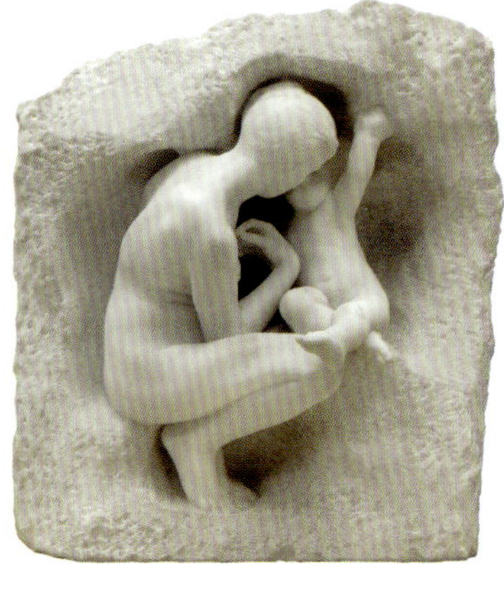

Auguste Rodin

(Paris 1840–Meudon 1917)

CAT. 84

Young Mother in the Grotto (Jeune mère à la grotte)

1891

Marble (carved by Jean Escoula)
H. 70.8 × W. 65.1; PR. 37 cm
Philadelphia Museum of Art, Pennsylvania: gift of Brook J. Lenfest, 2010. 2010-11-1

'Among these radiant canvases, stands a marble by M. Rodin': these were the words used to describe the only sculpture mentioned by Georges Lecomte in his book dedicated to Paul Durand-Ruel's Impressionist collection in 1892.[1] In his introduction, the author states his intention to devote several pages to Rodin, and, in the same way, to the work of Puvis de Chavannes, whose 'harmonious unity' and 'highest expressive ideals' he praises.

The *Young Mother* was created in around 1885, at the time of the great creative impetus sparked off by *The Gates of Hell* – for a while it was to be included in the upper left corner. It was at Durand-Ruel's that this subject was displayed for the first time in 1885, in a plaster version. Rodin did not often exhibit at the gallery, clearly favouring its competitor, Georges Petit. However, he maintained a significant business relationship with Durand-Ruel, as evidenced by the correspondence in the Musée Rodin and in the dealer's archives. The sculptor made several marble versions of the *Young Mother* from 1888. In a letter dated 30 January 1890,[2] Charles Durand-Ruel asked if Rodin would be willing to part with the example seen in his studio, explaining, 'it is to be kept at home' and would not be sold. Another letter (18 February) tells us that the marble had been delivered the day before and that Paul Durand-Ruel 'found it wonderful'. Although not the one that belonged to the Durand-Ruel collection, the marble displayed in this exhibition is very similar. It was commissioned in late 1890 by Mme Blum, from Geneva. It too was carved for Rodin by Jean Escoula, who was skilled at rendering the subtle effects of the flesh typical of the sculptor's marbles of the early 1890s. FB

1 Lecomte 1892, pp. 36–7, 163–7.
2 Paris, AMR.

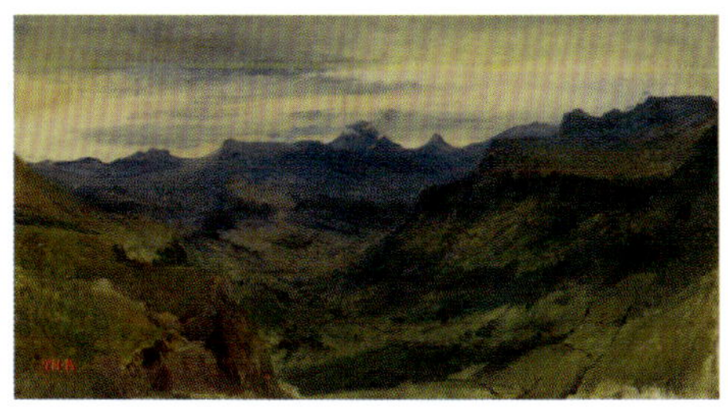

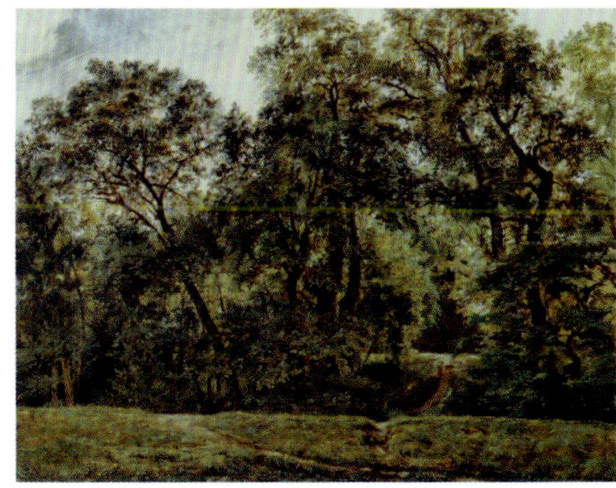

Théodore Rousseau

(Paris 1812–Barbizon 1867)

CAT. 85 [FIG. 42]

The Valley of Saint-Vincent (La Vallée de Saint-Vincent)

1830

Oil on paper laid on canvas, 18.2 × 32.4 cm
The National Gallery, London. Bought, 1918. NG3296
S 73
DR exhibition: Paris 1867, no. 15

In June 1830 Rousseau travelled to the Auvergne; the broadly and fluidly observed studies he produced of its wild beauty were seminal for his development as a painter. A number of these were set in and around the valley of Saint-Vincent at the foot of Puy Mary, the highest peak depicted here. Rousseau focused on the vertiginous drop from the foreground rocks, the sweep of the valley and the distant, menacing mountain range. Along with other Auvergne studies, the picture was sold by the artist to Durand-Ruel and Brame in 1867, who exhibited it soon after. It was bought in July 1869 by a Mr Ourdeki for 300 francs.[1] The painting was later in the collection of Edgar Degas, who purchased it at auction in 1899, 'by mistake', thinking, 'from a slight distance', that it was a Corot. Degas recalled: 'Durand-Ruel didn't want to take it back from me and assured me that it was an excellent picture, which is true.'[2] SH

1 Ourdeki may have been a misspelling for Hourquebie, a dealer who might have bought it on behalf of the next owner, Alfred Sensier.
2 Bought for 1000F at the Doria sale May 1899 (no. 221 '*Th. Rousseau. Etudes de Montagnes, vallée cantal*'). Unpublished notes, private collection. See London 1996, p. 67, note 223.

CAT. 86 [FIG. 45]

The Old Park at Saint-Cloud (L'Ancien Parc de Saint-Cloud)

About 1831–2

Oil on canvas, 66.6 × 82.5 cm
National Gallery of Canada, Ottawa.
Purchased 1977. Inv. 18904
S 91
Galerie Durand-Ruel, Recueil d'estampes gravées à l'eau-forte, 1873, vol. 2, pl. 84, engraved by Alfred Delauney

EXHIBITED IN PHILADELPHIA

CAT. 87 [FIG. 43]

View of Mont Blanc, seen from La Faucille (Vue du Mont Blanc, prise de La Faucille)

About 1863–7

Oil on canvas, 91.4 × 118.4 cm
Lent by the Minneapolis Institute of Arts, Minnesota.
The Putnam Dana McMillan Fund, 2010. Inv. 2010.62
S 678[1]

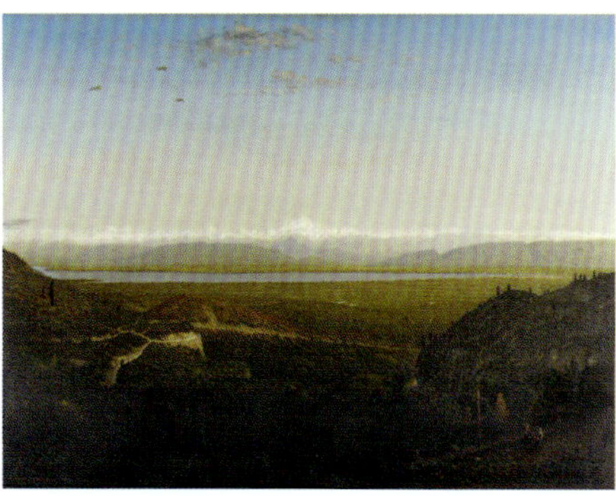

Rousseau's early, rapidly worked sketch, probably painted en plein air, represents a copse of trees in the former royal park of Saint-Cloud in the west of Paris. The gestural touch and the treatment of the sky suggest the influence of Richard Parkes Bonington. Paul Durand-Ruel acquired this painting from Alfred Sensier, Rousseau's friend and biographer, on 17 May 1872, for 4,500 francs. He sold it to the collector Szarvady on 12 November 1872 for 15,000 francs, a more than three-fold profit.[2] The dealer did not receive cash but an exchange of 23 landscapes by Georges Michel (1763–1843), and one still life by Philippe Rousseau (1816–1887).[3] The picture was reproduced in the 1873 *Galerie Durand-Ruel* catalogue (no. 84). By this time, it no longer belonged to Durand-Ruel and was included to promote the quality of work that passed through his gallery.

Rousseau's second painting represents a panoramic view of the Alps in which the foreground has been darkened in order to intensify the luminosity of the distant mountains. The artist used the meticulous touches of his late, proto-pointillist style, which attracted mixed reviews when the picture was shown at the 1867 Salon. The telegraph poles at bottom right are a rare example of modern iconography in Rousseau's work. The Alsatian collector Alfred Hartmann commissioned the painting in 1862 and sold it to Durand-Ruel, in partnership with Hector Brame, in February 1867 for 14,300 francs. Durand-Ruel and Brame sold the picture in the same month to the Chevalier Alfred De Knyff, the Belgian painter and collector, for 18,000 francs. On 16 December 1867, they bought it back for the same amount before selling it to Madame de Cassin (the future Marquise de Carcano), for 20,000 francs in April 1868.[4]

These two works reflect Durand-Ruel's interest in acquiring the full range of Rousseau's work from the early sketches to the very different late style. SK

1 Schulman 1999, no. 678 provides an incorrect image of the painting. See Kelly 2009.
2 The buyers were the Hungarian Frédéric Szarvady and his wife, the noted pianist Wilhelmina Szarvady.
3 The stock book indicates that the still life *Nature morte oeufs et laitue* (2121), was by 'Ch. Rousseau'. Since Charles Rousseau was born in 1862, this work was probably by Philippe Rousseau.
4 The dealer Francis Petit acted as the agent for Madame de Cassin in this transaction. The painting appears in the stock books with the title *Vue de Suisse* (*View of Switzerland*).

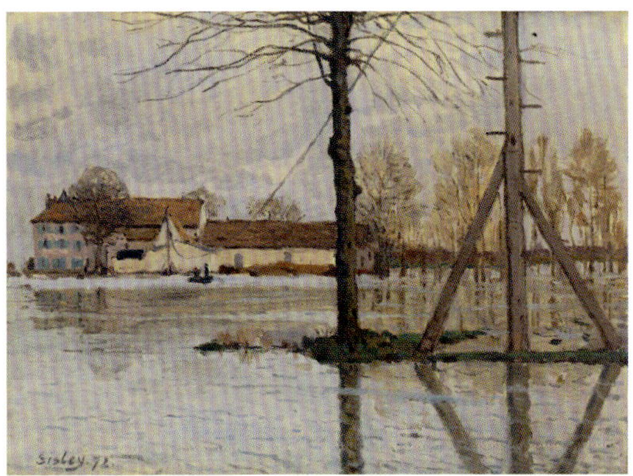

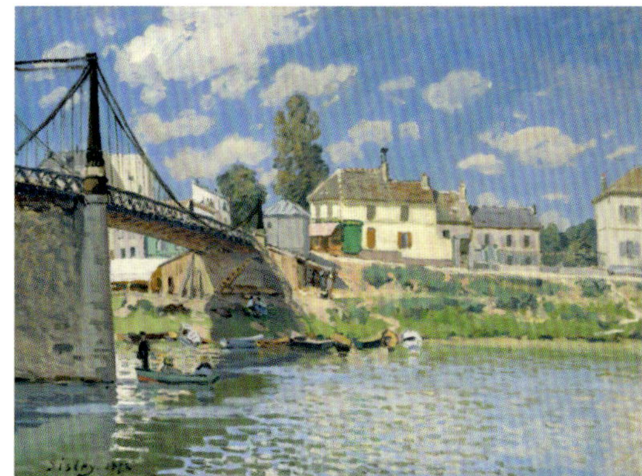

Alfred Sisley

(Paris 1839–Moret-sur-Loing 1899)

CAT. 88 [FIG. 80]

Ile de la Loge or The Flood (Le Bac de l'Ile de la Loge – Inondation)

1872

Oil on canvas, 45 × 60 cm
Ny Carlsberg Glyptotek, Copenhagen, acquired 1914.
MIN 1752
D 21
DR exhibitions: Paris 1874, no. 162; London 1883, no. 45; New York, 1886a and b, no. 235 (*'Le bac de l'Ile de la Loge'*);[1] Paris 1899, no. 45

The Seine at Port-Marly flooded in December 1872. One of four views of the inundation (D 21–24), Sisley's daring composition shows a small ferry pulled by cable across the swollen river. Its landing spot in the foreground is now merely a sliver of grass poking above the water. The painting was bought by Durand-Ruel for 200 francs on 21 January 1873. He lent it to the First Impressionist Exhibition in 1874, where the critic L. de Lora singled it out as 'among the best landscapes.'[2] In 1883 the dealer showed it at the Dowdeswell & Dowdeswell Gallery in London. By 1893 he had sold it to a major client, the Rouen collector François Depeaux.[3] In 1906 Depeaux was facing financial hardship and made plans to sell part of his collection at auction. Durand-Ruel wrote a heated letter on 10 February pointing out that this was one of four paintings from his private collection, including cat. 81, which he had sold on the express understanding that Depeaux would donate them to the museum at Rouen.[4] The sale went ahead and on this occasion the dealer's attempt to strategically place major works in a French public collection was stymied. CR

1 Durand-Ruel Godfroy 1992, p. 52: 'almost certainly exhibited by Durand-Ruel in New York in 1886.'
2 Ibid., p. 282.
3 Lespinasse 2010, p. 131.
4 Ibid., p. 150.

CAT. 89 [FIG. 59]

The Bridge at Villeneuve-la-Garenne (Le Pont à Villeneuve-la-Garenne)

1872

Oil on canvas, 49.5 × 65.4 cm
Lent by The Metropolitan Museum of Art, New York, gift of Mr and Mrs Henry Ittleson Jr., 1964. Inv. 64.287.
D 37
Galerie Durand-Ruel, Recueil d'estampes gravées à l'eau-forte, 1873, vol. 28, pl. 113, engraved by Charles Courtry

Sisley painted at this small town along the River Seine opposite the Ile Saint-Denis in the spring and summer of 1872. As the brilliant sunshine suggests, this is one of three paintings from the summer campaign. It shows an iron suspension bridge cutting diagonally into the picture space at the left, a motif and a dynamic composition to which the artist would return, for example when he painted the bridge over the Thames at Hampton Court during his English sojourn of 1875 (D 123). Durand-Ruel purchased the painting for 200 francs soon after completion, on 24 August 1872; it was one of three paintings he bought from the artist that day. The following year, on 15 April 1873, he sold it for 360 francs to the great Impressionist collector and patron of Sisley, Jean-Baptiste Faure. That Durand-Ruel thought highly of the work is suggested by the fact he had it engraved for an (unrealised) album of prints after the most beautiful paintings in the gallery's stock. CR

CAT. 90 [FIG. 8]

L'Ile Saint-Denis

1872

Oil on canvas, 50.5 × 65 cm
Musée d'Orsay, Paris, donated by Ernest May, 1923. RF 2435
D 47
Galerie Durand-Ruel, Receuil d'estampes graves à l'eau-forte, 1873, vol. 2, pl. 13 (*'La Rivière'*), engraved by Flameng
[See cat. no. 35]

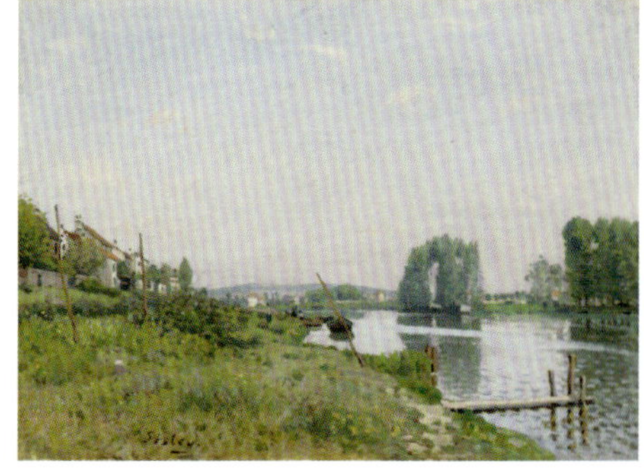

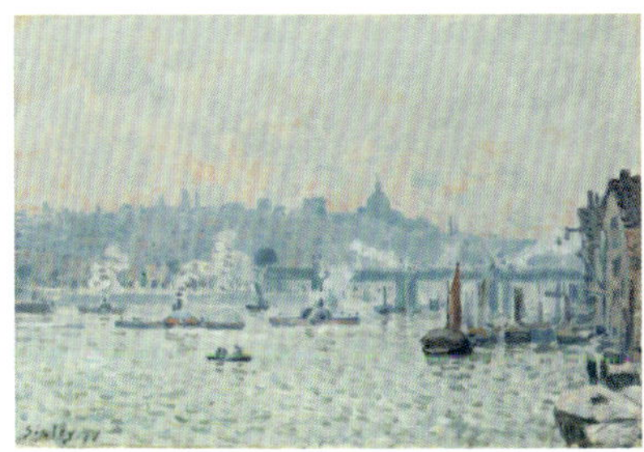

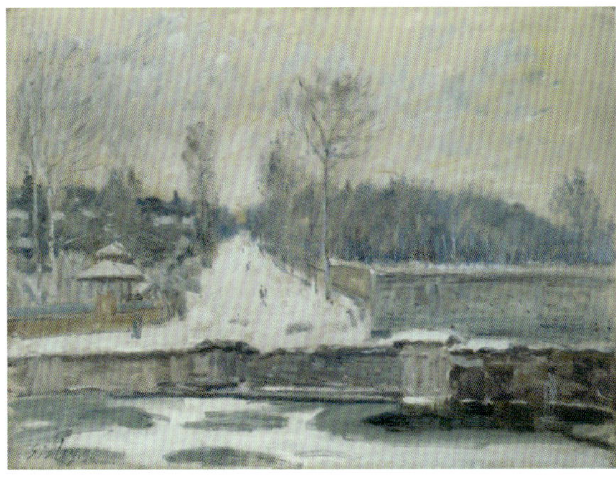

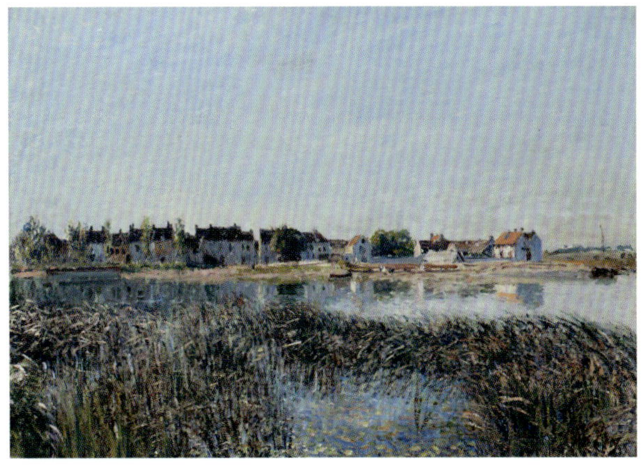

CAT. 91 [FIG. 121]

View of the Thames: Charing Cross Bridge (Vue de la Tamise et du pont de Charing Cross)

1874[1]

Oil on canvas, 33 × 46 cm
The Andrew Brownsword Arts Foundation. L986
D113
DR exhibitions: Paris 1899, no. 116; London 1905, no. 286

Sisley visited England with his patron, the singer Jean-Baptiste Faure, between July and October 1874. This view showing the distinctive dome of St Paul's Cathedral rising above busy river traffic – the strict geographical accuracy of the view has been questioned[2] – seems to be the only painting of some 14 Thames views from that year to depict central London. All others show the city's western suburbs. Durand-Ruel purchased the work from the artist in 1876, but seems not to have shown it publicly until he included it in an exhibition at his Paris gallery in 1899. Six years later he sent it to London for the Grafton Galleries exhibition of 1905. At a later date he sold it to a Swiss collector resident in Paris, Baron Louis de Chollet, in whose family it remained until recent times. CR

1 John Rewald first read the date as 1871 and discussed it as a work of exile created during the Franco-Prussian War in the first two editions of his *History of Impressionism*. Later acknowledging his mistake, Rewald pointed out that Durand-Ruel himself mistakenly told Félix Fénéon in 1920 that he had been introduced to Sisley by Monet in London at that time. Rewald 1973, p. 269, note 42.
2 Reed 2008, p. T9.

CAT. 92 [FIG. 88]

The Watering Place at Marly-le-Roi (L'Abreuvoir de Marly-le-Roi)

Probably 1875

Oil on canvas, 49.5 × 65.4 cm
The National Gallery, London.
Bought, Courtauld Fund, 1926, NG4138
D152
DR exhibition: Paris 1876, no. 240[1]

From 1875 to 1877, Sisley lived at Marly-le-Roi, where he painted the remains of Louis XIV's summer palace, destroyed in the Revolution. The final year of the date here is indistinct but a closely related painting of the same site (D 154) is clearly dated 1875. One of eight paintings by Sysley [sic] listed in the catalogue of the Second Impressionist Exhibition in 1876, it was lent by the dealer Pierre-Firmin Martin, known as 'Père' Martin, who was particularly interested in Barbizon and Impressionist paintings. The principal organiser of the 1876 exhibition, Durand-Ruel almost certainly arranged the loan, as well as that of three other Sisleys (nos. 237, 239 and 243), with his fellow dealer. Further suggesting a relationship between the two, the painting then entered the collection of one of Durand-Ruel's most assiduous clients for Impressionist paintings, the Rouennais François Depeaux, who also owned Sisley's *Ile de la Loge* (cat. 88). Depeaux sold the present work in 1901.[2] CR

1 In Washington and San Francisco 1986, no. 37, p. 186, the painting is associated with no. 240 in the Second Impressionist exhibition.
2 Sales cat. Paris 1901, no. 48.

CAT. 93 [FIG. 96]

View of Saint-Mammès (Vue de Saint-Mammès)

About 1881

Oil on canvas, 54 × 74 cm
The Carnegie Museum of Art, Pittsburgh, purchase 99.7
D 422

This tranquil image of a small town along the River Seine, full of closely observed light effects, reveals something of Durand-Ruel's American marketing strategies. He purchased it from the artist on 23 July 1881 (stock no. 1483, entitled *Village au bord de l'eau*), selling it to the New York merchant William L. Andrews on 16 October 1888. He subsequently bought it back and re-sold it to the important early American collector of Impressionism, A. W. Kingman, on 11 April 1892, from whom he re-purchased it on 5 March 1896. In 1898 he loaned it to the Third Annual Exhibition of the Carnegie Museum in Pittsburgh – the so-called Carnegie International, still on-going – an increasingly prestigious forum for modern art in a fast-growing, wealthy city. The Museum purchased the picture from the exhibition, and it thus became the first painting by Sisley to enter an American public collection. The sequence traces Durand-Ruel's efforts first to place 'his' artists with ever more prominent American private collectors and then, more ambitiously, to move such works from the private sphere into the burgeoning public collections of the United States.[1] CR

1 Exh. cat. London, Paris and Baltimore 1992, no. 51.

NOTES

Paul Durand-Ruel, an 'Unrepentant Risk-taker'

1 Rewald 1943, repr. in 1985, p. 197.
2 Durand-Ruel Godfroy 2011, p. 60.
3 Rothenstein 1931, p. 71.
4 Lecomte 1892, p. 36.
5 Signac to Bardur, 26 April 1899, Musée d'Orsay, Paris, Ruth Berson archive.
6 At that time, there were no Impressionist works in any British collections apart from one picture by Degas (cat. 17).
7 Lucy and House 2012, p. 25.
8 Chastel and Pomian 1987.
9 Becker 1988.
10 The business strategies employed by publishers and entertainment entrepreneurs, inseparable from the development of capitalism, are comparable in many respects to those of art dealers. See, for example, the work of Jean-Claude Yon on entertainment shows in France, and Yon 2008 in particular. Research into nineteenth-century publishing has been particularly extensive and we limit ourselves here to referring to the work of Mollier, to Mollier 1988. The more general work carried out by Christophe Charles and Pascal Ory on the cultural history of the period should also be cited.
11 Bibliothèque central des musées nationaux, Paris, and Musée d'Orsay.
12 Musée d'Aquitaine, Bordeaux, Goupil archive; Getty Research Institute, Los Angeles (GRI), The Dieterle Family Records of French Art Galleries, 1846–1986. See Penot-Lejeune 2012.
13 GRI; Institut national d'histoire de l'art, Paris (INHA). See Vignon 2010.
14 GRI.
15 National Gallery, London.
16 Among others, Preti-Hamard and Sénéchal 2005; Panzanelli and Preti-Hamard 2007; and the 'London and the Emergence of a European Art Market (c. 1780–1820)' conference, organised by the National Gallery, London and the Getty Research Institute, Los Angeles, at the National Gallery on 21 and 22 June 2013.
17 Dewhurst 1904, p. 41.
18 Lecomte 1892, p. 36.
19 Alexandre 1911, pp. 11–12.
20 Duret 1906b, p. 30.
21 Duret to Monet, 29 November 1884, Musée d'Orsay, Paris, Monet archive ODO 2007-1-29.
22 Quoted by Renoir 1981, p. 270.
23 Quoted by Alexandre 1911, pp. 10–11.
24 Elias 1912.
25 The memoirs have been republished by Paul-Louis Durand-Ruel and Flavie Durand-Ruel (Durand-Ruel and Durand-Ruel 2014) to tie in with this exhibition. This catalogue has been based on the 1939 publication since the new edition was not yet available.
26 Venturi 1939, I, pp. 5–112.
27 Ibid., p. 7.
28 Bellony 2005, p. 29. For the English edition of Rewald's history see Rewald 1973.
29 Moulin 1967, pp. 30–1.
30 White and White 1965. See White and White 1991 for the French translation.
31 National Gallery of Ireland, Dublin. O'Byrne 2000, p. 206.
32 Formerly *Don Evaristo Pérez de Castro*, RF 1476. AMN Comités consultatifs des Musées nationaux, IBB35, 29 January 1903.
33 Alexandre 1911, p. 16.
34 *L'Evénement*, 5 November 1885. [Trans. Assouline 2004, p. 182.]
35 Blanc 1869, p. XLII, quoted by Vottero 2012, p. 330.
36 *Abraham Banishing Hagar and Ishmael*, ADR, daybook, 12 April 1872.
37 Lafont-Couturier 1996; Penot-Lejeune 2012.
38 A systematic analysis of addresses in the *livrets* of the Salons between 1864 and 1892 has been carried out under the guidance of Isabelle Gaëtan.
39 Argencourt 1984 (who attributes to Paul Durand-Ruel that which relates to his father in the French catalogue), pp. 96–9.
40 Durand-Ruel to Monet, 20 June 1883, in sales cat. Paris 2006b, no. 61.
41 Durand-Ruel purchased a single Merle in 1879, ADR, daybook, 1 December (*'Head of a Young Girl'*; 2,000 francs).
42 ADR, daybook, 6 February 1800, and Patry, this book.
43 Noce 2007 expressed this regret with regard to the Vollard exhibition.
44 Durand-Ruel [1939], p. 186.
45 29 September 1894, BnF, Est., Arch. Pissarro microfilm.
46 Barye, see p. 162 for Carpeaux, Itasse etc.
47 Whiteley 1983, pp. 69–71.
48 Zola 1886, in Zola [1991], pp. 114. [Trans. D.W. Galenson, *Conceptual Revolutions in Twentieth-Century Art*, 2009, pp. 159–60.]
49 Monet to Alexandre, 6 December 1920, WL 2391; Nonne 2009.
50 ADR, daybook, 12 March–12 April 1872; stock book June 1872.
51 Bodelsen 1968, p. 333.
52 Durand-Ruel to Monet, 2 March 1876, in sales cat. Paris 2006a, no. 57.
53 ADR, account book.
54 Nonne 2009, pp. 369–70.
55 Fink 1978.
56 GRI, Goupil & Co, stock books 11 and 12.
57 Durand-Ruel to Cassirer, 5 January 1910, ADR, quoted by Durand-Ruel Godfroy 1999, p. 29.
58 The Musée de Nantes purchased one Delaunay in December 1883 (3,498 francs, ADR, daybook) and was assigned one of the two Maufras acquired from the dealer by the State in 1896 for 1,300 francs (AN, F 21 2414).
59 Dupré, *Morning* and *Evening*, deposited at the Musée de Nantes; Chronology, 23 May 1894, this book.
60 Boudin to Martin, 5 February 1881, INHA-Doucet, MS212. This commission was never fulfilled.
61 Durand-Ruel Godfroy 1991, p. 51.
62 See Houssais and Lagrange 2010.
63 Bibliophile Julien, 18 May [unknown year], AMR, in Le Normand-Romain 2007, I, p. 471, note 7.
64 Rathbone and Steele 1996, pp. 233–4.
65 p. 258.
66 Tabarant 1921, p. 529.
67 Cooper 1954, p. 28.
68 With Bernheim-Jeune and Paul Cassirer: see Gruetzner Robins 2010, p. 784.
69 *L'Evénement*, 5 November 1885.
70 Mirbeau 1884, p. 78.

Paul Durand-Ruel (1831–1922): A Portrait

1 Lecomte 1892, pp. 35–6, illustrated with 36 etchings.
2 Quoted by Félix Fénéon in *Le Bulletin de la vie artistique*, no. 10, 15 April 1920, p. 262.
3 Durand-Ruel and Durand-Ruel 2014, p. 161.
4 Jean Durand and Marie Ruel married on 11 October 1825, combining their surnames to form 'Durand-Ruel'. Their son would legalise the name 50 years later, and it was made official in 1896 by a Conseil d'Etat decree.
5 Durand-Ruel and Durand-Ruel 2014, p. 2.
6 Letter to a family member, 12 December 1916, private collection.
7 Undated letter, private collection. Trans. Assouline 2004 (US edn), p. 274.
8 Clemenceau 1928, p. 61. Trans. Assouline 2004 (US edn), p. 11.
9 Pissarro to Joseph Durand-Ruel, 18 September 1896, private collection. The Dreyfus Affair (1894–1906) was a political scandal involving a military cover-up. Captain Alfred Dreyfus, a young French artillery officer of Alsatian Jewish descent, was unjustly accused of selling French military secrets and sentenced to life imprisonment before he was eventually pardoned. French public opinion was split into two hostile factions, for and against Dreyfus.
10 Durand-Ruel and Durand-Ruel 2014, p. 146.
11 Spiritual testament, 23 June 1913, private collection.
12 Letter to his son-in-law, Albert Dureau, 3 January 1917, private collection.
13 See the article by Paul Durand-Ruel in *Le Figaro* on 31 October 1873, repr. in Durand-Ruel [1939], vol. II, p. 210.
14 In 1836, King Louis-Philippe reprimanded his son, the Prince de Joinville, for having purchased from Durand-Ruel a picture by Marilhat that had been rejected by the Salon. Joinville 1894, pp. 75–6.
15 Galerie Durand-Ruel 1845.
16 Plate no. 36.
17 Musée du Louvre, Paris.
18 Durand-Ruel and Durand-Ruel 2014, p. 6.
19 Ibid.
20 In the 1860s, the cost of hiring a work for one month varied from 3% of its value for the least important to 8% for the largest formats.
21 Paul Durand-Ruel was number 142 of the 241 students admitted to Saint-Cyr

(letter from the Minister for War, 31 October 1851, ADR).

22 Paul Durand-Ruel: 'Having been summoned to Saint Petersburg by Countess Grégoire Koucheleff early in 1869, in order to take all necessary measures prior to the sale of her collection of old masters, I profited from the occasion to make a thorough study of the Hermitage Museum. I returned with great enthusiasm.' (Durand-Ruel and Durand-Ruel 2014, p. 64).

23 Durand-Ruel and Durand-Ruel 2014, p. 19.

24 The records held by the Archives Durand-Ruel begin in the early 1860s.

25 Durand-Ruel and Durand-Ruel 2014, p. 104.

26 In order to make the most of his predominantly European clientele, Paul Durand-Ruel timed the work's journey to Vienna to coincide with the start of the International Exhibition, which opened its doors on 1 May 1873. He rented premises in the centre of Vienna, on Elizabethstrasse, and sent one of his employees to accompany the work. Unfortunately, there was a cholera outbreak in the city and the success he had hoped for did not materialise.

27 The London branch of the Durand-Ruel Gallery (1870–5) was located at 168 New Bond Street.

28 The 35 works by Delacroix on display included *The Death of Sardanapalus* (no. 141). At that time, the Durand-Ruel Gallery was located at 16, rue Laffitte, with another entrance at 11, rue Le Peletier and 16, rue Laffitte.

29 Number 73 in the exhibition entitled 'National Academy of Design, New York. Celebrated Paintings Brought from Paris, for Exhibition only' (25 May–30 June 1887).

30 'Vente de tableaux modernes', *Gazette des Beaux-Arts*, 5 April 1863, p. 1. Trans. Assouline 2004 (US edn), p. 75.

31 Fels 1929, p. 130.

32 Monet is quoted on 15 April 1870 in the first art review founded by Durand-Ruel, the *Revue internationale de l'art et de la curiosité*, in the preface to the Salon of 1870, signed by Jean Ravenel (Sensier's pseudonym), pp. 320–3.

33 Including *Entrance to the Port of Trouville*, purchased for 300 francs and exhibited at the Durand-Ruel Gallery in London, December 1870, no. 36 in the catalogue.

34 Paul Durand-Ruel to Pissarro, 21 January 1871, ADR (Durand-Ruel and Durand-Ruel 2014, p. 175). Including *Snow Effect*, purchased for 200 francs and exhibited at the Durand-Ruel Gallery in London, December 1870, no. 38 in the catalogue, unidentified.

35 Eva died on 27 November 1871.

36 Trans. Assouline 2004 (US edn), p. 173; Rewald 1986, p. 102. The sale was eventually entrusted to Durand-Ruel and Georges Petit.

37 Durand-Ruel and Durand-Ruel 2014, p. 110. The hospital at Charenton housed mentally ill patients.

38 Having only extremely limited capital at his disposal since starting his business in 1865, Paul Durand-Ruel operated on the credit he could obtain. He was unable to pay his bills in 1874 and 1884 but succeeded in convincing his creditors to agree to a moratorium and they were later reimbursed in full. He was not able to repay all his debts until 1894.

39 Another spectacular sale was *The Death of Sardanapalus* by Delacroix, purchased for 100,800 francs (hammer price and buyer's premium) in 1873 and sold for 50,000 francs in 1879.

40 Article of 3 April 1876. Durand-Ruel 2014, p. 134.

41 Durand-Ruel and Durand-Ruel 2014, p. 153.

42 See the essay by Anne Distel in this book and Distel 1989b.

43 Renoir to Paul Durand-Ruel, November 1885, ADR, repr. in Durand-Ruel Godfroy 1995, p. 47, and Durand-Ruel and Durand-Ruel 2014, p. 198.

44 Alexandre 1911, p. 6.

45 Monet to Durand-Ruel, 28 July 1885, ADR.

46 Durand-Ruel also sold pictures by the Barbizon School in the United States, including to Adolph E. Borie from Philadelphia from 1866; to Henry Probasco from Cincinnati from 1867; and to the New York-based dealers Samuel Avery and Herman Schaus from 1867 and 1869 respectively.

47 An example taken from *The Critic*, 1 April 1886: 'New York has never seen a more interesting exhibition'; in *Cosmopolitan*, June 1886, written by Luther Hamilton: 'One of the most important artistic events that ever took place in this country'.

48 Durand-Ruel and Durand-Ruel 2014, p. 158.

49 Such as A.W. Kingman, Catholina Lambert, Albert Spencer, Erwin Davis, William H. Fuller, and later Potter Palmer, Martin A. Ryerson, etc.

50 See the essay by John Zarobell in this book.

51 See the essay by Sylvie Patry in this book.

52 ADR, daybook.

53 Paul Durand-Ruel to Monet, 20 March 1882, private collection; Cornebois sale, Paris, ArtCurial, 13 December 2006, lot 59.

54 Durand-Ruel and Durand-Ruel 2014, p. 32.

55 Monet to Paul Durand-Ruel, 18 September 1882, private collection.

56 Paul Durand-Ruel to Monet, 18 September 1882, private collection.

57 Paul Durand-Ruel to Pissarro, 23 October 1884, ADR.

58 Paul Durand-Ruel to Monet, 18 September 1882, private collection.

59 Paul Durand-Ruel to Boudin, 17 August 1892, ADR.

60 Renoir to Paul Durand-Ruel, May 1884, ADR, repr. in Durand-Ruel Godfroy 1995, p. 42.

61 *Galerie Durand-Ruel. Recueil d'estampes gravées à l'eau forte*, 1873–5, 30 instalments.

62 The Archives Durand-Ruel holds 108 plates that were not published.

63 Exhibitions by Renoir in 1892; Guillaumin in 1894; Pissarro in 1896; Maufra in 1901, 1907, 1910 and 1912; Toulouse-Lautrec in 1902; Rouart in 1912.

64 Renoir exhibition in 1883.

65 Exhibitions by Monet in 1892 and Binet in 1902.

66 Pissarro exhibition in 1892.

67 Berthe Morisot exhibition in 1896.

68 Raffaëlli exhibition in 1889 in New York, among others.

69 Exhibitions by Pissarro in 1904 and Monet *Views of the Thames* in 1904.

70 Marcellin Desboutin exhibition in 1889.

71 See the essay by John Zarobell in this book.

72 For Durand-Ruel's relationship with America, see the essay by Jennifer A. Thompson in this book.

73 For Durand-Ruel's relationship with Germany, see the essay by Dorothee Hansen in this book.

74 *Pastels et aquarelles d'Edgar Degas*, November 1892.

75 Including Tadamasa Hayashi, who bought works from Durand-Ruel.

76 Among others these include: Les XX and La Libre Esthétique in Brussels, the Secession in Vienna and Munich, the Venice Biennale and several exhibitions in provincial cities in France and Germany.

77 Asmodée 1892.

78 Private collection, p. 330.

79 Barnes Foundation, Philadelphia, Daulte 292, Dauberville 215.

80 Private collection, DB 151.

81 Private collection.

82 The Phillips Collection, Washington, Daulte 292, Dauberville 55.

83 Hill-Stead Museum Farmington, Connecticut, RW 122.

84 Private collection, W 559.

85 Private collection, L 502.

86 The National Gallery, Washington, L 289.

87 The Phillips Collection, Washington, RW 55.

88 See Durand-Ruel Godfroy 2011.

89 Alexandre 1911. Durand-Ruel and Durand-Ruel 2014, p. 196.

90 Quoted by Félix Fénéon in *Le Bulletin de la vie artistique*, no. 10, 15 April 1920. Durand-Ruel and Durand-Ruel 2014, p. XI.

91 Elder 2010, p. 25; Durand-Ruel and Durand-Ruel 2014, p. 267, note 205.

Durand-Ruel and 'La Belle Ecole' of 1830

I would like to thank Paul-Louis and Flavie Durand-Ruel for their invaluable assistance during my visit to the Durand-Ruel Archive in Paris in December 2013 and in the months thereafter. Thanks also to Sylvie Patry for her valuable support.

1 See Durand-Ruel [1939], vol. 2, pp. 162 and 208.

2 There were 91 dealers listed in the Parisian *Annuaire du Commerce* in 1854, with most of these focusing on the Old Masters. Only a relatively small number

concentrated on contemporary art including blue-chip dealers such as Adolphe Goupil, known for his support of academic painting, and Francis Petit, a major supporter of Delacroix. Other prominent dealers at the time included Emmanuel Weyl, Alexis-Eugène Détrimont, Adolphe Beugniet, Georges Thomas and Tedesco, all of whom bought significant numbers of work by the School of 1830 artists in the 1850s and 1860s.

3 See Green 1987, pp. 62–87.

4 See Jensen 1994.

5 See Whiteley 1979, pp. 25–8, and 1996.

6 'pour son génie une admiration sans borne'. Durand-Ruel [1939], p. 156.

7 'un éclat incomparable'. Durand-Ruel [1939], p. 159.

8 See Durand-Ruel [1939], p. 163. Durand-Ruel subsequently often bought out Brame's share in their acquisitions.

9 Five paintings were acquired in June and four in July for an overall sum of 118,000 francs. *The Abduction of Rebecca* (ADR, stock 1868–1873, no. 10953) was acquired in June for 20,000 francs and sold on immediately to the collector Emile Gavet at a 50% profit for 30,000 francs.

10 Durand-Ruel bought work by Delacroix with Brame and another dealer, Alexis Febvre, with shares of 33% each.

11 ADR, stock 1868–1873, nos. 1056–9. Each work was priced at 12,500 francs.

12 ADR, stock 1868–1873, no. 2689. The purchase was 100,800 francs with buyer's premium. See Daniel Wilson Sale (1873). Durand-Ruel also bought major work by Dupré, including *Landscape Near Southampton* (fig. 6) (Musée d'art et d'histoire Louis Senlecq, L'Isle-Adam), Inv. 2011.1.1.) for 44,100 francs. In total, he acquired work at this sale for 148,000 francs (155,400 francs with buyer's premium). Thanks to Sylvie Patry for this information.

13 Durand-Ruel sent *The Death of Sardanapalus* to London on 25 April, 1873 and it was returned to him from Vienna on 8 January 1874. It was probably sent directly from London to Vienna. See email to author from Paul-Louis and Flavie Durand-Ruel, 31 March 2014.

14 On 10 May 1879, Durand-Ruel sold the painting to the Scottish collector James Duncan for 52,500 francs (ADR, daybook). ADR, stock 1868–1873, no. 2689 provides a figure of 50,000 francs. For the collectors Wilson and Duncan see Watson 2011, pp. 101–8.

15 See Durand-Ruel [1939], p. 156.

16 For *Macbeth*, see ADR stock 1868–1873, no. 3756, acquired for 6,000 francs in October 1867. In December 1867, Durand-Ruel bought eight views of France for a total of 4,200 francs. Durand-Ruel remembered that he also acquired Salon works such as *Lake Nemi* (Art Institute of Chicago) and *The Church of Marissel* (Musée du Louvre, Paris), but these do not appear in the stock books.

17 For this number, see email from Paul-Louis Durand-Ruel to author, 25 February 2014.

18 In the month of March 1872 alone, he purchased 37 paintings for around 77,000 francs.

19 ADR, stock 1868–1873, no. 938. *Rivière* [Pont de Mantes], January 1872, purchased from Brame for 1,200 francs. Other works were purchased from a range of dealers, including Cléophas, Détrimont, Tempelaere, Tedesco, Cadart and Luquet.

20 ADR, stock 1868–1873, no. 1202: *Incendie de Sodom*. Purchased from Corot in March, 1872. Sold to de Camondo in March 1872 for 18,000 francs.

21 ADR, stock 1868–1873, no. 844. Purchased from Emile Gavet. Sold to Laurent-Richard on 2 August 1872 for 13,000 francs. This painting was a later variant on *A Morning. The Dance of the Nymphs* (Musée d'Orsay, Paris), shown at the 1850–51 Salon.

22 See Durand-Ruel [1939], p. 203.

23 See also Kelly 1999 and Kelly 2014.

24 See Durand-Ruel [1939], p. 155.

25 See Durand-Ruel [1939], p. 157. Durand-Ruel exaggerated the extent to which the sale was a failure. Durand-Ruel *père* acquired five paintings at this auction.

26 'Brame & Durand-Ruel sont venus mardi dernier … on est venu les chercher pour déjeuner chez Rousseau.' See Millet to Sensier, 26 October 1866 in the Département des Arts Graphiques, Musée du Louvre, Paris. Aut. 2144. Cote BS. b14. L431.

27 *Dessous de bois avec vaches* (now known as *Intérieur de forêt*, Musée d'Orsay, Paris) (ADR, stock 1868–1873, no. 10,011, sold to the American collector Henry Probasco on 23 May 1867 for 8,000 francs.

28 ADR, stock 1868–1873, no. 10,522, *Port en bessin, grotte*, acquired June 1867 for 500 francs. Sold to Brame on 11 September 1872 for 2,500 francs.

29 'C'est vraiment la clef de tout son oeuvre qu'il vient de livrer au public en autorisant cette exhibition.' See Burty 1867.

30 ADR, stock 1868–1873, no. 10,674. The sale took place on 16 January 1868.

31 ADR, stock 1868–1873, no. 10,016. On 28 November 1866, Durand-Ruel and Brame acquired this painting from the collector Worms for 10,000 francs, and on the same day sold it to Khalil Bey for 14,000 francs.

32 They sold the painting in April 1868 to Madame de Cassin for 30,000 francs. Durand-Ruel's involvement with this painting continued until 1912, when he served as expert at the sale of the Marquise de Carcano [formerly Madame de Cassin], where the work was sold to the Louvre for 270,000 francs, another record for the artist.

33 They acquired a total of approximately 70,000 francs worth of paintings, watercolours and drawings from a total sale of only 160,000 francs. See Durand-Ruel [1939], p. 167.

34 Sensier 1872, p. 307.

35 ADR, daybook, 22 May 1869–4 January 1873, 12 April 1872.

36 *Revue internationale* (August 1870), pp. 25–40. The lecture was also included at the end of Sensier's *Souvenirs sur Th. Rousseau*.

37 Durand-Ruel purchased Brame's half-share of the painting for 12,000 francs (ADR, stock 1868–1873, no. 1060, February 1872). On 5 July, 1882, the painting was purchased by the Durand-Ruel company for 50,000 francs from Mr Durand-Ruel (See ADR, stock 1880–82, no. 2492) or from Jules Feder, the banker and Durand-Ruel's financial backer (see ADR, daybook, 5 July 1882). Between 1881 and 1883, Durand-Ruel had to repay the major loans from Feder's bank, then bankrupt. The paintings were used as collateral and the entries in the Durand-Ruel books for these years are not clear. See email from Paul-Louis and Flavie Durand-Ruel to author, 27 May 2014. Thanks also to France Daguet for her assistance here during my Phd. research in the Durand-Ruel Archives in the summer of 1993.

38 See Jean-François Millet to Alfred Sensier, Barbizon, 26 October 1866. Département des Arts Graphiques, Musée du Louvre, Paris. In 1860, Millet had signed a contract with the Belgian dealer Arthur Stevens for his exclusive production over a three-year period, a move he later regretted. Stevens represents a little known precedent for Durand-Ruel's monopolistic methods.

39 'Il ne m'est pas possible d'imaginer comment nous aurions pu vivre si Durand-Ruel ne m'avait pas demandé de la peinture. Il s'est trouvé notre Providence.' See MN, vol. 3, p. 69.

40 ADR, stock 1868–1873. The author's amount, based on accumulation of the stock book purchases of Millet's work in 1872.

41 *L'Angelus*, bought for 30,000 francs from Gavet in February 1872, and sold to Gauchez for John Waterloo Wilson ('Memoirs of Paul Durand-Ruel'), 8 July 1872 for 38,000 francs (ADR, stock 1868–1873, no. 993); *The Shepherd*, bought from Gavet for 32,000 francs in April 1872 and sold to Gibson on 9 July 1872 for 40,000 francs (ADR, stock 1868–1873, no. 1203); *Death and the Woodcutter*, bought from Brame in February 1872 for 16,000 francs (ADR, stock 1868–1873, no. 1001).

42 'Durand … expose dix ou douze de vos tableaux, parmi lesquels Oedipe, l'Angelus, la Mort et le Bucheron, Novembre, etc, etc … Ils sont tous très admirés.' Alfred Sensier to Jean-Francois Millet, Paris, 5 March 1872, Département des Arts Graphiques, Musée du Louvre, Paris.

43 The batch (also including 19 pastels) was valued at 116, 450 francs. *The Sower* [ADR, stock 1868–1873, 1545] was valued at 10,000 francs.

44 'I saw Durand-Ruel, and it is of course understood that everything you do is to his taste in advance, and that you can enlarge your subjects of dealer size, as far as seems reasonable to you and him ... he wants everything you do. ['J'ai vu Durand-Ruel, et il est bien entendu que tout ce que vous faites est d'avance à son goût, et que vous pouvez agrandir vos sujets de dimensions marchandes, jusqu'à ce qu'il vous semblera raisonnable pour vous et pour lui ... il désire tout ce que vous faites.'] Alfred Sensier to Jean-Francois Millet, Paris, 17 November 1871, Département des Art Graphiques, Musée du Louvre, Paris.

45 *Shepherdess Spinning* [*La Bergère Filant*] [AIC, no. 1922.414] was acquired for 10,000 francs in May 1872 from Millet (ADR, stock 1868–1873, no. 1477). *The Turkey Herder* [Metropolitan, 17.120.209] was sold to Mélas on 8 March 1873 (ADR, stock 1868–1873, no. 2592).

46 On 8 February 1873, Durand-Ruel sent *Mort et Bûcheron* and *Le Semeur* to the Musée de Cluny in Paris, where the Jury of the Vienna Universal Exhibition accepted them for the Vienna show. Both paintings were returned from Vienna to Durand-Ruel in Paris on 20 December 1873. See the email to the author from Paul-Louis and Flavie Durand-Ruel, 31 March 2014.

47 ADR, stock 1868–1873, no. 2786. *Woman by Lamplight* (Frick Collection, New York) was acquired from Millet on 20 August 1872 for 14,000 francs and sold to Laurent-Richard on the same day for 23,000 francs (ADR, stock 1868–1873, no. 1869).

48 'Durand a racheté vos deux tableaux. C'est Collombel qui les a fait pousser pour Durand, qui voulait faire une hausse ... ce brave Durand ne connait pas d'obstacles et il prétend que vos tableaux doivent monter aux prix de Meissonnier. Je n'y vois pas d'inconvénient, mais en aura-t-il la force?' Alfred Sensier to Jean-François Millet, Paris, 9 April 1873. Département des Art Graphiques, Musée du Louvre, Paris.

49 Courbet's painting depicted drunken clergy. ADR, stock 1868–1873, no. 1771. *Return from the Fair*. Purchased for 10,000 francs on 11 July 1872, and sold the next day to Dreyfus for 15,000 francs.

50 The total purchase amounted to 54,300 francs. *The Great Oak* (ADR, stock 1868–1873, no. 1412) was acquired for 3,000 francs and sold to Gibson for 6,000 francs on 30 August 1872. *The Wave* (ADR, stock, 1868–1873, no. 1423) was sold immediately to Carlin for 15,000 francs and it appeared in his auction sale on 29 April 1872.

51 The combined total was 39,000 francs. *The Grotto of the Source of Love* was purchased for 500 francs (ADR, stock, 1868–1873, no. 2527). Durand-Ruel delayed delivering payment for these works but did fulfil his obligations to pay the artist, despite his own financial problems.

52 Durand-Ruel sent Courbet's work to Vienna on 22 February 1873 and received them back on 15 July 1873. Eleven canvases were brought over from Paris by the dealer (including *The Burial at Ornans*) but only six were initially shown in the exhibition. See Huemer 2012.

53 'I am most grateful to you (and to M. Durand-Ruel as well, of course) for all you are doing for me.' Courbet to Alphonse Legrand, Ornans, 6 February 1873. Quoted in *Correspondence Courbet* [1996].

54 Durand-Ruel acquired five forest views from Diaz in 1867. He acquired Constant Troyon's *Cows* for 36,000 francs from Febvre in February 1872 (ADR, stock 1868–1873, no. 999).

55 See Durand-Ruel [1939], p. 186.

56 From 1868 until 1873, he bought 168 works by Dupré (see email to author from Paul-Louis Durand-Ruel, 25 February 2014). On 27 March 1870, he bought seven Duprés from Faure for 37,500 francs. In spring 1868, he acquired *Soleil couchant* [location unknown] from Dupré for 9,000 francs (ADR stock, 1868–1873, no. 323).

57 'L'on m'a écrit que des officiers prussiens avaient passé la nuit dans mon salon à faire de la musique du piano...', Jules Dupré to Paul Durand-Ruel, Cayeux-sur-Mer, 21 January 1871 in Venturi 1939, II, pp. 67–69.

58 'Continuez à m'écrire comme vous le faites, vos excellentes lettres me font du bien et me donnent du courage.' Ibid.

59 'J'en ai grand besoin car j'ai des jours de profonde tristesse'. Ibid.

60 Daubigny wrote in November 1870 that the dealer had just commissioned three paintings of Villerville from him. Daubigny's own account book (a copy of which is now in the Département des Arts Graphiques, Musée du Louvre, Paris) reveals several sales to Durand-Ruel.

61 No works by Millet, Rousseau and Delacroix were in the official display and only one by Courbet. There were 10 works by Corot, but these were badly hung in corners and separated from one another. Daubigny showed nine paintings.

62 See exh. cat. Paris 1878.

63 Durand-Ruel later argued that the display was more impressive than that organised by Antonin Proust at the 1889 Universal Exhibition in Paris. See Durand-Ruel [1939], p. 209.

64 Ibid.

65 This is evident from an overview of the 1873 catalogue of his stock, which contained 300 prints after paintings in his stock or which had recently passed through his gallery. There were 28 prints after Corot, 28 after Millet, 24 after Dupré, 20 after Rousseau, 10 after Troyon, seven after Courbet, eight after Diaz, 26 after Delacroix and 23 after Georges Michel. Few prints appeared reproducing the work of the Impressionists.

66 See Galenson and Jensen 2007.

Durand-Ruel and the Market for Modern Art from 1870 to 1873

I would like to thank Paul-Louis Durand-Ruel and Flavie Durand-Ruel for generously making the Durand-Ruel Archives available for research and for offering support through the process of developing this essay. I would also like to thank Sylvie Patry for her reading and assistance and two of her colleagues, Léa Saint-Raymond and Clémence Laurent. This essay is dedicated to my mentor and friend, Robert L. Herbert.

1 Green 1987 and Green 1989.

2 Jensen 1994.

3 Green 1987, p. 59. The Edwards sale (Lugt 31807) has recently been investigated in depth by Léa Saint-Raymond, who has graciously shared with me her research on and photographs of the catalogue and the *procès verbal* (report) in the collection of the Archives de Paris (reference: D42E3 53).

4 Durand-Ruel [1939], p. 171. Also see, for example: '*Le Bel Hamlet au cimetière* (*Hamlet et Horatio*) du catalogue; Delacroix le donna à Alexandre Dumas père, puis il fut acheté 100 francs par Durand-Ruel père (vous lisez bien cent francs!) Aujourd'hui, 21,000 francs en vente publique...', Ravenel 1870b pp. 236–7.

5 Green 1987, p. 66.

6 Isaac Péreire is given a page in the account book beginning in 1868, p. 206. He made some large purchases (46,000 francs) of paintings by Rousseau and Delacroix, among others.

7 Fletcher and Helmreich 2011.

8 Baetens, 2010. See also Whiteley 1983.

9 Baetens 2010, pp. 40–1.

10 Durand-Ruel [1939], pp. 166–71.

11 See Simon Kelly's essay in this book.

12 Jensen 1994, pp. 51–2.

13 The idea of entrepreneurial art dealers was first elaborated by Boime; see Boime 1976. This paradigm is further elaborated and qualified in Jensen 1994.

14 White and White 1965. See also Galenson and Jensen 2007.

15 This role is noted in Green 1987 and Jensen 1994 as well as Distel 1989b.

16 Palmade 1972, p. 125.

17 Ravenal 1870a.

18 ADR, stock 1872–1876, pp. 115–16.

19 Durand-Ruel [1939], p. 184.

20 See Palmade 1972, p. 141.

21 See Simon Kelly's essay in this book.

22 Kelly 2012, pp. 62–3.

23 'Benefices sera à partager entre lui et M. Durand s'il vend ce tableau'. ADR, daybook, 3 February 1872.

24 Helmreich 2011, pp. 65–84.

25 For more on Durand-Ruel's activities in London see the essay by Anne Robbins in this book.

26 Distel 1989b, p. 22.

27 Ibid., p. 24.

28 Duret 1906, pp. 129–31; Wilson-Bareau 2000, p. 163; Durand-Ruel and Durand-Ruel 2011, pp. 284–5; and Kelly 2012 pp. 57–69.
29 ADR, account book 1869–72, p. 170 (no date listed but the exchange was written in last).
30 Durand-Ruel and Durand-Ruel 2011, p. 285.
31 The correspondence with the Impressionists was published in Venturi 1939. See also *Correspondence Pissarro* [1980–1991].
32 Paul Durand-Ruel to Camille Pissarro, 21 January 1871, reproduced in Venturi 1939, pp. 247–8.
33 House 1978.
34 Pissarro (1980–1991], vol. 1, pp. 63–5.
35 The catalogue raisonné of Pissarro's work lists four pictures bought during this London period: one by Durand-Ruel and three by Jules Berthel, so perhaps Berthel was acting as an agent for Durand-Ruel and Pissarro is referring to these four pictures. PDRS 185 or 187, 189 and 192.
36 1871 'The First Annual Exhibition in London of Pictures. The Contribution of the Society of French Artists', ADR, p. 2.
37 House 1978, p. 637.
38 These accounts are first discussed in Wildenstein, 1974–91, I, p. 63 and later in Tucker 1995, p. 57 and Stuckey 1998. A more detailed assessment is provided by Simon Kelly and the figures are more or less confirmed by a perusal of Durand-Ruel's accounts. See Simon Kelly, 'Monet's Commercial Strategy' a talk given at the Musée d'Orsay symposium *Impressionism(s): new projects*, 10–11 December 2009. See also Kelly 2013.
39 Durand-Ruel and Durand-Ruel 2011, p. 284, lists only one Renoir but in fact two are listed in ADR, stock 1868–1873: no. 1131, *Vue de Paris. Pont des Arts*, bought from Renoir in March 1872 for 200 francs; and no. 1470, *Fleurs (pivoines et coquelicots)* bought from Renoir 23 May 1872 for 300 francs.
40 ADR, stock 1872–1876, pp. 99–102 (April 1872).
41 ADR, account book 1872–1876, pp. 186–7 (Monet: February–December 1872), pp. 224–5 (Pissarro: March–December 1872).
42 *Recueil d'estampes* 1873.

Durand-Ruel and the Impressionists' Solo Exhibitions of 1883

I would like to thank Paul-Louis and Flavie Durand-Ruel. I would also like to thank Anne Chaptout, Anne Distel, Isabelle Gaëtan, Simon Kelly, Clémence Laurent, Félicie de Maupeou, Monique Nonne, Edouard Papet, Léa Saint-Raymond, Marie-Claire Rodriguez, Camille Richer, Jennifer A. Thompson, John Zarobell and Coline Zellal.

1 Durand-Ruel to Monet, 22 February 1882, in Paris 2006a, no. 59.
2 Durand-Ruel to Monet, 22 January 1886, Paris, Musée d'Orsay, Paris. ODO 2007-1-19.
3 Dargenty 1883b.
4 The dates are derived from letters, daybooks, or the press (in square brackets), wherever they do not appear in the exhibition catalogues themselves: Boudin [1–25 February] with a preview on 31 January; Monet (1–25 March) with a preview on 28 February; Renoir (1–25 April), Pissarro (1–25 May); Sisley (1–25 June).
5 We have used the terms 'solo', 'individual' and 'monographic' exhibitions here as equivalents to denote exhibitions of works by the same artist, be they presentations of recent works or retrospectives.
6 Gauguin to Pissarro, January–February 1883, in *Correspondence Gauguin* [1984], no. 32.
7 Marriott 1883.
8 See the essay by Anne Distel in this book.
9 Pissarro to Monet, 12 June 1883, in *Correspondence Pissarro* [1980–1991], I, no. 158, p. 217.
10 As opposed to 'painters of the *Petit Boulevard*'. Vincent van Gogh to Theo van Gogh, 10 March 1888, in *Correspondence Van Gogh* [2010], no. 584.
11 Ward 1995.
12 'Assumed an unrivalled place in the historical and commercial construction of modernism' (Jensen 1994, p. 113).
13 Rewald only grants them two short paragraphs (1986b, pp. 309–10).
14 H. Flamans, in *La Vérité*, 20 February 1883, quoted by De Knyff 1976, p. 163.
15 As demonstrated by the archives of the Fondation Taylor, consulted by Marie-Claire Rodriguez. Also see Poggi 2008.
16 However, the 14 works by Manet were spread throughout the gallery's rooms (ibid., p. 33, note 37).
17 I owe these figures to Marie-Claire Rodriguez, who is preparing a thesis on the 'monographic retrospective: emergence of an exhibition form' under the supervision of Pascal Griener and myself (35 exhibitions between 1870 and 1879; email of 23 February 2014), and to Félicie de Maupeou (email of 10 March 2014), author of an unpublished thesis, *Claude Monet et l'exposition*, under the supervision of Frédéric Cousinié and Ségolène Le Men, University of Rouen – University of Paris-Ouest Nanterre La Défense, 2 vols, 2013. This work has identified 2,107 solo exhibitions in Paris between 1855 and 1921 (p. 109).
18 See *Chronique des arts et de la curiosité* of 19 November 1881, no. 36, p. 287: this reference, from Marie-Claire Rodriguez, corrects the date of early 1881, published by Daulte 1959, p. 342.
19 Renoir 1879.
20 Monet to Mme Charpentier, 27 June 1880, WL 186.
21 See Dixon 1998.
22 Signac to Monet, 31 May [1912], Musée d'Orsay, Paris, ODO 2007-1.
23 Monet to Murer, 3 July 1880, WL 189; Monet to Duret, 5 July 1880, WL 191.
24 According to Rewald, there were no sales at all, p. 306, note 14. The picture purchased by Ephrussi on 29 June does not seem to have come from this exhibition (WL 188).
25 Until 7 July. Alice Hoschedé to Ernest Hoschedé [about 23 June 1880], WL 46; Monet to Duret, 5 July 1880, WL 191.
26 Monet to Duret, 2 February 1881, WL 208.
27 Gauguin to Pissarro, 26 September 1879, in *Correspondence Gauguin* [1984], no. 11; ADR, daybook 18 and 25 September 1879, 18 October 1879–28 February 1881.
28 *Gil Blas* 1879; Ward 1995, p. 51.
29 Durand-Ruel Godfroy 1992, p. 48: Durand-Ruel sent 18 paintings by Sisley in 1881, ADR, daybook.
30 ADR, daybook 1 March–5 October 1881, 11 April 1881.
31 Melot 1988.
32 Twenty-five in the catalogue, probably at least two not in the catalogue (Isaacson 1986, p. 378).
33 Sisley to Durand-Ruel, 5 November 1882, quoted in Venturi 1939, II, pp. 56–7.
34 Monet to Durand-Ruel [3 December 1882], WL 305.
35 Monet to Durand-Ruel, 10 November 1882, WL 300.
36 Ibid.
37 Ibid.
38 Renoir to Monet, [1883?], in sales cat. Paris 2006b, no. 116.
39 Monet to Durand-Ruel, 10 November 1882, WL 300; Burty 1883a, p. 3; Alexandre 1892. I would like to thank Anne Roquebert for this last reference.
40 Renoir, quoted in Renoir 1981, p. 270.
41 For the relationship between the crises of the Salon, the development of the market and independent exhibitions, see the admirable analysis by Vaisse, 1995.
42 Sixty in 1881, 31 in 1882 and 73 in 1883, according to Manoeuvre 1998, pp. 189–90.
43 Of a total of 1,680 pictures listed in the 'Pictures Purchased 1877' register, ADR. For the Impressionists, pictures sold before November 1877 have been subtracted.
44 Sixty-eight in 1881 and 89 in 1882, according to estimates made from the daybooks and stock books. Unless otherwise stated, I owe these estimates to Paul-Louis and Flavie Durand-Ruel.
45 Sixty-one in 1881 and 34 in 1882.
46 Durand-Ruel Godfroy 1992, p. 47 (45 in 1881 and 43 in 1882).
47 Forty-four in 1881 and 43 in 1882.
48 Fourteen in 1881 and 24 in 1882.
49 [August or September 1881], in *Correspondence Gauguin* [1984], no. 17.
50 Boudin to Martin, 10 December 1881, Bibliothèque de l'INHA – Collections Jacques-Doucet, MS 212, Paris. The extracts from Boudin's unpublished letters kept at the INHA library and cited in this essay were transcribed by Isolde Pludemacher, who I would like to thank for her generosity.
51 See the essay by Simon Kelly in this book.

52 Boudin to Martin, 10 December 1869, in *Correspondence Boudin – Martin* [2011] no. III, 14, p. 214.
53 Boudin to Martin, 5 February 1881, INHA-Doucet, MS 212.
54 Boudin to Martin, 10 December 1881, INHA-Doucet, MS 212.
55 16 September 1878, WL 138. See Alice Hoschedé to Ernest Hoschedé, 24 and 26 December 1879, WL 39 and 40; Pissarro to Murer [1878] in *Correspondence Pissarro* [1980–1991], no. 54, p. 110.
56 Monet to Duret, 9 December 1880, WL 203: possibly *Apples and Grapes*, about 1879–80, Metropolitan Museum of Art, New York, W 545. On 9 December, Monet sold two still lifes for 1,400 francs.
57 If we include W 549; Monet to Petit, 11 June 1882, WL 276.
58 Durand-Ruel to Monet, 14 December 1883, in sales cat. Paris 2006a, no. 60.
59 Wildenstein 1996, I, vol. I, p. 184.
60 Durand-Ruel to Monet, 15 June 1883, in Paris 2006a, no. 61.
61 Durand-Ruel to Monet, 4 May 1884, ibid., no. 64.
62 See Thomson 1999, pp. 116–28.
63 ADR, daybook, 28 July, 7 and 9 August 1883. Durand-Ruel to Monet, 11 August 1883, in sales cat. Paris 2006a, no. 62.
64 Blanche 1931, p. 115.
65 ADR, daybook, 6 January 1879, 15 January, 15 April and 15 May 1880. In January 1882, the former premises of the Watercolour Painters were sublet to the Banque Nationale (AP, D1P4 636 1876, information provided by Monique Nonne).
66 Monet to Durand-Ruel [22 December 1882], WL 305.
67 Burty 1883a, p. 4. See also Ward 1991.
68 Durand-Ruel 1939, p. 213.
69 Monet to Durand-Ruel, 10 November 1882, WL 300.
70 Boudin to Martin, 17 December 1882, INHA-Doucet, MS 212.
71 Boudin to Martin, 7 January 1883, INHA-Doucet, MS 212.
72 Pissarro to Lucien, 23 April 1883, in Pissarro [1980–1991], I, no. 141, p. 198.
73 ADR, daybook 30 November 1883: the return of these decorations, which may not have been displayed alongside the Impressionists' works, whose exhibitions had closed before the summer!
74 Boudin to Martin, 7 January 1883, INHA-Doucet, MS 212.
75 Labarrière 1883.
76 Monet to Durand-Ruel [5 March 1883], WL 336. These cost the dealer almost 140 francs (ADR, daybook 23 April 1883).
77 Monet to Durand-Ruel, 10 December 1885, WL 638. Durand-Ruel appeared in the catalogue as the lender of four of the 10 works by Monet on display.
78 Sisley in 1888 and Monet in 1889 (with Rodin), exhibiting 145 works, including four lent by Durand-Ruel.
79 Monet to Durand-Ruel, 10 December 1885, WL 638.
80 Durand-Ruel 1939, p. 213.
81 We have been unable to find the Sisley exhibition catalogue and this section of our analysis is based on press reports.
82 I would like to thank Paul-Louis Durand-Ruel for pointing out these two purchases by De Bellio (Renoir, *Melon*, stock 1876, no. 517, no purchase date; Monet, *Chalets by the Water*, 15 October 1872, stock 1868–1873, no. 1140) and one purchase by Caillebotte (Monet, *View of Rouen*, stock 1876, no. 533, no purchase date, W 216).
83 Bergerat 1883.
84 Labarrière 1883.
85 'The attributions are fantasies apart from a few names' (repr. in De Knyff, 1976, p. 161).
86 From the gallery's archives and thanks to work by Claire Durand-Ruel in PDRS, 2005, III, p. 362.
87 Monet to Durand-Ruel, 10 February 1883, WL 322.
88 Monet to Durand-Ruel, 15 February 1883, WL 329.
89 ADR, daybook, 28 July 1883.
90 Boudin to Martin, 7 February 1883, INHA-Doucet, MS 212.
91 'Your presence is absolutely necessary', wrote Durand-Ruel to Monet on 7 February 1883 (ADR).
92 Pissarro to Lucien, 13 May 1883, in *Correspondence Pissarro* [1980–1991], I, no. 148, p. 206.
93 Boudin to Martin, 7 February 1883, INHA-Doucet, Paris, MS 212.
94 Geffroy 1883, p. 1 (55); Jacques 1883b ('about 60'). The estimate of 80 provided by Flavie Durand-Ruel is based on the movements of works registered in the archives but we do not know how many works were finally hung. The same is true of Renoir: 85 pictures were moved compared with 70 in the catalogue.
95 With the exception of Sisley, *The Forge at Marly-le Roi*, 1875 (Musée d'Orsay, Paris).
96 He contacted De Bellio (*Capucines*, not catalogued, W 548), Graff for *La Galette* and Delius (W 630 and 631).
97 Geffroy 1883, p.2.
98 Durand-Ruel to Pissarro, 18 December or October 1882, BnF, Estampes, Paris, Arch. Pissarro microfilm, partially published in Buffévent 2005, p. 19.
99 Sometimes intended as genuine retrospectives, such as Diaz in 1849, Rousseau in 1850 and Corot in 1858, for example, as pointed out to me by Simon Kelly.
100 Dargenty 1883a.
101 Bailey, in New York 2012, pp. 175–6.
102 Monet to Durand-Ruel, 9 February 1883, WL 320.
103 Durand-Ruel to Pissarro, 18 December or October 1882, BnF, Estampes, Paris, Arch. Pissarro microfilm, partially published in Buffévent 2005, p. 19.
104 Boudin to Alfred Stevens, 28 July 1891, recalling a conversation in 1880, in Honfleur 1998, p. 193.
105 Gauguin to Pissarro [January–February 1883], in *Correspondence Gauguin* [1984], no. 32.
106 Burty 1883b.
107 *The Gorge at Varengeville*, no. 33, lent by Berard, W 730.
108 Monet to Pissarro [June 1883], WL 357.
109 Durand-Ruel to Monet, 13 February 1883, ADR.
110 See for example ADR, daybook, 15 January 1883 (the sums varied by several hundred francs, but the general balance remained the same), and AP, D1P4 636 1876.
111 ADR, daybook, 17 February 1883.
112 Boudin to Martin, 7 February 1883, INHA-Doucet, MS 212. Estimated by Ward 1991, p. 617, note 60: 11,615 francs.
113 ADR, daybook, 28 February, 31 March, 30 April, 31 May and 26 June 1883.
114 Durand-Ruel to Monet, 6 March 1883, ADR.
115 17 February 1883, sold to M. Gallimard, 79, Rue Saint-Lazare, no. 12 in the catalogue: *Bacalan, View from the Quay*, sold for 800 francs, stock no. 225.
116 20 February 1883, *Deauville Harbour* (no. 126), purchased for 200 francs from the artist in December 1882, stock no. 1695, sold to Roll for 500 francs.
117 AP, 'Constitutions de sociétés', D31 U3 502, registered on 23 December 1881.
118 *The Pond, autumn*, sold on 27 March 1883 and paid for on 3 July, 300 francs, to M. Cotinaud: stock no. 1237. Possibly no. 35 in the exhibition.
119 Burty 1883a, p. 4.
120 Boudin to Martin, 10 April 1883, INHA-Doucet, MS 212.
121 ADR, daybook, 9 August 1883.
122 Pissarro to Monet, 12 June 1883, in *Correspondence Pissarro* [1980–1991], I, no. 158, p. 216.
123 Ibid.
124 ADR, invitation letter for the Boudin preview on 31 January, reproduced in De Knyff, 1976, p. 160.
125 Boudin to Martin, 4 March 1883, INHA-Doucet, MS 212.
126 Burty 1883b.
127 Hustin 1883a.
128 Boudin to Martin, 7 January 1883, INHA-Doucet, MS 212.
129 Boudin to Martin, 4 March 1883, INHA-Doucet, MS 212.
130 Quoted in De Knyff 1976, p. [165].
131 Geffroy 1883, p. 2.
132 ADR, daybook, 27 February 1883.
133 Hustin 1883b.
134 Durand-Ruel to Monet [March 1883], in sales cat. Paris 2006a, no. 60.
135 See Ganz and Kendall 2007, pp. 193–200.
136 This 'sketch' came back from the boulevard de la Madeleine on 2 July 1883 (ADR, daybook).
137 Durand-Ruel to Monet, 6 March 1883, in sales cat. Paris 2006a, no. 61.
138 Truffaut 1955.
139 De Baecque 1991, I, p. 155.
140 Durand-Ruel [1939], p. 158.
141 Ibid., p. 212.

142 Durand-Ruel to Monet, 21 and 23 February 1885, in sales cat. Paris 2006a, no. 65. See the key analysis on the subject in Bouillon 1986.
143 Pissarro to Durand-Ruel [late May–early June 1884], in *Correspondence Pissarro* [1980–1991], I, p. 303. We put forward this hypothesis on the basis of his drafts for the 'Société des Irrégularistes' (published in Herbert 2000).
144 For 3,000 francs he rented the '*grand salon* with access to the boulevard' from the brother of a painter who was holding an exhibition there (Durand-Ruel to Grenier, 19 November 1883, ADR), then 37,500 francs from a tailor (Durand-Ruel to Monet, 3 February 1884, in sales cat. Paris 2006a, no. 63).
145 Durand-Ruel to Monet, 25 February 1885, ibid., no. 65.
146 He had previously been on the third floor (AP, D1P4 973 1876).
147 Durand-Ruel to Monet, 15 March 1885, in sales cat. Paris 2006a, no. 65.
148 At Boussod & Valadon, Degas and Monet in 1888, then Monet in 1890, Sisley at Petit in 1888.
149 Arsène Alexandre, *Quarante années de vie artistique*, unpublished manuscript, Paris, BCMN, MS 0632, p. 90.
150 But between 1855 and 1921, Félicie de Maupeou counts fewer than 130 exhibitions for Durand-Ruel, compared with 370 for Petit, or rather 8% and 22% of the total number (Maupeou 2013, p. 120).
151 Haskell 1992.

Durand-Ruel and Impressionist Collectors in France

With this short essay, I would like to pay tribute to the memory of Charles Durand-Ruel, who granted me access to the family archives. This research, which focused initially on the history of works kept in public collections in France and on the career of Renoir, led me to write *Les Collectionneurs des impressionnistes* (Distel 1989b), a book that, completed by an embryonic bibliography, provides an introduction to the subject in question. I hope my immodest references to my own articles, for which I ask readers to forgive me, will demonstrate the extent of my debt to the Durand-Ruel Archives. I would also like to thank Paul-Louis Durand-Ruel for having welcomed me in turn, and for indulging my repeated requests, not to mention Flavie Durand-Ruel for the helpful assistance she so kindly provided. Precise references to the archives that already appear in the chronology will not be repeated here.

1 Zola [1986], p. 244.
2 This probably refers to Louis Gustave Mülhbacher, the head of a large vehicle manufacturing business founded by his grandfather. The sale of his estate (Galerie Georges Petit, Paris, 13–15 May 1907) only included earlier artworks, including French painting from the eighteenth century. He was a client of Durand-Ruel.
3 Paris, BCMN, donated by Mme Asselain, granddaughter of Roger Marx.
4 Musée Marmottan Monet, Paris. Monet's account book MM 5160 (1); according to Durand-Ruel's books, Hoschedé bought several lots of works by the future Impressionists on 17 February and 28 April 1873. Faure also bought works by Degas, Manet and Sisley in the spring of 1873.
5 In 1876, we can see the names of Faure, Chocquet and Dollfus, and of the dealers Durand-Ruel (the exhibition took place on his premises), Legrand, Mme Latouche, Martin and Poupin; Charpentier, De Bellio, Duret, Fromenthal and Manet in 1877; initials point with some certainty to Hoschedé, Caillebotte, Henri Hecht, Henri Rouart, Charles Haviland, Henri Vever and, in my opinion, Chocquet, who was already present in the form of his portrait by Cézanne. No dealer names appear in 1877; the exhibition was organised by the painters in a rented apartment.
6 See Valéry 1938.
7 Robida 1958; Rewald 1969; Niculescu 1970; Bonniot 1973; Callen 1974; Reiley-Burt 1975; Callen 1988; Distel 1989a.
8 See Bodelsen 1968. Hoschedé's first, voluntary, sale on 13 January 1874 shows De Bellio, Rouart, Baudry and Laurent-Richard; Durand-Ruel purchased works by Pissarro, Monet and Sisley through the intermediary Hagerman. The minutes of the sale organised by Monet, Morisot, Renoir and Sisley on 24 March 1875 lists Rouart, Arsène Houssaye, Hoschedé, Petitdidier (Emile Blémont), Arosa, Chesneau, Charpentier, Dollfus, Hecht and other names that remain obscure alongside those of the dealers, including Durand-Ruel, and the painters themselves.
9 I would like to thank Paul-Louis Durand-Ruel for this detail, taken from the *Memoirs* of Paul Durand-Ruel.
10 Hélène Adhémar, in Rewald and Weitzenhoffer 1984, pp. 5–71.
11 Distel 1981. According to his account book, Albert Hecht was a client of Durand-Ruel (he had purchased a Rousseau in 1872 for the sum of 5,000 francs, the most expensive of all the works he bought). However, his Manet paintings were purchased from the artist or at auction; his paintings by Degas and Monet from the artists; and his Pissarro paintings from the artist, from Latouche and at the 1878 Hoschedé auction, alongside a Sisley, all at prices cheaper than those offered by Durand-Ruel. His brother Henri Hecht had similar tastes as a collector.
12 Paper on Charles Hayem given by Benjamin Foudral, 14 June 2014, at the Société de l'histoire de l'art français (awaiting publication in the society's journal).
13 Distel 1997a.
14 Distel 2010.
15 Vauxcelles 1908.
16 Zola [1986], p. 245.
17 Theodore Haviland was also a client of Durand-Ruel.
18 Rewald 1986a.
19 Lespinasse 2010; Tellier 2010.
20 Durand-Ruel to Depeaux, 10 February 1906, Paris, ADR, quoted in Lespinasse 2010, p. 150.
21 Distel 2002.
22 Rewald 1953, p. 52 (22 April 1899).

Durand-Ruel and America

I am deeply grateful to Paul-Louis Durand-Ruel and Flavie Durand-Ruel for providing access to the Durand-Ruel Archives. Many other colleagues provided invaluable research assistance and support: Matthew Affron, Ashley Boulden, Melanie Bourbeau, Carolyn Carr, Kathryn Costello, Isabelle Gaëtan, Gloria Groom, Catherine Herbert, Adrienne Jeske, Kimberly Jones, Patrice Mattia, Monique Nonne, Sylvie Patry, Remi Poindexter, Joseph Rishel, Christopher Riopelle, Anne Robbins, Naina Saligram, Rick Sieber, Andrew Slavinskas, Susan Stein and Evan Towle.

1 Durand-Ruel to Fantin-Latour, 21 August 1886. Venturi, 1939, II, p. 252.
2 Cortissoz 1925, pp. 269–70.
3 Morton founded Morton Bliss & Co., represented New York State in Congress, and served as Minister to France, the 22nd Vice-President of the United States and the 31st Governor of New York.
4 ADR, daybook.
5 Morton's collection was sold at Leavitt Art Galleries, New York, 28 February–1 March 1882. He later commissioned paintings from Léon Bonnat, Carolus Duran and others. Toulouse 2003, p. 41.
6 Strahan 1872, pp. 221–6 and 1879–80, II, pp. 15–24.
7 Venturi 1939, II, p. 169 and Whiteley, 1996, Durand-Ruel and Durand-Ruel and Durand-Ruel 2014, pp. 53–4, 146.
8 Gibson's considerable acquisitions from Durand-Ruel in July 1872 fuelled art world gossip. Fidell-Beaufort and Welcher 1982, p. 54. Fell visited the gallery on 29 June 1869 with Borie and acquired paintings by Diaz, Dupré and Isabey for 23,000 francs; Borie purchased a book on Decamps for 20 francs. ADR, daybook.
9 *American Register*, vol. 51, 27 March 1869, p. 3, cited in Fidell-Beaufort, 2000, p. 105, note 22.
10 7 January 1870, Lucas 1979, vol. 2, p. 313 and PDRS 138.
11 PDRS 296 was bought by Cole for Angell on 2 January 1875 for 500 francs. ADR, daybook. For Angell and Cole, see exh. cat. London and West Palm Beach 2005, pp. 23, 126, 134.

12 Exh. cat., New York 1993, p. 203 and A215, A395.
13 Hirshler 1998, pp. 179–86.
14 Lindsay 1985, pp. 13–14 and Mathews 1984, p. 152.
15 The Monet, W 174, was purchased from Durand-Ruel on 9 April 1881. The Pissarro has not been identified.
16 Katherine Cassatt to Alexander Cassatt, 10 December 1880. Mathews, 1984, pp. 154–5.
17 On 31 March 1883, Durand-Ruel shipped their purchases to England: Monet (*Sunset*, W 328), Cassatt (*Woman Driving*, probably B 69), Renoir (*Head of a Young Girl*, likely D 639), and a Raffaëlli acquired from Georges Petit. ADR, daybook.
18 Another was Anna Riddle Cassatt, cousin of the Cassatts and widow of a Pennsylvania Railroad president, who purchased several Impressionist paintings with Mary Cassatt in 1883–4. Lindsay 1985, p. 15.
19 Mary Cassatt to Alexander Cassatt, 27 April 1884, Mathews, 1984, pp. 183–4. She acquired W 194 from Durand-Ruel for Thomson.
20 Mary Cassatt to Alexander Cassatt, 2 September 1886. Mathews 1984, pp. 200–2.
21 Cassatt's extensive activities as an advisor to American collectors are described in Hirshler 1998.
22 Curatorial files, Metropolitan Museum of Art and Weitzenhoffer 1981, p. 125.
23 Weitzenhoffer 1981, p. 126.
24 Pissarro and Venturi, 1939, I, p. 48.
25 Morton and King were members of the Stanley Club, an American society in Paris, and active in the subscription fund for the Statue of Liberty. ADR, letterbook 1884–5, Levi P. Morton Papers, Manuscripts and Archives Division, New York Public Library.
26 *Galignani's Messenger*, 21 May 1883. Scrapbook 5, 1881–4, Levi P. Morton Papers, NYPL.
27 A list of 72 paintings for 'Exposition en Boston' appears in the daybook for 30 May 1883. According to an undated list in a Durand-Ruel letterbook, eight additional works, including three gouaches by Pissarro, were also sent.
28 The gallery's expenses for the shipment were 13 francs, 12 June 1883, ADR, daybook
29 Durand-Ruel to Root & Tinker, 22 June 1883, ADR letterbook. Weitzenhoffer 1984, p. 75 suggests that Durand-Ruel travelled to Boston, but it has not been possible to document this trip.
30 Boston 1883, pp. 201–17.
31 *The Art Amateur*, vol. 9/no. 5, October 1883, p. 90.
32 *The Independent*, 20 September 1883, p. 7.
33 *The Chicago Tribune*, 16 September 1883, p. 7.
34 Monet to Durand-Ruel, 27 June and 28 July 1885, Venturi 1939, I, pp. 293–5.
35 Pissarro wrote to Lucien on 21 January 1886: 'Today they are making a selection from my works' and noted in an undated letter that Durand-Ruel was making visits to Guillaumin, Seurat and Signac, 'to ask for some canvases for the exhibition in America'. Pissarro [2002], pp. 65–6.
36 Durand-Ruel to Edmond Turquet, 18 September 1885. Archives Nationale, Paris F/21/4054B. I am grateful to Monique Nonne for this reference.
37 20 October 1885, ibid.
38 Paul and Charles Durand-Ruel, merchant and student aged 54 and 21, arrived in New York on 25 March 1886 on the S.S. *Amerique*. Documents from *ancestry.com* and Huth 1946, p. 239.
39 The American Art Association galleries were booked for its annual Prize Fund Exhibition in May.
40 *The Critic*, 17 April 1886, p. 195.
41 *Brooklyn Eagle*, 11 April 1886, p. 2.
42 *The Nation*, vol. 42/no. 1085, 15 April 1886, p. 328.
43 Venturi 1939, II, p. 160 and *The Evening Star*, 15 May 1886, p. 5.
44 Durand-Ruel recalled seeing Probasco's collection before it was shipped to New York for sale at the American Art Association on 18 April 1887, an auction that Durand-Ruel claimed to have arranged. Whiteley 1996. *New York Times*, 6 January 1887, p. 5 and *The Art Amateur*, vol. 22/ no. 2, January 1890, p. 30.
45 Information on sales provided by Paul-Louis Durand-Ruel in a lecture at the Frick Collection, 7 May 2012. The value of works sold was reported in *The Art Amateur*, vol. 16/no. 2, January 1887, p. 27. Included in this figure may be a 10,000 franc advance that Durand-Ruel received from the American Art Association on 4 February 1886 against future sales. Bolas, 1998, p. 215, note 33. Huth, 1946, p. 244 estimated sales around $18,000 based on a $5,500 tariff paid by Durand-Ruel.
46 Abel Williard Kingman and his son Alden Wyman Kingman were merchants. Alden travelled Europe in 1891–2 before moving to the western United States where he died in 1898, suggesting that his father was dually responsible for these acquisitions and their later sales via Durand-Ruel. Documents on *ancestry.com* and *New York Tribune*, 22 September 1898, p. 9.
47 Camille Pissarro to Lucien Pissarro, July 1886. Pissarro [2002], p. 77.
48 Twelve lists of paintings for the American Art Association in New York appear in the ADR daybook between 15 and 28 September 1886. Some changes may have been made: two Cassatt paintings were crossed off a list made on 28 September.
49 Durand-Ruel to Fantin-Latour, 21 August 1886. Venturi 1939, II, p. 252. One Fantin-Latour painting was in the spring 1886 exhibition.
50 Puvis refused to participate in the 1886 exhibition but lent seven works in 1887. Venturi 1939, II, p. 93 and 25 August 1886. ADR, daybook.
51 Duncan lent 20 works, including the two Delacroix canvases, *The Death of Sardanapalus* (fig. 20) and *Interior of a Dominican Convent* (cat. 18). Schnall provided 17, and Suzanne Manet lent the *Execution of Maximilian*. ADR, daybook.
52 See *The Critic*, 30 October 1886, p. 148 and *Chicago Daily Tribune*, 30 December 1886, p. 3.
53 Protests against the tax-free status accorded to Durand-Ruel started in November 1885. *New York Tribune*, 13 November 1885, p. 5 and 23 November 1885, p. 2.
54 *The Critic*, 28 May 1887, p. 271.
55 *The Art Amateur*, vol. 17/no. 1, June 1887, p. 2 and *The Studio*, vol. 2/no. 10, April 1887, pp. 177–8.
56 *The Studio*, ibid.
57 *The Durand-Ruel Collection of French Paintings*, Moore's Art Galleries, New York, 5–6 May 1887.
58 Nonne 2002, pp. 104–6.
59 *New York Times*, 6 May 1887, p. 8 and 7 May 1887, p. 5.
60 *The Art Amateur*, vol. 17/no. 1, June 1887, p. 2. An annotated copy of the catalogue in the Durand-Ruel Archives provides information on sales and the names of three buyers: Albert Spencer, Catholina Lambert and Theodore Haviland.
61 Royal Cortissoz in *Chicago Daily Tribune*, 11 June 1887, p. 13 and *The Studio*, vol. 3/no. 1, July 1887, pp. 1–6.
62 A list of paintings returning from New York appears in the ADR daybook for 1–2 September 1887.
63 He was in New York between 14 November 1887 and 3 March 1888 according to the passenger list for the S.S. *La Bourgogne* and a letter in the Durand-Ruel Archives indicating that he was expected back in Paris in early March.
64 Nothing sold at Moore's auction on 30 November–2 December 1887, but several works were purchased at the American Art Association on 21–3 February 1888, ADR Annotated auction catalogues. Each auction included pictures that were exhibited in 1887.
65 PDRS 688.
66 W 733. Andrews and Lambert also purchased three Sisleys apiece from the gallery in 1888. Durand-Ruel London, Paris and Baltimore 1992–1993, p. 55, note 77. PDRS 154, 252, 269, 270, 284, 298, 398, 658, 684, 687, 792, and 828.
67 Many remain in the Johnson collection, Philadelphia Museum of Art (cats 921, 1027, 1043, 1051, 1062 and 1063), but others were sold, including Puvis's *Autumn*, acquired from Durand-Ruel in summer 1888 and exchanged in November for four reductions of the Amiens murals.
68 The American and French operations were separate businesses that sold paintings to one another, kept independent books, and used different stock numbers.
69 He recalled making nine trips to America between 1886 and 1898. Durand-Ruel and Durand-Ruel 2014.
70 *The Collector*, vol. 2/no. 4, 15 December 1890, p. 44.
71 Venturi 1939, II, pp. 215–16. *New York Times*, 13 October 1892, p. 4.

72 See Smith 2009, pp. 81–94 for Harris Whittemore's purchases from various dealers.
73 Pissarro to Lucien, July 1886. Pissarro [2002], pp. 77–9.
74 In an 1895 letter to an unknown recipient, Durand-Ruel estimated that over 300 Monets were in America. 3 March 1895, ADR, letterbook. For Monet's reception in America, see Weitzenhoffer, 1984 and Zafran, New York 2007, pp. 81–151.
75 *The Art Amateur*, vol. 21/no. 4, September 1889, p. 88. *Old Masters on exhibition at Durand-Ruel's*, 1890, and *The Collector*, 1 November 1890, p. 4.
76 New York 1993, pp. 62–5.
77 The Havemeyer collection is richly described and documented in Weitzenhoffer 1986 and New York 1993.
78 New York 1993, pp. 208–9.
79 *New York Times*, 21 March 1894, p. 12. In 1899 when a gas explosion damaged the building, its upper floors were occupied by men's and women's tailors. *New-York Daily Tribune*, 6 August 1899, p. 12. A second fire broke out in the building in 1902, at which time the family had an apartment on the top floor. *Daily People*, 2 February 1902, p. 2.
80 For the Chicago exhibitions, see *Chicago Daily Tribune*, 20 May 1888, p. 27; 18 November 1888, p. 32; 26 February 1890, p. 8; and 5 March 1895, p. 9. The gallery lent 26 paintings by Monet (cat. 45), Pissarro, Renoir, Sisley, Degas and others to the 1890 Interstate Exposition. Jensen 2007, pp. 511–25. Twenty Monets were lent by the gallery to the Art Institute in 1895. *Daily Inter Ocean*, 24 February 1895, p. 23.
81 Weisberg 1997 and Neal 1996.
82 The exhibitions were noted in *The Pittsburg Bulletin* on 11 January 1896, p. 12; 14 November 1896, p. 12; 30 October 1897, p. 12; and 3 December 1898, p. 12.
83 Two Pissarros were lent to the 7th Annual St Louis Exposition in 1890 and at least 20 works to the *Trans-Mississippi and International Exposition* in Omaha, Nebraska in 1898.
84 Durand-Ruel lent Impressionist paintings to Boston dealer Eastman Chase in May 1888 and March 1891. Foxcroft Cole had introduced them by asking Chase to suggest a venue for Durand-Ruel's exhibitions. Cole to Chase, 23 November 1886, Archives American Art, microfilm 996 and *Boston Herald*, 6 May 1888, p. 12.
85 *The Denver Evening Post*, 19 November 1897, p. 9. This venture may have been recommended by gallery client Alden Wyman Kingman, who lived in Colorado in the 1890s.
86 Durand-Ruel reportedly visited the first Carnegie International in November 1896. *The Pittsburg Post*, 29 November 1896, p. 7.
87 Durand-Ruel and Georges arrived unannounced in Cleveland on 10 November 1893, visited the collections of Alfred A. Pope and Jeptha H. Wade II, and stayed for dinner with the Popes. A year later, Pope wrote to Whistler: 'We expect a visit from the old gentleman, Durand-Ruel, this week.' 27 November 1894, Glasgow University Library, MS Whistler, P640. I am grateful to Melanie Bourbeau of the Hill-Stead Museum for this material.
88 He arrived in New York on 23 October 1893 and travelled to Chicago to see the 'very interesting' Exposition. Durand-Ruel to Mary Cassatt, 9 February 1894, ADR, letterbook. Durand-Ruel saw Arthur J. Eddy on 2 December 1894 and John A. Lynch the following evening. Eddy to Whistler, 5 December 1894, Glasgow University Library, MS Whistler E7.
89 Hill's impressive Barbizon collection was formed with the help of several New York dealers, including Durand-Ruel. Joseph prepared a hanging plan for Hill's gallery in May 1891, and both brothers visited several times in the 1890s. Hancock 1991, pp. 23, 30, 52.
90 In August 1894 Durand-Ruel wrote to Hallowell that he was abandoning plans to open a branch in Chicago, a proposal they had discussed the previous year. Weitzenhoffer 1986, pp. 124–5.
91 Exh. cat. Boston 1905.
92 Works by Monet, Renoir, Cassatt, Sisley and Pissarro were shown at the Robert Lindsay Galleries in Philadelphia in April while 103 Impressionist paintings inaugurated the new Toledo Museum of Art building in November. Mary Cassatt's *The Child's Bath* (cat. 4) was lent to the Summer Exhibition in Worcester. For New Orleans: *Times-Picayune*, 28 December 1905, p. 9.
93 Venturi 1939, II, p. 219.

Durand-Ruel and Germany

I would like to thank Flavie Durand-Ruel, Paul-Louis Durand-Ruel, Ute Haug, Michael Mohr, Anncristin Scarlett Schlothauer and Jasper Warzecha for their support in my research.

1 Lichtwark to the Commission 14 January 1901, Lichtwark 1896–1920, vol. 9, p. 39.
2 For Lepke, see Walter-Ris 2003, p. 21.
3 ADR, stock 1866–1873.
4 See Walter-Ris 2003, p. 25f.
5 See Paul 1988 and Ludewig 2012.
6 Teeuwisse 1986, p. 107 and p. 284; note 209 wrongly gives a figure of 23 pictures.
7 See ADR, paintings on deposit 1875–1884.
8 See Paul 1988, p. 12, no source given.
9 See Paul, 1988, p. 14f.
10 See Ziegler 2001, p. 48 and Schlenker 2007, p. 235.
11 See Ziegler 2001, pp. 43–9, 59, notes 15–17. He bought Monet's *Le chemin de la cavée* (*Path between Hills*) (W 760) from Durand-Ruel on 13 January 1890 (but actually delivered before that date). The exact date for the sale of Monet's *Barque de la Seine à Jeufosse* (*Barge on the Seine at Jeufosse*) (W 915) is not known. ADR.
12 Heilbut 1890.
13 See Bastek 2001, p. 46f.
14 See Luckhardt 2001, p. 35f.
15 See Schlenker 2007, p. 235f. and p. 248.
16 See ADR, paintings on deposit 1881–1898.
17 Durand-Ruel to Behrens, letters of 15 October 1890, 12 December 1891, 22 February 1892, 1 March 1892, ADR.
18 For Degas, see letters of Durand-Ruel to Heilbut, 22 October 1891, 5 November 1891, 16 February 1892, 22 February 1892, 1 March 1892, ADR.
19 Degas, *Portrait of Joséphine Gaujelin* and *Portrait of Emma Dobigny*, see Bastek 2001, p. 50, fig. p. 98. See ADR, paintings on deposit 1884–1901.
20 Heilbut to Amsinck, 12 December 1889. Hamburger Kunsthalle, Kunstbibliothek, Archive No. 81. See Schlenker 2007, p. 260.
21 Heilbut to Amsinck, 18 December 1889. Ibid.
22 Durand-Ruel to Heilbut, 5 October 1892, ADR.
23 Durand-Ruel to Heilbut, 18 January 1893, ADR. He was even planning to expand to Berlin, but until now there has been no evidence of a mutual transaction in Berlin.
24 Ibid.
25 Lichtwark to the Commission, 1 June 1893, Lichtwark 1896–1920, vol. 2, p. 159.
26 See Lichtwark 1883a, b; Hopp 1986–7, p. 51f.; Howoldt 2013, p. 173.
27 See ADR, paintings on deposit 1881–1898. For the exhibition, see exh. cat., Hamburg 1895; Wallsee 1895; Schiefler 1985, p. 104; Kern 1989, pp. 79, 252.
28 See Walter-Ris 2003, pp. 26f.; Teeuwisse 1986, pp. 220–41.
29 Max Liebermann, 'Hugo von Tschudi' in Liebermann 1978, p. 117.
30 Ibid.
31 See Paul 1993, p. 356.
32 See ADR, paintings on deposit 1884–1901.
33 See Paul 1993, p. 357.
34 See ibid., p. 216 and Dorrmann 2001, p. 27 (W 776).
35 See Dorrmann 2001. For other collectors of French moderns see Pophanken/Billeter 2001.
36 See Paul 1993, p. 357.
37 See ibid., p. 358f.
38 See ADR, paintings on deposit 1884–1901; catalogue of the International Art Exhibition, Dresden 1897, catalogue no. 410, 486; See Paul 1993, pp. 359f (W 277, P 308).
39 See Paul 1993, pp. 109f.
40 Liebermann to Gustav Pauli, March 1908, in Liebermann 1995, p. 70.
41 See Faass 2013, p. 167 and exh. cat., Bremen 1995–1996.
42 For Degas, Manet and Courbet, see the sales dates in ADR, daybook 14 May 1897, 30 October 1897, 17 December 1897. For these works in the Max

Liebermann collection, see Haus/Hedinger 2013, nos. SL 17, 19, 40, 109 and also Janda Tatzkow 2013–14, nos. 17, 18, 42, 113.

43 Liebermann to Linde, 8 May 1897. In Liebermann 2012, vol. 2, p. 102. See ADR, paintings on deposit 1884–1901. Somewhat later, Liebermann also recommended to Linde Degas's *Place de la Concorde*; see Liebermann to Linde, 28 June 1897, in ibid., p. 124.

44 See Haug/Hedinger 2013, SL 19, ADR, paintings on deposit 1884–1901.

45 See Eberle 1995, No. 1882/1.

46 Liebermann to Graul, 12 November 1896, in *Correspondence Liebermann* 2012, vol. 2, p. 53.

47 See Hedinger 2013, p. 19. See also ADR, daybook, 8 July 1897.

48 Liebermann 1898, pp. 193–6, illustration without page number.

49 Durand-Ruel to Heilbut, 21 December 1896, ADR.

50 Durand-Ruel to Heilbut, 5 October 1892, ADR.

51 Durand-Ruel to Moritz Meyer, 2 November 1893, ADR.

52 'Commissionär' in the original German is defined as 'a person responsible for carrying out a task on behalf of a private client.' Meyer's office was at No. 2 Grosse Johannisstrasse, near the city hall market; see Hamburg address book for 1896, pp. 367 and 1029.

53 See ADR, paintings on deposit 1884–1901.

54 The location of the Berlin exhibition is unknown. The fact that the pictures were subsequently sent on to Berlin is established by a letter from Durand-Ruel's business partner Destrée to Lichtwark, 9 December 1896, Hamburger Kunsthalle Archive.

55 See ADR, paintings on deposit 1884–1901.

56 Sold on 9 December 1896 for 8,000 francs. See ADR, paintings on deposit 1884–1901.

57 See ADR, paintings on deposit 1884–1901. See Paul 1993, p. 357f.

58 See ADR, paintings on deposit 1884–1901. See Paul 1993, p. 357.

59 Elias 1912, p. 106. Julius Elias had known Durand-Ruel since 1890, and claimed that he was responsible for awakening his interest in hotel exhibitions. But in fact Durand-Ruel had already formulated the idea in a letter to Heilbut in 1892.

60 From 8 to 12 May, 29 pictures that had been delivered from Berlin could be viewed in Hamburg's Hotel de l'Europe. See ADR, paintings on deposit 1884–1901 and ADR, daybook, 1897.

61 See Leppien 1986, p. 129.

62 See Kessler 2004, vol. 3, p. 55. Lichtwark also gave an account of this visit to the Commission. Letter of 1 January 1897, Lichtwark 1896–1920, vol. 5, p. 89.

63 Seidlitz 1897, p. 60. Von Seidlitz had been in correspondence with Durand-Ruel since 1894. At the beginning of 1896, he had a picture by Degas sent to him at the *Pan* headquarters in Berlin, which he bought for his personal collection. Durand-Ruel to Seidlitz, 20 January 1896, ADR.

64 On 20 September 1897, he bought a garden picture by Sisley for 5,000 francs, ADR, daybook. For Stern and the Berlin collectors see Pucks 1996–7.

65 ADR, daybook 1897. Weidenbusch bought three pictures by Degas in 1897, one by Sisley and one by Renoir. See *Gemäldegalerie II. Abteilung des Privatgelehrten Hans Weidenbusch zu Wiesbaden*, Lempertz auctions, Cologne 1899, with illustrations.

66 See ADR, paintings on deposit 1884–1901. In addition, Theodor Behrens bought a picture by Zandomenghi from the exhibition.

67 See Voss 1897.

68 See ADR, paintings on deposit 1884–1901.

69 Durand-Ruel to Lichtwark, 31 January 1898. Hamburger Kunsthalle Archive.

70 See ADR, paintings on deposit 1884–1901, at a price of 8,750 francs. See also Durand-Ruel to Lichtwark 1 January 1898, Hamburger Kunsthalle Archive.

71 See ADR, paintings on deposit 1884–1901.

72 Lichtwark to the Commission, 27 September 1898, Lichtwark 1896–1920, vol. 6, p. 212.

73 In 1896 he got Durand-Ruel to send a Monet painting to the Berlin dealer Pächter, with the possible intention of a subsequent further deal. Durand-Ruel to Meier-Graefe, 21 January 1896, ADR.

74 Joseph Durand-Ruel to Meier-Graefe, 2 September 1898, ADR. See also Durand-Ruel 2007, p. 211.

75 See ADR, paintings on deposit 1884–1901.

76 See Echte and Feilchenfeldt 2011–13, vol. 1, pp. 39–68.

77 Durand-Ruel to Meier-Graefe, 28 September 1898, ADR.

78 See Berding 2012, p. 129ff., pp. 164, 486. For Durand-Ruel's deliveries See ADR, paintings on deposit 1884–1901.

79 See Negendanck 1998, p. 65f., and ADR, paintings on deposit 1884–1901.

80 See Echte and Feilchenfeldt 2011–13, vol. 1, p. 23f.

81 Ibid., vol. 1, p. 164f.

82 See ADR, paintings on deposit 1884–1901.

83 Ibid.

84 Echte and Feilchenfeldt 2011–13, vol. 1, pp. 165–7.

85 Ibid., p. 302.

86 See ADR, paintings on deposit 1901–1914. In 1905 he delivered 12 pictures to this address, ibid.

87 See Teeuwisse 1986, p. 256ff.

88 See Hansen 2005–6, p. 256f.

89 These were most important places, but there were other shows elsewhere. See ADR, paintings on deposit 1901–1914.

90 Meier-Graefe 1904, vol. 3, p. 40ff. See also Echte and Feilchenfeldt 2011–13, vol. 3, p. 30.

91 See Wolf 1913, p. 313.

92 Courbet's *Stormy Sea*, see Pauli 1913, p. 45 (sold in 1921); Monet, *Camille*, (W 65); Manet, *Portrait of Zacharie Astruc* (RW 92). The two paintings by Monet (W 411) and Renoir (DAUBERVILLE 378) were all lost in the war.

93 See Paul 1993, pp. 367, 368, 370, 379.

94 ADR, paintings on deposit 1901–1914.

95 Manet, *Faure as Hamlet* (RW 256) and *Portrait of Henri Rochefort* (RW 366).

96 Monet, *Le Déjeuner* (W 132) and Renoir, *La Fin de Déjeuner* (D 288).

97 Lichtwark to the Commission, 1 October 1904, Lichtwark 1896–1920, vol. 12, p. 203ff.

98 See Nierhoff 2002–3; Hansen 2002–3, pp. 186f.

99 See *Kampf um die Kunst* 1911.

100 See exh. cat. Cologne 2012.

101 See Elias 1912, p. 106.

102 See Alexandre 1911.

103 See Meier-Graefe 1913, p. 206.

Durand-Ruel's Conquest of London

The writing of this essay would not have been possible without the support and input of Christopher Riopelle, as well as Paul-Louis and Flavie Durand-Ruel at the Durand-Ruel Archives.

1 *The Times*, 17 January 1905; Flint 1984, p. 207.

2 *Athenaeum*, 4 February 1905, p. 129.

3 Monet to Durand-Ruel, 8 March 1905, Venturi 1939, II, p. 402.

4 'Sur le pavé de Londres ou la tempête nous avait poussés…' Moreau-Nélaton, 1925, p. 105.

5 ADR, daybook, 1870.

6 Durand-Ruel [1939], pp. 175–6.

7 Ibid.; Whiteley 1996, chap. 7, p. 36.

8 *Hamlet*, by Ambroise Thomas. Lunn 1870.

9 Durand-Ruel [1939], p. 177.

10 Fletcher and Helmreich 2012, p. 56.

11 The daybooks recall record sustained sales of reproductions of pictures to Victor Delarue, print publisher, based at 10 Chandos Street, London, as well as Paris.

12 Durand-Ruel [1939], p. 162.

13 ADR, daybook, 1 August 1864–1 April 1867; also daybook 2, 1 April 1867–22 May 1869.

14 Durand-Ruel [1939], p. 176. Wallis bought the lease of the French Gallery from Gambart in 1867. Maas 1975, p. 223.

15 A 'local provisoire'. Ibid.

16 Ibid., p. 175.

17 Moreau-Nélaton 1925, pp. 102–3. Moreau-Nélaton 1927, p. 75.

18 Daubigny to La Rochenoire, signed Lisle Street, Leicester Square, 15 October 1870: 'J'ai vu Durand-Ruel…'.

19 Moreau-Nélaton 1927, p. 75.

20 'Daubigny s'enflammait pour lui et, mis au courant des difficultés extrêmes de sa position, l'emmenait chez Durand-Ruel,

qu'il invitait d'autorité à accueillir sur le champ ses ouvrages. En déférant à l'injonction, le négociant sauvait la vie à Claude Monet. D'autres palettes du même bord que la sienne, et non moins déshéritées du sort, bénéficiaient bientôt de la même sollicitude agissante…', Moreau-Nélaton 1925, p. 105.

21 4 January 1871. See Moreau-Nélaton 1927, p. 75.

22 'bijou de musée'. Moreau-Nélaton 1927, p. 80.

23 All three artists signed in on Friday 25 November 1870 in the following order: 'Claude Monet'; 'A. Legros'; 'De la Rochenoire'. Visitor Book vol. III (21 June 1870–11 September 1871), MS Dulwich Picture Gallery Archive.

24 On 3 December 1870 in London, Monet gave a painting to an exhibition organised for the 'benefit of the distressed peasantry of France'. It was *Sea Shore at Trouville*. House 1978; Korn 2004, p. 192.

25 Moreau-Nélaton 1925, p. 105. The encounter presumably happened by early December 1870, since Daubigny was on the organising committee for the show in aid of the French peasantry, for which pictures had to be submitted by 3 December. See House 1978.

26 Monet and his wife first lived on Arundell Street, perhaps at no. 11, between Leicester Square and Piccadilly Circus. They later moved further west to 1 Bath Place (Mrs Theobald's), Kensington, now 183 Kensington High Street. House 1978, p. 641, note 22. Daubigny lived on Lisle Street, Leicester Square, before moving to 13 Canning Place, Kensington, by November 1870. Miquel 1975, III, p. 697.

27 Monet quoted by Thiébaut-Sisson, *Le Temps*, 26 November 1900, p. 23. See House 1978.

28 Soon after 21 January 1871. See House 1978, p. 637.

29 Kessler 2011, p. 311 (Paris, 28 November 1903, Saturday). The author is grateful to Christopher Riopelle for drawing her attention to this reference.

30 The Café Royal had been set up in 1865 at 68 Regent Street. It is now the Hotel Café Royal. Deghy and Waterhouse 1955.

31 Elder 1924, p. 24, on Daubigny: 'C'est grâce à lui que je suis rentré en relation avec Durand-Ruel, et ce jour-là j'eus la vie sauve. Voici comment : En [18]70, refugiés à Londres, nous fréquentions, Pissarro, moi et quelques autres, un café où les français tenaient assises: Daubigny s'y montrait parfois. Il apprit que nous étions des confrères, voulu voir notre peinture. Et le voilà qui s'exalte, s'emballe, jure de nous venir en aide, à Pissarro et à moi. "Je vais vous envoyer un marchand" dit-il. En effet, arrive bientôt le père Durand qui avait transporté sa boutique à Londres pour la durée de la guerre. Daubigny m'avait spécialement recommandé à lui. Nous ne fûmes pas longs à nous entendre…'.

32 Paul Durand-Ruel to Pissarro, 21 January 1871 in Durand-Ruel and Durand-Ruel 2014, p. 175. BnF, Est., Arch. Pissarro microfilm.

33 *Correspondence Pissarro* [1980–1991], I, pp. 63–4; also Venturi 1939, I, p. 27.

34 Consigned in the stock book in October 1872, Paris: two pictures purchased in January 1871, '*Sydenham*' and '*Norwood*'; two in June of the same year: Untitled and '*Effet de Neige*'.

35 Durand-Ruel to Pissarro, 21 January 1871 in Durand-Ruel and Durand-Ruel 2014, p. 175.

36 *Athenaeum*, 5 November 1870, no. 2245, p. 597.

37 Durand-Ruel erroneously writes '159 New Bond Street'. Durand-Ruel [1939], p. 176.

38 Starting in 1853. See *Art Journal*, June 1853, No. 180, 'Gallery of German Paintings'.

39 Fletcher and Helmreich 2011, pp. 303–4.

40 Rosa Bonheur (1858); William Holman Hunt (1860); Gustave Doré (1868).

41 Durand-Ruel [1939], p. 176.

42 *Athenaeum*, 8 November 1873, no. 2402, p. 601.

43 *Athenaeum*, 9 May 1874, no. 2428, p. 638.

44 Following the relocation of the Royal Academy to Burlington House in 1867, the area saw an ever-growing concentration of art galleries around Piccadilly, a couple of which (including the Doré Gallery) were already established on New Bond Street, a busy commercial street specialising in luxury goods. See Fletcher and Helmreich 2011, p. 56.

45 Ibid.

46 Ibid., p. 52.

47 Founded 1823, and one of the most established exhibiting institutions in England.

48 Durand-Ruel to Fromentin, 18 January 1871, 1995, *Correspondence Fromentin* [1995], p. 1627.

49 *Art Journal*, February 1871, pp. 43–4.

50 In first Society exhibition, second hanging: 1871 (London 1871a), no. 27, Greuze, 'From the Gallery of Count Koucheleff Besborodko' [1834–1862]; nos. 131 & 132, 'two works by M. Carot [sic]' from the Demidoff gallery (*Athenaeum*, 11 March 1871, no. 2263, p. 309). In the second show, 1871 (London 1871b), 71 pictures on loan from Laurent-Richard's collection, nos. 74–144.

51 Durand-Ruel to Fromentin, 18 January 1871. *Correspondence Fromentin* [1995], p. 1627.

52 See exh. cat. London 1871c 'Opinions of the press', *The Observer*: 'Perhaps we may be permitted to rejoice in the announcement that [the exhibition] is intended to be the first of an annual series, without accepting as an evil omen its present location in the so-called "German Gallery".'

53 Durand-Ruel to Fromentin, 18 January 1871. *Correspondence Fromentin* [1995], p. 1627.

54 Durand-Ruel to Fromentin, 20 January, Ibid., p. 1628.

55 London-based Jean-Baptiste Faure was also a lender; numerous English private collections contributed pictures.

56 No. 1273, *Repose*; no. 1274, *Entrance to Port of Vionville* [sic], both belonging to the artists; a third picture by Monet was exhibited, no. 1282, *Camille*, belonging to M. Luquet. See House 1978.

57 No. 1276, *Winter Scenery*, and no. 1277 *Upper Norwood*.

58 'By C. PISSARO [sic], two winter subjects of much natural truth' (*Art Journal*, September 1871, no. 33, p. 218).

59 Respectively nos. 167 and 552 in the French edition of the International Exhibition catalogue.

60 No. 1194, 'Delacroix, L'Amende Honorable, appartient à M.C. Edwards'.

61 *Athenaeum*, 11 March 1971, no. 2263, p. 309 (the second hanging of the first exhibition of the Society of French Artists). The Regnault that drew the attention of the critic was no. 108 in the catalogue (*The Summary Execution under the Moorish kings of Granada*), 1870, Musée d'Orsay, Paris.

62 *Athenaeum*, 17 December 1870, no. 2251, p. 808.

63 First exhibition of the Society of French Artists, first hanging, 1870 (London 1870): no. 26 Ingres, *Odyssey*, no. 29 *Iliad*. See *Athenaeum*, 17 December 1870, no. 2251, p. 808.

64 London 1871a: no. 27, Greuze; London 1871b: no. 74, Boilly; nos. 75 and 76, Chardin.

65 'Opinions of the Press', extract from *The Illustrated London News* in exh. cat. London 1871b.

66 London 1871a: no. 84, 'Louis David, *The Death of Marat*'.

67 'Eighth exhibition of the Society of French Artists', spring 1874 (London 1874a), no. 131.

68 'Sixth exhibition of the Society of French Artists', spring 1873 (London 1873a), no. 13, 'Delacroix, *Death of Sardanapalus*', *Art Journal*, June 1873, p. 176.

69 *Art Journal*, May 1873, p. 137.

70 See exh. cat. London 1873a, no. 13.

71 The pictures in the sixth exhibition were displayed in two rooms: the ground floor and 'First Floor Gallery', see London exh. cat. 1873a, p. 7. Nos. 13, 54, and 68 were on the ground floor.

72 London 1873a, no. 54. Musée d'Orsay, Paris.

73 Ibid., no. 68, Musée d'Orsay, Paris.

74 London 1872a, no. 26, 'Manet's Studio at Batignolles, Paris', Musée d'Orsay, Paris.

75 Lilley 2014.

76 Painter and potter (1841–1901). See exh. cat. London 1872a. The Durand-Ruel Archives record many instances of Bouvier ceramics being sent to London: see daybook no. 4, entries for 13 and 20 February 1873.

77 London 1873a, 'Pottery by Charles Cazin' (1841–1901).

78 London 1872a, nos. 123–7. Also no. 93 (Wilkie) and no. 84 (Hunter); nos. 1 and 97 (Edwards).

79 In September 1871.
80 Its first secretary (for the first and second shows) was Arthur A. Hutton, who had worked as a secretary for the French gallery in late 1860s (Maas 1975).
81 Ibid., p. 215.
82 See also GUW. Works by Whistler were shown in the winter exhibitions of 1872 and 1873. London 1872c, nos 30, 38 and 122; London 1873a, no. 110.
83 Lawrence Alma-Tadema, *A Picture Gallery in Roman Times*, 1874, Townley Hall Art Museum; commissioned by Gambart between 1871 and 1874. I am grateful to Prof. Elizabeth Prettejohn for drawing my attention to the painting and its connection with Durand-Ruel. See also Maas, 1975, p. 242.
84 London 1874a, no. 10 (see *Athenaeum*, 9 May 1874, no. 2428, p. 639). 'Ninth exhibition of the Society of French Artists' (London 1874b): nos. 8, 11, and 53, Mrs Alma-Tadema (see *Athenaeum*, 21 November 1874, no. 2456, p. 683).
85 London 1872c, nos. 30, 38, 122; London 1873a: nos. 109, 112; London 1873b: no. 110.
86 London 1872b, no. 77, Edwards, *London Bridge*; no. 96, Daubigny, *Old Chelsea*.
87 London 1874a: no. 41, Daubigny, *St Paul's from the Surrey Side*. The painting is now in the collection of the National Gallery, London. See reviews in *Athenaeum*, 9 May 1874, no. 2428, p. 639; *The Era*, 31 May 1874. I am grateful to Sarah Herring for alerting me to the latter review.
88 London 1872a, no. 113, *'Sydenham'*.
89 London 1872c, no. 9, Monet, *St Germain l'Auxerrois*; no. 31, Monet, *Green Park*.
90 London 1873a, no. 114, Monet, *Houses of Parliament*.
91 'I began ... by slipping a few canvases by these two painters into my exhibitions'. Durand-Ruel [1939], p. 180.
92 London 1871a: no. 36, Monet, *'Entrance to Trouville Harbour'*; no. 38, Pissarro, *'Snow Effect'*; No. 41, Pissarro, *'View in Upper Norwood'*.
93 *The Times*, 22 April 1873, p. 12. Quoted in Flint 1984, p. 34.
94 See John Zarobell's essay in this book.
95 Manets shown in London 1872a: nos. 15, 24, 31, 72, 105, 106, 110. In London 1872b: nos. 19, 36, 38, 91, 104, 127. In 1872c: no. 49.
96 *Athenaeum*, 24 February 1872, no. 2313, p. 247.
97 London 1872b, Degas: nos. 4, 95 (*Robert le Diable*, first version of cat. 13), Sisley: nos. 24, 28, 44, 83 (*Winter*; possibly the *'Effet de Neige'* bought by Durand-Ruel on 12 March 1872?).
98 London 1872c, no. 37.
99 London 1873b, no. 62, *Monisot (Mdlle)* [sic].
100 Durand-Ruel bought his first four Sisleys in March 1872, stock nos. 1173–75. House 1978, p. 637, note 13. Contrary to what was said, the dealer and the painter did not meet in London but in Paris after the Franco-Prussian War.
101 London 1873b, no. 111, *A Factory* (*The Robec Stream*, 1872, Musée d'Orsay, Paris). See Fowle 2006, pp. 142–3.
102 Works by Degas in London 1873a: no. 33, *Getting Ready for the Start*; no. 79, *A Race Course in Normandy*; no. 100, *Horses at Grass*. Korn 2004, p. 195. The transactions took place on 25 April and 7 May 1873. Exh. cat. Paris, Ottawa and New York, 1988–1989, p. 221. Faure had also purchased one Monet and two Pissarros from the gallery.
103 'The extreme realistic party in French painting ... will assemble in great force at M. Durand-Ruel's gallery [Deschamps had taken over] in April, with M. Degas at their head'. (*Art Monthly Review*, 29 February 1876, p. 15.) Korn 2004 argues that Degas may have been more successful in England because of more numerous and direct contacts with his British counterparts via Whistler.
104 London 1872c, not catalogued. Huth paid £168 for the painting on 7 December 1872 (ADR, stock 1824). Exh. cat. Paris, Ottawa and New York 1988–1989, pp. 176–7; Korn 2004, p. 194.
105 Ibid.
106 On Hill, see Pickvance 1962.
107 See Korn 2004, pp. 195–6. According to Pickvance 1963 and Korn 2004, the first Degas acquired by Hill was no. 9, *Scène de Ballet*, in the ninth exhibition (London 1874b). In the copy of the catalogue of the ninth exhibition kept in the National Art Library, London, no Degas is listed, and no. 9 is a picture by De Nittis. Hill was to acquire a Monet from Durand-Ruel, *Garden-Orchard Scene with Blossoms and with Poplars*, possibly as early as 1876.
108 Pickvance 1963, p. 258, note 20.
109 'We are informed that the Society of French Artists ... is now entirely under the directorship of the gentleman to whose judgment and lively sense of what is becoming it has owed so much of its individuality of late years.' (*Art Journal*, August 1875, p. 245), Flint 1984, p. 36 (described as referring to Durand-Ruel, while these lines describe Deschamps).
110 *Art Journal*, February 1875, p. 57.
111 *Pall Mall Gazette*, 28 November 1872: Korn 2004, p. 195.
112 *The Times*, 27 April 1874, p. 14.
113 '12th Exhibition of Pictures by Modern French Artists', Deschamps Galleries, April 1876 (London 1876).
114 'Paintings, Drawings and Pastels by Members of "La Société des Impressionnistes".' Dowdeswell Galleries, 20 April–July 1883 (London 1883). See Cooper 1954, p. 23, note 6.
115 The Dowdeswell and Dowdeswell Gallery (as it was known between 1880 and 1886), 133 New Bond Street, dealt in modern English painting, including Whistler. Fletcher and Helmreich 2011, p. 300.
116 'Exposition Impressionniste', White's Gallery, 13 King Street, July 1882 (London 1882), in Korn 2004, p. 208. See Wedmore 1883: 'M. Durand-Ruel ... held a little exhibition of the works of these artists last summer in a small room near St James's Street, but the gallery was not ample enough, and the representation of the men, though interesting, was inadequate, nor was it properly proportioned'. Quoted in Flint 1984, p. 48.
117 'England knows them [the Impressionists] only by scattered examples, and by the small and scarcely representative collection of their painting which M. Durand Ruel showed in England last summer'. (*The Artist*, 1 May 1883, pp. 137–8).
118 'An exhibition of pictures and sculpture, by a group of artists of the French School', Dudley Gallery, Egyptian Hall, Piccadilly, May 1884 (London 1884). In Korn 2004, p. 208.
119 No. 16, Monet, *Petit Bras à Argenteuil*, £160, Dowdeswell Galleries, April 1883.
120 Two Cassatts, three Morisots, seven Degas, seven Monets, eight Sisleys, eight Renoirs and 11 Pissarros (including three watercolours); also 10 Boudins, six John Lewis Browns and three Manets.
121 No. 46, Manet, *Le Pont de l'Europe* (*The Railway*, 1874, National Gallery of Art, Washington). The other picture priced at £400 was no. 6, Degas, *Courses de Gentlemen* (Musée d'Orsay, Paris).
122 Wedmore 1883; in Flint 1984, pp. 46–55.
123 'Exposition des œuvres de P.-A. Renoir', Galeries Durand-Ruel, Paris, 1883 (Paris 1883c).
124 No. 34, Monet, *Chemin de la Carée* [sic], £100.
125 'M. Manet ... in his Pont de l'Europe has painted a woman and child and a bunch of grapes, by no means in his best manner'. (*Daily News*, 3 May 1883, p. 3: cited in Locke 2010, pp. 781–2).
126 Three Renoirs had been seen in the Society of French Artists exhibitions: in the fifth show (London 1872c, no. 37) and the ninth, 1874b no. 12 and no. 75, *'A Ballet Dancer'*, see fig. 70).
127 'We do not see quite all we were hoping to see at the Messrs Dowdeswell's Exhibition ... what has become of Renoir's brilliant vision of a certain festival at Bougival?' (*Standard*, 25 April 1883, cited in Flint 1984, pp. 57–8).
128 'M. Renoir, some of whose work has come too late for cataloguing ...', *Daily Telegraph*, 26 April 1883, cited in Flint 1984, p. 59.
129 Exh. cat. New York 2012, p. 206. The picture was enthusiastically received; Durand-Ruel gave it a price of £600, making it the most expensive in the show.
130 See *The Morning Post*, 26 April 1883, cited in Cooper, p. 23. (According to Cooper, *The Morning Post* was leading the campaign of derision against the Impressionists.) See also *Punch*, 5 May 1883, p. 208.
131 See Flavie and Paul-Louis Durand-Ruel's essay in this book. Only one Degas was sold.
132 Manet died on 30 April 1883. 'M. Manet, whose death early this week at the age of fifty [sic] his brothers are now

mourning . . .' (*Daily News*, 3 May 1883, p. 3:, cited in Locke 2010, pp. 781–2).
133 'Pictures by Claude Monet', Goupil Galleries, London, April 1889 (London 1889).
134 From 1888.
135 From 1898.
136 In 1898, the International Society of Sculptors, Painters and Gravers borrowed pictures by Degas, Monet, Manet, including *The Execution of Maximilian*; in 1901, four pictures, including one Monet, were lent to the Glasgow International Exhibition, see Fowle 2006, p. 153.
137 *Saturday Review*, 26 January 1901, XCI, p. 106. D.S. MacColl, 'Impressionists in London' cited in Flint 1984, p. 159.
138 'Exhibition of Pictures by French Impressionists: Monet, Sisley, Pissarro, Renoir and other Masters', London, Hanover Gallery, spring 1901 (London 1901): 10 Pissarros, nine Renoirs, nine Sisleys, nine Monets, including *Lavacourt under Snow* (see cat. 41). The Durand-Ruel Archives record that the painting left in December 1900 and returned in March 1901.
139 Hanover Gallery, 47 New Bond Street, managed by Messrs Hollender and Cremetti. It had opened by 1880 and exhibited mostly continental art by artists such as Meissonnier, Bonheur and Bierstadt.
140 Monet to Durand-Ruel, 9 February 1901, in Venturi 1939, II, p. 380.
141 Monet to Durand-Ruel, 12 August 1904, in ibid., p. 396.
142 Ibid., I, p. 96, mentions 278 pictures but 315 works are listed in the catalogue.
143 Grafton Galleries, 8 Grafton Street, Bond Street West (see photographs BL24279/001 [façade] to BL24279/006 [restaurant], 1918, in English Heritage Archives). The building, almost completely rebuilt, is now next door to the Sprueth Magers Gallery, 7 Grafton Street.
144 'Paintings by Boudin, Cézanne, Degas, Manet, Monet, Morisot, Pissarro, Renoir, Sisley', Grafton Galleries, January–February 1905 (London 1905).
145 It included 35 Degas, 19 Manets, 55 Monets, 13 Morisots, 47 Pissarros, 59 Renoirs, 37 Sisleys, 10 Cézannes and 38 Boudins; among these 196 came from Durand-Ruel's private collection.
146 *Athenaeum*, 4 February 1905, no. 4032, p. 153.
147 See Waterfield 1991, p. 170.
148 'One of the most beautiful Dining Halls in London [The Grafton Galleries could be] hired for large dinners or for private concerts in the afternoon or evening. Catering arrangements in the hands of M. Benoist of Piccadilly who will give estimates for every class of entertainment'. Newspaper advertisement, 1896 (in Courtauld Institute Library).
149 'Painting and Sculpture, by British and Foreign Artists of the Present Day', Grafton Galleries, 18 February–31 December 1893 (London 1893).
150 'French Masters exhibition', Grafton Galleries, 1 May–July 1903 (London 1903); V. Benoist, Treasurer; N. Marchand, Business Manager; F.A. Lottin, Art Manager. The show included paintings by Carolus-Duran, Desvallières, Devambez, Dinet, Doré, Rouault, etc. and four Renoirs, nos. 152–5, Puvis de Chavannes's *Beheading of Saint John the Baptist*, no. 150, and *Toilet*, no. 151, were sent by Durand-Ruel. (They are now in the National Gallery London.)
151 Everard Meynell, *The Ladies' Field*, Saturday 28 January 1905, vol. XXVIII, no. 359, pp. 311–13.
152 Monet to Durand-Ruel, 28 July–12 August 1904, in Venturi 1939, II, p. 395.
153 Galerie Durand-Ruel, Paris, 9 May–4 June 1904.
154 Everard Meynell, *The Ladies' Field*, Saturday 28 January 1905, vol. XXVIII, no. 359, pp. 311–13.
155 'We have only one thing to regret in connection with the exhibition – namely, the time of its appearance . . . January days in London are often too dark for the proper seeing of pictures.' (*Athenaeum*, 4 February 1905, p. 153).
156 Cooper 1954, p. 28.
157 Rutter, *Sunday Times*, 26 March 1905, p. 5.
158 *Cliffs at Pourville, Sunrise*, 1896–7, (Fondazione Magnani-Rocca, Parma); Morisot, *The Jetty*. See Korn 2004, p. 201.
159 Degas, *Before the Curtain Call*, 1892, now in the Wadsworth Athenaeum, Hartford.
160 Degas, *Seated Dancer (Green Skirt?)* now in the Burrell Collection, Glasgow, and a pastel of dancers.
161 A.B. Hepburn purchased Monet's *Grainstack in Sunlight* (Kunsthaus, Zürich); Sir Hugh Shaw Stewart also bought a Monet, *On the Cliff near Dieppe*, 1897, W 1463. Fowle 2006, pp. 153–4.
162 Now in the National Gallery, London.
163 'A Selection from the Paintings by Boudin, Cézanne, Degas, Manet, Monet, Morisot, Pissarro, Renoir and Sisley', Grafton Galleries, London, January–February 1905.
164 Rutter, *Sunday Times*, 22 January 1905, quoted in Flint 1984, p. 215.

The Critical Fortunes of Paul Durand-Ruel

This brief essay would not have been possible without essential information from the archives about specific pictures but also from agreeable – and provocative – conversations with Paul-Louis and Flavie Durand-Ruel about Paul Durand-Ruel's taste and artistic values and how they evolved (or didn't) from the 1840s well into the twentieth century. I would also like to thank Ashley Boulden for her research assistance and Matthew Affron, Sylvie Patry, Susan Stein and Jennifer Thompson for their support.

1 *1803–1943: Exhibition Celebrating One Hundred Fortieth Anniversary*, 15 November–4 December 1943, Durand-Ruel Galleries.
2 Rewald 1985, p. 197.
3 See Rewald 1961, p. 574.
4 We have entered into the making of this exhibition on Durand-Ruel keenly aware of our fraternal relationship with the grand exhibition organised by the Metropolitan Museum of Modern Art, the Art Institute of Chicago and the Musée d'Orsay in 2006–7: *Cézanne to Picasso: Ambroise Vollard, Patron of the Avant-Garde*.
5 According to Rewald, Durand-Ruel's first Cézanne purchase was an unidentified picture, *Village*, in August 1891. Then in February 1894, he acquired two still lifes from Sara Hallowell in New York (R 426 and R 427). Rewald 1996, vol. I, pp. 285–7. See also Rewald 1989, pp. 12–13. Then in 1896 at the Chabrier estate sale, he acquired the pre-Impressionist still life *The Harvest*, about 1877 (R 301). See Rewald 1985, p. 185, note 92.
6 I am grateful to Flavie and Paul-Louis Durand-Ruel for sharing this insight from Durand-Ruel's memoirs. See Durand-Ruel and Durand-Ruel 2014, p. 117. For *The Hanged Man's House* (R 202) see Rewald, 1996, pp. 152–3.
7 On the relationship between Cézanne and Vollard and the circulation of Cézanne's work among collectors and artists before 1895 see Jensen 2006, pp. 29 and 41–2. On the role of Pissarro, see Rewald 1961, p. 573.
8 Following Rewald 1996, the 18 Cézannes that Durand-Ruel bought at the Chocquet sale are R 202 (not catalogued, for Camondo), R 220, R 275, R 277, R 296 (not catalogued), R 312, R 315, R 316, R 329, R 337, R 348, R 375, R 393, R 436, R 506, R 618, R 671 (not catalogued), and R 719. According to Rewald, Durand-Ruel kept six of the unsold pictures in his private collection at the recommendation of his son Joseph (R 275, R 316, R 329, R 348, R 296, and R 506). See Rewald 1996, p. 223 and Rewald 1989, p. 128, note 36.
9 Durand-Ruel sold *Mardi-Gras* (R 618) to Shchukin in 1904. Kostenevich 2006, p. 244.
10 *View of the Domaine Saint-Joseph* (R 612) was the only Cézanne sold from the 1913 Armory Show when the Metropolitan Museum of Art Purchasing Committee bought the painting from Vollard in March 1913. Rewald 1989, pp. 203–7.
11 I am grateful to Sylvie Patry for bringing this letter to my attention. Durand-Ruel to Renoir, 27 April 1908, *Correspondence Renoir – Durand-Ruel* [1995], II, p. 29. Durand-Ruel wrote regarding an exhibition he organised in April–May of that year with works by Monet, Cézanne, Renoir, Pissarro, Sisley, André and d'Espagnat. Of these, almost half were Renoirs. See p. 250, notes 118–19.
12 Ibid. [Trans. Ashley Boulden.] Such views were of course common; it is likely that

Mary Cassatt advised Mrs. Havemeyer in 1909 to divest herself of her Cézannes. See Weitzenhoffer 1986, pp. 191–3. In 1909, Joseph would buy two Cézannes (R 219 and R 623) on consignment from Mrs H.O. Havemeyer. Rewald 1989, pp. 122–5.

13 The 10 Cézannes Durand-Ruel exhibited at the Grafton in 1905 were all acquired at the Chocquet sale: R 220, R 275, R 296, R 312, R 316, R 329, R 337, R 348, R 506 and R 719.

14 Durand-Ruel 2013, p. 223. I am indebted to Flavie Durand-Ruel for providing me with her essay.

15 *Emil Gauguin, the Artist's Son*, about 1878–9 (Metropolitan Museum of Art, New York) was not in the exhibition catalogue. See Durand-Ruel 2013, p. 222.

16 For Durand-Ruel's discussion of the crash, see Durand-Ruel [1939], II, p. 213.

17 Gauguin wrote to his agent Daniel de Monfreid on 12 September 1893 to say he had been to see Durand-Ruel to discuss an exhibition. Frèches-Thory 2004, p. 84. Durand-Ruel and Gauguin corresponded in October and November to arrange the terms of the exhibition. Durand-Ruel produced the invitations, posters, and exhibition catalogues and took a commission on sales; in exchange, Gauguin agreed to leave some of the paintings on deposit after the exhibition. Durand-Ruel 2013, p. 225.

18 Cahn and Groom 2004, p. 345.

19 On the reactions to the exhibition in the press, see Frèches-Thory 2004, p. 86.

20 Gauguin 2003, p. 188, quoted in Frèches-Thory 2004, pp. 86–7. See also Durand-Ruel 2013, pp. 226–7.

21 Degas bought *Te faaturuma (The Brooding Woman)* and *Hina Tefatou (The Moon and the Earth)*. Cahn and Groom 2004, p. 345. The latter was acquired by Degas after the exhibition in an exchange with Gauguin. Durand-Ruel 2013, p. 226.

22 Durand-Ruel 2013, p. 227.

23 Ibid.

24 On 19 January 1895, Durand-Ruel wrote to Gauguin that it was 'absolutely impossible to consider the matter' and that 'business is bad at the moment and I am not buying anything'. Durand-Ruel 2013, p. 227. [Trans. Ashley Boulden.]

25 The preparatory canvas (R 116) was cat. 112 as '*Island Grande Jatte*'. *Bathers at Asnières* (R 98) was cat. 170 as '*Bathing*'. The drawings were listed collectively as cat. 133, '12 Studies'.

26 See for example the reviews 'French Impressionists,' *The New York Times*, 28 May 1886, where *Bathers at Asnières* is described as 'among the most distressing paintings shown,' and 'Paintings for Amateurs', *The New York Times*, 10 April 1886, where the figures are described as 'bags of boneless outline, and ugly outline at that.'

27 *Correspondence Pissarro* [1980–1991] II, no. 306, January 1886, pp. 15–16.

28 Ibid., no. 348, 30 July 1886, pp. 64–6. [Trans. Rewald 2002, p. 80.]

29 Ibid., no. 587, pp. 348–50. Letter to Esther, 5 May 1890. Pissarro wrote to his niece, 'Art is indeed the expression of thought, bought also of *sensation*, above all *sensation* ...' [Trans. Buffévent, in PDRS vol. I, p. 217. Buffévent's emphasis.]

30 PDRS no. 828. In 1887, Durand-Ruel borrowed the painting for *Les XX* exhibition in Brussels and bought it back from Davis in 1899. See pp. 544–5.

31 *Exposition Maximilien Luce*, 16 October–1 November 1899. The group show was *Exposition*, 10–31 March 1899.

32 For a good review of the state of Vincent's paintings immediately following his death, including the 10 canvases returned in 1895 to Theo's widow Johanna from Durand-Ruel, where they had been on consignment after the death of Père Tanguy in 1894, see Stein 2005, pp. 29–30. I am grateful to Susan Stein for this reference.

33 Theo van Gogh to Dr Gachet, Paris, mid-September 1890, Gachet 1953, n.p. Theo van Gogh had by this time fallen out with Boussod & Valadon. Theo received a definite answer from Durand-Ruel later that month and told Emile Bernard on 18 September that Durand-Ruel had refused. [Trans. Rewald 1956, pp. 412–13.]

34 Theo died on 25 January 1891.

35 For a discussion of Vollard's dealings with Van Gogh's work in 1890s, see Pascoe Pratt 2006, pp. 57–8.

36 I am grateful to Flavie and Paul-Louis Durand-Ruel for sharing this letter with me in the archives. Durand-Ruel to Pissarro, 17 October 1890. [Trans. Ashley Boulden.]

37 Galenson and Jensen 2007, p. 158.

38 Jampoller 1986, p. 51.

39 *Correspondence Pissarro* [1980–1991], II, no. 597, letter to Theo van Gogh, 7 October, 1890. See p. 359, note 1. [Trans. Ashley Boulden.] Theo had organised a Pissarro exhibition at Boussod & Valadon in February.

40 Halévy 1995, p. 204. [Trans. Ashley Boulden.] I am grateful to Sylvie Patry for bringing the diary and this excerpt to my attention.

41 These artists were not without merit, even if outside the canonical company we have come to exclusively associate with Durand-Ruel. Artists such as John Lewis Brown and Desboutin were among his early holdings. Loiseau, Moret, Zandomeneghi, D'Espagnat, André and Maufra appear frequently in his stock books and figured in the travelling exhibition that Durand-Ruel organised from 1905 to 1908 in Toledo, Cincinnati, Pittsburgh, St. Louis, and Buffalo. Caroline Durand-Ruel Godfroy's *Catalogue Critique Maxime Maufra* is forthcoming.

42 Kahnweiler and Crémieux 1971, p. 32. I am indebted to Sylvie Patry for bringing this part of the interview to my attention.

SELECT BIBLIOGRAPHY

Catalogues Raisonnés

[B] BERHAUT 1994
M. Berhaut, with S. Piétri, *Gustave Caillebotte. Catalogue raisonné des peintures et pastels*, Paris 1994.

[P] BROWN-PRICE 2010
A. Brown-Price, *Pierre Puvis de Chavannes*, 2 vols, New Haven and London 2010.

CACHIN 2000
F. Cachin, with M. Ferretti-Bocquillon, *Signac. Catalogue raisonné de l'oeuvre peint*, Paris 2000.

[CMR] CLAIRET, MONTALANT AND ROUART 1997
A. Clairet, D. Montalant and Y. Rouart, *Berthe Morisot, 1841–1895. Catalogue raisonné de l'oeuvre peint*, Montolivet 1997.

[D] DAUBERVILLE 2007–12
G-P. and M. Dauberville, with C. Fremontier-Murphy for vol. I, *Renoir. Catalogue raisonné des tableaux, pastels, dessins et aquarelles*, 4 vols, Paris 2007–12.

[D] DAULTE 1959
F. Daulte, *Alfred Sisley. Catalogue raisonné de l'oeuvre peint*, Paris 1959.

[DB] DOHME BREESKIN 1970
A. Dohme Breeskin, *Mary Cassatt: A Catalogue Raisonné of the Oils, Pastels, Watercolors, and Drawings*, Washington 1970.

[F] FERNIER 1978
R. Fernier, *La Vie et l'oeuvre de Gustave Courbet. Catalogue raisonné*, 2 vols, Lausanne and Paris 1978.

[H] HELLENBRANTH 1976
R. Hellenbranth, *Charles-François Daubigny 1817–1878, Catalogue raisonné*, Morges 1976.

[J] JOHNSON 1986–2002
L. Johnson, *The Paintings of Eugène Delacroix: A Critical Catalogue*, 5 vols, Oxford 1986–2002.

[L] LEMOISNE 1954
P-A. Lemoisne, *Degas et son oeuvre*, Paris 1954.

[MN] MOREAU-NÉLATON 1921
E. Moreau-Nélaton, *Millet raconté par lui-même*, 3 vols, Paris 1921.

[PDRS] PISSARRO AND DURAND-RUEL SNOLLAERTS 2005
J. Pissarro and C. Durand-Ruel Snollaerts, with A. de Buffévent and A. Champié, *Pissarro. Catalogue critique des peintures*, 3 vols, Milan and Paris 2005. (English edition: *Pissarro: Critical Catalogue of the Paintings*, Milan and Paris 2005.)

[R] REWALD 1996
John Rewald, with W. Feilchenfeldt and J. Warman, *The Paintings of Paul Cézanne: A Catalogue Raisonné*, 2 vols, New York 1996.

[ROBAUT] ROBAUT 1965
Alfred Robaut, *L'Oeuvre de Corot. Catalogue raisonné et illustré, precede de l'Histoire de Corot et de ses oeuvres par Étienne Moreau-Nélaton*, 5 vols, Paris 1965.

[RW] ROUART AND WILDENSTEIN 1975
D. Rouart and D. Wildenstein, *Edouard Manet. Catalogue raisonné*, 2 vols, Lausanne and Paris 1975.

[S] SCHULMAN 1999
M. Schulman, *Théodore Rousseau, 1812–1867. Catalogue raisonné de l'oeuvre peint*, Paris 1999.

[W] WILDENSTEIN 1996
D. Wildenstein, *Monet, le triomphe de l'impressionnisme*, Cologne and Paris 1996.

[WL] WILDENSTEIN 1974–1991
D. Wildenstein, *Claude Monet. Biographie et catalogue raisonné*, 5 vols, Lausanne and Paris 1974–1991.

Articles and Books

AHRENS 2013
A. Ahrens, 'Ein Präludium über Malerei. Frühe Begegnungen Max Liebermanns mit französischer Malkunst in Berlin und Weimar', in exh. cat. Berlin 2013, pp. 10–21.

ALEXANDRE 1892
A. Alexandre, 'Degas', *Paris*, 9 September 1892.

ALEXANDRE 1911
A. Alexandre, 'Durand-Ruel. Bild und Geschichte eines Kunsthändlers', in *Pan*, vol. 2, no. 4, 1911, pp. 115–22.

[ANONYMOUS] 1870a
[Anonymous], 'Nouvelles', in *Revue internationale de l'art et de la curiosité*, vol. III, no. 4, 15 April 1870, pp. 348–52, no. 12, 24 April 1870, p. 66, and no. 19, 8 May 1870, p. 75.

[ANONYMOUS] 1870b
[Anonymous], 'Nouvelles', in *Chronique des arts et de la curiosité*, no. 22, 29 May 1870, p. 87.

[ANONYMOUS] 1876
[Anonymous], 'Concours et expositions', in *Chronique des arts et de la curiosité*, no. 19, 6 May 1876, p. 171.

[ANONYMOUS] 1883
[Anonymous], 'À travers l'art', in *L'Art moderne*, 1883, p. 16.

[ANONYMOUS] 1884
[Anonymous], 'Le Congrès du canal de Suez', in *Le Monde illustré*, 21 February 1884, pp. 126–7.

[ANONYMOUS] 1885
[Anonymous], 'Les impressionnistes français', in *L'Art moderne*, no. 25, 21 June 1885, pp. 197–8.

[ANONYMOUS] 1886a
[Anonymous], 'The Impressionists. II', in *New York Mail and Express*, 10 April 1886, n.p.

[ANONYMOUS] 1886b
[Anonymous], 'Exhibition of the "Plein-Airistes",' in *The Nation*, 15 April 1886.

[ANONYMOUS] 1886c
[Anonymous], 'The Impressionist Pictures', in *The Studio*, New York, new series no. 21, 17 April 1886.

[ANONYMOUS] 1988
[Anonymous], 'Sammler der frühen Moderne in Berlin', in *Zeitschrift des deutschen Vereins für Kunstwissenschaft*, vol. 42, no. 3, Berlin 1988, pp. 47–62.

ARGENCOURT 1984
L. d'Argencourt, 'Bouguereau et le marché de l'art en France', in *William Bouguereau*, exh. cat. (Musée du Petit Palais, Paris, Musée des Beaux-Arts, Montreal and Wadsworth Atheneum, Hartford 1984–1985), Paris 1984, pp. 95–103.

ASMODÉE 1892
Asmodée, 'Profils et silhouettes, amateurs et marchands', in *Le Guide de l'amateur d'oeuvres d'art*, Paris, June 1892.

ASSOULINE 2002/4
P. Assouline, *Grâces lui soient rendues. Paul Durand-Ruel, le marchand des impressionnistes*, Paris 2002. (English edition: *Discovering Impressionism: The Life of Paul Durand-Ruel*, trans. W. Wood and A. Roberts, New York 2004.)

BAETENS 2010
J.D. Baetens, 'Vanguard Economics, Rearguard Art: Gustave Coûteaux and the Modernist Myth of the Dealer-Critic System', in *Oxford Art Journal*, vol. 33, no. 1, 2010, pp. 25–41.

BASTEK 2001
A. Bastek, 'Die Sammlung Erdwin und Anthonie Amsinck', in exh. cat. Hamburg 2001, pp. 46–51.

BECKER 1988
H. S. Becker, *Les Mondes de l'art*, Paris 1988.

BELLONY 2005
A. Bellony, *John Rewald. Histoire de l'art et photographie*, Paris 2005.

BERDING 2012
B. Berding, *Der Kunsthandel in Berlin für moderne angewandte Kunst von 1897 bis 1914*, Munich 2012.

BERGERAT 1883
E. Bergerat, 'Claude Monet', in *Le Voltaire*, 26 March 1883, n.p.

BIEDERMANN 2001
H. Biedermann, 'Die Sammlungen Adolf Rothemundt und Oscar Schmitz in Dresden', in Pophanken and Billeter 2001, pp. 209–34.

BIJVANCK 1892
W.G.C. Bijvanck, *Un Hollandais à Paris en 1891. Sensations de littérature et d'art*, Paris 1892.

BLANC 1869
C. Blanc, 'Salon de 1869', in *Le Temps*, 19 May 1869.

BLANCHE 1931
J.-E. Blanche, *La Troisième République. 1870 à nos jours. Les Arts plastiques*, Paris 1931.

BODELSEN 1968
M. Bodelsen, 'Early Impressionist Sales 1874–94 in the Light of Some Unpublished Proces-Verbaux', in *Burlington Magazine*, vol. CX, no. 783, June 1968, pp. 331–48.

BODELSEN 1970
M. Bodelsen 'Gauguin, the Collector', in *Burlington Magazine*, vol. CXII, no. 810, September 1970, pp. 590–4.

BOIME 1976
A. Boime, 'Entrepreneurial Patronage in Nineteenth-Century France', in E. Carter II, R. Forster and J.M. Moody (ed.), *Enterprise and Entrepreneurs in Nineteenth- and Twentieth-Century France*, Baltimore and London 1976, pp. 137–207.

BOLAS 1998
G.D. Bolas, *The Early Years of the American Art Association, 1879–1900*, Ph. D. diss., City University of New York 1998.

BONA 2012
D. Bona, *Deux soeurs. Yvonne et Christine Rouart, les muses de l'impressionnisme*, Paris 2012.

BONNIOT 1973
R. Bonniot, *Gustave Courbet en Saintonge*, Paris 1973.

BOUILLON 1986
J.-P. Bouillon, 'Sociétés d'artistes et institutions officielles dans la seconde moitié du XIXe siècle', in *Romantisme*, no. 54, 1986, pp. 89–113.

BROCKHOUSE 2008
R. Brockhouse, *The Royal Alexandra Theatre: A Celebration of 100 Years*, Toronto 2008.

BUFFÉVENT 2005
A. de Buffévent, 'A Painter and his Age: A Biography and Critical Reception', in Pissarro and Durand-Ruel Snollaerts 2005 (English edition), 'Un peintre et son époque. Biographie et fortune Critique' (French edition) I, pp. 95–322.

BURTY 1883a
P. Burty, 'Les Paysages de M. Eugène Boudin', *La République française*, 4 February 1883, pp. 3–4.

BURTY 1883b
P. Burty, 'Les Paysages de M. Claude Monet', *La République*, 27 March 1883.

CAHN AND GROOM 2004
I. Cahn and G. Groom, 'Chronology of Gauguin's Life: 1848–1903', in exh. cat. Paris and Boston 2003–2004, pp. 356–66.

CALLEN 1974
A. Callen, 'Faure and Manet', in *Gazette des Beaux-Arts*, March 1974, pp. 157–78.

CALLEN 1988
A. Callen, 'Degas et Faure', in exh. cat. Paris, Ottawa and New York 1988–1989, pp. 221–3.

CASTAGNARY 1872
J. Castagnary, 'Salon de 1872 (deuxième article)', *Le Siècle*, 18 May 1872.

CHASTEL AND POMIAN 1987
A. Chastel and K. Pomian, 'Les intermédiaires', *Revue de l'art*, no. 1, 1987, pp. 5–9.

CLEMENCEAU 1928
G. Clemenceau, *Claude Monet*, Paris 1928.

[COLLECTIVE] 1911
Im Kampf um die Kunst. Die Antwort auf den "Protest deutscher Künstler", mit Beiträgen deutscher Künstler, Galerieleiter, Sammler und Schriftsteller, Munich 1911.

COOLIDGE 1887
S. Coolidge, *A Short History of the City of Philadelphia from its Foundation to the Present Time*, Boston 1887.

COOPER 1954
D. Cooper, *The Courtauld Collection: A Catalogue and Introduction*, London 1954.

Correspondence Boudin – Martin [2011]
Eugène Boudin. Lettres à Ferdinand Martin, 1861–1870, ed. I. Pludermacher, in collaboration with L. Manoeuvre, Trouville-sur-Mer 2011.

Correspondence Courbet [1996]
Correspondance de Courbet, ed. P. ten-Doesschate Chu, Paris 1996.

Correspondence Degas – Durand-Ruel [1989]
'Lettres de Degas conservées dans les archives Durand-Ruel', ed. C. Durand-Ruel Godfroy, in *Degas inédit. Actes du colloque Degas, Musée d'Orsay, 18–21 April 1988*, Paris 1989, pp. 433–509.

Correspondence Fromentin [1995]
Correspondance d'Eugène Fromentin, 1859–1876, ed. B. Wright, Paris 1995.

Correspondence Gauguin [1946]
Lettres de Gauguin à sa femme et à ses amis, ed. M. Malingue, Paris 1946.

Correspondence Gauguin [1984]
Correspondance de Paul Gauguin, documents, témoignages, ed. V. Merlhès, Paris 1984.

Correspondence Liebermann [2012]
Max Liebermann. Briefe. II. 1896–1901, ed. Ernst Braun, Baden-Baden 2012.

Correspondence Mallarmé [1965–1985]
Stéphane Mallarmé, *Correspondance*, ed. H. Mondor and L. J. Austin, 11 vols, Paris 1965–85.

Correspondence Millet [2005]
Une chronique de l'amitié. Correspondance intégrale du peintre Jean-François Millet, ed. L. Lepoittevin, in collaboration with J. et B. Le Vast, 2005.

Correspondence Mirbeau [2009]
Octave Mirbeau, Correspondance générale, ed. P. Michel, 2 vols, Lausanne 2009.

Correspondence Morisot [1950]
Correspondance de Berthe Morisot, ed. D. Rouart, Paris 1950.

Correspondence Pissarro [1980–1991]
Correspondance de Camille Pissarro, ed. J. Bailly-Herzberg, 5 vols, Paris 1980–91.

Correspondence Proust [1976–1993]
Marcel Proust, Correspondance, ed. P. Kolb, 21 vols, Paris 1976–93.

Correspondence Renoir – Durand-Ruel [1995].
Correspondance de Renoir et Durand-Ruel, ed. C. Durand-Ruel Godfroy, 2 vols, Lausanne 1995.

Correspondence Seguin – O'Conor [1989]
Une vie de bohème. Lettres du peintre Armand Seguin à Roderic O'Conor, 1895–1903, ed. D. Sutton and C. Puget, in collaboration with C. Boyle-Turner, Pont-Aven 1989.

Correspondence Van Gogh [2009]
Vincent van Gogh. The Letters, 6 vols, ed. L. Jansen, H. Luitjen and N. Bakker, Arles, Amsterdam and The Hague, Huygens Institutes, 2009.

CORTISSOZ 1925
R. Cortissoz, *Personalities in Art*, New York 1925.

CROZET 1991
R. Crozet, *Les Instituteurs de Seine-et-Oise vers 1900*, Saint-Ouen-l'Aumône 1991.

DARGENTY 1883a
G. Dargenty, 'Exposition des oeuvres d'Eugène Boudin', in *Courrier de l'art*, 22 February 1883, p. 88.

DARGENTY 1883b
G. Dargenty, 'Exposition des oeuvres de M. P. A. Renoir', *Courrier de l'art*, 12 April 1883, pp. 171–2.

DAUNTON 2007
M. Daunton, *Wealth and Welfare: An Economic and Social History of Britain, 1851–1951*, Oxford 2007.

DAVIES 1970
M. Davies, *National Gallery Catalogues: French School*, London 1970.

DAWSON 2008
B. Dawson et al., *Hugh Lane: Founder of a Gallery of Modern Art for Dublin*, London 2008.

DAYER GALLATI 2000
B. Dayer Gallati, '1886: A Year of Transition', in *William Merritt Chase: Modern American Landscapes, 1886–1890*, exh. cat. (Brooklyn Museum of Art, Art Institute of Chicago, and Museum of Fine Arts, Houston, 2000–1), New York 2000, pp. 37–49.

DE BAECQUE 1991
A. de Baecque, *Histoire d'une revue. Les Cahiers du cinéma*, 2 vols, Paris 1991.

DECROOQ 2009
M.-C. Decrooq, 'Monet und Durand-Ruel: Die Finanzkrise und die 7. Impressionisten-ausstellung im Licht ihrer Korrespondenz (Januar bis März 1882) aus dem Archiv Cornebois', in *Claude Monet*, exh. cat. (Von der Heydt-Museum, Wuppertal, 2009–2010), Wuppertal 2009, pp. 55–9.

DEGHY AND WATERHOUSE 1955
G. Deghy and K. Waterhouse, *Café Royal: Ninety Years of Bohemia*, London 1955.

DE KNYFF 1976
G. de Knyff, *Eugène Boudin raconté par lui-même, sa vie, son atelier, son oeuvre*, Paris 1976.

DISTEL 1981
A. Distel, 'Albert Hecht, collectionneur (1842–1889)', in *Bulletin de la Société de l'histoire de l'art français*, 1981 (1983), pp. 267–79.

DISTEL 1985
A. Distel, 'Les Amateurs de Renoir. Le prince, le prêtre et le pâtissier', in exh. cat. London, Paris and Boston 1985–1986, pp. 28–44.

DISTEL 1989a
A. Distel, 'Charles Deudon (1832–1914), amateur et collectionneur', in *La Revue de l'art*, no. 86, 1989, pp. 58–65.

DISTEL 1989b
A. Distel, *Les Collectionneurs des impressionnistes*, Paris 1989.

DISTEL 1997a
A. Distel, 'Portrait de M. Clapisson en mécène', in exh. cat. Ottawa, Chicago and Fort Worth 1997–1998, pp. 77–86.

DISTEL 1997b
A. Distel, 'Les Carnets de Léon Clapisson', in exh. cat. Ottawa, Chicago and Fort Worth 1997–1998, pp. 346–56.

DISTEL 2002
A. Distel, 'Edward Bérend (1860–1897), un élève de Manet et un ami de Signac', in *Mélanges en hommage à Françoise Cachin*, Paris 2002, pp. 140–5.

DISTEL 2010
A. Distel, 'Un amateur insolite pour les impressionnistes: l'abbé Paul Gaugain (1850–1904)', in *Bulletin de la Société de l'histoire de l'art français*, 2010 (2011), pp. 249–61.

DISTEL 2014
A. Distel, *Pierre Auguste Renoir: un voyage en Espagne?*, conference paper given at the Prado in Madrid, 21 January 2014.

DIXON 1998
A. Dixon, 'The Marketing of Monet: the Exhibition at "La Vie moderne",' in exh. cat. Ann Arbor, Dallas and Minneapolis 1998, pp. 91–116.

DORRMANN 2001
M. Dorrmann, 'Unser bedeutendster und glücklichster Sammler von neuen Bildern. Die Entstehung und Präsentation der Sammlung Arnhold in Berlin', in Pophanken and Billeter 2001, pp. 23–40.

DORRMANN 2002
M. Dorrmann, *Eduard Arnhold (1849–1925). Eine biographische Studie zu Unternehmer- und Mäzenatentum im Deutschen Kaiserreich*, Berlin 2002.

DURAND-RUEL [1939]
'Mémoires de Paul Durand-Ruel', in Venturi 1939, II, pp. 143–220.

DURAND-RUEL 2007
F. Durand-Ruel, 'Paul Durand-Ruel. Freund und Händler der Impressionisten', in *Vienna – Paris. Van Gogh, Cézanne und Österreichs Moderne, 1860–1960*, exh. cat. (Vienna, Belvedere, 2007–8), Vienna 2007, pp. 205–13.

DURAND-RUEL 2013
F. Durand-Ruel, 'Exposer, exposer, exposer ... La première exposition monographique de Paul Gauguin à la galerie Durand-Ruel à Paris, novembre 1893', in *Voyage into the Myth: Gauguin and After*, exh. cat. (Seoul Museum of Arts, 2013), Seoul, 2013, pp. 222–9.

DURAND-RUEL AND DURAND-RUEL 2011
P.-L. Durand-Ruel and F. Durand-Ruel, 'Les premiers achats de Paul Durand-Ruel à Édouard Manet, 1872–3', in exh. cat. Paris 2011, pp. 284–5.

DURAND-RUEL AND DURAND-RUEL 2014
Paul Durand-Ruel, Memoirs of an Impressionist Art Dealer (1831–1922), ed. P.-L. Durand-Ruel and F. Durand-Ruel, Paris 2014.

DURAND-RUEL GODFROY 1992
C. Durand-Ruel Godfroy, 'Paul Durand-Ruel et Alfred Sisley: 1872–1895', in exh. cat. London, Paris and Baltimore 1992–1993, pp. 43–61.

DURAND-RUEL GODFROY 1999
C. Durand-Ruel Godfroy, 'Durand-Ruel's Influence on the Impressionist Collections of European Museums', in exh. cat. Atlanta, Seattle and Denver 1999, pp. 29–38.

DURAND-RUEL GODFROY 2000
C. Durand-Ruel Godfroy, 'Paul Durand-Ruel's Marketing Practices', *Van Gogh Museum Journal*, 2000, pp. 82–9.

DURAND-RUEL GODFROY 2009
C. Durand-Ruel Godfroy, 'Paul Durand-Ruel and Renoir: 47 Years of Friendship', in *Renoir Promise of Happiness*, exh. cat. Seoul Museum of Art 2009, Seoul 2009, pp. 275–9.

DURAND-RUEL GODFROY 2011
C. Durand-Ruel Godfroy, 'Les Oeuvres de Claude Monet dans la collection privée de Paul Durand-Ruel', in *Monet au musée Marmottan et dans les collections suisses*, exh. cat. Martigny, fondation Pierre Gianadda, 2011, Martigny 2011, pp. 59–63.

DURAND-RUEL SNOLLAERTS 2005
C. Durand-Ruel Snollaerts, 'Un peintre et un marchand: Camille Pissarro (1830–1903) et Paul Durand-Ruel (1831–1922)', in Pissarro et Durand-Ruel Snollaerts 2005, I, pp. 13–59.

DURET 1906a
T. Duret, *Histoire de Edouard Manet et de son oeuvre*, Paris 1906.

DURET 1906b
T. Duret, *Histoire des peintres impressionnistes: Pissarro, Claude Monet, Sisley, Renoir, Berthe Morisot, Cézanne, Guillaumin*, Paris 1906.

EBERLE 1995–6
M. Eberle, *Max Liebermann, 1847–1935. Werkverzeichnis der Gemälde und Ölstudien*, 2 vols, Munich 1995–6.

ECHTE AND FEILCHENFELDT 2011–13
B. Echte and W. Feilchenfeldt (eds), *Kunstsalon Bruno & Paul Cassirer: die Ausstellungen 1898–1901: 'Das Beste aus aller Welt zeigen'*, 3 vols, Wädenswil 2011–13.

ELDER 1924
M. Elder, *Chez Claude Monet à Giverny*, Paris 1924.

ELDER [2010]
M. Elder, *A Giverny chez Claude Monet*, Paris 2010.

ELIAS 1912
J. Elias, 'Paul Durand-Ruel (Aus dem Leben eines Kunsthändlers)', *Kunst und Künstler*, no. 10 (1912), pp. 105–7.

ENAULT 1876
L. Enault, 'Mouvement artistique: l'exposition des intransigeants dans la galerie de Durand-Ruel', *Le Constitutionnel*, 10 April 1876.

FAASS 2013
M. Faass, '"Haben Sie wirklich Geld für den Dreck gegeben?" Wie der Impressionismus nach Berlin kam', in exh. cat. Berlin 2013, pp. 162–71.

FELS 1929
M. de Fels, *La Vie de Claude Monet*, Paris 1929.

FÉNÉON 1970
F. Fénéon, *Oeuvres plus que complètes. I. Chroniques d'art*, ed. J. U. Halperin, Geneva and Paris 1970.

FIDELL-BEAUFORT 2000
M. Fidell-Beaufort, 'The American Art Trade and French Painting at the End of the 19th Century', *Van Gogh Museum Journal*, 2000, pp. 101–7.

FIDELL-BEAUFORT AND WELCHER 1982
M. Fidell-Beaufort and J. Welcher, 'Some Views of Art Buying in New York in the 1870s and 1880s', *Oxford Art Journal*, vol. 5, no. 1, 1982, pp. 48–55.

FINK 1978
L.M. Fink, 'French Art in the United States, 1850–1870. Three Dealers and Collectors', *Gazette des Beaux-Arts*, September 1978, pp. 87–100.

FLETCHER AND HELMREICH 2011
P. Fletcher and A. Helmreich (eds), *The Rise of the Modern Art Market in London, 1850–1939*, Manchester 2011.

FLINT 1984
K. Flint (ed.), *Impressionists in England: The Critical Reception*, London, Boston and Melbourne 1984.

FOURCAUD 1883
Louis de Fourcaud, 'Exposition d'oeuvres de M. Claude Monet, 9 boulevard de la Madeleine', *Le Gaulois*, 12 March 1883, p. 3.

FOWLE 2006
F. Fowle, 'Making Money Out of Monet: Marketing Monet in Britain 1870–1905', in Idem. (ed.), *Monet and French Landscape: Vétheuil and Normandy*, Edinburgh 2006, p. 141ff.

FRÈCHES-THORY 2004
C. Frèches-Thory, 'The Exhibition at Durand-Ruel', in exh. cat. Paris and Boston 2003–4, pp. 83–9.

GACHET 1953
P. Gachet, *Vincent van Gogh aux 'Indépendants'*, Paris 1953.

GALENSON AND JENSEN 2007
D.W. Galenson and R. Jensen, 'Canvases and Careers: The Rise of the Market for Modern Art in Nineteenth-Century Paris', in *Current Issues in Nineteenth-Century Art, Van Gogh Studies 1*, 2007, pp. 137–66.

GALERIE DURAND-RUEL 1845
Galerie Durand-Ruel, *Spécimens les plus brillants de l'École moderne*, 2 vols, Paris 1845.

GEFFROY 1883
G. Geffroy, 'Claude Monet', in *La Justice*, 15 March 1883, pp. 1–2.

GEFFROY [1980]
G. Geffroy, *Claude Monet. Sa vie, son oeuvre*, ed. C. Judrin, Paris 1980.

GÈNE-MUR 1876
Gène-Mur [Eugène Murer], 'Revue artistique : les impressionnistes', *La Correspondance française*, 16 April 1876.

GIDE [1996]
A. Gide, *Journal 1887–1925*, Paris 1996.

GIL BLAS 1879
[The editor], 'Le salon de Gil Blas', *Gil Blas*, 3 December 1879, p. 1.

GONCOURT [1989]
E. and J. de Goncourt, *Journal. Mémoires de la vie littéraire*, ed. R. Ricatte, 3 vols, Paris 1989.

GREEN 1987
N. Green, 'Dealing in Temperaments: Economic Transformation of the Artistic Field in France During the Second Half of the Nineteenth Century', *Art History*, vol. 10, no. 1, March 1987, pp. 59–78.

GREEN 1989
N. Green, 'Circuits of Production, Circuits of Consumption: The Case of Mid-Nineteenth-Century Art Dealing', *Art Journal*, spring 1989, pp. 29–34.

GRUETZNER ROBINS 2010
A. Gruetzner Robins, '"Manet and the Post-Impressionists": A Checklist of Exhibits', *Burlington Magazine*, vol. CLII, no. 1293, December 2010, pp. 782–93.

GUW
The Correspondence of James McNeill Whistler, 1855–1903, ed. M.F. MacDonald, P. de Montfort and N. Thorp, including *The Correspondence of Anna McNeill Whistler, 1855–1880*, ed. G. Toutziari (http://www.whistler.arts.gla.ac.uk/).

HALÉVY 1995
Daniel Halévy, *Degas parle*, Paris 1995.

HANCOCK 1991
J.H. Hancock et al., *The Art Collection of James H. Hill*, Saint Paul 1991.

HANSEN 2002
D. Hansen, '"Preistreiberei" oder "Brotkorbinteressen"? Kunsthandel, Preise und der Künstlerstreit', in exh. cat. Bremen 2002–2003, pp. 186–203.

HANSEN 2005
D. Hansen, 'Camille in Bremen – zur Rezeption Monets in Deutschland', in *Monet und Camille. Frauenportraits im Impressionismus*, exh. cat. (Kunsthalle Bremen, 15 October 2005–26 February 2006), Munich 2005, pp. 256–65.

HASKELL 1989
F. Haskell, 'Un Turc et ses tableaux dans le Paris du XIXe siècle', in Idem., *De l'art et du goût jadis et naguère*, Paris 1989, pp. 362–83.

HASKELL 1992
F. Haskell, *La Difficile naissance du livre d'art*, Paris 1992. (English edition: *The Painful Birth of the Art Book*, London 1988.)

HAUG AND HEDINGER 2013
S. Haug and B. Hedinger, 'Verzeichnis der Sammlung [Max Liebermann]', in Hedinger, Diers and Müller 2013, pp. 250–94.

HEDINGER 2013
B. Hedinger, 'Liebermann als Sammler', in Hedinger, Diers and Müller 2013, pp. 17–38.

HEDINGER, DIERS AND MÜLLER 2013
B. Hedinger, M. Diers and J. Müller (eds), *Max Liebermann. Die Kunstsammlung. Von Rembrandt bis Manet*, Munich 2013.

HEILBUT 1890
H. Helferich [Emil Heilbut], 'Claude Monet', *Freie Bühne für modernes Leben*, no. 1, 1890, pp. 225–30.

HEILBUT 1891–2
E. Heilbut, *Die Sammlung Eduard L. Behrens zu Hamburg*, 2 vols, Munich 1891–2.

HEILBUT 1895
E. Heilbut, 'Die große Kunst-Ausstellung in der Kunsthalle, V und VI. Die französische Abteilung', *Hamburgischer Correspondent*, no. 277, 21 April 1895, morning edition, and no. 301. 1 May 1895, morning edition.

HELMREICH 2011
A. Helmreich, 'The Goupil Gallery at the Intersection Between London, Continent and Empire', in Fletcher and Helmreich 2011, pp. 65–84.

HERBERT 2000
Nature's Workshop: Renoir's Writings on the Decorative Arts, ed. R.L. Herbert, New Haven 2000.

HIRSHLER 1998
E.E. Hirshler, 'Helping "Fine Things Across the Atlantic": Mary Cassatt and Art Collecting in the United States', in exh. cat. Chicago, Boston and Washington 1998–1999, pp. 176–211.

HOPP 1986–7
G. Hopp, 'Lichtwark und Frankreich', in exh. cat. Hamburg 1986–1987, pp. 47–64.

HOUSE 1978
J. House, 'New Material on Monet and Pissarro in London in 1870–71', *Burlington Magazine*, vol. CXX, no. 907, October 1978, pp. 636–41.

HOUSE 1994
J. House (ed.), *Impressionism for England. Samuel Courtauld as Patron and Collector*, London 1994.

HOUSSAIS AND LAGRANGE 2010
L. Houssais and M. Lagrange (eds), *Marché(s) de l'art en province (1870–1914)*, Bordeaux 2010.

HOWOLDT 2013
J.E. Howoldt, '"Wissen Sie, ... das Ding ist so gut, das kann nur ich oder ein Museum kaufen". Max Liebermann und Alfred Lichtwark als Sammler des französischen Impressionismus', in exh. cat. Berlin 2013, pp. 172–83.

HUEMER 2012
C. Huemer, '"Une exposition (in)complète": Courbet in Vienna', *Nineteenth-Century Art Worldwide*, vol. 11, no. 2, Summer 2012, pp. 1–9.

HUSTIN 1883a
A. Hustin, 'Exposition de Pissarro', *Moniteur des arts*, 11 May 1883, p. 166.

HUSTIN 1883b
A. Hustin, 'L'exposition de A. Sisley', *Moniteur des arts*, 5 June 1883, p. 209.

HUTH 1946
H. Huth, 'Impressionism Comes to America', *Gazette des Beaux-Arts*, April 1946, pp. 225–52.

ISAACSON 1986
J. Isaacson, 'The Painters Called Impressionists', in exh. cat. Washington and San Francisco 1986, pp. 373–89.

JACQUES 1883a
E. Jacques, 'Beaux-arts: exposition de M. Pissarro', *L'Intransigeant*, 14 May 1883.

JACQUES 1883b
E. Jacques, 'Beaux-Arts', *L'Intransigeant*, 13 June 1883, p. 3.

JAMPOLLER 1986
L. Jampoller, 'Theo Van Gogh and Camille Pissarro: Correspondence and an Exhibition', *Simiolus, Netherlands Quarterly for the History of Art*, vol. 16, no. 1, 1986, pp. 50–61.

JANDA AND TATZKOW 2013
K.-H. Janda, A. Janda and M. Tatzkow, 'Verzeichnis der Sammlung Liebermann', in exh. cat. Berlin 2013–2014, pp. 107–250.

JANSEN 2007
I. Jansen, *Franz Marc et l'art français*, Paris 2007.

JENSEN 1994
R. Jensen, *Marketing Modernism in Fin-de-siècle Europe*, Princeton 1994.

JENSEN 2006
R. Jensen, 'Vollard et Cézanne: anatomie d'une relation', in exh. cat. New York, Chicago and Paris 2006–7, pp. 29–47.

JENSEN 2007
K.M. Jensen, *The American Salon: The Art Gallery at the Chicago Interstate Industrial Exposition 1873–1890*, Ph. D. diss., The City University of New York 2007.

JENSEN 2012
K.M. Jensen, *Monets in the Castle: Building the Palmer Collection*, conference paper given at the Frick Collection, New York, 29 November 2012.

JOINVILLE 1894
Vieux souvenirs (1818–1848). Prince de Joinville, Paris 1894.

KAHNWEILER AND CRÉMIEUX 1998
D.-H. Kahnweiler and F. Crémieux, *Mes Galeries et mes Peintres: Entretiens avec Francis Crémieux*, Paris 1998. (English edition: *My Galleries and Painters*, London 1971.)

KELLY 1999
S. Kelly, 'The Landscapes of Théodore Rousseau and their Market', in A. Burmester, C.Heilmann and M.F. Zimmermann (eds), *Barbizon: Malerei der Natur – Natur der Malerei*, Munich 1999, pp. 419–36.

KELLY 2009
S. Kelly, 'New Discoveries: Théodore Rousseau's "View of Mont Blanc, Seen from la Faucille"', *Nineteenth-Century Art Worldwide*, vol. 8, no. 1 (spring 2009).

KELLY 2011
S. Kelly, 'Quel marché pour Manet?', in exh. cat. Paris 2011, pp. 57–69.

KELLY 2013
S. Kelly, 'Daubigny et Monet: le paysage de rivière, un produit commercial', in *Éblouissants reflets. Cent chefs-d'oeuvre impressionnistes*, exh. cat. (Musée des Beaux-Arts, Rouen 2013), Paris 2013, pp. 34–41.

KELLY 2014
S. Kelly, 'An Artist Focused on his Research: Théodore Rousseau and the Marketing of His Oil Sketches and Drawings', in *The Untamed Landscape. Théodore Rousseau and the Path to Barbizon*, exh. cat. (The Morgan Library and Museum, New York 2014), New York 2014, pp. 24–39.

KERN 1934
G.J. Kern, 'Louis Friedrich Sachse, der Begründer des Berliner Kunsthandels. Ein Beitrag zur Geschichte der neueren Berliner Kunst und Kultur', *Zeitschrift des Vereins für die Geschichte Berlins*, no. 1, 1934, pp. 1–12.

KERN 1989
J. Kern, *Impressionismus im Wilhelminischen Deutschland. Studien zur Kunstund Kulturgeschichte des Kaiserreichs*, Würzburg 1989.

KESSLER [2004]
Comte H. Kessler, *Das Tagebuch 1892–1897*, ed. R.S. Kamzelak and N. Ott, Stuttgart 2004.

KESSLER [2011]
H. Kessler, *Journey to the Abyss: The Diaries of Count Harry Kessler*, trans. and ed. L.M. Easton, New York 2011.

KORN 2004
M. Korn, 'Exhibitions of Modern French Art and their Influence on Collectors in Britain 1870–1918: the Davies Sisters in Context', in *Journal of the History of Collections*, vol. 16, no. 2 (2004), pp. 191–218.

KOSTENEVICH 2006
A. Kostenevich, 'Russian Clients of Ambroise Vollard', pp. 243–56 in exh. cat. New York, Chicago and Paris 2006–2007. (French edition: 'Vollard et les collectionneurs russes', pp. 258–71.)

KYSELA 1964
J. Kysela, 'Sara Hallowell Brings "Modern Art" to the Midwest', *The Art Quarterly*, no. 27, 1964, pp. 150–67.

LABARRIÈRE 1883
P. Labarrière, 'Exposition de Claude Monet', *Le Journal des artistes*, 16 March 1883, p. 1.

LACAMBRE 1994
G. Lacambre, 'Whistler et la France', in *Whistler 1834–1903*, exh. cat. (Tate Gallery, London, Musée d'Orsay, Paris, and National Gallery of Art, Washington, 1994–5), Paris, pp. 39–47 (English edition: London 1994).

LAFONT-COUTURIER 1996
H. Lafont-Couturier, 'La maison Goupil ou la notion d'oeuvre d'art originale remise en question', *Revue de l'art*, no. 112, 1996, pp. 56–69.

LECOMTE 1892
Georges Lecomte, *L'Art impressionniste d'après la collection privée de M. Durand-Ruel*, Paris 1892.

LEES, RAND AND WEBBER 2013
S. Lees, R. Rand and S.L. Webber (eds), *Nineteenth-Century European Paintings at the Sterling and Francine Clark Art Institute*, 2 vols, New Haven and Williamstown 2013.

LE NORMAND-ROMAIN 2007
A. Le Normand-Romain, *Rodin et le bronze. Catalogue des oeuvres conservées au musée Rodin*, 2 vols, Paris 2007.

LEPPIEN 1986
H.R. Leppien, 'Berichte von Taten, Pläne und Meinungen Alfred Lichtwarks. Pan: eine Zeitschrift für Deutschland', in exh. cat. Hamburg 1986–1987, pp. 129–31.

LESPINASSE 2010
F. Lespinasse, 'François Depeaux, une grande collection rouennaise', in *Une ville pour l'impressionnisme : Monet, Pissarro et Gauguin à Rouen*, exh. cat. (Musée des Beaux-Arts, Rouen, 2010), Paris 2010, pp. 124–65.

LICHT 1995
W. Licht, *Industrializing America: The Nineteenth Century*, Baltimore 1995.

LICHTWARK 1883a
A. Lichtwark, 'Gurlitts Herbstausstellung', *Die Gegenwart*, vol. 24, no. 43, 27 October 1883, p. 269ff.

LICHTWARK 1883b
A. Lichtwark, 'Kunstausstellungen. Die Pariser Impressionisten in Gurlitts Kunstsalon', *Die Gegenwart*, vol. 24, no. 51, 22 December 1883, p. 400ff.

LICHTWARK 1896–1920
Alfred Lichtwarks Briefe an die Commission für die Verwaltung der Kunsthalle, 20 vols, Hamburg 1896–1920.

LIEBERMANN 1898
M. Liebermann, 'Degas', in *Pan*, no. 4, 1898, pp. 193–6.

LIEBERMANN [1978]
Max Liebermann: Die Phantasie in der Malerei, Schriften und Reden, ed. G. Busch, Frankfurt 1978.

LIEBERMANN [1995]
Max Liebermann, 'Briefe an Gustav Pauli 1900–1913, kommentiert von Dorothee Hansen', in exh. cat. Bremen 1995–1996, pp. 61–95.

LILLEY 2014
E. Lilley, 'Manet and His London Critics Revisited', *Burlington Magazine*, vol. CLVI, no. 1333, April 2014, pp. 232–3.

LINDSAY 1985
S.G. Lindsay, 'Introduction: Mary Cassatt and Philadelphia', in *Mary Cassatt and Philadelphia*, exh. cat. (Philadelphia Museum of Art, 1985), Philadelphia 1985, pp. 9–32.

LOBSTEIN 2014
D. Lobstein, 'L'Actualité artistique parisienne', in *Paris 1900, la ville spectacle*, exh. cat. (Petit Palais, Musée des Beaux-Arts de la Ville de Paris, 2014), Paris 2014, pp. 360–81.

LOCKE 2010
N. Locke, 'Manet and His London Critics', *Burlington Magazine*, vol. CLII, no. 1293, December 2010, pp. 781–2.

LUCAS [1979]
Diary of George A. Lucas: An American Art Agent in Paris, 1857–1909, ed. L.M.C. Randall, 2 vols, Princeton 1979.

LUCKHARDT 2001
U. Luckhardt, 'Eduard L. Behrens und Theodor E. Behrens. Sammeln moderner Kunst in zwei Generationen', in exh. cat. Hamburg 2001, pp. 35–43.

LUCY AND HOUSE 2012
M. Lucy and J. House, *Renoir in the Barnes Foundation*, New Haven 2012.

LUDEWIG 2012
A.-D. Ludewig, '"Haben Sie wirklich Geld für diesen Dreck ausgegeben?" Die Sammlung Carl und Felicie Bernstein', in Ludewig, Schoeps and Soder 2012, pp. 90–103.

LUDEWIG, SCHOEPS AND SODER 2012
A.-D. Ludewig, J. Schoeps and I. Soder (eds), *Aufbruch in die Moderne. Sammler, Mäzene und Kunsthändler in Berlin 1880–1933*, Cologne 2012.

LUGT
F. Lugt, *Répertoire des ventes publiques intéressant l'art ou la curiosité…, 1e période: 1600–1825*, The Hague 1938; *2e période: 1826–1860*, The Hague 1953; *3e période: 1861–1900*, The Hague 1964; *4e période: 1901–1925*, Paris 1964.

LUNN 1870
H.C. Lunn, 'The London Musical Season', *The Musical Times and Singing Class Circular*, no. 14, 1 September 1870, pp. 583–6.

MAAS 1975
J. Maas, *Gambart, Prince of the Victorian Art World*, London 1975.

MANET [1987]
Julie Manet Journal 1893–1899, intro. by R. de Boland Roberts and J. Roberts, Paris 1987.

MANOEUVRE 1998
L. Manoeuvre, 'Biographie', in exh. cat. Honfleur 1998, pp. 179–96.

MARCHAND AND THÉLOT 1997
O. Marchand and C. Thélot, *Le Travail en France (1800–2000)*, Paris 1997.

MARRIOTT 1883
H. Marriott, 'Exposition de Claude Monet', *Le Journal des arts*, 6 March 1883, p. 2.

MATHEWS 1984
N.M. Mathews, *Cassatt and Her Circle: Selected Letters*, New York 1984.

MAUPEOU 2013
F. de Maupeou, *Claude Monet et l'exposition*, PhD thesis supervised by F. Cousinié and S. Le Men, université de Rouen–université Paris-Ouest Nanterre La Défense, 2 vols, 2013.

MEIER-GRAEFE 1904
J. Meier-Graefe, *Entwicklungsgeschichte der modernen Kunst. Vergleichende Betrachtung der bildenden Künste als Beitrag zu einer neuen Ästhetik*, 3 vols, Stuttgart 1904.

MEIER-GRAEFE 1913
J. Meier-Graefe, 'Handel und Händler II und III', in *Kunst und Künstler*, no. 11, 1913, pp. 104–9, 196–210.

MELOT 1988
M. Melot, 'Daumier and Art History', *The Oxford Art Journal*, vol. II, no. 1, 1988, pp. 3–24.

MÉRIGEAU 2012
P. Mérigeau, *Jean Renoir*, Paris 2012.

MIQUEL 1975
P. Miquel, *L'École de la Nature. Le paysage français au XIXe siècle, 1824–1874*, Maursla-Jolie 1975.

MIRBEAU 1884
O. Mirbeau, 'Notes sur l'art. Degas', *La France*, 15 November 1884, cited in Idem., *Combats esthétiques*, ed. P. Michel and J.-F. Nivet, Paris 1993, I, pp. 77–81.

MIREUR 1911
H. Mireur, *Dictionnaire des ventes d'art faites en France et à l'étranger pendant les XVIIIe et XIXe siècles: tableaux, dessins, estampes etc.*, 7 vols, Paris 1911.

MOLLIER 1988
J.-Y. Mollier, *L'Argent et les lettres. Histoire du capitalisme d'édition. 1880–1920*, Paris 1988.

MOREAU-NÉLATON 1921
E. Moreau-Nélaton, *Millet raconté par lui-même*, 3 vols, Paris 1921.

MOREAU-NÉLATON 1925
E. Moreau-Nélaton, *Daubigny raconté par lui-même*, Paris 1925.

MOREAU-NÉLATON 1927
E. Moreau-Nélaton, *Bonvin raconté par lui-même*, Paris 1927.

MOULIN 1967
R. Moulin, *Le Marché de la peinture en France*, Paris 1967.

NEAL 1996
K. Neal, *A Wise Extravagance: The Founding of the Carnegie International Exhibitions, 1895–1901*, Pittsburgh 1996.

NEGENDANCK 1998
R. Negendanck, *Die Galerie Ernst Arnold (1893–1951). Kunsthandel und Zeitgeschichte*, Weimar 1998.

NICULESCU 1970
Remus Niculescu, 'Georges De Bellio, l'ami des impressionnistes', *Paragone*, no. 247, September 1970, pp. 25–66, no. 249, November 1970, pp. 41–85.

NIERHOFF 2002
B. Nierhoff, 'Der Künstlerstreit 1911 – eine Chronologie', in exh. cat. Bremen 2002–2003, pp. 148–53.

NOCE 2007
V. Noce, 'Vollard et la manière', *Libération*, 23–4 June 2007.

NONNE 2002
M. Nonne, 'Les droits douaniers américains et les marchands de tableaux français au XIXe siècle', *48/14 La Revue du musée d'Orsay*, no. 14, spring 2002, pp. 102–8.

NONNE 2003
M. Nonne, 'Carolus Duran et les États-Unis', in *Carolus Duran, 1837–1917*, exh. cat. (Palais des beaux-arts, Lille and Musée des Augustins, Toulouse, 2003), Paris 2003, pp. 37–41.

NONNE 2009
Monique Nonne, 'Alfred Cadart (1828–1875), marchand de tableaux modernes', *Bulletin de la Société de l'histoire de l'art français*, 2009 (2010), pp. 363–73.

NORTON 1883
C.B. Norton, *Official Catalogue Foreign Exhibition*, Boston 1883.

O'BYRNE 2000
R. O'Byrne, *Hugh Lane, 1875–1915*, Dublin 2000.

O'SULLIVAN 1991
T. O'Sullivan, 'Showcase and Stronghold: The Art Gallery of the James J. Hill House', in *Homecoming: The Art Collection of James J. Hill*, exh. cat. (Saint Paul, James J. Hill House, 1991), Saint Paul 1991, pp. 45–61.

PALMADE 1961
G.P. Palmade, *Capitalismes et capitalistes français au XIXe siècle*, Paris 1961.

PALMADE 1972
G.P. Palmade, *French Capitalism in the Nineteenth Century*, trans. G.M. Holmes, Newton Abbot 1972.

PANZANELLI AND PRETI-HAMARD 2007
R. Panzanelli and M. Preti-Hamard (eds), *La Circulation des oeuvres d'art. The Circulation of Works of Art in the Revolutionary Era, 1789–1848*, Rennes 2007.

PASCOE PRATT 2006
J. Pascoe Pratt, 'Patron or Pirate? Vollard and Works of Vincent van Gogh', in exh. cat. New York, Chicago and Paris 2006–2007, pp. 49–59.

PAUL 1988
B. Paul, 'Drei Sammlungen französischer impressionistischer Kunst im kaiserlichen Berlin – Bernstein, Liebermann, Arnhold', *Zeitschrift des deutschen Vereins für Kunstwissenschaft*, vol. 42, no. 3, 1988, pp. 11–30.

PAUL 1993
B. Paul, *Hugo von Tschudi und die moderne französische Kunst im Deutschen Kaiserreich*, Mayence 1993.

PAULI 1913
Gustav Pauli, *Katalog der Gemälde und Bildhauerwerke in der Kunsthalle Bremen*, Bremen 1913.

PENOT-LEJEUNE 2012
A. Penot-Lejeune, *L'Internationalisation des galeries françaises Durant la seconde moitié du XIXe siècle. L'exemple de la maison Goupil (1846–1884)*, PhD. diss., supervised by D. Poulot, université Paris I Panthéon-Sorbonne, 2012.

PICKVANCE 1962
Ronald Pickvance, 'Henry Hill: An Untypical Victorian Collector', *Apollo*, vol. LXXVI, no. 10, December 1962, pp. 789–91.

PICKVANCE 1963
R. Pickvance, 'Degas's Dancers: 1872–6', *Burlington Magazine*, vol. CV, no. 723, June 1963, pp. 256–66.

PISSARRO [2002]
Camille Pissarro, *Letters to His Son Lucien*, ed. John Rewald, Boston 2002.

PISSARRO AND VENTURI 1939
L.R. Pissarro and L. Venturi, *Camille Pissarro. Son art, son oeuvre*, Paris, I, 1939.

POGGI 2008
J. Poggi, 'Les galleries du boulevard des Italiens, antichambre de la modernité', in *48/14 La Revue du musée d'Orsay*, no. 27, autumn 2008, pp. 22–33.

POPHANKEN AND BILLETER 2001
A. Pophanken and F. Billeter (eds), *Die Moderne und ihre Sammler. Französische Kunst in deutschem Privatbesitz vom Kaiserreich zur Weimarer Republik*, Berlin 2001.

PRETI-HAMARD AND SÉNÉCHAL 2005
M. Preti-Hamard and P. Sénéchal (eds), *Collections et marché de l'art en France, 1789–1848*, Paris and Rennes 2005.

PRETTEJOHN 1994
E. Prettejohn, 'Modern Foreign Paintings and the National Art Collections: Anthology of British Texts, 1905–1932', in House 1994, pp. 225–52.

PUCKS 1996
Stefan Pucks, 'Von Manet zu Matisse: Die Sammler der französischen Moderne in Berlin um 1900', in *Manet bis Van Gogh. Hugo von Tschudi und der Kampf um die Moderne*, exh. cat. (Nationalgalerie, Berlin and Neue Pinakothek, Munich 1996–1997), Munich and New York, 1996, pp. 386–90.

RATHBONE AND STEELE 1996
E.E. Rathbone and E. Steele, 'A History of Renoir's "Luncheon of the Boating Party",' in *Impressionists on the Seine: A Celebration of Renoir's Luncheon of the Boating Party*, exh. cat. (The Phillips Collection, Washington 1996–1997), Washington 1996, pp. 231–5.

RAVENEL 1870a
J. Ravenel [Alfred Sensier], 'Vente de la collection de M. Th. [sic] Edwards', *Revue de l'art et de la curiosité*, vol. III, no. 2, 15 February 1870, p. 106.

RAVENEL 1870b
J. Ravenel, 'Vente de la collection de M. Th. Edwards. Compte-rendu', *Revue internationale de l'art et de la curiosité*, vol. III, no. 3, 15 March 1870, pp. 236–7.

RECUEIL D'ESTAMPES 1873–5
Galerie Durand-Ruel. Recueil d'estampes gravées à l'eau-forte, edition of 30, Paris, London and Brussels 1873–5.

REED 2008
N. Reed, *Sisley on the Thames and the Welsh Coast*, London 2008.

REILEY-BURT 1975
M. Reiley-Burt, 'Le pâtissier Murer', *L'OEil*, no. 245 (December 1975), pp. 54–61, 92.

RENOIR 1879
E. Renoir, 'Notre exposition', in *La Vie moderne*, no. 1, 10 April 1879, pp. 14–15.

RENOIR 1981
J. Renoir, *Pierre-Auguste Renoir, mon père*, Paris 1981.

REWALD 1953
J. Rewald, 'Extraits du journal inédit de Paul Signac, III, 1898–1899', *Gazette des Beaux-Arts*, July 1953, pp. 27–57.

REWALD 1956
J. Rewald, *Post-Impressionism: From Van Gogh to Gauguin*, New York 1956.

REWALD 1961
J. Rewald, *The History of Impressionism*, New York 1961.

REWALD 1965
J. Rewald, *Histoire de l'impressionnisme*, Paris 1965.

REWALD 1969
J. Rewald, 'Chocquet and Cézanne', *Gazette des Beaux-Arts*, July–August 1969, pp. 33–96.

REWALD 1973
John Rewald, *History of Impressionism*, 4th revd. edn, London 1973.

REWALD 1985 (1943)
J. Rewald, 'Durand-Ruel: 140 Years, One Man's Faith', in Rewald 1985 (first published in *Art News*, vol. XLII, no. 14, 1–14 December 1943.

REWALD 1985
J. Rewald, *Studies in Impressionism*, ed. I. Gordon and F. Weitzenhoffer, New York 1985.

REWALD 1986a
J. Rewald, 'Theo van Gogh as Art Dealer', in Idem., *Studies in Post-Impressionism*, London 1986, pp. 7–115.

REWALD 1986b
J. Rewald, *Histoire de l'impressionnisme*, new revised and augmented edition, Paris 1986.

REWALD 2002
J. Rewald, *Camille Pissarro – Letters to his Son Lucien*, Boston 2002.

REWALD AND WEITZENHOFFER 1984
J. Rewald and F. Weitzenhoffer (eds), *Aspects of Monet: A Symposium on the Artist's Life and Times*, New York 1984.

REWALD AND WEITZENHOFFER 1989
J. Rewald with the assistance of F. Weitzenhoffer, *Cézanne and America: Dealers, Collectors, Artists, and Critics, 1891–1921. The A.W. Lectures in the Fine Arts, Princeton, 1979*, Princeton 1989.

ROBERT 1991
H. Robert, 'Le destin d'une grande collection princière au XIXe siècle: l'exemple de la galerie de tableaux du duc d'Orléans, prince royal', *Gazette des Beaux-Arts*, July–August 1991, pp. 37–60.

ROBIDA 1958
M. Robida, *Le Salon Charpentier et les impressionnistes*, Paris 1958.

ROESCHEL 2002
C. Roeschel, 'The Städtische Kunsthalle Mannheim', in exh. cat. Bremen 2002–2003, pp. 224–5.

ROTHENSTEIN 1931
W. Rothenstein, *Men and Memories: Recollections of William Rothenstein, 1872–1900*, New York 1931.

RUTTER 1905
F. Rutter, 'Round the Galleries', *Sunday Times*, 26 March 1905.

RUTTER 1933
F. Rutter, *Art in My Time*, London 1933.

SCHIEFLER 1985
G. Schiefler, *Einehamburgische Kulturgeschichte 1890–1920. Beobachtungen eines Zeitgenossen*, ed. G. Ahrens, Hamburg 1985.

SCHLAGENHAUFF 2000
A. Schlagenhauff, 'Delaroches "Hémicycle" vor dem Berliner Publikum. Der Kunsthändler Louis Friedrich Sachseund sein Einsatz für den künstlerischen Austausch zwischen Berlin und Paris', in U. Fleckner, T.W. Gaehtgens, M. Schieder and M.F. Zimmermann (eds), *Jenseits der Grenzen: französische und deutsche Kunst vom Ancien Regime bis zur Gegenwart: Thomas W. Gaehtgens zum 60. Geburtstag*, Cologne 2000, pp. 168–81.

SCHLENKER 2007
S. Schlenker, *Mit dem 'Talent der Augen'. Der Kunstkritiker Emil Heilbut (1861–1921). Ein Streiter für die moderne Kunst im Deutschen Kaiserreich*, Weimar 2007.

SEIDLITZ 1897
W. von Seidlitz, 'Degas', in *Pan*, no. 1, 1897, pp. 57–60.

SENSIER 1870
A. Sensier, 'Conférence sur le paysage', in *Revue internationale de l'art et de la curiosité*, August 1870, pp. 25–40.

SENSIER 1872
A. Sensier, *Souvenirs sur Th. Rousseau*, Paris 1872.

SENSIER AND MANTZ 2005
A. Sensier and P. Mantz, *La Vie et l'oeuvre de Jean-François Millet*, intro. G. Lacambre, Bricquebosq 2005.

SMITH 2009
A.Y. Smith, *Hidden in Plain Sight: The Whittemore Collection and the French Impressionists*, Washington 2009.

STEIN 2005
S. Stein, 'The Paper Trail: From Portfolios to Posterity', in *Vincent van Gogh: The Drawings*, exh. cat. (Van Gogh Museum, Amsterdam, and The Metropolitan Museum of Art, New York, 2005), New Haven and London 2005, pp. 21–39.

[STRAHAN] 1872
[E. Strahan], 'Private Art Collections of Philadelphia. V. Mr. A. E. Borie's Gallery', *Lippincott's Magazine*, vol. 10, August 1872, pp. 221–6.

STRAHAN 1879–80
E. Strahan, *The Art Treasures of America: Being the Choicest Works of Art in Public and Private Collections in North America*, 3 vols, Philadelphia 1879–80.

STUCKEY 1985
C.F. Stuckey (ed.), *Monet: A Retrospective*, New York 1985.

STUCKEY 1987
C.F. Stuckey, 'Berthe Morisot', in exh. cat. Washington, Fort Worth and South Hadley 1987–1998, pp. 15–185.

STUCKEY 1998
C.F. Stuckey, 'Love, Money and Monet's Debacle Paintings of 1880', in exh. cat. Ann Arbor, Dallas and Minneapolis 1998, pp. 41–64.

STUCKEY AND SCOTT 1987
C.F. Stuckey and W.P. Scott, *Berthe Morisot*, Paris 1987.

TABARANT 1921
Adolphe Tabarant, 'Le Congrès d'histoire de l'art chez Durand-Ruel', *Bulletin de la vie artistique*, 15 October 1921, pp. 527–9.

TEEUWISSE 1986
N. Teeuwisse, *Vom Salon zur Secession: Berliner Kunstleben zwischen Tradition und Aufbruch zur Moderne 1871–1900*, Berlin 1986.

TELLIER 2010
M.-H. Tellier, *François Depeaux (1853–1920), le charbonnier et les impressionnistes*, Rouen 2010.

THOMSON 1999
R. Thomson, 'Theo Van Gogh, un marchand entreprenant, un homme de Confiance', in exh. cat. Amsterdam et Paris 1999–2000, pp. 61–149. (English edition: 'Theo Van Gogh, 1857–1891: Art Dealer, Collector and Brother of Vincent'.)

TINTEROW 1988
G. Tinterow, 'The 1880s: Synthesis and Change', in exh. cat. Paris, Ottawa and New York 1988–1989, pp. 363–74.

TRUFFAUT 1955
F. Truffaut, 'Ali Baba et la politique des auteurs', *Les Cahiers du cinéma*, February 1955, pp. 45–7.

TUCKER 1995
P.H. Tucker, *Claude Monet, Life and Art*, New Haven 1995.

VAISSE 1995
P. Vaisse, *La Troisième République et les peintres*, Paris 1995.

VALÉRY 1938
P. Valéry, *Degas, danse, dessin*, Paris 1938.

VAN HEUGTEN AND STOLWIJK 1999
S. van Heugten and C. Stolwijk, 'Theo Van Gogh: the Collector', in Amsterdam and Paris 1999–2000, pp. 153–63.

VAUXCELLES 1908
L. Vauxcelles, 'La collection de M. Paul Gallimard', *Les Arts*, September 1908, pp. 2–32.

VENTURI 1939
L. Venturi, *Les Archives de l'impressionnisme. Lettres de Renoir, Monet, Pissarro, Sisley et autres. Mémoires de Paul Durand-Ruel. Documents*, 2 vols, Paris and New York 1939.

VIGNON 2010
C. Vignon, *Londres – New York – Paris. Le commerce d'objets d'art de Duveen Frères entre 1880 et 1940*, PhD diss. supervised by Alain Mérot, université Paris IV Sorbonne 2010.

VINNEN 1911
C. Vinnen, 'Quousque tandem', in *Ein Protest Deutscher Künstler*, Iéna 1911, pp. 2–16.

VOSS 1897
G.V. [Georg Voss], 'Kunst, Wissenschaft und Literatur', *National-Zeitung*, no. 689, 2nd supplement, 12 December 1897.

VOTTERO 2012
M. Vottero, *La Peinture de genre en France, après 1850*, Rennes 2012.

WALLSEE 1895a
H.E. Wallsee, 'Eröffnung der großen Kunstausstellung in der Kunsthalle', *Hamburger Nachrichten*, no. 63, 14 March 1895, evening edition.

WALLSEE 1895b
H.E. Wallsee, 'Zur Einführung', *Hamburger Nachrichten*, no. 66, 18 March 1895, evening edition.

WALTER-RIS 2003
A. Walter-Ris, *Die Geschichte der Galerie Nierendorf. Kunstleidenschaft im Dienst der Moderne 1920–1995*, Ph. D. diss., Freie Universität Berlin 2003.

WARD 1991
M. Ward, 'Impressionist Installations and Private Exhibitions', in *The Art Bulletin*, vol. 73, no. 4, December 1991, pp. 599–622.

WARD 1995
M. Ward, *Pissarro, Neo-Impressionism, and the Spaces of the Avant-Garde*, Chicago and London 1995.

WATSON 2011
A. Watson, 'Deux éminents collectionneurs écossais du XIXe siècle: Daniel Wilson et James Duncan of Benmore', *Société des Amis du Musée national Eugène Delacroix*, Bulletin, no. 9, 2011, pp. 101–8.

WEDMORE 1883
F. Wedmore, 'The Impressionists', *Fortnightly Review*, January 1883.

WEDMORE 1905
F. Wedmore, '"Impressionist" Figure Painters', *Standard*, 20 January 1905.

WEISBERG 1997
G. Weisberg et al., *Collecting in the Gilded Age: Art Patronage in Pittsburgh, 1890–1910*, Pittsburgh 1997.

WEITZENHOFFER 1981
F. Weitzenhoffer, 'First Manet Painting to Enter an American Museum', *Gazette des Beaux-Arts*, March 1981, pp. 125–9.

WEITZENHOFFER 1984
F. Weitzenhoffer, 'The Earliest American Collectors of Monet', in Rewald and Weitzenhoffer 1984, pp. 74–89.

WEITZENHOFFER 1986
F. Weitzenhoffer, *The Havemeyers: Impressionism Comes to America*, New York 1986.

WHITE AND WHITE 1965 and 1991
H.C. White and C.A. White, *Canvases and Careers: Institutional Change in the French Painting World*, New York 1965. French edition: *La Carrière des peintres au xixe siècle. Du système académique au marché des impressionnistes*, Paris 1991.

WHITELEY 1979
L. Whiteley, 'Accounting for Tastes', *Oxford Art Journal*, vol. 2, April 1979, pp. 25–8.

WHITELEY 1983
L. Whiteley, 'Art et commerce d'art en France avant l'époque impressionniste', *Romantisme*, vol. 13, no. 40, 1983, pp. 65–76.

WHITELEY 1996
L. Whiteley, *Painters and Dealers in Nineteenth-Century France, 1820–1878, with Special Reference to the Firm of Durand-Ruel*, Ph. D. diss., University of Oxford 1996.

WILSON-BAREAU 2000
J. Wilson-Bareau, *Manet by Himself*, London 2000.

WOLF 1913
G.J. Wolf, 'Französische Kunst in Deutschland. Zur Ausstellung "Französische Kunst des XIX. Jahrhunderts" in der Galerie Heinemann in München', *Deutsche Kunst und Dekoration*, no. 32, 1913, p. 313.

WOLFF 1876
Albert Wolff, 'Le calendrier parisien', *Le Figaro*, 3 April 1876.

YON 2008
J.-C. Yon, in collaboration with P. Goetschel (eds), *Directeurs de theater (XIXe-XXe siècles). Histoire d'une profession*, Paris 2008.

ZAFRAN 2007
E.M. Zafran, 'Monet in America', in *Claude Monet (1840–1926): A Tribute to Daniel Wildenstein and Katia Granoff*, exh. cat. (New York, Wildenstein & Co., 2007), New York, 2007, pp. 81–151.

ZIEGLER 2001
Hendrik Ziegler, 'Emil Heilbut, ein früher Apologet Claude Monets', in Pophanken and Billeter 2001, pp. 41–65.

ZOLA 1866
E. Zola, 'M. Manet', *L'Evénement*, 7 May 1866.

ZOLA 1876
E. Zola, 'Deux expositions d'art au mois de mai', *Messager de l'Europe*, Saint Petersburg, June 1876 (in Russian).

ZOLA [1986]
E. Zola, *Carnets d'enquêtes, une ethnographie inédite de la France*, ed. H. Mitterand, Paris 1986.

ZOLA [1991]
E. Zola, *Ecrits sur l'art*, ed. J.- P. Leduc-Adine, Paris 1991.

ZOLA [1996]
E. Zola, *Ecrits sur l'art*, Paris 1996.

Exhibition Catalogues

ALGIERS 1880
Société des Beaux-Arts, des Sciences et des Lettres d'Alger. Exposition de peinture, sculpture, gravure, architecture et des arts appliqués à l'industrie (Algiers 1880).

AMSTERDAM AND PARIS 1999–2000
Theo Van Gogh, 1857–1891: Art Dealer, Collector and Brother of Vincent (Van Gogh Museum, Amsterdam 24 June–5 September 1999; Musée d'Orsay, Paris 27 September 1999–9 January 2000). (French edition: *Theo Van Gogh, marchand de tableaux, collectionneur, frère de Vincent*.)

ANN ARBOR, DALLAS AND MINNEAPOLIS 1998
Monet at Vétheuil. The Turning Point (The University of Michigan Museum of Art, Ann Arbor, 25 January–15 March 1998; Dallas Museum of Art, 28 March–17 May 1998; Minneapolis Institute of Art, 30 May–26 July 1998).

ATLANTA AND MINNEAPOLIS 2001
Degas and America (High Museum of Art, Atlanta, 3 March–27 May 2001; The Minneapolis Institute of Arts, 16 June–9 September 2001).

ATLANTA, SEATTLE AND DENVER 1999
Impressionism: Paintings Collected by European Museums (High Museum of Art, Atlanta, 23 February–16 May 1999; Seattle Art Museum, 12 June–29 August 1999; Denver Art Museum, 2 October–12 December 1999).

BERLIN 1905
Ausstellung VIII. Jahrgang (Berlin, Paul Cassirer, 1905).

BERLIN 2001–2002
Im Streit um die Moderne: Max Liebermann, der Kaiser, die Nationalgalerie (Max Liebermann Haus, Berlin, 27 October 2001–27 January 2002).

BERLIN 2013
Max Liebermann und Frankreich (Liebermann Villa am Wannsee, Berlin, 21 April–12 August 2013).

BERLIN 2013–2014
Verlorene Schätze die Kunstsammlung Max Liebermanns (Liebermann Villa am Wannsee, Berlin, 24 November 2013–3 March 2014).

BOSTON 1891
The Impressionists of Paris: Claude Monet, Camille Pissarro, Alfred Sisley, from the Galleries of Durand-Ruel Paris and New York (Chase's Gallery, Boston, 17–28 March 1891).

BOSTON 1895
Claude Monet (St. Botolph Club, Boston, 4–16 February 1895).

BOSTON 1905
Loan Collection of Paintings by Claude Monet and Eleven Sculptures by Auguste Rodin (The Copley Society, Boston, 4 March–15 April 1905).

BREMEN 1995–1996
Max Liebermann, der deutsche Impressionist: 'Nichts trügt weniger als der Schein' (Kunsthalle Bremen, 16 December 1995–24 March 1996).

BREMEN 2002–2003
Van Gogh: Felder. Das Mohnfeld und der Künstlerstreit (Kunsthalle Bremen, 19 October 2002–26 January 2003).

BRUSSELS 1904
Exposition des peintres impressionnistes (Bruxelles, La Libre Esthétique, 1904).

CHICAGO, BOSTON AND WASHINGTON 1998–1999
Mary Cassatt: Modern Woman (Art Institute of Chicago, 10 October 1998–10 January 1899; Museum of Fine Arts, Boston, 14 February–9 May 1999; National Gallery of Art, Washington, 6 June–6 September 1999).

COLOGNE 2012
Mission Moderne. Die Jahrhundertausstellung des Sonderbunde (Wallraf-Richartz Museum, Cologne, 31 August–30 December 2012).

DRESDEN 1897
Internationale Kunstausstellung (Ausstellungspalast, Dresden, 1 May–17 October 1897).

HAMBURG 1895
Führer der Grossen Kunstausstellung des Kunstvereins in der Hamburger Kunsthalle (Hamburger Kunsthalle, March–April 1895).

HAMBURG 1970
Französische Impressionisten. Hommage à Durand-Ruel (Kunstverein, Hamburg, 28 November 1970–27 January 1971).

HAMBURG 1986–1987
Kunst ins Leben. Alfred Lichtwarks Wirken für die Kunsthalle und Hamburg von 1886 bis 1914 (Hamburger Kunsthalle, 9 December 1986–1 February 1987).

HAMBURG 2001
Private Schätze: über das Sammeln von Kunst in Hamburg bis 1933 (Hamburger Kunsthalle, 23 March–17 June 2001).

HONFLEUR 1998
Eugène Boudin en Normandie (Musée Eugène-Boudin, Honfleur, 4 July–4 October 1998).

LONDON 1870
First Exhibition of the Society of French Artists, First Hanging (The German Gallery, 168 New Bond Street, London, December 1870).

LONDON 1871a
The First Annual Exhibition, in London, of Pictures, the Contribution of the Society of French Artists, Second Hanging (The German Gallery, 168 New Bond Street, London, 6 March 1871).

LONDON 1871b
The Second Annual Exhibition, in London, of Pictures, the Contributions of the Society of French Artists (168 New Bond Street, London, April 1871).

LONDON 1871c
International Exhibition at South Kensington (South Kensington Museum, London, May 1871).

LONDON 1872a
Third Exhibition of the Society of French Artists (168 New Bond Street, London, February 1872).

LONDON 1872b
Summer [Fourth] Exhibition of the Society of French Artists (168 New Bond Street, London, summer 1872).

LONDON 1872c
Fifth Exhibition of the Society of French Artists (168 New Bond Street, London, November 1872).

LONDON 1873a
Sixth Exhibition of the Society of French Artists (168 New Bond Street, London, April 1873).

LONDON 1873b
Seventh Exhibition of the Society of French Artists (168 New Bond Street, London, November 1873).

LONDON 1874a
Eighth Exhibition of the Society of French Artists (168 New Bond Street, London, spring 1874).

LONDON 1874b
Ninth Exhibition of the Society of French Artists (168 New Bond Street, London, summer 1874).

LONDON 1876
Twelfth Exhibition of Pictures by Modern French Artists (Deschamps Galleries, London, April 1876).

LONDON 1882
Exposition impressionniste (White's Gallery, London, July 1882).

LONDON 1883
Paintings, Drawings and Pastels by Members of 'La Société des Impressionnistes' (Dowdeswell & Dowdeswell, London, 20 April–July 1883).

LONDON 1884
An Exhibition of Pictures and Sculpture, by a Group of Artists of the French School (Dudley Gallery, Egyptian Hall, London, May 1884).

LONDON 1889
Pictures by Claude Monet (Goupil Galleries, London, April 1889).

LONDON 1893
Painting and Sculpture, by British and Foreign Artists of the Present Day (Grafton Galleries, London, 18 February–31 December 1893).

LONDON 1901
Exhibition of Pictures by French Impressionists, Monet, Sisley, Pissarro, Renoir and Other Masters (Hanover Gallery, London, spring 1901).

LONDON 1903
French Masters Exhibition (Grafton Galleries, London, 1 May–July 1903).

LONDON 1905
Pictures by Boudin, Cézanne, Degas, Manet, Monet, Morisot, Pissarro, Renoir, Sisley Exhibited by Messrs. Durand-Ruel & Sons of Paris (Grafton Galleries, London, January–February 1905).

LONDON 1996
Degas as a Collector (National Gallery, London, 22 May–26 August 1996).

LONDON 2003
Pissarro in London (National Gallery, London, 14 May–3 August 2003).

LONDON AND EDINBURGH 1991–1992
Palaces of Art: Art Galleries in Britain, 1790–1990 (Dulwich Picture Gallery, London, 27 November 1991–1 March 1992; National Gallery of Scotland, Edinburgh, 12 March–3 May 1992).

LONDON, PARIS AND BALTIMORE 1992–1993
Alfred Sisley (Royal Academy of Arts, London, 3 July–18 October 1992; Musée d'Orsay, Paris, 28 October 1992–31 January 1993; Walters Art Gallery, Baltimore, 14 March–13 June 1993).

LONDON, PARIS AND BOSTON 1985–1986
Renoir (Hayward Gallery, London, 30 January–21 April 1985; Galeries nationales du Grand Palais, Paris, 14 May–2 September 1985; Boston, Museum of Fine Arts, 9 October 1985–5 January 1986).

LONDON AND WASHINGTON 2001–2002
Spirit of an Age: Nineteenth Century Paintings from the Nationalgalerie, Berlin (National Gallery, London, 8 March–13 May 2001; National Gallery of Art, Washington, 10 June–3 September 2002).

LONDON AND WEST PALM BEACH 2005–2006
Impressionism Abroad: Boston and French Painting (Royal Academy of Arts, London, 2 July–11 September 2005; Norton Museum of Art, West Palm Beach, 19 November 2005–5 March 2006).

LONDON AND WILLIAMSTOWN 2007
The Unknown Monet: Pastels and Drawings (Royal Academy of Arts, London, 17 March–10 June 2007; Clark Institute, Williamstown, 24 June–16 September 2007).

LYON, COLOGNE, LIVERPOOL AND AMSTERDAM 1994–1995
Maurice Denis (Musée des Beaux arts, Lyon, 29 September–18 December 1994; Wallraf-Richartz Museum, Cologne, 22 January–2 April 1995; Walker Art Gallery, Liverpool, 21 April–18 June 1995; Van Gogh Museum, Amsterdam, 7 July–17 September 1995).

MANNHEIM 1909
Ausstellung von Werken der Malerei des 19. Jahrhunderts (Kunsthalle zu Mannheim, December 1909).

NEW YORK 1886a
Works in Oil and Pastel by the Impressionists of Paris (American Art Association, New York, 10–25 April 1886).

NEW YORK 1886b
Works in Oil and Pastel by the Impressionists of Paris (National Academy of Design, New York, 25 May–30 June 1886).

NEW YORK 1887
Celebrated Paintings by Great French Masters (National Academy of Design, New York, 25 May–30 June 1887).

NEW YORK 1890
Old Masters on Exhibition at Durand-Ruel's (Durand-Ruel Gallery, New York, 1890).

NEW YORK 1895a
Paintings of Claude Monet (Durand-Ruel Gallery, New York, 12–17 January 1895).

NEW YORK 1895b
Exposition of Paintings, Pastels and Etchings by Miss Mary Cassatt (Durand-Ruel Gallery, New York, 16–30 April 1895).

NEW YORK 1895c
Exposition of Paintings by Edouard Manet (Durand-Ruel Gallery, New York, 1895).

NEW YORK 1898
Exhibition of Paintings, Pastels and Drypoints by Mary Cassatt (Durand-Ruel Gallery, New York, February–March 1898).

NEW YORK 1902
Exhibition of Paintings by Claude Monet (Durand-Ruel Gallery, New York, 11–25 February 1902).

NEW YORK 1903
Exhibition of Paintings and Pastels by Mary Cassatt (Durand-Ruel Gallery, New York, 5–21 November 1903).

NEW YORK 1943
1803–1943: Exhibition Celebrating One Hundred Fortieth Anniversary (Durand-Ruel Galleries, New York, 15 November–4 December 1943).

NEW YORK 1970
'One Hundred Years of Impressionism'. A Tribute to Durand-Ruel, for the Benefit of the New York University Art Collection (New York, Wildenstein, 2 April–9 May 1970).

NEW YORK 1980
Pablo Picasso: A Retrospective (The Museum of Modern Art, New York, 22 May–16 September 1980).

NEW YORK 1993
Splendid Legacy: The Havemeyer Collection (The Metropolitan Museum of Art, New York, 27 March–20 June 1993).

NEW YORK 2012
Renoir, Impressionism, and Full-Length Painting (The Frick Collection, New York, 7 February–13 May 2012).

NEW YORK, CHICAGO AND PARIS 2006–2007
Cézanne to Picasso: Ambroise Vollard, Patron of the Avant-Garde (The Metropolitan Museum of Art, New York, 13 September 2006–7 January 2007; The Art Institute of Chicago, 17 February–12 May 2007; Musée d'Orsay, Paris, 19 June–16 September 2007). (French edition: *De Cézanne à Picasso, chefs d'oeuvre de la Galerie Vollard*).

OTTAWA, CHICAGO AND FORT WORTH 1997–1998
Renoir's Portraits: Impressions of an Age, (National Gallery of Canada, Ottawa, 27 June–14 September 1997; The Art Institute of Chicago, 17 October 1997–4 January 1998; Kimbell Art Museum, Fort Worth, 8 February–26 April 1998). (French edition: *Les Portraits de Renoir. Impressions d'une époque.*)

PARIS 1867
Notice des études peintes par M. Théodore Rousseau exposées au Cercle des Arts (Cercle des arts, Paris, June 1867).

PARIS 1872
[Untitled] (Galerie Durand-Ruel, Paris, April 1872).

PARIS 1873
[Untitled] (Galerie Durand-Ruel, Paris, 1873).

PARIS 1874
Première exposition impressionniste (Société anonyme des artistes peintres, sculpteurs, graveurs, etc., 35, boulevard des Capucines, Paris, 15 April–15 May 1874).

PARIS 1876
Deuxième exposition de peinture (Société anonyme des artistes peintres, sculpteurs, graveurs, etc., Galerie Durand-Ruel, Paris, April 1876).

PARIS 1878
Exposition rétrospective de tableaux et dessins des maîtres modernes (Galerie Durand-Ruel, Paris, 1878).

PARIS 1882
Septième exposition des artistes indépendants (Salons du Panorama de Reichshoffen, Paris, 1882).

PARIS 1883a
Oeuvres de Eugène Boudin (Galerie Durand-Ruel, Paris, 1–25 February 1883).

PARIS 1883b
Exposition des oeuvres de Claude Monet (Galerie Durand-Ruel, Paris, 1–25 March 1883).

PARIS 1883c
Exposition des oeuvres de P. A. Renoir, (Galerie Durand-Ruel, 9, boulevard de la Madeleine, Paris, 1–25 April 1883).

PARIS 1883d
Oeuvres de C. Pissarro (Galerie Durand-Ruel, Paris, 1–25 May 1883).

PARIS 1884
Une collection particulière [collection de Mme de Cassin, marquise de Carcano] (Galerie Georges Petit, Paris, 1 October–10 December 1884).

PARIS 1889
Exposition de tableaux de Monet, Pissarro, Renoir & Sisley (Galerie Durand-Ruel, Paris, 1889).

PARIS 1892a
Camille Pissarro (Galerie Durand-Ruel, Paris, February 1892).

PARIS 1892b
Monet. Série des peupliers des bords de l'Epte (Galerie Durand-Ruel, Paris, 29 February–10 March 1892).

PARIS 1892c
Exposition A. Renoir (Galerie Durand-Ruel, Paris, May 1892).

PARIS 1893
Exposition de tableaux, pastels et gravures de Mary Cassatt (Galerie Durand-Ruel, Paris, 27 November–16 December 1893).

PARIS 1894
Manet (Galerie Durand-Ruel, Paris, December 1894).

PARIS 1896a
Berthe Morisot (Madame Eugène Manet) (Durand-Ruel, Paris, 5–21 March 1896).

PARIS 1896b
Oeuvres récentes de Camille Pissarro (Galerie Paris, Durand-Ruel, 15 April–9 May 1896).

PARIS 1899
Tableaux de Renoir, Monet, Pissarro et Sisley (Galerie Durand-Ruel, April 1899).

PARIS 1900
Exposition universelle (Champs-Élysées, Invalides, Champ de Mars, Palais étrangers, Trocadéro, Paris 1900).

PARIS 1904
L'Oeuvre de Camille Pissarro (Galerie Durand-Ruel, Paris, April 1904).

PARIS 1906
Dix-sept tableaux de Cl. Monet de la collection Faure (Galerie Durand-Ruel, Paris, 19–31 March 1906).

PARIS 1975
Jean-François Millet (Grand Palais, Paris, 17 October 1975–5 January 1976).

PARIS 1980
Hommage à Claude Monet (1840–1929) (Grand Palais, Paris, 8 February–5 May 1980).

PARIS 1989
Gauguin (Galeries nationales du Grand Palais, Paris, 14 January–24 April 1989).

PARIS 1991
De Corot aux impressionnistes, donations Moreau-Nélaton (Galeries nationales du Grand Palais, Paris, 3 May–22 July 1991).

PARIS 2011
Manet, inventeur du moderne (Musée d'Orsay, Paris, 5 April–3 July 2011). (English edition: *Manet: The Man who Invented Modernity.*)

PARIS AND BOSTON 2003–2004
Gauguin Tahiti (Galeries nationales du Grand Palais, Paris, 30 September 2003–19 January 2004; Museum of Fine Arts, Boston, 29 February–20 June 2004).

PARIS AND CHICAGO 1994–1995
Gustave Caillebotte, 1848–1894 (Galeries nationales du Grand Palais, Paris, 12 September 1994–9 January 1995; The Art Institute of Chicago, 15 February–28 May 1995).

PARIS AND GHENT 1997
Paris-Bruxelles, Bruxelles-Paris (Galeries nationales du Grand Palais, Paris, 18 March–14 July 1997; Museum voor Schone Kunsten, Ghent, 6 September–14 December 1997).

PARIS AND NEW YORK 1991–1992
Seurat (Galeries nationales du Grand Palais, Paris, 9 April–12 August 1991; The Metropolitan Museum of Art, New York, 24 September 1991–12 January 1992).

PARIS, OTTAWA AND NEW YORK 1988–1989
Degas (Galeries nationales du Grand Palais, Paris, 9 February–16 May 1988; National Gallery of Canada, Ottawa, 16 June–28 August 1988; The Metropolitan Museum of Art, New York, 27 September 1988–8 January 1989).

PITTSBURGH 1898
International Exhibition of Contemporary Painting (Carnegie Institute, Pittsburgh, 1898).

PITTSBURGH 1997
Collecting in the Gilded Age: Art Patronage in Pittsburgh, 1890–1910 (Frick Art and Historical Center, Pittsburgh, 1997).

PONT-AVEN 2001
Gustave Loiseau et la Bretagne, 1865–1935 (Musée de Pont-Aven, 30 June–1 October 2001).

VIENNA 1998–1999
Heiliger Frühling: Gustav Klimt und die Anfänge der Wiener Secession 1895–1905 (Albertina, Vienna, 16 October 1998–10 January 1999).

WASHINGTON, FORT WORTH AND SOUTH HADLEY 1987–1988
Berthe Morisot, Impressionist (National Gallery of Art, Washington, 6 September–29 November 1987; Kimbell Art Museum, Fort Worth, 12 December 1987–21 February 1988; Mount Holyoke College Art Museum, South Hadley, 14 March–9 May 1988).

WASHINGTON AND SAN FRANCISCO 1986
The New Painting: Impressionism, 1874–1886 (National Gallery of Art, Washington, 19 January–6 April 1986; Fine Art Museums, M.H. de Young Memorial Museum, San Francisco, 19 April–6 July 1986).

Sales Catalogues

COLOGNE 1899
Gemäldegalerie. II. Abteilung des Privatgelehrten Hans Weidenbusch zu Wiesbaden (Lempertz auction house, Cologne, 1899).

NEW YORK 1896
Catalogue of Paintings, Studio, Appointments, Curios etc. Belonging to William Merritt Chase (American Art Galleries, New York, 7 January 1896).

NEW YORK 1897
The Durand-Ruel Collection of French Paintings (Moore's Art Galleries, New York, 5–6 May 1887).

NEW YORK 2013
The Unknown Renoir (Heritage Auctions, New York, 19 September 2013).

PARIS 1868
Collection de tableaux anciens et modernes de S. Exc. Khalil-Bey (Hôtel Drouot, Paris, 16–18 January 1868).

PARIS 1873
*Collection de tableaux de M. D. W.*** Tableaux anciens et modernes, tapisseries du XVe siècle* (Hôtel Drouot, Paris, 21 March 1873).

PARIS 1901
Vente de tableaux modernes provenant de la collection d'un amateur (Hôtel Drouot, Paris, 25 April 1901).

PARIS 1906
Tableaux modernes, aquarelles, dessins (Galerie Georges Petit, Paris, 31 May–1 June 1906).

PARIS 1912
Catalogue de tableaux modernes. Aquarelles, dessins, pastels, sculptures, tableaux anciens, dessins anciens, objets d'art & d'ameublement appartenant à Madame la Marquise Landolfo Carcano (Galerie Georges Petit, Paris, 30 May–1 June 1912).

PARIS 1975
Archives de Camille Pissarro (Hôtel Drouot, Paris, 21 November 1975).

PARIS 2006a
Archives Claude Monet. Correspondance d'artiste Collection Monsieur et Madame Cornebois (Artcurial, hôtel Dassault, Paris, 13 December 2006).

PARIS 2006b
Lettres et manuscrits autographes, documents historiques (Paris, Piasa sale, 16–17 March 2006).

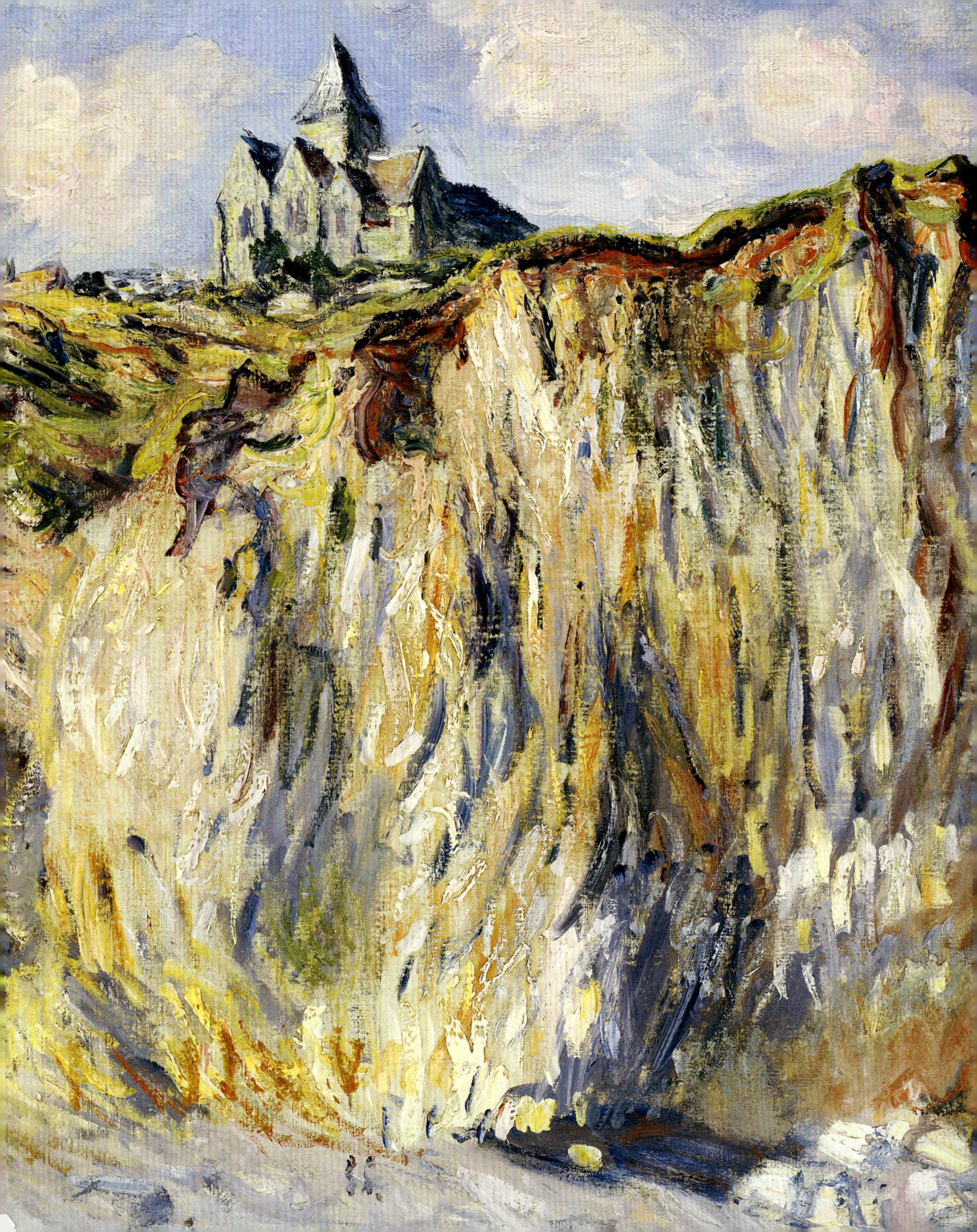

LIST OF LENDERS

This exhibition has been made possible by the provision of insurance through the Government Indemnity Scheme. The National Gallery would like to thank HM Government for providing Government Indemnity and the Department for Culture, Media and Sport and Arts Council England for arranging the indemnity.

BALTIMORE
The Walters Art Museum

BATH
Andrew Brownsword Arts Foundation

BERLIN
Alte Nationalgalerie

BOSTON
Museum of Fine Arts, Boston

CHICAGO
The Art Institute of Chicago

CINCINNATI
Cincinnati Art Museum

CLEVELAND
The Cleveland Museum of Art

COPENHAGEN
Ny Carlsberg Glyptotek

GENEVA
Musées d'Art et d'Histoire

THE HAGUE
The Mesdag Collection

HAMBURG
Hamburger Kunsthalle

LONDON
The Courtauld Gallery
The National Gallery
Tate Gallery
Victoria and Albert Museum

LYON
Musée des Beaux-Arts

MANNHEIM
Kunsthalle Mannheim

MINNEAPOLIS
Minneapolis Institute of Arts

NEW YORK
The Metropolitan Museum of Art

NORFOLK
Chrysler Museum of Art

OTTAWA
National Gallery of Canada

PARIS
Musée Marmottan Monet
Musée d'Orsay
Musée du Louvre

PHILADELPHIA
Philadelphia Museum of Art

PITTSBURGH
Carnegie Museum of Art

PRINCETON
The Henry and Rose Pearlman Foundation, on long-term loan to the Princeton University Art Museum

RICHMOND
Virginia Museum of Fine Arts

SAINT LOUIS
Saint Louis Art Museum

SHELBURNE
Shelburne Museum

TOKYO
Ise Cultural Foundation
National Museum of Western Art

TORONTO
Art Gallery of Ontario

WASHINGTON, DC
National Gallery of Art

WILLIAMSTOWN
Sterling and Francine Clark Art Institute

and all those private lenders who wish to remain anonymous.

INDEX OF NAMES

Locators in **bold** refer to the Notes section; those in *italics* refer to donors in the catalogue section.

PHOTOGRAPHIC CREDITS

All exhibited works are referred to by cat. number.
Comparative illustrations are referred to as figs.

BALTIMORE
© The Walters Art Museum, Baltimore, Maryland: cat. 28 (and detail, pp. 54–5), cat. 34.

BARCELONA
© Museu Picasso de Barcelona/Photograph: Gasull. Succession Picasso/DACS, London 2015: fig. 162.

BERLIN
© bpk/Zentralarchiv, Staatliche Museen zu Berlin: fig. 106.
Nationalgalerie, Staatliche Museen zu Berlin-Preussischer Kulturbesitz:
© Photo Scala, Florence/bpk, Bildagentur für Kunst, Kultur und Geschichte, Berlin/Photo: Klaus Goeken: cat. 6 (and detail, pp. 152–3); © Photo Scala, Florence/bpk, Bildagentur für Kunst, Kultur und Geschichte, Berlin/Jörg P. Anders: fig. 101 © Photo Scala, Florence/bpk, Bildagentur für Kunst, Kultur und Geschichte, Berlin: fig. 102.

BOSTON, MASSACHUSETTS
© 2014 Museum of Fine Arts, Boston: cats 44, 81 (and detail, p. 265).

BREMEN
Kunsthalle Bremen:
© Karen Blindow: fig. 107; © White Images/Scala, Florence: fig. 109.

BUDAPEST
Szépművészeti Múzeum:
© Bridgeman Images: fig. 56.

BUFFALO, NEW YORK
© 2014. Albright Knox Art Gallery/Art Resource, NY/Scala, Florence: fig. 130.

CHICAGO, ILLINOIS
© The Art Institute of Chicago, Illinois: cats 4, 60 (and detail, pp. 134–5), 75.

CINCINNATI, OHIO
© Cincinnati Art Museum, Ohio/The Bridgeman Art Library, London: cat. 7.

CLEVELAND, OHIO
© The Cleveland Museum of Art, Cleveland, Ohio: cat. 64.

COPENHAGEN
Ny Carlsberg Glyptotek:
© Ny Carlsberg Glyptotek, Copenhagen/Photo: Ole Haupt: cat. 33; © SMK Photo: cat. 88.

FRANKFURT AM MAIN
Städelsches Kunstinstitut:
© Artothek/Bridgeman Images: fig. 104; © Photo Fine Art Images/Heritage Images/Scala, Florence: fig. 110.

GENEVA
© Musée d'Art et d'Histoire, Ville de Genève, inv. no. 1915-33/Photo: Flora Bevilacqua: cat. 67.

GLASGOW
Glasgow Museums: Art Gallery and Museums, Kelvingrove:
© CSG CIC Glasgow Museums and Libraries Collections: fig. 132.

THE HAGUE
© The Mesdag Collection, The Hague: cat. 9.

HAMBURG
Hamburger Kunsthalle:
© Bridgeman Images: fig. 100; © Photo Scala, Florence/bpk, Bildagentur für Kunst, Kultur und Geschichte, Berlin: cat. 42.

L'ISLE-ADAM
Musée d'art et d'histoire Louis-Senlecq:
© Henri Delage: fig. 6.

LONDON
The Courtauld Gallery:
© SCT Enterprises Ltd: cat. 36.
© Mary Evans Picture Library 2013: fig. 112.
© The National Gallery, London: cats 3, 10, 16, 22, 26, 29, 31 (and detail, pp. 170–1), 41, 61, 62 (and detail, pp. 76–7), 85, 92; figs 131, 163.
© Tate, London 2014: cat. 55.
© Victoria and Albert Museum: cat. 13.

LYON
Musée des Beaux-Arts:
© RMN-Grand Palais/René-Gabriel Ojéda: cat. 82.

MANNHEIM
© Kunsthalle Mannheim/Margitta Wickenhäuser: cat. 69.

MELBOURNE
National Gallery of Victoria:
© Bridgeman Images: fig. 165.

MERION, PENNSYLVANIA
The Barnes Foundation:
© Bridgeman Images: fig. 139.

MINNEAPOLIS, MINNESOTA
© Minneapolis Institute of Arts: cat. 87.

MOSCOW
Pushkin State Museum:
© akg-images: fig. 161.

NEW YORK
© The Metropolitan Museum of Art, New York: cats 8, 20, 89; figs 47, 78, 93.
© Wurts Bros. (New York, N.Y.)/Museum of the City of New York: fig. 98.

NORFOLK, VIRGINIA
© Chrysler Museum of Art, Norfolk, Virginia: cat. 78.

OTTAWA, ONTARIO
© National Gallery of Canada: cat. 86.

PARIS
Archives Durand-Ruel © Durand-Ruel & Cie.: figs 16, 17 (and detail, pp. 194–5), 18, 19, 34, 60, 111 (and detail, pp. 30–1), 129, 134, 136–8, 148, 150–2, 154–60.
Bibliothèque de l'INHA, collections Jacques Doucet:
© INHA, Dist. RMN-Grand Palais/Martine Beck-Coppola: fig. 149.
© Bibliothèque Nationale de France, Paris: figs 144–6, 153.
Musée d'Orsay:
© RMN-Grand Palais (musée d'Orsay)/Hervé Lewandowski: cats 11, 12 (and detail, p. 239), 24, 35, 79 (and detail pp. 10–11), 80, 90 (and detail, pp. 2–3); figs 44, 48, 50, 55, 71 © RMN-Grand Palais (musée d'Orsay)/Gérard Blot: cat. 32; © RMN-Grand Palais (musée d'Orsay)/Jean-Gilles Berizzi: cat. 40 (and detail, pp. 98–9); © Musée d'Orsay, Dist. RMN-Grand Palais/Patrice Schmidt: cats 56, 72; figs 127, 135, 147, 164 (and detail, pp. 206–7); © RMN-Grand Palais (musée d'Orsay)/René-Gabriel Ojéda: cat. 63; © RMN-Grand Palais (musée d'Orsay)/Benoit Touchard/Michel Urtado fig. 87; © RMN-Grand Palais (musée d'Orsay)/Jean Schormans: fig. 142; © RMN-Grand Palais (musée d'Orsay)/Stéphane Maréchalle: fig. 143; © RMN-Grand Palais (musée d'Orsay)/Martine Beck-Coppola: fig. 166.
Musée du Louvre:
© RMN-Grand Palais (musée du Louvre)/Gérard Blot: cat. 19; © Musée du Louvre, Dist. RMN-Grand Palais/Angèle Dequier: figs 20, 39; © RMN-Grand Palais (musée du Louvre)/Thierry Le Mage: fig. 41; © RMN-Grand Palais (musée du Louvre)/Franck Raux: fig. 46.
© Musée Marmottan Monet, Paris, France/Giraudon/The Bridgeman Art Library: cat. 39.
Petit Palais, Musée des Beaux-Arts de la Ville de Paris:
© akg-images: fig. 126.

PASADENA, CALIFORNIA
© The Norton Simon Foundation: fig. 141.

PHILADELPHIA, PENNSYLVANIA
Philadelphia Museum of Art:
© Philadelphia Museum of Art, Pennsylvania: cats 1, 2, 5, 17, 18, 23, 30, 37, 45, 53, 58, 71, 84; fig. 133; © Art Resource/Scala, Florence: fig. 7.

PITTSBURGH, PENNSYLVANIA
© Carnegie Museum of Art, Pittsburgh: cats 65, 93.

PRINCETON
© Princeton University Art Museum/Art Resource NY/Scala, Florence/Photo: Bruce M. White: cat. 66.

PRIVATE COLLECTION
© The Andrew Brownsword Arts Foundation: cat. 91.
Archives Durand-Ruel © Durand-Ruel & Cie.: cats 46–50, 51 (and detail, p. 255), 52, 76, 77, 83 (and detail, p. 6).
© The Art Archive/Private Collection/Superstock: fig. 99.
© Christie's Images/Bridgeman Images: fig. 120.
© Christie's Images, London/Scala, Florence: cat. 43 (and detail, p. 296).
© Ise Cultural Foundation, Tokyo: cat. 54.
© Photo courtesy of the owner: cats 27 (and detail, p. 246), 73.
© Private collection: fig. 89.
Private Collection, Ireland:
© Photo courtesy of the owner: cat. 14.

RICHMOND, VIRGINIA
© Virginia Museum of Fine Arts/Photo: Katherine Wetzel: cat. 15.

SAINT LOUIS, MISSOURI
© The Saint Louis Art Museum, Missouri: cat. 21.

SAN FRANCISCO, CALIFORNIA
© Fine Arts Museums of San Francisco, California: fig. 36.

SHELBURNE, VERMONT
© Shelburne Museum, Shelburne, Vermont: cat. 25.

TOKYO
© National Museum of Western Art, Tokyo: cat. 57 (and detail, p. 256).

TORONTO, ONTARIO
© Art Gallery of Ontario, Toronto: cat. 68 (and detail, pp. 232–3).

WASHINGTON, DC
© Copley Society records, Archives of American Art, Smithsonian Institution: fig. 97.
National Gallery of Art:
© Image courtesy of the Board of Trustees, National Gallery of Art, Washington, DC: cats 38, 59 (and detail, pp. 120–1), 70.
The Phillips Collection:
© Bridgeman Images: fig. 33.

WILLIAMSTOWN, MASSACHUSETTS
Sterling and Francine Clark Art Institute:
© Bridgeman Images: fig. 140; © Sterling and Francine Clark Art Institute, Williamstown, Massachusetts, USA (photo by Michael Agee): cat. 74.